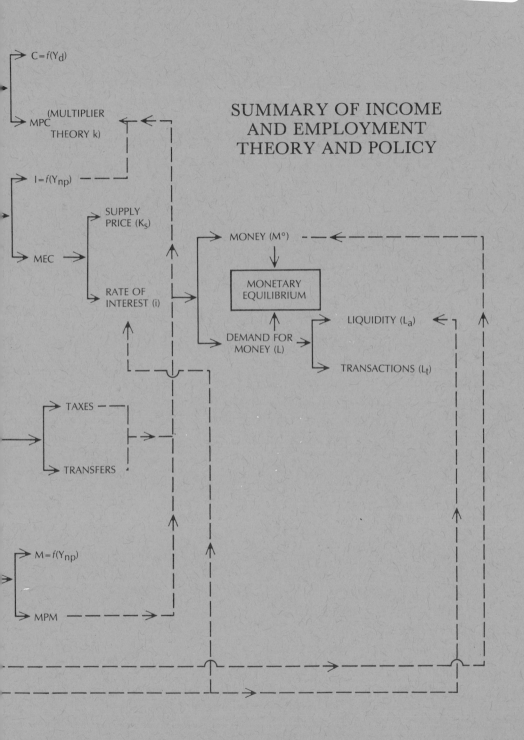

SUMMARY OF INCOME AND EMPLOYMENT THEORY AND POLICY

Income,
Employment,
and
Economic Growth

Fifth Edition

Supplementary to this text: *Study Guide to Accompany Wallace C. Peterson's* INCOME, EMPLOYMENT, AND ECONOMIC GROWTH, Fifth Edition, by Harold R. Williams

Wallace C. Peterson

UNIVERSITY OF NEBRASKA

Income, Employment, and Economic Growth

Fifth Edition

W.W. NORTON & COMPANY
New York London

FIFTH EDITION

The text of this book is composed in Baskerville, with display type set in Optima.
Composition by Vail-Ballou. Manufacturing by The Maple-Vail Book Manufacturing Group.

Library of Congress Cataloging in Publication Data
Peterson, Wallace C.
Income, employment, and economic growth.
Fifth Edition
Includes index.
1. Macroeconomics.   I. Title.
HB172.5.P453   1984   339   83-23635

W. W. Norton & Company, Inc.
500 Fifth Avenue, New York, N.Y. 10110
W. W. Norton & Company Ltd.
37 Great Russell Street, London WC1B 3NU

1 2 3 4 5 6 7 8 9 0

To Eunice

Contents

Part III   Alternative Approaches to Macroeconomics

Preface

A dozen years ago or so a broad consensus existed on the content and utility of macroeconomic theory. There was, to use Thomas Kuhn's terminology, an accepted "paradigm" that clearly defined the structure and boundaries of the subject. This is no longer the case. Today several diverse viewpoints are contending with one another for a dominant position in the field. This is not necessarily an unhealthy situation, but it does complicate the task of revising a textbook. In addition to sharpening the exposition of key ideas, principles, and concepts, I have worked hard to make certain that the text fully captures the diversity of approaches and ideas now characteristic of contemporary macroeconomics. The support given the text by so many teachers and students since its first appearance has made this task a labor of love.

As in all earlier editions, my primary aim is to set forth a clear and complete explanation of the forces that drive the aggregate economy. This is what macroeconomics is all about. A textbook should equip students to understand and apply economic principles with a minimum of outside help, thus freeing the instructor in the classroom to explore special facets of the analysis and important policy issues. The emphasis throughout is upon economics and understanding economics, not quantitative manipulation. As in prior editions, mathematics is used sparingly, although where appropriate there are mathematical appendices for those students interested in the derivation of key propositions.

In making this revision I have sought to keep intact the organizational structure, but at the same time thoroughly update all of the theoretical and empirical material relevant to contemporary macroeconomics.

• More stress than ever is placed upon making certain that the text reflects the real, important problems of our era. Every effort has been made to introduce significant policy issues early, as they arise in connection with the discussion of theory. Furthermore, wherever possible throughout the book, both theory and policy recommendations are tied to what is actually happening in the world today.

• Chapter 12, "The Rebirth of Classical Economics," is new. It is devoted to analysis of the "new classical economics," including its foundation in the theory of rational expectations and Walrasian general equilibrium theory, and supply-side economics, the approach to macroeconomics that provided much of the theoretical rationale for President Reagan's Program for Economic Recovery.

• Chapter 13, "Post Keynesian Economics," is also new. It examines the ideas and emerging theoretical contributions to macroeconomics of the Post Keynesians. These are a group of economists who challenge both the standard interpretation of Keynes, orthodox monetarism, and the supply-side economies.

The Plan of the Book

The fact that currently there is a significant amount of disagreement among economists with respect to the appropriate content of contemporary macroeconomic theory underscores another crucial point: Values enter into the perceptions economists have of how the world economy actually works. *All* of the different theoretical approaches to macroeconomics mentioned above carry ideological overtones. They do so because either explicitly or implicitly they embody policy implications that point not just to "what is" but "what ought to be." This is not necessarily bad; it is something embedded in the character of theoretical reasoning in the social sciences. A text must provide a thorough understanding of both the broad areas of agreement within the subject and the kinds of theoretical disagreements that exist. Furthermore, it must offer a reasoned judgment of the significance of such disagreements with respect to the overall development of the subject. This book is organized with these goals in mind.

The first three chapters, Part I, elaborate in detail the major measures used by economists to take the pulse of the economy. Measurement is the starting point for all scientific endeavor. Much of these chapters is devoted to income and its measurement, since income is fundamental to all of macroeconomics. However, additional in-depth material on employment and unemployment as well as the general price level is included.

In Chapters 4 through 10, Part II in the text, the theoretical ideas that constitute the core material for contemporary macroeconomics are developed in detail. Essentially, this core material deals with relationships involving consumption and investment spending, the impact that governmental and international economic transactions have on the economy, and the special role that money and interest rates play in determining output and employment levels. All the material in these chapters has been thoroughly reviewed and updated. The lineage of this core is and remains Keynesian. It is my strong conviction that no student can be adequately prepared in macroeconomics without a grounding in these core ideas: They provide the point of departure for ideas that have appeared recently.

Mastery of the core material brings us logically to areas where economists disagree. Thus, in Chapters 11, 12, and 13 we examine, in turn, the key theoretical ideas found in modern monetarism, the new classical economics, supply-side economics, and Post Keynesian economics. One of the important consequences to emerge from these schools— although not in the same way in each instance—has been the belief that standard, post–World War II macroeconomics neglected the role supply plays in the aggregate economic picture, especially with respect to inflation. Chapter 14 on "The Economics of Inflation" draws together several strands touched upon earlier in the text to derive an empirically based aggregate supply function, one which dovetails nicely with the important but too often neglected theory of the price level that Keynes developed in *The General Theory*. The chapter also includes an up-to-date discussion of the Phillips curve and its limitations, as well as an analysis of both the theory and practice of incomes policies. Closing out Part III is Chapter 15 on "Managing the Macroeconomy," which analyzes closely the links between theory and policy, and reviews critically the effectiveness of macroeconomic policies since the end of World War II. All postwar administrations, from Truman through Reagan, are subject to critical scrutiny in the light of concepts developed earlier in the book.

In Part IV we examine key dynamic aspects of macroeconomic behavior. Chapter 16, "Productivity and Growth," analyzes the phenomenon of economic growth, including discussion of the major theoretical approaches to this vital subject. New material has been added on the "productivity crisis," a major development that bears on the ability of the economy to grow at full employment without inflation. In the final chapter in the text, "Business Cycles and Forecasting," we deal with the business cycle, a major characteristic of advanced market systems. The material in this chapter, including the analysis of forecasting techniques, has been reviewed thoroughly and updated. This chapter is essentially self-contained. It may be assigned to be read along with Chapters 2 and 3 in Part I that deal with national income measurement and accounting. Some instructors prefer to deal with cycles early in the course, and given the discussion in Chapter 1 of the economy's basic instability, this would be appropriate.

Acknowledgments

As is the case with a textbook—especially one which has gone through several editions—the author can never fully acknowledge the many persons to whom he is indebted. There are, however, always a few to whom special thanks are due. Thus, I want specifically to express my thanks and appreciation to Professors John L. Bungum of Gustavus Adolphus College and Paul D. Bush of California State University–Fresno for their careful and detailed reviews of the fourth edition. Their comments have been extremely helpful to me in preparing this revision. Other colleagues who have offered helpful suggestions from time to time include Professors Hyman Minsky of Washington University and Warren J. Samuels of Michigan State University. Among my colleagues at the University of Nebraska–Lincoln, Professors Harish Gupta, Thomas Iwand, Campbell McConnell, Jerry Petr, and Ted Roesler were always willing to help with comments and suggestions as the revision progressed.

A special word of thanks is due W. Drake McFeely and Debra Makay for their skill and efficiency in editing the manuscript. I, of course, accept full responsibility for all errors. From the time I began the first edition, Donald S. Lamm, now president of W. W. Norton & Company, has been a major source of encouragement in the writing and revising of this text. This is appreciated.

Finally, I want to express deep appreciation to my wife, Eunice, for the strong support she has always given me, not just in this current revision, but in prior revisions and the first writing of the text.

As with earlier editions, Professor Harold R. Williams of Kent State University has developed a study guide especially designed for this text. Many instructors will find this workbook a valuable adjunct that enables students to review and undertake applications of the theoretical material found in the text.

Finally, for kind permission to quote from *The General Theory of Employment, Interest, and Money,* I wish to thank Harcourt, Brace & World, Inc., Macmillan & Co. Ltd., and the trustees of the estate of the late Lord Keynes.

Wallace C. Peterson

I

Introduction and Measurement

1

An Overview of Macroeconomics

Events in recent years have not been kind to the American economy—or to most other Western economies for that matter. Too much inflation, too much unemployment, sluggish growth, and lagging productivity are but a few of the troublesome problems that have plagued the economy. These and other problems are the concern of the branch of economics called *macroeconomics*. *Macro* comes from a Greek word meaning "large" or "big." Hence, macroeconomics is concerned with problems and behavior that embrace the entire economy. It focuses primarily on how the economic system performs in three major ways: (1) the total production of goods and services, including the growth over time in that production; (2) providing employment for the nation's work force; and (3) the overall behavior of prices.

No person, no family, no business firm, nor any governmental body is untouched by the performance of the economy. The new graduate seeking a job, the worker nearing retirement, the business firm contemplating building a new plant, the school district planning a bond issue for a new school, and the federal government looking for revenue to finance military spending have in common the basic fact that the success or failure of ambitions and plans depends heavily on the state of the economy's health. Understanding the forces that determine this health is the fundamental task of macroeconomic analysis.

It is not just the ordinary citizen who has a stake in how the economy performs. The economy's performance is of critical concern for the national government as well, not simply because the government's economic fortune, like those of the family and business concerns, is tied to the performance of the economic system, but because the federal government has a special responsibility to "promote the general welfare," as specified in the Constitution. The Employment Act, which Congress passed in 1946, stated more specifically that the federal government has a responsibility to "promote maximum employment, production, and purchasing power."[1] More recently another act, the Full Employment and Balanced Growth Act of 1978, has been even more explicit in prescribing the responsibilities of the federal government in the pursuit of such national goals as full employment, economic growth, and stable prices. Although the economy's performance in recent years has fallen far short of the goals embodied in these legislative acts, nevertheless they represent commitments that cannot be neglected indefinitely, even though recent administrations have all but ignored these goals. Their existence also means that the study of government policy, of the actions taken by the federal government in relation to production, employment, and the price level, is a legitimate part of macroeconomic analysis. Understanding the successes and failures of economic policy is one of the purposes of this text.

Macroeconomics is but one of the two large divisions into which economists divide their subject. The other is microeconomics. *Micro* also is derived from the Greek, meaning "small." What microeconomics does is focus on the behavior of the individual units of the economy, particularly the households, wage and salary earners, and business firms. Microeconomics seeks to understand how markets work in establishing individual and relative prices for the goods and services produced, how economic resources get allocated among different uses, and how payments are made to the owners of resources (land, labor, and capital) for the services the resources render in the production of goods and services. Although "micro" and "macro" are different and distinct branches of econommc science, they are closely interrelated. Since macroeconomics reflects the aggregate behavior of the many millions of primary economic units—households, firms, and governmental bodies—there is no essential conflict between these two fundamental branches of economics. They represent the analysis of economic activity from two different perspectives—perspectives that necessarily complement one another. Traditionally, the macro branch of economics is referred to as income and employment theory, whereas the micro branch is described as value and distribution theory. Until the late 1960s there was not much effort made to link macro- and microeconomic theories, but now there is a significant amount of research being devoted to the discovery of the microeconomic foundations of macroeconomics.

Measuring the Economy's Performance

One useful way to appreciate the essential nature of macroeconomics is to look at several key aggregates to which economists turn for measurement and evaluation of the economy's performance. *Aggregate* is a term

---

1. Employment act of 1946, Public Law 304, 79th Congress.

used to describe a variable that pertains to the entire economy. There are many such aggregates, but measures of total output, prices, and unemployment are of special significance. In Chapters 2 and 3 some of these measures are analyzed in greater depth; here a brief sketch of the well-known and widely used measures will help us understand the nature and scope of macroeconomics.

The National Output

Undoubtedly, the best-known measure of economic performance is the *gross national product,* or GNP as it is often called. Hardly a day passes without some reference to this figure in the nation's press or over the radio and TV airways. What is the gross national product? Simply put, it is the monetary value of all goods and services produced in the economy in a current time period. Normally, the latter is the calendar year, although GNP data are prepared and made available quarterly. In the United States, the responsibility for preparation and publication of gross national product data rests with the Bureau of Economic Analysis of the United States Department of Commerce.[2]

Nominal versus Real GNP

Essentially, the GNP is obtained by adding up the expenditures made for the vast variety of goods and services produced and sold in the economy in a given period of time. In Chapter 2 we shall examine the major types of spending which, when added up, give us an output total. At this point, however, let us note that an expenditure for a good or a service involves two things: the *quantity* of the good or service purchased and the *price* at which it is purchased. Thus, when the appropriate purchases of goods and services during a year are summed up to get the gross national product figure, the result is what economists call the *nominal* GNP.[3] Nominal GNP data measure output in current prices.

Nominal GNP figures are important and useful, but we cannot use them if we want to compare one year with another. The reason is that from year to year the nominal figures reflect changes in prices as well as actual changes in production. Thus, we might find that the nominal GNP

2. The U.S. Department of Commerce publishes a monthly magazine, *The Survey of Current Business,* which contains extensive data on the GNP and related income and product measures. Another monthly publication, *Economic Indicators,* published by the Joint Economic Committee of the Congress, contains a wealth of current statistical information about the economy, including the latest GNP figures.
3. "Appropriate" in this sentence refers to what economists define as "final" goods and services. This means that in the adding up to get GNP figures, intermediate products purchased by business firms are not counted since their value is included in the price of the goods and services destined for sale to the ultimate user. For example, bread is a "final" product and its price covers the cost of wheat and flour which in adding up purchases would result in "double-counting," and an overstatement of the amount of actual production taking place.

for a particular year was greater than the previous year only because prices had risen, there being no change in actual production. For comparisons over time we need a measure of GNP that has removed from it any changes in the prices of the goods services which enter into the output total. This is called the *real* gross national product. It is a measure of actual production that is not distorted by any change in prices. Each year expenditures are calculated in prices for a particular year, known as the *base year.* When this is done we have a GNP figure in constant prices, or a measure of real GNP.

To illustrate the difference between nominal and real GNP, consider the following figures for 1981 and 1982. In 1982, *nominal* GNP was $3,073 billion, a figure $119 billion higher than the *nominal* GNP of $2,954 in 1981. This looks like a rather impressive gain, but it is all due to the fact that prices in 1982 were 6 percent higher than in 1981. *Real* GNP figures show that what actually happened was a decline in output between 1981 and 1982. For example, *real* GNP in 1982, measured in the base year prices of 1972, was $1,485 billion, a figure slightly smaller than the *real* GNP of $1,514 billion (in 1972 prices) in 1981.[4] There was a sharp recession in 1982, which accounts for the fall in actual output, even though prices continued to climb during the year.

Potential GNP

There is yet another way to calculate national output that is of interest and value to economists. This is *potential* GNP. It is a measure (in *real* terms) of the goods and services that the economy would be capable of producing if the labor force were fully employed. There is no absolute or precise definition of "full employment," although it is generally interpreted as a situation in which people able and wanting to work are able to find jobs. In recent years labor has been regarded as fully employed if no more than 4 to 5.5 percent of the labor force is out of work. Thus, the measure of *potential* GNP will depend upon how "full employment" is defined. The question of the appropriate rate of unemployment for a "fully employed" economy is complex and controversial, as is the problem of computing an appropriate measure of potential output. We shall deal with these issues subsequently.

Potential GNP provides a useful benchmark against which we can evaluate the actual performance of the economy over a period of time. This is done in Figure 1–1, where *potential* GNP is shown as the solid, straight line, whereas *actual* GNP follows the broken line, a less stable path, characterized by ups and downs, or "boom" and "bust." The comparison between the paths of actual GNP and potential GNP indicates when there is slack in the economy, when the economy is overheated, and when the economy is growing in a nearly "normal" fashion. Figure 1–1, for example, shows clearly the effects of recessions, times when a

4. *Economic Indicators,* March 1983, p. 2.

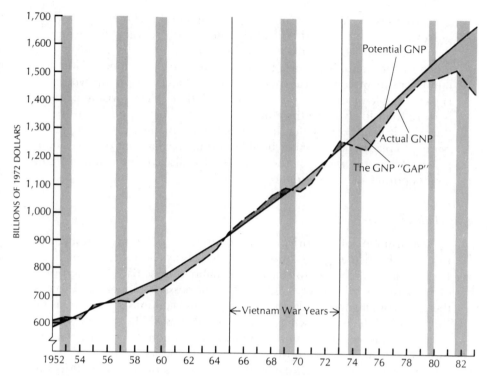

FIGURE 1–1. Actual and potential GNP: 1952–82

SOURCE: *Economic Report of the President,* 1977, 1981

sizable gap opens between actual and potential performance. In the figure the vertical shaded areas mark off the major recessions the economy has experienced since 1952. Equally evident from the diagram is the period of the Vietnam War, years in which *actual* output ran ahead of *potential.* This can happen for a short time because potential is not the economy's absolute maximum level of production; it is more like a norm that can be sustained year in and year out, given some growth in the labor force and regular improvement in productivity. In wartime it is always possible to extend the workweek, employ more shifts than in peacetime, and, in general, stretch productive capacity to its outer limits. But actual output cannot run ahead of *potential* output indefinitely.

The Price Level

A second major area of concern in macroeconomics involves prices. This is a matter of prices in general, not the prices for particular goods or services. The latter are the province of microeconomics. In recent years, interest in pricing behavior has focused on the inflation rate since a rising price level has existed in the American economy since the end of World War II. It has not always been this way; historically, there have been periods in American life when the general trend for prices was downward. In the second half of the nineteenth century, for example, the trend for prices was down, as it was during the 1920s. However, for much of the nation's history, the trend has been inflationary, and certainly for the immediate future it is not likely that the economy will experience a stable or declining price level. Inflation—that is, rising prices— is more than likely to be the rule rather than the exception. This being the case, it is important that economists not only measure what is happening to prices, but that they be able to explain what they observe about prices. Thus, the study of the price level is also an important part of contemporary macroeconomics.

Index Numbers

Measurement of the price level—in contrast to the measurement of prices for particular goods or services—has always presented difficulties. It is possible, of course, to collect reasonably precise data for the prices of particular goods or services. But it is not possible to measure directly the prices of all goods and services. To do this economists resort to using the statistical device known as an *index number*. Basically, an index number is a statistical device for comparing the amount by which one or more prices have changed over some specific period of time. As in the case of real GNP, a particular year is selected as the *base year*. Prices in all other years are measured as a percentage of the price in the base year. For example, suppose that in 1972—our assumed base year—the price of a bushel of wheat was $2.00, but we found that by 1982 this price had risen to $4.75 per bushel. To construct an index for the price of wheat, using 1972 as a base year, we divide the current year price ($4.75) by the price in the base year ($2.00) and multiply the result by 100. Thus, ($4.50 ÷ $2.00) × 100 = 237.5. The reason we multiply by 100 is to represent the price in the base year—1972 in this instance—as 100 (or 100 percent). The index tells us the relative change in a price (or prices) since the base year. To read an index number as a percentage change, simply drop 100 from the index for the year in question. In our example the 1981 index of 237.5 for a bushel of wheat means that wheat has gone up in price by 137.5 percent since 1972, the base year.

Construction of index numbers when a large number of prices are involved is a much more complex statistical problem, although the fundamental technique is essentially the same as just described. To construct an index for prices generally—the general price level—it is necessary to *weight* the various individual prices that enter into the index in accordance with their *relative* importance. Unless this is done, the resulting price index will not accurately reflect relative (or percentage) changes in the general level of all prices. For the construction of a complex price index such as that of the general price level, the two most important problems are these: First, there must be the proper selection of the individual goods and services (and their prices) that are to be included in the index;

second, appropriate weights must be assigned to each of the individual items making up the index. Once these knotty problems are solved, the actual computation of the index is relatively simple, even though the mathematics involved may be complex.

Consumer Price Index   Three major price indexes are used in the United States. They are reported on regularly by the press, including radio and television, and watched carefully by officials in government, key figures in business and industry, and ordinary citizens. The best known of these indexes is the *consumer price index*, or CPI. The CPI measures relative (or percentage) changes in the prices of a representative marketbasket of goods and services presumed to be typical of spending by approximately 80 percent of the population. This particular index has been in existence for more than 60 years, stretching back to a pioneer survey of expenditures by wage-earners and clerical workers made in 1917–19. Periodically, the index undergoes a major revision, the purpose being to update both groups included in the index and the marketbasket of goods and services purchased. The last such major revision took place in 1977–78, although there was another important revision in 1981. The latter changed the way in which housing costs enter into the index, a response to critics who argued that excessive weight was placed upon interest rates on new mortgages in computing the housing cost component in the index. This change went into effect in 1983, whereas the next major revision of the CPI is scheduled for 1985.

In 1982 the consumer price index was 289.1. This means that prices for the marketbasket of goods and services purchased by a consumer in 1982 were 189.1 percent higher than in the base year of 1967. To put it another way, this index tells us that it took, on the average, $289.10 in 1982 to purchase the same quantity of goods and services that $100 purchased in 1967. If prices rose by 189.1 percent between 1967 and 1980, it required an additional $189.10 over and above the original $100 necessary to get the same marketbasket of goods and services.

Producer Price Index   A second index, not quite so well-known as the CPI, but also important, is the *producer price index*. It measures, in fashion similar to the CPI, changes in prices for a vast array of commodities purchased, not by consumers or households, but by business firms. Typically, the commodities represented in the producer price index are raw materials entering into the manufacturing of other goods, capital equipment such as machinery and tools, or finished consumer goods acquired by business firms for ultimate resale to consumers and households. The producer price index covers prices for nearly 3,000 commodities, but unlike the CPI it does not include services. This index formerly was called the wholesale price index. Since prices for the commodities included in this index are reflected eventually in the prices of goods and services sold at retail, many economists view changes in producer prices as forerunners for later changes in the general level of consumer prices. This, though, is not a hard and fast rule.

Implicit GNP Deflator   The third important price index, also less well-known to the general public than the CPI, is called the *implicit GNP deflator*. This measure of price changes is obtained by dividing the nominal GNP figure in a particular year by its constant price value in the same year. The result tells us how much the prices of *all* the goods and services entering into gross national product have changed as compared to prices in the base year used in the determination of *real* GNP. For example, nominal GNP in 1982 was $3,073 billion; its value in 1972 prices was $1,485. The ratio of *nominal* to *real* value is 2.07, which means that prices for all the goods and services that make up the GNP figure rose by 107 percent between 1972 and 1982. Put another way, the implicit GNP deflator stood at 207 in 1982, using 1972 as 100. Because the gross national product is the most comprehensive measure of production we have, many economists regard the implicit GNP deflator as the best single measure of price changes available. However, it is neither as well-known nor as widely used as the consumer price index. It is the latter, for example, that is most often used in the process of "indexing" wage contracts, Social Security payments, and other transactions. *Indexing* refers to the process of adjusting the monetary value of a contractual obligation to reflect changes in the general price level. In many labor-union contracts it is common practice to provide for annual or semiannual adjustments in wage rates to reflect an increase in the cost of living as measured by changes in the consumer price index. These are called COLAs, an acronym for "cost-of-living adjustments."

Responsibility for compiling the consumer and producer price indexes rests with the Bureau of Labor Statistics in the U.S. Department of Labor. These indexes are issued monthly. When the Bureau of Labor Statistics issues its monthly report on consumer and producer prices, it not only reports on the most recent value for the index, it also reports the percentage change in the index over the preceding month. This figure is also reported on an annual rate, thereby giving the public some idea of how rapidly consumer and producer prices are changing at the time the figures are released.

Employment and Unemployment

The third major area of measurement for the economy's performance is employment and unemployment. As with output and pricing figures, economists use a variety of measures to determine how effectively the economy is performing in the realm of jobs. Ever since the catastrophic experience of the 1930s—the decade of the "Great Depression" more than half a century ago—the American public has worried about unemployment. Consequently, the federal government's Bureau of Labor Statistics produces an abundance of data on who is working and who is not working.

Unemployment Rate

The best-known measure of performance in the jobs area is the *unem-ployment rate*. This is the percentage of the civilian labor force actually unemployed at a particular time. Like the indexes for consumer and producer prices, this figure is computed by the Bureau of Labor Statistics and published on both a monthly and an annual basis. In 1982, to illustrate, the unemployment rate was 9.5 percent, which meant that on the average during the year approximately 10.7 million Americans were without jobs.

Labor Force Participation Rate

Unemployment depends not only upon the number of people who want jobs but are not working, but also on the size of the civilian labor force. To be in the labor force means to be working or actively seeking work. The size of the labor force is not a fixed figure, but depends ultimately upon the size and age structure of the nation's population. Economists regard the noninstitutionalized population of 16 years of age and older as the pool, so to speak, from which the labor force comes. The proportion of this population making up the actual labor force varies with time, circumstance, and custom. For example, women of all ages, including married women with children, are much more a part of the labor force now than was the case even a quarter of a century ago. Economic conditions also determine this proportion; in good times it may rise, and in bad times it may fall. The latter happens because the lack of jobs causes some people to drop out of the labor force. The Bureau of Labor Statistics calls such people "discouraged workers."

The proportion of the noninstitutionalized population aged 16 and over that is actually in the labor force at any particular time is called the *labor force participation rate*. In the post–World War II period there has been a persistent rise in this figure, climbing from 55.8 percent in 1946 to 64.3 percent in 1982. Primarily this has come about because of the increased participation by women in the labor force. In 1946, their *labor force participation rate* was 31.2 percent, but by 1982 it had reached 52.6 percent. In the same time span the rate for men declined from 82.6 to 76.6 percent.

Charting the Economy's Performance

The foregoing measures of output, prices, and unemployment provide the statistical basis for a series of graphic representations that show, sometimes quite dramatically, how the American economy has actually performed both recently and over the whole of this century. Note has already been taken in Figure 1–1 of the "gap"—sometimes negative but mostly positive—which opens up from time to time between the economy's potential for production and what it actually produces. Figure 1–1 also shows that the time path of real output is never smooth and, although we progress in the sense that real output grows over time, this progress is irregular, characterized by ups and downs. This is shown even more forcefully in Figures 1–2 and 1–3, both of which plot data on the national output since the beginning of the century.

Growth of GNP

Figure 1–2 traces *real* and *nominal* GNP from 1900 through 1980. Real GNP is measured in 1972 prices, the base year now used by the Department of Commerce. Note again that the course of growth is not smooth for either nominal or real GNP, both measures being marked by year-to-year fluctuations. Figure 1–2 also shows greater fluctuations in the

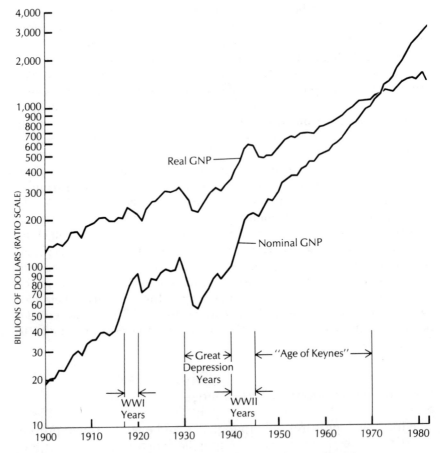

FIGURE 1–2.   Real and Nominal Gross National Product: 1900–82

SOURCE: *Historical Statistics of the United States* and *Economic Report of the President,* 1981

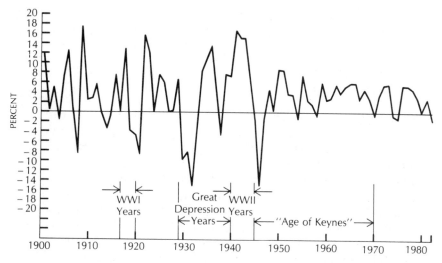

FIGURE 1–3. Annual Percentage Change in Real Gross National Product: 1900–82

SOURCE: *Historical Statistics of the United States* and *Economic Report of the President,* 1981

year-to-year values for *nominal* as compared to *real* GNP, something expected since the nominal figure includes price changes as well as actual output changes. Note also that prior to 1972 the nominal GNP curve lies *below* the real GNP line, which tells us that before 1972 the prices used to measure nominal GNP were lower than prices in 1972. After 1972 prices each year were higher than those of the 1972 base year.

In Figure 1–3 we look at the path of *real* GNP over the course of this century from a different perspective. These data tell us something important about the overall stability of the economic system. In this figure, annual rates of change in real GNP are plotted for every year since 1900. The figure is instructive in two respects. First, it shows more dramatically than either Figure 1–1 or 1–2 the extremes of year-to-year fluctuations in output that have been characteristic of the American economy's long-term performance. In some years output jumped by more than 15 percent, whereas in other years it dropped by almost as large a percentage. Second, it is clear from this figure that there has been a noticeable dampening down in the cyclical behavior of the economy in the post–World War II period. Whether or not this is the result of the active use of policy measures based upon the kind of macroeconomic knowledge and principles that are the subject of this text is disputed by some economists. Nevertheless, now there is more stability in the economy than there was before World War II. It is also worth noting that in the post–World War II period negative changes in *real* GNP were much less frequent and much less severe than in the pre-war era. This reflects the long post–World War II boom, a time when recessions were relatively mild and when prices, though moving up, did so at a relatively slow pace—at least until the 1970s. These years have been called the "Age of Keynes" by the distinguished British economist and Nobel laureate Sir John Hicks.[5]

Pattern of Price Changes

What happened to prices in the United States during this century? Like *real* output, they have been subject to turbulence and change, but the pattern of price changes differs significantly from that of the gross national product. Figures 1–4 and 1–5 tell the story of the price level over the past 80 years, using the *implicit GNP deflator* for this purpose. Long-term trends are shown in Figure 1–4, which plots the index of the implicit GNP deflator from 1900 through 1980; in this series, 1972 equals 100. Unlike the pre-1940 period for *real* GNP, prices were relatively stable during most of the 40 years from 1900 to 1940. World War I brought a sharp burst in the inflation rate, as have all previous wars in American history. This was followed by a collapse in prices after the war, although they did not fall entirely back to their pre-war level. The war, in other words, had a ratcheting effect on the price level.

The relative stability of pre-1940 prices ended with World War II. As Figure 1–4 shows in dramatic fashion, prices began rising in 1940 and they have continued to rise ever since. As a matter of fact, there was only one year (1949) in this 40-year span that the GNP deflator showed a decline—and this was less than 1 percent. If the 1930s can be characterized as the years of the Great Depression, it is possible to characterize the years after World War II, especially the 1970s, as the years of the "Great Inflation." Between 1940 and 1980 prices in the United States (as measured by the GNP deflator) underwent a sixfold increase. According to British economic historian E. H. Phelps Brown, there was only one other period in the last 1,000 years of economic history in Western nations when a comparable price explosion occurred. This was in the sixteenth century, an age characterized by the disintegration of feudalism, by the beginnings of capitalism and a commercial economy, and, above all, by a vast influx of gold and silver into Europe from the newly discovered lands of the Western Hemisphere.[6]

If we look at the inflation rate on an annual basis, however, we find similarities to the behavior of *real* GNP as shown in Figure 1–3. Annual percentage changes in the inflation rate (measured by the GNP deflator) are shown in Figure 1–5. These data, which tell much the same story as told by Figure 1–4 but from a different perspective, suggest several things. First, it is apparent there has been little year-to-year stability in prices, as is the case with *real* output. Second, before World War II there were enough downward movements offsetting upward movements in the price level so that—except for the experience of World War I—there was a

5. Sir John Hicks, *The Crisis in Keynesian Economics* (New York: Basic Books, 1974), p. 1.
6. E. H. Phelps Brown and Sheila V. Hopkins, "Seven Centuries of the Prices of Consumables Compared with Builders' Wage-Rates," *Economica*, November 1956, p. 305.

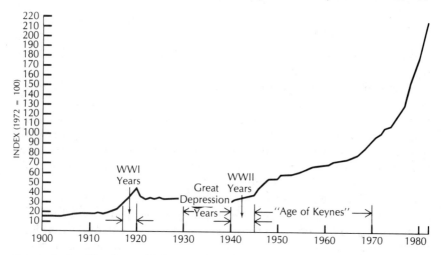

FIGURE 1–4. The General Price Level: 1900–82

SOURCE: *Historical Statistics of the United States* and *Economic Report of the President,* 1981

As measured by the implicit GNP deflator

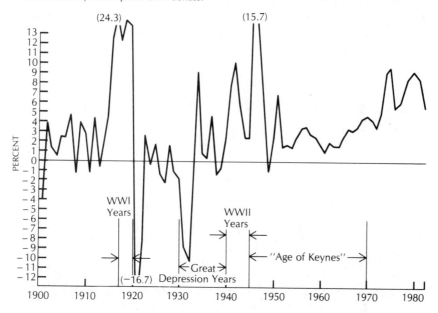

FIGURE 1–5. Annual Percentage Change in the Inflation Rate as measured by the Implicit GNP Deflator: 1900–82

SOURCE: *Historical Statistics of the United States* and *Economic Report of the President,* 1981

As measured by the implicit GNP deflator

rough overall stability in prices. Finally, Figure 1–5 shows that, since World War II, instability in pricing behavior still exists in the economy, but all the instability is upward. These data reinforce what is shown in Figure 1–4: a sharp acceleration in the inflation rate in the 1970s.

Fluctuation and Unemployment

Finally let us look at the economy's record on unemployment, in both the long and short term, and for specific groups within the economy. Figure 1–6 shows the unemployment rate for the civilian labor force from 1900 to 1980. Like all the other statistical series we have reviewed that relate to the economy's overall performance, this rate has fluctuated widely from year to year. Beyond this, however, these data underscore dramatically the impact of the Great Depression and war on jobs in the United States. At the depth of the depression in 1933, unemployment reached the staggering level of 24.9 percent of the nation's work force, a level of joblessness experienced neither before nor since in American history. Even in the worst post–World War II recession—the 1981–82 slump—unemployment never got over 11 percent. The other development noted by these data is that it has been primarily during wartime that unemployment has fallen below the band in the figure labeled "Full-Employment Zone." For most peacetime years, both before and after World War II, the unemployment rate has been higher than the 4–5 percent range designated by this band. Finally, these data show that since about 1950 there has been a slow, upward drift in the unemployment rate. This is shown by the dashed line in the figure labeled "Post–World War II Secular Trend."

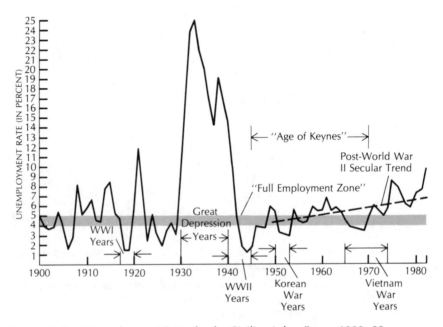

FIGURE 1–6.   Unemployment Rates for the Civilian Labor Force: 1900–82
Unemployment Rates (in percent)

SOURCE: *Historical Statistics of the United States* and *Economic Report of the President,* 1981

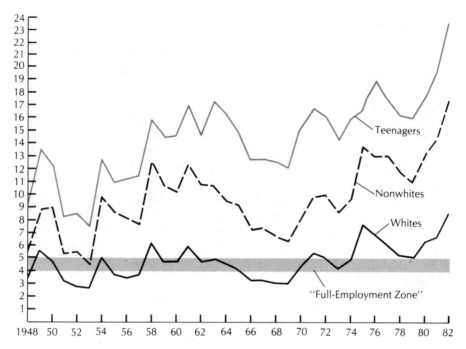

FIGURE 1–7.   Unemployment Rates for Whites, Non-Whites, and Teenagers: 1948–82

Source: *Economic Report of the President, 1981*

Designating unemployment in the range of 4–5 percent as the "Full-Employment Zone" raises a fundamental conceptual and policy question. Is there any agreed-upon measure among economists of full employment? A tentative answer is no, but this is a matter that we shall explore further in Chapter 3. If we accept for the moment the notion that "full employment" lies between 4 and 5 percent as shown in Figure 1–6, another fact emerges from data on unemployment. This is that certain segments of our society have never experienced anything remotely resembling "full employment," by whatever standard it is measured. Even the most conservative economists would hesitate to call unemployment rates in excess of 6 percent "full employment." Yet for blacks and other minorities, not to mention teenagers, this has been the reality throughout the post–World War II period. Figure 1–7 compares unemployment rates since 1948 for whites, nonwhites, and teenagers.

The Meaning of the Data

What conclusions can we draw about the performance of the American economy from our examination of the foregoing data on output, prices, and unemployment? First, examination of these data show clearly that turbulence is the rule in American economic life. It is true, of course, that the economy has been buffeted by noneconomic developments throughout the century, especially by two world wars. But in spite of wars and other upheavals, such as the Arab oil embargo of the early 1970s, the path of the economy is rarely smooth. This is our first conclusion. Second, a close reading of the data shows that recently a new and highly disturbing development has entered the picture. Beginning approximately in the mid 1960s, the economy experienced *simultaneously* high levels of inflation and high levels of unemployment, a condition often described by the ugly word "stagflation," meaning a stagnant economy with rising prices. Throughout the 1970s, this situation worsened as both the underlying basic inflation and unemployment rates drifted upward. Figure 1–8 shows this development. Its persistence is one of the unsolved and challenging problems confronting contemporary macroeconomic theory. Inflation, it is true, was down sharply in late 1983, a consequence of the 1981–82 recession. There is no assurance, however, that the rate will not rise again, once another economic boom is under way.

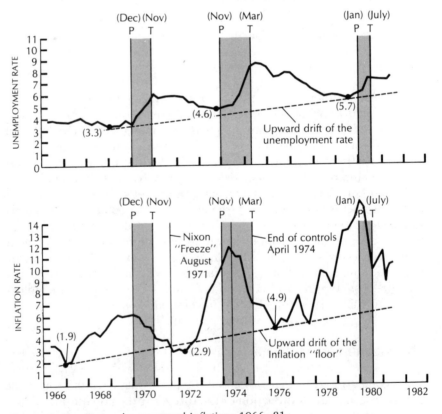

FIGURE 1–8. Unemployment and Inflation: 1966–81.

SOURCE: *Economic Report of the President* and *Business Conditions Digest*

This brings us back to the nature of our subject—what macroeconomics is all about. What we are seeking are answers to the problems suggested by the trends we have just examined. Why is it that the economy behaves in such an irregular fashion? What are the causes of simultaneous inflation and unemployment? What can we do about these conditions? Can the economy's performance be improved?

We look to macroeconomic theory to provide us with some answers and some guides to workable policy decisions. Since macroeconomics is an organized body of knowledge pertaining to an important area of human activity, it is essential that we understand clearly the kind of knowledge that we are dealing with. Put succinctly, macroeconomic theory entails a quest for scientific knowledge, for the discovery of broad and enduring principles which truly explain the facts that we have observed.

On the Nature of Science

There is no exact, absolute definition for the word *science*. In its most general sense, science has to do with the process of knowing; the Latin root *scire* of our modern English word *science* means "to know." But "to know" implies understanding, which means "to be able to explain." This definition of science, while technically correct, does not go far enough; we need to know in a more specific way how science seeks to achieve understanding.

Classification

Understanding involves, first, the classification of things, or phenomena, and second, the discovery or observation of uniformities among the phenomena so classified. Classification, the oldest form of scientific activity, attempts to bring order to the universe by seeking out similarities between things and placing them in groups, each group being designated by a name or symbol which is representative of all things brought into it. Classification is a necessary first step toward understanding; it provides the basis for the creative act of finding relationships between phenomena, which lies at the heart of all scientific activity. Professor Jacob Bronowski describes this creative act as being the discovery of hidden likenesses in facts or experiences that are separate. In such facts or experiences the scientist "finds a likeness which had not been seen before; and he creates a unity by showing the likeness."[7]

Generalization

The act of discovery means the establishment of meaningful generalizations (that is, general statements) pertaining to relationships between

7. J. Bronowski, *Science and Human Values* (New York: Julian Messner, 1956), p. 35.

phenomena. Such generalizations are meaningful in the sense that they attempt to explain phenomena in the world by linking them together in a cause and effect relationship. The construction of such generalizations, or laws, is the essence of scientific activity.

Scientific laws are formulated as "if . . . , then . . ." propositions, which is to say that they assert that some event or thing will happen if certain conditions are present or satisfied. Scientific generalizations, in other words, explain because they describe a causal relationship between phenomena. A note of caution is in order here: Causation should not be confused with correlation, although this happens at times. Correlation is a statistical concept that involves a relationship between two variables such that the value of one is *uniquely* related to the value of the other. It is well known, for example, that a correlation exists between the price of a good and the quantity sold (the economic "law" of demand). Correlation, however, does not reveal anything about the reasons (that is, the causes) for a relationship. Causation is nearly always complex and difficult to ascertain. Even though an observable statistical relationship may exist between phenomena, the causal significance of such a relationship is not always readily apparent. In the last analysis, attributing a particular cause to a particular effect requires the exercise of the most careful kind of judgment. For example, in the matter of the relationship between price of a good and quantity sold, causation tends to run from price to sales. How do we know? Only careful study of the actual behavior of buyers in real markets indicates that buyers generally respond to price and not the other way around.

To say that scientific laws are essentially "if . . . , then . . ." propositions means that all such laws consist of two parts. The if part implies that scientific laws rest upon certain assumptions concerning the data under investigation. For example, it is a well-accepted principle of physics that all bodies fall at a constant rate of acceleration: approximately 32 feet per second. But this is true only if the body is falling freely in a vacuum. In this instance the assumption serves to specify the conditions under which the physical law of falling bodies is valid.

The second part of any scientific law consists of the conclusion derived by the process of logic from the basic assumption or postulates. Mathematics often enters the picture at this point, since all sciences use mathematics to some degree in the process of drawing conclusions from a set of assumptions. The use of mathematics, though, should not obscure the fact that the essential activity at this stage of the scientific process involves logic.

Validity

How do we determine whether or not a particular scientific law is valid? Validity depends upon the correct use of logic in deriving conclusions from a given set of assumptions. If the rules of logic are not applied correctly, a generalization will not have validity, irrespective of the merit of its underlying assumptions. More important, a generalization must succeed in explaining that which it sets out to explain. Its conclusions must be compatible with the observed behavior of the data under investigation. Empirical observation is, in other words, the final test of the validity, or truth, of any scientific theory. This means that a scientific principle should predict what will happen under a stipulated set of circumstances, but it does not mean that such a principle must be an exact and detailed mirror of the real world. Experience can never conclusively prove a generalization to be absolutely right; there will always remain the possibility that a different generalization might explain better the situation under investigation. What empirical observation does show is that the conclusions reached in a scientific principle are (or are not) in accordance with the facts of reality.

Realism in the Assumptions

Does the validity of the principle require that its assumptions be realistic? This, unfortunately, is a question that cannot be given a categorical yes or no answer. In one sense, the answer is no, for, as we have already seen, the formal validity of the principle is a matter solely of its logical derivation from the underlying assumptions, irrespective of the degree of realism present in the latter. Moreover, the question of exactly what constitutes realism is not easily resolved. To illustrate, let us recall once again the physical principle that governs the acceleration of falling bodies. Strictly speaking, the underlying assumption of the principle can hardly be termed realistic, as we rarely find a vacuum existing in the real world. But we know that conditions approximating this assumption often do exist in the real world; therefore the principle does explain the behavior of the falling bodies. What we seek is reasonable accuracy in both assumptions and generalizations.

Economics as a Science

What is the basis for the claim that economics is a scientific discipline? The primary objective of economic study is development of generalizations—or theories—that explain relationships between economic phenomena. Like all scientific generalizations, economic theories are basically "if . . . , then . . ." statements to which a causal significance is imparted. Thus, given our contention that the key characteristic of scientific activity is the discovery of generalizations that explain the why of things, economics is entitled to scientific standing.

Since economics concerns itself with human behavior, some may wonder if it is really possible to have a science of economics. Is it not true that human behavior is, more often than not, wholly capricious? Many persons would argue that man is a free agent and thus uniquely different from all other natural objects, living or inanimate. Under such circumstances, how can useful predictions be made about such an uncertain thing as human behavior?

At first it might seem that the obvious answer is that one cannot make such predictions, but a little reflection should convince us that such an answer is too glib and superficial. It is possible to generalize about human behavior because when human beings live together in organized society they behave most of the time in orderly—and predictable—ways. If they did not, chaos would result and civilized living as we know it would be impossible. Think about the extent to which the successful completion of your daily activities depends upon the assumption that the scores of people you have contact with each day will behave in a predictable fashion. A simple example is the use of red, green, and yellow lights to control the flow of automobile traffic.

The behavior patterns characteristic of civilized societies manifest themselves in a multitude of ways, ranging from simple customs, or folkways, such as the wearing of particular types of clothing, to highly complex organizational arrangements for achieving the political, economic, or religious ends of a society. Whether the behavior patterns of a society are simple or complex, it is the business of the economist, as well as other social scientists, to develop generalizations that seek to describe and explain these patterns of behavior.

A useful notion that pervades most economic analysis is that of *maximizing* behavior. Essentially, it means that human beings will act in such a way as to maximize what they perceive as their economic well-being. Thus, the businessman tries to maximize profits, the worker his or her wages, and the consumer the satisfaction to be obtained from the consumption of goods and services. Adam Smith, the founder of modern economic analysis, commented on this propensity a long while ago. "Every individual," he said, "is continually exerting himself to find out the most advantageous employment for whatever capital he can employ. It is his own advantage, indeed, and not to that of society which he has in view."[8] Smith's language is a bit quaint, coming as it does from the eighteenth century, but the meaning is unmistakable. If the word "resources" (including labor power) is substituted for Smith's "capital" in the foregoing sentence, we have a clear statement of the maximizing idea. A *caveat* is in order, however. The maximizing notion is one of those assumptions found so frequently in economics that have a useful role to play, but which are not literally true (recall our discussion on realism in assumptions earlier in this chapter).

Before leaving this question, it is necessary to say something about the problems posed for economics as a science by the assumption that a human being is a free agent. We cannot resolve the philosophical problem of

8. Adam Smith, *The Wealth of Nations* (New York: Random House, 1937), p. 421.

whether or not people possess free will. We need to recognize as a practical matter, however, that people are thinking beings and that this has some vital consequences for economic study. Because we have the power of thought, and because, too, we can learn from experience, we are able to bring about change in society. Put differently, humans do establish new behavior patterns. Therefore, a given set of conditions may not produce the same response at one time and place as they do at another.

The foregoing makes prediction in economics and the other social sciences inherently more risky than it is in the natural or physical sciences, but it precludes neither the fact that there are uniformities in human behavior nor the possibility that such uniformities can be discovered. Economics must develop generalizations concerning economic behavior and make use of the predictive character of all such generalizations. The student of economics should remember that humans, because they possess the power to think, can if they so choose take cognizance of the predictive element embodied in a generalization and by so doing modify the outcome. This fact does not change the basic character of economics as a scientific discipline, but it does mean that economics is much less exact than such sciences as physics and chemistry.

Abstraction and Economics

The object of all scientific inquiry is to understand, not simply to reproduce or reconstruct reality. The world of reality is a complex of forces so vast that no one could possibly comprehend all their interrelationships. If progress is to be made toward the understanding of reality, it is essential to simplify the complexities of the real world. We can do this by directing our investigation toward the forces, or factors, believed to be of strategic importance for an understanding of how things do work in the real world. This is nothing less than the process of abstraction. Thus, economic theories are not detailed, photographically faithful reproductions of a portion of the real world, but are, rather, simplified portraits whose purpose is to make the real world intelligible.

It is important to understand that abstraction is a characteristic of theory in any discipline, including the biological and physical sciences. The major difference between the social sciences and the natural sciences is not in the degree of abstraction, but in the fact that the social sciences are generally unable to resort to a laboratory to determine the validity of their principles. We shall return to a discussion of this point shortly.

Functional Relationships in Economics

An important characteristic of economic generalizations concerns the form in which these generalizations or principles are presented. Since the economic aspects of human behavior usually are reflected in economic quantities, such as prices, outputs, incomes, and wage rates, economic principles can be stated in mathematical form. The most common practice in this respect is to express the principles of economics in the form of a *functional relationship* between economic variables.

The idea of a functional relationship between economic quantities is essential to an understanding of the nature of economic analysis. In fact, this is perhaps the most important concept the reader can grasp. If one fully and clearly understands the nature of the functional idea, the way to a thorough comprehension of economic analysis is open. A *functional relationship exists between two variables when they are related in such a way that the value of one depends uniquely upon the value of the other.* Such a relationship can be expressed in equation form as follows:

$$y = f(x). \tag{1-1}$$

An equation of this form reads "*y* is a function of *x*." It means, simply, that the variable represented by the letter *y* is related in a systematic and dependable way to the value of the variable represented by the letter *x*.

The concept of a functional relationship enables us to express symbolically (that is, in mathematical form) the essence of a particular economic theory. For example, the economic law of demand can be expressed in equation form as

$$Q_d = f(P), \tag{1-2}$$

which means that the quantity demanded for a particular commodity is a function of its price. By itself the above equation does not tell us anything more than that quantity and price are linked together in a systematic and dependable relationship. Knowledge of the exact nature of the relationship between these two variables requires more information than can be obtained from the equation alone, a point to which we shall return subsequently.

Although the functional concept is an important tool for economic analysis, there are limitations inherent in the concept that must be appreciated if it is to be used effectively. In the first place, the fact that two variables are related to one another in a functional sense does not mean that the one is the *cause* of the other. Cause is not easily determined. To determine cause requires keen judgment and a broad knowledge of the situation under study. The law of demand provides an excellent example of the need for the careful exercise of judgment. The mathematical expression of this law simply tells us that the variables, quantity demanded and price, have a measurable and dependable relationship to one another. For a clear understanding of the nature of this relationship we must be aware of the behavior of buyers in a market situation More precisely, we must know whether the quantity demanded varies as the price varies or, conversely, whether price varies as quantity demanded varies. If we can answer this, we will be in a position to say something about the *causal* relationship that may exist between these variables. Since we are discussing the behavior of buyers in a market situation and not the behavior of suppliers of the commodity in question, the reasonable conclusion is that buyers vary their purchases in accordance with changes in price. But this says that, in the equation, quantity demanded (Q_d) is the dependent variable, and price (P) is the independent variable. Quantity demanded varies (inversely) with price and not the other way around. If we say this, does it not also mean that we have identified price as the immediate—although not necessarily sole— *cause* of the quantity demanded by buyers? In a common-sense meaning of the word *cause* the answer to this question obviously is yes.

A second important aspect of the functional idea is that a particular variable may be a function of a number of other variables. For example, to say that the quantity demanded of a commodity is a function of its price does not mean that the quantity demanded cannot at the same time be a function of variables besides price. In the case of the law of demand, many things besides price affect a buyer's decision as to the amounts of any specific good he will purchase at any particular time. Thus, we might say that the quantity demanded of a good is a function not only of price, but of the buyer's income, the price of other goods, the buyer's expectations as to future prices, and a host of other factors.

The fact that an important economic magnitude may be functionally linked to a number of variables presents a difficult problem for economic analysis, particularly when some of the variables cannot be quantified. The usual way in which economists solve this problem is to resort to the device of *ceteris paribus,* "other things are equal." This procedure involves analysis of the relationship between two or more variables on the basis of the assumption that all other variables that might influence the outcome of the situation remain constant. This is a kind of intellectual equivalent to the laboratory procedure that is commonly followed by the physical or biological scientist. The investigator seeks to analyze in isolation the relationship between the variables or factors believed to have the most strategic significance in determining the value of the phenomena under investigation. A clear exposition of the nature of *ceteris paribus* is found in the following statement by Alfred Marshall:

> It is sometimes said that the laws of economics are "hypothetical." Of course, like every other science, it undertakes to study the effects which will be produced by certain causes, not absolutely, but subject to the condition that *other things are equal,* and that the causes are able to work out their effects undisturbed. Almost every scientific doctrine, when carefully and formally stated, will be found to contain some proviso to the effect that other things are equal: the action of the causes in question is supposed to be isolated; certain effects are attributed to them, but only on the hypothesis that no cause is permitted to enter except those distinctly allowed for.[9]

Verification in Economics

Earlier we pointed out that the ultimate test of *any* scientific generalization is reality—an appeal to the facts of experience. This applies to

9. Alfred Marshall, *Principles of Economics,* 8th ed. (London: Macmillan, 1925), p. 36.

economics no less than it does to all sciences. In many of the biological and physical sciences it is possible to test the validity of a scientific proposition by controlled experiments in a laboratory setting. The merit of the controlled experiment is that, by rigidly regulating the conditions under which a particular event takes place, the investigator can isolate the effects of a change in any one of the factors that enter into the situation under study. Verification of a particular hypothesis is achieved through the repetition of the experiment until sufficient experience is accumulated to either sustain or disprove the hypothesis.

In the sciences that concern themselves with the group behavior of human beings, the strict application of the controlled experiment as a means of verifying hypotheses is usually impossible. This is because the social scientist normally cannot bring a part of society into the laboratory and re-create experience over and over again under strictly identical conditions. In the social sciences, consequently, evidence for the validity of a generalization depends most of the time, as John Stuart Mill said, on "the limited number of experiments which take place (if we may so speak) of their own accord, without any preparation or management of ours; in circumstances, moreover, of great complexity and never perfectly known to us."[10] Mill's "limited number of experiments" are to be found in recorded facts of human experience, statistical and historical, and it becomes the task of the economist or social scientist to search patiently through the complex fabric of events of the real social world for necessary evidence to verify his generalizations. This task is not as hopeless as it may first appear, for, as Professor Milton Friedman has pointed out, experience does provide us with an abundance of evidence, although the interpretation of this evidence is at once more difficult and less dramatic than that arrived at by the controlled experiment.[11] In spite of the difficulties that economics may present with respect to verification, the final and necessary test of the validity of any economic generalization is observed reality.

The Use of Models in Economic Analysis

When a number of economic generalizations expressed as functional relationships are brought together, the result is an economic *model*. Most people are familiar with the idea of a model as a physical representation,

10. John Stuart Mill, *Essays on Some Unsettled Questions of Political Economy* (London: Longmans, Green, 1877), p. 147. Experimentation is not wholly impossible in economics, however. During the first half of the 1970s the federal government sponsored a series of experiments to determine the effect of a guaranteed income (a "negative income tax") on work incentives and the reduction of poverty. Findings indicated no significant reduction in the number of family heads holding jobs or seeking work because of an income guarantee. This was not a controlled, laboratory experiment in the strict sense of the term, but controls were in effect during the experiment. They were designed to isolate as nearly as possible the effects of an income guarantee on work incentives.
11. Milton Friedman, *Essays in Positive Economics* (Chicago: University of Chicago Press, 1953), p. 10.

a replica in miniature of something that exists or can be observed. Anyone who has visited a planetarium has seen a model of the solar system. Almost everyone is familiar with model airplanes and model cars. Less familiar, perhaps, is the idea of a nonphysical representation, or model, of something as large, complex, and intangible as the economic system. Yet, this is quite possible, and, increasingly, models of varying degrees of complexity are being used to represent many facets of the economy, including the entire national economy.

What is an economic model? As the term suggests, it is a representation of all or part of the economy. An economic model usually involves representation in mathematical form of the way in which the various parts of the economy are interrelated. The mathematical form for a model may be either geometric or algebraic. The kind of diagram found in any elementary text that shows how an equilibrium price is established by the intersection of supply and demand schedules is an example of a simple economic model presented in geometric form. In this case, the model is that of the market process.

An economic model is expected to show the relationships that exist between measurable economic magnitudes. These are called *variables* because they are capable of changing. Any magnitude which is assumed to remain constant is termed a *parameter*. Such models should have the ability to predict the change in a particular economic variable as a result of change in one or more other economic variables.

Technically, the mathematical equations which show the relationships believed to exist between the economic variables constitute the *structure* of the model. Specific numerical values for any of the constants (or parameters) which appear in the equations are estimated from actual, historical data. For example, econometric models that depict the whole economy usually show that consumption spending is a fixed proportion of income. The coefficient (parameter) which shows this proportion is estimated from the ratio between consumption and income in the past.[12]

In macroeconomics, econometric models have grown rapidly in number and complexity in recent years. Some of the econometric models now in use are of such complexity that they may include three hundred or more equations. What is important to understand, though, is that the role of equations in an econometric model is to specify in algebraic terms the relationships that make up the model. In the United States, econometric models of the American economy have been developed by such diverse groups as the Federal Reserve Board, the President's Council of Economic Advisers, the Bureau of Economic Analysis of the U.S. Department of Commerce, the Brookings Institution (a private research organization in Washington, D.C.), and academic economists at many of our major public and private universities.

Irrespective of their complexity, all econometric models have certain

12. This does not mean that consumption spending cannot be related to other variables besides income. The relationship that may exist between consumption and any other variables would have to be estimated separately, again using actual, historical data.

features in common. First, and no matter how many equations they embrace, they are still abstractions—simplifications of the real world. Putting more equations into a model does not change this basic fact. Second, the variables in an econometric model are characterized as either *exogenous* or *endogenous*. An exogenous variable is one whose value is determined by relationships which lie outside the model, whereas an endogenous variable is one whose value is determined by the relationships that lie within the model. Finally, an econometric model may be *closed* or *open*. It is closed in a mathematical sense if the number of equations and the number of variables are equal, but it is open whenever the number of equations is less than the number of variables. When the number of equations and the number of endogenous variables are equal, the model can be solved mathematically by the method of simultaneous equations. For models with a large number of equations, the use of a computer is an obvious necessity.

The elements of an economic model can be illustrated simply by an example from elementary economics: the well-known proposition that the price of any good or service is determined by the interaction between demand and supply schedules. Such a model of market price determination can be formulated in terms of the following equations:

$$Q_d = f(P),\qquad\qquad (1-3)$$
$$Q_s = f(P),\qquad\qquad (1-4)$$
$$Q_d = Q_s.\qquad\qquad (1-5)$$

The first two equations specify the relationships involved in the model, namely, that quantity demanded is a function of price and quantity supplied is a function of price. The third equation specifies that in equilibrium the market will be cleared, which is to say that there is some price at which quantity demanded and quantity supplied are equal. Since there are three equations and three unknown endogenous variables—Q_d, Q_s, and P—the model is complete and capable of solution.

The use of models in economic analysis—especially mathematical models—is fraught with several dangers. Since the relationships specified in the model depend upon what happened in the past, a model may suggest a continuity in economic events that does not really exist. Statistical trends are necessary and useful for understanding the past and forecasting ahead, but we should not lose sight of the fact that they are in a sense artificial. History is not a smooth trend line; it is a series of discontinuous and unique events. Second, a model may give a misleading impression of greater constancy in economic relationships than experience justifies. Economic generalizations—or theories—do show us what will happen under specific circumstances, but we must not forget that in the real world economic circumstances are never exactly the same because the economy moves forward through time. Finally, models may become "frozen" as reality moves on and the model remains unchanged.

For an economic model to be useful, it must reflect the reality of the economic structure.

Let us add one further word of caution with respect to the use of the functional concept and models in economic analysis. Reducing economic generalizations to the form of a functional relationship between quantitative magnitudes suggests more precision in our knowledge of economic behavior than is really the case. Mathematics is a precise discipline, and its use in conjunction with economic analysis may be misleading. We have already observed that the generalizations of economics and the social sciences are usually less exact than those of the physical or biological sciences. This does not prevent us from using mathematics in economic analysis, but it does require that we guard ourselves against the temptation to view the principles of economics as a set of exact relationships akin to the laws of physics or chemistry. We should also be on guard against another danger, which is the temptation to view the medium—mathematics—in which the economy's structure often is explained as the reality. Models are sometimes elegant in their construction and design, but we should not try to force reality into the confines of a model simply to preserve that elegance.

Economic Analysis, Economic Policy, and Value Judgments

Any discussion of the nature of economics would be inadequate without consideration of the policy aspects of economics. The word *policy* refers to some course of action that is designed to realize or bring about some specific objective or end. Policy is concerned with what we want and how we get it. Economic policy thus has to do with the means that individuals, groups, or a whole society may utilize to achieve ends or objectives that are primarily of an economic nature.

Since economic policy is concerned with the ends or objectives of society, it involves *value judgments;* it is concerned with questions of what ought to be. It is important that the significance of value judgments be recognized, for individuals and groups usually have deeply held convictions about the economy and how things ought to be, and such convictions profoundly affect their behavior. Value judgments concerning the proper ends of economic activity are important, too, because they are the source of much that is controversial in economics. Disagreement in economics stems not so much from disagreement over the economic objectives being sought, but over the appropriate means for the realization of these ends.

With this understanding of the nature of economic policy and its significance as a source of controversy in economics, we are prepared to discuss the relation of economic analysis to economic policy. Once again a word of warning is in order, for economists are not in agreement among themselves as to the manner in which these two facets of economics are related to one another. This being the case, we shall begin by describing briefly the major positions that economists hold with respect to the relationship between economic analysis and economic policy.

Positive versus Normative Economics

At one extreme of the spectrum of possible attitudes is the positivist view that economic analysis and economic policy are two separate aspects of economics which simply cannot be mixed. This particular point of view asserts that economics is a positive science, which means it is an activity that concerns itself *only* with the discovery of generalizations of the kind we described earlier; it is completely divorced from any consideration of values. John Neville Keynes, in his classic work *The Scope and Method of Political Economy*, defined a positive science as "a body of systematized knowledge concerning what is," and contrasted it with a normative, or regulative, science, which he defined as "a body of systematized knowledge discussing the criteria of what ought to be, and concerned therefore with the ideal as distinguished from the actual."[13] Professor Friedman asserts that "positive economics is in principle independent of any particular ethical position or normative judgments."[14] In sum, the positivist view holds that the economist must, if he is to retain his claim to scientific objectivity, confine his activities to the discovery of significant relationships among economic phenomena and remain scrupulously neutral toward ends or goals of society.

It is doubtful that all economists today accept without reservation the positivist view of the nature and scope of economics. For one thing it is argued that values cannot be separated from analysis because economics is a social science and the social sciences possess significance only to the extent that they contribute to the solution of real social problems. If this is a valid contention, it means that economists and other social scientists can hardly avoid becoming involved in some fashion with the ends or goals of the society of which they are a part. The reader will recognize, of course, that this particular attitude is itself a value judgment, but it is one, nevertheless, that many competent economists share. For example, the late Professor John H. Williams, a former president of the American Economic Association, once stated, "Economic theorizing seems to me pointless unless it is aimed at what to do. All the great theorists, I think, have had policy as their central interest, even if their policy were merely laissez faire."[15]

A viewpoint like that of Williams does not necessarily refute the posi-

13. John Neville Keynes, *The Scope and Method of Political Economy* (London: Macmillan, 1891), p. 34. J. N. Keynes was the father of John Maynard Keynes.
14. Friedman, *Essays in Positive Economics*, p. 4.
15. John H. Williams, "An Economist's Confessions," *American Economic Review*, March 1952, p. 10.

tivist position that economic analysis can be neutral in the sense of being completely detached from value judgments, but it suggests that such an economics, if it really could exist, might be a barren discipline.

The phrase "if it really could exist" brings us to the second major reason why some economists assert that economic analysis cannot truly be free of value judgments. The more fundamental objection to the positivist viewpoint is that values are inevitably a part of the analytical techniques employed by the economist. Value judgments are, so to speak, built into economic analysis to such an extent that it is vain to expect that economics can be a science completely detached from all value considerations.

The questions raised concerning relationships between economic analysis and economic policy are difficult ones for which no final or definitive answers exist. Objectivity and the role of values in economic analysis are matters that should not be taken lightly. It is important to keep in mind that economic theory—especially macroeconomic theory of the kind discussed in this text—always involves perceptions of how the economic world actually works. Most economists strive to be objective, to be scientific, but the fact remains that there are different ways of approaching the subject, that economists vary in their perspectives. The viewpoint favored in this text is that economics is not a *pure* science, detached from the great issues of public policy in our time. In itself this also is a value judgment. But it arises out of the conviction that economics is worthwhile and deserving of public support *only* to the extent that it can contribute in a meaningful way to the solution of real and pressing human problems.

Origins of Contemporary Macroeconomic Theory

Economists are in much less agreement today than they were 10 to 15 years ago on the nature of the theoretical relationships that explain the aggregate behavior of the economy. Economic turbulence in recent years plus the absence of a consensus on the kind of policies necessary to cope with inflation, unemployment, and sagging productivity have led to a search for new explanations, new insights into the workings of the economy.

The antecedents of modern macroeconomic theory stretch well back into the nineteenth century—and even earlier. It is not correct to say that a formal body of macroeconomic analysis existed prior to the mid-1930s, but it is correct to say that important ideas existed before then about how the economy in the aggregate worked. Two such ideas are of special significance, particularly because they have reappeared in recent years in modern dress as important challenges to what was until relatively recently the dominant theoretical approach in macroeconomics.

These ideas are Say's "Law of Markets" and the classical quantity theory of money. A brief explanation of each is in order.

Say's Law of Markets

Say's "Law of Markets" is named after Jean Baptiste Say, a French economist of the early nineteenth century who disseminated and popularized the ideas of Adam Smith in France and elsewhere on the European continent. His law is the formal expression of the idea that widespread and involuntary unemployment because of general overproduction is impossible. To put the matter slightly differently, there cannot be any involuntary unemployment because of a deficiency of total demand. The simplest possible statement of this doctrine is that "supply creates its own demand." The meaning of this statement is that in some sense the whole of the costs of production must necessarily be spent in the aggregate, directly or indirectly, on purchasing the product. Every producer who brings goods to the market (that is, creates supply) does so in order to exchange them for other goods (that is, creates demand). Consequently, every act of production must necessarily represent the demand for something.

The conclusion that follows from the assertion that all supply is potentially the demand for something is that there cannot be any general overproduction or deficiency of total demand for the economy as a whole. True, there may be some misdirection of production and therefore an oversupply of some commodities, but the pricing mechanism will correct this and cause some entrepreneurs to shift their output to other and more profitable lines. But such oversupply cannot be the case for the whole economy because the act of production always creates sufficient value or purchasing power to take off the market all goods and services produced. If there cannot be deficiency of total demand in the economy, it also follows that involuntary unemployment because of overproduction is impossible. Say's law is of more than historic interest because it is also the foundation of contemporary supply-side economics, a part of the theoretical foundation for the Reagan administration's program for economic recovery.

Quantity Theory of Money

The second idea of importance is the quantity theory of money, one whose ultimate lineage can be traced back to Jean Bodin (another Frenchman) in the sixteenth century and which runs almost straight down to the 1980s and the contemporary monetary views of Milton Friedman. Simply put, the quantity theory of money (nineteenth-century version) holds that the prime determinant of the price level is the supply of money. In equation form, the quantity theory says that $p = f(M)$, p being the general level of prices and M being the money supply. The classical quantity theory is a natural corollary to Say's law of markets, because if the economy works so that full utilization of resources is the normal state of affairs, the only economic variable that the money supply can affect is the price level. There is more to the quantity theory than this, as we shall see subsequently, but the link between money and the price level is its essential message. As suggested earlier, these two ideas do not represent a fully developed explanation of macroeconomic performance, but their general widespread, and often tacit, acceptance by economists in the nineteenth century and early part of the twentieth century largely had the effect of removing macroeconomic problems from the theoretical agenda of economists. If the economy performed well most of the time in terms of output and employment, there was little need for macroeconomic theory.

All this changed drastically with the crash of 1929 and the deep depression that engulfed Western economies during the 1930s. The collapse of output and prolonged underemployment swept away faith in the validity of Say's law of markets. Furthermore, at a time when prices (including money wages) plunged to historic lows, the classical quantity theory, with its traditional stress on the inflationary dangers inherent in too much money in circulation, was equally irrelevant to the problems of the moment. What was clear to most economists and the general public was that these ideas no longer sufficed to explain what was happening to the economy. New ideas and a new theory were needed.

Keynesian Theory

The new ideas and the new theory were supplied by the British economist John Maynard Keynes, one of the most influential economic thinkers in the twentieth century. Keynes is the "father" of modern macroeconomics. In 1936 he published *The General Theory of Employment, Interest and Money*, a work destined to change the manner in which people thought about the working of the economic system in advanced Western nations. The impact of Keynes on theory has been so great that few would disagree with John Kenneth Galbraith in calling *The General Theory* "the most influential book on economic and social policy in this century. . . . By common, if not yet quite universal agreement, the Keynesian revolution was one of the great modern accomplishments of social design."[16] As another observer has said, "finance ministers around the world approach the problems of economic management through an analytical framework which, perhaps for want of a better word, commentators rightly call Keynesian."[17]

What kind of a book is *The General Theory?* Basically, Keynes set out to explain the forces which shape and determine the level and rate of growth

16. John Kenneth Galbraith, "Came the Revolution," *New York Times Book Review,* May 16, 1965.
17. D. E. Moggridge, *Keynes* (London: The Macmillan Press, Ltd., 1967), p. 9.

of national production and employment, a subject not well understood by either economists or the layman prior to the catastrophic depression of the 1930s. In this he succeeded exceedingly well; *The General Theory* laid the basic foundation for what has become a highly developed body of economic theory and policy directed toward the most pressing problems of the economy as a whole—output, employment and unemployment, economic growth, and inflation.

Keynesian ideas continue to occupy a central place in the body of modern macroeconomic theory. In this connection, three points are crucial. First, Keynes established the basic conceptual framework within which contemporary economists of every persuasion approach and analyze the problems of the macroeconomy. This is the framework of aggregate demand and aggregate supply, the essentials of which are developed in Chapter 4. Second, the primary stress of Keynesian economics—at least as his ideas were largely interpreted in the quarter century after World War II—has been on understanding what determines the level of total demand for the economy's output over relatively short periods of time. For this reason, the Keynesian analysis is usually described as an "income-expenditure" approach to macroeconomic theory. The policy counterpart of this approach is the concept of "demand management," that is, the belief that through fiscal and monetary action the central government can manage the level of aggregate demand and bring about a high level of production and employment without excessive pressure on the price level. To an important degree, an "income-expenditure" perspective is the natural consequence of the fact that Keynes wrote *The General Theory* during the depths of the worst economic collapse in the history of Western market economies. Because not all of today's macroeconomic problems—such as the persistence of inflation when there is serious slack in the economy—are readily explained by either an excess or a deficiency of total demand, economists are seeking new theoretical insights into the economy's overall behavior. Nevertheless—and this is the third point—the aggregate demand and supply framework and the relationships which Keynes and succeeding economists developed within that framework remain as the essential core of modern macroeconomics. As a body of theory, it has been subjected to more testing and rigorous analytical scrutiny than any competing approaches. Many of the major econometric models widely used in forecasting are Keynesian in the sense that their key equations embrace variables derived from the income-expenditure approach to aggregate economics.

The Major Schools of Contemporary Macroeconomics

Alternative approaches to macroeconomic analysis have gathered substantial support within the economics profession. Broadly speaking, there are three different and major approaches—or "schools of thought"—which now compete with each other as well as the basic Keynesian theory. Two of these schools look back to pre-Keynesian, or classical, economics both for inspiration and for key intellectual concepts, a fact which has lead them to be described as part of a "Keynesian Counter-revolution." The third school is different. Describing itself as "Post Keynesian," it looks primarily to Keynes's *General Theory* for inspiration, but argues that the post–World War II interpretation of Keynes which dominated macroeconomics in the 1960s (the income-expenditure approach) is faulty because it neglected or glossed over key ideas in *The General Theory* which explain why advanced market economies are inherently unstable.

Monetarism: The Modern Quantity Theory

Clearly the most influential challenge to Keynesian ideas in the post–World War II era has come from Professor Milton Friedman, Nobel laureate and for many years member of the economics department at the University of Chicago. In a monumental work published in 1964,[18] Professor Friedman, in collaboration with Anna Jacobson Schwartz, developed the basic thesis that the money supply is the single most important, strategic variable that determines in the short term the level of nominal gross national product and the level of employment. Friedman's theories, which are cast in a Keynesian framework even though they stress different variables, are described either as "monetarism" or the "modern quantity theory." Both terms reflect Professor Friedman's intellectual indebtedness to the quantity theory of money mentioned earlier. Among the important ideas which have emerged from the monetarist school is, first, the belief that since it is primarily the money supply that affects current spending, there is neither need nor justification in trying to influence output and employment through changes in government spending and taxes. Contemporary monetarism, in other words, rejects the idea that fiscal policy (the use of taxes and government expenditures to influence the economy) is an appropriate tool for economic stabilization. Second, the monetarists see variations in the stock of money as being chiefly responsible for the upheavals and fluctuations that have characterized American economic life throughout our history. A market system, they believe, is inherently stable and may be subject to shocks brought about by monetary mismanagement. Consequently, their primary policy recommendation is that the money-creating authority—in the American case, the Federal Reserve System—be required to keep the money supply growing at a constant rate. The latter should be determined by growth in the economy's underlying real factors, such as the rate of technological change and growth in the labor force, plus a mar-

18. Milton Friedman and Anna Jacobson Schwartz, *A Monetary History of the United States* (Princeton: Princeton University Press, 1964).

gin that allows people to hold a fraction of their wealth as money balances in a growing economy. Basically, the monetarists seek to limit the government's discretionary power to manage the economy.

New Classical Economics and Rational Expectations

More recently there has emerged a more radical, more far-reaching challenge to Keynesian theory. Known as the "new classical economics," this movement embraces two diverse but related sets of ideas. Although both have deep roots in classical economics, they differ in important ways. From the standpoint of analytical elegance, the most important development is the *theory of rational expectations.* In a nutshell, this theory argues that because people are rational they correctly anticipate the results of actions and behave accordingly. When combined with a Walrasian[19] general equilibrium model which shows that markets always clear, rational expectations theory holds that a market system, *if free from government intervention,* will quickly and efficiently achieve an equilibrium at full employment. Rational expectationists maintain that *no* macroeconomic policy whatsoever can significantly alter the real course of the economy. In this respect, they go well beyond monetarists in arguing against any positive policy acts whatsoever; the monetarists believe at least that the path of the economy can be influenced by following a monetary rule for a fixed rate of growth in the money supply.

Supply-Side Economics

The other offshoot which belongs under the label of the new classical economics is much better known to the public, although its theoretical foundation is more vague than that of the rational expectations stream. This is "supply-side economics," a view of how the economy works that was the basis for the Reagan administration's massive cuts in federal and corporate income taxes approved by Congress in the late summer of 1981. Inspiration for contemporary supply-siders comes from Say's law of markets, because adherents to this school see the source of today's economic problems as insufficient output, not insufficient demand. They believe strongly that the basic argument of Say's law that "supply creates demand" is essentially correct; what holds back supply is excessively high taxes. Thus, we have the rationale for large tax cuts, since taxes impair incentives and depress production. The architect for the notion that excessively high tax rates impair incentives to work, save, and invest is Arthur Laffer, an economist at the University of Southern California.

19. Leon Walras was a nineteenth-century French economist who developed mathematically a model of a multi-market economy in which he demonstrated how markets could clear and there could be a simultaneous equilibrium in all markets. Walras's analysis is usually described as a theory of general equilibrium, "general" in this sense meaning the entire economy.

What monetarism, the rational expectations school, and supply-side economics have in common are the following; (1) an aversion to governmental action coupled with a belief that governmental intervention into the economy, even with the best of intentions, will fail, and (2) a strong faith in the efficacy of the market and the inherent stability of the economic system when left alone. Since these were the basic ideas of the classical economics challenged by Keynes, it is understandable why the phrase the "Keynesian Counter-revolution" is used to describe these theories.

Post Keynesian Economics

The approach of the third school of thought to understanding macroeconomic behavior takes a sharply different tact. Operating under the label "Post Keynesian economics," adherents of this viewpoint argue, first, that the interpretation of Keynesian theory that became standardized after World War II [20] was seriously deficient because it had the practical effect of pushing Keynes's contributions back into a classical mold. Second, the "Post Keynesians," who have their own scholarly journal (*Journal of Post Keynesian Economics*), maintain that contemporary macroeconomic theory is deficient because it fails to integrate into the theory key insights into aggregate behavior that are either explicit in *The General Theory* or strongly suggested by the tone and temper of this classic economic work. The most significant of these center on uncertainty and its impact upon economic decisions, the fact that the economic process takes place in real, historic time, and, finally, the crucial role that economic and political institutions play in determining outcomes in the real economic world. In connection with the latter point, the Post Keynesians are especially critical of economic theory that neglects the impact that market power has on economic behavior, particularly in the explanation of inflation. Although there is agreement among the "Post Keynesians" on the foregoing points, they have not yet developed an agreed-upon macroeconomic model of the economy.

Summary

1. Macroeconomics is concerned primarily with analysis and measurement of the overall performance of the economy. It concentrates on such key variables as total production, employment and unemployment, and the general level of prices.

---

20. Professor Paul Samuelson of MIT coined the term "the neoclassical synthesis" to describe this view of Keynesian economics, the reason being that it combined Keynesian principles relating to aggregate demand with traditional—or "classical"—ideas about how demand and supply forces operating in competitive markets allocate resources and distribute income. See Paul Samuelson, *Economics, An Introductory Analysis*, 6th ed. (New York: McGraw-Hill, 1955), p. 337.

2. Gross national product, measured in both current prices (*nominal* GNP) and constant prices (*real* GNP), is the most widely used single measure of economic performance.

3. Prices in general are measured through indexes. The three basic indexes used in macroeconomics are the consumer price index, the producer price index, and the GNP deflator.

4. Employment and unemployment are strategic measures of the economy's performance. They are closely tied to the general level of production. Unemployment is the proportion of the labor force without jobs.

5. Analyses of statistics of output, employment, and prices over the long period show that the economy grows, but that growth is never smooth. Volatility is a basic characteristic of the American economy.

6. Economics, like other sciences, observes, establishes relationships among things observed, and predicts what will happen under specific circumstances. Tests of predictions are the ultimate test of the validity of all science, including economics. Unlike many of the natural sciences, however, economic hypotheses cannot be tested in laboratories.

7. Economic theories are abstractions, expressed often as functional relationships. Models are developed by combining several functional relationships.

8. Economic policy is concerned with the economic goals of society, including such things as full employment, price stability, and growth. Much economic policy develops from economic theory.

9. Modern macroeconomics is no longer a unified body of theory. Several interpretations of the way the economy works are contending with one another for dominance. These include the income-expenditure approach, monetarism, the "new" classical economics, and Post Keynesian economics.

2

Principles of National Income Accounting

One of the great accomplishments of macroeconomics in the last half-century has been the development of sophisticated statistical techniques for measuring the national output (income) and employment and unemployment. In this chapter we shall examine some of the basic concepts that underlie the measurement of the national output. In the next chapter we shall look at specific measures of income and output now in use and examine the ways in which employment and unemployment are measured.

The Nature and Uses of National Income Accounting

The techniques of national income accounting developed in the United States and other nations during the last half-century are not fundamentally different from the accounting systems developed for and utilized by business firms. Many readers are familiar with the typical accounts employed by the business firm, like the balance sheet and the profit and loss statement. These accounts provide a numerical record of the activities of the business firm. To conduct the affairs of his firm successfully, the businessman must have at his disposal accurate and current information concerning sales receipts, expenditures, and the profit of his firm. From information provided by the firm's accounting system, the businessman judges the state of economic health of his enterprise.

National income accounting is designed to do for the economy as a whole what more traditional forms of accounting do for the business firm. That is to say, the basic objective of a system of national income accounting is to provide a systematic and factual record of the performance of the economy during a specified period of time.[1]

Responsibility for compilation of the statistical data that go into the accounts of the system rests with the Bureau of Economic Analysis (BEA) of the United States Department of Commerce. The statistics of national income are published at periodic intervals in the *Survey of Current Business,* a monthly publication of the Department of Commerce. In the February 1981 *Survey* an explanation of the national income and product accounts was published under the title "The National Income and Product Accounts of the United States: An Overview." Another document, *Readings in Concepts and Methods of National Income Statistics, 1976,* has gathered together all BEA publications from 1954 to 1976 that contain information on the conceptual framework and methodology used in national income accounting. In December 1980 the BEA completed a massive revision and updating of all the national income and product data back through 1929. This was published in September 1981 as a special supplement to the *Survey* under the title *National Income and Product Accounts of the United States, 1929–76.* Revised data for 1976 through 1981 were published in the July 1982 *Supplement* to the *Survey.*

The most important use of national income accounting[2] is in the formulation of economic policy, primarily by governments, but also by business firms and labor organizations. Since the great stock market crash of 1929 there has been a vast expansion in the role played by government (federal, state, and local) in the economy; between 1929 and 1982, for example, the purchases of goods and services by all levels of government rose from 8 percent of national output to 21.1 percent.[3] As a consequence, public policies relating to taxes and expenditures have become one of the most strategically important determinants of the overall performance of the economic system. Given the growing complexity of the modern economy, detailed statistical information on the performance of the economy as provided by systems of national income accounting is indispensable in developing intelligent and workable public policies.

1. In the United States, national income accounting got a major start in 1920, when the National Bureau of Economics Research, a private research organization, began extensive work on the measurement of national income. After the onset of the Great Depression and as a result of a 1932 Senate resolution, the U.S. Department of Commerce began to compile national income statistics for the American economy. Professor Simon Kuznets, the fourth economist awarded a Nobel Prize in this field, directed the early work of the National Bureau on national income measurement and worked closely with the Department of Commerce in preparing its first estimates. These latter were published in 1934 as a report, *National Income 1929–32.* For a more detailed review of the history of national income accounting, see John W. Kendrick, *Economic Accounts and Their Uses* (New York: McGraw-Hill, 1972), Chap. 2.
2. National income accounting is a broad and descriptive term covering a wide variety of economic accounts that apply to the economic system. The best known of these include national income and product accounts (the subject of this and the following chapter), flow of funds accounts, input-output analysis, balance of international payments accounts, and statements of national wealth. For a detailed discussion of various forms of national income accounting see Kendrick.
3. Joint Economic Committee, U.S. Congress, *Economic Indicators,* September 1983, p. 1.

Another important application of national income accounting is to trace fluctuations and growth in total activity, as described in Chapter 1. Aggregate data of this nature provide us with useful information about the use and availability of resources in the economy. When national income data are broken down into different sectors and industries, we are able to gain important insights into the structure and anatomy of the economic system. Such information is invaluable in analyzing the effect of specific policies on prices, production, and employment in different parts of the economy. Furthermore, interrelationships between different parts of the economy are clarified. Business firms, too, make use of national income data, especially as a background for important business decisions pertaining to production, purchasing, borrowing, and capital spending.

The usefulness of national income data reaches beyond the domestic economy. Important comparisons between nations can be made on the basis of their respective national income accountings systems, especially because the terminology and conceptual framework for such systems are becoming increasingly standardized. National income accounting as developed in this and the following chapter is the most widely used frame of reference for making forecasts and projections of economic activity.

Income and Wealth

Having sketched out the nature of national income accounting, we shall analyze, first, the concept of income and, second, the meaning of income in reference to the whole society. A similar discussion on wealth will follow; then we shall discuss the relationship between income and wealth.

The Concept of Income

There are a number of different ways in which income can be defined, but the one thing common to all definitions is the idea that income is a *flow* phenomenon. By a *flow* is meant something that is *measured over time.* For the individual, the income flow is usually thought of in terms of money received between two points of time, although one might just as readily—and correctly—conceive of it as a flow of satisfactions during a period of time. The business firm, too, usually thinks of income as money received over time. But no matter how we choose to define income from the point of view of the individual or the firm, the crucial element in our definition is that of flow.

This last statement brings us to the question of what we mean when we talk in terms of the income of the whole society—what, in short, is the meaning of *national income*? We emphasized that the basic purpose of national income accounting is to provide a factual record of the performance of the economy. Since economic activity aims at satisfaction of human wants, and since satisfaction of wants results from consumption of goods and services, the performance of the economy must be measured in terms of the amount of productive activity taking place in a period of time. Productive activity, however, culminates in the output of valuable goods and services; thus, income from the standpoint of the whole society is a *flow of output over a period of time.* Let us inject a word of caution: The income of the whole society, even though normally measured in money terms, is not the same as the aggregate of all money incomes received by persons in the economy. Flows of money income do not always represent or correspond to output flows, and increases in money flows do not always mean that there has been an increase in output flows. We shall develop the reasons for this in greater detail subsequently.

The basic definition of income in a social sense as a flow of output presents a difficult problem in measurement. Output consists of a vast and heterogeneous quantity of goods and services that cannot be added together unless they can be reduced to a common unit of measurement. As a practical matter, the only way in which we can add together all the different kinds of goods and services produced by the economy during a period of time is by reducing them to their money value. Money value is the common denominator that enables us to sum up and reduce to a single figure the complex aggregation of goods and services contained in the economy's flow of output during some definite period.

It is possible to reduce the economy's flow of output to its monetary valuation because in a market economy practically all productive activity will be reflected in money transactions. Most activities that are productive—which lead to the creation of goods and services—are carried on through the mechanism of the market and will thus carry a price tag. If a way can be found to summarize all the monetary transactions that reflect productive activity, it becomes possible to measure in money terms the total income, or flow of output, of the society.

Although, in principle, the summing of money transactions describes the technique by which the output of the whole society is measured, several qualifications to the above statement should be noted. For one thing, all monetary transactions do not necessarily reflect current productive activity; this is the case with sales of secondhand goods or the purchase and sale of various financial instruments, such as stocks and bonds. Second, some productive activity does not pass through the mechanism of the market and thus is not reflected in a monetary transaction. The labor of the homemaker is a case in point. Finally, money itself is not a stable unit of measure since the value of money fluctuates as the general level of prices changes. This problem as we saw in Chapter 1, is corrected by measuring output in constant prices.

The Circular Flow of Income and Product

Income, as we have stressed, is a flow phenomenon. But it is important to note the *circular* character of this flow. This basic concept is illustrated in Figure 2–1. Output originates in the producing units of the economy—including the government as a producing entity—and moves from them to the economy's households, which are not only the ultimate users of the economy's output, but also the owners and suppliers of the economic resources that enter into the creation of output. The existence of a flow of output means there must be a corresponding flow of inputs, for the essence of the productive process is the transformation of the services rendered by the economic resources of land, labor, and capital into economically useful goods and services. Thus, as shown in Figure 2–1, the underlying real economic process consists of a continuous, circular process whereby inputs of resources are transformed by the economy's production units into goods and services.

Figure 2–1 presents a simplified view of the matter because it lumps all goods and services together and assumes that all of the output is directed toward the households or the consumer of the economy. Actually some of the output consists of capital or investment goods, for which firms rather than households are the ultimate users. Moreover, households do not spend all of their income, as some is saved and some is taxed. These exceptions, though, should not cloud our understanding of the basically circular character of the economic process.

The input and output flows that constitute the essence of the economic process are matched by two flows of money—one of income and one of expenditure. According to Figure 2–1, which outlines the productive process in a market economy wherein resources are privately owned and most production decisions are privately made, resource owners exchange the service of their resources for money incomes, while the producing entities of the economy exchange their output of goods and

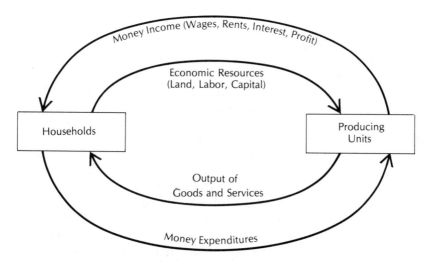

FIGURE 2–1.   The Circular Flow of Economic Activity

services for the flow of expenditures originating in the households of the economy. The flow of income and expenditure matching the real flows of the economy is seen to be circular in the same sense that the underlying flows of product and services of economic resources are circular.

The circular flow diagram, though oversimplified, illustrates a number of important propositions relating to the economic process and the flow of income. First, the diagram shows that income (or output) creation involves an interaction between the two basic kinds of markets that exist in the economy. Exchanging the services of economic resources for money incomes, depicted in the top half of the diagram, reflects transactions taking place in the resource (factor) market, whereas the expenditure of money income for the economy's output, depicted in the lower half of the diagram, represents the total of transactions taking place in the economy's market for goods and services. Second, the circular flow diagram aids in understanding why the flow of income, the flow of output, and the flow of expenditures for output are necessarily equal, *once they have taken place.* The reason for this equality is that all of these flows are different measures of the same thing—the volume of productive activity in the economy. Since the circular flow analysis reveals that the total flow of current income is always equal to the value of current output, this means that the productive process will always generate sufficient total money income to purchase the current output of the economy. This does not mean, however, that all the income so generated will be spent by those who first receive it, as some may be saved and some may be taxed. There may be spending by business that offsets saving and by government that offsets taxes, but this does not necessarily have to happen.

The Concept of Wealth

Wealth and income are concepts so closely related that it is easy to confuse them and not see that they are distinct entities. As a starting point, let us define *wealth* as all material things that possess economic value. Wealth, in other words, consists of goods that can command other goods and services in exchange. Several aspects of this definition should be noted. First, our definition limits wealth to tangible or material things, which is to say that intangibles (for example, services) are excluded. Second, wealth is a *stock* phenomenon in contrast to income, a *flow* phenomenon. Wealth is a concept that relates to the total material things existing at a moment of time. Contrast this with the income concept, which has to do with the flow of output or money over a period of time.

The basic difference between wealth and income is reflected in the way in which the two are measured: Income can be measured only by reference to some distinct period of time such as the day, the week, the month, or the year, whereas wealth can be measured only by reference to a specific moment of time, such as the final day of the week, the month, or the year. This difference can be illustrated with reference to the balance sheet and the profit and loss statements of the business firm. The balance sheet is analogous to the wealth concept; it reveals the position of the firm in terms of its assets and liabilities at a given moment of time, usually the close of business on the last day of the year. The profit and loss statement, on the other hand, is analogous to the income concept; it depicts the receipts and expenditures flowing into and out of the firm during a specific period of time, usually one year.

Finally, it is important to note that wealth, because it involves a stock of goods, is exhaustible, whereas income, because it is a flow, is capable of being continuously renewed. Wealth, in other words, can be wholly used up. The corollary to this is that the renewal of wealth used up in production must come out of what is produced. It is also true, of course, that within a specific period most income is normally used up, but the income flow will be renewed in the next period as long as the economic resources that are the basic source of income are not destroyed.

The distinction between a stock and a flow extends beyond income and wealth to other economic variables. The labor force, for example, is a stock variable, but the income a worker gets from being employed is a flow variable. Much of the time there is a stock counterpart to a given flow—as in the relationship between wealth and income—but not always. No hard and fast rule exists to tell whether a stock component exists for any particular flow—only common sense and a careful examination of the flow variable in question can determine this.

Problems in the Measurement of Wealth

In any discussion of wealth, particularly in reference to the economy as a whole, distinction must be made between *wealth* and *claims to wealth*. Wealth consists of material things of economic value, whereas claims to wealth are, in effect, evidences of ownership—stocks or deeds or claims that do not necessarily involve ownership, such as bonds, paper money, and other debt instruments. From the viewpoint of the individual, the distinction between wealth and claims to wealth is not critical; the individual, in reckoning his personal wealth position, usually counts both the material items of wealth in his possession, such as a house or land, as well as intangible claims in the form of bonds, shares of stock, and money in the bank. This is a logical position as far as the individual is concerned because for any single individual both the material wealth and claims to wealth that he owns possess exchange value and can, if necessary, be converted into purchasing power.

For the economy as a whole, however, the distinction between wealth and claims to wealth is vitally important. When we are trying to measure or get an inventory of the material wealth of the society, it would be illogical to add up all goods and all claims to goods as well. This would give us a total in which everything has been counted twice. In the economy as a whole, the value of all material things would just equal the sum total of all claims possessing exchange value because every material item of wealth must be owned by an individual, a group of individuals, some type of business entity such as the corporation, or by some kind of governmental unit.

In taking inventory of the wealth of a community or the nation, there is an immensely difficult and complex problem of valuation. Wealth can be measured only if valued in some such common denominator as money. Normally items of wealth are valued in money terms as a result of their purchase and sale in a market, but for many items of wealth that ought to be included in a national inventory this method of valuation is simply not possible. What, for instance, is the value of a great public library or hospital? A national park or forest? Or an ancient building of great historical significance? For items of wealth such as these and, perhaps, for resurces which are bought and sold only infrequently, there can only be an arbitrary judgment as to their real value.

Our discussion of the nature of wealth would not be complete without comment on the basic categories of material wealth existing in any society. The most fundamental classification distinguishes between natural resources and resources that are man-made. In the first category we find all natural wealth, which is to say land and the values inherent in land—fertility, mineral deposits, and climatic characteristics. These things are basically gifts of nature, even though their economic value over time may be modified by man's actions. Within the category of man-made resources it is necessary to distinguish between wealth possessed by consumers or households, which is often thought of as nonproductive, and wealth possessed by firms, which is regarded as productive (because its services are employed in the production of future output). It is not literally true, of course, that items of personal wealth—for example, automobiles, refrigerators, washing machines, and other household appliances—are nonproductive, since they render services to their owners. Granted this, it is still desirable to distinguish items of consumer wealth from the society's stock of productive instruments in the form of buildings and various types of capital equipment. In determining the productive potential of any society, it is wealth in the form of productive instruments that is of critical importance. Wealth in the form of capital goods represents a dynamic and procreative element in modern society because the real function of such goods is to produce other goods and services.

How much tangible wealth is there in the United States? It has been estimated that at the end of 1975 the nation's net *real* wealth (corrected for changes in the value of the dollar) totaled $5,684 billion—a staggering sum that amounted to an average of $26,560 for every man, woman, and child residing in the United States. If the nation's *real* wealth grew between 1975 and 1982 as rapidly as the nation's *real* output, national wealth in 1982 would total $6,820 billion, or $29,396 per capita. The latter may be compared to the nation's *real* output (GNP) per capita in 1982 of $6,367. The 1975 estimates, which are the most recent available, show that 36.5 percent of the nation's tangible wealth consisted of equipment, 44.9 percent structures, 10.1 percent land, and 8.5 percent stocks of goods on hand (inventories). It is unlikely that these percentages have changed significantly since 1975. Since the nation was founded in 1776, *real* wealth per person has, on the average, about doubled every 50 years.[4]

The Concept of Human Wealth

In recent years some economists have applied the wealth concept to the investment by human beings in skills and knowledge. The skills, education, and knowledge that human beings acquire is in a broad sense a form of capital that contributes in a significant way to the process of production. Professor Theodore W. Schultz, Nobel laureate and an early advocate of the idea that economic analysis should take into account human as well as material capital, points out that not only does wealth in the form of human skill and knowledge require investment for its creation, but this form of wealth has grown in Western societies at a much faster rate than other, nonhuman types of capital. Furthermore, Professor Schultz says, the growth of human capital may be the most distinctive feature of the modern economy, contributing more to the growth of output over the long run than conventional forms of wealth.[5]

Measurement of the economic value of human capital presents formidable statistical difficulties, although, roughly speaking, the net worth of an individual's human capital depends on the income that person expects to earn over his or her working life. (Chapter 6 discusses the problem of how the current economic value of any item of wealth, or capital, which produces an income is determined.)

Aside from statistical difficulties in measuring human capital, there is a reluctance—and perhaps even a repugnance—among economists and others to suggest even remotely that human beings might be looked upon as capital goods. As Professor Schultz points out, to regard human beings as capital that can be augmented by investment runs counter to deeply held values, primarily because of the long struggle of Western man to rid society of any form of slavery or indentured service.[6] Nevertheless, economists have continued to refine the concept of human capital and to measure its value. In the 1960s the concept provided a rationale for more spending on education, since it was widely held that investment in human capital would contribute as much or more to the growth of the economy than other sources of wealth. Second, it appeared that spending for education might work to lessen inequality in income distribution,

---

4. John W. Kendrick, "Measuring America's Wealth," *Morgan Guaranty Survey*, May 1976, pp. 6, 10.
5. Theodore W. Schultz, "Investment in Human Capital," *American Economic Review*, March 1961.
6. Ibid.

since studies showed a high correlation between income earned and educational levels attained. Raising the educational level of persons at the lower end of the income scale would thus tend to lessen inequalities.

Hope for the latter outcome has largely vanished, in part due to the fact that income distribution has not changed significantly in recent decades. This is the case in spite of substantial increases in high school graduation rates and in the ratio of college graduates to nongraduates. The issue of the payoff for education appears more complex than seemed to be the case a decade and a half ago, and the basic assumption of an important correlation between educational attainment and income has been challenged.[7] Nonetheless, it should be understood that low-income groups and minorities often do not have a fair opportunity to make the kind of long and costly personal investment needed to improve their skills and knowledge.

Interactions of Income and Wealth

We have outlined some of the basic differences between income and wealth; it is important also to have a clear understanding of the way in which they are linked together.

Our fundamental definition of income from the point of view of the whole society is that of a flow of goods and services. Given this definition, a key question is: What use or disposition is made of the economy's income? The simplest answer is that whatever the economy produces in any particular period of time must be either consumed or not consumed. To consume output means, of course, to use up goods and services in the satisfaction of human wants. If a good or service can satisfy a human want it is said to have utility. Consumption, therefore, involves the using up of utilities as wants are satisfied. Production, on the other hand, involves the creation of utilities so that wants can be satisfied.

But what happens to the output that is not consumed during the income period in which it is produced? This output becomes an addition to the existing stock of wealth of the economy. Here we have the essential relationship between income and wealth; whenever current income exceeds current consumption the stock of wealth automatically is increased, and whenever current consumption is in excess of current income the stock of wealth will automatically be reduced. The relationship between the flow of income and consumption and the stock of wealth may be likened to a reservoir of water, in which the water level (that is, the stock of water) depends upon the rate at which water flows into the reservoir as compared to the rate at which water flows out of the reservoir. If the rate of inflow is greater than the rate of outflow the water level within the reservoir will rise, whereas if the rate of outflow is greater than the rate of inflow the water level will drop.

If some part of the current output of an economy is not consumed

7. See, for example, Christopher Jencks et al., *Inequality: A Reassessment of the Effect of Family and Schooling in America* (New York: Basic Books, Inc., 1972).

during the period in which it is produced, *saving* has taken place. Two things about saving should be noted. First, saving, like income, is a flow phenomenon. The assets (real and monetary) of both a nation and an individual may increase because of saving. Second, saving is a negative act, since basically it represents the *nonconsumption* of current output.

There is, however, another facet to the nonconsumption of current output. The addition to the economy's existing stock of wealth that is the inevitable consequence of the act of saving is also defined as *investment*. In a fundamental sense, investment means a net addition to the stock of wealth of the economy. As we probe further into national income measurement and analysis, we shall see that it is necessary for practical reasons to modify this definition, but this does not change the important underlying idea that the act of investment always involves something *real*, in the sense that it has to do with changes in the economy's stock of wealth. Another word of caution is in order here: This overly simple definition will have to be modified when we consider the difference between net and gross additions to the economy's stock of wealth.

The relationship between output and wealth should be viewed in another way. Not only is it true that the stock of wealth is augmented when the economy does not consume all of current output, but it is also true that output is a flow having its origins in the size, quality, and use made of the economy's stock of both material and human wealth. The act of investment (discussed below) is essential if a society is to maintain intact—or increase—its stock of wealth. Unless the society makes provision for investment, the income flow will be imperiled.

Whenever we discuss or measure saving and investment in an *ex post*,[8] or after-the-fact sense, they are necessarily equal. This follows from the way in which we have defined these phenomena: If some part of the economy's current output is not consumed, we say that saving has taken place, but by the same token we say that this represents investment because an act of nonconsumption will add to the economy's stock of wealth. The notion that investment and saving are identical when defined in this manner is highly important in economic analysis and one that will be encountered frequently in subsequent chapters.

Basic Components of National Income

Our discussion of the relationship of income and wealth provides the foundation for understanding the major categories of output and expenditure actually employed in national income measurement and analysis. Before we examine the major measures of national income and product currently constructed by the Department of Commerce, it is

8. Economists use the term *ex post* to refer to values (spending, saving, etc.) that are measured by looking back after an event has happened. *Ex ante* is used to refer to values that involve looking forward to what is intended or planned to happen. For a further discussion of the concepts see p. 58.

essential to have a clear understanding of the kinds of output that enter into these aggregates. The broad concepts discussed in the previous section must be translated into specific categories that are capable of measurement and practical use in a national income accounting system.

Consumption Goods and Services (C)

In most societies the largest proportion of current output will consist of consumer goods and services. These may be defined as goods and services designed to satisfy human wants. The usual method for measurement of the economy's output of consumer goods and services is through adding up the expenditures made by all households and private nonprofit institutions. Beyond this it is customary in national income accounting to break this category down into three subcategories: expenditures for consumer durables (automobiles, household appliances, household furnishings, etc.), nondurables (mostly food and clothing), and services. (In all subsequent discussion and analysis we shall designate this particular component of the national output by the capital letter C.)

The durable goods component of consumption expenditures presents us with a problem of measurement. A durable good (like an automobile) is essentially a consumer capital good. Typically such goods have a life span of a number of years, and their real economic value lies in the fact that they render a service to the consumer during this life span. In the case of an automobile, the service is that of transportation; in the case of a refrigerator, that of food storage and refrigeration. Since the basic purpose of national income accounting is to measure the amount of productive activity taking place in the economy during a specific period, the logical procedure would be to count the services rendered to the consumer during each income period by a durable good, such as an automobile, as a part of the income (or output) of that income period. This logical procedure has not been followed, however, because of the near impossibility of measuring statistically the rate at which the economy's enormous stock of consumer durable goods delivers services to consumers. As a result, national income accountants and statisticians resort to the convenient fiction that all consumer goods, including consumer durables, are consumed during the income period in which they are purchased. The only important exception to this procedure is consumer housing, for purchases of new houses are treated as investment rather than consumption expenditures. This point will be discussed in the following section.

Investment Goods (I)

In a broad sense the investment goods category of the national output should consist of all additions to the economy's stock of wealth; this was the basic meaning we gave to the term *investment* in our previous discussion. From the standpoint of national income accounting, however, it has been necessary to modify this fundamental approach, primarily because it is impractical and statistically impossible to include all additions to the economy's stock of wealth in the investment goods category. (The capital letter *I* will be used in this and later chapters to designate the investment component of output.)

The usual practice in national income accounting is to measure the economy's output of investment goods by the expenditures made during the income period by the end-users (generally business firms) for goods of this type. The Department of Commerce classifies the following as domestic investment expenditure:

1. All purchases by business firms of new construction and durable equipment
2. All purchases of new houses, that is, all residential construction
3. All changes in inventories held by business firms

The rationale for this particular structure of classification warrants explanation. The first category, producer's plant and equipment, obviously consists of additions to the economy's stock of productive instruments. It is less clear, though, why purchases of new houses should be considered as investment goods. Actually the decision to include residential construction in the investment goods category is arbitrary, because one could argue with justifiable logic that the purchase of a durable item like a house, which renders a service to its owner over its lifetime, is basically no different from the purchase of other durable consumer goods such as automobiles, stoves, and refrigerators. The logic of such a position would be almost irrefutable if all newly constructed houses were sold to consumers or households. On the other hand, it would be equally logical to treat houses as a productive *capital* instrument if all houses were sold to business firms and then rented to the consumer, for in this case the house would clearly be a means for the provision of a service for which the consumer would pay. Actually this is what is assumed in national income accounting and measurement, even though a very large portion of the nation's houses are occupied by their owners. The basic reason for this procedure is that the much longer life of houses as compared to other consumer durables would make the fiction of the consumption of durables in the income period in which they are produced and sold quite absurd if applied to housing. The purchase of new houses, therefore, is treated as an investment expenditure in the income period in which the purchase is made, and a rent is imputed to the owner of the house in the case of owner-occupied housing during subsequent income periods. This imputed rent presumably represents the value of the service provided by the house to its owner over its useful life and thus becomes a part of the economy's output of consumption goods and services.

The inclusion of all changes in the volume of inventories held by business firms in the investment goods category is in accord with our earlier discussion of the fundamental nature of the investment process. Consumer goods, including those in process, and quantities of raw materials produced but not sold or used up during an income period necessarily represent an addition to the economy's stock of wealth. Such goods and raw materials represent a net increase in the inventories—or stocks of goods on hand—of the business firms of the economy. Thus, changes in inventories properly belong in the investment goods category of the national output.

Note, at this point, that a question arises: What happens if the stock of all types of goods held by business firms is drawn down during an income period? If this takes place, there has been *disinvestment* insofar as inventories are concerned. Whenever the net change in inventories is negative, sales are being made from stocks rather than current output. This implies that expenditures reflect not only current output but output from some previous period. Thus, if we hope to measure current output by expenditures, it is necessary to deduct expenditures that represent the using up of past output. Broadly, the process of disinvestment means that the economy has consumed more than it has produced during an income period; consequently there will be a reduction in the economy's existing stock of wealth. From an *ex post* viewpoint, disinvestment is conceptually identical with *dissaving*, as the latter takes place whenever current consumption exceeds current output.

Gross and Net Investment   In a discussion of the investment goods category of the economy's output it is important to distinguish between investment that is gross and investment that is net. Once the reader understands the difference between gross and net investment there will be no difficulty in understanding the difference between gross and net output, a distinction that is useful in economic analysis. Basically, gross investment refers to the output of *all* goods in the investment goods category during an income period. This total is gross because it includes capital goods for replacement and for additions to the economy's stock of physical wealth. It is logical that some part of the economy's current total output of investment goods should constitute replacement for the portion of the economy's existing stock of productive wealth used up in the course of producing the current output. The productive process requires use of capital instruments in conjunction with other resources in order to secure an output, and whenever capital equipment is used it will experience wear and tear. Thus, in any income period some part of the total stock of capital equipment or productive wealth is exhausted and must be replaced. The share of the total investment goods output that serves to replace worn-out capital instruments is termed *replacement investment*. There are serious statistical problems with respect to measurement of this magnitude, but we shall defer any discussion of these to a later point.

If we subtract from the total output of investment goods in any income period the amount representing replacement investment, we are left with a total *net investment*. This total is net because, if our figure for replacement purposes is accurate, the difference between this figure and the total must represent the amount by which the economy's stock of productive wealth has increased during the current income period. Thus, net investment refers to the process by which a society increases its stock of productive capital instruments. If, during an income period, net investment is positive, the economy will have experienced an absolute increase in its physical stock of productive wealth, which means that its ability to produce goods and services has been enlarged. On the other hand, if net investment is negative, there has been a reduction in the economy's total stock of productive wealth, a development that normally implies an impairment of productive capacity.

Government Purchases of Goods and Services (G)

Up to this point we have discussed two major categories of output: consumption goods and services, and investment goods. In general, it is the practice in national income accounting to measure the amount of output in each of these categories by the expenditures made during the income period by the end-users of each kind of output, namely, households and other nonprofit institutions (if consumption goods and services are involved), and business firms (if investment goods are involved). This is possible because the bulk of the goods and services that fit into these categories are produced and sold on a private basis through the mechanism of the market; consequently, expenditure totals are a good indicator of output.

The above classification, however, is incomplete, because it leaves out a third important category—the output of the public (or government sector) of the economy. Use of the word *output* in connection with the activities of government may at first glance strike some readers as strange, yet this is a perfectly appropriate and proper use of the term. The public sector of an economy produces a vast array of economically valuable goods and services, ranging from material things like highways, parks, dams, and schools to intangibles like police and fire protection, the services of judicial systems, and the activities of regulatory bodies, such as the Federal Communications Commission. Output originating in the public sector differs from output originating in the private sector primarily because it has a collective character. Public sector goods and services also differ from privately produced goods and services because the decision to produce the former is a political one—made through government—whereas the latter is private, that is, made by individual producers in response to the quest for profit.

In general, the output of the public sector consists of goods and services that normally would not be produced by private firms or, if they were produced, would not be produced in sufficient quantities. Such goods and services are collective in the sense that they are indivisible, that is, their benefits accrue to society as a whole. The individual, to be sure, benefits from their production, but only by virtue of the fact that he is a member of the society in which such goods are being produced. The nation's judicial system is a case in point. All members of a nation receive some benefit, intangible though it may be, from the existence of a system of courts, yet there is no practical way to measure the amount of this benefit that accrues to each citizen. And if the benefit cannot be measured individually, then it is impractical to attempt to produce the good or service privately.

The basic distinction between collective and private goods and services can be seen through application of the *exclusion principle*. If there is no practical way to exclude a person from obtaining the benefits of a good or service—as in the instance of flood control—the good or service is clearly collective in nature. On the other hand, if persons not willing to pay directly for the benefit are excluded from the use of the good or service, it is clearly of a private and individual character. This latter point does not mean that such a good or service could not be produced and sold on an individual basis by a government unit. Packages, for example, are delivered by the government (the Postal Service) and by private, profit-making firms (such as the United Parcel Service).

Of course, not all the goods and services produced by the public sector are clearly of a collective and indivisible character. Education, for example, can be—and is—produced and sold on an individual basis. In spite of this, the greater portion of education is produced collectively. If our system of public education were entrusted to private enterprise for production at a profit, there would not be an adequate supply of educational services. The well-being of the whole society would be endangered. The same is true with respect to other goods and services produced by the public sector, such as highways, parks and recreational areas, dams, and many different types of services. The private production and sale of such goods and services are not impossible, but in most instances the private plus the social benefit would be small as compared to the benefit that results when such goods are produced on a collective basis.

In addition to their social character, goods and services produced in the public sector differ from privately produced goods and services in another important way. In the private sector of the economy, output is normally disposed of by sale to the end-user of the output, but in the public sector the usual procedure is to distribute this output without charge to the society as a whole. Governments, in other words, normally do not sell on an individual basis the collective goods and services which it is their responsibility to provide. This means that we cannot measure the value of the output of the public sector in the same way that we measure the value of the private sector, namely, by the total of expenditures made by those who purchase the different categories of output.

Since the output of the government sector is distributed free to all or most members of the community, the only practical measure of the value of this output is in terms of what it costs to supply it to the community at large. For the public sector to carry out its function of providing the economy with an array of collective goods and services, it must obtain economic resources; generally, it does this either directly through the hire of labor or indirectly through purchase of part of the output of the private sector. Therefore, the public sector's purchases of goods and services constitute the input of resources necessary to the output of collective goods and services. In national income accounting, government purchases of goods and services are used as a measure of the portion of the total output that originates in the public sector. (It is the usual practice to designate this category of output by the capital letter G.)

Transfer Expenditures (TR) and Taxes (TX)

It is necessary to distinguish another, and important, type of government expenditure that does not enter directly into the computation of output totals. These expenditures, which occur at all levels of government, are called *transfer payments,* primarily because they involve transfers of income by the government from group to group rather than the acquisition of resources necessary to the production of governmental output. Transfer expenditures, in other words, provide income (real or monetary) to the recipients of such expenditures, but the government unit does not receive either goods or services in return. Old-age pensions, unemployment compensation, aid to dependent children, and various forms of aid to war veterans are common forms of transfer payments. Insofar as the national economy is concerned, interest on the public debt and subsidies to business firms are considered to be transfers. Transfer expenditures may be viewed in another way, too, for they are, in a sense, negative taxes. Just as the recipient of a transfer payment does not directly provide the government unit making the payment with an equivalent value of either goods or services in exchange, neither does the government, in collecting taxes, provide each citizen individually with an immediate and equivalent value of goods or services in exchange. Transfer expenditures, in other words, are a one-way flow of income from the government to the individual or business firm; taxes, on the other hand, are a one-way flow of income from the individual or the business firm to the government. It is in this sense that we can also speak of taxes as being negative transfers. (In subsequent discussion in this text we shall designate transfer expenditures by the symbol TR and taxes by the symbol TX.)

Net Exports (I_f)

The category of national income known as net exports is equal to the difference between a nation's exports of goods and services and its imports of goods and services. If there are no *transfers* of income to or from foreign residents, net exports may also be identified as *net foreign invest-ment,* designated as I_f. This latter definition is subject to a number of qualifications, but for the moment it will serve as a working definition of foreign investment. A nation's exports represent expenditures for its output that originate outside the nation's borders, whereas a nation's imports represent spending by its residents for output that originates in foreign countries. If a nation's exports of goods and services exceed its imports of goods and services, net foreign investment is positive. On the other hand, if imports of goods and services are in excess of exports of goods and services, net foreign investment is negative. Positive net for-eign investment increases the claims of the residents of a country against residents of other countries; negative net foreign investment does the reverse.

Since we seek in our discussion to link the various categories of the national output to expenditures made by end-users for each of these categories, it is important to understand the sense in which net exports constitute an expenditure category. If exports of goods and services exceed imports, the difference should be counted as an addition to the other categories of expenditure, the total of which is a measure of the national output. On the other hand, if imports of goods and services exceed exports, the difference should be subtracted from the sum of the other categories of expenditure. Expenditures by the nation and its residents for imported goods and services are normally included in the other cat-egories of expenditure, since there is no practical way to distinguish the exact portion of expenditures for imports in each category. Conse-quently, total expenditures by residents for imported goods and services should be deducted in order to avoid counting them as output. This will be done automatically by making the net foreign investment category negative whenever imports of goods and services exceed exports of goods and services.

Net foreign investment is similar in its economic effects to expendi-ture for investment goods. Expenditure leading to production of capital goods has the effect of creating money income within the economy equal to the amount of the expenditure. But there is not created in the same income period an offsetting volume of consumer goods and services, owing to the durable character of capital goods that produce value equal to their cost in the form of consumer goods only over their entire life—which usually encompasses several income periods. An excess of exports over imports (positive net foreign investment) will have the same eco-nomic effect, because the production of goods and services for export creates money income in the national economy, but no offsetting volume of goods and services for domestic purchase is available. If imports fall short of exports, an excess of money income over the total of goods and services available for purchase during the income period exists. This excess is equal to the difference between exports and imports. On the other hand, an excess of imports over exports means that the physical volume of goods and services available for purchase by the nation and its residents is in excess of the amount of money income created by the process of producing the national output. Expenditures on imported goods and services, it may be noted, are similar in their economic effects to saving, because use of any part of current income to finance the purchase of imported goods means that a part of current income is not being spent on domestically produced output. This is the same thing that takes place when some part of current income is saved. Thus, in an economic and conceptual sense, imports of goods and services are a counterpart of saving, whereas exports of goods and services are a counterpart of domestic investment.

Fundamental Identities among National Income Components

The manner in which the various component parts of the national output fit together can be expressed symbolically and summarized in a series of *identity equations*. An identity equation defines one variable in terms of other variables; it is an equation asserting an equality that is true by definition. Such equations are normally derived by taking a total (or aggregate) and expressing it as the sum of its parts. Identity equations are to be contrasted with *behavior equations*, which express a relationship between variables. Behavior equations are not necessarily true in the same sense as identity equations. They are a mathematical statement of a hypothesis concerning economic behavior and, consequently, the relationships involved in such equations are causal in nature. If we say, for example, that total consumption expenditures equal expenditures for consumer durables plus expenditures for consumer nondurables plus expenditures for consumer services, we would have an identity equation, because these three forms of consumer expenditures represent the component parts of the total consumer purchases of goods and services. If we let C stand for total consumption, C_d spending for consumer durables, C_n spending for nondurables, and C_s spending for services, the identity equation reads as follows[9]:

$$C \equiv C_d + C_n + C_s.$$

In such an equation, the right and left sides are equal by definition—they cannot be unequal. The equation is always true for all values of C_d, C_n, and C_s.

On the other hand, if we assert that total consumption expenditures are a function of (that is, depend upon) current income, this would be a behavior equaton, because it expresses a hypothesis about economic behavior. Such a hypothesis might be expressed in equation form as follows (see Chapter 5 for a more detailed analysis):

$$C = a + bY.$$

9. Since these are identity equations we shall use the identity sign $\equiv$ instead of the equality sign $=$.

This is a behavior equation that says that total consumption spending is determined by the particular values assigned to *a, b,* and *Y. In this equation, a* and *b* are parameters, that is, economic magnitudes whose values are *fixed.* There is only one unique value for *C,* depending on the values assigned the parameters and *Y* (the symbol used for income).

For our series of identity equations that describe how the component parts of the national output fit together, we will use the following symbols:

Y = the national output, or national income

I = investment expenditures (output of investment goods)

I_f = net foreign investment (net exports)

C = consumption expenditures (output of consumer goods and services)

S = saving

G = government expenditures for goods and services (output of communnity or collective goods)

X = export expenditures (domestic output that is exported)

M = import expenditures (foreign output that is imported)

TR = transfer expenditures

TX = taxes

Let us start with an imaginary but highly simplified economic system that has no government and no economic ties with any other nation. In this hypothetical system, the origin and disposition of income can be expressed symbolically as follows.

$$Y \equiv C + I, \tag{2-1}$$

$$Y \equiv C + S. \tag{2-2}$$

Equation (2–1) states that output (income) originates from expenditures for consumption goods and services and investment goods. Equation (2–2) expresses the idea that income created in the productive process must be either consumed or not consumed (that is, saved).

From these equations we can derive a third equation showing the identity between saving and investment. Since income and consumption are common terms in both of the above equations, it follows that investment and saving must be equal to one another. Thus,

$$I \equiv S. \tag{2-3}$$

The above identities are *ex post* equations because they are descriptive of that which exists or is actual; they do not in any way describe economic behavior in an intended, planned, or *ex ante* sense. It should be recognized that these two magnitudes must be identical in an *ex post* sense because of the way in which they are defined, but this does not mean that the amounts saved and the amounts invested in the economy in any specific income period always coincide with the amounts that firms or persons *intended* to save and invest. The latter is an entirely different matter, which we will analyze thoroughly at a later point in the text.

We can proceed closer to reality in the development of our identity equations by dropping the assumption of an economy without a government. We will retain for the moment, however, the assumption that our economy has no relationships with other economies; in other words, it is a closed economy. Let us assume, too, that the only function of our government is to provide for collective goods and services; it does not engage in transfer expenditures. On the basis of this set of assumptions we would have the following identities:

$$Y \equiv C + I + G, \tag{2-4}$$

$$Y \equiv C + S + TX, \tag{2-5}$$

$$S + TX \equiv I + G, \tag{2-6}$$

$$S \equiv I + (G - TX). \tag{2-7}$$

Equation (2–4) means that output consists of consumption goods and services, investment goods, and collective goods. Equation (2–5) relates to the disposition of income and shows that with the introduction of government a third alternative is now available for the disposition of current income, namely, taxes. The economic effect of taxes is similar to saving because taxes also represent a nonexpenditure of current income for consumption goods and services.

Equation (2–6) is a modification of the saving-investment identity. It is made necessary by the introduction of government expenditures and taxes. Saving plus taxes, both of which are leakages from the current income stream, are equal to investment plus government expenditures for goods and services. Reversing the identity, investment and government expenditures are offsets to leakages in the form of saving and taxes. Equation (2–7) transfers taxes to the right-hand side of the equation, showing that saving is equal to investment *plus* the government deficit or *minus* the government surplus.

The terms *deficit* and *surplus* as used here do not in any way refer to the budgetary situation of the federal government. Rather, these terms refer to the current income and product transactions of all governmental units (federal, state, and local) in the economy. For example, if the current expenditures of the public sector for goods and services are in excess of total taxes collected, then the public sector has incurred a deficit on its income and product transactions. Insofar as the public sector is concerned, dissaving has taken place because governmental units have spent more than their income, the latter being derived from taxation. If $G - TX$ is placed on the right-hand side of Equation (2–7), it must be positive, because the total saving of the economy must cover investment expenditure plus the amount of the deficit of the public sector.

On the other hand, if the tax collections of the public sector are in excess of the current expenditures of government units, then there is a surplus in the income and product transactions of the public sector. This would be a form of governmental saving, for expenditures are less than current receipts. Again, if $G - TX$ is placed on the right-hand side of the same equation, it should be negative, as the total saving, S, of the economy is now less than investment expenditure and must be augmented by governmental saving.

We are now able to drop the last of the simplifying assumptions with which we started our discussion: those of a closed economy and of no transfer expenditures. When we drop these assumptions, our structure of identity equations becomes realistic, describing accurately how the component parts of the national output fit together. We now have the following series of identity equations.

$$Y \equiv C + I + G + X - M, \tag{2-8}$$

$$I_f \equiv X - M, \tag{2-9}$$

$$Y \equiv C + I + G + I_f, \tag{2-10}$$

$$Y \equiv C + S + TX - TR, \tag{2-11}$$

$$S + TX - TR \equiv I + G + I_f, \tag{2-12}$$

$$S \equiv I + G + I_f - (TX - TR). \tag{2-13}$$

Equation (2–8) is essentially the same as Equation (2–4), except that we have now added expenditures for exports and subtracted expenditures for imports. Since the difference between exports and imports is equal to net foreign investment, as in Equation (2–9), the basic identity equation describing the origin of output and income takes the form shown in Equation (2–10).[10]

The existence of transfer expenditures means that we must modify the equation describing the disposition of income to take such transfers into account. This is done in Equation (2–11), in which transfer expenditures are subtracted from taxes. Since transfers are, in effect, negative taxes, they offset taxes as a leakage from the current income stream. Moreover, once we have introduced transfers into the system, they must be deducted from the components on the right-hand side of the disposition of income equation, or else they would be counted twice. This is the case because transfer expenditures are income to the recipients of such expenditures, and as such can be a source of consumption expenditures, saving, or tax payments just as much as income derived from the process of production. Thus, transfer expenditures will be reflected in consumption, saving, and taxes, in Equation (2–11), showing the disposition of current income.

Finally, the basic saving-investment identity is modified to take into account net foreign investment, which offsets not only saving and taxes in the same manner as investment and government expenditures, but also the effect of transfer expenditures, on the deficit or surplus of the public sector with respect to income and product transactions. Thus, saving plus *net* taxes $(TX - TR)$ is equal to investment plus net foreign investment and government expenditures for goods and services in Equation (2–12). If net taxes are shifted to the right-hand side of this

10. This assumes no transfers to or from the rest of the world.

equation, the basic identity equation relating saving and investment takes the form shown in Equation (2–13).

Current Data and Identity Equations in an Open Economy

The identity equations that pertain to an open economy with transfers may be verified by fitting to them actual data from the national income and product accounts for the United States for 1982. The data have been both simplified and rounded to the nearest whole number; therefore, the details may not add to the totals. First, we have the equation for the origin of gross national product:

$$Y \equiv C + I + G + X - M, \tag{2–14}$$

$$\$3,\!058 \equiv \$1,\!972 + \$422 + \$647 + \$350 - \$333. \tag{2–15}$$

These data are in billions of dollars in current prices and are obtained from the 1983 *Economic Report of the President*.[11] Note that in 1982 the United States had a small surplus in its foreign trade, $X - M$.

The equation for the disposition of the GNP may be written

$$Y \equiv C + S + T_{\mathrm{n}}. \tag{2–16}$$

In the above equation, T_{n} is equal to *net* taxes and is the difference between total taxes, *TX*, and transfers, *TR*. When the data for 1982 are fitted to this identity showing the disposition of the gross national product, we have

$$\$3,\!058 \equiv \$1,\!972 + \$535 + \$551. \tag{2–17}$$

The basic saving-investment (Equation 2–13) identity now becomes

$$S \equiv I + I_{\mathrm{f}} + G - T_{\mathrm{n}}. \tag{2–18}$$

In the above equation, I_{f} is equal to the difference between exports X and imports M.

With 1982 data fitted to the equation, we now have

$$\$535 \equiv \$422 + \$17 + \$647 - \$551. \tag{2–19}$$

This equation shows that in 1982 there was a deficit on the income and product transactions of the public sector, which is an offset to saving.

Summary

1. The comprehensive system of national income and product statistics developed over the last half-century has been a major achievement of macroeconomics.

---

11. The GNP total from the 1983 *Economic Report of the President* differs slightly from the figure for nominal GNP given in Chapter 1 because the *Economic Report* figures for 1982 were preliminary and subsequently modified.

2. Income and wealth are distinct concepts: Income is a *flow* phenomenon, measuring what happens over time, and wealth is a *stock* phenomenon, measuring the amount of material things in existence at a point in time.

3. The concept of wealth as applied to human beings involves seeing the education, knowledge, and skills possessed by people as a form of human capital.

4. The basic relationship between wealth and income is that, to add to the stock of wealth, a part of income must be saved and invested. This is true for all societies.

5. The nation's total income (or production) is measured by four major expenditure categories: (1) consumption; (2) investment; (3) government purchases of goods and services; and (4) net exports.

6. The relationship between these categories is expressed in a fundamental identity equation: $Y \equiv C + I + G + X - M$, where Y equals output, C equals consumption, I equals investment, G equals government purchases of goods and services, X equals exports, and M equals imports.

3

Measuring Output and Employment

In the last chapter we analyzed the fundamental principles that underlie most systems of national income accounting. Now we turn, first, to a discussion of some of the specific measures for output and income now in use in the United States, concentrating on the five aggregate measures now in wide use: (1) gross national product, (2) net national product, (3) national income, (4) personal income, and (5) disposable income. We follow this with an examination of concepts and problems involved in measuring employment and unemployment. We shall be especially concerned with the meaning and measurement of "full employment," a concept of vital importance in modern macroeconomics.

Gross National Product

Gross national product, also called gross national income or gross national expenditure, is the best-known and most widely used of the various statistical measures developed to gauge the economy's performance. Formally, it is defined as *the current market value of all final goods and services produced by the economy during an income period.* The normal income period for most national income accounting systems, including that of the United States, is the calendar year. As an expenditure total, gross national product (or GNP as it is usually called) represents the total purchases of goods and services by consumers and governments, gross private domestic investment, and net foreign investment. As an income total, GNP shows both the total income created as a result of current productive activity and the allocation of this income. The output total included in the GNP figure is described as gross because it does not take into account capital goods that have been consumed or worn out during the process of production. It is termed national because it refers to the productive activities of the nationals of a particular nation, including the contribution to current output of property resources owned by these nationals. Table 3–1 shows GNP data for selected years for the United States during the period 1929–82.[1]

TABLE 3–1.   Gross National Product or Expenditure; Selected Years, 1929–82 (in billions of current dollars)

Year	Gross National Product	Personal Consumption Expenditure	Gross Private Domestic Investment	Government Purchases of Goods and Services	Net Exports of Goods and Services
1929	$ 103.4	$ 77.3	$ 16.2	$ 8.8	$ 1.1
1933	55.8	45.8	1.4	8.2	0.4
1940	100.0	71.0	13.1	14.2	1.8
1945	212.4	119.5	10.6	82.8	−0.5
1950	286.5	192.0	53.8	38.5	2.2
1955	400.0	253.7	68.4	75.0	3.0
1960	506.5	324.9	75.9	100.3	5.5
1965	691.1	430.4	113.5	138.4	8.8
1970	992.7	621.7	144.2	220.1	6.7
1975	1,549.2	976.4	206.1	339.9	26.8
1980	2,631.7	1,668.1	401.9	537.8	23.9
1982	3,073.0	1,991.9	414.5	649.2	17.4

Source: *Economic Report of the President,* 1983, p. 163, and *Economic Indicators,* September 1983, p. 1.

Final and Intermediate Goods and Services

In defining GNP, we stated that it is a measure of the economy's output of final goods and services during an income period. In national income accounting, it is necessary to distinguish between *final goods and services,* which are the end products of the economy, and *intermediate goods and services,* which normally are thought of as goods and services purchased for resale. We must make this distinction to avoid double-counting. Intermediate goods and services enter into the production of final goods and services. Therefore, if we added up expenditures for final goods and services as well as expenditures for intermediate goods and services, we would count the same goods and services twice. This would give us an exaggerated total for GNP. For example, the production of bread involves several stages and several transactions. Wheat is produced by the farmer and sold to the miller, who in turn processes the

1. As an identity equation *GNP* or *Y* equals $C + I + G + X - M$.

wheat and produces flour, which is sold to the baker, who uses it to produce bread. In this simple example wheat and flour are intermediate products, whose value will be reflected in the value of the final product, bread. This being the case, it would be an error to add separately the value of the wheat produced by the farmer, the value of the flour produced by the miller, and the value of the bread produced by the baker.

There is no exact rule by which we can clearly determine whether a good or a service is an intermediate or final product. In our example, flour is an intermediate product because it is sold to the baker for further processing. But if flour were sold directly to a homemaker it would be classified as a final product, since the homemaker is the ultimate user of the product (as contrasted to the baker, who clearly is not the ultimate user). To distinguish between intermediate and final products in national income measurement, the Department of Commerce has adopted the working definition that a final product is one that is not resold, whereas an intermediate product is one that is purchased with the normal intention that it be resold.[2] Thus, in the example cited, wheat sold to the miller and flour sold to the baker constitute intermediate products, because in both instances the products will be resold, although in altered form. Bread purchased by the homemaker normally will not be resold and therefore can be considered a final product.

Monetary Transactions and Productive Activity

Since GNP is a measure of productive activity, the basic technique for its measurement is through the summation of all monetary transactions that reflect productive activity. There is a problem here because, as pointed out in Chapter 2, some monetary transactions do not represent current productive activity, while certain types of productive activity, on the other hand, will not show up in any monetary transaction. The most common monetary transactions that are not measures of current output are (1) those involving the purchase and sale of used or secondhand goods, because such goods constitute part of the output of a previous income period; (2) those involving purchase and sale of various financial instruments, such as bonds and equities; and (3) transfer payments, both public and private. All of these transactions should be excluded from any monetary measure of current productive activity.

For productive activity not reflected in a monetary transaction, the homemaker's activities can again serve as an example. If she bakes her own bread, no monetary transaction reflecting the sale of a final product is involved, although there will be such a transaction if she buys her bread in the bakery or grocery shop. Yet in both instances productive activity has taken place. The same sort of thing takes place if a house-

---

2. U.S. Department of Commerce, *National Income,* 1954, p. 30. This document states the official position of the U.S. government on concepts and methods used in national income accounting in the United States.

holder chooses to paint his own house rather than hire a professional painter to do the job. When the householder paints his house, productive activity occurs that is not reflected in the current GNP. But if a painter is hired, the resulting productive activity involves a monetary transaction and hence appears in the current output figures.

Ideally, GNP should be a measure of all current productive activity in the economy, whether or not the activity is reflected in a market transaction. But as a practical matter it is quite impossible to measure with any degree of statistical accuracy the total value of all the "do-it-yourself" types of productive activities and other nonmarket transactions that occur in the economy. The U.S. Department of Commerce limits its data to economic production. The basic criterion used for classifying an activity as economic production is whether it is reflected in the sales and purchase transactions of the market economy. The only exception to this is that the Department of Commerce makes estimates of certain income and product flows that are not reflected in transactions in the market. The most important of these *imputations* (estimates of nonmarket production) are wages and salaries paid in kind rather than money, fuel and food produced and consumed on the farm, and the rental value of owner-occupied homes.[3] Aside from these imputations, the Department of Commerce does not attempt to measure and record productive activity that is of a nonmarket character. The decision as to what nonmarket production ought to be included in national income and product measures is necessarily an arbitrary one. There is no logical reason, for example, to include the rental value of owner-occupied homes and to exclude the value of the labor of the homemaker.

An Alternative Technique for Measuring Gross National Product

An alternative approach to the measurement of GNP is through a summation of charges against the output total or, in other words, through the allocation of the gross income created in the process of producing the economy's current output of final goods and services. (Allocations and charges are different names for what is basically the same technique of measurement.)

Table 3–2 summarizes the two techniques by which GNP can be measured. The right-hand side of the table shows the *expenditure* or *flow-of-product* approach to the measurement of gross output. It is a summation of expenditures for the four major categories of goods and services produced by the economy during the income period. The left-hand side of the table represents the *charges* or *allocations* approach to the measurement of output. It summarizes the total of charges levied against the income total, or shows the allocation of the total income.

Contemporary national income accounting practice recognizes two major types of charges against the value of GNP. The first of these is

3. Ibid.

factor costs, or *income charges*, which consists of income received by the owners of economic resources in the form of wages, salaries, and other kinds of employee compensation; rents; interest payments; and profits. The other is *nonincome charges* and consists of capital consumption allowances and indirect business taxes.

Factor Costs   Basically, factor costs consist of necessary payments that have to be made in either money or kind in order to secure the services of the factors of production. The utilization of the services of these factors makes possible the production of goods and services. Items 1 through 7 in Table 3–2 are the factor costs for the gross national product of the American economy in 1982. Each of these is explained as follows.

Compensation of employees consists primarily of all wages and salaries and income in kind paid in return for the services of labor and, in addition, certain supplements to wages and salaries. These latter are contributions made by employers under the Social Security system (contributions by employees are included in the figure for wages and salaries), employer contributions to private pension plans, and various minor forms of labor income, such as compensation for injuries and pay for individuals in the military reserve.

TABLE 3–2.   Sources and Allocations of the Gross National Product, 1982 (in billions of dollars)

Allocations of Gross National Product		Origins of Gross National Product	
1. Compensation of employees	$1,855.9	1. Personal consumption expenditures	$1,972.0
2. Proprietors' income	120.1	2. Gross private domestic investment	421.9
3. Corporate profits tax liability	58.8	3. Government purchases of goods and services	647.1
4. Dividends	70.3		
5. Undistributed profits*	32.0	4. Net exports of goods and services	16.5
6. Rental income of persons	34.1		
7. Net interest	265.3		
National Income	**$2,436.5**		
8. Indirect business taxes	258.8		
9. Business transfer payments	13.7		
10. *Less:* Subsidies less current surplus of government enterprises	8.3		
11. Statistical discrepancy (+)	0.1		
Net National Product	**2,700.8**		
12. Capital consumption allowances	356.8		
Gross National Product	**3,057.5**	**Gross National Product**	**3,057.5**

SOURCE: *Economic Report of the President,* 1983, pp. 184–87.
*Includes inventory valuation and capital consumption adjustment.

Proprietors' income is a measure of the monetary earnings and income in kind accruing to all unincorporated business enterprises in the economy. This item is primarily a measure of the profits of sole proprietorships, partnerships, and producer cooperatives.

Corporate profits tax liability consists of the total of federal and state taxes levied against the earnings of all corporations in the economy.

Dividends represents the amount of corporation profits paid out to shareholders during the current income period.

Undistributed profits constitute the part of corporate profits neither paid out to the shareholders as dividends nor collected as taxes by federal and state governments. The sum of this item and the previous two items gives total corporate profits in the income period.

Rental income of persons equals the money income received by individuals from the rental of real property, such as buildings and land.

Net interest is a measure of income in the form of interest payments received by individuals in the economy, with the exception of interest payments by government (federal, state, and local) and by consumers. The Department of Commerce states that interest on the public debt and interest paid by consumers are not a part of current production; hence, they should not be treated as a factor cost.

It may be noted that the sum of Items 1 through 7 in Table 3–2 is labeled national income. This is so because, fundamentally, the term *national income* refers to the factor costs of the goods and services produced by the economy. We shall discuss this particular measure in more detail shortly.

Nonincome Charges   Indirect business taxes constitute the first type of non-income charge against GNP. The major types of taxes included in this category of nonincome charges are sales, excise, and real property taxes paid by business firms.[4] These taxes are called indirect because it is assumed they are treated by business firms as a part of the cost of doing business; thus, they will be included in the sale price of final goods and services produced. If such taxes are shifted forward to the consumer, as the Department of Commerce believes, they will be reflected in the expenditure totals for the various component parts of GNP and, consequently, they must appear, too, on the allocations side of current GNP. But the total of indirect taxes cannot appear as a factor cost because they accrue to the government, and it is not the present practice in United States national income accounting procedures to treat government as a factor of production.

Capital consumption allowances, the other major nonincome charge against GNP, ideally should measure the physical wearing-out of capital equipment during the year. Capital goods are a part of the economy's stock of productive resources and their use in the productive process will inevitably entail a gradual wearing-out of such assets. The amount by which

---

4. Ibid., p. 33.

the economy's stock of real capital has been used up (or consumed) during the current income period is what we try to measure through capital consumption allowances.

It is the practice of the Department of Commerce to measure capital consumption allowances by the sum of depreciation charges by private business firms against their current incomes, plus accidental damage to fixed capital occurring during the income period. The basic difficulty with this procedure is that charges by the business firm for depreciation do not accurately reflect the physical wearing-out of capital goods, for the purpose of depreciation charges from an accounting viewpoint is to allow the individual producer to maintain intact the money value of his equipment. For the most part, allowances made by the business firm for depreciation are based on various arbitrary formulas that have little relationship to either the actual physical life of the asset or its use in any particular year. In spite of these deficiencies, the Department of Commerce continues to use business charges for depreciation as the best available measure at the present time of the economy's consumption of real capital during the income period.

Two Minor Charges   Two minor charges against the output totals remain to be explained. These appear in Table 3–2 as the items *business transfer payments* (Item 9) and *subsidies less current surplus of government enterprises* (Item 10). Business transfer payments are transfers from business to persons; they embody charges against the output total for which no return in the form of factor income is received. Most consist of corporate gifts to nonprofit institutions and consumer bad debts. "Subsidies less current surplus of government enterprises" is really a combined entry. In moving from national income to GNP in Table 3–2, it is necessary to deduct subsidies from the national income total. They are factor costs on the assumption that they constitute a form of payment necessary to secure the services of particular factors, although they are not reflected in the market price of final goods and services. The current surplus—or profit— of government enterprise is not, on the other hand, a factor cost, because government is not regarded as a factor of production; yet the value of goods and services produced by government enterprise and sold through normal market channels will be reflected in the value of final product totals. Electric power produced and sold by a municipal power and light plant is an example of this type of entry. It is the current practice of the Department of Commerce to combine these two relatively minor charges against the output totals into a single item on the allocations side of GNP.

Other Measures of Product and Income

We have devoted a relatively large amount of space to discussion of GNP not only because it is the most widely used national income aggregate, but also because it is the best point of departure for consideration and understanding of the other aggregates that make up the Department of Commerce's five-family series of national income and product measures.

Net National Product

Net national product (NNP) is defined by the Department of Commerce as the market value of the *net* output of final goods and services produced by the economy during the relevant income period.[5] In a theoretical sense it is a measure of the nation's output after allowance has been made for the consumption of capital in the current process of production. NNP is derived by subtracting capital consumption allowances from GNP. If business reserves for depreciation and the other items that enter into capital consumption allowances accurately reflected the real depreciation of the nation's stock of physical capital, net national product would measure exactly the amount of output that the nation could use for consumption, for the public sector, or for adding to the existing stock of capital without any impairment of productive capacity because of a failure to provide for the replacement of consumed items of real capital. Unfortunately, though, existing measurement techniques do not permit an accurate measurement of real capital consumption, so the net national product figure is not widely used.

National Income

We have already defined national income as the sum of the factor costs incurred during production of the economy's current output. More specifically, the Department of Commerce defines national income as the aggregate earnings of labor and property that arise from the production of goods and services by the nation's economy.[6] This measure is also described as the *net national product at factor cost* because it is a measure of the factor costs of the net output total. The national income is a concept of fundamental importance; it represents for the economy as a whole the amount of income earned by the owners of economic resources (land, labor, and capital) in return for supplying the services of these resources to the productive units of the economy. As such, it is the major source of money income or spending power for the purchase of most of the national output. The national income figure can be derived either by summing up the total of factor costs incurred in producing the current output or by deducting indirect business taxes and the other minor charges from the net national product total. It should be noted that the national income is both a measure of product (in the sense that it represents the factor cost of the current output) and a measure of money income earned by the factors of production.

5. Ibid., p. 56.
6. Ibid.

Personal Income

Although the national income aggregate is a measure of income earned by the owners of economic resources through participation in the productive process, it does not measure money income actually received by persons and households during the current income period. The reason is that some parts of earned (or factor) income are not actually received as money income by persons or households, whereas some households and persons receive money income that is not earned through supplying the services of economic resources to the productive process. The latter consists of transfer payments and interest income from consumers and government. Although the Department of Commerce defines personal income as the current income "received" by persons from all sources,[7] this is not strictly correct. The Department of Commerce normally measures personal income on a before-tax basis, but since some income taxes are withheld from wage and salary income, such income is not actually received. The intent, though, is to show the money income that persons are entitled to from all sources.

The usual procedure for obtaining the personal income measure is to deduct from national income the major categories earned (or factor) income that are not actually received as money income by persons or households, and then add to this figure the total of transfer incomes received from both government and business. The major deductions are (1) contributions to social insurance, (2) corporate profits tax liability, and (3) undistributed corporate profit. The chief forms of government transfer payments that must be added in are (1) interest on the public debt, (2) pensions paid to retired persons, (3) unemployment compensation, (4) various forms of relief payments, and (5) benefits extended to war veterans.

Disposable Income

The final, widely used measure of income is that of disposable income, which the Department of Commerce defines simply as the income remaining to individuals after deduction of all taxes levied against their income and their property by all governmental entities in the economy.[8] It is obtained by deducting such taxes from the personal income total, and it represents a measure of the after-tax purchasing power at the disposal of persons or households. Disposable income less personal consumption expenditures gives the total of personal saving in the economy. Gross private saving consists of this figure plus corporate saving (undistributed corporate profits) and capital consumption allowances.

The manner in which the five aggregate of both product and income are linked together is shown in Figure 3–1. Not only does this schema

7. Ibid.
8. Ibid.

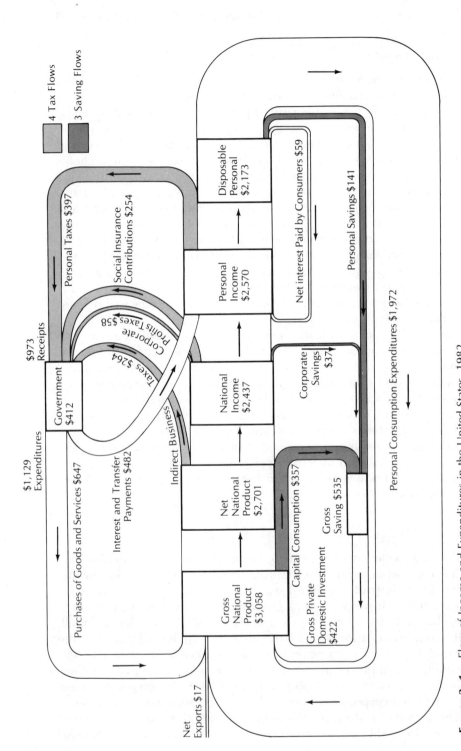

FIGURE 3–1. Flow of Income and Expenditures in the United States, 1982

SOURCE: *Economic Report of the President*, 1983

show the interrelationships existing with respect to these product measures, it also underscores the *flow* character of the gross national product
and its various components and serves to demonstrate this flow of product (income) and expenditures through the major sectors of the economy—households, businesses, and governments, as well as to the rest of
the world. This figure should be studied carefully.

Price Indexes and Comparisons over Time

The practice of the Department of Commerce is to report the money
value of national income and product statistics in terms of the prices
prevailing during the reporting period. Thus, GNP data for 1983 are
reported in prices of 1983. If we are interested only in the statistics of
income or output for a particular year, this does not create a special
problem; but if we want to make comparisons between a number of years,
then it is necessary to correct for changes in the general level of prices.
This must be done because changes in the monetary value of product
totals may result from either a change in the physical quantity of production or a change in the prices at which physical output is valued. The
latter type of change is a distortion insofar as comparisons over time are
concerned. If such comparisons are to be used meaningfully, it is desirable that we compare *real* changes rather than changes in value due to
changes in price. Thus, the effect of price-level changes must be eliminated if income and product data for different years are to reflect real
changes.

The procedure for eliminating the effect of price-level changes from
income and product data is to divide the data value in current prices by
an appropriate price index. This has the effect of converting the data to
a constant-price basis, thus making possible comparisons of real changes
over time. The underlying reason for dividing data valued in current
prices by a price index in order to get data valued in constant prices can
be explained by means of an example. Let us assume that we want to
convert GNP data for 1983 to 1972 prices so we can compare the actual
physical change in GNP between these two dates.[9] Since, by definition,
GNP is a measure of the monetary value of the current output,

$$GNP_{1983} = O_{1983} \times P_{1983}. \tag{3-1}$$

This equation means that the value of current 1983 output is equal to
the actual output *(O)* times the prices *(P)* at which the output is sold in
that year. From our prior discussion of price indexes, it also follows that
the index of prices for 1983, using 1972 as the base year, is equal to the
ratio of 1983 prices to 1972 prices. Thus,

$$\text{price index for } 1983 = \frac{P_{1983}}{P_{1972}}. \tag{3-2}$$

9. The Department of Commerce uses 1972 as its base year for constructing GNP price
deflators, i.e., indexes used to convert GNP data to constant dollars.

If we divide the GNP data for 1983 by the above price index, the result will be a measure of the physical output of 1983 valued in the prices of 1972. The following equations show algebraically why this is true.

$$\frac{GNP_{1983}}{P_{1983}/P_{1972}} = \frac{P_{1983} \times O_{1983}}{P_{1983}/P_{1972}}. \tag{3-3}$$

From Equation (3-3) it follows that

$$\frac{GNP_{1983}}{P_{1983}/P_{1972}} = (P_{1983} \times O_{1983}) \times \frac{P_{1972}}{P_{1983}}. \tag{3-4}$$

In Equation (3-4) the two expressions for 1983 prices, P_{1983}, on the right-hand side cancel out, and thus we have

$$\frac{GNP_{1983}}{P_{1983}/P_{1972}} = O_{1983} \times P_{1972}. \tag{3-5}$$

By dividing GNP measured in current (1983) prices by the current (1983) price index, the GNP data are converted to a figure which values the current output in prices for a selected base year. Table 3-3 shows the United States GNP in both current and constant dollars (or prices) for selected years since 1929. The table also includes in Column (3) the price indexes used to deflate the current dollar amounts.

TABLE 3-3.   Gross National Product and Constant Dollars; Selected Years, 1946–83 (in billions of dollars)

(1) Year	(2) GNP in Current Dollars	(3) Price Index* 1972 = 100	(4) = (2) ÷ (3) GNP in Constant Dollars
1948	259.5	53.0	489.8
1950	286.5	53.6	534.8
1955	400.0	60.8	657.5
1960	506.5	68.7	737.2
1965	691.1	74.4	929.3
1970	992.7	91.5	1,085.6
1975	1,549.2	125.6	1,274.7
1980	2,633.1	178.6	1,474.0
1982	3,057.5	207.2	1,475.5

SOURCE: *Economic Report of the President,* 1983, pp. 163–66.
*Implicit GNP deflator.

Limitations Inherent in Aggregate Measures of Income and Product

Athough GNP and the other aggregates are used extensively to measure the material performance of the economy, they are subject to a number of limitations, particularly with respect to economic welfare (material performance and welfare are not always identical). The most important of these limitations can be briefly summarized.

Economic versus Social Values

National income and product figures measure the economic rather than the social value of current productive activity. These data are largely limited to a measurement of economic value in terms of the market prices that different types of goods and services may command. But the market price of a good or a service may not accurately reflect the value to the society of the good or service in a more fundamental, philosophical sense. A society, for example, might spend identical sums on education and tobacco, and yet one would hesitate to assert that the social, as distinct from the economic, value of these two types of expenditures is the same. As Professor Robert Lekachman put it, "the national income expert totals not only the value of oil pumped up from the Santa Barbara channel [from oil spills] or the Gulf coast but also the expenses of cleaning up beaches and salvaging fishing grounds in the wake of oil-well blowouts. . . . By current criteria, gross national product rises when auto sales increase, regardless of what may be happening to the quality of the enjoyments these arrogant chariots generate or the variety of adverse side effects for which they are responsible."[10] The basic problem here is that the social value of the national output is necessarily a subjective matter, dependent upon individual judgments concerning what ought to be. It follows that there are no simple, direct, or objective criteria for measurement of the social value of the national output. It is desirable, nevertheless, that the distinction between economic and social value be clear—that is, the former is not always representative of the latter.

Economic versus Social Costs

Much of what we have said about economic and social values applies equally to economic and social costs. There is no necessary identity between the economic costs of producing the current national output and the social costs of the output. Economic costs include items such as factor costs, capital consumption allowances, and indirect business taxes—elements identified earlier as charges against GNP, and for which a monetary valuation is available. Social costs, on the other hand, relate to subjective and intangible phenomena such as the general deterioration of the physical and social environments as a result of current productive activity. For example, the beauty of the countryside may be irreparably marred, as has often happened in mining and industrial areas; rivers and the atmosphere may be contaminated through the disposal of indus-

10. Robert Lekachman, *National Income and Public Welfare* (New York: Random House, 1972), p. 7.

trial wastes; and disease and crime-infested slums may result as a by-product of industrial growth and urbanization. These costs are not measured directly by gross national product figures. Nevertheless, social costs are as much a part of the real cost of the national output as the more readily measurable economic costs, but because of their subjective nature there are no obviously certain criteria for judging their magnitude. Their existence, though, should be recognized by the serious student of economics.[11] Later in this chapter we shall discuss a pioneering effort to incorporate some social costs into the conventional measure of GNP.

There are, however, indirect ways in which social costs will be reflected in gross national product and other output measures. First, the money spent for workers and other resources needed to repair environmental damage from the past will be reflected in the output figures for the period in which such expenditures are made. Unhappily, as Professor Lekachman suggests, existing techniques for national income accounting and measurement cannot—or do not—distinguish between expenditures of this type and other expenditures that reflect newly created goods and services. Second, the expenditures that must be made to prevent further environmental deterioration or pollution also enter into gross national product accounting, although these expenditures do not directly increase either the quantity of goods and services we consume or our stock of capital instruments. Expenditures of this nature will probably grow rather than decrease in the future. One estimate put a $271 billion price tag on pollution-control costs over the decade ending in 1985.[12] Finally—and much more subtly—the social cost of environmental deterioration may show up in the higher wages needed to attract workers to deteriorating areas, and growing congestion and higher taxes in areas to which people flee to escape depressing surroundings.

The Value of Leisure

In any analysis of the economic welfare or well-being of a nation the amount of leisure time at the people's disposal should rank high in importance; yet the national income and product statistics do not measure directly the value of leisure to society. Over the last half-century the length of the standard workweek has fallen from sixty to seventy hours to fewer than forty hours, a development that represents a drastic improvement in welfare. What this means, in part, is that people have been willing to "exchange" relatively fewer goods and services for more leisure. One needs to be careful on this point, however, for no simple "trade-off" is involved. The reason, of course, is that the productivity of the work force—what an average worker can produce in a unit of time—

11. A leading proponent of this viewpoint is the British economist E. J. Mishan. See his *The Cost of Economic Growth* (New York: Praeger, 1967). See also Robert Lekachman, *National Income and the Public Welfare*, Chaps. 5, 6, and 7.
12. *U.S. News and World Report*, February 7, 1977, p. 43.

has also gone up, so it is possible to work less and yet enjoy the same or even a larger bundle of goods and services as compared to an earlier time. It is in this sense that GNP figures do not—they cannot—measure directly the value of leisure to a society. Nonetheless, not many would question the proposition that a society that is able to produce a larger volume of material goods and services with an equal or even smaller expenditure of human effort is in a real sense better off.

Qualitative Changes in the National Output

In the discussion of price indexes in Chapter 1, we pointed out the necessity for eliminating the distortion produced by changes in the prices of goods and services entering into the national income product statistics if comparisons were to be made of the national output at different points in time. Unfortunately, it is not possible to make the same adjustments for changes in the quality of goods and services. It is possible, for example, that the economy might spend (in terms of constant dollars) about the same amount today as it did ten years ago for television sets, but today's set is in a qualitative sense a vastly different product from one produced ten years ago. In some instances, qualitative changes may be so great that for all practical purposes no basis exists for comparing the value of a product now being produced with the value of the same or similar product in an earlier period. In the present stage of development of national income accounting no satisfactory technique exists for taking into account qualitative changes in the income and product totals.

The Composition of Output

The various aggregates that we have been discussing are limited as measures of economic welfare because they do not tell us very much about the composition of the national output, except in the broad terms of consumption, investment, and government expenditure. The welfare implications of an increase in the national output (in constant dollars) cannot be assessed without some knowledge of the composition of that output. For example, *real* GNP in the United States rose sharply during World War II, yet it would be ridiculous to say that the whole of this increase represented an increase in our well-being. Moreover, over long periods of time the composition of the national output may change drastically. Today, transportation by air is commonplace; sixty to seventy years ago, this kind of service did not exist. Thus, to evaluate fully the welfare implications of an increase in a society's real national product, it is necessary to know the composition of the product total and changes that may have taken place in this composition over relatively long periods of time.[13]

13. Lekachman, Chap. 3.

The Distribution of the National Output

Although national income and product data serve as highly useful measures of the economy's overall productive performance, they do not tell us how the output total is distributed among the members of society. It may be noted that the data indicate how the national income is distributed with respect to various forms of income—that is, wages, rents, profits, and so on—but not how it is distributed to persons. It is impossible, though, to ignore the distribution of output (and income) in any analysis of the welfare implications of a given level of economic activity. There are no wholly objective or purely scientific criteria for proper distribution of output and income in a society. One reason is that economists have, for reasons that probably don't make a lot of sense to the lay person, largely taken themselves out of the "theoretical-philosophical question of how income ought to be distributed."[14] Nevertheless, those economists who feel that greater equality in the distribution of the national income is to be preferred to less equality tend to argue along these lines: that society's welfare will be increased if, for example, a thousand dollars is taken from a rich man and given to a poor sharecropper with four or five children. The difficulty in this is that there are no objective criteria to tell us how far to push such a proposition.[15] In any event, some knowledge of the actual distribution of income in society, and some concept of how income ought to be distributed is necessary for an evaluation of the economy's performance in terms of economic welfare.[16]

Income and Output per Capita

Finally, it is necessary to take into account changes in population as well as changes in real output totals if meaningful comparisons of economic welfare are to be made over time. A rise in real income will not bring an improvement in the material level of well-being if population grows at a faster rate than the output total. For many purposes it is desirable that the aggregate data of national output and income be reduced to a per capita basis before comparisons are made. For example, between 1945 and 1982 *real* GNP grew by 163 percent, whereas per capita GNP grew by only 159 percent.

The shortcomings described are not the only limitations involved in the use of national income statistics. The careful reader, who understands that such limitations exist, will exercise caution in drawing welfare conclusions from the performance data recorded in national income and product statistics. National income data are of great value for the measurement of the economy's performance, but they must be interpreted correctly.

14. Alice M. Rivlin, "Income Distribution—Can Economists Help?" *The American Economic Review,* May 1975, p. 5.
15. Ibid., p. 6.
16. Lekachman, Chap. 4.

The Search for Improved Measures of Product and Welfare

The limitations of currently used measures of national income and product have not gone unnoticed by national income theoreticians and statisticians. In recent years two approaches to the problem have emerged that aim to establish better and more refined measures of output and well-being. The objective of one is to have statistics on economic output reflect social benefits, social costs, and leisure. The objective of the other is more far-reaching: It seeks to measure the social health of the nation in the same way that national income accounts have measured its economic health. Both of these are worthy of our attention.

Professors James Tobin and William Nordhaus of Yale University have developed an experimental *measure of economic welfare*—termed MEW—which is designed to convert the conventional GNP figure into one that measures economic welfare.[17] As they point out, the major shortcoming of GNP is that it is an index of production, not consumption. Since presumably the main purpose of economic activity is consumption, any measure of economic welfare ought to be oriented toward consumption more than production. Their experimental MEW represents essentially a rearrangement of conventional national income data to reflect this point of view.

The necessary adjustments to GNP data fall into three basic categories[18]: (1) reclassifying GNP expenditure totals so as to get more accurate measures of consumption, investment, and intermediate products; (2) making estimates—*imputations*—for the value of the services of consumer and public capital, for leisure, and for household work; and (3) adding a correction that reflects some of the disamenities—that is, social costs—of urbanization.

In reclassifying GNP final expenditures as normally reported in the U.S. national income accounts, Professors Tobin and Nordhaus adjusted capital expenditure figures in two ways. First, they enlarged the capital consumption category to include estimates of capital consumption for three additional types of capital: the stock of privately held consumer durables, government capital, and human capital (see Chapter 2, p. 47). This logically follows from their reclassification of some government expenditures as capital expenditures (housing, education, transportation, for example), the treatment of all outlays for consumer durables as gross investment, and the classification of private expenditures for educational and medical purposes as investment in human capital. Second, they develop an estimate of the additional investment in all forms of

17. James Tobin and William Nordhaus, "Is Growth Obsolete?" in *Economic Growth* (New York: National Bureau of Economic Research, 1972). Professor Tobin received the Nobel Prize for economics in 1981. Professor Nordhaus was a member of the President's Council of Economic Advisers in 1977 and 1978.
18. Ibid., p. 5.

public and private capital needed to sustain per capita consumption with a growing population and improving technology. This they term the growth requirement. The underlying assumption is that, if population growth and technical progress are present, then the economy's stock of capital must also grow.

In addition to the adjustments in the capital expenditures category, GNP data were adjusted to change some expenditures now classified as final output to an intermediate, or instrumental, category. These include such public expenditures as police services, sanitation, road maintenance, and national defense, the rationale being that most government expenditures—other than those of a capital goods nature—are necessary overhead costs in a modern nation.[19] Private expenditures reclassified as intermediate included a portion of personal transportation expenditures and all personal business expenses.

As pointed out earlier, national income procedures now in use include an imputation for rent on owner-occupied homes as a part of consumption and income. But no allowance is made for the value of leisure. This tends to understate economic welfare. Consequently, Professors Tobin and Nordhaus introduce into the calculation of MEW estimates of the value of leisure and nonmarket productive activities (housework and other home-produced services). These, of course, have a positive value.

The two final adjustments made by Tobin and Nordhaus to transform GNP into MEW involve estimates of some of the social costs, or disamenities, associated with urbanization, and of the value of services provided by government and private capital held by consumers. The main disamenities included in their calculations are pollution, litter, congestion, noise, insecurity, and buildings and advertisements offensive to taste that are characteristic of urban life. These they attempt to measure by calculation of a disamenity premium, which is based upon estimates of the additional income required to induce people to live in densely populated cities rather than in smaller communities and rural areas.[20]

Although the MEW concept still awaits refinement, it is at least a start. Not nearly so much progress has been made in efforts to construct a comprehensive system of social accounts that would measure the nation's social health in the same way that economic accounts measure the nation's material health. Some impetus in this direction was given by the release in 1969 of a report from what was the Department of Health, Education and Welfare before the Carter administration established a separate Department of Education. This report urged the development of a set of social indicators and an annual *Social Report* on the model of the annual *Economic Report* of the President's Council of Economic Advisers.[21] Legislation was introduced into the Congress establishing a Council of Social Advisers and requiring the publication of an annual *Social Report,* to be transmitted by the president to the Congress. But there has been little support in recent years for such legislation.

What would a social report and social accounting attempt to do? Specifically, it would measure, via a set of social indicators, social progress or retrogression. According to *Toward a Social Report,* this would require the development of quantitative measures of the factors that help (or hinder) the individual citizen to live a full and healthy life within a decent social and physical environment. Among such factors are health and illness, the extent of social mobility, the quality of the physical environment, the extent and incidence of poverty, conditions of public order and safety, the availability of educational and cultural opportunities, and the existence and extent of alienation in society.

Obviously, formidable difficulties confront any effort to construct a set of social accounts comparable to the economic accounts now in use. Not only are many of the social factors inherently subjective in nature, but they do not lend themselves readily to quantification in index form. But the task is not impossible. In areas like health, education, and crime, for example, statistical data are being compiled and used in a manner that reflects improvement or retrogression. Slow but persistent progress can be expected in the development of statistical indicators in such areas. What is not likely, though, is the development of a single, unified statistic comparable to GNP that would be a barometer of the nation's social health. As the HEW report said, "It would be utopian even to strive for a Gross Social Product, or National Socioeconomic Welfare, figure which aggregated all relevant social and economic variables. There are no objective weights, equivalent to prices, that we can use to compare the importance of an improvement in health with an increase in social mobility. . . . Thus the goal of a grand and cosmic measure of all forms or aspects of welfare must be dismissed as impractical, for the present at any rate."[22]

Employment and Unemployment

Let us now turn our attention to the matter of defining and measuring employment—especially "full employment"—and unemployment in the economy. Historically, it was the enormous scarcity of jobs during the Great Depression of the 1930s that led Keynes and others to develop theories to explain aggregate economic behavior. For many people, the primary criterion of whether or not the economy is performing well is the availability of jobs for all persons seeking work. Consequently, the meaning of *employment* and *unemployment* needs to be examined carefully and fully.

The idea that full employment is a proper and desirable objective of

22. *Toward a Social Report,* p. 99.

public policy gained widespread acceptance in the United States and most of the nations of Western Europe during and immediately following World War II. In the United States, the Employment Act of 1946 gave legislative sanction to the view that the federal government has a direct responsibility for the level of employment and income prevailing in the economy. The act specifically stated:

> The Congress hereby declares that it is the continuing policy and responsibility of the Federal Government to use all practicable means consistent with its needs and obligations and other essential considerations of national policy, with the assistance and cooperation of industry, agriculture, labor, and State and local governments, to coordinate and utilize all its plans, functions, and resources for the purpose of creating and maintaining, in a manner calculated to foster and promote free competitive enterprise and the general welfare, conditions under which there will be afforded useful employment opportunities, including self employment, for those able, willing, and seeking work, and to promote maximum employment, production, and purchasing power.[23]

The qualifying phrases found in the Employment Act suggest, on the one hand, that full employment is not a social goal to be achieved at all costs and, on the other, that the federal government has other obligations ranking in importance with that of full employment. Increasingly, economists believe that stability of the general price level is a goal equal in importance to full employment. They believe this because they fear that continuous upward pressure on the price level not only dissipates the gains resulting from full employment, but jeopardizes the economy's ability to maintain conditions of full employment of for any significant period of time. These fears have been given a concrete policy expression in the Full Employment and Balanced Growth Act of 1978, which amended the Employment Act to include "reasonable price stability" as a major policy objective. More will be said shortly about this 1978 act.

Although the Employment Act made maximum or full employment an objective of public policy it did not define exactly what constitutes a fully employed labor force. Yet without some conception of what is meant by full employment, administration of the act in any practical sense is impossible. The simplest definition of full employment is a situation in the economy characterized by an absence of *involuntary unemployment.* The latter exists when members of the labor force are willing to work at prevailing wages in their trade or occupation but are unable to obtain employment. If we let N' be representative of the labor force and N stand for the actual level of employment, then full employment exists in the society as $N' - N$ approaches zero.

It should be noted that we used the phrase *approaches zero* rather than *equals zero.* The reason for this is that absolute full employment of the labor force, which would prevail if $N' - N$ were equal to zero, is a condition that is seldom, if ever, attained in practice. In almost any society there is likely to be a varying amount of *frictional unemployment,* which

23. Public Law 304, 79th Congress, Employment Act of 1946.

results whenever persons in the labor force are temporarily out of work because of imperfections in the labor market. At any given time some workers will be in the process of changing jobs or occupations; others will be experiencing temporary layoffs caused by the seasonal nature of the employment, by shortage of materials in some industries, or by shifts in demand that reduce the need for some types of workers and increase the need for others. Many other similar factors cause some proportion of the labor force to be out of work for short periods of time.

Quite early in the history of the implementation of the Employment Act a 4 percent unemployment rate emerged as a rough measure of full employment in the American economy. Full employment not only means that frictional unemployment is at a minimum, but that the economy can attain such a level without the risk of serious inflation.

Increasingly in recent years some economists have been using the term the "natural rate of employment" to define a situation in which not only the demand and supply of labor are in balance, but it is impossible to increase employment without causing more inflation. Critics dislike this terminology in part because the word "natural" may imply to some something that is beyond social—that is, public—control. Furthermore, application of the concept of a "natural rate of unemployment" to the situation of the last ten to fifteen years leads to acceptance of levels of unemployment that once would have been regarded as wholly unaccept-able. Since the unemployment rate has gone up along with the inflation rate, the implication is that the "natural rate" of unemployment has been rising. Why this has happened will be clearer as we continue the story of the search for a more precise measure of full employment in the American economy.

In the foregoing observation that a 4 percent unemployment rate was regarded as an appropriate measure of "full employment" in the early days of the Employment Act, the use of the adjective "rough" was delib-erate. This is because between 1946 and 1961 the President's Council of Economic Advisers strongly resisted using any explicit figure to measure full employment. In January 1955, for example, Council member Arthur F. Burns told the Joint Economic Committee of the Congress that "although 4 percent of the labor force is widely regarded as an approx-imate measure of the average amount of frictional and seasonal unem-ployment, the Council has not favored this or any other rigid figure to serve as a trigger to governmental action or as a measure of good per-formance."[24]

It was not until the Kennedy administration that an explicit figure for full employment was agreed upon. In the January 1962 *Economic Report of the President,* the Council explicitly set a 4 percent unemployment rate as an interim goal, the expectation being that ultimately an even lower target figure could be established:

---

24. *Economic Report of the President: Hearings,* 84th Congress, 1st Session (Washington, D.C.: U.S. Government Printing Office, 1955), p. 45.

> In the existing economic circumstances an unemployment rate of about 4 percent is a reasonable and prudent *full employment target for stabilization policy* [emphasis added]. If we move firmly to reduce the impact of structural unemployment, we will be able to move the unemployment target steadily from 4 percent to successively lower levels.[25]

Under the Johnson administration, 4 percent continued to be accepted as an appropriate target, although no attempt was ever made to lower the figure. For a while the Vietnam war made the question academic, since unemployment dipped below 4 percent for the four years 1966 through 1969.

During the Nixon and Ford administrations, references to a specific target for unemployment practically vanished from the reports of the president's economic advisers. As inflation picked up steam in the 1970s, some economists began to abandon the idea that 4 percent represented even a satisfactory interim goal. In its 1972 report, the Council argued that 5 percent rather than 4 percent unemployment would be a more suitable benchmark,[26] mainly due to the fact that women and teenagers constitute a growing portion of the labor force. In 1948, for example, 33 percent of the labor force consisted of women and teenagers; in 1980 these two groups accounted for 47 percent of the labor force.[27] Since both teenagers and women have higher unemployment rates on the average than men, this tends to pull the overall unemployment rate up. In the final report for the Ford administration, Alan Greenspan, chairman of the Council, reported that the outgoing Council believed the appropriate full employment rate for joblessness was 4.9 percent, but warned that inflationary pressure might set in even at an unemployment rate of 5.5 percent.[28] When the Ford administration left office, unemployment was running close to 8 percent.

During the Carter presidency, the concept of full employment was given a more explicit definition in the Full Employment and Balanced Growth Act of 1978. In addition to amending the Declaration of Policy of the 1946 Employment Act to include "reasonable price stability" as one of the goals of the act, the 1978 legislation established as a goal—to be reached within five years after passage of the act—reduction of the unemployment rate for all persons over twenty years of age to 3 percent, and for teenagers an unemployment rate no greater than 4 percent. In terms of a goal, then, it may be said that full employment overall is defined

25. *Economic Report of the President* (Washington, D.C.: U.S. Government Printing Office, 1962), p. 46.
26. Ibid., 1972, pp. 108 ff.
27. Ibid., 1981, pp. 264, 266. The above figures represent the total of teenagers and women as a percentage of the total labor force. They should not be confused with the labor force participation rate for these two groups individually. The latter represents the proportion of members of a particular group in the labor force. For example, in 1980, the labor force participation rate for women was 51.6, which means that 51.6 percent of *all* women eligible for the labor force actually were a part of the labor force.
28. Ibid., 1977, p. 56.

as an unemployment rate slightly less than 4 percent, depending on the number of teenagers in the labor force. Unfortunately, the 1978 act had little to say of practical importance as to how the government should reach this goal. More important, perhaps, the act contains a major loophole, because it permits a president to modify both the timetable for attaining the goals of the act and the goals themselves if economic conditions are such that the president does not believe the goals can be obtained. The Carter administration, even though professing a belief in full employment as a goal, was quick to take advantage of this feature of the act. In its 1980 *Economic Report,* the administration said that it was no longer practicable to attempt to reach a 4 percent unemployment rate and a 3 percent inflation rate by 1983, the target date set originally in the act.[29]

The Reagan administration, like the Nixon and Ford administrations earlier, has avoided a commitment to any specific level of unemployment as representing full employment. In its *Program for Economic Recovery,* submitted to the Congress in February 1981, the administration said that 13 million new jobs would be created in the economy by 1986, a development that it forecast would bring the unemployment rate down to 5.6 percent by then.[30] The latter rate is about where the Ford administration defined the "natural" or modified "full employment" level, but well above the interim target set earlier in the Kennedy-Johnson years.

If we accept as a working hypothesis that full employment lies somewhere between no more than 4 and 5 percent of the civilian labor force without jobs, then it appears that unemployment has been high in the American economy for most of the years since World War II.

Figure 1–6 in Chapter 1 traces unemployment in the American economy since 1900. For the period 1946 through 1980 unemployment averaged 5.1 percent of the civilian labor force, although in more than half of those years (19) it rose above 5 percent. If we look at the data more closely, the record is uneven, for it was only during the years affected by the Korean war (1950–53) and the Vietnam war (1966–69) that average unemployment got below the Kennedy target of 4 percent. It is only in contrast with the devastating experience of the 1930s that the post–World War II employment record looks exceptionally good. In 1933, which was the low point of the Great Depression, unemployment totaled 24.9 percent of the civilian labor force—one worker out of every four was jobless. Even as late as 1939, ten years after the crash of 1929, unemployment still stood at 17.2 percent of the labor force.[31]

The problem with averages such as the overall unemployment rate is that they often exclude as much as they reveal. Some segments of our

29. Ibid., 1980, p. 93.
30. The White House, *A Program for Economic Recovery* (Washington, D.C., February 18, 1981), pp. 1, 25.
31. *Historical Statistics of the United States,* Bicentennial Edition, Vol. 1 (Washington, D.C.: U.S. Government Printing Office, 1975), p. 135.

society have never experienced anything that remotely resembles "full employment," by whatever standard it is measured. Blacks and other nonwhite minorities as well as teenagers are in this category. The overall situation for women is not as bad as for these two other groups, but most of the time they have found it tougher to get jobs than have adult white males. The bleak fact is that most of the time during the years of high prosperity after World War II nonwhite minorities and teenagers actually confronted depressionlike conditions in the nation's job markets (see Figure 1–7, p. 17).

Why this condition persists in good times and bad for these two groups (there is obviously some overlap) is by no means readily apparent. It has been suggested that somehow teenagers and minorities are less attached to the labor force and the idea of working, one reason being that many of the jobs available to both groups are not only low paying, but "dead end."[32] In a formal sense this view is embodied in the "dual labor market hypothesis," which holds that the nation's labor market really consists of two basic markets—a *primary* sector and a *secondary* sector.[33] In the primary sector are the better-paying, preferred jobs, characterized by good working conditions, reasonable employment stability, and opportunities for advancement. Unemployment in this sector, when it occurs, is usually described as *cyclical* or "Keynesian," in that it comes about when the economy falls into a recession or depression. In the secondary sector, the situation is quite different; there we find low pay, poor working conditions, frequent layoffs, high turnovers, and little opportunity for advancement. Workers in this sector frequently drift from one low-paying job to another. The kind of unemployment found in the secondary sector is called *structural,* a broad term which has come to mean unemployment that is not frictional and that persists even when times are good. Economists are by no means in agreement on the extent of such unemployment—obviously not all minority and teenage unemployment is of this nature—but there is considerable consensus that such unemployment is much more difficult to cure than the "Keynesian" variety. The fact that there have been such high rates of joblessness for minorities and teenagers in good times and bad ever since World War II attests to this.

Employment and Output

In the foregoing paragraphs we stressed that full employment for the nation's labor force has become a public policy objective of major significance in contemporary American society. It is equally important to

32. Martin Feldstein, "The Economics of the New Unemployment," *The Public Interest,* Fall 1973, p. 14.
33. Peter B. Doeringer and Michael J. Piore, "Unemployment and the 'Dual Labor Market,' " *The Public Interest,* Winter 1975, p. 70.

understand that a close link exists between the employment level and the output level. In other words, we can expect the amount of employment to vary more or less directly with the volume of production. Since the latter constitutes the real income of society, it follows that the employment level serves as an indicator of the economy's overall performance. Conversely, the output level is a good indicator of the prevailing employment situation in the economy. This, of course, applies to the overall average, not the specific employment situation for any particular segment of the labor force at any given time.

The link between real income and the employment level is important for economic analysis because it embraces a number of simple, but fundamental, economic relationships. Basic to an understanding of the determinants of the level of production and employment is the concept of the economy's productive capacity. In Chapter 1 we described this as potential GNP. At any time there exists for the economy as a whole a given productive capacity, that is, a potential for the production of goods and services. Even in the short run the economy's productive capacity is not an exact or unvarying magnitude, for in practically all economies there is some flexibility in the maximum output that can be obtained over short periods of time. Nevertheless, all economies have an upper limit to the amount of goods and services that can be produced, and this upper limit will necessarily constitute an economy's short-run maximum capacity to produce. Over time, of course, this may change as the process of economic growth brings about expansion in the economy's productive capacity. A *dynamic economy* is characterized by a continuously expanding capacity for production.

What determines the productive capacity of the economy? This is one of the most complex of all economic problems, yet the basic factors in the process can be readily identified. In the simplest sense, productive capacity depends upon first, the quantity and quality of resources available to the economy and, second, the skill and efficiency with which these resources are brought together for the purpose of production. The latter involves technology, for in its broadest meaning technology refers to the overall level of effectiveness attained by an economy in combining resources together in the productive process.

The statements in the foregoing paragraph can be summarized symbolically by the following equation:

$$Q = f(N', H', R', K'\ T) \tag{3-6}$$

In this and the following equations the symbols used have the following meanings:

Q = the economy's productive capacity (*potential GNP*)
N' = the economy's labor force
H' = the standard hours of work per year
R' = the economy's stock of known and economically useful natural resources

K' = the economy's stock of capital or man-made instruments of production

T = the level of technology prevailing in the economy

The meaning of equation 3–6 is that the economy's productive capacity is a function (the symbol f in the equation) of the basic determinants
listed above: the quantity of labor, the standard hours of work, natural
resources, capital, and the level of technology. Note that the equation
does not in any way specify the exact proportions in which the determinants of capacity are brought together, but merely states that productive
capacity depends on these things. Because technology is not a stock, as
are labor, capital, and natural resources, it is separated from the other
variables by a semicolon. Technically, it is a *parameter,* whose value determines the output potential associated with specific quantities of the other
three determinants.

The productive capacity of the economy can be defined, too, in terms
of the fully employed labor force, N', and the average productivity of
labor, P_r. The productivity of labor, or average output per worker-hour
(or some other time unit such as worker-year), does not refer to the
degree of skill possessed by labor in general, but rather to the efficiency
with which labor power is employed in the productive process. Since the
latter depends upon the quantity and quality of capital equipment and
natural resources used in conjunction with labor, the following is a correct statement of the relevant relationships:

$$P_r = f(R', K', T). \tag{3–7}$$

The equation states that the productivity of labor is a function of the
quantity of natural resources and capital equipment, given the level of
technology. This being the case, it follows that the economy's productive
capacity is equal to the fully employed labor force, N', times the normal
hours of work per year, H', times the average productivity of labor, P_r.
When so stated, P_r represents *output per worker-hour.* Thus, we have the
equation

$$Q = (N' \times H \times P_r). \tag{3–8}$$

If we let P_r' represent *output per worker-year,* the equation would simply
be

$$Q = (N' \times P_r'). \tag{3–9}$$

Just as the economy's productive capacity depends upon the quantity
and quality of available resources, the actual level of output is determined by the extent to which these resources are being used. Output
results from the utilization of productive capacity. In economics the
physical relationship that exists between the input of resources and the
output of goods and services in any given period of time is termed the
production function. Stated in other terms, the production function embodies

a functional relationship between the quantity of input and the quantity of output. In the short run it may take the following form:

$$Y = f(N, R', K', T). \qquad (3-10)$$

This equation means that—*given the stock* of natural resources and capital, as well as the level of technology—output is determined by the labor input *(N)*. It is also true that output can be defined as the product of the actual labor employed and the average productivity of labor. For example, if P_r' represents output per worker-year, then we have:

$$Y = N \times P_r'. \qquad (3-11)$$

The concept of the production function is depicted graphically in Figure 3–2, which shows output on the vertical axis and labor input (people at work) on the horizontal axis. The output curve will eventually level off because of diminishing productivity. On the curve labeled Y_a, an increase in the income level from Y_1 to Y_2 results when employment increases from N_1 to N_2. The same increase in income may be obtained with no change in employment if the entire production function shifts upward to the level depicted by the curve Y_b. This would result from a change in the stock of capital and natural resources, a change in technology, or a combination of the two.

The foregoing discussion provides a basis for understanding the close relationship which exists between employment and output over short periods of time, during which it is assumed that the quantity of capital,

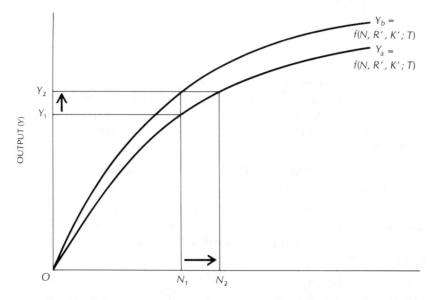

FIGURE 3–2. The Production Function

natural resources, and the level of technology remain relatively fixed. By implication, then, productive capacity is also relatively fixed.

There is no way to define precisely the length of real time involved in the short run, although a satisfactory working definition is that it is long enough to permit some cyclical fluctuations in income and employment, but not sufficiently long to show a definite trend. The significant factor for our analysis is that the short run is not a long enough period of time to permit any really significant changes in the economy's productive capacity. Consequently, we may assume that the underlying determinants of capacity in Equation (3–6) have relatively fixed magnitudes, although the extent to which they are actually utilized in production is variable. This is particularly true with respect to the labor force, because the level of employment, N, can quite obviously depart rather widely at times from the size of the labor force, N'. For the economy as a whole, the output level, Y, in the short run will tend to vary directly with the employment level N. Thus, a good workable hypothesis is as follows:

$$Y = f(N). \tag{3–12}$$

In this formulation the level of employment, N, has meaning not only in relation to the overall supply of labor, N', but also as a barometer of the extent to which the economy's productive capacity is actually being utilized. In the chapters that follow we will make frequent use of this simple but important notion that over relatively short periods of time employment and real income move together.

Summary

1. Gross national product (GNP) is defined as the current market value of all final goods and services produced by the economy during an income period. It can be measured both from the summation of the kinds of final output that enter into GNP and from the summation of charges against the output total.

2. Net national product (NNP) is obtained by subtracting capital consumption allowances from the GNP.

3. The national income (NI) is defined as the factor cost of the net national product. It can be obtained by summing up all factor costs—wages, interest, rents, and profits—or by deducting indirect business taxes from the NNP.

4. Personal Income (PI) is the sum of money income from all sources that goes to persons or households. It is obtained by subtracting from the national income earned by the factors of production, but not actually paid out, and adding in transfer payments.

5. Disposable Income (DI) is equal to personal income less all taxes

paid by persons and households. It measures income available for consumption or saving.

6. All income measures are subject to important limitations, including the fact that they measure only economic gains and costs. They do not adequately measure the value of leisure, the quality of output, or the distribution of the national output.

7. The Employment Act of 1946 was a watershed measure that explicitly made the federal government responsible for attaining satisfactory levels of employment and minimizing unemployment.

8. "Full employment" is an important concept and is usually defined in terms of a percentage of the labor force not working. There is no agreement among economists on the precise percentage of the labor force unemployed that represents "full employment."

II

The Basic Theory of Income and Employment

4

A General Model of
the Economic System

It is now time to turn our attention to the basic theory that explains why the economy behaves in the way it does. Specifically, in this chapter we shall develop a broad and general model within which we can fit the basic forces that determine the level of output, employment, and prices in the modern economy. This model will provide us with a point of departure for examination of the principal theoretical relationships that enter into contemporary macroeconomic theory.

In constructing our basic model, we shall draw upon two of the oldest and most important theoretical concepts known to economics, namely, those of demand and supply. We shall consider supply and demand in the context of the economy as a whole, rather than in the context of a single market for a single commodity or service. Developing a general model of the economy around supply and demand concepts does not require the mastering of something entirely new. Rather, it requires drawing upon familiar ideas, but using them in a different way. To put it slightly differently, the reader will find the ideas in this chapter to be familiar, but the perspective will be different.

The Essence of the
Income-Employment Problem

It will be recalled that capacity is the economy's potential for the production of goods and services. If we begin with the concept of capacity, certain consequences logically follow. First, output will depend upon the extent to which this capacity is being utilized. This will be true up to the limits of capacity. Second, output will depend upon the level of employment as long as all resources other than labor are fixed. This brings us to the key question of modern employment theory: *What is it that determines the extent to which the economy's productive capacity is being utilized?*

In a sense the answer to this question is deceptively simple, for it is the *expectation* of the businessman that he will be able to sell what he produces that leads him to make use of the productive capacity at his disposal. The presumption here is that the output will be sold at prices that cover costs of production. Stated in more formal terms, productive capacity will be brought into use (or production will take place) whenever there exists the expectation that demand for the output will be sufficient to clear the market of what is being produced. Note carefully two points. First, this statement describes the conditions under which productive capacity will be utilized in a market economy, that is to say, an economy in which the basic decisions about what is to be produced and in what quantities are made by private individuals rather than public authorities. Second, the key word in the statement is *expectation,* which is a way of stressing the fact that production in a market economy is carried on, for the most part, in anticipation of demand.

Assuming that the expectation of demand is the essential condition required to bring productive capacity into use, it follows that *the theory of income determination in the modern economy is basically a theory of aggregate demand.* In other words, if we are to understand how the level of output and employment is actually determined, it is necessary that we understand how demand for the output of the whole economy is determined. In sum, aggregate demand is the crucial determinant of the level of income and employment during short periods when productive capacity is assumed to be relatively fixed. This is the central theme of Keynes's *The General Theory.*

At this point we must add an important proviso. As indicated in Chapter 1, the dismal experience of recent years, in which prices kept rising in spite of levels of unemployment that have been excessive by historic standards, led some economists to look more to supply rather than demand factors for an explanation of why an increase in total spending—that is, aggregate demand—does not always lead readily to an equivalent change in output. As we have also noted, "supply-side" economics provided the theoretical rationale for the economic programs of the Reagan administration. Subsequently (see Chapters 11 and 12) we shall give due attention to these developments. But they should not cause us to forget or neglect what is, perhaps, the most fundamental working principle of a market system: No matter how great productive capacity may be, *no* business firm operated for profit will produce anything for sale unless it expects that sooner or later someone will buy what is produced. Demand ultimately does determine the extent to which productive capacity is used. There is no escape from this fundamental fact. Of course, in the long run, the relationship between capacity, output, and employment is more complex. The reason is that, in the long run, the economy's productive capacity changes. Thus, in the long run the theory of income and employment determination must explain, first, changes in the economy's productive capacity over time and, second, how aggregate demand adjusts over time to such changes. This is the essential problem of growth theory, which we shall examine in Chapter 16.

The Aggregate Supply Schedule

The idea that there exists for the economy a given productive capacity that will be utilized in greater or lesser degree according to the aggregate of expectations held by entrepreneurs is represented by the concept of an aggregate supply schedule or function. The aggregate supply schedule for the whole economy is very much like the supply schedule for any individual commodity. A typical supply curve for a commodity has a positive slope—that is, it slopes upward to the right—and shows the prices at which various amounts of the commodity will be forthcoming. It is an *ex ante* concept in the sense that it depicts the intended response of the suppliers of the commodity to varying circumstances. It shows that more of any commodity will be brought to the market as the price increases. The schedule is, in effect, a series of *supply prices* for varying amounts of the commodity. The supply price for any particular quantity of a commodity is that price which will just induce the producer or supplier to continue to offer that quantity of the commodity on the market; thus, the *supply schedule* shows the amounts of the commodity that will be forthcoming at any and all possible prices. The aggregate supply schedule represents not the response of a single producer supplying the market with a particular commodity, but the summation, in effect, of the responses of all producers supplying the whole of the output of the economy. It seeks to show, in other words, the conditions under which varying amounts of total output will be supplied or produced.

The Keynesian Aggregate Supply Function

Early in *The General Theory* Keynes defined the aggregate supply price of the output of a given amount of employment as "the expectation of proceeds which will just make it worth the while of the entrepreneur to give that employment."[1] What Keynes had in mind was a schedule that would show for any and all possible levels of employment the volume of receipts from the sale of output that would justify the varying quantities of employment. The receipts would have to be sufficient to cover all costs incurred by the entrepreneur plus a profit. Keynes believed that entrepreneurs sought at all times to maximize their profits. The receipts—or expected proceeds—must cover costs plus profits for the economy's

---

1. John Maynard Keynes, *The General Theory of Employment, Interest and Money* (New York: Harcourt, Brace & World, First Harbinger ed., 1964), p. 24.

total employment in the same way that price must cover costs and a unit profit for the supply of a particular good or service. Such a schedule shows the amount of employment that entrepreneurs in the aggregate can be expected to offer on the basis of any and all possible volumes of proceeds from the sale of the output resulting from the different amounts of employment. In *The General Theory* Keynes linked employment, rather than output or real income, to expected proceeds because at the time he was writing (1936) statistical techniques for the accurate measurement of important aggregates such as GNP were not highly developed. He thought that employment constituted the best single measure of total or aggregate economic activity.

A highly simplified version of the Keynesian aggregate supply function is illustrated by the hypothetical data in Table 4–1, which relate employment and expected proceeds. For the sake of simplicity we assume that labor is the only resource, and thus the only cost of production to be covered in the aggregate by the sales proceeds are labor costs. It is further assumed that the normal workweek is forty hours, and that workers are employed for fifty-two weeks each year. In the table there are two schedules: Schedule A and Schedule B. Schedule A is based upon the assumption that the money wages of workers remain constant at $6.50 per hour, regardless of the actual level of employment or demand for labor. Schedule B is based upon the assumption that the money wage will rise as more employment is offered. This implies that, as the demand for labor increases, its price—that is, the money wage—will rise. Note, too, that money wages rise in Schedule B at different rates as the employment level increases.

TABLE 4–1. The Aggregate Supply Function

Employment (N) (in millions of workers)	Schedule A		Schedule B	
	Money Wages (w) (per hour)	Aggregate Supply Price (Z) (in billions of dollars)	Money Wages (w) (per hour)	Aggregate Supply Price (Z') (in billions of dollars)
96	$6.50	$1,298	$6.50	$1,298
98	6.50	1,325	6.70	1,366
100	6.50	1,352	6.95	1,446
102	6.50	1,379	7.25	1,538
104	6.50	1,406	7.60	1,644
106	6.50	1,433	8.00	1,764
108	6.50	1,460	8.45	1,898
110	6.50	1,487	8.95	2,047

Note: A 40-hour workweek and a 52-week work-year are assumed. Thus, each employee works 2,080 hours per years. To get the aggregate supply price for any level of employment, this figure is multiplied by the average hourly wage and then by the total number of workers employed (N). If H equals annual hours worked, then $Z = H \times (w) \times N$.

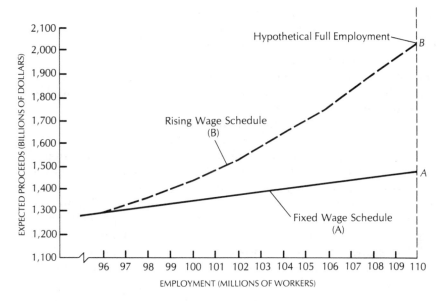

FIGURE 4–1.   The Keynesian Aggregate Supply Function: Employment and Proceeds

Let us examine each of these schedules in a little more detail. Schedule *A* shows what the minimum expected sales proceeds must be for entrepreneurs to offer employment to specified numbers of workers. For example, if employers in the aggregate are to offer employment to 96 million workers, the expected proceeds from the sale of the output produced by these 96 million workers must at a minimum equal $1,298 billion. Why is this? The $1,298 billion represents the total money costs of this amount of product that must be covered by sales proceeds if entrepreneurs in the aggregate are to continue to offer this amount of employment. Thus, the $1,298 billion is the aggregate supply price of this amount of employment. In Schedule *B* the aggregate supply price for each level of employment subsequent to 96 million is higher because of the assumption that the money wage will rise from $6.50 per hour to $8.95 per hour as the total volume of employment climbs from 96 to 110 million workers.

Figure 4–1 illustrates graphically the Keynesian aggregate supply function.[2] In the figure, employment is plotted on the horizontal axis, and expected sales proceeds on the vertical axis. If we then plot the data of Table 4–1 we get the two curves shown in the figure. The one labeled

2. The student should not confuse the above curves with the production function, which normally shows the relationship between employment and output. The supply schedule as depicted could be made more "realistic" by the addition of a "markup" factor to total labor costs, which would represent the entrepreneur's profit. This does not change the basic principle involved, however. The aggregate supply "price" still must cover all the necessary costs associated with a given amount of employment.

A is the aggregate supply schedule based upon a fixed money wage of $6.50 per hour, whereas the schedule labeled *B* reflects the fact that the money wage may rise as the level of employment rises. The more rapidly the money wage rises (in percent) with actual changes in the level of employment, the less responsive is the employment level to any given change in expected proceeds. Technically, this means that, as the elasticity of the employment level decreases, the money wage becomes more sensitive to any increase in the demand for labor. The aggregate supply schedule will become perfectly inelastic with respect to expected proceeds at the level of employment that represents full employment of the existing labor force. If, for example, the employment level of 110 million workers is the upper limit to the labor supply in our hypothetical economy, then the two curves, *A* and *B*, will terminate at this point. Since no more workers are available once employment has reached the 110-million level, actual employment cannot exced this amount, irrespective of what happens to expected proceeds. This is shown in Figure 4–1 by the dashed line extending vertically upward at the 110-million mark on the horizontal axis.

Alternative Concepts of Aggregate Supply

The Keynesian aggregate supply function just examined linked employment to expected proceeds primarily because Keynes thought employment to be the most satisfactory measure of changes in the current output of the economy. Since publication of *The General Theory*, various alternative measures for determining total output have been developed. The extensive and rapid development of national income accounting has provided the economist with excellent techniques by means of which the heterogeneous complex of goods and services produced by the economy can be reduced to a single aggregate. Procedures for measurement of real changes in this aggregate over time are similarly well developed. Consequently, the aggregate supply function can be formulated in terms of total output (or real income) rather than the level of employment; this has become the standard practice in modern employment theory.

Such a formulation of the aggregate supply schedule is shown in Figure 4–2. The aggregate supply schedule is represented by the line *OZ*, which, it should be noted, bisects the origin at an angle of 45°. (Generally in modern income theory the aggregate supply function is depicted by a 45° line.) To understand the significance of the 45° line, the reader should recall that the aggregate supply schedule consists of a series of points, each one of which represents the supply price for the output associated with different amounts of employment. The aggregate supply schedule must show the conditions under which entrepreneurs in the aggregate will produce a particular volume of goods and services and, more important, will continue to produce that volume. This is what the 45° line in Figure 4–2 attempts to do.

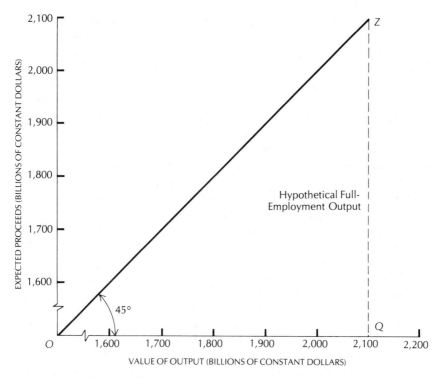

FIGURE 4–2. The Aggregate Supply Schedule: Expected Proceeds and Value of Output in Constant Prices

Real income is measured on both the vertical and horizontal axes of the figure, but the sense in which we are measuring real income differs for each of the two axes. The horizontal axis measures the money value in constant prices of the economy's current output of goods and services; but this also is equivalent to the total cost—including a normal profit—incurred by entrepreneurs in the aggregate in producing any given output. Statistically and in the aggregate, the value of any given quantity of physical output must be equal to the costs of producing that output. Thus, we can interpret the horizontal axis of the figure as a measure of current output seen from the viewpoint of the costs that entrepreneurs incur when they decide to produce a particular volume of goods and services. Specifically, the costs involved are those listed earlier (Chapter 3) in the discussion of the allocations side of the gross national product: wages, rents, interest, profits, capital consumption allowances, and indirect business taxes.

Since the aggregate supply schedule, or function, must show the conditions under which any particular level of production will continue, it follows that entrepreneurs in the aggregate must receive a return flow of expenditures equal to the costs they incur if they produce any given aggregate of goods and services. Since Figure 4–2 measures real income (output valued in constant prices) on both the horizontal and vertical axes, the only possible line that will conform to the conditions described above is the 45° line that bisects the point of origin. In other words, if the vertical axis is viewed as measuring the flow of expenditures or expected proceeds in constant prices, then the 45° line must of necessity be the aggregate supply schedule, for each point on such a schedule represents the amounts that entrepreneurs must receive back as receipts (as measured on the vertical axis) if they are to continue to produce varying amounts of output (as measured on the horizontal axis).

As was the case with the Keynesian aggregate supply function, there will be some level of output that represents full employment for the 45° aggregate supply schedule. This may be represented by a point upon the horizontal axis, for once the economy has achieved full employment (capacity production) no further increases in output are possible. In Figure 4–2 this point is represented by the vertical line ZQ. It is possible, though not customary, in modern income analysis to combine the Keynesian aggregate supply schedule with the 45° aggregate supply schedule by measuring employment as well as output or real income on the horizontal axis. This can be done because each possible level of output will correlate with a specific amount of employment. Because of the law of diminishing returns, however, employment will not necessarily vary in the same proportion as output, a fact that makes it difficult to compute the exact amount of employment which might be associated with each and every possible level of real output (see Footnote 2). As a consequence, most modern income theorists have been content to measure real income on only the horizontal axis and simply assume—correctly—that employment will vary more or less directly with changes in the level of real income.

One serious drawback to this formulation of the aggregate supply schedule is that the general level of prices "disappears." It disappears because of the use of deflated values for both output and expected proceeds. When Keynes wrote *The General Theory* this was not a serious problem because there was little concern in the depths of the depression of the 1930s about prices rising too rapidly when output expanded. In recent years, however, this has not been the situation. We have frequently had rising prices (inflation) both when output is falling and when it is expanding.

Prices can be brought into the aggregate supply schedule if we change the vertical axis in our diagram from a measure of output in constant prices to a measure of output in *current* prices. This is done in Figure 4–3. In the figure, we still measure real income on the horizontal axis. But the vertical axis now measures the current market value of output, which is its value in present prices. The aggregate supply function now takes on the shape of the curve ZZ. This curve shows that the general level of prices will rise with successive rises in real income.[3] As a conse-

---

3. This increase in the price level may be accounted for by an increase in unit costs of production as output expands because of diminishing returns, as well as an increase in wage rates and other money costs that ensue when production increases.

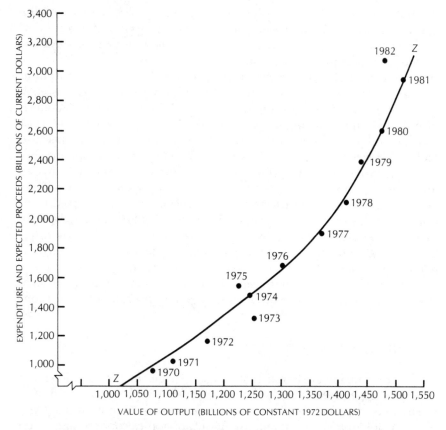

FIGURE 4–3.   The Aggregate Supply Schedule: Expected Proceeds in Current
             Prices and Value of Output in Constant Prices

SOURCE: *Economic Report of the President, 1983*

quence, the flow of expected proceeds that entrepreneurs must receive
to induce them to continue to produce at varying levels must increase
proportionally more than the increase in output. The closer the economy gets to full-employment and full-capacity output, the sharper will
be the increase in the general price level—hence the steeper the rise in
the aggregate supply curve ZZ. When the full-employment output level
is attained, the curve becomes completely inelastic. Output will no longer
respond to changes in the flow of expenditures. All that can happen
from this point is a further upward shift in the general level of prices.
The curve ZZ in Figure 4–3 was constructed from actual GNP data for
the period 1970 through 1982. Values of GNP in both constant (1972)
and current prices for each year are given by the dots next to each year
shown. It may be observed that the fit of the ZZ curve, though not perfect, clearly reflects the concepts just discussed. The curve also reflects
the increasing vulnerability of the economy to inflation in recent years.

Thus far we have considered three different formulations of the aggregate supply function—Keynes's original proposition linking employment and expected proceeds, a 45° schedule in which the values of both output and proceeds are shown in constant prices, and a schedule showing expected proceeds in current prices and the value of output in constant prices. Which one is best? No one is necessarily best, as each formulation has its uses in connection with different aspects of modern income and employment analysis. The concept we shall use in Part II of this text (Chapters 4–9) is the 45° aggregate supply schedule because Part II focuses upon the core material of modern macroeconomic theory. This core material rests upon important theoretical relations involving consumption, investment, and government spending, as well as international economic transactions. These relationships are derived from *real*, not *nominal*, values for the variables involved. Thus, it is appropriate that we examine them initially within the context of a model cast in *real* terms. We do not intend to ignore changes in the price level, a crucial matter for contemporary macroeconomic theory and policy. Once the core material has been mastered, the complications resulting from a changing price level can be introduced logically and with less confusion.

The Aggregate Demand Schedule

The second major analytical tool in modern income and employment theory is aggregate demand. Just as aggregate supply is conceived of as a schedule showing the expected proceeds necessary to induce a given quantity of employment or amount of output in the economy, aggregate demand is also conceived of as a schedule showing the amounts the major spending units in the economy are prepared to spend at each and every possible level of real income. It is a schedule that links real income and spending decisions for the economy as a whole. The idea that the aggregate demand schedule involves a relationship between decisions to purchase the different categories of output and the level of output itself is gross oversimplification of a concept that is quite complex. But such a definition of the aggregate demand schedule is, nevertheless, a good point of departure for our analysis.

Figure 4–4 depicts the relationship described above. The line *DD* is the aggregate demand schedule. As in Figure 4–2, the vertical axis measures income as a flow of expenditure, and the horizontal axis depicts income as a flow of output. Thus, the curve *DD* can be said to represent the spending decisions associated with any and all possible levels of output, or real income.

Since the aggregate demand schedule seeks to show how much the economy is disposed to spend for the various categories of output at different levels of real income, it is therefore an *ex ante* phenomenon. The aggregate demand schedule does not represent any particular level

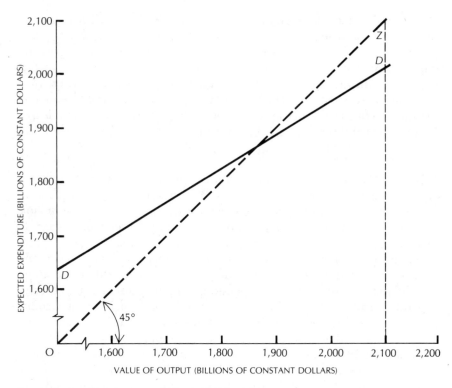

FIGURE 4–4. The Aggregate Demand Schedule

of statistical demand, but rather the demand·that will prevail if certain conditions are satisfied. The notion of an aggregate demand schedule is important for our analysis because it underscores the fact that those who make the decisions to spend are not necessarily the same individuals or groups who make the decisions for production and employment. This will become fully apparent when we examine the process by which the income and the employment level is actually determined.

The Origin of Spending Decisions

Where do the spending decisions of the economy originate? Or, stated in different terms, who or what are the spending units in the economy? This question concerns the component parts of the aggregate demand schedule, and a complete answer depends upon the discussion to follow in the next several chapters. But a brief answer can be given here that will serve to outline the basic problem involved in the analysis of demand for the output of the whole economy.

If we ignore for the moment any economic ties the economy may have with other nations, decisions to purchase a portion of the current output of the economy must originate in one of three major economic sectors:

(1) the household, or consumer sector, which is the purchaser of consumer goods and services; (2) the business, or firm, sector, which is the purchaser of capital, or investment, goods; and (3) the public, or government sector, which is the point of origin for decisions relating to the economy's output of government, or collective, goods and services. In a symbolic sense, then, the schedule of aggregate demand will be equal to the sum of consumption, C, investment, I, and government expenditure, G, for goods and services. In other words,

$$DD = C + I + G. \tag{4-1}$$

Since the aggregate demand schedule represents the spending intentions of the major spending units in the economy, a corollary question concerns the source of spending power at the disposal of these major spending units. In a monetary economy, spending power requires access to a quantity of money, and thus the question pertains to the source of supply of money for the economy's spending units. Fundamentally, there are three possible sources of spending power for an individual spending unit in the economy. First, a spending unit may finance its current expenditures by drawing upon assets accumulated during past income periods. These may be in the form of holdings of money or in the form of other assets that can be converted into money. A household, for example, might finance some of its current expenditures by drawing down a savings account, or perhaps by the sale of some of its holdings of stocks or bonds. Second, current expenditures may be financed out of current income. For the household, or consumer, sector of the economy and for the bulk of government purchases of goods and services, this is the typical pattern. Most individuals have to depend upon current money income to finance the major portion of their current expenditures.

In the past, the more usual practice in the business sector of the economy was to finance capital expenditures by borrowing, rather than by using current and internal resources. Increasingly, however, business firms are resorting to internal financing for major items of capital expenditure; moreover, the firm can, like the consumer, draw upon assets accumulated in past income periods to finance current outlays. But borrowing remains important as the third and final source of spending power for current expenditures. Consumers usually resort to loans for financing large items of expenditures, such as houses, automobiles, and other durable goods, whereas it is quite commonplace for government units in the economy to borrow to meet a portion of their current expenditures. National governments, we may note in passing, possess the unique distinction of having the power to create money.

These remarks about the source of the money that provides the basis for spending power in a monetary economy apply to the whole economy much in the same way as they apply to individual spending units within the economy. For the aggregate of all spending units, in other words, spending, or purchasing, power can be derived from current income, by borrowing, or by drawing down previously accumulated cash balances. If all spending units resort to the latter two sources for some portion of their purchasing power, new or additional quantities of funds are injected into the economic system. How this comes about will be examined in greater detail later.

These various sources of purchasing power rule out the possibility of any simple and direct relationship between the spending decisions embodied in the aggregate demand schedule and the income level. One major component of aggregate demand, consumption, can be related functionally to the real income level, but this is not necessarily the case with the other two components. To repeat, the kind of schedule shown in Figure 4–4 is a simplification. Such a schedule, though, is an extremely valuable analytical tool; what counts from the standpoint of the income and employment level is the willingness of the entrepreneur in the economy to make use of the economy's productive capacity. And this is directly tied to his expectations concerning demand, which, in turn, depend upon the decisions made by the major spending entities in the economy.

The Equilibrium Level of Income and Employment

The schedules of aggregate supply and aggregate demand take us directly to the heart of modern income and employment theory. The basic—and in many respects simple—idea that Keynes put forth in *The General Theory* is that the aggregate supply and demand schedules of the economy between them determine the level of income and employment. According to Keynes, "the volume of employment is given by the point of intersection between the aggregate demand function and the aggregate supply function. . . . This is the substance of the General Theory of Employment."[4]

The way in which aggregate supply and aggregate demand, considered together, determine the income and employment level is shown in Figure 4–5. As in Figures 4–2 and 4–4, real income is shown on both the vertical and horizontal axes. Again the 45° line OZ is the aggregate supply function, while the schedule DD represents the aggregate demand function. Given these two schedules, the volume of income and employment will inevitably adjust to the level found at the point of intersection of these two schedules. This is represented by the income level Y_e, which is both the equilibrium income level and the equilibrium employment level.

The reason income and employment must of necessity adjust to the level represented by Y_e and why this particular level represents income

4. Keynes, p. 25.

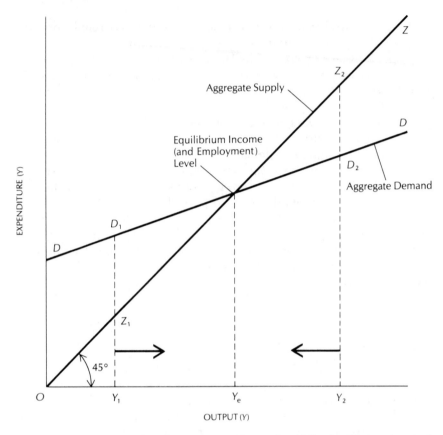

FIGURE 4–5.   Aggregate Supply, Aggregate Demand, and the Equilibrium Level of Income

and employment equilibrium can best be understood if we analyze what will happen assuming for the moment that some other income level exists in the economy. Let us assume that business firms (in the aggregate) anticipate or expect sales equal to Y_1Z_1; therefore, they will produce that amount of goods and services, paying out in the process income to owners of economic resources equal to OY_1. What is the situation with respect to aggregate demand? The current income level, Y_1, is not an equilibrium income level, because at this particular level aggregate demand, *DD*, exceeds aggregate supply, *OZ*. This is an unstable, or *disequilibrium*, condition that cannot be sustained; instead it will drive the economy toward higher levels of income and employment.

Let us look more closely at what is taking place in the current income period. In the first place, additional purchasing power over and above the amounts generated by current income is being injected into the economy's income stream. Diagrammatically, this is represented by the distance Z_1D_1, since the excess of aggregate demand over aggregate supply is a measure of the amount of purchasing power required beyond that being generated by the process of production. For our immediate purposes the exact source of this purchasing power does not matter; what does matter is that new spending power is being injected into the income system. If the distance Z_1D_1 is a measure of the excess of current spending intentions over current (actual) output, how will the spending plans of the economy's spending units be satisfied? Since our analysis is in real terms, we have precluded any increase in the general level of prices as a result of the excess of aggregate demand. But if we rule out price changes, and if current supply falls short of demand, there remains only one other alternative: The excess of aggregate demand must be satisfied by sales out of existing stocks (*inventories*) of goods. The distance Z_1D_1 represents not only the excess of aggregate demand over aggregate supply in the current income period, but also the amount by which current inventories of goods must be drawn down to satisfy this demand. From the standpoint of the whole economy, the distance represents *unintended (unplanned) disinvestment* in stocks. Such disinvestment is unintended because it results solely from the failure of production or output plans to coincide with spending plans in the curent income period.

How does the situation that we have been describing appear from the point of view of the business firms of the economy? Typically, in this situation business firms will find their sales running ahead of current production; consequently they will revise their production plans upward for the next income period in the belief that the existing demand is a reliable indicator of demand in subsequent income periods. If most firms in the economy act accordingly, then output and employment will rise throughout the whole economy. This process of adjustment will necessarily continue until a situation is achieved in which output and spending decisions coincide. In Figure 4–5 this is the situation depicted by the intersection of the aggregate supply and aggregate demand schedules.

The foregoing analysis serves not only to show the essentials of the process by which income and employment adjust toward equilibrium values, but should also underscore the fact that disequilibrium—which always implies change—occurs whenever expected, or *ex ante*, values diverge from actual, or *ex post*, values. In the analysis we have been pursuing, entrepreneurs expected demand to be at the level Y_1Z_1, which originally led them to produce output at the rate Y_1. But aggregate demand turned out to be at the level Y_1D_1, reflecting the spending intentions of consumers, business firms (for investment), and governments. Changes in the income and employment levels in subsequent income periods stem from this initial divergence between expected and actual values. There is no inherent reason why expected and actual values should always coincide. Modern income and employment theory stresses that spending and output decisions are made by different groups or persons, so there is no reason to expect the two values to be always equal. The reader should note this carefully, for it is basic to the explanation of the *why* of changes in income and employment levels in the modern economy.

To round out our present discussion of the equilibrium income level, let us postulate a situation just the opposite of the one we have considered. Let us assume that in the current income period the supply of output is in excess of the demand for that output. In Figure 4–5 this is depicted at the income level Y_2, as measured on the horizontal axis. At this income level the aggregate supply schedule, OZ, lies above the aggregate demand schedule, DD. Output in the current income period equals Y_2Z_2, but spending decisions or current demand for that output only add up to the distance D_2Y_2, with the consequence that, for the income period in question, *there is unintended (unplanned) investment* in stocks or inventories. More money income or purchasing power is being generated by current output than is being spend on that output; once more, a disequilibrium situation exists.

The typical business firm sees this as an unhappy situation in which sales fall short of current production and the firm suffers losses. Unless an immediate change to a better sales position is anticipated, the firm will have no choice but to revise downward its production plans for subsequent income periods. As most firms in the economy do this, output and employment levels for the whole economy will decline. Such a downward adjustment of income and employment must continue until a point is reached at which the supply of output is no longer in excess of current demand for the output. This, again, is the situation shown in Figure 4–5 by the intersection of the aggregate supply and aggregate demand schedules.

A Numerical Example

The process of adjustment of income and employment to an equilibrium level can be illustrated by means of a simple arithmetical example that employs a set of hypothetical data pertaining to employment, aggregate demand, and aggregate supply. Table 4–2 provides these data. In Column (1) are shown the varying amounts of employment associated with different levels of aggregate output (or national income) for our imaginary economy. The various possible levels of national output are given in Column (2), which is the aggregate supply schedule. For each of these various output levels, producers will incur costs exactly equal to the value of the output produced. Column (3) is the aggregate demand schedule and shows the amounts that spending units are prepared to spend at each possible income or output level shown in Column (2). Column (4) tells us which direction income and employment can be expected to change in response to the various levels of aggregate supply and aggregate demand. Column (5) shows the unplanned inventory changes that result when DD and OZ are unequal.

In Table 4–2 there is only one possible income level at which total spending in the economy is just equal to the value of current output. This condition occurs at an output level of $2,000 billion and an employment level of 104 million. At all other possible values for income and

TABLE 4–2.   The Equilibrium of Income and Employment

(1) Employment (N) (in millions of workers)	(2) Aggregate Supply or National Income (OZ) (in billions of dollars)	(3) Aggregate Demand (DD) (in billions of dollars)	(4) Direction of Change in Income and Employment	(5) Unplanned Inventory Change (in billions of dollars)
96	$1,600	$1,800	Rise	$ − 200
98	1,700	1,850	Rise	− 150
100	1,800	1,900	Rise	− 100
102	1,900	1,950	Rise	− 50
104	2,000	2,000	**Equilibrium**	—
106	2,100	2,050	Fall	+ 50
108	2,200	2,100	Fall	+100
110	2,300	2,150	Fall	+150

output disequilibrium is present. Suppose, for example, that current output, is equal to $1,700 billion. At this level the aggregate demand schedule, Column (3), shows that spending units in the aggregate intend to spend at a rate of $1,850 billion. Total spending, in other words, will run ahead of total output by an amount equal to $150 billion. Under these circumstances, and in view of our explicit assumption that prices remain constant, there can be only one possible outcome—employment and production must rise. Under these circumstances, the $150 billion of excess demand represents the amount by which stocks of goods will be drawn down during the income period so that the spending intentions of the spending units can be satisfied.

Just the reverse will hold true if output in any income period rises above the equilibrium level of $2,000 billion. If production proceeds, say, at an annual rate of $3,200 billion, producers are doomed to disappointment because at this particular income level the total of spending decisions in the economy amount to only $2,100 billion. Producers will find that inventories of unsold goods are accumulating at an unwanted rate of $100 billion per year. The reader should note carefully that the economy has not failed through its current productive activity to generate enough purchasing power to clear the market of all goods and services produced, but rather it has failed to spend this purchasing power at the same rate at which it is being created.

Characteristics of the Income Equilibrium

The analysis so far attempts to explain how, in a most fundamental sense, aggregate demand and aggregate supply are the key determinants of income and employment levels. This is the crux of modern employment theory, for if the schedules of aggregate supply and aggregate demand are known, it is possible to determine both the income and employment level for the economy.

But—and this is a point of critical importance—the equilibrium level of income and employment brought about by the interaction of aggregate demand and aggregate supply will not automatically be one of *full employment*. Since decisions to produce and decisions to spend are made independently, it is largely a matter of chance whether or not they happen to coincide at a level of output that represents full employment of the economy's labor force. The economic forces embodied in the analytical concepts of aggregate supply and aggregate demand must of necessity drive the economy toward an equilibrium position, but there is nothing special in these forces that will in any way make full employment the normal state of affairs for the economy.

In fact, one basic lesson of modern income and employment analysis is that *any* level of employment may be normal in the sense that it may be sustained over a considerable period of time. For example, during the whole decade of the 1930s large-scale unemployment was the normal situation in the American economy. If there is a deficiency of aggregate demand relative to a full-employment output, the economy will experience a *deflationary gap* and may reach equilibrium at less than full employment. On the other hand, if aggregate demand persistently runs ahead of full-employment aggregate supply, there will be an *inflationary gap*. The latter situation is characterized by strong upward pressure on the price level and the percentage of the labor force unemployed will fall below the level normally thought of as full. The essential point to remember is that, in the short run, the economy can achieve equilibrium of income and employment at levels that represent full employment, less than full employment, or even "overly" full employment. This last is made possible through inventory adjustments, that is, drawing down of inventories. No one level is in any sense inherently more normal than any other level. The economy does not automatically move through market processes toward such an equilibrium. It all depends upon the relationship existing at any given time interval between aggregate supply and aggregate demand.

But one should not assume that the use of equilibrium concept as a technique for analyzing change means that the economy necessarily settles down into a steady situation with respect to income and employment. The main thrust of Keynes's great work is instability—not just the failure of the economy to attain full employment much of the time, but the inherently unstable nature of a market economy. The basic reason is that the economic forces that lie behind aggregate demand—especially investment spending—are unstable, a subject which we shall develop in greater depth subsequently. Thus, the economy may be tending toward an equilibrium as depicted in Figure 4–5 and Table 4–2, but before it reaches a stable situation, the aggregate demand schedule may change. How this type of change affects the system is discussed in the next section.

Changes in Income and Employment

Besides explaining how the level of employment is determined, the foregoing analytical framework serves to illuminate clearly the how and the why of change within the economic system. The vital principle running through our analysis is that change is the inevitable outcome of a situation in which expected and actual events do not agree, which is to say that change will occur whenever *ex ante* and *ex post* values do not coincide. Insofar as income and employment are concerned, this means that these magnitudes will be changing whenever aggregate supply and aggregate demand are not equal.

It is necessary to note, however, that within this rather broad analytical framework two distinct kinds of change can be envisaged. In the first instance, change may come about because, with given schedules of aggregate supply and aggregate demand, actual output or income fails to correspond to the demand for that output. This is the kind of situation depicted in Figure 4–5. The resultant change is the adjustment of the income and employment level toward equilibrium values that are based upon a given position for the schedules of aggregate supply and aggregate demand. Changes of this type originate with the producing units of the economy because they come about as a result of the failure of entrepreneurs to judge accurately the level of demand for the output of the whole economy.

Change is also involved in the movement of the economic system from one equilibrium level to another. In the short run, such change results from a shift in the position of the aggregate demand schedule that occurs when the spending units of the economy are predisposed to spend more (or less) on current output at any and all levels of income. This shift in the position of the aggregate demand schedule will disturb a previously existing equilibrium between spending and output decisions and thereby set in motion all of the forces involved in the adjustment of the economy toward equilibrium values for income and employment.

The latter type of change is illustrated in Figure 4–6. Schedule DD represents the original position of aggregate demand; output will adjust to the level Y_e, which is the intersection of the aggregate supply schedule, OZ, and the aggregate demand schedule DD. If, however, aggregate demand shifts to the level represented by schedule $D'D'$, then the existing equilibrium income level, Y_e, is disturbed. The immediate consequence of this shift is to create a new situation in which aggregate demand at Y_e, exceeds aggregate supply or output. This will set in motion forces making for change; income and employment will rise until a new equilibrium obtains at the level Y'_e. The important thing to note is that the original impetus for this type of change came from the spending rather than the producing units in the economy. One consequence of this type of change is that the increase in output may be greater than the shift in

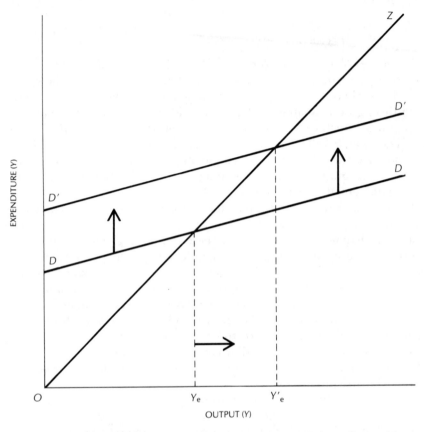

FIGURE 4–6.   Aggregate Supply, Aggregate Demand, and Shifts in the Equilibrium Level of Income

the aggregate demand schedule. Thus, there may be a *multiplier effect* associated with such shifts, a topic to be discussed in the following chapter.

Statics and Dynamics

The previous paragraph concerns a particular type of economic change, namely, the shift from one equilibrium position to another. Technically, this is described as an exercise in *comparative statics*. In economic analysis the term *statics* applies to a situation in which the motion of the system is toward an equilibrium position, as in the examples discussed earlier of the movement toward an income equilibrium. Such a situation is deemed static because all of the underlying determinants of the schedules involved—the aggregate demand and supply schedules in the material we have been discussing—are "givens" (or parameters). The motion takes place in response to the economic forces embodied in these schedules—

schedules whose positions are presumed known. When one of the schedules changes, as is shown in Figure 4–6, the system will shift to a new equilibrium position, but it still represents an essentially static situation because no further change can take place until there is a new disturbance. Hence the term *comparative* statics.

Dynamics, on the other hand, is a term that connotes continuous change and movement. Equilibrium diagrams of the kind discussed earlier in this chapter are not suitable for the discussion of constant change. One reason is that if change is continuous, then time must become a part of the analysis. But the usual supply and demand types of diagrams so widely used in economic analysis do not embody time.[5] A dynamic approach will view the behavior of the economy as essentially a process taking place through time, whereas a static approach will look at the economy's behavior as a system that tends toward a state of balance. Neither approach is the only correct approach; both have their uses in helping us to understand real world economy.

The Model Summarized

The essential elements of the general model developed in this chapter may be summarized as follows:

1. In the short run, defined as a period of time in which productive capacity is fixed, the employment level will vary directly with the extent to which productive capacity is being utilized.

2. In the private sector of the economy the extent to which productive capacity is actually utilized depends upon the entrepreneur's expectation that his sales proceeds will be sufficient to cover the costs incurred in the production of any given volume of output. The aggregate supply schedule represents the formal, analytical expression of this idea, because it is a schedule showing the expected proceeds necessary to induce entrepreneurs in the aggregate to offer on a continuing basis a given amount of employment or produce a given output of goods and services.

3. The aggregate demand schedule associates spending decisions with differing levels of real income. It shows, in other words, the amounts that will be spent for output at each and every possible income level.

4. Given the aggregate supply and aggregate demand schedules for the economy, the equilibrium level of income and employment will be determined by the intersection of these two schedules. There is nothing inherent in these forces of aggregate supply and aggregate demand to assure that this equilibrium will be one of full employment.

5. Change in the economy's level of income and employment results from the failure of the output and spending plans embodied in the

5. This comment applies to both supply and demand diagrams used to explain individual price behavior (microeconomic analysis) and aggregate supply and demand diagrams of the type discussed in this chapter (macroeconomic analysis).

schedules of aggregate supply and demand to coincide. In the short run such changes may take the form of a movement toward an equilibrium position, given an initial imbalance between output and spending, or a movement from one equilibrium position to another. This latter type of change is contingent upon a shift in the schedule of aggregate demand.

A Concluding Comment

The "model" of output and employment determination developed in this chapter and summarized above is usually described as an "income-expenditure" model, the reason being the emphasis it places upon the level of aggregate demand as a key to the output and employment level. It is a fairly straightforward interpretation of Keynes's *The General Theory*, a fact which makes it the ideal point of departure for serious study of all the many factors that enter into such a complex problem as the determination of output, employment, and the price level in the modern economy. It is, of course, not the whole of contemporary macroeconomic analysis—only a starting point. The rationale for beginning with a simple model and proceeding from it to situations of greater complexity was well-stated by Keynes.

> The object of our analysis is, not to provide a machine, or method of blind manipulation, which will furnish an infallible answer, but to provide ourselves with an *organised and orderly method of thinking out particular problems* [italics added]; and, after we have reached a provisional conclusion by isolating the complicating factors one by one, we shall have to go back on ourselves and allow, as well as we can, for the probable interactions of the factors among themselves. *This is the nature of economic thinking* [italics added].[6]

This brief passage will serve as a useful direction-finder as we make our way through the complexities of modern economics.

Summary

1. Aggregate demand is the key determinant of the extent to which the economy's productive capacity is used in the short run.

2. The aggregate supply schedule shows levels of output associated with the proceeds entrepreneurs require in order to produce any particular level of output.

3. The aggregate supply schedule (function) can be shown in various ways, depending upon whether required proceeds are measured in current or constant prices.

4. The aggregate demand schedule is the counterpart of the aggregate supply schedule and shows the amount of spending by major

6. Keynes, p. 297.

spending units—households, firms, and governments—associated with different income levels.

5. The equilibrium level of income (output) and employment is determined by the intersection of the aggregate demand and aggregate supply schedules.

6. Changes in output (and the employment level) come about either because the economy is not yet at the level of equilibrium as determined by the intersection of the aggregate demand and supply schedules or because of a shift in the aggregate demand schedule.

7. The difference between *static* and *dynamic* changes in output (and the employment level): Static changes are associated with movements toward an equilibrium position as determined by aggregate demand and aggregate supply. Dynamic changes involve a continuous change in output over time.

5

Consumption, Saving, and the Multiplier

In the preceding chapter, the fundamental point was made that in the short run aggregate demand is the key determinant of the level of income and employment. The reason is that aggregate demand determines the extent to which the economy's production capacity will be utilized. The aggregate demand schedule is a summation of decisions to use the economy's output, that is, a demand for the various categories of goods and services that enter into the national output. Structurally, aggregate demand (in a closed economy) consists of the sum of expenditures for consumer goods and services, C, investment (or capital goods), I, and government (or collective goods and services), G. In an open economy it is necessary to take into account net foreign investment, I_f.

Given the underlying assumption that output and employment in the short run depend primarily upon the level of aggregate demand, our basic task is to understand the forces that enter into the determination of the demand for the output of the whole economy. Since we have already identified the component parts of the economy's structure of total demand, the logical procedure is to understand the determinants of each part, following this with an analysis of how the parts link together to form a schedule of demand for the economy's whole output. We begin with consumption, taking up investment and government spending in the two following chapters.

The Determinants of Consumption Expenditure

Keynes's basic hypothesis with respect to the volume of consumption expenditure in the economy is that *income is the prime determinant of con-*

sumption expenditure. This is the case for the individual and for the economy as a whole. Keynes stated that "aggregate income . . . is, as a rule, the principal variable upon which the consumption constituent of the aggregate demand function will depend."[1] To say that income is the prime determinant of consumption expenditure is not to say that there may not be other determinants. For the moment, however, we shall put aside any other possible determinants and concentrate on the variable of income.

Which particular measure of income is appropriate for our analysis? Should we regard consumption as a function of GNP, national income, personal income, or some other income measure? Since we are concerned primarily with consumer behavior, the income concept most appropriate to our analysis is one that most nearly approximates the idea of take-home pay. If there is validity to the hypothesis that income is a prime determinant of consumption expenditure, income in this context must mean the income which is wholly at the disposal of the consumer for consumption expenditure. Within the framework of national income aggregates, the particular measure that meets this requirement is *disposable income,* which is defined as the income remaining to individuals after deduction of all personal taxes. It is the closest approximation to take-home pay at the national level. Accordingly, contemporary income and employment theory has generally formulated the consumption function in terms of the relationship between disposable income and consumption expenditure. Consumption is thus held to be a function of disposable income.

If we assume that all saving other than capital consumption allowances originates in the household sector, disposable income will be equal to the net national product minus taxes and plus transfer payments. In equation form we have

$$Y_d = Y_{np} - TX + TR. \tag{5-1}$$

In the discussion which follows in this and ensuing chapters *net national product* (Y_{np}) will be used as our basic income measure rather than gross national product, primarily because use of the latter in the algebraic models require making the extreme assumption that saving even in the form of capital consumption allowances originates in the household sector. Use of net national product does not in any way change the basic analysis or principles.

The Consumption Function

In *The General Theory* Keynes established two basic ideas concerning the relationship between consumption and income. These ideas are the underpinning of the modern theory of consumption and saving. First,

---

1. John Maynard Keynes, *The General Theory of Employment, Interest and Money* (New York: Harcourt, Brace & World, First Harbinger ed., 1964), p. 96.

Keynes asserted that consumption expenditure is related to income in a systematic and dependable way. Symbolically, we have the equation

$$C = f(Y_d). \tag{5-2}$$

Keynes defined the functional relationship between a given level of income and the consumption expenditure out of the level of income as *the propensity to consume*.[2] (It may be noted that the functional relationship posited by Keynes is one that concerns real consumption and real income.)

The second key idea is known as Keynes's fundamental psychological law.

> The fundamental psychological law, upon which we are entitled to depend with great confidence both *a priori* from our knowledge of human nature and from the detailed facts of experience, is that men are disposed, as a rule and on the average, to increase their consumption as their income increases, but not by as much as the increase in their income.[3]

Basically what Keynes meant is that when an individual's income increases he will spend more for consumption because of the increase, but he will not spend the whole of the increase. Some portion of the increase, in other words, will be saved. Keynes believed that this was especially true in the short run, for our consumption standards tend to become habitual, and are not quickly adjusted either upward or downward. If income rises, spending, and our standard of consumption, may not immediately adjust upward to a new and higher level. The reverse, it may be noted, will be the case when income falls.

In modern income and employment theory these two Keynesian ideas with respect to income and consumption are brought together in the concept of the *consumption function,* which may be defined as a *schedule showing the amounts that will be spent for consumer goods and services at different income levels.* The nature of the consumption function is shown in Figure 5–1. Aggregate real income is measured on the horizontal axis and real consumption expenditure on the vertical axis. The curve $C = f(Y_d)$ represents the consumption function; this curve shows the amount of consumption expenditure forthcoming at any and all income levels.

The notion of the consumption function as a schedule follows logically from Keynes's definition of the *propensity to consume* as the functional relationship between income and consumption. This functional relationship can be represented by a schedule that shows the range of values over which the dependent variable (consumption) moves as a result of changes in the independent variable (income).

It should be noted that, *as a concept,* the consumption function is quite similar to the ordinary demand curve. The latter is the graphic representation of a schedule showing the amounts of a commodity or service

2. Ibid., p. 90.
3. Ibid., p. 96.

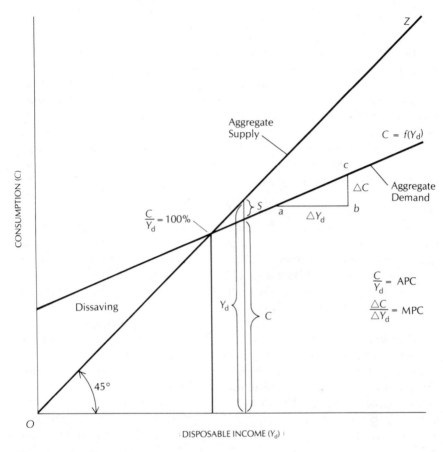

Figure 5–1.   The Consumption Function

that buyers are willing to purchase at any and all possible prices within a specified period of time. The ordinary demand schedule embodies the idea that quantity demanded is a function of price. Thus, it is correct to state the law of demand in the form of an equation, such as $q = f(p)$, in which q represents quantity demanded and p represents the price of a good or service. So it is with the consumption function, except that the two variables are disposable income (the independent variable) and consumption expenditures (the dependent variable).

The income-consumption schedule, like all similar schedules in economic analysis, is an *ex ante* phenomenon. The schedule shows intended values, that is, the levels to which consumers plan to adjust their consumption expenditures on the assumption that any particular income level is achieved and maintained for a reasonable period of time. The consumption function is presumed to define the normal relationship of consumption to income.

Technical Attributes of the Consumption Function

The consumption function has two key attributes, the average propensity to consume and the marginal propensity to consume. The *average propensity to consume* (APC) is the ratio of consumption to income, C/Y_d, at a specific level of income. It is the proportion of a given income that is spent for consumption purposes. This is the first significant attribute of the function. The average propensity to consume may vary as the income level varies. In Figure 5–1, for example, the average propensity to consume is 100 percent at the point at which the consumption function $C = f(Y_d)$ crosses the aggregate supply function, *OZ*. At this point, consumption is exactly equal to income. To the left of this point, the average propensity to consume will be more than 100 percent because at every possible income level intended consumption is greater than income. Thus, the ratio C/Y_d will be greater than 100 percent. To the right of the point of intersection, on the other hand, the average propensity to consume will be less than 100 percent because, at every income level above that at which consumption and income are equal, intended consumption is less than income.

The second important attribute of the consumption function is the *marginal propensity to consume* (MPC). This concept is the formal expression of Keynes's fundamental psychological law, which, the reader will recall, states that people are disposed to increase or decrease their consumption by less as their income increases or decreases. We may define the marginal propensity to consume as the ratio of a change in consumption, ΔC, to a change in income, ΔY_d. With an increase in income, the marginal propensity to consume gives, in percent, the amount by which consumption will increase. If income declines the marginal propensity to consume measures—again in percent—the amount by which consumption expenditure will decline. If we assume, for example, that the marginal propensity to consume of the economy is 0.75 (i.e., 75 percent), consumption expenditure will increase by $0.75 with every increase of $1.00 in the income level and fall by the same amount with every $1.00 decline in the income level.

In Figure 5–1 the marginal propensity to consume is measured by the slope of the consumption function, because, in mathematical terms, the slope of a line is determined by the ratio of the vertical distance to the horizontal distance (when movement takes place horizontally). Since consumption, C, is measured on the vertical axis and income, Y_d, on the horizontal axis, the marginal propensity to consume must necessarily be the same thing as the slope of the curve. In Figure 5–1 the marginal propensity to consume can be depicted by reference to the triangle *abc*. The vertical side of the triangle is the change in consumption expenditure ΔC, and the horizontal side is equal to the change in income, ΔY_d. The reader should note carefully that as long as the consumption function is assumed to be linear—that is, drawn as a straight line—the marginal propensity to consume will have a constant value. The basic reason for this is that all triangles formed by ΔY_d and ΔC will be similar (in a geometric sense) to the triangle *abc*, and consequently the ratio of their vertical sides to their horizontal sides will always be the same. The marginal propensity to consume and its constant value are to be contrasted to the changing value of the average propensity to consume.[4]

In an analytical sense, Keynes's functional psychological law establishes limiting values for the slope of the consumption function. In *The General Theory* Keynes held that normally the marginal propensity to consume is positive, but its value is less than unity. This means that the slope of the consumption function will normally be less than 1. The marginal propensity to consume relates to consumption expenditure that is *induced* by a change in income. Such a change can be viewed geometrically as a movement along a known consumption function, and should not be confused with the change that may come about as a result of a shift in the consumption function itself. Keynes assumed that normally the consumption function is stable, so that most changes in consumption are induced by income changes. This means that fluctuations in the income and employment level are not likely to have their origins in the consumption component of the aggregate demand schedule.[5] Whether or not this particular conclusion is warranted remains to be seen; for the moment, though, our chief concern is with the marginal propensity to consume as a phenomenon having to do with induced changes in consumption expenditure. The analytical significance of the idea of induced consumption expenditures is that we find in such phenomena the basis of the theory of the multiplier, an aspect of modern income and employment theory that we shall develop in full detail later in this chapter.

Our discussion of the consumption function would not be complete without the algebraic expression of this relationship. If we assume the function is linear, as we did in Figure 5–1, the consumption function can be stated as

$$C = C_0 + aY_d. \tag{5-3}$$

In the above expression, C is the level of consumption; C_0 is the amount of consumption when income is zero; and a is the marginal propensity to consume. Geometrically, C_0 is the point at which the consumption

---

4. The above remarks do not necessarily imply that the income-consumption relationship must be linear. The consumption function may have a shape such that both marginal and average propensities to consume decline as the income level rises. For reasons of simplicity in analysis, however, most economists operate on the assumption that the consumption function is linear.

5. This comment needs to be qualified. Contemporary policy-makers clearly understand that one way to influence consumption spending (and with it the overall level of economic activity) is by changing taxes. A tax reduction, for example, will increase disposable income (Equation 6–1), which should lead to higher consumption spending. The Kennedy-Johnson administration did this in 1964, as did the Ford administration in 1975, the Carter administration in 1977, and the Reagan administration in 1981. The mechanics of tax changes and the income and employment effects are analyzed in Chapter 7.

function cuts the vertical axis, and *a* is the slope of the consumption function. The value of C_0 at zero income is wholly hypothetical, as there is no known instance of zero income for an entire society for any significant period of time. Students of algebra will recognize this equation for the consumption function as the formula for a graph of a straight line of the type depicted in Figure 5–1. A consumption function which has the characteristics of Equation 5–3 is usually described as a *cyclical* function, the reason being that the pattern of actual data for the short term fits such a schedule (see Figure 5–3).

The Saving Function

The counterpart to the consumption function is the *saving function,* which we may define as a *schedule showing the amounts that income recipients intend to save at different levels of income.* Saving is the nonconsumption of current income; because we are not at the moment concerned with any disposition of income other than consumption or saving, it logically follows that saving, too, is a function of income. In algebraic terms,

$$S = f(Y_d). \qquad (5-4)$$

Since we are assuming for the moment that consumption and saving are the only alternative uses of income, the saving schedule can be derived directly from the consumption function. At each income level intended saving will equal the difference between the aggregate supply function and the consumption function, and these are the amounts that should be plotted to derive a schedule as shown in Figure 5–2.

Since the saving function is conceptually similar to the consumption function, it is characterized by similar technical attributes. Thus, the *average*

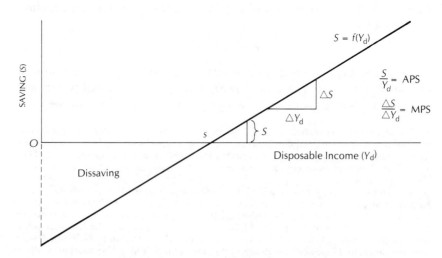

FIGURE 5–2.   The Saving Function

propensity to save (APS) may be defined as the ratio of saving to income, S/Y_d, at a given level of income. It is the proportion of any given income that is saved. Like the propensity to consume, the ratio of saving to income may vary as the income level changes. At the intersection of the saving function and the horizontal axis (point s in Figure 5–2), the volume of saving is zero; hence the average propensity to save is zero. To the left of this point, the saving function drops below the horizontal axis, which means that saving is negative, or that dissaving is taking place. If this is the case, the saving-income ratio, S/Y_d, will be negative, which is as it should be, since the consumption-income ratio, C/Y_d and S/Y_d must add up to unity. To the right of point s, the average propensity to save is not only greater than zero, but increases in value as the income level rises. The proportion of income saved increases as the income level increases.

The counterpart of the marginal propensity to consume is the *marginal propensity to save* (MPS). It is defined as the ratio of a change in saving, ΔS, to a change in income, ΔY_d. Analogous to the representation of the consumption function, the marginal propensity to save is depicted graphically by the slope of the saving schedule. If this schedule is assumed to be linear, the marginal propensity to save will have a constant value. Numerically, the marginal propensity to save is equal to 1 minus the marginal propensity to consume. This is true only so long as we adhere to our assumption that all income must be either consumed or saved. A marginal propensity to consume of 0.75 would mean a value of 0.25 for the marginal propensity to save because, if $0.75 is spent for consumption purposes out of an additional $1.00 of income, the balance of $0.25 is by definition saving. The ratio $\Delta S/\Delta Y_d$ must equal 0.25.

Empirical Verification

Up to this point in our analysis we have advanced two general propositions. The first of these is that consumption (and saving) is primarily a function of income, and the second is that the functional relationship between consumption (and saving) tends (in the short run) to assume the shape and character depicted by the schedules shown in Figures 5–1 and 5–2. But how well do these propositions accord with the facts of experience? In other words, do the statistical data pertaining to income and consumption expenditures tend to confirm the existence of the kind of behavior pattern embodied in the notion of the consumption function? Table 5–1 gives data on disposable income and personal consumption expenditures for the American economy for the period 1929–82. The table also shows the percentage of disposable income spent for consumption goods and services in each of these years. The data are computed in 1972 prices; thus, we are dealing with real income and real consumption expenditures. A careful inspection of the data reveals a rather general tendency of consumption expenditure to conform to the pattern suggested by the Keynesian hypothesis. For example, from 1929

TABLE 5–1.   Disposable Income and Personal Consumption Expenditure: 1929–
(in billions of 1972 dollars)

	(1)	*(2)*	*(3)*	*(4) = (3) ÷ (2)*
			Personal	*Average Propensity*
		Disposable	*Consumption*	*to Consume*
	Year	*Income*	*Expenditure*	*(in percent)*
	1929	$229.5	$215.1	93.7
	1930	210.6	202.8	96.3
	1931	201.9	194.8	96.5
	1932	174.4	176.5	101.2
	1933	169.6	170.5	100.5
	1934	179.8	179.1	99.6
	1935	196.8	189.9	96.5
	1936	220.5	208.8	94.7
	1937	227.7	216.5	95.1
	1938	212.6	211.5	99.5
	1939	229.8	219.8	95.6
	1940	244.0	229.9	94.2
WW II Years	1941	277.9	243.6	87.7
	1942	317.5	241.1	75.9
	1943	332.1	248.2	74.7	WW II Years
	1944	343.6	255.2	74.3
	1945	338.1	270.9	80.1
	1946	332.7	301.0	90.5
	1947	318.8	305.8	95.9
	1948	335.8	312.2	92.9
	1949	336.8	319.3	94.8
	1950	362.8	337.3	92.9
	1951	372.6	341.6	91.7
	1952	383.2	350.1	91.4
	1953	399.1	363.4	91.1
	1954	403.2	370.0	91.8
	1955	426.8	394.1	92.3

to 1933 disposable income declined, but the average propensity to consume rose. This is the type of behavior pattern for consumption expenditure suggested by the consumption function in Figure 5–1. From 1933 to 1941, a period in which disposable income was rising, the average propensity to consume underwent a decline. Between 1941 and 1945 the figures lose much of their value, since these were war years, and consumption expenditures as a percentage of disposable income fell sharply because of wartime rationing, cutbacks in the production of consumer durables, pressures on the consumer to save and purchase war bonds, and general shortages of consumer goods and services. For the postwar period, beginning in 1946, disposable income has risen in relatively steady fashion. Consumption expenditure too has increased, but the average propensity to consume has shown, particularly in recent years,

TABLE 5–1.   (continued)

(1)	(2)	(3)	(4) = (3) ÷ (2)
		Personal	Average Propensity
	Disposable	Consumption	to Consume
Year	Income	Expenditure	(in percent)
1956	446.2	405.4	90.9
1957	455.5	413.8	90.8
1958	460.7	418.0	90.7
1959	497.7	440.4	91.8
1960	489.7	452.0	92.3
1961	503.8	461.4	91.6
1962	524.9	482.0	91.8
1963	542.3	500.5	92.3
1964	520.8	528.0	90.9
1965	616.3	557.5	90.5
1966	646.8	585.7	90.6
1967	673.5	602.7	89.5
1968	701.3	634.4	90.5
1969	722.5	657.9	91.1
1970	751.6	672.1	89.4
1971	779.2	696.8	89.4
1972	810.3	737.1	90.9
1973	865.3	768.5	88.8
Recession ⌈1974	858.4	763.6	88.9⌉ Recession
Recession ⌊1975	875.8	780.2	89.0⌋ Recession
1976	906.7	823.1	90.8
1977	942.9	864.3	91.7
1978	988.8	903.2	91.3
1979	1,015.7	927.6	91.3
1980	1,018.0	930.5	91.4
Recession ⌈1981	1,043.1	947.6	90.8⌉ Recession
Recession ⌊1982	1,055.2	957.0	90.7⌋ Recession

SOURCE: *Economic Report of the President,* 1983.

a greater tendency toward a constant value than was true of the prewar years. Note that in 1970 and 1971 the average propensity to consume fell slightly, a consequence some economists believe of the temporary surtax on the personal income tax in effect at that time. Between 1972 and 1976 the propensity to consume also fell slightly, even during the 1974–75 recession. Some economists believe that continued inflation in these years led to a somewhat higher savings ratio. Somewhat the same seemed to happen in 1981–82, another recession period, but also one of high inflation, at least in 1981. During 1982 the inflation rate was coming down. Nevertheless, the postwar data appear to be roughly in line with the consumption function hypothesis.

A better view of the extent to which actual data conform to the Keynesian hypothesis can be obtained if we plot the data of Table 5–1 on a graph. This is done in Figure 5–3, wherein disposable income is measured on the horizontal axis and personal consumption expenditures on the vertical axis. When all the points representing consumption expenditure associated with disposable income for specific years are plotted, we have what statisticians term a *scatter diagram*. Such a diagram is highly useful for it helps us to determine whether or not values for two variables are related. If they are independent, then the value of one of the variables will be associated equally with large and small values for the other variable. In such a case the points will spread over the scatter diagram as if they were thrown there at random. On the other hand, if the value of one of the variables is uniquely determined by the value of the other variable, the points will lie on a line or curve that represents the *perfect* relationship between variables.[6] Such a line or curve is said to describe a perfect relationship in the sense that this would be the way in which the two variables are related if the value of one of the variables was determined solely by the value of the other variable. This, of course, is rarely the case with any two variables in the real world.

The data plotted in Figure 5–3 fall into three distinct periods: 1929–41 (the depression years); 1947–82 (the post–World War II era); and 1929–82 (the entire period). World War II was an abnormal period, as consumption expenditures as a percentage of disposable income dropped well below pre-war averages, the prime reason being the lack of consumer durables during the war. Thus, it is appropriate to look at the pre- and postwar periods separately. Keynes argued that the stability of the consumption function depended upon the existence of normal conditions, by which he meant the absence of wars, revolutions, or any form of social upheaval that might seriously distort the income-consumption relationship.

If we fit curves to the pre- and post–World War II data of Figure 5–3 we obtain two distinct schedules, one appropriate to each of these periods. Inspection of these curves shows, first, that the fit is not perfect, as all the points do not lie on the curves but, second, that there is a tendency for the actual data to be in accord with the consumption function hypothesis.[7] The general shape and slope of the curves are similar to those of the hypothetical consumption function of Figure 5–1. The fact that the fit of the curves is not perfect suggests that other factors besides income play a role in the determination of the level of consumption expenditure in the economy. Actually, there is nothing surprising in this, for neither Keynes nor any other modern economic theorist seriously maintains that income is the sole determinant of consumption expenditure. When we posit the notion of a functional relationship

6. R. G. D. Allen, *Statistics for Economists* (London: Hutchinson House, 1953), p. 120.
7. In Figure 5–3 the schedules are fitted to the plotted data by simply drawing them in such a manner that they pass as closely as possible to all the dots. There are, of course, more exact and specialized statistical techniques for fitting a curve to data, but the approximation method employed here is adequate for our purposes. The lines which relate consumption to disposable income are called *regression lines*. Expressed as an equation, they take the form $C = C_0 + aY_d$ (Equation 5–3). The empirical consumption functions for the three periods calculated from the data in Table 5–3 are shown in the figure.

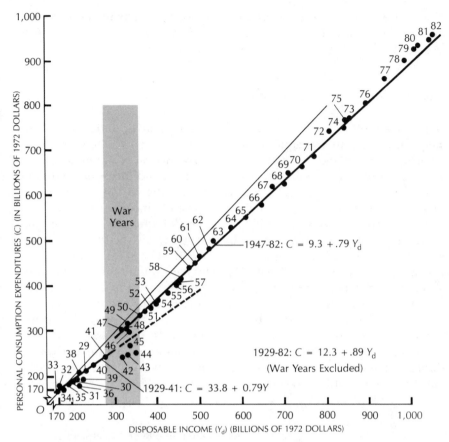

FIGURE 5–3.   Consumption Expenditure and Disposable Income, 1929–82

between income and consumption we are saying in effect that, of the many factors that probably influence the level of consumption expenditure, income is of the most strategic significance. Later on we shall analyze some of the other factors.

Before we conclude our discussion of the empirical validity of the consumption function hypothesis, let us consider an additional fact revealed by the data plotted in Figure 5–3. It is apparent that these two curves differ from each other in both level and slope. In order to compare the curves, we have extended the straight-line curve which best fits the data for 1929–41 beyond the period to which the data apply (dashed lines in Figure 5–3). Note that the extension lies below the curve fitted to the data for 1947–82. What is the significance of this? One possible answer is that the empirical data suggest that the consumption function tends to shift upward over time. The 1947–82 curve, for example, lies above the extended 1929–41 schedule. There are good, logical reasons why this may happen, but we shall defer any further consideration of this point until later in this chapter when we discuss recent theoretical efforts to deal with the apparent phenomenon of the shifting consumption function. If we calculate the consumption-disposable income relationship for the entire period, 1929–82, excluding the war years (1940–45), the resulting schedule shows that $C = 12.3 + 0.89Y_d$.

The Equilibrium Income Level

The consumption function is important as an analytical tool because it helps us determine the equilibrium income level. To see how this relationship comes about, let us examine a hypothetical economy in which there are only two categories of output or expenditure, consumption and investment. Table 5–2 gives data pertaining to this hypothetical economy. Column (1) in this table lists possible income levels for the economy (from 0 to $2,500 billion), while Column (2) represents the economy's consumption function, in that it reveals the intended consumption associated with these income levels.[8] The consumption function in this model is $C = \$450 + 0.75Y_d$. This consumption function is also shown graphically in Figure 5–4. The 45° aggregate supply function (OZ in the figure) shows that the analysis is in real terms because output in constant prices is measured on both the horizontal and the vertical axes.

We shall assume that investment expenditure is autonomous with respect to the income level, that is, that the amount of investment expenditure is independently given—not determined by any of the other variables that enter into our hypothetical economic system. We are not

TABLE 5–2.   The Process of Income Determination (in billions of constant dollars)

(1) Income Y_{np}	(2) Planned Consumption C	(3) Planned Saving S	(4) Planned Investment I	(5) Aggregate Demand C+I	(6) Unplanned Inventory Change
$ 0	$ 450	$ – 450	$100	$ 550	$ – 550
1,600	1,650	– 50	100	1,750	– 150
1,700	1,725	– 25	100	1,925	– 125
1,800	1,800	—	100	1,900	– 100
1,900	1,875	25	100	1,975	– 75
2,000	1,950	50	100	2,050	– 50
2,100	2,025	75	100	2,125	– 25
2,200	2,100	100	100	2,200	—
2,300	2,175	125	100	2,275	25
2,400	2,250	150	100	2,350	50
2,500	2,325	175	100	2,425	75

8. Since the hypothetical economy has only the two categories of output, consumption and investment, there are neither taxes nor transfer expenditures. Consequently, net national product and disposable income are identical: $Y_{np} = Y_d$. The consumption function is constructed such that the marginal propensity to consume has a value of 0.75.

implying that economic analysis has nothing to say about the determinants of investment spending. Rather, for the sake of convenience and analytical simplicity, we assume its value as given in the same sense that the schedule for the consumption function is given. Furthermore, we assume that the amount of investment expenditure will not change as the income level changes. Column (4) of Table 5–2 is this autonomous investment schedule. The term *schedule* is used deliberately here because the values shown are *ex ante*.

Since the schedule of aggregate demand consists of the sum of *ex ante* consumption and *ex ante* investment expenditure, we can construct this schedule for our hypothetical economy by adding an amount equal to autonomous investment to the consumption function. In Table 5–2 the results of this procedure are shown in Column (5). In Figure 5–4 we derive the aggregate demand function diagrammatically by drawing $C+I$ parallel to the consumption function and at a distance equal to the assumed value for autonomous investment expenditure. Thus, aggregate demand is equal to the consumption function plus autonomous investment. We can express this idea algebraically in the form of an equation:

$$DD = (C_0 + aY_d) + I. \tag{5–5}$$

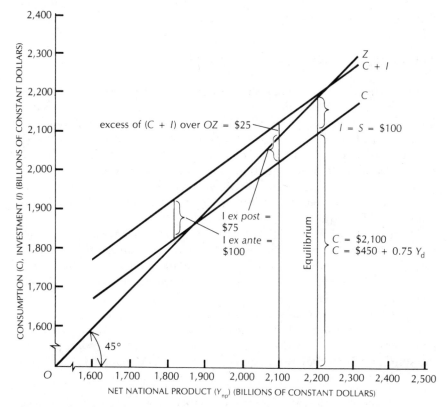

FIGURE 5–4.   The Process of Income Determination

Given the fact that we have established an aggregate demand schedule, $C+I$, for this hypothetical economy, the process by which an equilibrium income level is attained is as described in Chapter 4. The equilibrium income (and employment) level is to be found at the point of intersection of the aggregate demand and aggregate supply schedules. On the basis of the data contained in Table 5–2 the income equilibrium is $2,200 billion.[9] It is at this income level that the aggregate demand schedule of Figure 5–4 intersects the aggregate supply schedule. If actual income is below the $2,200-billion level in any income period, a disequilibrium situation in which aggregate demand is in excess of aggregate supply will result. This will set in motion forces that tend to drive the income level higher. As long as aggregate demand is in excess of aggregate supply, income and employment will continue to rise toward the equilibrium position. Conversely, an income level above $2,200 billion cannot be sustained because aggregate supply then runs ahead of aggregate demand, a condition that will lead to unwanted inventory accumulation and eventual cutbacks in output. A downward adjustment in income and employment levels would continue until output is once again in balance with total demand. Equilibrium is a situation in which producing and spending intentions coincide and, given the assumed schedules of consumption and investment for this hypothetical economy, the only income level at which such coincidence is possible is $2,200 billion.

The Identity of Saving and Investment

In the discussion of the relationship between income and wealth in Chapter 2, the statement was made that saving and investment are necessarily identical when conceived of in an *ex post* sense. This *ex post* equality (or accounting identity of saving and investment as it is sometimes called) logically follows from the way in which we defined saving and investment. The basic identity equations for a single economy in which consumption and investment are the only categories of output permit us to demonstrate that saving and investment must be equal. This equality holds true all the time.

There is, however, a condition in which saving and investment are not necessarily always equal. This is when saving and investment are conceived of in an *ex ante* sense, which means planned saving and investment. The claim that in one sense saving and investment are always equal, and that in another sense they are not necessarily equal, may at first glance seem to be logically impossible. For a number of years after the publication of Keynes's *The General Theory* lively controversy raged among professional economists over the exact meaning of these concepts and the sense in which they were equal or not equal. Actually, however, it is not difficult to reconcile the seemingly contradictory claims.

---

9. See the appendix to this chapter for construction of a simple algebraic model of income determination and its use to obtain the $2,200-billion equilibrium figure.

Let us assume that the economy in Table 5–2 and Figure 5–4 has not yet attained an equilibrium income level. Income in the current period, let us say, is at the level of $2,100 billion. We know that this particular level cannot be maintained, but for the moment that is not of primary concern to us. We want to understand what is taking place during the current income period, irrespective of how income may change in subsequent periods. Consumption will be $2,025 billion. This is planned consumption expenditure, since the consumption function is an *ex ante* phenomenon. If planned consumption is $2,025 billion, then it follows logically that *ex ante* saving must equal $75 billion, because the saving function is the counterpart of the consumption function and is derived (in this hypothetical economy) by subtracting the consumption function from the aggregate supply schedule. But since the actual income level must always lie on the aggregate supply schedule, this is tantamount to saying that the *ex ante* saving is equal to the distance between actual income and *ex ante* consumption.

But what of investment? Column (4) of Table 5–2 has already been described as the autonomous investment schedule. This means that the unchanging level of *ex ante*, or planned investment expenditure, is $100 billion. But if investment *ex ante* is equal to $100 billion, while saving *ex ante* is equal to $75 billion, we have a situation in which these two entities are not equal. The failure of *ex ante* saving and investment to be in balance is a prime indicator of the existence of a disequilibrium condition with respect to the income and employment level; the income equilibrium must be defined in terms of equality between *ex ante* saving and *ex ante* investment.

There is nothing mysterious about the notion that saving and investment *ex ante* are not always equal, because there is no inherent reason that the intentions or plans of savers in the economy should always coincide with the intentions or plans of those undertaking investment expenditure. They may coincide, of course, although it is more likely that they will not.

Returning now to the idea that saving and investment *ex post* must always be equal, let us see how this concept of the identity between saving and investment can be explained through reference to the data of Table 5–2. By definition, saving is the nonconsumption of current income, so in this hypothetical economy saving *ex post* (or actual) must also be equal to $75 billion at the income level of $2,100 billion. Investment has been defined as the net addition to the economy's stock of wealth that results when the whole of current income (i.e., output) is not consumed. Thus, actual investment in an income period is the difference between income and consumption. In the income period that we have under consideration, actual, or *ex post*, investment equals current income ($2,100 billion) minus current consumption ($2,025 billion), or $75 billion. This is the same as *ex post* saving during the income period.

At this point the reader may wonder how to reconcile *ex post* investment of $75 billion with *ex ante* investment of $100 billion. Since our analysis is constructed to rule out any change in the general level of prices, if planned investment runs ahead of actual investment, the difference between planned *(ex ante)* and actual *(ex post)* investment represents the portion of total demand that is satisfied through sales from *existing* stocks of goods. In Figure 5–4 it can be seen that at the $2,100-billion level of income this difference of $25 billion between investment *ex ante* and investment *ex post* is the identical amount by which the aggregate demand schedule exceeds the aggregate supply schedule. This $25 billion represents the amount of inventory *disinvestment* that has taken place in the income period because aggregate demand is in excess of aggregate supply. This inventory disinvestment is unplanned and comes about primarily because producers (in the aggregate) have underestimated the level of aggregate demand. It is *unplanned* investment or investment in stocks that is the balancing item between planned and actual investment.[10] Column (6) in Table 5–2 shows this magnitude for all income levels.

From the foregoing discussion we emerge with the important conclusion that equilibrium requires that saving and investment *ex ante* be equal. Equilibrium also means that *ex ante* and *ex post* values coincide. Disequilibrium exists if saving and investment are not equal in an *ex ante* sense, and, whenever this is the case, forces are set in motion that make for a change either upward or downward in the income and employment level.

The Theory of the Multiplier

In Chapter 4 we pointed out that changes in the income and employment level can be of two distinct types. In the one instance, we have the kind of change just discussed that involves adjustment toward a specific equilibrium level, given known positions for the schedules that enter into the structure of aggregate demand. There is also the kind of change that takes place when an existing equilibrium situation is disturbed as a result of a shift in the position of the aggregate demand schedule. A change of this type can be brought about by a shift in any of the schedules that constitute the aggregate demand schedule. This includes the consumption function, although most economists believe it to be highly stable under normal conditions. The implications of shifts in the aggregate demand schedule lead us into consideration of one of the most significant facets of modern income and employment theory, the *multiplier* process.

Let us assume, using data for the consumption function from Table 5–2 and Figure 5–4, that the autonomous investment schedule shifts upward by $25 billion. This means simply that at all the relevant income

10. It is possible that there can be unplanned saving as well as unplanned investment. Unplanned saving may come about if consumption expenditure lags behind changes in income. In our analysis, however, we are assuming that consumption expenditure adjusts immediately to any change in income. This is not necessarily the case in reality.

levels businessmen are prepared to spend for investment goods at an annual rate of $125 billion rather than $100 billion. Table 5–3 contains data for this new situation. Inspection of this table reveals that the effect of this increase in autonomous investment expenditure has been to shift the aggregate demand schedule upward by a like amount, namely, $25 billion. These new data for our hypothetical economy are plotted in Figure 5–5.

What has been the consequence for the income equilibrium of this upward shift in the schedule of autonomous investment expenditure and the upward shift in the aggregate demand schedule? If we look at the numerical data of Table 5–3 and the graphic presentation of these data in Figure 5–5, we are struck by the fact that the equilibrium income level has risen not by $25 billion, but by $100 billion. Here is a clear illustration of the multiplier process: An autonomous change in one of the variables that enters into the structure of aggregate demand has brought about a change in the income level several times greater than the amount of the initiating change. Technically, the multiplier can be defined as the *coefficient* which relates an increment of expenditure to an increment of income.[11] Keynes discussed the multiplier process entirely in terms of an *investment multiplier*, which he designated by the symbol k. The investment multiplier "tells us that, when there is an increment of aggregate investment, income will increase by an amount which is k times the increment of investment."[12] In algebraic form this idea is expressed as

$$\Delta Y_{np} = k\Delta I. \tag{5–6}$$

From this equation it follows that we can define the investment multiplier as a ratio of a change in income ΔY_{np} to a change in investment, ΔI. Thus,

$$k = \frac{\Delta Y_{np}}{\Delta I}. \tag{5–7}$$

Although Keynes analyzed the multiplier process almost entirely in terms of the relationship between changes in investment and changes in income, the reader should not be misled into thinking that the multiplier effect is limited to changes in investment expenditure. Actually it is a coefficient that links *any* autonomous shift in aggregate demand to the consequent change in income. This point is emphasized because it is usually most convenient to introduce and discuss the theory of the mul-

---

11. Basically the multiplier process is concerned with real changes. We are assuming that any change in expenditure for either consumption or investment goods leads to a corresponding increase in the output of these goods. This does not mean that a multiplier effect in purely monetary terms cannot take place in the economy. If, for example, there would be an increase in expenditure when the economy is at a level of full employment, the multiplier would still come into play, but the ensuing income changes would be wholly the result of changes in the general level of prices.

12. Keynes, p. 115. The net national product, Y_{np}, equals disposable income, Y_d, for in the simple system under discussion, which has neither taxes nor transfers, the two measures of income are identical.

TABLE 5–3.   Increased Investment and the Income Equilibrium
(in billions of constant dollars)

(1) Income Y_{np}	(2) Planned Consumption C	(3) Planned Saving S	(4) Planned Investment I	(5) Aggregate Demand C+I	(6) Unplanned Inventory Change
$ 0	$ 450	$– 450	$125	$ 575	$– 575
1,600	1,650	– 50	125	1,775	– 175
1,700	1,725	– 25	125	1,850	– 150
1,800	1,800	—	125	1,925	– 125
1,900	1,875	25	125	2,000	– 100
2,000	1,950	50	125	2,075	– 75
2,100	2,025	75	125	2,150	– 50
2,200	2,100	100	125	2,225	– 25
2,300	2,175	125	125	2,300	—
2,400	2,250	150	125	2,400	25
2,500	2,325	175	125	2,450	50

tiplier through analysis of changes in the investment component of the aggregate demand structure.

What lies behind the fundamental idea of the multiplier that any change in the expenditure rate for any of the component parts of the aggregate demand schedule will have magnified effects upon the overall income level? To answer this, let us go back and trace what happens in the economy when, as is assumed in Table 5–3, there is an increase in the rate of investment expenditure equal to $25 billion. For the moment we need not be concerned with the means by which this extra $25 billion of investment expenditure is financed; all that interests us is that businessmen have increased their spending for investment goods by $25 billion.

When this happens, the first discernible result is that the producers or suppliers of investment or capital goods will find that their incomes have risen by $25 billion, because increased spending for investment goods will lead to an increase in their production and, as more output is generated, incomes will rise. Thus, the primary effect of the increased spending for investment goods will be to create an equal amount of new income (in the form of wages, rents, interest, and profits) which will accrue to resource owners in the capital goods producing sector of the economy. What will happen after this? For the answer to this question we return to Keynes's assertion that whenever income increases there will be a strong tendency for the beneficiaries of such increases to step up their expenditures for consumption goods and services. In the case of our hypothetical economy, the beneficiaries of the initial increase in spending are those engaged in the production of investment goods. Since the members of this group have experienced a rise in their incomes, it is to be expected that they will spend some part of this additional income for consumption goods and services. There will be, in other words, *induced*

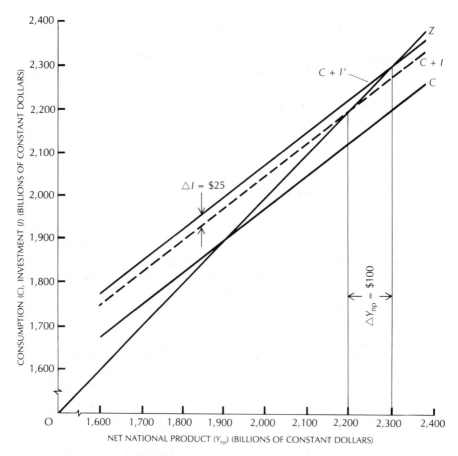

FIGURE 5–5. Multiplier Effect of a Shift in the Investment Function

changes in consumption expenditure. These induced changes can be described as a *secondary* effect flowing from the increased spending for investment goods.

We have been able to isolate and describe two major effects associated with an increase in expenditure of the kind that leads to an increase in output and increased incomes for the producers of the output. These effects are a *primary*, or initial, effect, which is associated with the initial change in income, and a *secondary*, or induced, effect, which arises out of the fact that the original recipients of the increased income will in turn spend some portion of this increase for consumer goods and services. It is in this secondary effect that we have the real key to the multiplier process, because, in the absence of any induced or secondary changes in spending, the impact of increased investment expenditure (or any other form of spending) on the income level could be no greater than the amount of the initial change in income. The multiplier effect results from the sum of the initial and induced changes in expenditure (and output) that ensue from a change in the rate of expenditure for any of the component parts of the aggregate, demand structure.

What, however, determines the amount of induced spending? The answer is quite simple: the *marginal propensity to consume.* Once we know what proportion of an increment of income will be spent for consumption goods and services, we are in a position to determine how great will be the secondary or induced effects resulting from autonomous increases in expenditure. The marginal propensity to consume thus provides the analytical key to the increases in secondary spending and, consequently, to the numerical value of the multiplier.

The Formal Multiplier Process

To understand the multiplier process clearly, the first step is to trace in detail the effects of the increase in investment expenditure of $25 billion. The hypothetical consumption function presented in Tables 5–2 and 5–3 is constructed in such a way that it has a slope of 0.75, which means that the marginal propensity to consume, a, is 0.75; out of every $1.00 increment of income, $0.75 will be spent for consumption. On the basis of this and given our assumed increase in investment outlays of $25 billion, we have constructed Table 5–4 to show how this initial increment in investment expenditure will generate a whole chain of respendings. The first column, which contains only the figure of $25 billion, represents the *initiating* increase in expenditure. The second column represents groups of income recipients, designated by numbers, while the third column records the increments of income that accrue to each of these groups as a result of successive rounds of spending. The fourth column shows the *induced* consumption spending that results from the income increases experienced by each successive group. The fifth

TABLE 5–4.   The Multiplier: With a Single Initiating Increase in Investment Expenditure (in billions of constant dollars)

(1) Initiating Increase in Expenditure ΔI	(2) Income Recipients	(3) Income Changes ΔY_{np}	(4) Induced Consumption ΔC	(5) Algebraic Derivation of ΔC
$25.00	1st Group	$ 25.00 ⟶	$18.75	ΔIa
	2nd Group	18.75	14.06	ΔIa^2
	3rd Group	14.06	10.55	ΔIa^3
	4th Group	10.55	7.91	ΔIa^4
	5th Group	7.91	5.93	ΔIa^5
	6th Group	5.93	4.45	ΔIa^6
	7th Group	4.45	3.34	ΔIa^7
	8th Group	3.34	2.50	ΔIa^8
	9th Group	2.50	1.86	ΔIa^9
	nth Group	1.86	1.40	ΔIa^n
$25.00		$\Sigma = 100.0*	$\Sigma = 75.0*	

*After an infinite number of spendings and respendings.

column shows the algebraic derivation of the change in consumption for each group, based upon the initiating increase in investment expenditure of $25 billion. Breaking the process of income change down into separate groups of income recipients is an artificial simplification, but it does enable us to analyze clearly how an initial increase in spending has multiple effects.

The initial increase in investment expenditure accrues as income to the first group, which then increases its consumption expenditures by $18.75 billion (75 percent of $25 billion). The spending will accrue as income to the suppliers of these consumption goods and services, namely, the second group, which also increases its consumption expenditures by 75 percent of the rise in its income, providing additional income for yet a third group. And so forth. We can thus see that the initial increase in expenditure will generate a series of spendings and respendings, which, if carried far enough, will raise income by some multiple of the original increment. The data in Table 5–4 show that ultimately the sum of induced consumption expenditure will total $75 billion, which, with the original increase in investment expenditure of $25 billion, will add up to a total increase in income of $100 billion, or four times the initiating increase. The value of the multiplier in this case is 4. Students familiar with mathematics will recognize that the total change in income (ΔY_{np}) involves a geometric progression of infinite sequence in which the change in investment (ΔI) is the first term and the marginal propensity to consume (a) is the common ratio or fixed number by which each preceding number in the sequence is multiplied.

Two further aspects of Table 5–4 should be noted. First, the multiplier has a time dimension, since it would be quite impossible in reality for the whole series of spending and respending to occur simultaneously. This point is stressed because in theoretical analysis we often ignore, for reasons of simplicity, the time element in the multiplier process. Second, the data of Table 5–4 show only what happens with a single, nonrecurring increment of investment expenditure. If we extended our example over a greater time span, income, which at first rose, would gradually fall back to its original level. The total increase in income spread over the whole time period in which the multiplier process was at work would, of course, equal the $100 billion shown in Table 5–4, but this would not be a permanent change. In order for the equilibrium income level to rise permanently to a new and higher level—which is the situation depicted in Table 5–3 and Figure 5–5—the increase in expenditure that initially triggers the expansion must be a *sustained* increase. Investment expenditure would have to expand from $75 billion to $100 billion and remain at that level if an enduring increase in the income level from $2,200 to $2,300 billion were to be brought about.

The nature of the multiplier process, given the assumption of a sustained increase of $25 billion in investment expenditure, is shown in Table 5–5. The data shown for Period 0 pertain to the equilibrium existing prior to the increase in investment expenditure by $25 billion. In

TABLE 5–5.   The Multiplier: With a Sustained Increase in Investment Expenditure (in billions of constant dollars)*

(1)	(2)	(3)	(4)	(5)	(6)	(7)	(8)†
			Actual	Planned	Induced	Planned	Actual
	Aggregate	Aggregate	Increase	Consump-	Consump-	Invest-	Invest-
	Demand	Supply	in Output	tion	tion	ment	ment
Period	$C+I$	Y_{np}	ΔY_{np}	C	ΔC	I	I'
0	$2,200	$2,200	—	$2,100	—	$100	$100
1	2,225	2,200	—	2,100	—	125	100
2	2,244	2,225	$25	2,119	$19	125	106
3	2,258	2,244	19	2,133	14	125	111
4	2,269	2,258	14	2,144	11	125	114
5	2,277	2,269	11	2,152	8	125	117
6	2,283	2,277	8	2,158	6	125	119
7	2,288	2,283	6	2,163	5	125	120
8	2,292	2,288	5	2,167	4	125	121
	2,300	2,300	—	2,175	—	125	125

*For simplicity, all numbers have been rounded to the nearest whole number.
†Actual (ex post) investment is the difference between aggregate supply (Column 3) and planned consumption (Column 5).

Period 1 investment expenditure increases by $25 billion, a development which amounts to a shift upward in aggregate demand from $2,200 billion to $2,225 billion. In this table we are operating on the assumption that output cannot respond instantaneously to an increase in expenditure; consequently, output does not rise to the level of aggregate demand of Period 1 until Period 2. In Period 2 the actual increase in output of $25 billion—Column (4) in the table—induces additional consumption expenditure in the amount of $19 billion as shown in Column (6). This is because the assumed value for the marginal propensity to consume is 0.75. Aggregate demand in Period 2, therefore, is equal to the total of planned consumption expenditure ($2,100 billion plus $19 billion) and planned investment expenditure ($125 billion). Output in this period has risen in response to the level of aggregate demand of the previous period, but aggregate demand has risen even higher because of the phenomenon of induced consumption expenditure. Gradually, though, the increments of induced consumption become smaller and smaller as the new equilibrium level of $2,300 billion is approached. In theory, this level will be reached only at the expiration of an infinite number of income periods, but, as a practical matter, the increments of both income and consumption expenditure will become insignificantly small after a finite number of periods. Once the new equilibrium income level has been attained, consumption expenditure will total $2,175 billion and investment expenditure will be $125 billion. There has been a multiplier effect of 4, because the initial increase of $25 billion in investment expenditure has brought about a total increase in income of $100 billion.

Algebraic Statement of the Multiplier

Now that we have examined by means of a numerical example the multiplier process, let us formalize the concept by stating it in terms of some relatively simple algebraic formulas. From our investigation of the multiplier process we have discovered that the magnitude of the multiplier effect depends upon the sum of initial and secondary effects. We saw that the key to the magnitude of the secondary effect is the marginal propensity to consume. Let us begin our algebraic analysis with the basic identity.

$$Y_{np} = I + C = Y_d. \tag{5-8}$$

The above equality is true because we are assuming the absence of taxes and transfer payments (see Footnote 8). In the following algebraic discussion, the multiplier is defined in relation to net national product, which is the same as disposable income, given the foregoing assumption. From the above identity it follows that

$$\Delta Y_{np} = \Delta I + \Delta C. \tag{5-9}$$

In the preceding analysis it was concluded that induced consumption expenditures depend upon the value of the marginal propensity to consume. In Equation (5-3) the marginal propensity to consume out of disposable income ($\Delta C/\Delta Y_d$) was designated as a. Since Y_d and Y_{np} are assumed to be equal, we can substitute $a\Delta Y_{np}$ for ΔC in Equation (5-9). We now have

$$\Delta Y_{np} - a\Delta Y_{np} = \Delta I. \tag{5-10}$$

Let us manipulate this equation algebraically as follows:

$$\Delta Y_{np} - a\Delta Y_{np} = \Delta I, \tag{5-11}$$

$$\Delta Y_{np}(1 - a) = \Delta I, \tag{5-12}$$

$$\Delta Y_{np} = \Delta I \times \frac{1}{1-a}, \tag{5-13}$$

$$\frac{\Delta Y_{np}}{\Delta I} = \frac{1}{1-a}. \tag{5-14}$$

The left-hand side of Equation (5-14) is what was defined in Equation 5-7) as the multiplier, the ratio of a change in income to a change in investment. From this we may conclude that in a formal, mathematical sense the multiplier is equal to the reciprocal of *1 minus the marginal propensity to consume*.[13] In our simple and hypothetical economy the mul-

---

13. The theoretical limits to the value of the multiplier are 1 and infinity (∞). If the value of the marginal propensity to consume is zero (0), then the multiplier will have a value of 1; if, on the other hand, the value of the marginal propensity to consume is 1.00 (100 percent), the multiplier will have a value of infinity (∞). The reader should work out the simple arithmetic to convince himself that it is true.

tiplier would also be equal to the reciprocal of the marginal propensity to save, for as long as saving and consumption are viewed as the only alternatives for the disposition of income, it is a simple matter of arithmetical truth that one minus the marginal propensity to consume, $1 - \Delta C/\Delta Y_d$, equals the marginal propensity to save, $\Delta S/\Delta Y_d$. But one must be careful here not to generalize that the value of the multiplier is always equal to the reciprocal of the marginal propensity to save. It is equal to this only in the absence of taxes and foreign trade.

Now that we have defined the multiplier algebraically, we shall review the process and apply the formula to the data of our hypothetical economy. Originally, the income equilibrium level was $2,200 billion, given the consumption function and a level of investment expenditure of $100 billion (Table 5–2). The marginal propensity to consume is 0.75, which yields a numerical value for the multiplier of 4. All that is necessary is to apply this coefficient to the change in investment expenditure, $25 billion. A change of investment expenditure of this amount will cause income to rise by $100 billion ($k \times \Delta I = 4 \times \$25$ billion $= \$100$ billion). As a result of this $100-billion increase in income, consumption expenditure will rise by $75 billion.

Summary Remarks on the Theory of the Multiplier

Before we discuss other important aspects of consumption theory, it is important to summarize the salient features of the multiplier concept.

First, the multiplier is a device for explaining why a change in spending may have cumulative effects upon the income level. The multiplier is associated with any autonomous change in expenditure in the economic system; it is not limited, as in our example, to changes in investment expenditure.

Second, the multiplier is properly regarded as an aspect of consumption theory, since its value depends upon induced consumption spending.[14] The amount of induced, or secondary, consumption spending that will ensue depends upon the marginal propensity to consume, the slope of the consumption function.

Third, the magnitude of the multiplier effect is inversely related to the total of *leakages* from the current income stream. Income that is not spent for currently produced consumption goods and services may be regarded as having *leaked out* of the income stream. Most economists regard the marginal propensity to consume as normally having a value of less than 1, because it is felt that some leakages are bound to be present. In this chapter, saving represented the only form of leakage from the income stream. In reality, though, there are other forms of leakages. Tax collections and expenditures for imported goods and services can be considered as leakages, as we shall see subsequently. A leakage is any-

14. It should be noted that consumption expenditure is not the only type of expenditure that may be induced through a change in income. It is possible for investment expenditure, too, to be induced. This is a matter that we shall discuss in the following chapter.

thing that reduces the tendency toward the spending or respending of income on currently produced domestic goods and services; the greater such leakages, the smaller will be the multiplier effect. It is for this reason that we cannot claim that the multiplier is always equal to the reciprocal of the marginal propensity to save. If we could determine and measure all leakages as marginal propensities, then we could state comprehensively that the multiplier has a value equal to the reciprocal of the sum of all leakages.

Finally, we must be very careful to note that the computation of a numerical value for the multiplier depends upon accurate knowledge of the economy's consumption function and marginal propensity to consume. The empirical data examined earlier suggest that consumers tend to behave in the fashion indicated by the consumption function hypothesis, but this does not mean that it is easy to construct a statistical consumption function that will determine the exact value of the multiplier for the economy. In the mid-1960s, the Council of Economic Advisers estimated a value of 2 for the multiplier effect of a contemplated tax cut. This estimate turned out to be approximately correct. In essence, we are cautioning against an overly simple interpretation of the multiplier phenomenon. If we recognize and understand this limitation, we are still left with a concept of great value for analysis of the process of change in the income and employment level.

Income, Consumption, and Saving in the Long Run

There is another aspect of the income-consumption relationship that has intrigued economists for a number of years. The consumption function depicted in Figure 5–1 is one in which the average propensity to consume falls as the income level rises. The slope of a function of this type is such that it intersects both the aggregate supply function and the vertical axis. Since this schedule pertains to the behavior of consumption expenditure over relatively short periods of time, it is usually described as a short-run, or cyclical, function. The statistical data shown in Table 5–1 and plotted in Figure 5–3 tend to confirm the existence of this type of relationship.

However, a dilemma is created by the fact that statistics on income, consumption, and savings for very long periods of time show that the consumption-income ratio, C/Y, tends to be constant. In some pathbreaking studies published just after World War II, Nobel laureate Simon Kuznets showed that, for approximately 60 years (1869 to 1929), the ratio between consumption and income tended to be constant.[15] Kuz-

15. Simon Kuznets, *Uses of National Income in Peace and War* (New York: National Bureau of Economic Research, 1941), p. 31, Table 2, and p. 35, Table 6. See also Kuznets, *National Product since 1869* (New York: National Bureau of Economic Research, 1946), p. 119. Similar results were found by Raymond Goldsmith; see his *A Study of Savings in the United States* (Princeton: Princeton University Press, 1955), pp. 22, 78.

nets's data are shown in Table 5–6. Also shown in this table are data for three post–World War II decades, 1950–59, 1960–69, and 1970–79. These data are not strictly comparable with the earlier data developed by Kuznets, primarily because he computed consumption as a percentage of net national product, whereas the postwar figures relate consumption to disposable income. Furthermore, Kuznets employed definitions of both the net national product and consumption different from those currently used by the Department of Commerce. Nevertheless, both the pre- and post–World War II data show that over long periods of time the ratio between consumption and income (however defined) tends to be constant. The only exception to this for the period covered by the data in Table 5–6 is the decade 1929–38 (Kuznets's data), when the ratio of consumption to income rose to nearly 100 percent. The reason for this is that this period includes the years of the Great Depression.

The upshot of all this is that, over the long run, consumers spend about the same proportion of their income, even though they have experienced a steady rise in the level of real income. As a matter of fact, in the years covered by Kuznets's data when the propensity to consume remained practically constant, *real* income rose nearly eightfold. Diagrammatically,

TABLE 5–6.   Net National Product and Consumption Expenditures in the Long Run (in billions of 1929 dollars)

(1) Decade	(2) Net National Product	(3) Consumption Expenditures	(4) Average Propensity to Consume (3) ÷ (2)
1869–78	$ 9.3	$ 8.1	87.1
1874–83	13.6	11.6	85.2
1879–88	17.9	15.3	85.5
1884–93	21.0	17.7	84.2
1889–98	24.2	20.2	83.5
1894–1903	29.8	25.4	85.2
1904–13	45.0	39.1	86.9
1909–18	50.6	44.0	86.9
1919–28	69.0	62.0	89.8
1924–33	73.3	68.9	94.0
1929–38	72.0	71.0	98.7
1950–59*	421	383	91.5
1960–69*	594	546	91.1
1970–82*	919	827	90.2

Source: Decades for 1869–78 through 1929–38 from Simon Kuznets, *National Product since 1869* (New York: National Bureau of Economic Research, 1946), p. 119. Decades 1950–59, 1960–69, and 1970–79, *Economic Report of the President* (Washington, D.C.: U.S. Government Printing Office, 1983), p. 191.
*1950–59, 1960–69, and 1970–82 data are for disposable income rather than net national product and are in 1972 dollars. The income and consumption figures are rounded to the nearest whole number.

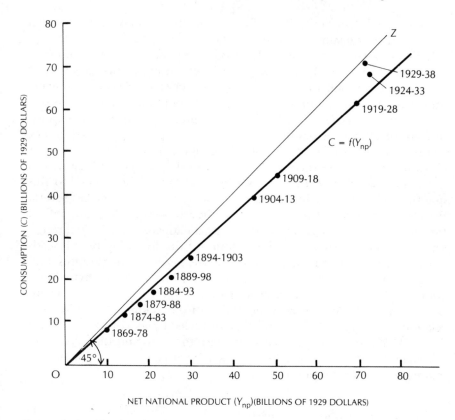

FIGURE 5–6. The Secular Consumption Function

the long-term (or *secular*) consumption function appears as a straight line whose slope is such that the marginal and average propensities to consume are equal. Such a consumption function is shown in Figure 5–6. The Kuznets data are also shown in this figure. It is called a secular function because it pertains to the behavior of consumption expenditures in relation to income over long periods of time.

The dilemma faced by economists is how to reconcile statistical evidence on the long-run constancy of the average propensity to consume with equally worthy statistical evidence which shows that in the short run the consumption-income ratio is not a constant. Actually, we have already suggested one solution to this dilemma, for in our earlier discussion of the empirical validity of the consumption function hypothesis we pointed out that the short-run data on income and consumption suggest that over time the consumption function may actually be shifting upward. The secular upward "drift" of the consumption function, as it has been called, is clearly seen in Figure 5–3, when we extrapolate data from the 1929–41 period into the post–World War II era. The extrapolated curve (the dashed line extensions in Figure 5–3) lies below the curve that fits the measured data in the 1947–82 period. Thus, it may be argued that the measured consumption function has shifted upward.

This, however, is not the only possible explanation of the observed differences between the consumption-income ratio in the long run as compared to the short run. It may also be argued logically and convincingly that the *real* relationship between consumption and income is one of proportionality (as revealed by the long-term data), but that short-term—or *cyclical*—factors distort this relationship, giving us the kind of consumption-income pattern displayed in Figure 5–3. What is the proper explanation for these differences in empirical findings? Unfortunately, contemporary income theory does not have a precise answer to this question. Rather, there has emerged from the research of the last several decades three general hypotheses—or theories—which seek to explain the ratio of consumption to income and what happens to this ratio through time. We may classify these theories under the following broad headings: the *absolute* income hypothesis; the *relative* income hypothesis; and the *permanent (life-cycle)* income hypothesis. The first two hypotheses embrace the idea that the measured short-term consumption function shifts upward through time, whereas the third hypothesis views the basic relationship as one of proportionality, distorted by short-term or cyclical factors.[16] We shall examine each of these theories, and then conclude this chapter with a brief discussion of some variables other than income that influence consumption.

The Absolute Income Hypothesis

The thesis developed earlier in this chapter to the effect that the average propensity to consume declines with an increase in income (Figure 5–1) has come to be known as the absolute income hypothesis. This is the theory that stems most directly from Keynes's analysis in *The General Theory*. Its basic tenet is that it is the absolute level of a family's income that, above all else, determines its consumption spending; hence, the designation absolute income hypothesis.

Inherent in this thesis is a basic difficulty; namely, it implies that a society will save an increasing proportion of its income, a conclusion denied by the long-term evidence on the income-consumption and income-saving ratios. However, the absolute income hypothesis is compatible with the idea that over time the cyclical function drifts upward, but as theory it does not offer an explanation for this phenomenon.

What this means is that we must look to a change in one or more variables other than income to account for this shift. In the analysis of consumer spending, the general practice is to treat all influences on consumption other than income as *parameters*, whose values determine the

---

16. Strictly speaking, the third category involves two separate theories, the *permanent* income hypothesis *and* the *life-cycle* hypothesis, but their basic ideas are so similar that there is ample justification to put them into a single category for purposes of explanation and exposition.

level and slope of the consumption function.[17] If there are changes in the parameters, then the position of the consumption function will shift. What kinds of influences might account for the secular upward drift of a consumption function of the type $C = C_0 + aY_d$?

Several such factors have been identified by economists as capable of exercising this kind of influence, although no conclusive statistical evidence exists showing a strong correlation between them and consumer spending. Among the most important of these parameters are household wealth, the distribution of income, the introduction of new consumer goods, urbanization, changes in the age structure of the population, and a decline in the number of self-employed persons in the economy. For example, with an increase in household wealth, there might be a greater willingness to spend out of current income, thus raising the average propensity to consume. Urbanization might have the same effect because there is some evidence that saving propensities are higher among farmers than for city-dwellers. In like fashion, a more equal distribution of income could raise the propensity to consume because of the fact that family budget studies generally show a decline in the income-saving ratio as income declines. Goods that were once regarded as luxuries sooner or later become necessities, another development that, over time, tends to keep the income-consumption ratio constant. The same effects might result from an increase in the proportion of people in the retirement age category in the population, simply because their incomes are likely to decline much more rapidly than their consumption patterns change. Self-employed persons normally save a higher proportion of their income than do wage-earners, so a decline in the proportion of self-employed in the working population would also tend to raise the average propensity to consume.

Changes in some of these parameters will be analyzed more fully in the closing section of this chapter. Here it is sufficient to stress again that changes of the kind just described in these parameters may have enough force to keep the income-consumption ratio constant through time, assuming that the absolute income hypothesis has validity. Empirical evidence on this point, though, is inconclusive.

The Relative Income Hypothesis

An alternative to the absolute income hypothesis was developed initially by Professor James S. Duesenberry of Harvard University and a former member of the President's Council of Economic Advisers.[18] Unlike

17. Parameters are magnitudes whose values are assumed to be constant. As such, they determine the position of the function. The parameters of the consumption function are C_0 and a; changes in other factors influencing the consumption decision operate to change the value of these constants.

18. James S. Duesenberry, *Income, Saving and the Theory of Consumer Behavior* (Cambridge, Mass.: Harvard University Press, 1949), pp. 17–46. See also Duesenberry, "Income-Consumption Relations and Their Implications," in *Income, Employment and Public Policy: Essays in Honor of Alvin H. Hansen* (New York: Norton, 1948), pp. 54–81.

the absolute income hypothesis, this theory does not depend upon changes in the value of parameters to account for the long-term stability of the C/Y ratio. Duesenberry's relative income hypothesis is based upon two key ideas: First, consumer preferences are interdependent, which means that the level of consumption of a family or household depends upon its income *relative* to other families and households. Consumption spending, in other words, is *emulative*, which is to say that it depends upon the spending of families on a higher rung of the income distribution ladder. Second, consumer spending does not depend upon the level of current income alone, as the absolute income hypothesis views it, but on a relationship between current income and the highest income that the family or household has previously experienced. Let us examine by means of a diagram the relative income hypothesis as developed by Professor Duesenberry.

In Figure 5–7 the curve labeled C_s is the secular, or long-term, consumption function, whereas the curves labeled C_1, C_2, and C_3 represent

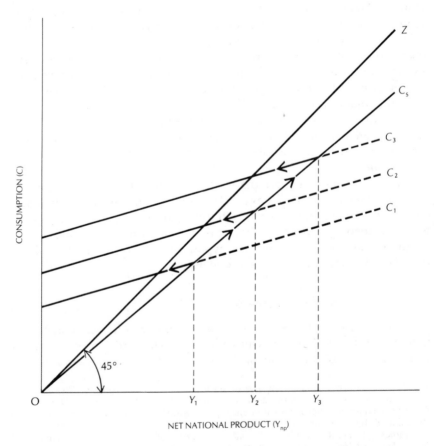

Figure 5–7.   The Upward Drift of the Cyclical Consumption Function

a series of cyclical, or short-term, consumption functions. Let us assume that initially the income level is given by Y_1, and that this represents the highest level of income yet achieved in the economy. We are at the peak of a cycle. What will happen now if income falls from the level of Y_1? On the diagram this is, of course, a movement to the left. According to Duesenberry's theory, consumption will move along the short-run path represented by the function C_1, because the most immediate and strongest influence on consumption will be the recent experience of achieving an income level equal to Y_1. Consumers, having become accustomed to this level during the boom, will strongly resist any reduction in their standard of consumption. Consumption will decline, of course, but more slowly than income. This is exactly the kind of behavior pattern envisaged by Keynes, since he thought that the most important influence at work is the consumer's habitual standard of life. The movement of consumption spending along the C_1 curve also means that the average propensity to consume will rise and the average propensity to save will fall. As the income level moves back to its original position, which will come about as the economy moves out of a recession, consumption will rise again along the path of C_1, at least until restoration of the previous high peak of income is achieved. As the income level moves back toward its prior peak, consumers will want to restore the earlier relationship between consumption and saving, and consequently the saving-income ratio, S/Y, will rise and the consumption-income ratio, C/Y, will fall.

What will happen once the economy regains the level Y_1 and, in a surge of growth, moves on toward Y_2, a new and higher income level? In this instance, consumption will rise along the path of the secular function, C_8, until the new peak level, Y_2, is achieved. Consumption increases proportionally to income. Why? For one thing, the prior income peak, Y_1, no longer exercises its influence over consumer behavior, since the economy is moving toward a new peak. In such a situation increments to income will be allocated between spending and saving in a constant ratio, the latter being the ratio regarded as normal at the prior highest income level. The relative income hypothesis holds that the average propensity to consume for the economy as a whole will not change as long as the distribution of income does not change. During the period when the economy is moving toward a new peak income level, there is no reason that the pattern of income distribution should change. All spending units will enjoy a higher absolute level of income because the income level of the whole economy has risen, but the *relative* position of each group will not necessarily change. Therefore, the average propensity to consume for the whole economy will not change. One important implication of the relative income theory is that there is a *ratchet effect* at work, tending to boost consumption spending to ever-higher levels of what consumers come to regard as normal.

Much the same conclusion concerning the relationship between the cyclical and secular consumption functions was reached independently by another economist, Professor Franco Modigliani.[19] He also suggests that the ratio between income and saving (or consumption) has to be linked not merely to current income but to a ratio or index that embodies both current income and the highest income level previously reached. In this respect his analysis is quite similar to Duesenberry's. In the Modigliani analysis, consumption will also follow a Keynesian path when the income level goes below the highest level yet achieved. He attributes this not only to consumer resistance to a reduction in acquired consumption habits, but to the growth in unemployment in the downward phase of the cycle and to the redistribution of income that occurs when the income level falls. With respect to the growth of unemployment, Modigliani's thesis asserts that even if there is a long-run tendency for employed persons to consume a constant proportion of their income, the ratio of consumption to income will rise when there is growing unemployment because unemployed persons consume even though they have no incomes. The redistribution of income that occurs in the downward phase of the cycle is likely to be in favor of groups having the highest propensity to consume. This is because the greatest income squeeze in a recession or depression is on profits. All these factors taken together account for the rise in the average propensity to consume when the income level falls, and the reverse when the income level is rising. With respect to the long-run picture, Modigliani agrees with Duesenberry that a constant proportion of income will be consumed once the economy moves beyond the highest income level previously achieved. But he explains this by the continuous appearance of new products and the improvement of old commodities. Portions of the income increments that accrue to all groups as a result of the long-term rise in the real income of the whole economy are absorbed by new goods and services that gradually become available. This is the basic reason offered by Modigliani for the long-term constancy in the consumption-income or saving-income ratio.

The Permanent (Life-Cycle) Income Hypothesis

The two major theories in this category have in common the primary idea that the consumer plans his consumption *not* on the basis of income received currently, but on the basis of long-term or even lifetime income expectations. Thus, the fundamental theoretical relationship between consumption and income is one of proportionality, although short-term (or cyclical) factors can cause departures of the average propensity to consume from the long-term norm. We shall now examine these ideas.

The best-known exposition of the permanent income hypothesis is that developed by Professor Milton Friedman, formerly of the University of

19. Franco Modigliani, "Fluctuations in the Saving-Income Ratio: A Problem in Economic Forecasting," in *Studies in Income and Wealth*, Vol. 11 (New York: National Bureau of Economic Research, 1949), pp. 379 ff.

Chicago, also the foremost proponent of the modern monetarist approach to the determination of the level of economic activity (see Chapter 10).[20]

The key concept in Friedman's hypothesis is that of *permanent* income. Permanent income is roughly akin to lifetime income, based upon the real and financial wealth at the disposal of an individual plus the value of one's human capital in the form of inherent and acquired skills and training. The average expected return on the sum of all such wealth at the disposition of an individual would be his permanent income.

The foregoing is the concept. Measurement is something else. The income that an individual actually receives in a year is what Professor Friedman calls *measured* income. Over a lifetime, measured income ought to coincide with permanent income, but in any one year measured income as a result of cyclical fluctuations and because of other random changes may depart from permanent income. But the best way to measure permanent income, according to this hypothesis, is through a weighted average of past and present measured income, with less weight being attached to measured income the farther it lies in the past. In any one year the difference between measured income and permanent income is called *transitory* income. It may be positive or negative, but over an individual's lifetime it is necessarily zero.

Professor Friedman's essential thesis is that an individual's permanent consumption is proportional to his or her permanent income. In other words, the consumer or household expects over its life to save a fixed proportion of its lifetime—or permanent—income. Practically, this thesis means that saving will increase (or decrease) whenever there is an increase (or decrease) in the transitory component of income. This is what accounts for short-term fluctuations in the saving-income (or consumption-income) ratio as depicted in the short-term, or cyclical, function. The idea that all transitory increases in one's income are saved may seem contrary to ordinary observation, as people often use windfall gains in current income to buy some kind of a durable consumer good, such as a car, color TV set, or stereo outfit. But, in concept at least, this difficulty disappears if durable goods purchases are viewed as additions to private wealth and their services viewed as consumption.

The essential idea of the permanent income hypothesis may be illustrated with a simple diagram, like that in Figure 5–8. In the diagram Y_p represents permanent income, C_p permanent consumption, and Y_m measured (or current) income. The difference between Y_p and Y_m is transitory income. The diagram shows the path over time of these three variables. Starting at the point in time t_1, current or measured income expands. As it rises from its starting level to a peak at time t_2, the ratio between permanent consumption C_p and measured income will decline.

20. Milton Friedman, *A Theory of the Consumption Function* (Princeton: Princeton University Press, 1957).

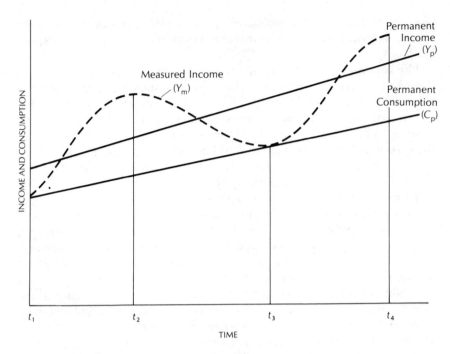

FIGURE 5–8. The Permanent Income Hypothesis

This is the ratio that may be observed from actual or current data. As measured income starts a decline from this peak, the measured (or observed) propensity to consume will increase. This will continue until measured income bottoms out at time period t_3, following which it will begin to climb once again. Thus, over the course of cyclical fluctuations in measured income, the average propensity to consume derived from observed data will follow the pattern found in the cyclical consumption functions discussed earlier. It is the assumption that consumption expenditures are tied in proportional fashion to permanent income and, thus, do not fluctuate as measured (or observed) income fluctuates.

Why should people behave in this fashion? The roots of Professor Friedman's theory trace back to the ideas of one of America's greatest economists from an earlier era, Irving Fisher.[21] Given the fact that households may desire to build up their stock of wealth through saving and given, too, the fact that people may save because of uncertainty and for anticipated future needs, how will they manage the relationship between saving and income over their lifetimes? A rational household seeking to maximize the utility it gets from both consumption and saving for the aforementioned objectives would try to arrange its affairs so that over its life it neither saved more nor less than the desired amount. This

21. Irving Fisher, *The Theory of Interest* (New York: August M. Kelly, 1961), Chaps, 4, 5.

means, though, that the household would have to save any income that was above its lifetime average—or permanent—income and dissave when its income fell below this figure. This is essentially what the permanent income hypothesis says will happen.

Both the life-cycle hypothesis and the permanent income theory suggest that consumers adjust their consumption patterns to the total resources which they can draw on for spending over their lifetimes. These resources consist of both wealth and the present value of expected income (the value of the human capital at an individual's disposal.)[22] The life-cycle hypothesis differs from the Friedman theory, however, in that the propensity to consume of an individual will vary with age as well as wealth. The basic relationship in the hypothesis is one of proportionality between the individual's lifetime income as determined by total resources (material wealth and human capital), but the observed relationship between consumption and income at any time will depend on the age of the consumer. Since the individual consumer's observed income is relatively low at the beginning and end of his or her life, the proportion of income consumed out of measured income will be high at these times. In his or her middle years, income will be high and the propensity to consume will be lower. Over the consumer's lifetime, however, consumption will be a fixed proportion of total income. The essential point of both theories is that the long-term proportion of permanent income consumed is independent of the consumer's income in a particular period. Transitory income changes do not have any significant impact upon current consumption. Thus, short-term changes in the observed consumption-income ratio are the result of transitory shifts in income.

Which Theory?

Which of the above theories offers the best—or most appropriate—explanation of consumer behavior? Unfortunately, no precise answer can be given to this question, as each represents a hypothesis that is reasonably in accord with observed experience. There are elements of truth in all these approaches to understanding the relationship between income and consumption (or savings). Probably what is most crucial is the realization that both theoretical analysis and empirical observation point strongly to the conclusion that income is the dominant factor in explaining consumption behavior in the national economy. Furthermore, the *observed* relationship between income and consumption seems to adhere to a Keynesian-type path over the short term, even though this relationship is a proportional one when a longer span of time is taken into consideration.

22. For details of the life-cycle hypothesis, see F. Modigliani and Richard Brumberg, "Utility Analysis and the Consumption Function: An Interpretation of Cross-Section Data," in K. Kurihara, ed., *Post Keynesian Economics* (New Brunswick, N.J.: Rutgers University Press, 1954), and A. Ando and F. Modigliani, "The Life-Cycle Hypothesis of Saving," *The American Economic Review*, March 1963.

Other Influences on Consumption

In the discussion of the support that empirical data concerning income and consumption offer the consumption function hypothesis, we pointed out that few economists believe that income is the only determinant of consumption spending. Let us now briefly examine some other variables that influence consumer expenditures. As already stressed, the general practice in analysis of consumer spending is to treat variables other than income as *parameters,* whose values determine the level and slope of the consumption function. Analytically, this means that changes in the value of any of these parametric factors will result in a shift in the position of the entire schedule, rather than a movement along it. Although parametric factors are generally recognized to influence the level of consumption expenditure, many of them are not subject to quantification and precise measurement. This being the case, we have to depend in part upon deduction to arrive at dependable conclusions concerning the way in which such variables influence consumer expenditures.

Attitudes toward Thrift

In a general way, we can group together in the category of thrift the psychological attributes of human nature that lead people to save rather than spend some part of current income, as well as various business practices and institutional arrangements of a society that make for saving. Cultural factors that condition a society's attitudes toward thrift and spending are deeply rooted in its past and not readily subject to change. In the United States, the Puritan tradition with its stress on the intrinsic virtues of work and frugality operated in times past to create a social climate more favorable to saving than to spending. Today, though, developments such as consumer credit and time-payment plans have a countereffect, although the impact of such phenomena on the position of the consumption function is by no means a simple or one-way affair.

Installment purchasing and other forms of borrowing that raise the propensity to consume are to some extent offset by developments of modern life which tend to raise the propensity to save. The twentieth century, in fact, has witnessed a powerful tendency toward the institutionalization of saving through commitments of income to life insurance, private pension plans, and long-term mortgages on private homes. Recently changes in the income tax laws have been made that are designed to increase savings by individuals and families. For example, since 1981, any wage-earner may open an Individual Retirement Account (an "IRA"), which permits the wage-earner to exempt from income taxation the first $2,000 of earned income. For a married couple who both work, up to $4,000 of income can be "sheltered" from the personal income tax. For a married couple with only one working spouse, the limit is $2,250. IRAs may be opened by any wage-earner, irrespective of other retirement or pension schemes in which the wage-earner is involved. Since saving is the nonexpenditure of current income for currently produced goods and services, these institutional arrangements create a continuous flow of quasi-compulsory saving that does not change simply because the income level has changed. The average person does not usually think of premiums on the life insurance, payroll deductions for a pension plan, or monthly amortization of home loans as forms of saving, yet they represent saving from the viewpoint of the whole economy. Moreover, most saving of this type is contractual in nature, and thus cannot readily be changed.

Asset Holdings by the Consumer

Another factor believed by many economists to exercise a powerful influence on consumer spending patterns has to do with assets held by the consumer, including both financial assets in the form of cash on hand, bank accounts, bonds, stocks, and other claims and physical assets in the form of stocks of durable goods in possession of the consumer.

Financial Assets   The most plausible hypothesis that we can advance regarding the influence of financial assets on expenditures is simply that spending will vary directly with the value of private holdings of financial assets. Such holdings, particularly if they are easily converted into purchasing power, constitute a reserve of spending power that the consumer can draw on in emergencies. As a consequence there is less need to save out of current income in order to build such a reserve. This means that an increase in holdings of liquid assets by consumers would, other things being equal, shift the consumption function upward. Moreover, households possessing stocks of liquid assets are more willing and more able to finance consumption spending by borrowing.

The hypothesis of a direct relationship between consumer spending and holdings of financial or liquid assets is subject to some reservations. For one thing, the distribution of ownership of liquid assets will have a bearing upon their overall impact on consumer spending. If, for example, ownership is concentrated in the upper-income groups, it is doubtful that the size or value of such holdings will have much influence upon the level of consumption for the whole economy, since high-income earners as a group tend to save a large proportion of their income at all times. If this viewpoint is valid, then holdings of liquid assets will not necessarily tend to raise the consumption function.

In addition to the distribution of ownership, changes in the real value of liquid assets may exercise an influence on the consumer's spending-saving decisions. For example, if the general price level rises, the real value of financial assets in the form of bank deposits, bonds, and other financial resources may decline. If this happens consumers may be induced to save more out of their current income in order to recoup a desired position with respect to asset holdings. The possibility of a unique relationship between the real value of the stock of liquid assets, the general level of prices, and the position of the consumption function is known as the *Pigou effect,* after A.C. Pigou, a noted British economist.[23] Pigou argued that a fall in the general level of prices would stimulate the economy by tending to shift the consumption function upward. The price drop would increase the real value of the consumer's financial assets and thereby lessen his need to save. We shall encounter the Pigou effect again in our later discussion of the general price level, but it is doubtful if many economists today take it very seriously. It is more in the nature of an exercise in abstract logic than an attempt to deal with forces that operate in the real-world economy.

Stocks of Durable Goods   The second type of asset that may effect the spending-saving pattern of the consumer consists of the stock of durable goods in his possession. As a general proposition, a large stock of durable goods in the hands of consumers may, other things being equal, have a tendency to depress consumption spending. Such goods represent a capital investment for the consumer, and they provide a stream of services as long as the goods are in existence. The man who owns an automobile for example, need not spend much of his income for other forms of transportation. Similar results flow from the ownership of other types of durable goods, such as television sets and radios, home laundry equipment, and various other household appliances. It should be recognized, though, that ownership of durables may stimulate other expenditures. The owner of an automobile, for example, must purchase large quantities of gasoline, new tires, and spare parts. He is, moreover, a purchaser of insurance and other services that stem directly from his ownership of an automobile. On balance, it is difficult to say which of these influences is the strongest.

The chief conclusion we can draw concerning the influence of the stock of consumer durables on consumer spending is that such goods by their very durability introduce elements of uncertainty into consumer spending. Beyond this it is difficult to say more with certainty because economists have yet to accumulate sufficient empirical data to indicate any precise relationship between the stock of consumer durables and consumption expenditure.

The Distribution of Income

Economists regard the distribution of money income of a society as one of the important parametric determinants of the consumption-income relationship. This particular influence on consumption is thought to be

---

23. A. C. Pigou, "The Classical Stationary State," *Economic Journal,* December 1943, and "Economic Progress in a Stable Environment," *Economica,* August 1947. The latter is reprinted in *Readings in Monetary Theory* (Philadelphia: Blakiston, 1951), pp. 241–51.

stable, as the pattern of income distribution in any society is determined by a complex of institutional factors, including the structure of property rights, the distribution of ownership of productive assets, the tax system, and the social security system, all of which appear to change with relative slowness.[24] Insofar as the pattern of income distribution has an influence upon the level and slope of the consumption function, some economists believe that, other things being equal, a movement toward more equality in the distribution of income will raise the level—and possibly, too, the slope—of the consumption function, whereas any movement toward greater inequality in the distribution of income will have the opposite effect. This deduction is based on the fact that studies of income and its disposition at the level of the household show that families in the lower-income brackets have a higher average propensity to consume than families in the upper-income brackets. Such studies are less conclusive with respect to the marginal propensity to consume of the two income groups, although economists have tended to assume on *a priori* grounds that the marginal propensity to consume would be low for the upper-income groups and high for the lower-income groups.

Let us consider the presumed relationship between differences in the average propensity to consume for families in different income brackets, the overall distribution of income, and the level of the consumption function. If the distribution of income in a society is relatively unequal, families in the upper-income brackets receive a large proportion of the total income. If this is the case, the average propensity to consume for the whole society will be low, irrespective of the level of total income of the society, since the upper-income groups tend, on the average, to consume a comparatively low percentage of their income. On the other hand, if the distribution of income is relatively equal, families or spending units in the lower-income brackets will receive the largest proportionate share of the income total. Since the average propensity to consume for these groups is high, the ratio for the society as a whole will also be high, regardless of the level of total income. Thus, greater equality in the distribution of income tends to raise the level of the consumption function, whereas more inequality has the opposite effect.

This analysis, buttressed by the assumption that the marginal as well as the average propensity to consume is higher for spending units in the lower-income brackets, leads to the conclusion that the consumption function could be raised if steps were taken to bring about a greater degree of equality in the distribution of money income. Taxation and transfer expenditures are the policy means by which the federal government could achieve this goal, assuming that it was desirable to increase the proportion of income spent. For example, if Group A with an assumed marginal propensity to consume of 0.50 had its disposable income reduced by $100 through taxation, and this sum was transferred to Group B,

24. Available statistical evidence indicates little change in the United States in the pattern of personal income distribution since 1929.

which has a marginal propensity to consume of 0.75, the result would be a net increase in consumption spending of $25. Note that this argument is concerned with changing the average propensity to consume by changing the distribution of income; it is not addressed to the question of whether the distribution of income should be more or less equal.

This means of bringing about an upward shift in the consumption function has been challenged in two ways. First, some statistical evidence exists to suggest that the differences in the marginal propensity to consume between the upper- and lower-income groups are much smaller than differences in the average propensity to consume. If this is the case, a redistribution of income from the upper- to the lower-income groups might not appreciably affect consumption spending. The decline in consumption spending resulting from a reduction in the disposable income of households in the upper brackets would approximately equal the increase in spending that would occur as households in the lower-income brackets experienced an increase in their disposable income. This would be the initial effect, but if redistributional measures were continued, a permanent alteration would occur in the pattern of income distribution in the direction of greater equality. Once this has taken place, the average rather than marginal propensity to consume should hold sway.

The idea that the consumption function can be raised by fiscal and other measures that bring about a redistribution of personal income faces a second challenge. It is argued that income redistribution theory is valid only upon the assumption of the absolute income hypothesis, which asserts that a consumer's preferences for goods and services are formed independently of the preferences of other consumers. If a family moves into a different income bracket—as a result, say, of measures designed to redistribute income—they will assume the income-consumption pattern of prior occupants of the bracket.

But the relative income hypothesis, which holds that consumer preferences are interdependent, implies that the level of consumption of a family depends upon its income relative to other families. This means that consumption standards are emulative, in that the amount an individual spends upon consumption does not depend simply on his own income, but also on the consumption patterns of families or spending groups on a higher rung of the income distribution ladder. If consumer preferences are interdependent and consumption standards emulative, this leads to the conclusion that a redistribution of income in the direction of greater equality may not increase consumption expenditure; on the contrary, such a redistribution could even lower consumption. In an interdependent and emulative society, reduction in the income and consumption of groups in the upper-income brackets might tend to reduce the pressure toward consumption spending for groups situated at lower levels on the income distribution scale. The standards of consumption that the latter groups emulate have been lowered, and thus their own consumption standards will follow suit.

In the face of these arguments, any conclusion about the probable effects of income redistribution measures on the level of the consumption function cannot be anything but nebulous. Most economists agree that the prevailing pattern of income distribution is an important determining factor of the level and slope of the consumption function. But economists do not agree upon either the extent to which income distribution can be changed in the short run or the immediate effects, if any, of such changes on the level of the consumption function.

The Rate of Interest

At one time many economists would have been inclined to list the rate of interest as probably the most important determinant of consumption and saving. According to pre-Keynesian thought, to save is to exchange present satisfactions (gained from consumption) for future satisfactions, but a price must be paid to persuade people to make such an exchange. This price is interest. The higher the price, the greater the willingness of people to postpone consumption; the lower the price, the smaller their willingness. As a consequence, interest was regarded as a prime determinant of the amount that families and spending units would save out of their income.

Today many economists do not believe that the rate of interest exercises any appreciable effect one way or the other on the level of consumption or saving. From a deductive point of view it is possible to show that increases in the level of interest rates may actually reduce saving. A rise in interest rates means that, if people save in order to amass a sum designed to yield them some specific annual income, a smaller absolute sum would yield an identical annual income at higher interest rates as a larger sum at lower rates. If, for example, the rate of interest rose from 10 to 15 percent, a saver would have to amass only $13,333 rather than $20,000 in order to obtain an annual interest income of approximately $2,000. A rise in the rate of interest also may tend to reduce some types of contractual saving, such as life insurance. At higher interest rates a *fixed* amount of life insurance requires smaller premiums.

Price Changes and Consumer Expectations

Changes in the general level of prices and shifts in consumer expectations for the future are two additional and related factors that economists recognize as potential influences on spending and saving levels. Our knowledge of the impact of these variables is more speculative than empirical. There is a presumption that a rise in the level of all prices will raise the average propensity to consume, assuming (somewhat tenuously) that money income does not change in the same degree. The increase in prices leads real income to decline, causing a higher consumption-income ratio. It is also possible, in the face of a falloff in real income, that consumers will attempt to maintain the same absolute level of real consumption. This would result in a shift upward of the consumption function, for consumption spending would absorb a higher proportion of an absolutely lower real income level.

A few pages back, we touched briefly on the Pigou effect, which concerns a shift in the consumption function brought about by a change in the real value of the consumer's liquid assets. This suggests that a rise in the general level of prices would tend to shift the consumption function downward rather than upward, the reason being that the fall in the real value of assets increases the propensity to save. This is exactly the opposite outcome from that discussed in the preceding paragraph. The inflationary experience of the 1970s does not throw much light on these questions. In the earlier part of the decade, as inflation mounted, the proportion of income saved rose, suggesting, perhaps, that consumers were responding in the Pigou manner. But as the decade progressed and as inflation worsened, the opposite took place, suggesting that as real incomes declined consumers were trying to maintain real consumption levels.

Consumer expectations concerning future prices may also influence the position and slope of the consumption function. It is possible, for instance, that widely held expectations that prices will continue to rise will lead consumers to devote a higher proportion of their current income to consumption purchases than would otherwise be the case. However, it is also possible that expectations that inflation will continue would lead people to retrench and save more, given the uncertainty which may cloud the future in an inflationary environment. About the only thing that can be said for certain is that if people expected inflation so uncontrollable that the value of money was completely destroyed—the case of "hyper"-inflation—then all saving would end. But within the context of the kind of inflation the American economy has experienced in recent years, there is no clear-cut statistical evidence supporting either of the above possible impacts that expectations of future prices may have on current income-consumption relationships.

Consumer expectations concerning future income may also be of significance, affecting the slope rather than the level of the consumption. The slope of the function is the marginal propensity to consume, which specifies the way in which consumers react to a change in their incomes. Logically, one would expect that an individual (or spending unit) would react differently to an increase (or decrease) in income, depending upon whether or not the change was expected to be permanent. To illustrate, if a change in income is seen as temporary, consumption spending probably would not change to the same degree as it would if the income change were viewed as permanent. In 1968 the Johnson administration belatedly enacted an increase in the income tax in the form of a surcharge on individual tax liabilities. This, of course, had the effect of reducing disposable income, but because the tax increase was widely advertised as a temporary measure made necessary by the Vietnam war, consumption spending did not decline to the extent that it might have if the tax increase had been permanent. The net effect was to reduce the saving ratio during 1968 and 1969, years in which the surcharge was in effect.

Consumer Credit

The significance of consumer credit on consumption is readily apparent; the availability of credit permits more spending for consumption purposes than would be possible if current income were the only source of purchasing power. The practical importance of consumer credit as a factor in consumer expenditure in the United States is enormous. In 1981 the volume of outstanding consumer credit of all types was over $413 billion, an amount that had grown 16 times since 1950. Moreover, the volume of credit extended to consumers has increased in nearly every post–World War II year, irrespective of the recessions of 1949, 1954, 1958, and 1970. The only exceptions were 1974 (a recession year), when the total fell slightly, and 1980, another recession year in which credit outstanding fell sharply.[25] The reason for the latter was stringent action by the Carter administration in the late winter and early spring to limit consumer borrowing, especially borrowing based upon credit cards. Clamping down on consumer credit was a part of the Carter administration's overall policy of monetary stringency to control inflation.

The obvious fact concerning consumer credit is that borrowed funds represent additional financial resources that can be used for current consumption expenditures. If consumers borrow sufficiently so that the total of their indebtedness increases—that is, new borrowings exceed repayments—the consumption function would tend to shift upward. Total consumption spending would rise relative to income, since borrowing has given the consumer control over financial resources greater than the amount represented by current income. It is interesting to note that ever since 1946 consumers have added to their borrowings at a greater rate than they have repaid their obligations. Consumer credit in this period thus created upward pressure on the consumption component of aggregate demand.

Although it is true that an initial extension of credit to the consumer tends to raise the propensity to consume, it is equally true that the subsequent effects of such credit extension may depress consumption expenditure. Such loans must be repaid. If Mr. Jones, for example, borrows $5,000 to help finance the purchase of a new automobile, his expenditure of the proceeds of the loan will take an item of current output off the market. Subsequently, though, a portion of Mr. Jones's current income will no longer be available to spend for currently produced goods and services, since he must repay the loan. If he arranges to repay the $5,000 at the rate of $167 a month, then for a period of

25. *Economic Report of the President,* 1981, p. 310, and *Current Economic Indicators,* November 1981, p. 27.

thirty months (ignoring interest and other charges connected with the loan) the amount of current income that he can spend for currently produced goods and services will be $167 less than usual.

What lesson does this hypothetical example hold for the economy as a whole? Unless there are new borrowings sufficient to offset the repayment of old borrowings, any stimulus to consumption expenditure that came from an extension of credit to the consumer will be short-lived. If borrowing by the consumer tends to raise the level of the consumption function, repayment of loans has the opposite effect. Economists interested in the influence of consumer credit on consumption expenditure are more concerned with the relationship between the rate of new borrowing and the rate of repayment than with the absolute amount of consumer credit outstanding at any particular time.

The rate at which consumers increase their indebtedness is no doubt in some way tied in with expectations. Again there is scant empirical evidence to help us determine the precise nature of this relationship. It does not require any great feat of the imagination to see how disastrous it could be for the economy if consumers decided all of a sudden to reduce drastically their rate of new borrowing. The result would be a precipitate fall in the level of the consumption function.

A Concluding Comment

In this chapter we have examined in detail the findings of modern economic analysis with respect to the determinants of consumption expenditure. The impetus for study and analysis of this key component in the structure of aggregate demand comes from Keynes's *The General Theory*. Keynes's belief in the existence of a functional relationship between real income and real consumption has been formalized in the concept of the consumption function. This has become one of the key analytical tools of modern income and employment theory. In retrospect, we can say that, although economists are no longer as sure as they once were of either the stability or simplicity of the consumption-income relationship, they do regard its embodiment into the formal body of economic analysis as one of the major achievements of economic science within the last several decades.

Appendix

Formal algebraic proof that the value of the multiplier k is equal to $1/1-a$

The value of the multiplier depends upon the sum of the initial injection of funds into the system plus the ensuing induced expenditures. The multiplier effect of an additional $1 of investment expenditure can be expressed in equation form as shown below. In the equations, *a* is the marginal propensity to consume and n represents the number of income periods.

(1) $k = 1 + a + a^2 + a^3 + a^4 + \ldots + a^a$

(2) $ak = a + a^2 + a^3 + a^4 + a^5 + \ldots + a^{n+1}$

(3) $(k - ak) = (1 - a^{n+1})$ [Equation (2) subtracted from Equation (1).]

(4) $k(1 - a) = 1 - a^{n+1}$

(5) $k = \dfrac{1 - a^{n+1}}{1 - a}$

(6) When the number of income periods, n, is very large, the value of a^{n+1} will be so small as to be negligible, if $0 < a < 1$. Therefore, we conclude that

$$k = \frac{1}{1 - a}$$

Algebraic proof that a equals the marginal propensity to consume

(1) $C = C_0 + aY_a$

(2) $C + \Delta C = C_0 + a(Y_d + \Delta Y_d)$

(3) $C + \Delta C = C_0 + aY_d + a\Delta Y_d$

(4) $\Delta C = a\Delta Y_d$ [Equation (1) subtracted from Equation (3)]

(5) $a = \dfrac{\Delta C}{\Delta Y_d}$

Algebraic determination of the equilibrium income level

(1) $Y_{np} = C + I$ The basic identity

(2) $C = C_0 + aY_d$ The consumption function

(3) $C = C_0 + aY_{np}$ This follows because $Y_d = Y_{np}$ when taxes and transfers are zero

(4) $I = I_0$ Autonomous investment

(5) $Y_{np} = C_0 aY_{np} + I_0$ Substitution Equations (3) and (4) into (1).

(6) $YN_{np} - aY_{np} = C_0 + I_0$

(7) $Y_{np}(1 - a) = C_0 + I_0$

(8) $Y_{np} = \dfrac{1}{(1 - a)}(C_0 + I_0)$

(9) $Y_{np} = k(C_0 + I_0)$

Using the data from Table 5–2 in which $C_0 = \$450$ and $I_0 = \$100$ we can find the value of Y_{np} as follows. The multiplier $k = 4$

(1) $Y_{np} = 4(\$450 + \$100) = \$2,200$ (All data are in billions.)

Summary

1. The consumption function, a fundamental principle, holds that consumption, other things being equal, is determined primarily by income.

2. There are two important technical attributes of the consumption income relationship: (1) the *average* propensity to consume (C/Y) and (2) the *marginal* propensity to consume ($\Delta C/\Delta Y$).

3. The marginal propensity to consume reflects Keynes's fundamental "psychological" law, which states that when income changes consumption changes, but not as much as does income. This is the basis for the theory of the multiplier.

4. The theory of the multiplier relates any exogenous change in one of the spending components—such as investment—to a total and larger change in income. The multiplier results because any initial or exogenous change induces additional changes in consumption and investment.

5. The value of the multiplier depends directly upon the *marginal* propensity to consume (and its converse, the *marginal* propensity to save), and it is equal to the reciprocal of 1 minus the marginal propensity to consume.

6. Several theories have been developed that expand upon the basic income-consumption relationship. These include the *absolute* and *relative* income hypotheses, as well as the *permanent* income and *life-cycle* hypotheses.

7. There are also other important influences upon consumption, including attitudes toward thrift, asset holdings by consumers, the distribution of income, the rate of interest, and expected prices.

6

Investment and Finance

In this chapter we turn to the second major category of expenditure entering into aggregate demand: investment expenditure. There are three basic reasons why investment expenditure occupies a highly significant role in the functioning of the economy. First, the demand for investment goods is a large and important part of the total demand picture. In 1982, for example, gross private domestic investment was $420.3 billion, an amount equal to 13.7 percent of GNP. Investment expenditures play an especially strategic role in the economy, because changes in both income and employment are more likely to result from fluctuations in spending for capital goods than from fluctuations in spending for consumer goods. Changes in spending for consumer goods generally come about as a result of changes in the income level, rather than the other way around. In Keynes's *The General Theory* investment expenditures are volatile. In 1980, for example, investment spending dropped by 5 percent from the 1979 level, but in the latter year it had jumped by nearly 11 percent over the level of 1978. Students of change and growth have long been aware that fluctuations in capital goods production are more violent than fluctuations in the production of consumer goods and services. This is true both in a relative sense and in an absolute sense. Investment expenditures not only initiate change in income and employment levels, but also act to exaggerate the effects. As Keynes saw it, the basic reason for the volatility of investment is that it depends upon our expectations about the future. But the future is something about which we know very little.[1]

Finally, investment expenditures are significant because of their impact on the economy's productive capacity. Investment expenditures involve

1. John Maynard Keynes, "The General Theory of Employment," *Quarterly Journal of Economics,* February 1937, p. 221.

the acquisition of capital goods, the procreative element in an industrial society. Their function is to produce other goods and services. This means that even though investment expenditures play a key role in determining current levels of income and employment, their influence reaches beyond the present by means of their impact upon capacity. Investment expenditures thus are vital factors in economic growth, which depends to a great extent upon how rapidly productive capacity is being enlarged.

The Investment Decision

There is one basic fact about investment spending in a market system that one should never forget: Business firms invest in equipment and buildings in order to make money. It is as simple as that. All investment expenditure is undertaken in the expectation of profit. In actuality it is often difficult in an enterprise to separate expectations of profit from actual (or current) profitability, which is dependent upon current levels of output, sales, and costs. Expected profits obviously will be influenced by current profits, as well as other variables. This is good common sense. But it does not mean that investment will take place only when current profits are satisfactory, because in many instances firms with low profit margins will invest in money-saving equipment in an effort to reduce costs.[2]

Generally speaking, there are two ways to which investment in capital will improve the profitability of the firm's operations. First, investment in new and improved equipment is a means of reducing production costs. Capital equipment is productive partly because it can supplement or take the place of other resources, particularly labor. Capital goods are tools. Through their use the effectiveness in production of both labor and natural resources may be enormously enhanced. It is estimated, for example, that machines in a modern factory supply from thirty to seventy times as much energy as could be provided by human muscle. Capital is also productive because it frequently represents the means by which new methods or techniques of production are introduced into the economic process.

The second way in which investment in capital equipment may improve the profitability of the firm's operations centers on market conditions. Frequently, the firm will be confronted with an opportunity to increase its profits either by introducing a new product or by expanding the output and sales of existing products. In either case, added capacity may be required if the firm is to exploit fully the profit potential of a favorable market situation; investment in new equipment and plants is necessary to provide this added capacity. In the quest for greater profitability, many firms engage extensively in product research and sales promotions. Both

2. Walter W. Heller, "The Anatomy of Investment Decisions," *Harvard Business Review,* March 1951.

these activities frequently force a firm to invest in more plant and equipment.

Now that we have examined briefly the reasons investment expenditure cannot be separated from profitability in the operation of the firm, let us examine the nature of the investment decision. How does the entrepreneur look upon an item of capital equipment? What factors does he have to take into account when he is contemplating the purchase of additional capital equipment? These questions lie at the heart of the investment decision, and investment theory, if it is to be meaningful, must provide at least tentative answers to them.

Investment and Expected Income

Since the entrepreneur undertakes investment expenditure in the expectation that it will be profitable, he sees an item of capital equipment essentially as a stream of expected income, or, as Keynes described it, "a series of prospective returns, which he expects to obtain from selling its output, after deducting the running expenses of obtaining that output, during the life of the asset."[3] To the businessman, the value of a capital good lies in the stream of net income that the asset is expected to yield over its life. What the businessman does in essence is convert money (his own or borrowed money) into capital goods (equipment and buildings) that are expected to generate a cash flow over their lifetime. The investment process in a market society is one that moves from money to goods and back to money. The stream of income—or cash flow—is an *expected* stream primarily because capital is durable and thus yields value to its user only over a relatively long period of time. The size of the expected income stream depends upon, first, the physical productivity of the capital instrument; second, the price at which the output produced with the aid of the capital equipment can be sold (which is primarily a matter of future demand and market conditions); and, finally, the nature and amount of other expenses in the form of wages and material costs that may be incurred from the use of additional amounts of equipment. These expenses, too, depend upon future market conditions. Keynes said that the considerations upon which "expectations of prospective yields are based are partly existing facts . . . and partly future events which can only be forecasted with more or less confidence. . . . The *outstanding fact is the extreme precariousness of the basis of knowledge on which our estimates of prospective yields have to be made.* Our knowledge of the factors which will govern the yield of an investment some years hence is usually very slight and often negligible."[4] Here in a nutshell is why investment spending is so much less stable than consumption spending, why expectations are subject to sudden and frequent change.

In analyzing the investment decision the usual practice is to think of

---

3. John Maynard Keynes, *The General Theory of Employment, Interest and Money* (New York: Harcourt, Brace & World, First Harbinger ed., 1964), p. 135.
4. Ibid., pp. 147, 149 (italics added).

the stream of expected income associated with the use of additional amounts of capital as being net of all other expenses that the firm may incur as a result of using more capital. Added expenditures for labor and materials, as well as any other additional operating expenses, are deducted from the contemplated income stream or prospective returns on the capital good. This is done because the entrepreneur is primarily interested in what the equipment will yield him in the way of income over and above any additional expenses that may be involved in its operation.

Having stripped the stream of expected income of all costs incidental to the process of producing additional output, the entrepreneur is faced with the question of whether the investment is worthwhile. Will it, in other words, be profitable? As has just been stressed, the businessman in modern industrial society obtains a profit by converting money, which is the most liquid of all assets and which can always be loaned out at interest, into a less liquid form, that of a capital asset. Through the sale of its output, the capital asset is converted back to monetary form. This movement from money to capital asset and back to money will be profitable to the entrepreneur only if the asset yields him more than the cost of its acquisition. Here is the nub of the investment decision. The entrepreneur will find an investment worthwhile if it yields him a stream of income greater than what he must pay to acquire the asset. The investment decision involves balancing expected gain against the costs of acquiring the gain.

The Costs of Investment

What are the costs that the entrepreneur has to take into account in estimating the profitability of an investment expenditure? If we ignore momentarily the element of risk present in the acquisition of any capital asset, we can distinguish two fundamental types of costs that enter into the investment decision: the cost under current market conditions of the capital asset itself and the cost involved in the use of money or funds to acquire the asset.

The cost of the capital good under current market conditions is called the *supply price* of the asset. This is the price that would induce the manufacturer of any particular type of capital asset to produce one additional unit of the capital asset in question. The supply price for a particular capital asset is not the current market price of existing assets of that kind, but, basically, the cost of producing a new unit. It is the price that lies somewhere on a supply curve for the kind of capital equipment under discussion. From a monetary standpoint this represents what the entrepreneur must spend in order to acquire the asset. It also represents the absolute, irreducible minimum that the entrepreneur expects to get back from the purchase and utilization of a capital good. In a world dominated by the profit motive no entrepreneur would contemplate the purchase of a new capital asset unless he believed that the asset would yield a stream of income whose present value, in the very least, would be equal to the supply price of the asset. In actuality, he would expect more, but this notion of a kind of irreducible minimum gives us a point of departure.

The above statements would be all that need be said if the use of money did not involve any costs. Then we could say that it would be profitable to acquire a capital asset whenever the value of the stream of expected income was greater than the current supply price. This, though, is not the case. In a monetary society there is always a cost involved in the use of money. The entrepreneur contemplating the acquisition of a capital asset has two choices open to him. Since he cannot obtain the asset without money, he must either borrow the necessary funds to finance its purchase or else draw upon his own accumulated reserves. If he borrows, he must pay the current market rate of interest appropriate to a loan of the type and duration necessary. The interest rate reflects the *financial cost* of the investment decision. Even if the entrepreneur uses his own funds to finance his purchase of capital equipment, the interest rate reflects financial cost. In this event, the financial cost is implicit, since by using his own funds for the purchase of a capital instrument, the return on which is uncertain, the entrepreneur foregoes the possibility of securing a return on these funds equal to the current market rate of interest, which he could get by lending his funds. It is only proper for the entrepreneur to treat such foregone interest income as a cost element in the acquisition of a capital asset. The market rate of interest is a measure of the opportunity cost involved in the use of funds to purchase an item of capital in preference to lending such funds to someone who is willing to pay the going rate to secure their use.

The essential point of the foregoing paragraph is that capital assets, no matter what their physical nature or durability, must be financed, which is to say that business firms have to acquire money before they can acquire more capital assets. Where do firms get the money? Essentially they may get it from their earnings (ploughing a part of profit back into new capital), by selling additional shares in the stock market (equity financing), or by borrowing (through bank loans or by issuing bonds or other types of debt instruments). In all three cases the current rate of interest represents either the implicit or explicit cost to the firm in using money however obtained to purchase additional capital assets.[5] Borrowing to obtain funds is not only a common practice, but presents for the business firm problems of a different sort than it may encounter when

---

5. In the case of the use of internal funds, the firm would expect to get back through the profitability of the capital a return at least equal to what the firm could have obtained by lending. If shares are sold, the purchasers will also expect a return in the form of dividends that also is at least equal to what they could have obtained by lending their money. There is no guarantee that the firm will earn such a return from the capital assets so acquired, but this is the expectation.

it uses its own resources or sells shares to obtain money.[6] The reason is that a loan arrangement sets up a stream of cash payments that have to be met in order to pay off the loan. Normally this cash flow of required payments is contractual in nature, which means the firm is legally committed to make payments to its creditors until the loan is paid off or refinanced with a new loan. When funds are obtained internally or by the sale of shares, no such contractual pledge exists, although the owners will expect a return on the money (i.e., dividends) they have put into the firm by the purchase of its shares. As we shall see subsequently, the size of the contractual flow of payments that confronts a firm as a result of debt financing of new capital assets may affect significantly its willingness to invest in such assets.

The Basic Framework of Investment Theory

Now that we have examined the essential character of the investment decision, let us develop a formal framework for investment theory. In the preceding discussion the point was emphasized that an excess of expected revenues from the use of a capital good over its supply price means that the good yields a prospective profit. This is true, regardless of the financial costs of the investment, as long as the expected income stream is greater than the supply price. The excess of the expected yield over the cost of the capital can be expressed as a rate; more specifically, this excess is a rate of return over cost, in which the net return per unit of time is shown as a percentage of the original cost. For example, a machine might cost an entrepreneur $10,000 and yield him a net annual return of $1,000. Without at this moment considering the question of the useful life of the machine, we can say that such a machine yields *an annual rate of return over cost* of 10 percent.

The rate of return over cost relates the expected yield of a capital good to its supply price. It is this relationship that Keynes, in *The General Theory*, called the *marginal efficiency of capital*.

> The relation between the prospective yield of a capital asset and its supply price or replacement cost, i.e., the relation between the prospective yield of one more unit of that type of capital and the cost of producing that unit, furnishes us with the *marginal efficiency of capital* of that type. More precisely, I define the marginal efficiency of capital as being equal to that *rate of discount* [italics added] which would make the present value of . . . the returns expected from the capital asset during its life just equal to its supply price.[7]

The above definition emphasizes the word *marginal.* We are interested in the expected rate of return on additional units of capital, not the rate

---

6. It is estimated that more than three-quarters of investment expenditure (equipment, buildings, and inventories) that is financed externally is financed by borrowing. See Frank J. Jones, *Macrofinance* (Cambridge, Mass. Winthrop Publishers, Inc., 1978), pp. 263 ff.
7. John Maynard Keynes, *The General Theory*, p. 135.

of return now being earned on existing capital. Keynes defined the marginal efficiency of capital as a rate of discount; specifically, as the rate of discount that will make the present value of the income stream derived from the capital good just equal to its supply price. What is a rate of discount? It is a rate used to determine the present value of a sum that will not be received until sometime in the future. For example, $100 due one year from today is worth less than $100 now on hand, the reason being $100 on hand can be loaned at interest. Thus, in one year the $100 will be worth more than $100 because of interest. Therefore, $100 due in a year must be worth less than $100 in hand. When we allow a sum to grow over time at a fixed rate of interest this is known as compounding—that is, growing at a constant rate. Discounting is just the opposite of compounding. It means shrinkage at a constant rate.

The Discount Formula

The discount formula is a mathematical formula for finding the present value of an expected future income. It applies a rate to some expected future sum that will cause it, as it were, to shrink in value. The usual procedure for determining the present value of some expected income stream is to discount it at the current rate of interest. To see how this works, let us assume that we have an asset that will yield an income of $3,000 per year for a three-year period ($9,000 over its total life span). We want to know the present value of this asset. The discount formula for finding the present value of a future income is

$$V_p = \frac{R_1}{(1+i)} + \frac{R_2}{(1+i)^2} + \cdots + \frac{R_n}{(1+i)^n}, \qquad (6-1)$$

Where V_p is present value; $R_1, R_2, \ldots R_n$ is the expected income stream in absolute amount; and i is the current rate of interest. The numerical subscript appended to each R represents the year in which each of the specific sums that are a part of the total is due. If we assume that the current rate of interest is 10 percent, we can apply the above formula to find the present value of our asset.

$$V_p = \frac{\$3,000}{(1.10)} + \frac{\$3,000}{(1.10)^2} + \frac{\$3,000}{(1.10)^3}.$$

And, clearing fractions,

$$V_p = \$2,727 + \$2.479 + \$2,288 = \$7,494.$$

The present value of the series is thus $7,494, an amount less than the sum of the absolute amounts to be received in the three years. The process we have just described is also called *capitalization*. When we use the rate of interest to find the present value of an income stream we are said to have "capitalized" the income stream. Present value is found, in other words, by capitalizing expected cash flows.

Our example shows that the more remote the date in the future at which the income is expected, the less its present value; $3,000 due in three years, for example, has a lower present value than $3,000 due in one year. Again leaving aside any question of uncertainty, simple arithmetic tells us that if we lend the sum of $2,727 for a period of one year at a rate of interest of 10 percent, we will get back $3,000, which includes the original sum and interest. This being the case, no one would be willing to pay more than $2,727 for an asset that would yield a total return of $3,000 one year hence. By the same reasoning, if we lend $2,479 for a period of two years at a rate of interest of 10 percent we will get back $3,000, for $2479 compounded at a rate of 10 percent for two years equals $3,000. Thus, no one would be willing to pay more than $2,479 for an asset that yields a total return of $3,000 two years hence. The same reasoning applies to the third sum in our series, namely, $2,288, if it is made available as a loan for a three-year period at the rate of 10 percent.

Examination of the process of discounting shows that there must be a rate of discount that will make the present value of prospective returns from a capital good equal to its supply price. This is the rate that Keynes calls the marginal efficiency of capital, which we shall designate by r. Let us now modify the foregoing discount formula by substituting the current supply price of the capital instrument for present value, V_p, and also by substituting the marginal efficiency of capital, r, for the current rate of interest i. The formula now appears as

$$K_s = \frac{R_1}{(1+r)} + \frac{R_2}{(1+r)^2} + \cdots + \frac{R_n}{(1+r)^n}. \tag{6-2}$$

The expected income stream (or series of Rs) is the same as in Equation (6-1). The current supply price, K_s, is a known value in contrast to the unknown present value, V_p, in the earlier equation. In the above formulation the unknown is the marginal efficiency of capital, r, or discount rate, which will make the present value of the expected income stream R_1, R_2, ... R_n equal to the supply price, K_s. The equation must be solved for the unknown r.

As long as the computed value of the marginal efficiency of capital is positive, we know that the capital asset in question will yield some rate of return. This means the income stream expected from the use of the capital asset is at least large enough to cover the supply price. But, the current supply price of the asset represents only a part of the cost of acquiring an added unit of capital. In addition to the supply price, there is the financial cost that arises from the use of money funds in the acquisition of the asset. Since this cost element is measured by the current rate of interest, we can compare it directly with the marginal efficiency of capital; both are rate phenomena.

If such a comparison is made and we find that the marginal efficiency of capital is greater than the current rate of interest, the situation is favorable to investment. The income stream expected from the use of an additional unit of capital exceeds the costs of acquiring the capital. Consequently, the capital instrument will be purchased. Of course, an entrepreneur may use his resources to purchase a financial asset rather than an item of capital equipment, and presumably he will do so whenever the marginal efficiency of capital falls below the current rate of interest.

The idea that, other things being equal, investment expenditure will take place whenever the marginal efficiency of capital is greater than the current rate of interest is the key element in the theory of investment. It is the formal, theoretical expression of the view that profitability is the dominant factor in the investment decision. Unless the prospects are such that the expected yield of a new item of capital exceeds its supply price plus financial cost, it will not be purchased by the business firm. When we say that the marginal efficiency of capital, r, is greater than the rate of interest, i, we are also saying that the present value, V_p, of the capital asset (which is obtained by discounting its expected income at the current rate of interest) is greater than its supply price K_s.

The Demand for Capital

At the level of the firm and industry the demand for capital must be formulated in relationship to the stock of capital goods. When a firm undertakes investment expenditures because the marginal efficiency of capital is greater than the current rate of interest, it will add more units of capital to its current stock. Thus, the first step in developing a theory of investment expenditure applicable to the economy as a whole is to examine the character of the demand for capital at the firm level in order to see how this can be translated into investment spending. There is a paradox to be resolved, for what is of interest to the firm is its stock of capital, including additions and subtractions from that stock, but what is of paramount concern with respect to income and employment levels for the economy as a whole is the overall flow of investment spending.

Figure 6–1 depicts the demand for capital as seen by the firm. The vertical axis measures present value, V_p, and the horizontal axis the quantity of capital, K. For the firm, present value is the same as the price it is willing to pay for each additional unit of capital. For each possible level of the rate of interest there exists a single down-sloping demand curve for capital. In Figure 6–1 three curves are shown. It should be noted that, other things being equal, the lower the rate of interest, the higher will be the level of the demand curve. The reason for this can be seen by reference to Equation (6–1); for any given income stream $(R_1, R_2, \ldots R_n)$, present value must be larger the lower is the rate of interest. This is a matter of mathematics.

The fundamental explanation for the negative slope of any single demand curve for capital lies in the principle of diminishing productivity. Given the rate of interest, and with all else held constant, including

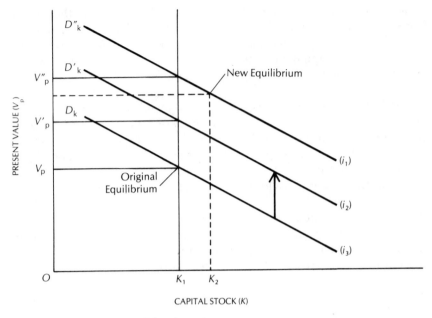

FIGURE 6–1.   The Demand for Capital

demand for the final product, the expected profitability of each successive increment to the capital stock must decline. In the terms of the variables of Equation (6–1), the expected income stream will decline as the
capital stock is enlarged. To put the matter differently, the *marginal efficiency of capital* will decline as the firm acquires more units of capital. In
this context it is crucial to note and understand that net investment takes
place in the economy whenever firms are in the process of adding to
their capital stock; net disinvestment results whenever the reverse process takes place, which is to say whenever firms reduce their stock of
capital instruments.

The Role of the Interest Rate

The effect of a change in the rate of interest is to shift the position of
the demand curve for capital. If the rate of interest is lowered, the curve
will be shifted upward. The economic reason for this is that a fall in the
rate of interest will increase the present value of the firm's marginal unit
of capital, making it more profitable for the firm to utilize additional
capital. From the viewpoint of the firm, the consequence of a fall in the
rate of interest is to increase the capital intensity of production, that is,
to cause firms to use more capital per unit of labor and other resources.
If all firms in the economy are affected in similar fashion by a decline in
interest rates, what will be the overall result? This is the question to which
we must now turn.

Let us begin the analysis with the assumption that, prior to the reduction in the interest rate, firms in the aggregate were in an equilibrium position with respect to their use of capital. This means that present value and the supply price are equal. This is also to say that, on balance, they were neither increasing nor decreasing the amount of capital used in the production process. This assumption means, too, that the total stock of capital of the economy is fixed. All investment expenditure at this point is replacement investment. The equilibrium stock of capital is depicted by K_1 in Figure 6–1. In technical terms capital is momentarily in completely inelastic supply.

Let us assume further that the rate of interest declines from i_3 to i_2. Under these circumstances the demand curve for capital will move to the level D'_k. The immediate consequence of this is to raise the present value of existing capital stock from V_p to V'_p; this is because we have had an increase in demand for a resource whose supply is temporarily fixed. This will also lead to an increase in the current price of capital goods, which will evoke a supply response. Capital goods production increases, because the suppliers of capital goods respond to an increase in the price of their product in the same manner as any other supplier, namely, by increasing output. Because it was assumed prior to this change that the economy was in equilibrium with respect to the quantity of capital employed in production, additional output of capital results in net investment. Our analysis, thus leads us to associate a fall in the rate of interest with an increase in the rate of investment, assuming initially an equilibrium position in the use of capital. A rise in the rate of interest would lead to opposite results.

If we start from an equilibrium position, the actual volume of net invesment that we can associate with a different rate of interest is determined by the output response of capital goods production to the change in the rate of interest. This is a matter of the reaction of the industries supplying capital goods to the change in the price of capital goods which results from the shifts in the demand curve for capital. This point means, in effect, that supply conditions in the capital goods sector are a prime determinant of the level of net investment for the economy as a whole in any given time period.

The Investment Demand Schedule

The foregoing discussion brings together the key elements involved in decisions at the firm level to increase the use of capital relative to other resources. The problem now confronting us is to derive a schedule that will relate the rate of investment expenditure to the rate of interest. If this can be done, we shall have the rudiments of a theory of investment which can be incorporated into our broader frame of reference, the theory of aggregate demand.

Figure 6–2 shows the relationships involved in the derivation of this schedule. In Part A of the figure, the 45° line represents equality conditions between present value and the supply price of newly produced

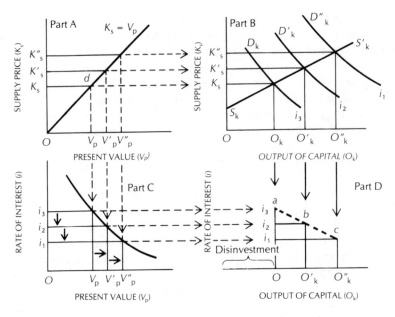

FIGURE 6–2.   The Rate of Interest and the Output of Capital

units of capital, K_s. The latter are represented on the horizontal and vertical axes, respectively. Part B contains a supply schedule for capital goods output, showing the latter on the horizontal axis and the supply price on the vertical axis. This curve has the usual positive slope characteristic of a supply curve, indicating that more output will be supplied only as the price increases. Part C of the figure contains a curve, R, which relates present value to the rate of interest. This curve, which is based upon expected proceeds, depicts graphically the relationship inherent in Equation (6–1), namely, present value, V_p, will vary inversely with the rate of interest. Part D contains the schedule that relates the net output of capital goods to the rate of interest. This schedule is the one in which we are most interested and it is derived from the relationships depicted in the other three parts of this diagram.

Let us begin our analysis by assuming the economy is initially in equilibrium with respect to the use of capital. The stock of capital equals K_1 (Figure 6–1), and the rate of interest is i_3. In equilibrium, present value and the supply price must be equal. This equilibrium is shown in Part A of Figure 6–2 at the point d on the 45° line showing equality between V_p and K_s. By projecting the equilibrium supply price to the right (Part B), we can determine from the supply schedule $S_k S'_k$ the output of capital goods associated with this price. This is O_k in Part B. By projecting the equilibrium present value downward (Part C), we can show that V_p is associated with the interest rate i_3. If we now project the output of capital goods O_k (Part B) downward, and the rate of i_3 (Part C) to the right, we find they will intersect at point a in Part D of the figure. Thus, we have established a point that relates the net output of capital to the rate of interest. Net output of capital goods at the interest rate i_3 is zero because our beginning assumption was that the economy had attained equilibrium with respect to its use of capital.

We shall now examine what will transpire with a fall in the rate of interest. Note carefully that the diagrams contained in Figure 6–2 are of such a nature that they can only depict effectively the end result of a disturbance to equilibrium; they cannot show the process through which change takes place. This is a consequence of their static nature. We begin by assuming a fall in the rate of interest from i_3 to i_2. The fall in the rate of interest increases the present value of the existing stock of capital, assuming no change in the series of expected proceeds. This change is shown in Part C, wherein present value rises to V'_p as the rate of interest falls to i_2. Momentarily we find that present value exceeds the current supply price (Part B) and, as a consequence, it will be profitable for firms to increase their use of capital. Because the capital goods sector cannot respond instantly to the increased demand for capital, the current market price for existing capital goods will rise. This leads, in turn, to an increase in the output of capital goods. For the economy this results in net investment, because additional capital goods output will, under the circumstances assumed in our analysis, increase the stock of capital. Output of capital expands until it reaches the level given by O'_k in Part B of Figure 6–2, for at this level of production present value and the current supply price of capital are once more in balance.

It is now necessary to repeat our previous process and project the output of capital O'_k (Part B) downward and the rate of interest i_2 (Part C) to the right to get an additional point of intersection. This is point b in Part D of the figure. We now have a second point relating the net output of capital goods to the rate of interest. If the rate of interest falls still further to the level i_1, the process just described will ensue once again, and we shall get still a third point c in Part D of the figure relating capital goods output to interest.

If we connect these three points (the dashed line in Part D) we have, in effect, constructed a schedule that shows how the rate of capital goods production (net investment) is linked to the rate of interest. What is of significance concerning this schedule is that it postulates, *ceteris paribus*, an inverse relationship between the rate of interest and the demand for units of newly produced capital goods, which will be added to the capital stock. The schedule shown in Part D of Figure 6–2 may be called the *marginal efficiency of investment*, because it is the theoretical basis for construction of an aggregate investment demand schedule which makes total investment expenditure an inverse function of the rate of interest. In *The General Theory* Keynes stated it was possible to construct such a schedule directly upon the basis of relationships embodied in Equation (6–2) because increased investment in any type of capital would lead to a decline in the marginal efficiency for capital of that type. The difficulty with this approach is that it overlooks the fact that the demand of the firm is for a fixed quantity of capital to be employed in conjunction with other resources in the production process. Thus, it is really not possible to construct a schedule relating investment expenditure to the rate of interest without at the same time bringing the stock of capital into the analysis. This is what is done in Figure 6–2.

To construct an investment demand schedule for the economy as a whole on the basis of the relationship shown in Part D of Figure 6–2 it is necessary to translate the rate of output shown on the horizontal axis of the diagram into a rate of investment expenditure. Conceptually this can be done by multiplying the output data shown by the current supply price of the newly produced capital goods to get an expenditure total for capital appropriate to each level of the interest rate. The results should then be deflated by an appropriate price index so as to reduce investment expenditures to real terms. A schedule derived in this manner is depicted in Figure 6–3, in which the rate of net investment expenditure is shown on the horizontal axis and the rate of interest measured on the vertical axis. This is an investment demand schedule of the type that Keynes envisaged in *The General Theory,* and which we have defined as the *marginal efficiency of investment* schedule. The investment demand schedule and the marginal efficiency of investment schedule are essentially identical because they both relate the rate of interest to the volume of investment study.

In algebraic terms the relationship embodied in the investment demand schedule is given by the equation

$$I = I_0 - ci, \tag{6–3}$$

where I_0 is investment expenditure that will take place at zero rate of interest and c is the coefficient relating investment expenditure to the rate of interest. The fact that c has a negative value reflects the inverse correlation between investment and the rate of interest, which is to say that the greater the value of i, the smaller will be the value of I.

At this point the student should note carefully the similarity of our treatment of investment expenditure with our earlier analysis of consumption expenditure. Compare, for example, Equation (6–3) with Equation (5–3). What this means, essentially, is at this point investment is made a function of a single variable, namely, the rate of interest. This does not mean, however, that other variables are not also important as determinants of the aggregate level of investment demand function. This procedure is identical to what we followed in the analysis of the consumption function and is a standard analytical technique in economics.

Shifts in the Investment Demand Schedule

As is true for any demand schedule, the investment demand curve depicted in Figure 6–3 is subject to either upward or downward shifts. These shifts are to be explained in terms of the fundamental determinants which lie behind the schedule. To clarify this, let us refer once

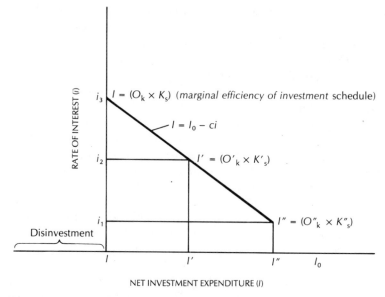

RATE OF INTEREST (*i*)

i_3 | $I = (O_k \times K_s)$ *(marginal efficiency of investment schedule)*

$I = I_0 - ci$

i_2 $I' = (O'_k \times K'_s)$

i_1 $I'' = (O''_k \times K''_s)$

Disinvestment

I I' I'' I_0

NET INVESTMENT EXPENDITURE (*I*)

FIGURE 6–3.   The Investment Demand Schedule

again to Equations (6–1) and (6–2). They serve to underscore the two major sources of a shift in the investment demand schedule. When we speak of a shift in a demand curve it means that there will be more or less of the variable shown on the horizontal axis associated with any specific value for the variable shown on the vertical axis. In the case of investment demand, it means more investment spending for a given rate of interest if the demand schedule shifts upward, and less when it shifts downward.

The two major sources of a shift in the curve are a change in the expected yield of capital [the R series in Equations (6–1) and (6–2)] and a shift in the supply curve for capital goods. Suppose there is a sharp decrease in expected yields for new capital (the R series in the equations), resulting from a wave of pessimism sweeping over the business community. In terms of Equation (6–1) this would reduce the present value of any capital asset a firm contemplated acquiring, assuming no change in market rates of interest, and in terms of Equation (6–2) it would reduce the marginal efficiency for that type of capital. But since it assumed that interest rates are unchanged, this latter change would cause the marginal efficiency of investment schedule (the investment demand schedule (Figure 6–3) to shift to the left. Similar results would follow from a shift in the supply curve for newly produced capital goods. A shift in the supply curve means that the schedule of prices for all possible quantities of capital the capital goods industry can produce will change, either upward or downward. If the supply curve shifts upward, it means in terms of Equation (6–2) a rise in the value of K_s, the current supply price. But with no change in the expected income stream (the series of R's), the marginal efficiency of capital must decline. This is tantamount to a shift to the left of the investment demand schedule. At any given rate of interest, there will be less investment.

This, then, is the formal model of investment spending found as developed originally in Keynes's *The General Theory*. But the abstract, formal model doesn't capture the full spirit of how Keynes thought about investment spending. What really counts is the volatility of the investment demand schedule—it is a highly unstable function, depending on expectations of the yield to be derived from capital goods whose useful life may stretch far into an uncertain future. As was pointed out earlier, Keynes believed that the basis of the knowledge on which the businessmen form their expectations of prospective yields is extremely precarious, subject to sudden and unforeseen changes as the climate of business opinion fluctuates. The world is little different today in this respect than it was when Keynes wrote in the 1930s. In *The General Theory* Keynes devoted an entire chapter to this theme,[8] a chapter in which he reminds us that "human decisions affecting the future, whether personal or political or economic, cannot depend upon strict mathematical expectation, since the basis for making such calculations does not exist; and that it is our innate urge to activity which makes the wheels go round, our rational selves choosing between the alternatives as best we are able, calculating when we can, but often falling back for our motive on whim or sentiment or chance."[9] Developing a schedule in which we link investment spending to a single variable like the rate of interest is a highly useful analytical technique, but we must not allow our preoccupation with the technique itself to cause us to lose sight of the more fundamental economic forces at work in any economic situation. Often the latter are not readily reduced to a quantitative, functional relationship.

The Shape of the Investment Demand Schedule

Even though the Keynesian investment demand schedule may be subject to frequent and unpredictable shifts, economists are also interested in its shape. Technically, this is a matter of the *interest elasticity* of investment expenditure, by which we mean the responsiveness of aggregate investment expenditure to a change in the rate of interest. Specifically, the interest elasticity of the investment demand schedule, which we shall designate as e_i, is equal to the ratio of a percentage change in investment expenditure to a percentage change in the rate of interest. In algebraic terms the interest elasticity of the investment demand schedule is given by the following formula:

$$e_i = \frac{\Delta I / I}{\Delta i / i} = \frac{\Delta I}{I} \times \frac{i}{\Delta i} = \frac{\Delta I i}{I \Delta i} . \tag{6–4}$$

8. Ibid., Chap. 12, "The State of Long-Term Expectation," pp. 147–64.
9. Ibid., p. 162.

An investment demand schedule that is relatively *elastic* will have a coefficient of elasticity whose absolute value is greater than 1, whereas an investment demand schedule that is relatively *inelastic* will have a coefficient of elasticity whose absolute value is less than 1.

The question of how investment spending responds to a change in the rate of interest is an important one, especially for policy purposes. Monetary policy, for example, works through changes in the money supply which, in turn, may affect the rate of interest. Whether investment spending responds to such changes is, therefore, an important policy consideration. Basically, two sets of circumstances determine how responsive investment spending may be to changes in the rate of interest, one of which is external to the business firm and the other internal. Let us examine these, using Equations (6–1) and (6–2) as our frame of reference. We shall assume a decline in interest rates.

A decline in interest rates, *ceteris paribus*, should favor more investment spending because after the decline the marginal efficiency of capital momentarily becomes greater than the rate of interest. A decline in interest rates also increases the present value (V_p) of any capital asset which the firm contemplates purchasing (Equation 6–1). Thus, investment spending should increase, but how much investment spending actually increases depends in part upon a factor external to the business firm. This is the elasticity of the supply schedule for the production of new capital rises, the supply price (K_s) normally rises also. But as Equation (6–2) shows, a rise in the supply price (K_s) will, *ceteris paribus*, cause the marginal efficiency of capital *(r)* to fall. This is where the elasticity of the supply schedule for capital goods becomes crucial. The more *elastic* this schedule, the more the production of capital assets can be increased without a sharp rise in their price—therefore, the more investment spending can respond to any given decline in the rate of interest. On the other hand, if the supply schedule for capital goods is *inelastic*, then any increase in demand for such goods will cause their prices to move up sharply, thus limiting the effectiveness of a decline in interest rates on investment spending. In sum, elasticity in the supply schedule for capital assets makes for elasticity in the investment demand schedule, and inelasticity in the supply schedule for capital assets makes for inelasticity in the demand schedule for capital.

The other factor that governs the elasticity of the investment demand schedule is essentially internal in that it pertains to the physical life of the capital asset that the firm contemplates purchasing. The effect of physical life on investment spending can readily be seen by examining the variables in Equation (6–1). The longer the physical life of a unit of capital, the smaller will be the expected net return on the asset in any single year $(R_1$ in the equation, for example). But the smaller the net return in a single year, the more pronounced is the impact on present value (and hence the marginal efficiency of capital) of a given change in the rate of interest. It follows from this that the more durable the capital asset—that is, the longer its expected physical life—the more sensitive investment spending for that type of asset will be to changes in the rate of interest. The less durable the asset, the less will be the response of investment spending to any change in the rate of interest.

The practical import of the foregoing is that business structures and residential construction, since they are relatively long-lived, are most likely to be sensitive to changes in the rate of interest. Equipment is normally less long-lived than structures, and inventories are the least durable of all forms of business investment. Thus, logically, it follows that the demand schedules for structures—both business and residential—should be more elastic than the schedules representing demand for either equipment or inventories. Undoubtedly, the latter are the least sensitive to interest rate variations of any of the forms of investment spending.

Thus, we have the theory, but what of the reality? Does investment spending, in other words, actually respond significantly to changes in the rate of interest? Unlike statistical findings with respect to the income-consumption relationship, the results of empirical research in this area have not been either highly fruitful or conclusive. An early and classic British study which took the form of asking businessmen about the influence of the rate of interest on their investment decisions found that, in general, changes in short-term interest rates did not directly affect either inventory or other forms of investment. But there was some indication that, in the manufacturing industry in particular, investment in equipment and structures is influenced by changes in the long-term rate of interest.[10] The latter is usually measured by the rate on corporate bonds of high quality. An early American study, for example, found an interest elasticity coefficient for investments in plant and equipment equal to −0.65. This means that investment spending would change by 6.5 percent for every 10 percent change in the rate on long-term bonds. This does not show much sensitivity to the interest rate. A more recent study computed the interest elasticity of investment in equipment for the entire economy at −0.36, a figure representing an even lower elasticity of demand for investment.[11] Housing may be the most sensitive of all forms of investment spending to changes in the rate of interest. In the five years from 1978 to 1982, for example, housing starts dropped by 47 percent, whereas mortgage interest rates rose by 58 percent during the same interval.[12]

The foregoing studies are useful in that they point to the fact that the sensitivity (i.e., elasticity) of investment spending to changes in interest rates increases the more long-lived the type of investment—as with hous-

10. T. Wilson and P. W. S. Andrews, ed., *Oxford Studies in the Price Mechanism* (Oxford: The Clarendon Press, 1951) pp. 27 ff.

11. Edwin Kuh and John R. Meyer, "Investment, Liquidity, and Monetary Policy," in *Impacts of Monetary Policy*, Commission on Money and Credit (Englewood Cliffs, N.J.: Prentice Hall Inc., 1963), p. 381, and Charles W. Bischoff, "Business Investment in the 1970s: A Comparison of Models," *Brookings Papers on Economic Activity*, Vol. 1 (Washington, D.C.: Brookings Institution, 1971), p. 30.

12. *Economic Indicators*, March 1983, pp. 19, 30.

TABLE 6–1.   Interest Rates and Investment Activity: 1977–82

Year	Nominal Prime Rate	Real Prime Rate	Equipment Investment (in billions)	Nominal Mortgage Rate	Real Mortgage Rate	Housing Starts (in thousands)
1977	6.83%	0.03%	$140.8	9.02%	2.22%	1,987
1978	9.06	0.06	170.2	9.56	0.56	2,020
1979	12.76	−0.63	191.9	10.78	−2.52	1,745
1980	15.27	2.87	198.6	12.66	0.26	1,292
1981	18.87	8.90	216.4	14.70	5.80	1,084
1982	14.86	10.96	206.5	15.14	11.24	1,062

SOURCE: *Current Economic Indicators,* March 1983, pp. 19, 24, 30.

ing. But they are limited because they simply do not reflect the unprecedented rise in interest rates that has taken place since the mid-1960s. Between 1965 and 1982, for example, the rate of interest on long-term corporate bonds of the highest quality (AAA) rose by 240 percent, while the rate of interest on prime commercial paper—a good measure of the cost of short-term borrowing by business firms—rose by 171 percent. These sharp increases came following a period of relative stability in interest rates, both for the short and the long term. They are also limited because they do not reflect changes in the *real* rate of interest, the difference between nominal rates and the inflation rate. If we look at *real* interest rates in recent years and investment in equipment and housing, the results are mixed. Table 6–1 below shows nominal and *real* values for the prime rate and for mortgage rates as well as the dollar volume of investment spending for equipment and housing starts for the years 1977 through 1982.

No dramatic and wholly clear-cut conclusion follows from these data, but it does appear that housing is sensitive to nominal as well as *real* rates, at least more so than is investment spending for equipment. The latter continued to rise until 1982, when the sharp increase in *real* short-term rates began to be felt. It is possible, too, that businessmen are more sensitive than home buyers to *real* as compared to nominal changes. Perhaps the soundest conclusion is that rising interest rates, both nominal and real, will ultimately choke off investment spending, but the degree of sensitivity (i.e., elasticity) of investment spending to interest rate changes remains uncertain.

Current Income and Investment Expenditure

Although the central idea in the standard Keynesian theory of investment is the inverse relationship between investment expenditure and the rate of interest, many economists argue that *income* is a major determinant of investment expenditure. This approach involves the phenomenon of *induced* investment, which we shall designate as I_i. In the algebraic terms $I_i = f(Y)$. This equation should be interpreted to mean that investment outlays will increase as income increases. The income measure appropriate to this relationship is the net national product.[13]

In Equation (6–3), it was stated that $I = I_0 - ci$. Let us designate $I_0 - ci$ as I'_0 and define it as all investment expenditure that is autonomous with respect to the income level. We can then postulate the following identity:

$$I = I'_0 + I_i. \tag{6–5}$$

This equation simply states that total investment consists of the two major categories of autonomous and induced investment. Since the latter is a direct function of income, we can transform the Equation (6–5) into the following form:

$$I = I'_0 + bY_{np}. \tag{6–6}$$

In the above expression b is the *marginal propensity to invest*, which algebraically we may define as

$$b = \frac{\Delta I_i}{\Delta Y_{np}}. \tag{6–7}$$

The student will note that we defined the marginal propensity to invest in a fashion analogous to the marginal propensity to consume and the marginal propensity to save, namely, as the ratio of a change in investment to a change in income (net national product). The marginal propensity to invest concept implies that some portion of any increased income will be directed toward investment expenditure, a logical outcome of the assumption that current investment expenditure is linked functionally to the current income level. The marginal propensity to invest also measures the slope of the schedule that relates induced investment to income. A schedule of this type is displayed in Figure 6–4. Net national product is measured on the horizontal axis and investment on the vertical axis. Because investment is an increasing function of income the schedule slopes upward to the right. The level at which the schedule intersects the vertical axis equals I'_0, investment which is independent of the income level.

The assumptions embodied in this relationship are, first, that investment depends upon profitability and, second, that profitability is directly linked to the current income level. There is a sound empirical basis for the second assumption, as is demonstrated in Figure 6–5. The figure contains a scatter diagram showing a close correlation between the level of the nation's gross national product and corporate profits for the period 1946–82. As the level of the GNP rose, there were parallel increases in the level of corporate profits. The latter are a good proxy for all profits in the economy. In *The General Theory* Keynes explained that, in general, there is a strong tendency within the business community to assume that

---

13. Net national product Y_{np} and disposable income Y_d remain equal because we are still assuming that neither taxes nor transfer payments are present in the system.

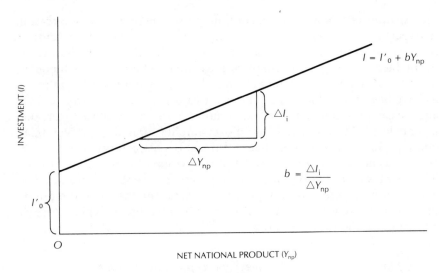

FIGURE 6–4.   Investment and the Income Level

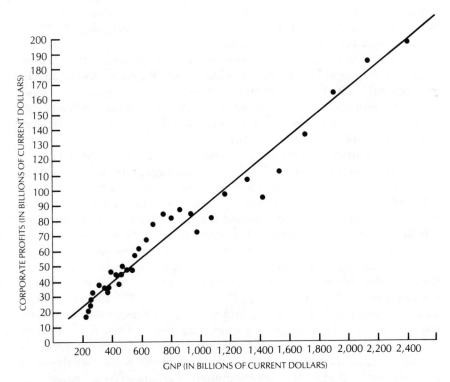

FIGURE 6–5.   Corporate Profits and Gross National Product 1946–82

SOURCE: *Economic Report of the President, 1981*

the existing state of affairs will continue, *unless* there is a specific reason to expect a change. This, Keynes said, constitutes a kind of convention that enables businessmen to cope with the reality that their knowledge of the factors that govern the prospective yield on a new investment "is usually very slight and often negligible."[14] Consequently, if current profits have been favorable, expectations for future profits will be favorable, and we can expect investment expenditure to rise in response to a rising income level. This, of course, is an oversimplification of a complex relationship. But the proposition that investment is a direct function of income enables us not only to deal with the phenomenon of induced investment in a direct way, but also to incorporate investment expenditure into the equilibrium income determination process and the theory of the multiplier far more readily than when we consider investment expenditure as a function of the rate of interest.

The Marginal Propensity to Invest and Equilibrium Income

Let us examine how the concept of the marginal propensity to invest may be incorporated into our formal equilibrium diagram. In Figure 6–6 the 45° line OZ again represents the aggregate supply function; the schedule labeled C is the consumption function. The basic difference between this figure and Figure 5–4 (p. 131) is that the aggregate demand schedule does not lie parallel to the consumption function; investment expenditure is not autonomous with respect to the income level, but increases as the income level increases. We construct the aggregate demand schedule by adding an investment schedule of the kind shown in Figure 6–4 to the consumption function. Equilibrium is attained at the point of intersection of the schedules of aggregate demand and aggregate supply. However, because we have included induced investment, the equilibrium level is higher than otherwise would be the case.

This can be seen clearly by contrasting an aggregate demand schedule, constructed with an autonomous investment function, with the aggregate demand schedule constructed with a function involving induced investment. In Figure 6–6 the dashed line $C+I'_0$ is an aggregate demand schedule of the former type whereas schedule $C+I'_0+I_i$, on the other hand incorporates the phenomenon of induced investment. $C+I'_0+I_i$ intersects the aggregate supply schedule at a higher income level than $C+I'_0$, and it should be noted that the slope of $C+I'_0+I_i$ is greater than the slope of $C+I'_0$. The slope of $C+I'_0+I_i$ is equal to the sum of the marginal propensity to consume and the marginal propensity to invest; the sum of these two marginal propensities can be defined as the *marginal propensity to spend,* a concept particularly relevant to multiplier analysis because, as was shown earlier, the value of the multiplier depends upon the amount of additional spending that is *induced* by an exogenous change in spending.

14. Keynes, *The General Theory,* p. 149.

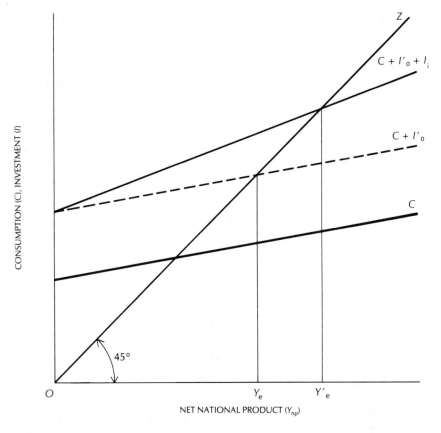

FIGURE 6–6. Induced Investment and Aggregate Demand

Induced Investment Expenditure and the Multiplier

Let us explore how induced investment expenditure may be incorporated into multiplier theory. To facilitate the exposition, we shall break the investment component of the aggregate demand schedule into two subcategories: autonomous investment, which we have already designated as I'_0 in Figure 6–6, and induced investment, represented symbolically by I_i. We assume that investment and consumption are the only expenditure categories and that changes in the income level are initiated as the result of shifts in the autonomous investment function. Given these basic assumptions, we can postulate the following two definitional equations:

$$Y_{np} = I'_0 + I_i + C, \qquad (6-8)$$

$$k' = \frac{\Delta Y_{np}}{\Delta I'_0}. \qquad (6-9)$$

Equation (6–8) is the basic identity equation, which states that income (net national product) is equal to the sum of consumption and investment, except that investment is broken down into its two subcategories. Equation (6–9) is the basic definition of the multiplier, k, except that in this instance we are using the symbol k' to indicate the multiplier because we incorporate into it the phenomenon of induced investment.

From Equation (6–8) we get the following identity pertaining to a change in the income level:

$$\Delta Y_{np} = \Delta I'_0 + \Delta I_i + \Delta C. \tag{6–10}$$

Since the change in induced investment expenditure, ΔI_i, depends upon the value of the marginal propensity to invest, b, and since the change in consumption expenditure depends upon the value of the marginal propensity to consume, a, we have

$$\Delta I_i = b \times \Delta Y_{np} \tag{6–11}$$

and

$$\Delta C = a \times \Delta Y_{np}.^{15} \tag{6–12}$$

If we substitute the above values for ΔI_i and ΔC in Equation 6–10 we have

$$\Delta Y_{np} = \Delta I'_0 + b\Delta Y_{np} + a\Delta Y_{np}. \tag{6–13}$$

This equation can be manipulated algebraically as follows:

$$\Delta Y_{np} = -a\Delta Y_{np} - b\Delta Y_{np} = \Delta I'_0, \tag{6–14}$$

$$\Delta Y_{np}(1 - a - b) = \Delta I'_0, \tag{6–15}$$

$$\Delta Y_{np} = \Delta I'_0 \times \frac{1}{1-a-b}, \tag{6–16}$$

$$\frac{\Delta_{np}}{\Delta I'_0} = \frac{1}{1-a-b}. \tag{6–17}$$

Thus, we can define k', the effective multiplier, as the reciprocal of 1 minus the marginal propensity to consume and the marginal propensity to invest. A quick examination of the algebra shows that by introducing an additional kind of induced spending into our analysis—induced investment spending—we will get a larger ultimate increase in spending for any initial exogenous increase in spending. As a parenthetical note, k' is sometimes called the supermultiplier.

In the foregoing discussion we assumed a constant value for the marginal propensity to invest, b, which in turn enables us to compute an exact value for the multiplier k'. Reality is not so accommodating, and it is most unlikely that the marginal propensity to invest will have a constant value for any significant length of time. This particular approach to induced investment rests on the assumption that current profits are sufficient to engender favorable expectations with respect to the profit-

15. $\Delta Y_{np} = \Delta Y_d$ when taxes and transfers are zero.

ability of additional capital equipment. If the current profit picture is not satisfactory, however, there is no reason to believe that any amount of investment expenditure will be induced by the current income level. Thus, there is no real assurance that the value of the marginal propensity to invest will remain stable, and, for that matter, there is no positive assurance that it will remain above zero.

The Acceleration Principle

A much more complex and dynamic analysis of the phenomenon of induced investment is based on the *acceleration principle*. In its original and earliest formulation, the principle asserted that net investment is a function of the *rate of change* in final output rather than of the absolute level of output. This is an important distinction. This concept of the acceleration principle was developed in 1917 by Professor John Maurice Clark in a renowned article, "Business Acceleration and the Law of Demand: A Technical Factor in Economic Cycles."[16] Clark set out to show, first, that a special and technical relationship exists between the demand for a final product and the demand for the capital equipment necessary to produce the final product and, second, that this technical relationship is of such a character that it can be employed to explain not only the nature of the demand for new capital instruments, but also why the demand for capital fluctuates much more violently than the demand for final goods. Since the publication of Clark's historic article, many economists have analyzed and refined this principle, using it to explain the apparent cyclical nature of much economic activity.

In our discussion of the acceleration principle we shall use the income symbol Y to designate *output of final goods and services*, and the symbol K to designate the capital stock. The technical relationship existing between a given level of output and the quantity of capital necessary to produce that output is defined as the *capital-output ratio*. We shall designate this ratio by the capital letter A. Thus, we have

$$A = \frac{K}{Y}. \tag{6-18}$$

If we assume no change in the technical condition under which resources are combined in order to obtain a given output, it is reasonable to assume that an increase in output once full capacity has been achieved will require additional capital equipment in the proportion indicated by the capital-output ratio. For example, if we find that, on the average, it requires capital equipment in the amount of $3.00 for each $1.00 of output, then, as long as there is no change in the technical conditions under which capital is combined with other resources in the productive process, every $1.00 increase in output above the level of existing capacity will require

16. Reprinted in *Readings in Business Cycle Theory* (Philadelphia: Blakiston, 1944).

$3.00 worth of additional capital equipment. Formally, we may say that, given constant technical conditions of production, the marginal capital-output ratio will equal the average capital-output ratio. When the average and the marginal capital-output ratios are equal,

$$A = \frac{K}{Y} = \frac{\Delta K}{\Delta Y}. \tag{6-19}$$

By definition, though, the change in the capital stock, ΔK, is the same thing as net investment in the economy, I_n. Substituting I_n for ΔK in the algebraic formula and transposing ΔY to the left-hand side of the expression, we have the following:

$$A = \frac{I_n}{\Delta Y}, \tag{6-20}$$

$$I_n = A \times \Delta Y. \tag{6-21}$$

Equation (6–21) is the formal algebraic expression of the acceleration principle. It tells us that there exists some coefficient A which, when multiplied by the change in output, will yield the required net investment expenditure. To put the matter the other way around, we can say that, if output is to increase by an amount equal to ΔY, then additional capital equipment in the amount I_n is required. This is necessary because, as can readily be seen from the formula, the larger the absolute change in output, the larger the amount of induced investment, assuming that initially capacity was fully utilized.

If we set this analysis within a time sequence, it is relatively easy to see why the acceleration principle makes induced investment expenditure a function of the *rate* at which output is increasing (or decreasing). Net investment in the current income period (designated by the symbol t) is equal to the different between the capital stock of the current period, K_t, and the capital stock of the previous period, K_{t-1}. Thus,

$$I_t = K_t - K_{t-1}. \tag{6-22}$$

The change in income in the current period, ΔY_t, is equal to the difference between current income, Y_t, and the income of the previous period, Y_{t-1}. Therefore, we have

$$\Delta Y_t = Y_t - Y_{t-1}. \tag{6-23}$$

The rate at which income (or output) changes between one period and the next is measured by the ratio of ΔY_t to Y_{t-1}. For example, if income in constant dollars rose by $45 billion between the present and the past income periods, and if Y_{t-1} was $900 billion, then the rate of income increase, $\Delta Y_t/Y_{t-1}$, will be 5 percent. The importance of this is that the rate of change in income depends upon the absolute change in income in a period relative to the income level of the previous period. The larger the absolute change relative to income of the previous period, the larger will be the rate of change. But the acceleration formula, Equation (6–21), shows that, given a fixed technical relationship between capital and output, the amount of induced investment will vary directly with the size of the absolute change in output. Consequently, the acceleration principle means that *induced net investment is a function of the rate of change of final output.*

A Practical Use for the Acceleration Principle   There is one highly important practical implication flowing from the acceleration principle. The principle helps to explain a phenomenon long observed by economists, namely, that the output of capital instruments fluctuates much more violently than the output of goods in general. The exaggerated impact of an increase (or decrease) in demand for final output on the demand for capital goods can be illustrated by means of a simple arithmetical example. Let us imagine a hypothetical industry whose output of final goods is 100 units per income period (see Table 6–2). The capital-output ratio for this industry is assumed to be 3, which means 300 units of capital are required to produce this output. These units of capital have an average economic life of 10 income periods, so the normal replacement demand for capital equipment is 30 units per income period. Let us now see what will happen if, first, there is a 10 percent increase in demand for the final product. A 10 percent increase in demand will mean the production of 10 additional units of final product per income period. But if the industry is operating at its capacity level prior to this increase in demand, then the production of 10 additional units of final product per income period will require 30 additional units of capital. Now if this increase in demand of 10 percent for the final product is presumed to take place within the confines of a single income period, the demand for capital goods will increase by 100 percent in this same income period. The reason for this is that the 30 units of capital needed to provide an additional 10 units of output are added to the normal replacement demand of 30 units, thus making a 100 percent increase in demand for capital goods in Period 2.

Let us go on to Period 3, in which the demand for final output is still

TABLE 6–2.   The Acceleration Effect and the Demand for Capital

Income Period	Capital Stock	Output	Replacement Demand	Demand for New Capital	Total Demand for Capital
1	300.0	100.0	30.0	0.0	30.0
2	330.0	110.0*	30.0	30.0	60.0
3	346.5	115.5†	30.0	16.5	46.5
n‡	346.5	115.5	34.6	0.0	34.6

*A 10% increase in final demand.
†A 5% increase in final demand.
‡When capital added in Periods 2 and 3 begins to be replaced.

rising, but at a slower pace than earlier. In this period the increase in final demand is 5 percent. Assuming that the capital stock was adjusted upward in the prior period to reflect the change in final demand, what happens now? Since demand has increased once again, more capital is needed, but not so much as in the previous period. Net investment will again increase, but the absolute amount will be less than in Period 2. Thus, we find that the *total* demand for capital will be smaller than previously. This is because the *rate* of increase in final demand between Periods 2 and 3 has slowed down. Total investment will rise to a peak and then fall back to a level determined wholly by replacement needs. Net investment will rise from zero to a peak and then fall back eventually to zero.

Our hypothetical example demonstrates the most important single fact about the acceleration principle: There will be induced investment expenditure only so long as final demand is increasing. Once the latter stabilizes at a new and higher level, induced investment expenditure will cease. Expressed in formal terms, the absolute level of induced net investment will enlarge as long as final demand is increasing at an increasing rate; once the rate of increase of final demand begins to slow down, the absolute level of induced net investment will decline. The reader should also note that the more durable the capital instrument, the greater will be the fluctuation in the demand for capital instruments relative to the demand for final output. If, in our hypothetical example, the capital units had an average economic life of 20 rather than 10 income periods, a 10 percent increase in demand for final output would have brought about a 200 percent increase in demand for capital instruments (15 replacement units plus 30 additional units of capital). This would be true as long as the capital-output ratio remained equal to 3.

Limitations of the Acceleration Principle   The foregoing analysis of the acceleration principle is sometimes described as the "simple" accelerator. Although it is useful in explaining the cyclical and sharp fluctuations in capital goods spending, the accelerator model that relates net investment spending to changes in the rate of output is subject to several important limitations. For one thing, most economists recognize that the acceleration principle is too mechanical to serve as an explanation of such a complex phenomenon as the investment process in a modern economy. One criticism is that the acceleration principle has little or no motivational content. The entrepreneur is presumed to act like a thermostat, noting when capacity is overtaxed and then taking the necessary steps to overcome this deficiency. A more serious criticism concerns the matter of productive capacity. In a strict sense, the acceleration principle is effective only when an industry or the economy as a whole is operating at a level of full utilization of existing capacity. Since the principle is based upon a technical relationship between capital and output, it logically follows that additional capital will not be required to make possible additional output unless existing productive capacity is being fully utilized. If surplus capacity exists in the economy, the principle breaks down because added output can be supplied from the untapped capacity. This has led some economists to conclude that, insofar as business-cycle analysis is concerned, the principle may have validity during the upswing (when rising demand eventually presses hard against existing capacity), but not in the downswing or depression phase of the cycle (when excess and idle capacity is one of the most common features of the economy).

A related objection concerns the sticky matter of the definition of capacity. There is little, if anything, in the voluminous literature that has grown up around the acceleration principle that attempts to define precisely the meaning of such terms as *capacity* and *surplus capacity*. In a literal sense, the acceleration principle asserts that net investment is induced, or more capital is created, because output has risen. Because of the technical relationship between capital and output fundamental to the acceleration principle, additional output can be forthcoming only if the stock of capital has already been increased. This is the dilemma that faces us if we interpret both the acceleration principle and its underlying assumption of full-capacity production quite literally. The only way out of this dilemma is to interpret the notion of capacity somewhat freely and suggest that at some point the entrepreneur will reach the conclusion that his existing facilities will be overtaxed if he attempts to provide for an expected demand without expansion.

The Flexible Accelerator Hypothesis   In terms of formal theory, the foregoing problem has led to the development of a less restrictive, a more relaxed, version of the accelerator. This is called the *flexible accelerator hypothesis*. Simply put, this version of the accelerator links investment spending to a gap between the desired capital stock and the actual capital stock, but recognizes that it is unlikely that this gap will be wholly closed in a single income period. As one analyst phrased it:

> In a situation of short capacity a tendency of plant expansion may be expected. But an immediate full adjustment is neither technically necessary nor considered possible or advisable from an economic point of view. There may be checks from the side of finance or the lumpiness of capital goods. Moreover, the high level of output may be expected to be temporary, in which case a "wait and see" policy will be followed.[17]

In equation form, the flexible accelerator hypothesis is expressed as follows:

$$I_n = \alpha(K^* - K_{t-1}), \qquad (6-24)$$

where the coefficient α represents the proportion of the gap between the desired capital stock (K^*) and the capital stock of the past income

17. L. M. Koyck, *Distributed Lags and Investment Analysis* (Amsterdam: North Holland, 1954), p. 63.

period (K_{t-1}) that can be closed in the current income period. Thus, it reflects the point stressed above, namely, that it is neither likely nor particularly desirable that net investment in a single income period increase by the full amount of the shortfall in the desired stock of capital. What the flexible accelerator hypothesis suggests is that the adjustment process involved when there is a change in demand that requires more capital goods will be spread over a number of income periods. There is still an accelerator effect, but there is also a lagged response of investment to the change in output.

Theory and Reality

From the foregoing discussion of investment theory three variables emerge as prime determinants of investment spending in the economy. They are, first, the rate of interest; second, the level of income; and third, the quantity of capital required to produce a particular level of output. The most basic idea, of course, is that investment spending is undertaken in the expectation of profit, and that such expectations are always tied to an elusive and unknown future. Formal investment theory attempts to cut through the difficulties involved in dealing with the uncertainties that surround expectations and tie investment spending to variables which are observable and measurable. The basic question, then, is which theoretical approach has the greatest validity?

In spite of the enormous—and growing—volume of economic literature that embodies empirical investigations into the determinants of investment spending,[18] no definitive answer to this question has emerged. As we found true in the case of different theories of consumption spending, there are elements of value in each of the foregoing approaches to the complex problem of investment behavior. Nevertheless, the empirical evidence now available offers support for the theoretical ideas discussed in this chapter. In these studies real output emerges as the most important single determinant of investment expenditure. This ties in with the theoretical analysis of induced investment spending. In manufacturing industries, for example, it was found that a 1 percent change in output led to a 1.5 to 2 percent change in investment spending within a two-year period.[19] Further, in practically every empirical study in which the interest rate was included as a variable, interest was found to be of some significance.

As we saw earlier in this chapter, although there is no agreement on

18. For a recent survey of this literature, see Dale W. Jorgenson, "Econometric Studies of Investment Behavior: A Survey," *Journal of Economic Literature*, December 1971, pp. 1111–47. In the bibliography which is a part of this survey, 109 articles and books dealing with the investment question are listed.
19. Michael K. Evans, *Macroeconomic Activity: Theory, Forecasting, and Control* (New York: Harper & Row, 1969), p. 138. See also Peter K. Clark, "Investment in the 1970s: Theory, Performance, and Prediction," *Brookings Papers on Economic Activity*, Vol. 1 (Washington, D.C.: The Brookings Institution, 1979), p. 103.

the value of the coefficient of elasticity of investment spending in relation to the interest rate, there is agreement that interest rates are a factor in determining the level of investment, especially in capital which is long-lived. Evidence on the validity of the accelerator is at best mixed, some studies finding support for such a relationship and others rejecting it. In general, however, empirical studies support the flexible rather than the simple version of the accelerator principle. Although it is encouraging that empirical research (to date) tends to support the basic ideas about the determinants of investment spending that emerged from *The General Theory*, it is unlikely that even the most painstaking econometric research will uncover the definitive investment function. The reason is rooted in the uncertainty and precariousness that surround *all* efforts to gauge the income stream that a new item of capital will yield. This is unlikely to change, no matter how sophisticated our econometric techniques.

The Financing of Investment

Investment spending, as we have seen, is an unstable component in the structure of aggregate demand in a market economy, the basic reason being the uncertainty that surrounds estimating the present value of an expected income stream. This is the essence of the contemporary view of investment. The instability may be exaggerated by how a business firm finances its acquisition of new capital assets, making it important to pay careful attention to the financing side of the investment decision, a topic to which we now turn.

Earlier it was pointed out that there are basically three sources from which firms can get the money needed to purchase new capital assets. These are (1) retained earnings (the internal cash flow of the firm); (2) selling of shares in the firm (equity financing); and (3) borrowing (issuing of bonds or other forms of debt). Although the first two sources of investment finance are not in any sense "problem-free," the funds obtained through borrowing are of major significance in linking finance to the volatility of investment spending. Thus, we shall concentrate most of our analysis upon this type of finance. Some idea of the magnitude of debt financing is found in the fact that in 1980 net new security issues of all types of American corporations totaled $83.8 billion, of which $53.2 billion (or 63 percent) were either bonds or short-term notes (promises to pay).[20]

Financial Instruments and Real Capital Assets

Professor Hyman Minsky suggests that it is necessary to adopt a Wall Street perspective if we are to understand fully the crucial role that finance

20. *Federal Reserve Bulletin*, May 1983, p. A-36. This does not measure the amount of debt financing for new capital assets, as it includes borrowings for all purposes by corporations, not just the acquisition of new physical capital.

plays in investment behavior.[21] By such a perspective he means that we are dealing not only with a monetary economy with highly sophisticated financial institutions, but one in which money and debts are the key instruments through which ownership or control of *real* capital assets is acquired. Thus, the instruments of finance (including money) become in their own right a powerful factor in the investment equation, especially because a market system attaches values—that is, prices—to such instruments just as it does to real capital assets as well as goods and services in general. Keynes described this intermingling of money, the instruments of finance, and real capital as follows:

> There is a multitude of real assets in the world which constitute our capital wealth—buildings, stocks of commodities, goods in the course of manufacture and of transport, and so forth. The nominal owners of these assets, however, have not infrequently borrowed *money* in order to become possessed of them. To a corresponding extent the actual owners of wealth have claims, not on real assets, but on money. A considerable part of the "financing" takes place through the banking system, which interposes its guarantee between its depositors who lend it money, and its borrowing customers to whom it loans money wherewith to finance the purchase of real assets. The interposition of this *veil of money* [italics added] between the real asset and the wealth owner is a specially marked characteristic of the modern world.[22]

Keynes wrote that in 1931. If anything, it describes more accurately the contemporary paper world of money and finance than it did the conditions when first set into print.

What happens when a firm borrows to finance purchase of real capital?[23] Basically by issuing debts (bonds) the firm gets the cash necessary to buy the desired capital asset. By issuing bonds the firm creates for itself a contractual obligation not only to repay the sum borrowed at some future date, but to meet periodically the interest payments on the debt. The firm, in other words, obliges itself to a flow of cash payments which stretch into the future, such payments lasting for the lifetime of the debt. Over and against this cash-flow commitment the firm must balance the expected cash inflow which stems from the assets purchased with the proceeds of the loan. Professor Minsky says that the fundamental speculative decision of a business firm centers on how much of the firm's income from normal operations can be pledged to pay the interest and principal on the liabilities incurred in order to acquire income-producing (capital) assets.[24] The firm, in adding to its liability structure, is

21. Hyman P. Minsky, *John Maynard Keynes* (New York: Columbia University Press, 1975), p. 73. This section draws heavily upon Professor Minsky's analysis of the role of debt finance in the investment decision.

22. John Maynard Keynes, "The Consequence to the Banks of the Collapse of Money Values," in *Essays in Persuasion* (New York: Norton, 1963), p. 169.

23. The analysis to follow applies primarily to investment in long-term capital—plant and equipment. Inventories are normally turned over in a very short time; hence, immediate sales prospects are the key factor in the investment in inventories decisions.

24. Minsky, p. 86.

"betting that the ruling situation at the future dates (when payments come due) will be such that the cash commitments can be met; it is estimating that the odds in an uncertain future are favorable."[25]

Pricing Financial Assets

To understand how the firm makes this fundamental speculative decision we must look again at the discount (capitalization) process. As we saw earlier, the investment decision in its most basic sense involves comparing the present value of the expected income stream produced by a capital asset with its supply price. When we introduce a contractual cash flow commitment into the picture, the comparison has to be between the present value of the expected income stream and the present value of the contractual cash flow. The latter covers both the supply price of the capital—what the firm has to pay for a newly produced unit—and the interest charges on the borrowed money.

Present value, let us recall, is determined by capitalizing a payments flow at *some* rate of interest. Unless a firm experiences a complete financial collapse, its long-term obligations (bonds) are secure because they are contractual. Thus, the present value for the debts issued by a firm normally would be found by discounting their contractual cash flows at the prevailing market rate of interest.[26] If the world were free of risk and the future not characterized by uncertainty, the same capitalization (or discount) rate could be applied to the stream of income expected from the capital assets whose purchase is being contemplated. Then it would be necessary only to compare two present values: if present value for the expected income stream were greater than present value for the cash-flow commitment from a newly issued debt, then the investment decision could be positive.

But the world is not like this. Risk is present and the future is uncertain. This means that much greater certainty attaches to income derived from a contractual cash commitment such as a bond provides than to income derived from a newly produced item of capital. But the less certain the future income stream, the less its present value. Since greater uncertainty (and risk) attaches to the prospective yield on capital, a higher rate of discount must be used to determine its present value as compared to the going rate for money loans. The difference between these two rates must in logic reflect the state of uncertainty existing at any particular time. The key question thus becomes: what determines this uncertainty?

In *The General Theory* Keynes dealt with this question by distinguishing between two types of risk: borrower's risk and lender's risk. As Keynes phrased it:

25. Ibid., p. 87.
26. This would also be the rate of interest that the bond pays, since the decision or comparison being discussed is made when new debt is being issued.

Two types of risk affect the volume of investment which have not commonly been distinguished, but which it is important to distinguish. The first is entrepreneur's or borrower's risk and arises out of doubts in his own mind as to the probability of his actually earning the prospective yield for which he hopes. If a man is venturing his own money, this is the only risk which is relevant.

But where a system of borrowing and lending exists, by which I mean the granting of loans with a margin of real or personal security, a second type of risk is relevant which we may call the lender's risk. This may be due to either a moral hazard, i.e., voluntary default or other means of escape, possibly lawful, from the fulfillment of the obligation; or the possible insufficiency of the margin of security, i.e., involuntary default due to the disappointment of expectation.[27]

Borrower's risk is essentially subjective, existing primarily in the mind of the borrower, never appearing explicitly in a contract. Lender's risk, on the other hand, is objective and shows up in various ways in financial contracts—higher interest rate, shorter terms to maturity, or the pledge of specific assets as collateral for a loan.[28] Borrower's risk is the key to the difference between the discount rate appropriate to a firm's debt structure and the rate used to determine present value for uncertain yields from new capital assets. Borrower's risk, in other words, is the focal point through which uncertainty makes itself felt.

Basically, the process works as follows. As a firm increases the proportion of new capital assets financed by debt relative to either internal funds or equities, the firm's basic financial position becomes increasingly risky. The reason is simply that it finds itself in a situation in which the cash-flow obligations it must meet because of its debt structure grow while the prospective yields become less and less certain as the firm continues to acquire new capital assets. Thus, the discount rate used to determine the present value of expected yields must rise to reflect the increasing uncertainty that follows from a rise in the ratio of debt to other forms of financing. But this means, of course, that the demand price for new capital will decline as uncertainty increases.[29] But as the demand price for capital (the present value of the expected yield) falls, the less favorable are the prospects for continued investment spending, particularly since normally the supply price for new capital assets is positive. Since borrower's risk is highly subjective, it may increase quite suddenly, thus causing a collapse in the demand price for capital, followed by a sharp drop in investment spending.

Boom Conditions, Asset Values, and Investment Spending

Boom conditions may provide a setting for this sequence of events. A factor that strongly influences borrower's risk is the past performance of the economy. Thus, in the early stages of a boom, when the economy is picking up steam, borrower's risk is likely to be low; furthermore, the

27. Keynes, *The General Theory*, p. 144.
28. Minsky, p. 110.
29. Ibid., p. 109.

debt-financing ratio may be low. In a boom period past estimates of the prospective yield for capital assets may turn out to have been too low—actual yields are higher than anticipated. This leads to capital gains—increases in the value of the firm and the firm's assets because of the higher than anticipated earnings on newly acquired assets. As a consequence both borrower's and lender's risks are reduced, a development which pushes the firm further into debt financing. As the boom proceeds, firms become more and more willing to resort to debt financing. Boom conditions lead to a "layering" of debt, which means using actual or anticipated capital gains as a source of more borrowing power. But as this process continues the firm's cash commitments due to its liabilities (debts) may begin to mount faster than the income the firm gets from its operations and assets it may own. In terms of the factors that enter into the investment decision, the cash-flow commitments from newly issued debt begin to outpace the proceeds expected from the capital assets financed by the debt. The optimism of the boom often leads a firm to overcommit itself to debt financing, the result being a situation in which its cash-payment obligations exceed the cash receipts flowing in from current operations. If the firm gets itself into this situation, both borrower's risk and lender's risk will rise sharply—especially borrower's risk. The consequence is a drastic fall in the demand price for new capital relative to its supply price, followed by a collapse in investment spending. With the latter, the boom will also collapse. A process of debt deflation may follow, a period in which firms attempt to scale down their debt structure, using whatever internal funds they can muster to service existing debts. They will try and reduce their cash-flow commitments by replacing short-term debt with long-term debt as the former matures, a process called refunding. It doesn't reduce the total debt-based cash commitments of the firm, but it can reduce the size of the more immediate, short-term cash obligations confronting the firm. During the debt deflation process borrower's risk remains high, a development which keeps investment spending for new capital low and the economy in a depressed condition.[30]

30. The American economy has not experienced a serious debt-deflation-induced depression since the 1930s, but Professor Minsky believes that the economy has come close on at least four occasions in recent years—in 1966, in 1970–71, in 1974–75, and in 1980. In each of these periods trouble developed in the financial sector of the economy because too many leading financial institutions had used short-term debt to finance their holdings of longer-term assets which could not be readily sold to meet short-term cash commitments. They engaged, in other words, in speculative finance, expecting to be able continuously to renew ("roll over" is the term the financial community uses) short-term debt as it came due. When this proved difficult, they found themselves in deep trouble. What saved the economy from going through the wringer of a full-blown debt deflation and the ensuing depression was the high level of government spending which sustained incomes and the willingness of the Federal Reserve System to provide the funds necessary to prevent collapse in the financial system. The efforts now under way by the Reagan administration to shrink significantly the size of the federal government relative to the GNP may increase the susceptibility of the economy in the future to an old-style debt-deflation type of depression. See Hyman P. Minsky, "Financial Markets and Instability, 1965–1980," *Nebraska Journal of Economics and Business,* Autumn 1981, pp. 5–16, and "How 'Standard' Is Standard Economics?" *Society,* March/April 1977, pp. 24–29.

The Supply Curve for Finance

Before we look briefly at some other factors that may influence the business firm's investment decision, some comments are in order on how firms typically view the costs of alternative forms of finance. The prior discussion centered around debt finance, primarily because this particular type of financing plays a crucial role in the volatility of investment spending. But firms also finance new capital assets from retained earnings and from issuing additional shares of the stock of the firm. The explicit or implicit cost of funds obtained from the three possible sources of finance is an important factor in the investment decision. For the typical firm contemplating the purchase of real capital assets, the supply curve for finance appears as shown in Figure 6–7.

Essentially, the supply schedule for finance has three segments, each one of which relates to the different source of finance. In the figure the first segment (designated A) is retained earnings. There is no lender's risk involved in getting funds from this source, and if we assume that borrower's risk is a constant, then the rate appropriate for funds from this source is the interest rate foregone by not lending (i.e., purchasing securities) the retained earnings. Thus, this segment of the curve is perfectly elastic (horizontal) at the current rate for outstanding long-term debts (i.e., bonds). The next segment (designated B) represents funds obtained by borrowing. This portion of the curve slopes upward to the right, reflecting the fact that, as the firm borrows more, the cost of borrowing will rise. This is primarily due to lender's risk, since this will get larger the more heavily indebted the firm becomes. Finally, there is a

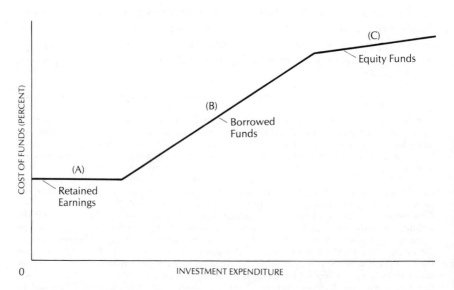

FIGURE 6–7.   The Supply Curve for Finance

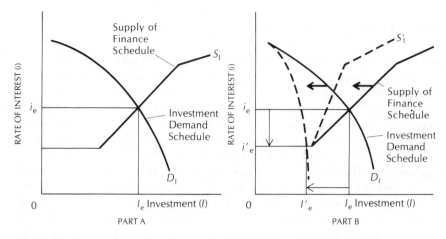

FIGURE 6–8. Investment Demand and the Supply of Finance Schedule

range in which the firm will resort to equity financing, which is to say it will issue new ownership shares to obtain the money needed to finance investment outlays (Segment C in Figure 6–7). This type of financing is generally regarded as more costly than borrowing, even though there is no obligation to pay out dividends to the shareholders. The reason for this is the differential treatment under the income tax laws for interest and dividend payments. Interest is a deductible expense in computing the tax liability of a business corporation, whereas dividends are not. The equity portion of the finance curve also slopes upward. This is because if a firm issues new shares, the increased supply of its stock will depress the market price of shares outstanding, thus causing their yields to rise.[31]

If we bring together the supply curve for finance shown in Figure 6–7 and the investment demand curve developed earlier (Figure 6–3), we can show how the interaction between the marginal efficiency of capital and the cost of finance determines the rate of investment. This is done in Figure 6–8, Part A. We can also use this diagram to show the impact of a change in both borrower's and lender's risks on the rate of investment. This we find in Part B of Figure 6–8. In this part of the figure the original demand and supply curves shift to the positions indicated by the dashed curves in the diagram. The investment demand schedule collapses because of a rise in borrower's risk. The impact of increased lender's risk is shown by an upward shift in the supply of funds curve. The resulting outcome—investment outlays decline to I'_e—is one in which investment spending is limited by the amount of internal finance available, the reason being firms hesitate to resort to debt financing of capital outlays until they have reorganized and scaled down their debt structure.

31. The foregoing analysis of the supply schedule for finance is drawn primarily from the approach found in Michael K. Evans, *Macroeconomic Activity*, pp. 86 ff.

Other Influences on the Investment Decision

Within the basic analytical framework of the capital and investment demand schedules, other determinants of investment are treated as parametric factors whose basic role is to determine the position of these schedules. Changes in the value of any of these factors cause a shift in their position or slope. As was true with the consumption function, many of these factors are subjective and hence not capable of exact quantitative measurement. But there is a growing amount of empirical investigation into the investment decision, and many of the conclusions economists have reached concerning determinants of investment expenditure have a sound basis in fact, even though the way in which such determinants are linked to investment expenditure cannot be reduced to a precise mathematical formula. The investment determinants discussed at this point in no sense represent all the factors other than interest and income that bear on the level of investment, but rather those that are believed to have the most telling effects.

The Role of Government

There has been an enormous expansion in the role and influence of the public sector in this century, a development that could not help but have far-reaching repercussions on the investment decision and the level of investment expenditure. Government units purchase an important part of the final output of goods and services in the economy and, as we have seen, demand for final output has a direct effect on investment outlays.

The public sector may exert a less obvious influence on investment activity through transfer payments. Transfer expenditures and the taxes that finance such expenditures affect both the distribution of personal income in the economy and the pattern of consumption expenditures. Changes in the latter will affect the demand for final goods and services and thus, indirectly, the demand for investment goods.

Probably the most important influence that public activity has on investment expenditure operates through taxes and the tax laws. The marginal efficiency of capital is concerned with the profitability of additional amounts of capital to the business enterprise, so it is to be expected that the businessman or entrepreneur would be acutely aware of the influence of anything as direct as taxation on the expected rate of return on capital assets. Investment expenditure depends upon the expected rate of return over cost, and it can thus be presumed that taxes, because they lower the expected returns, will lower investment expenditures. High taxes, to put it differently, impinge on incentives, and therefore adversely affect the investment decision.

Specifically, two techniques have been used by the federal government in recent years to influence investment spending in the economy. These are accelerated depreciation accounting, and the investment tax credit. We shall examine each of these briefly.

Accelerated depreciation is an administrative technique that permits a firm to depreciate a capital asset at a more rapid pace than usual. Since the Internal Revenue Service allows business firms to treat depreciation as an expense of doing business, acceleration will reduce the taxable income of the firm during the earlier years of the asset's life. Overall, taxes should not be changed, only deferred. But this will have two advantages for the firm. First, it will get for a time the use of money that would otherwise go to the government. Second, reduced taxes in the early years of the asset's life will increase its present value during those years, the reason being that its net after-tax income will be higher. Later, of course, the net after-tax income will go down, but since a dollar of expected income in the near future is worth more than a dollar due in the more distant future, the present value of the asset should be greater. Thus, accelerated depreciation should stimulate investment spending.

The investment tax credit as a device to stimulate investment spending was first introduced in 1962 by the Kennedy administration. An investment tax credit allows a firm to deduct a certain percentage of its investment outlays from its income tax liability. What this does, in effect, is to lower the supply price for a new item of capital, thereby raising its effective marginal efficiency [the r of Equation (6–2)]. When first introduced the tax credit was 7%. The investment tax credit was suspended in 1966, put back into effect in 1967, terminated by the Tax Reform Act of 1969, and reinstated again in 1971. In the spring of 1975 the rate was raised to 10% as part of a tax package designed to bring the economy out of the 1974–75 slump. It has remained at this level since that time.

The Role of Technology and Innovation

Among the possible factors that enter into the investment process, probably a majority of economists would rate changing technology and innovation near the top in terms of influence and importance. This is true even though technology and innovation are concepts that cannot be measured with precision or clearly distinguished from one another. Moreover, there is much obscurity in economic analysis with respect to the specific manner in which the investment decision is affected by these forces.

The concept of innovation as a significant force in economic life is most closely associated with the work of the late Professor Joseph A. Schumpeter. As a result of his analysis, innovation has come to be connected with the idea of change and the introduction of new commodities and resource combinations into the economic process. In his classic work, *The Theory of Economic Development,* Schumpeter defined innovation in terms of a change falling into one or more of the following categories:

1. The introduction of a new good, or of a new quality of an existing good
2. The introduction of a new method of production
3. The opening of a new market
4. The conquest of a new source of supply
5. The establishment of a new organization of industry[32]

Technology as a concept is generally construed as dealing more with the productive process than with the introduction of new goods or substantial changes in the quality and style of an existing good. The usual definition of *technological change* is a change involving a shift in the production function.[33] The production function, it will be recalled from Chapter 3, concerns the technical relationship between inputs of economic resources in the form of land, labor, and capital, and the output of product. Any particular combination of economic resources will embody a particular level of technology, and a change in technology means either more product from the same quantity and combination of resources or else the same amount of product with a smaller quantity of resources. If a change in technology involves a shift in the production function, it follows that innovations which lead to a reduction in costs and new ways of producing old goods cannot, in practice, be distinguished from changes in technology. On the other hand, innovations that have to do with the introduction of new goods may not involve new or different production techniques, and thus need not necessarily be construed as a change in technology. In any event, the reader is reminded that any real distinction between innovation and technological change is a subtle thing. In reality it is difficult to imagine a change in techniques of production that will not, sooner or later, affect at least the quality of existing goods, and thus ultimately become innovational in character. In our discussion of the impact of these two phenomena on the investment decision, we shall try to keep them separate; but the student should keep in mind that this is an arbitrary procedure, done primarily for analytical purposes.

Innovation and Investment   Introduction of a new product or development of a new market may or may not require new investment; there is no inherent reason why these kinds of innovation should require a drastic change in the physical quantity of any particular resource, such as capital. As Schumpeter pointed out, economic development results primarily from the employment of existing resources in a different way, or in doing new things with them rather than in increasing their quantity.[34] Thus, innovation may simply lead to a readjustment in existing capital equipment rather than an increase in the physical quantity utilized by

32. Joseph A. Schumpeter, *The Theory of Economic Development* (Cambridge, Mass.: Harvard University Press, 1951), p. 66.
33. Yale Brozen, "Determinants of the Direction of Technological Change," *American Economic Review*, May 1953.
34. Schumpeter, p. 68.

the firm. If this happens, it is necessary to look to conditions affecting the demand for the product in question before we can say anything about the probable effect of the innovation on investment expenditure. One possibility, of course, is that the introduction of a new product will be followed by such a rapid rise in demand for the product that the original introducer of the product, as well as his imitators, will have to expand capacity. In this case more investment will be forthcoming. In general, we can say that the manner in which the introduction of a new product or development of a new market will affect investment demand will depend largely upon the competitive character of the industry or market involved. Other things being equal, we might expect that the firm which introduces a new product in a highly competitive industry would gain a momentary advantage over its rival that could lead to more investment.

Technological Change and Investment How does technological change affect the demand for capital instruments? The traditional view is that technological change is highly favorable to investment spending. Some would argue that because capital goods are the physical embodiment of new production techniques, the latter cannot be introduced without at the same time creating more capital. It is also maintained that the adoption of techniques which shift the production function requires that the ratio of capital to other resources be increased, and that technological change renders existing capital goods obsolete. Both of these tendencies, if present in the economy, would link the demand for capital very closely to the rate of technological change.

Although many economists would agree that technological change is an important factor in the investment decision, there are reasons to doubt that the relationship between technological change and the investment decision is as simple and as direct as suggested by the traditional view. Howard R. Bowen, for example, questions the view that technological change will require more capital relative to other resources and that technologically induced obsolescence will increase the demand for capital.[35] Does technological change raise the capital-output ratio? If it does, then clearly technological change will increase the demand for capital. But, as Bowen points out, many innovations of a technological character are capital saving in the sense that they reduce the capital-output ratio. If technological change tends to be capital saving rather than capital using, its effects on the demand for capital may be reduced.[36] Bowen

---

35. Howard R. Bowen, "Technological Change and Aggregate Demand," *American Economic Review*, December 1954.
36. If the amount of capital required per unit of output is reduced, it does not necessarily follow that the demand for capital has been reduced. A reduction in the capital-output ratio means that the productivity of capital has been increased, and this may lead to an increase in the demand for capital. On this point see especially the article by Robert Eisner, "Technological Change and Aggregate Demand," *American Economic Review*, March 1956. See also John LaTourette, "Sources of Variations in the Capital-Output Ratio in the United States Private Business Sector, 1909–1959," *Kylos*, Fasc. 4, 1965.

also argues that a rapid rate of technological change may be inimical to a high level of investment expenditure because it increases the risk of obsolescence. If technological change makes existing capital obsolete, it may create a demand for new capital. But because obsolescence raises the element of risk in all investments, the entrepreneur may demand higher rates of return from prospective capital investments than otherwise would be the case. Thus, it is entirely possible that technological change can inhibit, as well as spur, investment expenditure.

Some studies cast doubt upon the assumption that technological change must necessarily be embodied in new capital instruments. These studies sought to determine the relative importance of different types of resource inputs—labor, capital, etc.—and of technological change in determining the nation's economic growth over the long run. For example, Benton F. Massell found that 90 percent of the increase in output per worker-hour between 1915 and 1955 in the United States should be attributed to technological change and only 10 percent to an increase in the physical quantity of capital employed per worker-hour.[37] Studies like Massell's should not be interpreted to mean that technology and technological change have no impact on investment expenditure, but rather that a distinction can be made between changes in technology and changes in the capital stock. They suggest that economists should give close attention to the factors that govern the rate at which new technological developments take place within the economic system.

The Role of Market Structures

The term *market structures* is used in reference to the kind and degree of competition characteristic of the industrial environment within which the firm functions. Traditionally, economists have argued that a competitive economic environment is highly conducive to both economic progress and a high rate of investment expenditure. This view rests upon the assumption that, since business firms seek to maximize profits, a major way of achieving this objective is to reduce production costs. In an environment of rigorous competition firms will be forced, if they are to survive, to seize every opportunity for the introduction and exploitation of cost-reducing innovations. Since innovation may lead to investment expenditure, it follows that a competitive market structure may be favorable to a high level of investment activity.

The reasons for the belief that monopoly is inimical to both investment expenditure and economic progress are summarized in a classic article by Evsey Domar.[38] When the business firm is confronted with a

37. Benton F. Massell, "Capital Formation and Technological Change in United States Manufacturing," *Review of Economics and Statistics,* May 1960. See also Robert M. Solow, "Technical Change and the Aggregate Production Function," *Review of Economics and Statistics,* August 1957; and Edmund S. Phelps, "Tangible Investment as an Instrument of Growth," in *The Goal of Economic Growth* (New York: Norton, 1962), pp. 94–105.

38. Evsey D. Domar, "Investment, Losses, and Monopolies," in *Income, Employment, and Public Policy* (New York: Norton, 1948), pp. 33–53.

technological or innovational change that requires additional investment in capital equipment, it must reach a decision with respect to two different and possible developments. In the first place, investment in new equipment often leads to the scrapping of older equipment that has become obsolete; the firm must balance the gain from the introduction of new equipment against the capital losses involved in scrapping older equipment. If the industry is competitive, the individual firm really has no choice. Inevitably, other firms in the industry will introduce the new equipment, and the individual firm faces capital losses because its equipment has become outmoded. A monopoly, on the other hand, can avoid the capital losses involved in the acquisition of new equipment by introducing new production techniques at a more leisurely pace and financing the necessary investment from internal sources. The capital losses that result from the scrapping of obsolete equipment are part of the price that a competitive economy must pay for both a rapid rate of technological change and a high rate of capital formation.

The second possibility confronting the firm concerns its market position. Domar argues that a technological or innovational development that leads to a reduction in costs or the introduction of a new product may present the firm with the opportunity to enlarge its share of the total market. This is most likely in oligopolistic industries. In the purely competitive type of industry, such as exemplified by agricultural production, no single firm can ever command more than a negligible portion of the total market. But in markets that are dominated by a relative handful of firms (the automobile industry is perhaps the best example), the share of each particular firm in the overall market is a subject of concentrated and continual interest on the part of management. Under these circumstances, innovation and investment may be a particularly attractive means for enlarging the firm's share of the total market. Monopoly would not lead to this result, for the monopolist does not have to worry about his firm's relative position in the market.

Some economists maintain that monopoly may be just as conducive as competitive oligopoly to innovation, technological change, and a high rate of investment expenditure. The ability, for example, of a firm to innovate and invest depends to a large degree on its entrepreneurial and managerial capacity and its financial power. If this is true, the monopolistic firm will be better off than the typical small firm in a highly competitive industry, the small firm having neither the ability to attract outstanding entrepreneurial talent nor the financial power to undertake the investment that is often necessary for the introduction of new techniques. It can be argued that only financially powerful firms, found in industries characterized by monopoly and oligopoly, can afford to underwrite the extensive, formalized research that is the necessary prelude to new developments in production and products in a world of rapid technological change.

We can best sum up this discussion of market structures and investment by pointing out that the traditional view that an economy domi-

nated by the competition of many small units is most conducive to
economic progress is not particularly appropriate in a world in which
research and technological change have become dominant factors in the
competitive position of the firm. Competition remains necessary and
desirable, but it is a different type of competition than that envisaged in
the model of a purely competitive market economy. It is, rather, the
competition of a relatively few large economic units with the ability and
power to bring together the human talent and other resources necessary
for performing the increasingly specialized functions of research and
introduction of the fruits of research into the economic process.

A Summary View

We have sought in this chapter to examine and analyze the most important things that contemporary economic theory has to say about the
determinants of investment expenditure. The investment decision remains
one of the most involved problems relating to the operations of the modern economy, chiefly because the factors that enter into it are more varied and less predictable than, say, those that enter into the consumption-
saving decision. In the area of consumption theory the economist has at
least the solid fact of income upon which to build his analysis; no matter
what other influences may be involved, it is impossible to ignore or overlook the dominant role that income plays as a determinant of consumption expenditure. In investment theory, however, there is no such prime
determinant to provide a foundation for analysis. In the early days of
Keynesian analysis, economists believed that the rate of interest could
occupy the same role in investment theory that income occupies in consumption theory, but research into the mechanics of the investment
decision has tended to undermine faith in this view. Modern investment
theory is cast in the framework of the capital and investment demand
schedules. But, at best, this approach is a device to organize our thinking, a means of getting started, not a complete theory that adequately
explains the fluctuating phenomenon of investment. Many of the more
important determinants are to be found in the area that we have labeled
"other influences" and the major difficulty here is not that their existence and importance go unrecognized, but that they are highly subjective. Most of the time these other determinants cannot be measured
quantitatively, and there is no easy way to assess their relative impacts
on the level of investment expenditure.

Appendix

*Algebraic determination of the income level with the inclusion of
induced investment*

(1) $Y_{np} = C + I'_0 + I_i$ The basic identity
(2) $C = C_0 + aY_d$ The consumption function
(3) $C = C_0 + aY_{np}$ This is correct when taxes and transfers are zero
(4) $I'_0 = (I_0 - ci)$ Investment expenditure which is independent of the income level
(5) $I_i = bY_{np}$ Induced investment
(6) $Y_{np} = C_0 + aY_{np} + I'_0 + bY_{np}$ Substitution of Equations (3) and (5) into Equation (1)
(7) $Y_{np} - aY_{np} - bY_{np} = C_0 + I'_0$
(8) $Y_{np}(1 - a - b) = C_0 + I'_0$
(9) $Y_{np} = \dfrac{1}{1 - a - b}(C_0 + I'_0)$
(10) $Y_{np} = k'(C_0 + I'_0)$ (k' = the supermultiplier)

Summary

1. Investment is a key determinant of the income level and a major source of instability in the economy. It is volatile because it depends upon uncertain expectations about the future.

2. The investment decision involves weighing the expected gains from the acquisition of more capital (structures and equipment) by the firm against the costs of acquiring the capital, including the finance costs.

3. The marginal efficiency of capital concerns the formal theory of investment and is a percentage measure of the rate of return over cost expected from new investment. It is compared to the rate of interest to determine if the investment should be made.

4. The expected rate of return on capital can be expressed as a schedule, called the investment demand schedule, showing how the rate of return declines as the volume of investment output is increased. This schedule is subject to sudden and unforeseen shifts because of changes in expectations with respect to the expected profitability of new capital.

5. Investment expenditure may be linked to income as well as to the rate of interest. This is done through the concept of the *marginal* propensity to invest and the accelerator. Both concepts add to theoretical understanding of the investment process.

6. In addition to the income level, another key factor in the determination of investment spending is the source of finance. Financing may be a source of instability, particularly when it involves debt financing.

7. Investment is also influenced by many other factors, including government policy, technology and innovation, and the kinds of markets in which the business firms operate.

7

Public Expenditures, Taxes, and Finance

In this chapter our focus is on how government expenditures, taxes, and other sources of finance for government activities affect the economy's aggregate demand function. Government purchases of goods and services exert a direct influence on the level of the aggregate demand schedule because they are a part of the demand for final output; government transfer expenditures and taxes exert an indirect influence as their impact is on the nongovernmental components of the schedule, consumption and investment.

Government Purchases of Goods and Services and the Income Level

To show how the purchase of goods and services by government units enters into the structure of aggregate demand, let us again make use of data pertaining to a hypothetical economy, as was done in Chapter 5.[1] These data for our hypothetical economy are shown in Table 7-1. Our economy is still closed, which is to say it has no economic ties with any other nation, but now we have assumed that there are three, rather than merely two, categories of output (or expenditure): consumption, C; investment, I; and government, G. The consumption function is given in Column (2) and shows the intended consumption expenditures at income levels ranging from 0 to \$2,700 billion. The marginal propensity

---

1. Chapter 5, pp. 130–32.

to consume of this schedule is 0.5, or ½. Investment expenditure, shown in Column (3), includes both autonomous and induced investment outlays. The marginal propensity to invest is 0.1, or ⅒. Government purchases of goods and services are shown in Column (4). For the sake of analytical simplicity we assume that government expenditures are autonomous with respect to the income level. Although it is likely that government expenditures increase as income increases, the nature of any such relationship is not known exactly.

Once we have assumed values for the investment function and autonomous government expenditures, the aggregate demand schedule is obtained by adding these to the consumption function, the position and slope of which are given by the parameters C_0, consumption at zero income, and a, the marginal propensity to consume. The parameters for the investment function are I'_0, investment expenditure that is autonomous with respect to the income level, and b, the marginal propensity to invest.[2] The results of this addition are given in Column (5), which now shows the aggregate demand schedule, $C+I+G$.

TABLE 7–1.   A Closed Economy with Three Categories of Output
(in billions of constant dollars)

(1) Net National Product Y_{np}	(2) Consumption C	(3) Investment I	(4) Government Expenditures (G)	(5) Aggregate Demand $(C+I+G)$
$ 0	$ 450	$100	$330	$ 880
1,600	1,250	260	330	1,840
1,700	1,300	270	330	1,900
1,800	1,350	280	330	1,960
1,900	1,400	290	330	2,020
2,000	1,450	300	330	2,080
2,100	1,500	310	330	2,140
2,200	1,550	320	330	2,200
2,300	1,600	330	330	2,260
2,400	1,650	340	330	2,320
2,500	1,700	350	330	2,380
2,600	1,750	360	330	2,440
2,700	1,800	370	330	2,500

This is shown graphically in Figure 7–1. The aggregate demand schedule, $C+I+G$, or DD, is derived by adding to the consumption function the appropriate values for investment and government expenditures. The process of income determination that results from the

2. Chapter 5, pp. 122–23, and Chapter 6, p. 184.

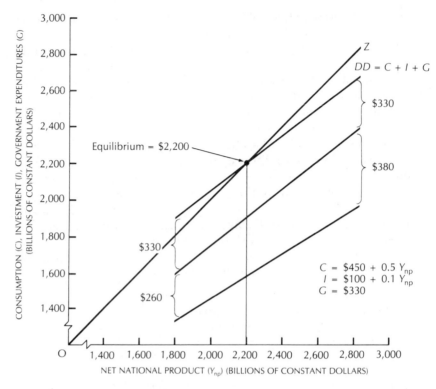

FIGURE 7–1.   The Process of Income Determination: Government Expenditures and Aggregate Demand

construction of an aggregate demand schedule which includes government expenditures is identical to the process discussed in earlier chapters. Equilibrium income is at the point of intersection of $C+I+G$, the aggregate demand schedule, and OZ, the aggregate supply schedule. In this instance, equilibrium is at $2,200 billion. This is the only output level at which the three major expenditure categories will add up to an amount identical with aggregate supply. At any output level greater than $2,200 billion $C+I+G$ would fall short of output, and we would have a disequilibrium situation in which aggregate supply, OZ, would be greater than aggregate demand, DD. Consequently, the income level would fall. At any income level below $2,200 billion the reverse would be the case. Aggregate demand, DD, would run ahead of aggregate supply, OZ, and the income level would rise.

The reader will recall that an income equilibrium is defined not only in terms of an equality between aggregate demand and aggregate supply, but also as a situation in which saving and investment *ex ante* are equal.[3] It is possible, given the data assumed for our hypothetical economy, to construct saving and investment schedules and show why the point at which they intersect must necessarily be the equilibrium income level.[4] When we include government purchases of goods and services in the analysis, the definition of an equilibrium in terms of equality between saving and investment must be modified to take into account these purchases. This is done in Table 7–2.

In Table 7–2, Column (3) is the sum of the investment and government expenditure totals of Table 7–1. Column (2) is obtained by subtracting intended consumption as shown in Table 7–1 from each income level. The difference between income and consumption we shall still define as saving, simply because at the moment we are not concerned with the matter of taxes. They will be brought into our analysis shortly. It may be noted, however, that taxes are similar to saving in their economic effects because they also represent a leakage from the current income stream.[5] In a closed economic system income not consumed must be disposed of either as saving or as taxes. Consumption, saving, and taxes are the only three alternatives for the disposition of income in a closed economy. In an open economy the purchase of imported goods and services is a fourth alternative. Returning to Table 7–2, we see that the equality between S and $I+G$ exists when income is $2,200 billion.

TABLE 7–2. Equilibrium of S and $I+G$ (in billions of constant dollars)

(1)	(2)	(3)
		Investment plus
Net National Product	Saving	Government Expenditures
Y_{np}	S	$I+G$
$ 0	$ − 450	$430
1,600	350	590
1,700	400	600
1,800	450	610
1,900	500	620
2,000	550	630
2,100	600	640
2,200	650	650
2,300	700	660
2,400	750	670
2,500	800	680
2,600	850	690
2,700	900	700

3. Chapter 5, pp. 132–34.
4. See Figure 5–4, p. 131.
5. Chapter 5, p. 142.

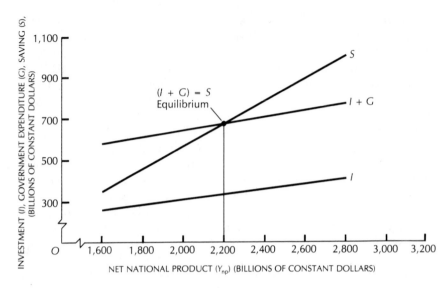

FIGURE 7–2.   Equilibrium of $I + G$ and S

The data of Table 7–2 are plotted graphically in Figure 7–2. The equilibrium level of income is determined by the intersection of the two schedules. At the equilibrium income level of $2,200 billion, $I + G$ *ex ante* is equal to S *ex ante*. Leakages out of the current income stream through saving are just being offset by expenditures for investment goods and government purchases of goods and services. This being the case, income must be in equilibrium.[6]

Government Expenditures and the Multiplier

Since the public sector buys a part of the national output in the same manner as consumers and business firms, the economic impact of government expenditures for goods and services is essentially the same as that associated with either consumption or investment expenditure. Consequently, a change in government purchase of goods and services will shift the level of the aggregate demand function in exactly the same manner as either an autonomous change in investment spending or an autonomous shift in the consumption function. It follows logically that there will be a multiplier effect associated with a change in government expenditures that is identical in concept with the general multiplier effects discussed earlier.

In Table 7–3 we have assembled another set of data pertaining to our hypothetical economy. The only difference between these data and those

6. The manner in which G is financed is discussed later.

of Table 7–1 is that the level of autonomous government expenditures, G, has risen from \$330 billion to \$410 billion. It is now labeled G'. We leave aside temporarily the question of how these increased government expenditures are being financed; for the moment it suffices to point out that if, prior to this change, saving was equal to the sum of investment and government expenditures, the expansion of government expenditures by the amount of \$80 billion means that new funds are being injected into the income stream. The data of Table 7–3 shows that the increase in government expenditure by this amount has, *ceteris paribus*, brought about a rise in the equilibrium level of income to \$2,400 billion. There is an increase of \$200 billion in the income total as a result of an autonomous change in government expenditures of \$80 billion. Thus, we have a multiplier of 2.5. Figure 7–3 shows these results graphically.

The underlying logic of the multiplier effect associated with changes in government expenditures is the same as that of the multiplier effect in conjunction with changes in investment expenditure or autonomous shifts in consumption.[7] The multiplier effect results from the combined impact of the initial (or primary) change in spending (which in this instance is the amount by which government purchases of goods and services have increased) and the induced (or secondary) spending that is a consequence of the increased income resulting from the original increase in expenditures. Induced spending is in the form of purchases of consumer goods and services and additional investment outlays.

TABLE 7–3.   Results of an Expansion in Government Expenditures (in billions of constant dollars)

(1) Net National Product Y_{np}	(2) Consumption C	(3) Investment I	(4) Government Expenditures G'	(5) Aggregate Demand $(C+I+G')$
\$ 0	\$ 450	\$100	\$410	\$ 960
1,600	1,250	260	410	1,920
1,700	1,300	270	410	1,980
1,800	1,350	280	410	2,040
1,900	1,400	290	410	2,100
2,000	1,450	300	410	2,160
2,100	1,500	310	410	2,220
2,200	1,550	320	410	2,280
2,300	1,600	330	410	2,340
2,400	1,650	340	410	2,400
2,500	1,700	350	410	2,460
2,600	1,750	360	410	2,520
2,700	1,800	370	410	2,580

7. Chapter 5, especially p. 135.

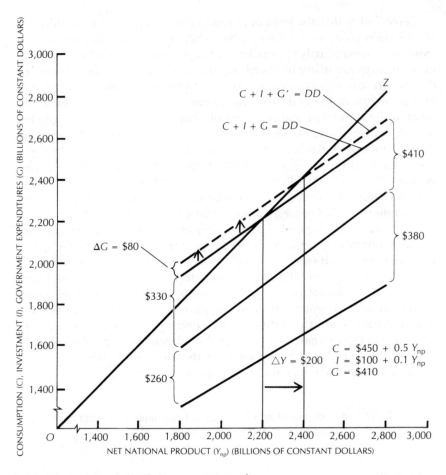

FIGURE 7–3.   Increase in Government Expenditure

The multiplier effect associated with the change in government expenditures can be explained through a series of simple algebraic formulas. In a formal sense, and as was the case with investment changes, we define the multiplier as the ratio of a change in income, ΔY_{np}, to a change in government expenditures for goods and services, ΔG. As the income variable relevant to our analysis is net national product, we have

$$k' = \frac{\Delta Y_{np}}{\Delta G}. \tag{7-1}$$

In a closed economy, output consists of three categories: consumption, C; investment, I; and government purchases of goods and services, G. Consequently, we begin with the following identity:

$$Y_{np} = C + I + G. \tag{7-2}$$

From the above it follows that a change in income must be composed of either a change in government expenditures, ΔG, a change in consumption expenditures, ΔG, a change in investment expenditures, ΔI, or some combination of all three. This gives us the additional identity

$$\Delta Y_{np} = \Delta C + \Delta I + \Delta G. \tag{7-3}$$

Since the change in government expenditures is the autonomous change, it follows that changes in either consumption expenditures or investment expenditures will be of an induced nature. Induced consumption depends upon the value of the marginal propensity to consume, whereas induced investment depends upon the value of the marginal propensity to invest. The former, it will be recalled, is designated by a and the latter by b. Induced consumption, ΔC, will be equal to $a \times \Delta Y_{np}$, on the assumption that taxes and transfers are still zero, and induced investment, ΔI_i, will be equal to $b \times \Delta Y_{np}$. If we substitute these values for ΔC and ΔI_i in Equation (7-3) we have

$$\Delta Y_{np} = \Delta G + a\Delta Y_{np} + b\Delta Y_{np}. \tag{7-4}$$

This expression may now be manipulated algebraically as follows:

$$\Delta Y_{np} - a\Delta Y_{np} - b\Delta Y_{np} = \Delta G, \tag{7-5}$$

$$\Delta Y_{np} [1 - a + b] = \Delta G, \tag{7-6}$$

$$\Delta Y_{np} = \Delta G \times \frac{1}{1 - (a+b)}, \tag{7-7}$$

$$\frac{\Delta Y_{np}}{\Delta G} = \frac{1}{1 - (a+b)} = k'. \tag{7-8}$$

Equation (7-8) tells us that the value of the multiplier in a closed system, with investment and government spending for goods and services, is equal to the reciprocal of 1 *minus* the marginal propensity to consume plus the marginal propensity to invest. It should be noted at this point that the mathematical expression $1 - (a+b)$ is a measure of leakages expressed as marginal propensities. The formal mathematical statement of the multiplier relationship just developed underscores once again the fundamental idea that the overall magnitude of the multiplier effect associated with any shift in the aggregate demand function depends upon the total secondary spending induced by such a shift.

Transfer Expenditures and the Income Level

Unlike government purchases of goods and services, which are a part of the aggregate demand function, transfer expenditures exert an indirect influence on aggregate demand. It is primarily by their impact on the volume of consumption expenditures that transfer payments influence the level of aggregate demand. To a lesser degree they may affect investment expenditures as well, but our analysis is directed basically toward the manner in which they affect expenditures for consumer goods and services.

To understand the influence of transfer expenditures on aggregate demand, it is necessary, first, to recall that the crux of the income-consumption relationship is that the amount of spending for consumption purposes is determined by the income level. In our discussion of the empirical validity of the consumption function hypothesis, we concluded that the most meaningful income measure appropriate to this relationship is that of *disposable income*.[8] Since we assumed a linear relationship between income and consumption, the consumption function in equation form is as follows:

$$C = C_0 + a(Y_d). \tag{7-9}$$

Disposable income was defined in Chapter 5 as the net national product less taxes (direct and indirect) paid by the owners of economic resources plus transfer payments received by individuals and households. Since we assumed that all saving (other than capital consumption allowances) originates with individuals or households and that government is the only source of transfer payments, disposable income was defined as follows:

$$Y_d = Y_{np} - TX + TR. \tag{7-10}$$

In Equation (7–10), Y_{np} is the net national product; TX, the total of all taxes, including indirect taxes; and TR the total of all transfer expenditures. The consumption function can now be written as

$$C = C_0 + a\,(Y_{np} - TX + TR). \tag{7-11}$$

It is apparent from Equation (7–11) that transfer expenditures influence consumption expenditure and thus indirectly the level of aggregate demand by affecting the amount of disposable income in the hands of individuals and households. A change in transfer expenditures will bring about a change in disposable income, which in turn will induce a change in consumer spending, since the amount of disposable income constitutes the point of origin of spending for consumer goods and services. Schematically, the chain of causation appears as follows:

$$\Delta TR \longrightarrow \Delta Y_d \longrightarrow \Delta C.$$

Let us refer once again to the data of the hypothetical economy for a demonstration of how this chain of causation may work. To show the relationships involved, we shall turn to Table 7–4 and Figure 7–4, confining the analysis initially to the impact of transfer expenditures on the consumption function. In Column (2) of Table 7–4 the consumption function for the hypothetical economy is as set forth in Table 7–1. This

8. Chapter 5, p. 119.

schedule appears as the solid line *C* in Figure 7–4. We may note that Table 7–1 contained no transfer expenditures, and consequently net national product and disposable income were the same. In Table 7–4 net national product and disposable income are equal prior to the introduction of transfer expenditures. They appear in Column (1).

What impact does the introduction of transfer expenditures into the analysis have on the level of consumption? Let us assume that the government of our hypothetical economy undertakes transfer expenditures of $80 billion. (We shall not concern ourselves at this point with the manner in which this new expenditure is financed.) The immediate effect of this new expenditure is to increase disposable income at all possible income levels, as shown in Column (4) of the table. This is the same at all income levels because the assumed increase in transfer expenditures of $80 billion must have the same effect on disposable income *irrespective of the actual income level.* The impact of this increase in disposable income on consumption expenditure depends upon the value of the marginal propensity to consume. Our original consumption function was drawn with a slope such that the marginal propensity to consume has a value of 0.5. If we assume that the introduction of transfer expenditures into the analysis in no way affects the slope of the schedule, it follows that consumption expenditures at each and every possible level of income will increase by $40 billion, one-half of the increase in disposable income.

TABLE 7–4. Results of an Increase in Transfer Expenditures (in billions of constant dollars)

(1) Net National Product* Y_{np}	(2) Consumption C	(3) Change in Disposable Income† ΔY_d	(4) Disposable Income Y_d	(5) Change in Consumption‡ C	(6) New Level of Consumption C'
$ 0	$ 450	$80	$ 80	$40	$ 490
1,600	1,250	80	1,680	40	1,290
1,700	1,300	80	1,780	40	1,340
1,800	1,350	80	1,880	40	1,390
1,900	1,400	80	1,980	40	1,440
2,000	1,450	80	2,080	40	1,490
2,100	1,500	80	2,180	40	1,540
2,200	1,550	80	2,280	40	1,590
2,300	1,600	80	2,380	40	1,640
2,400	1,650	80	2,480	40	1,690
2,500	1,700	80	2,580	40	1,740
2,600	1,750	80	2,680	40	1,790

* Net national product = disposable income when taxes and transfers are zero.
† This is equal to the increase in transfer expenditures.
‡ The marginal propensity to consume is 0.5.

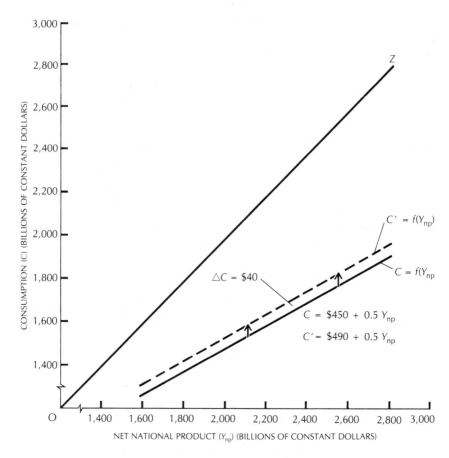

FIGURE 7–4. Shift in the Consumption Function

This change is shown in Column (5) of Table 7–4. The overall impact of the introduction of transfer expenditures may be described as *a shift in the position of the consumption function.* The consumption function has shifted upward because of the added factor of transfer expenditures. As a consequence, consumption expenditures are higher at all levels of the net national income. This shift is shown graphically in Figure 7–4. The new and higher consumption function is labeled C'. Thus, transfer expenditures constitute one of the key factors that influence the level of the consumption function. In a technical sense transfers exercise their influence through the parameter C_0, which determines the level of the function. A change in transfer expenditures will, therefore, bring about a shift in the position of the schedule, and in this way affect consumption spending and the level of aggregate demand.[9]

9. It is possible, too, that a change in transfers may affect the slope of the function, but this is precluded in our example.

Let us refer once again to the data of Table 7–1 and the income equilibrium level associated with these data. On the assumption that government expenditures for goods and services totaled a constant $330 billion, the equilibrium income is $2,200 billion, given the original position of the consumption function as shown in Column (2) and the investment function shown in Column (3) of Table 7–1. What will happen to the equilibrium income if an additional $80 billion in government transfer expenditures are injected into the picture? The immediate result is to shift the consumption function upward as we have done in Table 7–4. This means, in turn, an equal upward shift of the aggregate demand schedule. The immediate (or initial) increase in spending that this change entails is equal to the amount by which both the consumption function and the aggregate demand schedule have shifted upward. This is $40 billion, and if we multiply this change by the general multiplier of 2.5, we find that the new equilibrium level will be $100 billion higher than previously. This value of 2.5 for the general multiplier is based upon our assumed value of 0.5 for the marginal propensity to consume and 0.1 for the marginal propensity to invest. The effect on the income level of a change in transfer expenditures is shown numerically in Table 7–5 and graphically in Figure 7–5. In the table the original position of the consumption function is given by Column (3), its position after the intro-

TABLE 7–5. Transfer Expenditures and Aggregate Demand
(in billions of constant dollars)

	Before Transfers				After Transfers*		
(1)	*(2)*	*(3)*	*(4)*	*(5)*	*(6)*	*(7)*	*(8)*
Net National Product Y_{np}	*Disposable Income* Y_d	*Consumption* C	*Aggregate Demand* $C+I+G$†	*Net National Product* Y_{np}	*Disposable Income* Y_d	*Consumption* C'	*Aggregate Demand* $C'+I+G$†
$ 0	$ 0	$ 450	$ 880	$ 0	$ 80	$ 490	$ 920
1,600	1,600	1,250	1,840	1,600	1,680	1,290	1,880
1,700	1,700	1,300	1,900	1,700	1,780	1,340	1,940
1,800	1,800	1,350	1,960	1,800	1,880	1,390	2,000
1,900	1,900	1,400	2,020	1,900	1,980	1,440	2,060
2,000	2,000	1,450	2,080	2,000	2,080	1,490	2,120
2,100	2,100	1,500	2,140	2,100	2,180	1,540	2,180
2,200	2,200	1,550	2,200	2,200	2,280	1,590	2,240
2,300	2,300	1,600	2,260	2,300	2,380	1,640	2,300
2,400	2,400	1,650	2,320	2,400	2,480	1,690	2,360
2,500	2,500	1,700	2,380	2,500	2,580	1,740	2,420
2,600	2,600	1,750	2,440	2,600	2,680	1,790	2,480
2,700	2,700	1,800	2,500	2,800	2,880	1,890	2,590

*Transfers = $80.
†$I+G$ are the same as in Table 7–1.

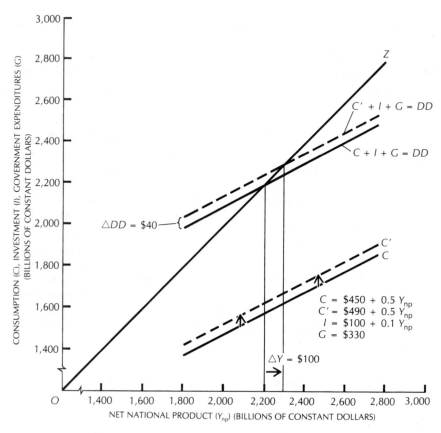

FIGURE 7–5.   Aggregate Demand and a Shift in the Consumption Function

duction of transfer expenditures by Column (7). The aggregate demand function, $C'+I+G$, at the new and higher level of the consumption function is shown in Column (8). The new equilibrium income level is $2,300 billion.

Transfer Expenditures and the Multiplier

There is a multiplier effect associated with a change in the level of transfer expenditures similar in a fundamental conceptual sense to all of the multiplier effects previously discussed. An increase (or decrease) in transfer expenditures will lead to an increase (or decrease) in the income level that is some multiple of the initial change in consumption resulting from the change in transfers. This is identical to what takes place when there is an autonomous change in investment outlays or government purchases of goods and services. But there is an important difference between the multiplier effect associated with transfers and that associated between the multiplier effect associated with transfers and that associated with the *G* or *I* components of the aggregate demand schedule. Normally, the multiplier effect associated with transfer expenditures will be *smaller* than the multiplier effect of a change in either investment or government expenditures. Let us see why this is true.

The multiplier phenomenon results from the combination of initial and induced changes in spending. But a change in transfer expenditures does not operate directly on the aggregate demand function in the same way as does a change in either investment expenditures or government purchases of goods and services. Additional transfer expenditures trigger, first, a change in disposable income, then, via the marginal propensity to consume, a new level of consumption spending. But so long as Keynes's fundamental psychological law holds true—that is, that normally the marginal propensity to consume is less than 100 percent—consumption cannot rise (or fall) by the full amount of the change in transfer expenditures. Consequently, *the shift in the aggregate demand function*, which is the initial or primary change in spending that gives rise to the multiplier process, *must always be smaller than the change in transfer expenditures*. It follows that, if the initial effect of any given change is smaller, then the induced effect will also be smaller. Thus, the multiplier effect will be smaller for transfers than for investment or government expenditures.[10]

Taxes and the Income Level

Our detailed analysis of the way in which transfer expenditures affect the income level by their influence on disposable income and consumption spending makes it relatively easy for us to consider the impact of taxes on the income level. Once we realize that taxes are, in a sense, nothing more than negative transfers, it can be seen that they will affect the income level in a manner exactly the reverse of transfers. Taxes, *ceteris paribus*, have the effect of reducing disposable income, as we saw in Equation (7–10). Thus an increase in taxes would tend to reduce consumption spending because it would reduce disposable income. On the other hand, a decrease in taxes would have the opposite effect of increasing consumption spending because it would increase disposable income. The foregoing remarks apply primarily to a situation in which taxes increase (or decrease) by a specific amount. Changes in taxation that may accompany changes in the income level present a more complex problem, as we shall see shortly.

In view of the above similarities between the impact of transfers and taxes on the income level, let us assert as a general principle that the absolute level of taxes is a factor which, like the absolute level of transfer expenditures, influences the level of the consumption function. This

---

10. See the Appendix to this chapter for an alternative treatment which develops a multiplier that can be applied directly against the entire change in transfer expenditures (or taxes) to derive the total change in income.

statement applies to that part of the tax total that is independent of income level. Given this general principle, it follows that any increase in taxes that is autonomous with respect to the income level will, *ceteris paribus*, shift the consumption function downward. On the other hand, an autonomous reduction in the level of taxation will, *ceteris paribus*, shift the consumption function upward. As is the case with transfer expenditures, the amount by which the consumption function shifts as a result of a change in taxation depends upon the value of the marginal propensity to consume. Taxes change disposable income, and consumption spending will change in accordance with whether the value of the marginal propensity to consume is high or low.

Let us refer once again to the data of our hypothetical economy to analyze the impact of an introduction of taxes into the system. We shall assume that a flat total of taxes in the amount of $160 billion is imposed. The effect of this change on disposable income and the consumption function is shown in Table 7–6. Essentially, the effect of new taxes in the amount of $160 billion is, first, to reduce disposable income by a like amount at all levels of the net national product and, second, to reduce consumption spending in accordance with the value of the marginal propensity to consume. This value is 0.5, which means, in effect, that at all levels of the net national product consumption spending will decline by $0.5 \times \Delta TX$. This is $80 billion; thus, we have an autonomous downward

TABLE 7–6. Results of the Introduction of Taxes (in billions of constant dollars)

(1) Net National Product Y_{np}	(2) Consump- tion* C'	(3) Change in Disposable Income† ΔY_d	(4) Disposable Income Y_d	(5) Change in Consump- tion C	(6) New Level of Consump- tion C''
$ 0	$ 490	$ − 160	$ − 80	$ − 80	$ 410
1,600	1,290	− 160	1,520	− 80	1,210
1,700	1,340	− 160	1,620	− 80	1,260
1,800	1,390	− 160	1,720	− 80	1,310
1,900	1,440	− 160	1,820	− 80	1,360
2,000	1,490	− 160	1,920	− 80	1,410
2,100	1,540	− 160	2,020	− 80	1,460
2,200	1,590	− 160	2,120	− 80	1,510
2,300	1,640	− 160	2,220	− 80	1,560
2,400	1,690	− 160	2,320	− 80	1,610
2,500	1,740	− 160	2,420	− 80	1,660
2,600	1,790	− 160	2,520	− 80	1,710
2,700	1,840	− 160	2,620	− 80	1,760

*Same as Column (6) of Table 7–4.
†This is equal to the increase in taxes ($160 billion) and is applied against the disposable income shown in Column (6) of Table 7–5.

shift in the consumption function in the amount of $80 billion. The new position of the consumption function is shown in Column (6) of Table 7–6.

The data contained in Table 7–7 indicate the effect of the introduction of taxes into the system upon aggregate demand and the equilibrium income level. Prior to this change, the equilibrium income was $2,300 billion and the position of the consumption function was given by Column (7) of Table 7–5. The initial impact of the added taxes is to reduce autonomously the consumption function by $80 billion—as we have just seen—and, if it is assumed that no change in either government purchases of goods and services or the investment function follows, this means, too, that the aggregate demand function shifts downward by $80 billion. When the general multiplier of 2.5 is applied against this shift, the ultimate decline in the net national product is $200 billion. Thus, the new equilibrium position is depicted in Table 7–7 as being at the $2,100 billion level. These changes are depicted graphically in Figure 7–6.

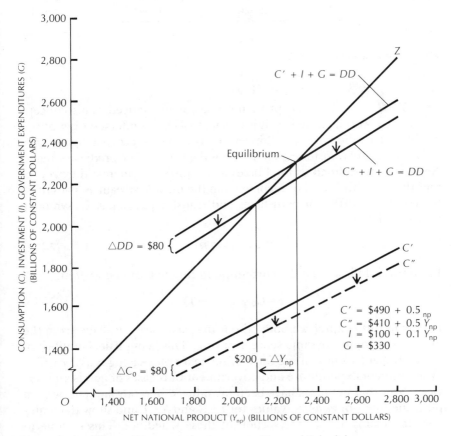

FIGURE 7–6.   Effect of Taxes on the Aggregate Demand Schedule

TABLE 7–7.   Taxes and Aggregate Demand (in billions of constant dollars)

(1) Net National Product Y_{np}	(2) Net Taxes T^*	(3) Disposable Income Y_d†	(4) Consumption C'	(5) Aggregate Demand $C'' + I + G$‡
$ 0	$80	$ − 80	$ 410	$ 840
1,600	80	1,520	1,210	1,800
1,700	80	1,620	1,260	1,860
1,800	80	1,720	1,310	1,920
1,900	80	1,820	1,360	1,980
2,000	80	1,920	1,410	2,040
2,100	80	2,020	1,460	2,100
2,200	80	2,120	1,510	2,160
2,300	80	2,220	1,560	2,220
2,400	80	2,320	1,610	2,280
2,500	80	2,420	1,660	2,340
2,600	80	2,520	1,710	2,400
2,700	80	2,620	1,760	2,460

*T = net taxes = $(TX − TR)$.
†$Y_d = Y_{np} − T$.
‡$I + G$ is the same as in Table 7–1.

In Table 7–7 the concept of net taxes is introduced. This concept should be carefully noted, as it is crucial to a clear understanding of the algebraic derivation of the multiplier in a system that incorporates changes in *both* taxes and transfer expenditures as the net national product changes. Net taxes are defined as total taxes less transfer payments; they represent the net withdrawal of income from the income stream as a result of the combined effect of both taxes and transfer payments. In symbolic terms, we have

$$T = (TX − TR). \qquad (7–12)$$

From this it follows that the consumption function can be written

$$c = C_0 + a(Y_{np} − T). \qquad (7–13)$$

Earlier in this chapter we pointed out that taxes are a leakage from the income stream in the same sense as saving. This being true, equilibrium requires that leakages in the form of net taxes plus saving must be offset by investment expenditure and government purchases of goods and services. Now that net taxes have been introduced into our analysis, we can plot schedule—or *ex ante*—values for $I + G$ and $S + T$ and show that equilibrium obtains at the intersection of these schedules. This is done in Figure 7–7.

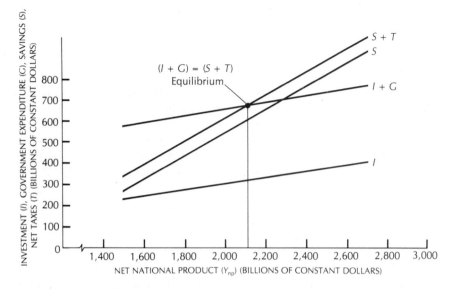

FIGURE 7–7.   Equilibrium of *I* + *G* and *S* + *Tf*

Transfers, Taxes, and the Multiplier

We shall now proceed to derive algebraically the multiplier in a system which includes both transfers and taxes, as well as induced investment. In Equation (7–12) we defined net taxes T as the difference between total taxes and transfer payments. We may also define net taxes as follows:

$$T = T_0 + tY_{np}. \qquad (7-14)$$

In this equation, T_0 represents net taxes that are independent of the income level, while t may be defined as the net marginal propensity to tax out of net national product. It is equal to $\Delta T/\Delta Y_{np}$. The value of t may increase, remain the same, or decline as Y_{np} rises, depending upon the nature of the rate structure for the tax system, a topic we shall discuss shortly. Equation (7–14) is the net tax function.

The consumption function shown in Equation (7–13) can be further modified by the substitution of the net tax function given above for T in the equation. This gives the following:

$$C = C_0 + a[Y_{np} - (T_0 + tY_{np})], \qquad (7-15)$$

$$C = C_0 + aY_{np} - aT_0 - atY_{np}, \qquad (7-16)$$

$$C = C_0 - aT_0 + (a - at)Y_{np}. \qquad (7-17)$$

We shall designate $(C_0 - aT_0)$ as C'_0. This represents consumption that is independent of the level of the net national product. The expression

$(a - at)$ is the marginal propensity to consume out of the net national product.[11] We shall designate this as a'. We now have the equation

$$C = C'_0 + a'Y_{np}. \tag{7-18}$$

Since both transfer payments and taxes have been introduced into our analysis, there no longer is equality between disposable income and the net national product. The multiplier formula must take this into account. We shall continue to designate the multiplier, which reflects the effect of both transfers and taxes as well as induced investment, as the *effective* multiplier, again using k' as the symbol for the multiplier. Recall, too, that k' is sometimes called the supermultiplier. Algebraically, the effective multiplier is

$$k' = \frac{\Delta Y_{np}}{\Delta D}. \tag{7-19}$$

In the equation, ΔD refers to any autonomous shift in the aggregate demand function. To complete our analysis, let us assume that it is an increase in government purchases of goods and services that is the source of an autonomous shift in the aggregate demand function. Then $\Delta G = \Delta D$. If this happens, it follows that

$$\Delta Y_{np} = \Delta G + \Delta C + \Delta I. \tag{7-20}$$

By substitution we have

$$\Delta Y_{np} = \Delta G + a'\Delta Y_{np} + b\Delta Y_{np}, \tag{7-21}$$

$$\Delta G = \Delta Y_{np} - a'\Delta Y_{np} - b\Delta Y_{np}, \tag{7-22}$$

$$\Delta G = \Delta Y_{np}(1 - a' - b). \tag{7-23}$$

If we substitute the right-hand portion of Equation (7-23) for ΔD in Equation (7-19) we get

$$k' = \frac{\Delta Y_{np}}{\Delta Y_{np}(1 - a' - b)} = \frac{1}{(1 - a' - b)}. \tag{7-24}$$

When a' is replaced with $(a - at)$ in the above expression, the equation defining the effective multiplier becomes

$$k' = \frac{1}{1 - (a - at) - b} = \frac{1}{1 - a + at - b}. \tag{7-25}$$

By careful examination of the above equation the student can see clearly the effect of both transfer payments and taxes on the value of the multiplier and hence on income changes as a result of an autonomous shift in aggregate demand. Any development that increases the value of the net marginal propensity to tax, t, will have the effect of reducing the size of the effective multiplier; any development that reduces t will have the opposite effect.

---

11. See the Appendix for algebraic proof that $a' = (a - at)$.

Putting Theory into Practice: The Record since World War II

The ideas discussed to this point about government's role in the economy are Keynesian in the sense that they look to changes in government spending and taxes as a means of influencing the level of aggregate demand and thereby the performance of the economy. This suggests two questions: First, to what extent have American governments in the post–World War II era resorted to tax and expenditure changes as a part of a strategy for economic management? Second, how successful have their efforts been?

From an examination of the policies of all of the post–World War II administrations, one fact clearly emerges. This is that tax changes rather than changes in government spending have become the primary fiscal instrument for influencing the economy's short-term behavior. The reasons for this are not wholly certain, although it is probable that tax changes, especially tax reductions, are politically more feasible than expenditure changes, either upward or downward.

1945–60

In the fifteen years from the end of World War II to the election of John F. Kennedy as president (1945–60), there was little effort by either the Truman or Eisenhower administration to apply the ideas of Keynesian economics to the overall management of the economy. This was the case in spite of the fact that the economy passed through four measurable recessions in this period and that the Employment Act was passed in 1946. This act, it will be recalled, clearly stated that it was the responsibility of the federal government to "promote maximum production, employment, and purchasing power."

In the spring of 1948, however, the Congress passed, over the veto of President Truman, the first of a series of major reductions in income taxes carried out during the post–World War II period. This particular tax reduction was not undertaken for Keynesian reasons, which is to say that its primary purpose was not to stimulate the economy. But it turned out fortuitously to be the right thing to do at the time. The reason was that later in the year the economy slid into the first of the mild postwar recessions it was to undergo between 1946 and 1960. President Truman believed at the time that inflation was a much more serious threat than deflation, so much so that he asked for a substantial tax increase in his 1949 budget message, even though by then the economy had definitely turned down. It was not until mid-year that the administration recognized that a recession was under way. In its mid-year economic report the request for a tax increase was withdrawn. The president also gave up his hope for a balanced budget, suggesting that a deficit would be a source of support against the factors making for decline in the economy.[12] The deficit was the result of the recession, not a policy-inspired deficit. No major fiscal policy measures were called for to deal with the recession, which reached a trough in the fourth quarter of 1949. Expansion got under way in the spring of 1950 and the Korean war boosted the economy into boom conditions through 1953.

The Eisenhower administration, which took office in January 1953, was even more committed to a balanced budget philosophy than its predecessor. In his 1960 *Economic Report*, President Eisenhower said that the appropriate budget policy is one that "not merely balances expenditures with revenues, but achieves a significant surplus for debt retirement."[13] This statement fairly well sums up the budget philosophy characteristic of the Eisenhower years. Behind this view appears to have been a persistent fear of inflation coupled with a belief that budget deficits were the prime source of inflation. There is no evidence that the Eisenhower administration understood—or wanted to understand—how Keynesian ideas might be used for effective economic management. The result was three more recessions—1953–54, 1957–58, and 1960–61—of which at least the first was probably the direct result of the administration's near-continuous preoccupation with a balanced budget. In an effort to cut down on the deficits incurred during the Korean war (1950–53), the new Eisenhower administration sharply curtailed federal spending in 1953–54. As a result, the federal budget became sharply restrictive and the economy in mid-1953 dropped into a second postwar recession. Unemployment rose from a Korean war low of 2.9 percent in 1953 to 5.5 percent in 1954. Once again a fortuitous development helped bail the economy out, as both individual and business taxes were cut in 1954. But these tax reductions were not put into effect as an anti-recession measure; they had been planned and scheduled earlier as a part of the administration's efforts to reduce the size of the federal budget.[14] In the last two recessions of the Eisenhower years, primary blame for the recessions cannot be laid at the door of the federal government. The administration did not, however, initiate vigorous policy measures in either 1957–58 or 1960–61[15] to get the economy out of the recessions.

1960–80

By far the most highly publicized Post–World War II "experiment" in demand management through tax changes was the 1964 tax cut pushed through by the Kennedy-Johnson administration. Originally proposed

12. Wilfred Lewis, Jr., *Federal Fiscal Policy in the Postwar Recessions* (Washington, D.C.: The Brookings Institution, 1962), p. 113.
13. *Economic Report of the President* (Washington, D.C.: U.S. Government Printing Office, 1960), p. 54.
14. Lewis, p. 182.
15. By 1961 the Eisenhower administration was out of office. In his last budget message, sent to the Congress in January 1961, President Eisenhower took an optimistic view of the state of the economy (unemployment in 1960 was 5.5 percent) and said that it was essential to maintain fiscal integrity. He continued to argue the need for a budget surplus.

to Congress by President Kennedy in 1963 to stimulate a sluggish econ-omy, the reduction legislation was not passed until the spring of 1964, some months after President Kennedy's assassination. It is worth noting that the 1963 *Economic Report of the President* contains a textbook-like explanation of the way in which a tax cut would work, including an anal-ysis of its expected multiplier effects.[16] Interestingly enough, the Coun-cil of Economic Advisers concluded that for each additional dollar of *direct* spending generated by the tax cut, there would be an additional $0.50 of induced consumption spending. In other words, the CEA esti-mated that the marginal propensity to consume out of the GNP was 0.5, a value similar to the one assumed in the numerical examples developed earlier in this chapter.

Did the 1964 tax cut work? Three years later, the Council of Economic Advisers concluded that the overall impact (original stimulus of about $11 billion plus the multiplier effects) was around $30 billion.[17] In the eyes of many economists the 1964 tax cut was a watershed event, as it seemed to demonstrate quite conclusively that tax cuts could be used successfully to move the economy out of a sluggish state and toward full employment. The 1964 "experiment" also was taken as proof of the pub-lic acceptance of one of the key ideas of Keynesian economics, namely, that through fiscal policy (changes in taxes and/or expenditures) the gov-ernment could affect aggregate demand and thereby the general level of economic activity, especially the employment level.

Later actions involving tax changes have been less certain in their eco-nomic effects. Belatedly, in 1968 the Johnson administration and the Congress raised taxes in an effort to stem the inflationary pressures that began to build following the rapid growth in military outlays after the 1966 escalation of the Vietnam war. Professional economic opinion was nearly unanimous that taxes should have been raised in 1966, once the war buildup began, but neither the administration nor the Congress was willing to act until two years later.[18] The 1968 tax increase was a fiscal counterpart to the tax reductions of 1964, but its overall effectiveness was less clear-cut. Prices did not stop going up after the tax increase was enacted, but the increase may have caused enough of a slowdown in consumer spending to help nudge the economy into a recession in late 1969. The late Arthur M. Okun, a former chairman of the Council of Economic Advisers, concluded in a 1971 study that the tax increase put the brakes on consumer spending, but not sufficiently to end the infla-tion.[19]

---

16. *Economic Report of the President* (Washington, D.C.: U.S. Government Printing Office, 1963), pp. 45–51.
17. *Economic Report of the President* (Washington, D.C.: U.S. Government Printing Office, 1966), p. 34.
18. The tax increase took the form of a 10 percent surcharge on personal and corporate income taxes. The rate dropped to 5 percent during the first half of 1970, and expired completely on June 30, 1970.
19. Arthur M. Okun, "The Personal Tax Surcharge and Consumer Demand, 1968–70," *Brookings Papers on Economic Activity,* No. 1, 1971.

In the spring of 1975 and again in the spring of 1977 taxes were once again cut as a stimulative measure. In 1974 the economy had plunged into its worst slump since the 1930s, a recession in which unemployment reached 8.9 percent of the labor force. In late March 1975 the Congress passed tax cuts proposed by the Ford administration, a package bill involving rebates on 1974 personal income taxes, tax credits for nearly all taxpayers, and reductions in corporate tax liabilities. Overall, the cuts contained in the Tax Reduction Act of 1975 amounted to about $15 billion, or an estimated 5 percent of the federal government receipts that would have been forthcoming in the absence of a tax cut.[20] Once again the results were not clear-cut. Probably the tax cut helped as the economy began to recover in the second half of 1975, but all through 1976 the recovery was sluggish and unemployment remained stubbornly high, standing at 7.7 percent of the labor force at year's end.

High unemployment and the nation's slow economic recovery were key issues in the presidential contest, as candidate Jimmy Carter continuously attacked the economic record of the Ford administration. As president, Carter proposed in early 1977 an array of tax cuts for consumers and business which were to total about $31 billion over a two-year period. As inflationary fears mounted in the spring of 1977 the reduction finally approved by the Congress was about half the sum originally proposed. Nevertheless, the Carter administration continued trying during 1978 to stimulate the economy through further tax cuts. Initially, a tax cut package totaling $25 billion was proposed, to take effect late in the year, but once again growing inflationary fears in the Congress led to a substantial scaling back in the cuts by the time the Revenue Act of 1978 was passed.[21] After 1978 the Carter administration became almost wholly preoccupied with fighting inflation, dropping consequently any further moves to cut taxes. During 1977 and 1978 changes in personal taxes were achieved primarily by lowering the schedule for individual rates (1978), increasing the personal exemption (1978), and raising the personal standard deduction (1977). In spite of the tax-cut strategy pursued by the Carter administration, unemployment remained high, declining to only 6.0 percent of the labor force in 1969, a level well above the 4 percent "full employment" rate attained in the Kennedy-Johnson years. Meanwhile, the inflation rate continued to climb, reaching 11.3 percent in 1979. Continued high unemployment and high inflation proved to be the Carter administration's undoing in the 1980 presidential election. As candidate Carter had done four years earlier in attacking the Ford administration, candidate Reagan used the combination of the

20. *Economic Report of the President* (Washington, D.C.: U.S. Government Printing Office, 1976), p. 51.
21. *Economic Report of the President* (Washington, D.C.: U.S. Government Printing Office, 1979), p. 93.

inflation and unemployment rates—the so-called "misery index"—with devastating effectiveness in his successful presidential campaign in 1980.[22]

The Reagan Program

Undoubtedly the most far-reaching and controversial post–World War II tax cut was the one engineered by the Reagan administration in the summer of 1981. This massive tax cut, which, by some estimates, would reduce federal revenues by more than $700 billion from 1981 to 1986, was the centerpiece in the president's *Program for Economic Recovery*, first made public in February 1981. Basically, the tax-cut portion of the Reagan program was an application of the theory of supply-side economics (see Chapter 12), especially as interpreted in the Congress by Representative Jack Kemp of New York and Senator William Roth of Delaware. For several years prior to the Reagan administration, the Kemp-Roth bill, calling for a 30 percent "across-the-board" reduction in tax rates over a three-year period, had been introduced in the Congress, but had always failed to pass until the Reagan administration adopted the tax-cut philosophy of Kemp-Roth as its own. In a nutshell, the economic argument underlying the proposed tax cut was that tax rates—especially marginal rates, or the tax on additional income—had become so high that incentives to work and save were badly impaired. As a consequence, the Reagan administration argued that a large and permanent tax cut was essential to get people to work more, to save more, and to get business firms to invest. The "pure" supply-siders like Representative Kemp maintained that only a tax cut was needed, nothing more. The effect of lower taxes on incentives would be so immediate and dramatic that output would rise sufficiently to more than offset the revenue loss which initially resulted from lowered rate of taxation. The Reagan administration was not convinced of the validity of the extreme supply-side view, choosing also to cut back social spending drastically in the federal budget (military spending was increased) and looking to the Federal Reserve System to keep a tight rein on money and credit until such time as the full supply-side effects of the tax cut became effective. The key role accorded a slow but steady growth in the supply of money and credit in the president's program was a tacit admission that basically the fiscal parts of the program (tax cuts plus changes in both military and social spending) would be, in the short term at least, inflationary.[23] After a long and bitter debate in the

22. The "misery index" is the sum of the unemployment and inflation rates. Carter invented the term, which came back to haunt him in the 1980 campaign. In 1976 the "index" stood at 12.5, but by 1980 it had climbed to 19.5.
23. For full details on the Reagan program see *A Program for Economic Recovery* (Washington, D.C.: The White House, February 18, 1981). An excellent summary and evaluation of the Reagan program is found in the September 1981 issue of the *Economic Review* of the Federal Reserve Bank of Atlanta, "The Reagan Program for Economic Recovery: Economic Rationale."

Congress in the spring and summer of 1981, the Reagan administration got almost everything it asked for in the way of tax legislation.[24] The major features of the "Economic Recovery Tax Act of 1981" are summarized in the following box (Table 7–8):

Although the ultimate effects of the Reagan "Program for Economic Recovery" will not be known for many years, the immediate impact was quite the opposite of what the administration had expected. Instead of the tax-cut features of the president's program unleashing a torrent of production through more work and a renewal of business confidence, the stringent monetary side of the program dominated the economy during 1981, especially in the first half of the year. Consequently, rising interest rates pushed the economy during the second half of the year into another recession, the fourth since 1969–70, and one more severe than the 1974–75 recession. The overall impact of the Reagan program during its first two years is discussed in Chapter 15, "Managing the Macroeconomy."

The Federal Budget

The combination of theoretical ideas of an essentially Keynesian nature concerning taxes and government spending in combination with post–World War II experience with actual policy measures has enlarged significantly our understanding of how the federal budget affects the economy. To the extent that we look to tax and expenditure changes at the national level as a means of influencing output and employment, the federal budget is the instrument for the exercise of fiscal policy. There are three important concepts to examine in this context: (1) the "full"- or "high"-employment budget; (2) automatic (or "built-in") stabilizers; and (3) the balanced budget thesis.

The mechanics of fiscal policy are relatively simple. If we let G^* represent *federal* spending for goods and services and T^* *net federal* taxes (total federal taxes minus federal transfers), then the federal budget is in deficit when $G^*>T^*$ and in surplus when $T^*>G^*$. As a general proposition, a deficit has an expansionary or inflationary effect, the reason being that with a deficit the federal government is putting more money

24. To pressure the Congress into accepting all of the major features of the tax act, the Reagan administration undertook what was probably the most intensive and expensive media "blitz" in favor of pending legislation that the Capitol had ever seen. As a consequence and because of the president's persuasive TV personality, opposition to the tax cut, particularly among conservative Democrats, virtually collapsed. An unexpected outcome, and one not initially sought by the administration, was a scramble by both Democrats and Republicans to outbid one another in offering tax concessions to a wide variety of special interests. As a consequence, the tax bill that finally passed was tilted heavily toward the upper-income groups, had the practical effect of virtually eliminating the corporate income tax as a significant source of federal revenue, and made it possible to transfer very large estates from generation to generation practically tax free.

TABLE 7–8. The Economic Tax Recovery Act of 1981, Major Provisions

Individual Income Taxes	*Business Taxes*

Individual Income Taxes

1. *Tax Rates:* Individual rates were reduced "across the board" 5% beginning October 1, 1981; 10% July 1, 1982; and 10% July 1, 1983. This was not quite the 30% reduction over three years found in Kemp-Roth, but a compromise that preserved most of the Kemp-Roth approach.

2. *Top Bracket:* The marginal tax rate on additions to income for families and individuals in the top income bracket was reduced from 70 to 50%.

3. *Capital Gains:* Top rate reduced from 28 to 20%.

4. *Estate and Gift Taxes:* By 1987 the first $600,000 of any estate will be exempt from tax and the entire estate irrespective of size will be exempt from taxation *if* the entire estate is deeded by a husband to his wife.

5. *Individual Retirement:* Beginning in 1982 any wage-earner can set up an Individual Retirement Account (IRA) for which the first $2,000 in contributions is not taxable ($2,250 for a married couple with only one working spouse). Only wage or salary income can be contributed to such an IRA, but an employee may set one up even if he or she is a member of a group retirement plan or has a Keogh plan.

6. *Indexing:* Beginning in 1985 the tax system will be "indexed" by adjusting tax brackets, exemptions, and deductions to take inflation into account. The purpose is to end the so-called "bracket creep," which is the putting of a taxpayer into a higher tax bracket because of a raise, even though the raise may be no greater than the inflation rate.

Business Taxes

1. *Depreciation:* The rate at which business firms can write off new investments in equipment and structures was accelerated. The new schedule is 15 years for buildings, 10 years for public utility property, 5 years for machinery and equipment, and 3 years for most motor vehicles.

2. *Investment Tax Credits:* For investments written off in three years, 6% of the cost of the capital may be deducted from the firm's tax liability. For other investments, except buildings, the rate remains at 10%.

3. *Windfall Profits Tax:* The rate of this tax, originally passed to capture some of the enormous "windfall" profits that accrued to oil companies from the decontrol of oil, is to be cut from 30 to 15% by 1986.

4. *Leasing:* Firms that have little or no profit are permitted to "lease" their investment credits and depreciation benefits to other firms. Critics say this is one of the most scandalous of all the special interest provisions found in the 1981 tax bill, calling it "food-stamps for needy corporations."

into the income stream through its spending than it is pulling out through taxes. If there is a surplus, the effect is the opposite, namely, tending toward contraction or deflation—more money is being pulled out of the income stream than is being put in.

The foregoing analysis is correct as far as it goes, but the fact that at any particular time the federal budget is in either deficit or surplus does not tell us whether or not the government is pursuing an active fiscal policy. In other words, a deficit or surplus may be a wholly *passive* development, in that it comes about because of changes in the general level of economic activity, not because the government is trying through spending or tax changes to influence the level of economic activity. The growing deficits that the Reagan administration wrestled with in the winter and spring of 1982 are a prime example. They came about because the recession caused spending to rise (more unemployment and welfare payments) and tax revenues to fall. The deficit was not deliberately engineered as a way to stimulate the economy.

The Full (High)-Employment Budget

In the early 1960s a technique emerged for determining whether or not a particular surplus or deficit was the result of deliberate policy actions—whether, in other words, the surplus or deficit was the consequence of an *active* fiscal policy. This technique led to the concept of the full-employment (or high-employment) budget, an idea developed for policy purposes in the early days of the Kennedy administration. The man most responsible for this development is Walter Heller, currently Professor of Economics at the University of Minnesota and a former chairman of the Council of Economic Advisers under President Kennedy. In explaining how the administration developed this concept, Heller said:

> As part of the reshaping of stabilization policy, then, our fiscal policy targets have been recast in terms of "full" or "high" employment levels of output, specifically the level of GNP associated with a 4-percent rate of unemployment. *So the target is no longer budget balance every year or over the cycle* [italics added], but balance . . . at full employment. And in modern stabilization policy . . . even this target does not remain fixed.[25]

Simply put, the full (or high)-employment budget does not measure the actual budget surplus or deficit in any single year; rather, it is a measure of the surplus or deficit that would exist *if* the economy were actually operating at a full employment level. This will give a much bet-

---

25. Walter W. Heller, *New Dimensions of Political Economy* (New York: Norton, 1967), p. 66. What Heller meant by the full employment target not being fixed was that the economy would grow over time, since a growing labor force and a rising productivity for the labor force would increase continuously the output level associated with a 4 percent unemployment rate.

ter indication of the active fiscal influence of a particular budget. For example, if the calculations show that at full employment a proposed budget will be in deficit, this is a clear indication that the budget will be expansionary (or inflationary). Note that deficit or surplus figures in the full (or high)-employment budget are hypothetical, not realized. They are the deficit or surplus figures that will be realized only if the economy reaches the full-employment level. Measuring the full (or high)-employment deficit or surplus requires, first, estimating the economy's full-employment output potential (see Chapter 3) and, second, determining the amount of revenue the federal tax system will generate at this level of output, as well as the amount of expenditures forthcoming. The basic rationale for this budget concept is that the true inflationary or deflationary potential of any proposed federal budget is apparent only when the economy is at full employment. Figure 7–8 illustrates the concept of the full (or high)-employment budget.

In the figure, real output as measured by net national product is shown on the horizontal axis and possible budget deficits or surpluses are shown in dollar amounts on the vertical axis. Two schedules are shown in the figure, one labeled Budget "A" and the other Budget "B." These schedules are obtained by subtracting actual expenditures for goods and service by the federal goverment $(G*)$ at various output levels from the net

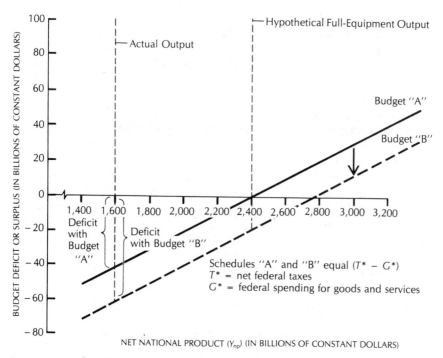

NET NATIONAL PRODUCT (Y_{np}) (IN BILLIONS OF CONSTANT DOLLARS)

FIGURE 7–8.   The Full (or High)-Employment Budget Concept

taxes *(T*)* appropriate to each income level. The schedules slope upward to the right because, with a fixed level of expenditures and a fixed rate structure for the federal government, net taxes *(T*)* will automatically rise as output rises, thus leading to a surplus (or a smaller deficit) at higher levels of income and the reverse at lower levels of income. In the figure the schedule labeled Budget "A" represents a combination of taxes and expenditures designed to balance at the full-employment output of $2,400 billion. If the actual output falls below the full-employment level, the budget will be in deficit, but the deficit will be of a *passive* nature, induced by the failure of the economy to attain full employment. In the figure actual output is shown at $1,600 billion, the result being a deficit of $40 billion. This will be the measured budget deficit found in the national income accounts. What the schedule labeled Budget "B" represents is a deliberately engineered full-employment deficit, the purpose of which is to provide the economy with a strong fiscal stimulus. The schedule will shift down either because expenditures are increased with no change in taxes or because taxes are reduced with no change in expenditures. In either case the effect will be to create a deficit under full (or high)-employment conditions, a development that sends a clear signal to policy-makers that fiscal policy has turned *active*. It should be noted parenthetically that the level labled "Hypothetical Full-Employment Output" in the figure is not fixed. As the economy grows, this will shift upward—to the right on the graph—and as this happens Budget "A" will generate automatically a surplus. We shall return to this possibility later (see Chapter 16).

Table 7–9 compares actual and full-employment spending, taxes, and deficits (there were no surpluses during these years) from 1970 to 1980. The amounts in the table illustrate clearly the differences between a budget deficit that is passive and one that results from an active fiscal policy. Examine, for example, what happened between 1972 and 1975, keeping in mind that 1974 and 1975 were recession years. Between 1973 and 1975 the actual budget deficit rose sharply, reaching $69.3 billion in 1975, a figure which was the largest on record until the deficits of the Reagan administration more recently. The full-employment deficit, however, was in decline between 1972 and 1974, a fact that reflects the restrictiveness of actual budget policy during these years. In these years the change in the budget deficit (or surplus) position as recorded in the last column of the table gives a clue to the direction that fiscal policy is moving. For the full-employment figures, the swing from a minus $12.3 billion in the column in 1972 to a positive $10.6 billion in 1974 reflects a shift from an expansive to a restrictive stance as far as the federal budget is concerned. The $69.3-billion actual deficit recorded in 1975 is of a passive character, since it came about because federal spending rose and taxes fell as a result of the recession.

The direction of change recorded in the last column of the full-employment portion of the table tells us whether or not the budget is

TABLE 7–9. Actual and Full-Employment Federal Government Receipts and
Expenditures: 1970–80 (billions of current dollars)

Calendar Year	Receipts	Expenditures	Surplus or Deficit (−) Amount	Surplus or Deficit (−) Change
Actual				
1970	$192.1	$204.2	$ − 12.1	$ − 20.6
1971	198.6	220.6	− 22.0	− 9.9
1972	227.5	244.7	− 17.3	4.7
1973	258.6	264.2	− 5.6	11.7
1974	287.8	299.3	− 11.5	− 5.9
1975	287.3	356.6	− 69.3	− 57.8
1976	331.8	384.8	− 53.1	16.2
1977	375.1	421.5	− 46.4	6.7
1978	431.5	460.7	− 29.2	17.2
1979	494.4	509.2	− 14.8	14.4
1980	538.9	601.2	− 62.3	− 47.5
Full-Employment				
1970	201.0	203.6	− 2.6	6.3
1971	210.0	219.1	− 9.2	− 6.6
1972	222.1	243.6	− 21.5	− 12.3
1973	252.7	264.0	− 11.3	10.2
1974	296.9	297.6	− 0.7	10.6
1975	315.8	344.9	− 29.1	− 28.4
1976	354.7	374.8	− 20.1	9.0
1977	390.7	413.8	− 23.1	− 3.0
1978	441.1	456.8	− 15.7	7.4
1979	504.2	506.5	− 2.2	13.5
1980	573.2	591.6	− 18.3	− 16.1

SOURCE: *Economic Report of the President,* 1977, 1981.
Note: Detail may not add to totals because of rounding.

becoming more or less restrictive (or expansionary). Positive values in
this column, especially for the full (or high)-employment budget, mean
that the deficit is declining or the surplus (if one exists) is increasing
under full-employment conditions. When this happens the budget is restrictive. We can easily trace, for example, the policy changes of the Carter
administration by looking at these data. In 1977, President Carter's first
year in office, the administration pursued a mild expansionary policy,
since they believed that their primary objective ought to be to get the
unemployment rate down. Thus, there was a slight increase ($3.0 billion)
in the full-employment deficit in this year. Thereafter, and as inflation
began to supercede unemployment as an administration priority, the
budget became more restrictive. Between 1977 and 1979, the full-
employment deficit dropped from $23.1 to $2.2 billion, an exceedingly

sharp shift from an expansionary to a restrictive budget stance. As with the Ford administration in 1974, this shift in budgetary policy by the Carter administration was a factor in the recession of 1980. The enormous jump in the actual deficit between 1979 and 1980 (from $14.8 to $62.3 billion) again reflects a *passive* budgetary change, brought on by the recession.

Built-in Stabilizers

The foregoing discussion pertains primarily to recent experience with *deliberate* changes in taxes as a technique for economic management by the federal government. But there is another way in which both taxes and transfer payments may play an important role in the functioning of the economy: Both taxes and transfer payments may vary (or change) as a consequence of changes in the income level. Changes of this type are the basis for *passive* budgetary shifts, but they are also the basis for *built-in stabilizers*, also called automatic fiscal stabilizers. The term *stabilizers* is used because these features of the economic system operate in a manner that counteracts fluctuations in economic activity. They are described as built-in because they come into play automatically as the income level changes. These built-in stabilizers do not depend, in other words, upon discretionary action by the monetary and fiscal authorities.

To illustrate, taxes may act as a stabilizing influence upon the economic system if the tax structure is designed so that the amount of taxes collected by the government rises with an increase in the net national product. If this is the case the effect will be to lessen the expansion in disposable income that accompanies any autonomous shift in the aggregate demand function. From a stabilizing point of view the consequence of this will be a less rapid rise in induced consumption spending than would be the case in the absence of this tax system. If the tax system is constructed so that the percentage of income going to taxes increases with an increase in net national product, the stabilizing impact will be even greater. This situation will prevail if the rate structure for the tax system is progressive, because then the effective rate at which income is taxed increases as the level of income increases. In terms of our analysis (see p. 238) such a system is one in which the value of the net marginal propensity to tax is an increasing function of the income level. Stabilizing effects of a reverse character come into play when the income level declines. The fiscal system, in short, operates in a countercyclical or stabilizing fashion if its overall effect is to insulate to a degree disposable income from changes in the net national product.

The foregoing analysis is predicated on prices being reasonably stable, because sharp and continued inflation can cause the stabilizers to work in a perverse fashion. One of the unhappy consequences of the serious inflation the nation experienced in the 1970s (annual rates from 3.3% to double-digit levels) was to thrust many families into a higher bracket, even though their money incomes were not rising any faster than the price level. Thus, the combination of inflation and a progressive tax structure brought them an actual decline in *real* income, not just a slowing down in the rate at which their income was rising. In both 1974 and 1980 *real* per capita disposable income actually declined, a factor that contributed to the recession in both these years. As mentioned in Table 7–8 (p. 235), the movement of a taxpayer into a higher tax bracket solely because of income gains which merely keep pace with inflation is known as "bracket creep." The purpose of indexing the tax system is to end such a phenomenon.

The above discussion of built-in stabilizers has concentrated on taxes, but the reader should be aware that various forms of transfer expenditures affect the economy in a similar countercyclical fashion. If transfer payments are to have a stabilizing effect, they must decrease in absolute amount when the net national product (or national income) increases and increase when the reverse happens. Transfers in the form of unemployment compensation payments provide a good example of this kind of behavior. When output and employment are falling, payments to the unemployed automatically increase, thus insulating disposable income to a degree from a decline in earned income. When unemployment declines with a recovery from a recession or depression, transfer payments fall off and, thus, disposable income does not rise as rapidly as would be the case otherwise.

How effective are the built-in stabilizers? It is instructive to look at some figures from four recent recessions, 1969–70, 1974–75, 1980, and 1982. These are given in Table 7–10, which shows the percentage changes in both federal tax receipts and transfers to persons for the period 1968 through 1982. They are derived from current dollar figures, not data corrected for changes in the price level. According to the theoretical propositions set forth in this chapter, we should expect the rate of tax collections to fall off and the rate of transfer outlays to rise during a recession. This is exactly what happened. There was a mild recession in 1969–70 (unemployment rose to 4.9 percent of the labor force in 1970 as compared to 3.6 percent in 1968), a sharp recession in 1974–75 (when unemployment hit 8.9 percent), another sharp but short recession in 1980, and a severe recession in 1982. In the latter year, unemployment was 9.7 percent of the civilian labor force. In the 1970 and 1974 recessions federal revenues actually declined, while in 1980 and 1982 their rate of increase fell off sharply. These figures on tax collections also reflect the phenomenon of "bracket creep," the reason being that in 1974–75 and 1980 the inflation rate was much higher than in 1970. In 1980 in particular a high inflation rate helped sustain growth in federal tax revenue, even though the rate of growth fell off from prior years. The data in the table also show clearly that transfer expenditures behaved in the expected countercyclical fashion, rising sharply during the recession years and falling back to more moderate rates of gain in the nonreces-

TABLE 7–10.   Changes in Federal Tax Receipts and
Transfer Payments to Persons: 1968–82
(annual percentage change)

Year	Tax Receipts	Transfers to Persons
1968	15.8%	14.7%
1969	12.9	10.0 ⎫ Recession
1970	−2.5	21.1 ⎭
1971	3.5	18.6
1972	14.6	10.7
1973	13.7	15.9
1974	11.3	22.7 ⎫ Recession
1975	−0.2	27.8 ⎭
1976	15.5	8.5
1977	13.1	6.8
1978	15.0	7.2
1979	14.6	12.7
1980	9.4	19.5 Recession
1981	15.6	14.0
1982	0.5	12.6 Recession

SOURCE: *Economic Report of the President,* 1983.

sion years. For the nonrecession years shown in the table, tax receipts grew at an annual average rate of 13.4 percent and transfers at an annual average rate of 11.0 percent. These averages should be compared to the figures for the recession years, both for taxes and transfers.

The behavior of the built-in stabilizers has been analyzed by many economists. One study of the experience of the 1950s concluded as follows:

> On the average a fall in national income has led to a rise in transfer payments and a fall in tax collections, totaling a swing of approximately 50 percent of the decline in national income. During upswings the automatic stabilizers have exhibited a swing to increases in national income of slightly less than 30 percent on the average. Thus, assuming a $10 billion increase in national income, disposable income will rise by $2.8 billion less than it would have had automatic stabilization been inoperative. Had national income fallen by $10 billion, the induced drop in disposable income would have been $5.1 billion less as a consequence of the presence of automatic stabilizers.[26]

Another study estimated the extent to which the stabilizers reduced the potential change in income during three recessions and three expansions. In this instance it found that the stabilizers are capable of reducing

26. M. O. Clement, "The Quantitative Impact of Automatic Stabilizers," *Review of Econommcs and Statistics,* February 1960, p. 60.

declines in the national income by about 50 percent, if the values for the marginal propensity to consume out of disposable income and the marginal propensity to invest out of retained corporate earnings are close to 0.9 and 0.5, respectively. (Note that the higher the value of the marginal propensity to consume out of disposable income, the greater is the impact of transfer expenditures in maintaining disposable income in the face of a decline in the national income.) It was also found that during expansions the stabilizers would prevent over 40 percent of the potential increase in income if the values for the marginal propensity to consume out of disposable income and the marginal propensity to invest out of retained corporate earnings were as above and, furthermore, if government spending upon goods and services remained unchanged.[27]

In 1963 the Council of Economic Advisers had the following comments about built-in stabilizers:

> Thus the tax-and-transfer response narrows fluctuations in income caused by irregularities in the strength of demand. The sharper the response of tax collections to changes in GNP, the stronger the stabilization effect. Although the tax-and-transfer response cannot prevent or reverse a movement in GNP, it can and does limit the extent of cumulative expansions and contractions. At least with respect to contractions, this is clearly an important service to the economy.
>
> Automatic fiscal stabilizers have made a major contribution in limiting the length and severity of postwar recessions. Each of the four postwar recessions—1948–49, 1953–54, 1957–58, and 1960–61—has been both short and mild.[28]

Few economists would argue that the stabilizers by themselves can smooth out fluctuations in income and employment in the complex economy characteristic of a modern nation, but most would probably agree that they are a vital and effective complement to discretionary action. Perhaps the best evidence in support of this is the fact that only once (1949) during the whole post–World War II period did disposable income decline, and even then the amount of the decline was negligible. Without the impact of built-in stabilizers it is unlikely that the economy could have gone this long without a major depression.

The Balanced Budget Thesis

Discussion of the impact of government expenditures, taxes, deficits, and surpluses on the level of output and employment would not be complete without consideration of a special case in which an increase (or decrease) in government expenditures for goods and services is matched

27. Peter Eilbott, "The Effectiveness of Automatic Stabilizers," *American Economic Review,* June 1966, p. 463. See also George E. Rejda, "Unemployment Insurance as an Automatic Stabilizer," *Journal of Risk and Insurance,* June 1966, pp. 195–208.
28. *Economic Report of the President* (Washington, D.C.: U.S. Government Printing Office, 1963), p. 67.

by an equal increase (or decrease) in taxes. This is a special situation because, contrary to what one might think at first glance, a tax-financed increase in such expenditures *may* be expansionary. This possibility has come to be known as the *balanced budget thesis*. It is derived from the fact that the multiplier effect associated with changes in both taxes and transfers is normally smaller than the multiplier effect associated with changes in government expenditures for goods and services.

To illustrate the nature of this thesis, let us refer once again to the data of Table 7–3. We made the assumption there that government exhaustive expenditures had increased by $80 billion. Let us now assume further that taxes are simultaneously increased by an equal amount so that the new and higher level of government expenditures can be financed. Our problem is to determine how the combined impact of the increase in both government expenditures and taxes will affect the income level. Contrary to what might be assumed at first, a change of this type is not neutral in its effects on the income level.

The effect of simultaneous change in both government expenditures and taxes depends upon the combined impact of the increase in government expenditures and the increase in taxes upon the aggregate demand function. In our example let us assume, as earlier, that the marginal propensity to consume out of disposable income, a, is 0.5; the marginal propensity to invest, b, is 0.1; and the marginal propensity to tax, t, is 0.2. The value of the effective multiplier, according to Equation (7–25), is thus 2. The shift in the aggregate demand function will equal the increase in government expenditure, ΔG, less the autonomous shift downward in the consumption function which results from the tax increase. This latter shift is designated as ΔC_0. In algebraic terms we have

$$\Delta D = \Delta G - \Delta C_0. \qquad (7\text{--}26)$$

But ΔC_0 depends upon the value of the marginal propensity to consume (out of disposable income) and the change in disposable income. The latter is the same as the increase in taxes. Thus, we have

$$\Delta C_0 = a\Delta Y_d = -a\Delta TX.$$

Given a value of 0.5 for a, we find that ΔC_0 is equal to minus $40 billion. The combined effect of the increase in government purchases of goods and services and the increase in taxes will be to shift the aggregate demand function upward by $40 billion. When the effective multiplier of 2 is applied against this increment in aggregate demand, the final change in the net national product is $80 billion, which is just equal to the amount by which government expenditures for goods and services increased. The significant point to note is that the expansion of these expenditures, even though accompanied by an equal increase in taxes—the balanced budget thesis—was not neutral with respect to its impact upon the output level. In other words, an expansion of government purchases of goods and services under balanced budget conditions may cause a rise in the output level; if the expansion were to occur with full-employment conditions the result would be a significant increase in pressure on the price level.

In the foregoing example the student will note that the net national product increased by an amount just equal to the increase in government expenditures, namely, $80 billion. If the marginal propensity to tax, t, were zero rather than 0.2, the increase in the net national product would have been $100 billion rather than $440 billion. On the other hand, if the value of the marginal propensity to tax is greater than 0.2 the increase in the net national product will be less than $80 billion, but will still be greater than zero. It would be a useful exercise to compute, assuming different values for the marginal propensity to consume out of a disposable income, a, how large a tax increase would have to be to prevent any increase in the net national product, given an $80 billion increase in government outlays. The student should note carefully, too, that the shift in the aggregate demand function, given the amount of the tax increase, is governed by the value of the marginal propensity to consume out of disposable income, whereas the size of the ultimate change in the net national product, given both the increase in taxes and the value of a, depends upon the value of the marginal propensity to tax, t.

The Role of Finance

In our earlier discussions in this chapter of the impact upon output and employment of an increase in government expenditures (or the reverse) or a decrease in taxes, questions pertaining to how the government finances added expenditures or how it responds to a revenue loss following a tax cut were deferred. Now it is appropriate to deal with these questions. As we have just seen, if government expenditures are increased and the added expenditures are financed by an equal increase in taxes, there will be some impact on output and employment, but the effect will be minimal. Much the same will be true if a tax cut is accompanied by an equal reduction in government expenditures, leaving the overall budget position of the government unchanged.

Finance enters the picture when the government either increases its expenditures without an offsetting tax increase or reduces taxes without cutting back on its outlays. Then a deficit is created, or an existing deficit is enlarged. In either event the government will have to resort to more borrowing—the deficit must be financed. This is the crucial point, for the ultimate impact of the fiscal action—increasing government expenditures or cutting taxes—will depend on how the deficit is financed.

Assuming that the government will not simply resort to the printing press to finance its deficit, it has basically two choices: (1) It can borrow from the public (this is done by selling government bonds to the public)[29] or (2) it can borrow directly from the central bank (the Federal Reserve System in the United States). We shall examine each of these alternatives.

Borrowing and the Crowding-Out Phenomenon

When the government obtains funds by borrowing directly from the public, the effect may be to lessen the stimulative impact of either an increase in spending or a reduction in taxes. This may happen either because households and business firms decrease some of their spending for goods and services in order to buy government bonds—the bonds are not purchased at the expense of either household or business saving—or because increased demand by government for credit causes interest rates to rise. This would lead to a reduction in private borrowing with a subsequent decline in private spending. It is possible in principle that private spending would fall sufficiently to nullify wholly the economic impact of more public spending or a tax cut.

If this happens, then the economy will have experienced the phenomenon known as *crowding out*. This term refers to the failure of any expansionary fiscal action by government (spending increases or tax cuts) to stimulate overall the level of economic activity. The "crowding-out" thesis originated with a paper published in 1968 by the Federal Reserve Bank of St. Louis.[30] Essentially, the thesis argues that, overall, the level of aggregate demand remains unchanged, the reason being that the stimulus coming from government action (more spending or a tax cut) will be offset by unplanned reductions in private spending elsewhere in the economy. As suggested above, the latter may result from higher interest rates or a decrease in spending slowing down the sale of bonds to the public. In either case, the expansionary effects are nullified. Since it was first formulated about a decade ago, the "crowding-out" thesis has generated considerable controversy among economic theorists, plus no small amount of empirical research, but no agreement has been reached on either the magnitude or certainty of this effect.[31]

Monetizing the Debt

A different picture emerges if the government chooses to finance its deficit by borrowing from the central bank (the Federal Reserve System). Technically, the U.S. government is limited by law in the amount the treasury can borrow directly from the Federal Reserve—the limit is $5

---

29. The term "public" includes banks, insurance companies, and other firms, as well as persons.
30. See "Crowding Out and Its Critics," *Review,* Federal Reserve Bank of St. Louis, December 1975.
31. For full details on the development and course of the controversies surrounding the "crowding-out" effect see the Federal Reserve Bank of St. Louis article just cited.

billion. But there is a way around this because there is no limit on the amount of Treasury debt (bills and bonds) that the Federal Reserve can buy in the open market for government securities. When the Federal Reserve purchases treasury obligations in the open market this, of course, increases the supply of money and credit. In effect, the Federal Reserve is indirectly financing the government's deficit through an expansion of the money supply. If the deficit is financed in this fashion—described as "monetizing" a part of the government's debt—there will not be the same pressure on interest rates as occurs when the government borrows directly from the public. In fact, the added supply of money and credit could cause lower rates, thus leading to an increase in private spending. The upshot of all this is that private spending is much less likely to be curtailed if this is the route chosen by the government for the financing of its deficit.

Budget Surpluses

To this point the discussion has centered on the financing problems associated with a deficit that results from either increased public expenditures or a tax cut. But, as the analysis undertaken earlier in this chapter suggests, fiscal action may move in either direction. That is, the government also may reduce its expenditures or increase its taxes. If expenditures are reduced without a corresponding cut in taxes, or taxes increased without an increase in expenditures, the government will have a surplus.[32] A surplus obviously does not pose a financing problem, as does a deficit, but it may have consequences for the general level of economic activity. Other things being equal, a surplus tends to be deflationary, the reason being that its existence means the government through taxes is taking more out of the income stream than it is putting back in through expenditures. But the impact of the surplus on aggregate demand will depend on the disposition the government makes of its surplus.

In principle, two options are available to the government. First, it may elect to use the surplus to retire debt held by the public. If it does this, it is, in effect, transferring the surplus revenues received to the public, which may or may not spend them. If the funds received by the public when debt is retired are spent, then the deflationary impact of the government's surplus is reduced. It is not too likely that this will happen, however, as many of the holders of government obligations are in the upper-income brackets; they will probably use the checks they receive from the government to purchase other securities. The alternative to debt retirement is for the government simply to continue to hold the surplus funds idle; then there cannot be any offsetting private expenditures at all. This is possible in principle, but the chances that it would actually happen are exceedingly remote.

32. Discussion of the economic effects of a budget surplus may seem academic, as there have been only four years since 1960 when the federal government had a surplus. These years were 1960, 1963, 1965, and 1969.

Appendix

Transfers, Taxes, and the Multiplier: An Alternative Treatment

Some writers prefer to treat the multiplier effects associated with both transfer payments and taxes in a different fashion. Rather than develop, as done in the text of this chapter, a general multiplier which can be applied against a shift in the aggregate demand function, and which, too, embodies the effect of both transfers and taxes, they prefer to speak of a transfer or tax multiplier as such. This multiplier coefficient, when multiplied by the change in either transfer payment or taxes, yields the resulting change in income (net national product). It should be understood clearly that in no sense does this approach involve a different type of multiplier than discussed to this point; rather, it is simply a different way of approaching the multiplier effects associated with either transfers or taxes. To illustrate this we shall derive algebraically a transfer expenditure multiplier. A tax multiplier could be derived in identical fashion, except that its value would be negative.

(1) $k_{tr} = \dfrac{\Delta Y_{np}}{\Delta TR} =$ a formal definition of the transfer multiplier

(2) $\Delta Y_{np} = \Delta C_0 + \Delta C_i + \Delta I$ (The increase in the net national product will be equal to the increase in autonomous consumption, ΔC_0, plus the induced changes in consumption and investment. This equation is an identity.)

(3) $\Delta C_0 = a \Delta TR$ (The increase in autonomous consumption—i.e., the shift in the consumption function—depends upon the increase in transfers and the value of the marginal propensity to consume out of disposable income, a.)

(4) $\Delta Y_{np} = a \Delta TR + \Delta C_i + \Delta I$ (By substitution.)

(5) $a \Delta TR = \Delta Y_{np} - \Delta C_i - \Delta I$ [From (4) above.]

(6) $\Delta TR = \dfrac{\Delta Y_{np} - \Delta C_i - \Delta I}{a}$ [From (5) above.]

(7) $k_{tr} = \dfrac{\Delta Y_{np}}{(\Delta Y_{np} - \Delta C_i - \Delta I)/a} = \dfrac{a \Delta Y_{np}}{\Delta Y_{np} - \Delta C_i - \Delta I}$

(8) $k_{tr} = \dfrac{a}{1 - \dfrac{\Delta C_i}{\Delta Y_{np}} - \dfrac{\Delta I}{\Delta Y_{np}}} = \dfrac{a}{1 - a' - b}$

$\dfrac{\Delta C_i}{\Delta Y_{np}} = a' =$ the marginal propensity to consume out of net national product

(9) $k_{tr} = \dfrac{a}{1 - a + at - b}$ since $a' = (a - at)$

Since a (the marginal propensity to consume out of disposable income) is normally less than unity, this formula for the transfer multiplier means that its numerical value will be smaller than the effective multiplier developed in the text. The tax multiplier can be derived in the same fashion, but its value will be negative.

Formal proof that $(a - at) = a'$, *the marginal propensity to consume out of net national product*

(1) $a = \dfrac{\Delta C}{\Delta Y_d}$ = the marginal propensity to consume out of disposable income

(2) $a' = \dfrac{\Delta C}{\Delta Y_{np}}$ = the marginal propensity to consume out of net national product

(3) $t = \dfrac{\Delta T}{\Delta Y_{np}}$ = the net marginal propensity to tax out of net national product

(4) $(1 - t)\dfrac{\Delta Y_d}{\Delta Y_{np}}$ = the net marginal rate of retention of income. This is derived as follows:

   (a) $Y_{np} = Y_d + T$

   (b) $\Delta Y_{np} = \Delta Y_d + \Delta T$

   (c) $1 = \dfrac{\Delta Y_d}{\Delta Y_{np}} + \dfrac{\Delta T}{\Delta Y_{np}}$ Divide both sides of (b) by ΔY_{np}.

   (d) $\dfrac{\Delta Y_d}{\Delta Y_{np}} = 1 - \dfrac{\Delta T}{\Delta Y_{np}} = (1 - t)$

(5) $(1 - t) \times a = \dfrac{\Delta C}{\Delta Y_{np}} = a'$ This is derived as follows:

   (a) $\dfrac{\Delta Y_d}{\Delta Y_{np}} \times \dfrac{\Delta C}{\Delta Y_d} = \dfrac{\Delta C}{\Delta Y_{np}} = a'$ (By substitution.)

   (b) Therefore: $a' = a(1 - t) = (a - at)$

Algebraic determination of the equilibrium income level using the effective multiplier

(1) $Y_{np} = C + I + G$ = the basic identity

(2) $C = C'_0 + a'Y_{np}$ = the consumption function

(3) $I = I'_0 + bY_{np}$ = the investment function

(4) $Y_{np} = (C'_0 + I'_0 + a'Y_{np} + bY_{np} + G)$ [Substitution of (2) and (3) into (1).]

(5) $Y_{np} - a'Y_{np} - bY_{np} = (C'_0 + I'_0 + G)$

(6) $Y_{np}(1 - a' - b) = (C'_0 + I'_0 + G)$

(7) $Y_{np} = \dfrac{1}{(1 - a' - b)} \times (C'_0 + I'_0 + G)$

(8) $Y_{np} = \dfrac{1}{1 - a + at - b} \times (C'_0 + I'_0 + G)$

(9) $Y_{np} = k'(C'_0 + I'_0 + G)$

Summary

1. Government expenditures for goods and services are a major element in the aggregate demand function. As with investment expenditure, there is a multiplier effect associated with changes in government spending for goods and services.

2. Transfer expenditures are basically different from the purchase of goods and services by government because they do not enter directly into aggregate demand. They do so indirectly by their effect upon disposable income.

3. The multiplier effect associated with changes in transfer expenditures is smaller than the multiplier associated with the direct purchase of goods and services by government. This is because changes in transfer expenditures first affect disposable income and only then is total spending affected through the consumption function.

4. Taxes affect the income level in the same manner as do transfers, except in the opposite direction. They affect disposable income first and then indirectly affect consumption. As with transfers, there is a multiplier effect smaller than the multiplier effect associated with a change in government spending for goods and services.

5. The full (high)-employment budget calculates what the federal surplus or deficit would be under full (or high)-employment conditions; it emerged in the 1960s as an important analytical tool for policy-makers. It has been used in varying degrees by recent administrations, depending in part on their activist propensities.

6. Built-in stabilizers are the features of the tax and transfer structure of the federal government that come into play automatically during cyclical swings and tend to either dampen down or stimulate the economy, depending upon the stage of the business cycle in which the economy finds itself.

7. The balanced budget thesis shows how a balanced budget may be expansionary because of the fact that expenditure for goods and services have a greater direct effect upon aggregate demand than do taxes.

8. The financing of government expenditures plays an important role in the impact of the government's actions on the economy's performance. Under some circumstances, spending financed by borrowing may "crowd out" private borrowing, and thus be less expansionary than expected.

8

International Transactions

Up to this point in our analysis we have assumed a "closed" economy, an economy that does not have any economic transactions with other nations. In this chapter we shall drop this assumption and undertake an analysis of the manner in which the international economic transactions of a nation interact with income and employment levels in the domestic economy. This pertains to an "open" economy. Specifically, we shall examine, first, how changes in the international economic position of a nation affect its internal economy and, second, how internal economic changes may affect the nation's international economic position. Our approach will be primarily in terms of relationships existing between international economic transactions and the aggregate demand function. Before we begin, however, it is necessary to sketch out the essential elements that enter into a nation's international transactions and how they are measured.

The Nature of a Nation's Foreign Balance

A nation's international economic balance involves all of the economic transactions that residents of the nation enter into with residents of all other nations during some specific period of time. The most important tool for analysis of the internal economic position of a nation is the balance-of-payments statement.[1] This accounting statement records (in

1. For the purpose of balance-of-payments accounting the word "residents" is interpreted to mean not only physical persons, but also business firms, governments, and international agencies. Persons are considered residents of the country in which they normally reside. Residents are not necessarily or always citizens. In the United States balance-of-payments statistics are compiled by the Department of Commerce.

principle) all of the economic transactions that residents of one country make with residents of foreign countries during a given period of time, normally the calendar year. Since an economic transaction generally consists of a payment or a receipt in exchange for a good, service, or some type of financial asset, the balance-of-payments statement constitutes a record of payments made by residents of a country to foreigners and payments made by foreigners to residents of the country in question.

In balance-of-payments accounting practice, transactions that require foreigners to make payments to residents of the domestic economy or, alternatively, provide residents of the domestic economy with the means to make payments to foreigners are treated as *credit* entries in the balance-of-payments statement. Thus, an export of merchandise by an American firm to the United Kingdom and a loan extended by a British bank to American residents would be credit entries in the American balance-of-payments statement. On the other hand, transactions that require residents of the domestic economy to make payments to foreigners or, alternatively, provide foreigners with the means to make payments to residents of the domestic economy are treated as *debit* entries in the balance-of-payments statement. Imports and loans extended to foreigners would fall into the category of debit transactions in the balance-of-payments statement of the domestic economy.[2] Balance-of-payments accounting is often confusing and complex. However, if the following key rule is kept in mind, it will be easier to understand:

A credit (+) is any transaction that results in a receipt from residents in the rest of the world (foreign residents) and a debit (−) is any transaction that requires a payment be made to residents in the rest of the world.

The Structure of the Balance-of-Payments Statement

A nation's balance of international payments statement normally consists of several component parts, sometimes called accounts. There are basically two major "accounts" plus one or more measures of the nation's external balance. The latter vary with individual governments and the particular national purposes that balance-of-payments statements may be designed to serve. In the United States the most important parts of our balance-of-payments statement consist of the *current* account, the *capital* account, and the *balance of official reserve transactions* segment of the statement. Table 8–1 contains balance-of-payments data for the United States in 1982. We shall interpret some of these data following discussions of the major parts of the balance-of-payments statement.

2. For a more extended discussion of the mechanics of balance-of-payments accounting see Peter H. Lindert and Charles P. Kindleberger, *International Economics* (Homewood, Ill.: Richard D. Irwin, Inc., 1982), Chaps. 13, 14.

The Current Account

The current account section of the balance of payments records all *current* transactions, which are transactions that involve either the export or import of goods (i.e., merchandise) and services. Under "services" are grouped income from transportation, banking, and insurance; income in the form of interest and dividends from various financial assets; and expenditures by tourists. Transactions involving services are sometimes described as *invisible* items, whereas transactions in goods or merchandise are classified as *visible* items. In general, goods and services exported by the domestic economy are a part of the national output, but goods and services imported constitute a form of dispostion of the national income. There are exceptions to this principle, but they are for the most part of minor significance. The current account section also includes unilateral (one-way) transfers by private individuals and governments (see below).

The difference between the export (or credit) items and the import (or debit) items in the current account represents its net balance. If the credit transactions exceed the debit transactions, it is customary to describe the current account balance as *active*. On the other hand, an excess of debit over credit transactions is usually spoken of as a *passive* balance on the current account. In Chapter 2 we pointed out that the net foreign investment component of the national output (GNP) can be *approximately* defined as the net difference between a nation's exports of goods and services and its imports of goods and services, because any excess of receipts from exports over payments for imports—or vice versa—reflects a net change in the international asset position of the nation concerned. The word "approximately" is emphasized because the Department of Commerce defines net foreign investment as the difference between exports and imports *plus* transfer payments to foreign residents.

The current account has special significance for the purposes of this text. This is because the transactions recorded in this portion of the balance-of-payments statement are linked closely to the determination of the national output and the employment level. Exports of goods and services enter directly into the aggregate demand schedule and hence become one of the determinants of output in an open economy. Imports of goods and services are, on the other hand, a form of disposition of the national income, analogous in their economic effects to saving and transfers.

Special mention needs to be made of one type of transaction normally found in the current account. This is the category of "unilateral transfers." Included in this category are all transfers, gifts, or donations, both public and private, made either by U.S. residents to the rest of the world or by foreign residents to the United States. The United States, for example, gives military and economic aid to some foreign nations. This is a unilateral transfer (government) from this country to the rest of the world. In the current account, the amount of such a transfer in any one year would be recorded as a debit (−) item, and the goods or services that were exported because such a transfer was made would be recorded as a credit (+) item. The latter presumes that the proceeds of the transfer were spent by the recipient country.

The Capital Account

The capital account represents the financial counterpart of transactions involving currently produced goods and services that are recorded in the current account. Let us assume, for example, that a nation has in the current income period an excess of exports (of goods and services) over imports. Since exports generate payment claims against domestic residents, it can readily be seen that the export surplus increases the claims of the domestic economy against the rest of the world. An import surplus would, of course, have just the opposite effect. Within the context of the current income period, settlement of the net export surplus can be effected in a number of ways. Foreigners, for example, may borrow the needed funds from residents of the domestic economy. If this is done, there will be a net increase in the foreign claims or internationally held assets of residents of the domestic economy. A transaction of this type is called a *capital export,* and in the balance-of-payments statement of the domestic economy it is recorded as a debit item since it provides foreign residents with the means to make payments to residents of the domestic economy. Alternatively, it is possible that foreign residents may finance the aforementioned export surplus of the domestic economy by drawing down bank balances they may hold in the banks of the domestic economy. If this is done, it means there has been a *net decrease* in the liabilities owed by domestic residents to foreign residents because a bank deposit is a liability of the bank.

The capital account section of the balance-of-payments statement basically reflects the net change during the accounting period in the claims and liabilities (real and financial) of the domestic economy *vis-à-vis* the rest of the world. But this net change can take the form of capital export, an increase in claims (or decrease in the liabilities) of domestic residents relative to foreign residents; conversely, it can take the form of a capital import, a decrease in the claims (or increase in the liabilities) of domestic residents relative to foreign residents.

International Equilibrium and the Balance of Payments

As an accounting instrument, the balance-of-payments statement must necessarily be in balance; for every credit entry there has to be an offsetting debit entry. But this does not mean that an *equilibrium* exists with respect to a nation's international economic position. Although there is no clear-cut and universally accepted method of determining economic equilibrium with respect to a nation's international payments position, the state of a nation's international "reserves" is a good indication of its international economic situation. For the nation, international reserves consist primarily of gold, national currencies widely accepted as money in international transactions (the U.S. dollar has been such a currency throughout most of the post–World War II period), special drawing rights, and other borrowing rights in the International Monetary Funds.[3] An important measure of the international economic position of the United States is the *balance of official reserve transactions,* the third important component in the nation's balance of international payments structure. This indicates the net change in the country's international reserves, including its holdings of gold, foreign currencies, and borrowing rights in the International Monetary Fund.

The common-sense meaning of an international equilibrium for a nation is that it is "paying its way" internationally, which is to say that it is obtaining sufficient foreign exchange on a sustainable basis to meet its needs to make payments abroad. Normally a nation obtains foreign exchange through its exports or by borrowing abroad on a long-term basis. But increasingly since World War II grants by governments and international agencies have become important as sources for certain currencies, particularly the dollar. Disequilibrium in a nation's balance of payments implies a condition that is not sustainable; one or more items in either the current account or the capital account must undergo change if an equilibrium condition is to be restored, and this can affect income and employment levels in the domestic economy.

Changes in the current or capital account may be described as either autonomous or induced. An *autonomous* change in the current account is one that is not the consequence of a change in the capital account; an *induced* change in the current account is one that follows from a change in the capital account. For example, a nation may find as a result of events abroad that its exports increase, and an export surplus develops in the current account. If imports remain unchanged, then this development requires an offsetting transaction in the capital account. This offsetting transaction, which will take the form of an outflow of capital, is properly described as *induced* because it is a consequence of a change that has already taken place in the current account. On the other hand, a nation may undertake lending operations abroad (i.e., a capital export) quite independently of any current account developments. If such *autonomous* capital transactions take place, they must be followed by offsetting transactions in the current account. In this event, changes in the current

---

3. For the United States, of course, dollars would not count as a part of its international reserves, but they would for other nations because the dollar is widely accepted as an international medium of exchange. Foreign currencies held by the United States do count, however, as a part of the nation's international reserves.

account would be of an induced nature. From an examination of the statistical data contained in a balance-of-payments statement it is not always possible to determine whether the recorded changes are autonomous or induced, but these concepts are nonetheless useful for economic analysis.

Table 8–1 below contains a simplified statement of the balance of international payments for the United States for 1982. The student should study these data carefully, although a few comments on particular items in the statement are in order. Overall, there was a deficit in the current account in 1982. One item of particular interest in the capital account is the large sum ($41.9 billion) labeled Statistical Discrepancy. Although there is no way to account for precisely all international economic transactions, this particular item reflects a large movement of financial capital into the United States in search of safety, given the turbulent conditions

TABLE 8–1.   Balance of Payments of the United States in 1982 (in billions of current dollars)

Item	Credits (+) (Receipts)	Debits (−) (Payments)	Balance
Current Account			
Trade in Goods*	$223.6	$259.3	$− 35.7
Investment Income	23.7	5.6	18.1
Current Services†	40.6	33.8	6.8
Other Private and Government Receipts	62.2	51.6	10.7
Unilateral U.S. Grants	—	7.9	− 7.9
Balance on Current Account	$350.1	$358.2	− 8.1
Capital Account			
Capital Outflows (net increase in U.S. assets abroad)			
1. U.S. Official Reserves‡		$ 5.0	
2. Other U.S. Government Assets		5.8	
3. Private Assets		107.5	
		Total $118.3	
Capital Inflows (net increase in foreign assets in the U.S.)			
1. Foreign Official Assets	$ 3.0		
2. Private Assets	81.5		
3. Statistical Discrepancy	41.9		
	Total $126.4		
Balance on International Financial Transactions			$ 8.1

SOURCE: U.S. Department of Commerce, *Survey of Current Business*, March 1983.
*Includes military spending.
†Includes travel, transportation, insurance, and other private services.
‡Includes gold, special drawing rights in the International Monetary Fund (IMF), convertible currencies, and U.S. reserves in the IMF.

that prevail in much of the world. The other item of major interest in the table is the financing of the current account deficit in the U.S. balance in 1982. Simply put, the financing of the deficit was done by foreigners increasing their holdings of assets in the United States ($126.4 billion) by an amount ($8.1 billion) greater than Americans increased their holdings of foreign assets.

The Exchange Rate

Besides knowledge of the balance of payments, some understanding of foreign exchange rates is needed for a full appreciation of the manner in which international economic transactions interact with the domestic economy. The rate of exchange is simply the price of one national currency measured in terms of another national currency. For example, the dollar-pound rate of exchange in early March 1982 was $1.82 = £1, which meant that it cost American residents $1.82 to obtain one unit of British currency. The exchange rate is important because exports, imports, and all possible financial transactions are affected not only by the levels of real income and prices that prevail in different countries, but also by the prices at which their currencies exchange for one another. To illustrate, Americans might increase their imports from Great Britain because, for one reason or another, the prices for certain goods in Britain were lower than in America. Or they might buy more from the United Kingdom because British currency had fallen in price in terms of American dollars.

Exchange rates may be either *fixed* or *flexible* (floating). A fixed exchange rate system is one in which the rate—or price—at which different currencies exchange for one another simply does not change, or at most changes infrequently. The gold standard system of the nineteenth century worked in this way. For the first 28 years (1945–73) of the post–World War II period, exchange rates between the major world currencies were relatively fixed. This was the Bretton Woods system, so named because of the 1944 wartime conference held in Bretton Woods, New Hampshire, which led to the establishment of the International Monetary Fund. Under the initial agreement, exchange rates were set using the U.S. dollar as the key—or benchmark—currency. Signatories also agreed to rather stringent conditions for changes in exchange rates, the latter to be carried out under the auspices of the International Monetary Fund. The individual currencies were linked to gold by virtue of the fact that the U.S. dollar maintained a basic gold parity ($35 per ounce), and the U.S. government agreed to convert dollars held by foreign "official" holders (foreign central banks and international organizations like the IMF) into gold at this price. Thus, dollars were regarded as "good as gold" and, for this part of the post–World War II period, nations were content to hold their international monetary reserves as dollars.

The alternative to a fixed exchange rate system is one in which rates are free to fluctuate (or float) on the basis of the interplay of demand and supply forces for different currencies. In any system in which exchange rates are not tied to gold or some other standard (such as the U.S. dollar), there are two basic possibilities. One is that rates be *absolutely* free to fluctuate in accordance with market forces. This would be a true *flexible* exchange rate system. The other alternative is for the exchange rate to be free of any tie to gold or another currency, but for governments to intervene in the market for exchange rates and attempt to keep fluctuations moderate or within a desired range. If this happens, the system is characterized as one with a *managed* or *dirty* float. For most countries this has been the kind of system in effect since 1973. Central banks all over the world intervene almost daily in foreign exchange markets to damp down fluctuations in the rate of exchange for their currency.

It is worth noting that the present system of flexible exchange rates with a managed (or dirty) float did not come into existence by design, but because of the gradual breakdown of the Bretton Woods system of fixed exchange rates caused by imbalances in the international economic accounts of the United States throughout the post–World War II period. During most of this period the outflow of dollars from the United States due to combined impact of our import purchasing, our lending, and our unilateral transfers (one-way grants) exceeded the inflow derived from exports and loan repayments. In the 1950s—the era of the worldwide "dollar shortage"—most nations were content to have dollars as international reserves and see their dollar holdings grow. But not so from the 1960s onward. As the dollar outflow continued because of international economic disequilibrium, more and more nations became uneasy, worrying about the convertibility into gold of their growing stock of U.S. currency. Thus, they increasingly exercised their right to convert official holdings into gold, the result being a drastic drain of gold from the United States. From a peak of $25 billion in 1949, the U.S. gold stock dropped to near $10 billion at the end of the 1960s. The continued pressure on the dollar and unceasing gold loss led President Nixon on August 15, 1971, to abandon all convertibility of the dollar into gold. Thus, the cornerstone of the Bretton Woods system crumbled. From there it was but a short step to the present system of fully *flexible* exchange rates. In December 1971 the dollar was devalued in terms of gold (its official price was raised from $35 to $38 an ounce), and most of the major currencies were revalued in terms of the dollar. But this arrangement lasted only until February 1973, when once again the dollar was devalued in terms of gold (the price went to $42.22 per ounce), and shortly thereafter all efforts to maintain fixed exchange rates between the major currencies were ended.

Our backdrop is now complete, and we can turn our attention to the main theme of this chapter—to analyze how changes in a nation's international economic position affect its domestic economy and vice versa.

Exports, Imports, and the Structure of Aggregate Demand

To analyze the manner in which exports and imports of goods and services fit into the structure of aggregate demand, let us begin by a review of the basic identity equations appropriate to an open economy. In an open economy, exports of goods and services enter directly into the aggregate demand function because they represent the portion of the demand for the national output that originates abroad. The demand for a nation's exports, X, is as much a part of the demand for its output as is the demand for consumption goods and services, C, investment goods, I, or social goods, G. In an open system, M is the domestic demand for imports. Thus, the origin and component parts of the net national output can be summed up in the following identity equation.[4]

$$Y_{np} = C + I + G + X - M. \qquad (8\text{--}1)$$

What determines the level of exports for a nation? We shall not try to answer this question at this point, but only make the assumption that expenditures for exports are autonomous with respect to output and employment levels in the domestic economy. This is not an unrealistic assumption, although we shall need to modify it later in the analysis. Since export expenditures constitute demand for domestic output originating outside the nation, their level will not be significantly affected by changes in the domestic income and employment levels. Thus, the export function may be shown as a horizontal line, as in Figure 8–1.

A nation's imports of goods and services do not represent expenditure for any part of the domestic or national output, but they do represent a form of disposition of the money income created as a consequence of current productive activity—specifically, the part of the domestic income that is directed toward the purchase of the output of other nations. In this sense, imports are a form of leakage from the domestic income stream and analogous in their economic effects to saving and taxes.

With respect to the level of imports, M, we are on somewhat surer ground than with exports. Since imports are a form of disposition of domestic income, the most reasonable hypothesis that we can advance is that the level of imports of a nation is basically a function of the general level of economic activity within the nation. Specifically, this means that imports are a function of the income level, as in the following equation:

$$M = f(Y_{np}). \qquad (8\text{--}2)$$

In most societies an important share of the import total will consist of consumer goods and services. Given this, we would expect a society's expenditures on imported consumption goods to rise as its income level

4. See the earlier discussion on identities in Chapter 2, p. 57.

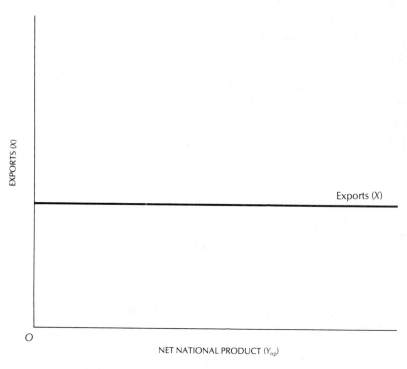

FIGURE 8–1. The Export Function

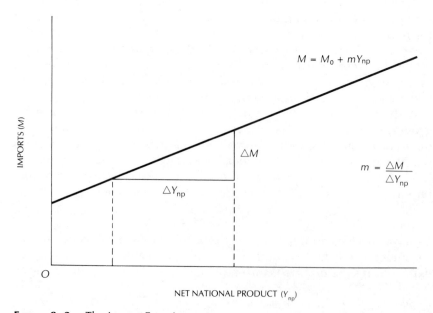

FIGURE 8–2. The Import Function

rises. Equation 8–2 is therefore nothing more than an extension of consumption theory to the situation of an open economy. Beyond this it is not unreasonable to expect that expenditures for imported goods which enter into the investment and government expenditures components of aggregate demand will rise along with rising levels of income and employment.

Since imports are analogous in their economic effects to saving and taxes, it follows that the import-income relationship can be expressed as a schedule. This is done in Figure 8–2. Income is shown on the horizontal axis, and imports on the vertical axis. For the sake of simplicity the import function, $M = f(Y)$, is presented as a straight line, although in reality the relationship between imports and the national income is not necessarily linear. The point at which the import function crosses the vertical axis indicates the amount of expenditures on imports at a zero income level. This, of course, is primarily a theoretical rather than a practical proposition. Algebraically the import function may be defined as

$$M = M_0 + mY_{np}. \tag{8–3}$$

The technical attributes of this function are conceptually similar to those associated with both the consumption and the saving function. M_0 represents import expenditures at zero income. The ratio between the level of imports, M, and the level of income, Y, at any and all possible income levels is the *average propensity to import*. This ratio shows the proportion of any given income level that is being spent for imported goods and services. Like the average propensity to consume and its counterpart, the average propensity to save, the ratio M/Y will vary as the income level varies. The ratio of a change in imports, ΔM, to a change in the income level, ΔY, is the *marginal propensity to import*. This ratio measures the slope of the import function (as shown in Figure 8–2) and indicates how (in percentage terms) imports will vary as the income level shifts. From the standpoint of the impact of changes in the export-import balance on the level of income and employment in the domestic economy, the marginal propensity to import, m, is a vital concept.

Income Equilibrium in an Open Economy

Determination of the equilibrium level in an open economy is essentially a matter of fitting both exports and imports into the kind of analytical structure that we have developed in earlier chapters. Table 8–2 gives data pertaining to a hypothetical economy. These data are similar to those in Chapter 7, except that now included is a column representing the value of the economy's exports. For the moment we shall assume that imports are zero. The export figures shown in Column (6) are the same for all income levels because of the autonomous nature of exports

TABLE 8–2. Exports, Aggregate Demand, and Equilibrium Income
(in billions of constant dollars)

(1) Net National Product Y_{np}	(2) Consump- tion* C''	(3) Invest- ment I	(4) Government Expen- ditures G	(5) Aggregate Demand $(C''+I+G)$	(6) Exports X	(7) Aggregate Demand $(C''+I+G+X)$
$ 0	$ 410	$100	$410	$ 920	$80	$1,000
1,600	1,210	260	410	1,880	80	1,960
1,700	1,260	270	410	1,940	80	2,020
1,800	1,310	280	410	2,000	80	2,080
1,900	1,360	290	410	2,060	80	2,140
2,000	1,410	300	410	2,120	80	2,200
2,100	1,460	310	410	2,180	80	2,260
2,200	1,510	320	410	2,240	80	2,320
2,300	1,560	330	410	2,300	80	2,380
2,400	1,610	340	410	2,360	80	2,440
2,500	1,660	350	410	2,420	80	2,500
2,600	1,660	360	410	2,480	80	2,560
2,700	1,760	370	410	2,540	80	2,620

*From Table 7–7, Chapter 7.

relative to the net national product. Investment and government purchases of goods and services are the same as in Table 7–3, while the
consumption function is drawn from Table 7–6. The aggregate demand
function for this hypothetical—and open—economy is obtained by adding the stated values for investment, government expenditures, and
exports to consumption at each indicated level of the net national product. This result is shown in Column (7). Given this aggregate demand
schedule, we find that the equilibrium income level for this open system
is $2,500 billion. Notice that Table 8–2 also contains an aggregate demand
schedule for a closed economic system—that is, no exports or imports.
This is shown in Column (5). In the absence of exports, the equilibrium
level of the net national product is $2,300 billion. The upward shift of
the aggregate demand function by $80 billion—the amount of the
exports—has the effect of increasing the equilibrium value of the net
national product by $200 billion. Thus, a change in the foreign balance
can exercise a multiplier effect upon the domestic economy. We shall
discuss shortly the operation and value of the multiplier in an open system.

The process of income determination is shown graphically in Figure
8–3. The aggregate demand schedule, *DD*, now includes exports, *X*, as
well as the other components of output included heretofore. As in our
previous analysis, the income equilibrium is determined at the point of
intersection of the aggregate demand, *DD*, and aggregate supply, *OZ*,
functions. This, according to the figure, is an income level of $2,500
billion. Given the position of the aggregate demand schedule, it is the

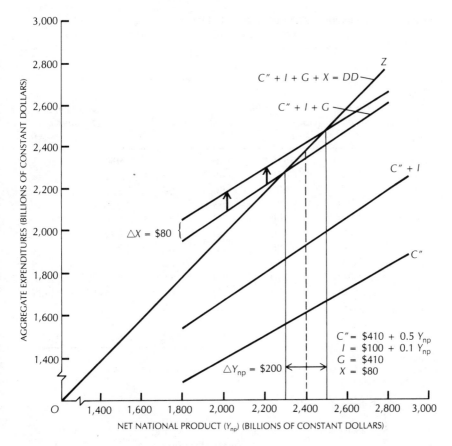

FIGURE 8–3.   Exports and Aggregate Demand

only possible income level at which our four major expenditure categories will add up to an amount equal to aggregate supply.

For simplicity's sake we assumed in the foregoing example that imports were zero. We can now make our hypothetical model more realistic by introducing an import function into the analysis. This is done in Table 8–3, in which the import function is shown in Column (5). In our example, imports, M, are equal to $16 billion plus $0.02 Y_{np}$. M_0, in other words, is equal to $16 billion and the marginal propensity to import, m, equals 2 percent (0.02). The aggregate demand function now becomes the sum of the four expenditure categories contained in Table 8–3 less imports $(C'' + I + G + X - M)$. This new aggregate demand schedule is shown in Column (6) of Table 8–3. Since imports constitute, in effect, a leakage of income from the domestic income stream, the effect of the introduction of an import function is to lower overall the level of the aggregate demand function. A comparison of the data in Tables 8–2 and 8–3 will show that at each possible value for aggregate supply—Column (1) in

TABLE 8–3. Exports, Imports, Aggregate Demand, and Equilibrium Income (in billions of constant dollars)

(1) Net National Product Y_{np}	(2) Consumption* C''	(3) Investment and Government Expenditure $I+G$	(4) Exports X	(5) Imports† M	(6) Aggregate Demand $(C''+I+G+X-M)$	
$ 0	$ 410	$510	$80	$16	$ 984	
1,600	1,210	670	80	48	·1,912	
1,700	1,260	680	80	50	1,970	
1,800	1,310	690	80	52	2,028	
1,900	1,360	700	80	54	2,086	
2,000	1,410	710	80	58	2,142	
2,100	1,460	720	80	60	2,200	
2,200	1,510	730	80	62	2,258	
2,300	1,560	740	80	64	2,316 ⎱	Equilibrium at
2,400	1,610	750	80	66	2,374 ⎰	$2,341 billion
2,500	1,660	760	80	68	2,432	
2,600	1,710	770	80	70	2,490	
2,700	1,760	780	80	72	2,548	

*Same as Table 8–2.
†$M = \$14 + 0.02\,Y_{np}$.

TABLE 8–4. Equilibrium of $(I+G+X)$ and $(S+T+M)$ (in billions of constant dollars)

(1) Net National Product Y_{np}	(2) Investment, Government Expenditures, and Exports $(I+G+X)$	(3) Saving, Net Taxes, and Imports $(S+T+M)$
$ 0	$590	$ – 394
1,600	750	438
1,700	760	490
1,800	770	542
1,900	780	594
2,000	790	648
2,100	800	700
2,200	810	752
2,300	820	804
2,341	824	824
2,400	830	856
2,500	840	908
2,600	850	960
2,700	860	1,012

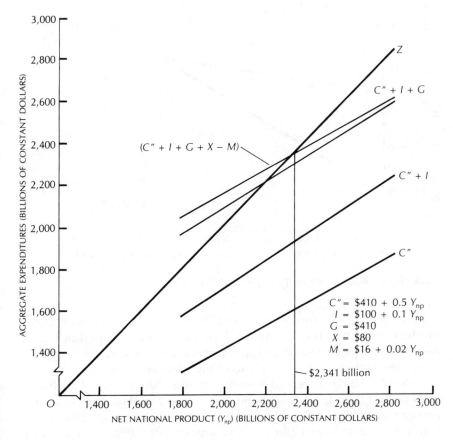

FIGURE 8–4.   Exports, Imports, and Aggregate Demand

each table—aggregate demand is less in Table 8–3 than it is in Table 8–2.

The data of Table 8–3 are plotted in Figure 8–4. A comparison of this diagram with Figure 8–3 shows clearly that the introduction of the import function shifts the level of aggregate demand function below the position given by the data of Table 8–2. The equilibrium level of net national product is now $2,341 billion rather than $2,500 billion. (See the Appendix to this chapter for the algebraic formula for determination of the income level in an open economy.)

The equilibrium level of the net national product in our open system can also be explained in terms of schedules which represent *ex ante* values for expenditures other than consumption (investment, government purchases of goods and services, and exports) and leakages out of the domestic income stream (saving, net taxes, and imports). Equilibrium exists at the point at which these expenditures $(I+G+X)$ just offset the leakages from the current income stream $(S+T+M)$. The sum of the expenditures items $(I+G+X)$ is shown in Column (2) of Table 8–4 and the sum of leakages $(S+T+M)$ is given in Column (3) of the same table.

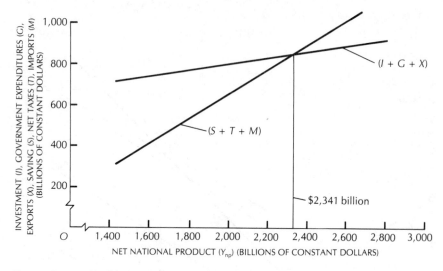

FIGURE 8–5.   Equilibrium of $(I+G+X)$ and $(S+T+M)$

Equality between the two exists at the $824 billion level of the net national product. Schedules for the sum of these variables are plotted in Figure 8–5, which depicts graphically the determination of the equilibrium level of the net national product in terms of the schedule values for $(I+G+X)$ and $(S+T+M)$. Income equilibrium requires that *ex ante* values for all leakages be offset by *ex ante* expenditures. At any level of the net national product at which $(S+T+M)$ is greater than $(I+G+X)$, aggregate supply will be in excess of aggregate demand, and output will fall. If the reverse situation prevails, output and employment will rise.

Foreign Trade and the Multiplier

An important implication of the preceding analysis is that income equilibrium in an open economy also means that equilibrium exists in the nation's balance-of-payments situation. Equilibrium in the nation's international economic position does not require that exports and imports be exactly in balance, but it does require that any imbalance between exports and imports be offset by other international transactions, such as loans or grants. (See the discussion of the role of the capital account in the discussion of the balance of payments in the beginning of this chapter.) A change in a nation's international economic position affects the export-import balance either directly or indirectly. When this happens the position of the aggregate demand function is altered. As we know from our previous study, a change in the position of the aggregate demand schedule will have a multiplier effect upon the income and employment levels within the domestic economy. Since a change in the export-import balance affects the position of the aggregate demand function, there will be a multiplier effect associated with such a change. Some writers prefer to talk of the *foreign trade,* or the *open system,* multiplier when discussing this phenomenon, but actually what is involved is nothing more than the application of the general theory of the multiplier to shifts in the aggregate demand function that have their origin in a change in the nation's international economic position. We saw in Table 8–2 that an autonomous increase in exports in the amount of $80 billion led to an ultimate increase in the net national product of $200 billion. Of course, an autonomous increase in imports—that is, an upward shift of the import function—could have the opposite effect.

To derive algebraically the multiplier in an open system, let us begin, as in Chapter 7, with our basic definition of the effective multiplier, k'. This is

$$k' = \frac{\Delta Y_{np}}{\Delta D}. \tag{8–4}$$

In an open economy it follows from Equation (8–1) that

$$\Delta Y_{np} = \Delta C + \Delta I + \Delta G + \Delta X - \Delta M. \tag{8–5}$$

By substitution we then have

$$\Delta Y_{np} = a'\Delta Y_{np} + b\Delta Y_{np} + \Delta G + \Delta X - m\Delta Y_{np}. \tag{8–6}$$

If we assume that $\Delta G = 0$, we then have

$$\Delta X = \Delta Y_{np} - a'\Delta Y_{np} - b\Delta Y_{np} + m\Delta Y_{np}, \tag{8–7}$$

$$\Delta X = \Delta Y_{np}(1 - a' - b + m). \tag{8–8}$$

Since the change in aggregate demand, ΔD, is the same as the change in exports, ΔX, we can substitute the right-hand portion of Equation (8–8) for ΔD in Equation (8–4). We thus get

$$k' = \frac{\Delta Y_{np}}{\Delta Y_{np}(1 - a' - b + m)} = \frac{1}{(1 - a' - b + m)}. \tag{8–9}$$

Equation (8–9) gives us the value of the multiplier in an open system. It includes not only the marginal propensity to import, but also the marginal propensity to tax. The latter is the case because $a' = a - at$. By further substitution, we can define the multiplier in an open system as

$$k' = \frac{1}{(1 - a + at - b + m)}. \tag{8–10}$$

Graphic Illustrations of the Multiplier in an Open System

Figure 8–6 depicts the effects on the net national product and imports that result from an autonomous change in exports. We assume a simplified economy that has neither investment and saving nor government

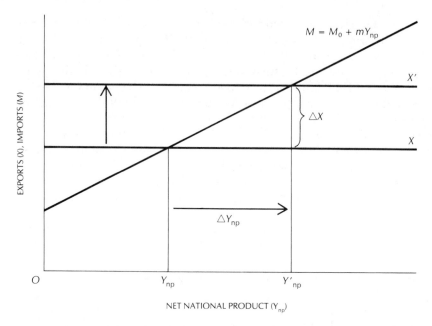

FIGURE 8–6. Foreign Trade and the Multiplier (*I, G, S,* and *T* omitted)

expenditures and taxes. In such a system the necessary condition for equilibrium is that exports *ex ante* and imports *ex ante* be equal, because only when they are equal will leakages, represented by imports, *M*, be just offset by expenditures originating outside the economy, that is, exports, *X*. In Figure 8–6 the equilibrium income level is determined by the intersection of the schedule of *ex ante* exports (depicted by the lower horizontal line) and the import function, $M = M_0 + mY_{np}$. At this income level, exports and imports are in balance.

A shift upward in the export function from X to the new level X' causes a movement of the equilibrium net national product from Y_{np} to Y'_{np}. The magnitude of this change depends upon the value of the multiplier, which in this instance is determined solely by the value of the marginal propensity to import, m. The important point to note is that, as the multiplier process works itself out and the income level rises, the volume of imports will also continue to rise. This is true because we have assumed a positive value for the marginal propensity to import. In our hypothetical system, in which there are no leakages other than expenditures for imports, the import level will have to continue to rise until once again it is equal to the volume of exports. The autonomous increase in exports disturbed a preexisting balance in the current account of our hypothetical economy, but the increase in income that was generated by the change in exports induced a significant rise in imports to restore the export-import balance. At the new equilibrium income level, exports and imports are once again in balance. Changes in the opposite direction would of course, take place if the economy experienced a decline in exports.

A more realistic picture results if we reintroduce both investment and saving as well as government expenditures and taxes into the analysis. This is done in Figure 8–7. The initial income equilibrium, Y_{np}, is at the point of intersection of the $I+G+X$ schedule and the $S+T+M$ schedule. The diagram is drawn so that, at the initial equilibrium, income level exports X and imports M are in balance, although it should be noted that this does not necessarily have to be the case. From the standpoint of the income equilibrium, all that is required is that $I+G+X$ *ex ante* be just equal to $S+T+M$ *ex ante*, not that I be exactly offset by S, G be exactly offset by T, or X be exactly offset by M.

Let us examine the impact on the economy of an increase in exports. This change will shift the entire $I+G+X$ schedule upward. The new position of the schedule is given in Figure 8–7 by the line labeled $I+G+X'$. The increase in exports, ΔX, will, via the multiplier process, drive income to the new and higher equilibrium level of Y'_{np}. The rise in the income level brought about by the increase in exports also induces in this instance not only an increase in imports, but additional saving and taxes as well. At the new and higher income equilibrium Y'_{np}, the sum of $I+G+X'$ is again in balance with the sum of $S+T+M$. Imports have not risen sufficiently to restore equality in the nation's export-import balance because leakages in the form of both taxes and saving also rise as the income level rises. The amount by which exports and imports differ at the new

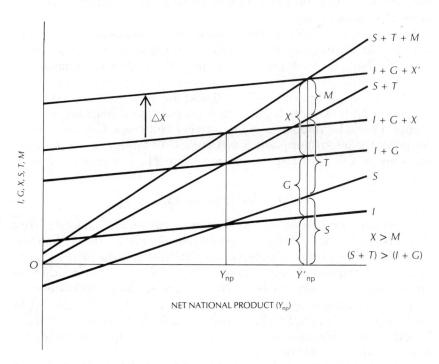

Figure 8–7. Foreign Trade and the Multiplier (I, G, S, and T included)

and higher income level will be just offset by the difference between domestic investment and saving or government expenditures and taxes, or both. Since $X>M$, then $S+T$ must be greater than $I+G$ by a like amount.

The Foreign Repercussion Effect

Up to this point we have not been concerned with the impact of a change in the international balance of the domestic economy upon foreign economies. This is a possibility that must be considered, because the imports of one nation are the exports of another. Consequently, the levels of income and employment in different economies may be linked together through their international economic transactions. The possibility that a change in the international economic position of the domestic economy can have repercussions abroad that, in turn, reverberate back to the domestic economy is described as the *foreign repercussion effect.* Such an effect exists only when the economy of one nation is relatively large as compared to the economy of other nations. Changes in the export-import balance of a very small nation are not likely to affect significantly the income and employment levels of other nations. However, a change in the imports of the United States, for example, could significantly affect the national income of one or more countries because of the sheer size of the American economy.

The nature of the foreign repercussion effect can readily be described. For the sake of simplicity in the analysis we shall assume only two countries. We shall call the domestic economy A, the foreign economy B. Let us assume, first, that there is an autonomous shift upward in the investment demand schedule in A. This will start the usual multiplier sequence in motion and not only bring with it an increase in income, but also induce additional imports as well as saving and taxes. For our present purposes the important point is that the rise in income in the domestic economy, A, will cause imports to rise as well. The sequence of events is as follows:

$$\Delta I_A \longrightarrow \Delta Y_A \longrightarrow \Delta M_A.$$

The foreign repercussion is concerned primarily with the ultimate effect that this change has on income and employment levels in the domestic economy. The increase in imports in A consequent to the increase in A's income is, given our assumption of only two countries, the same thing as an increase in the exports of B. But B experiences an increase in its exports, its domestic income and employment level will be affected by the foreign trade multiplier. Furthermore the increase in income in B can be expected to increase its imports as well. Thus, for country B, the sequence of events will be

$$\Delta X_B \longrightarrow \Delta Y_B \longrightarrow \Delta M_B.$$

The above increase in B's imports will reverberate back to the economy of A and cause its income to rise more than would be the case if domestic investment alone had changed. More exports by A will further stimulate its economy. The economy of A is linked to the economy of B through its exports; in identical fashion the economy of B is linked to the economy of A.

The essential character of the foreign repercussion effect can be demonstrated by a relatively simple geometric diagram such as Figure 8–8. The income of the domestic economy, A, is shown on the horizontal axis[5]; the income of the foreign economy, B, on the vertical axis. The curve $A = f(B)$, which slopes upward to the right, shows how the income level of A will vary directly with changes in the income level in B. The position of the curve depends on the strength of the other determinants of income within the domestic economy, such as domestic investment, government expenditures, and the consumption function. The curve $B = f(A)$ shows the same thing for the foreign economy, that is, the manner in which the income level in B will vary with changes in the income level in A.

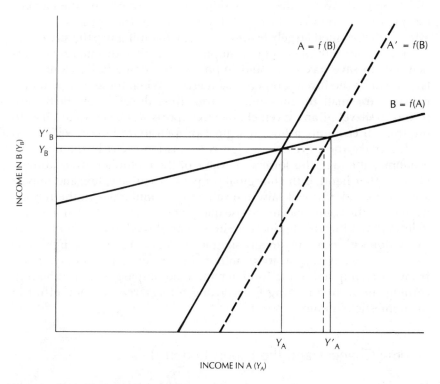

FIGURE 8–8. The Foreign Repercussion Effect

5. Romney Robinson, "A Graphical Analysis of the Foreign Trade Multiplier," *Economic Journal*, September 1952, pp. 546–64.

The point of intersection of the two schedules represents a condition of equilibrium with respect to the income levels of the two nations and their trade with each other. At this point neither the export-import balance nor the income level of A or B shows any disposition to change. There is equilibrium in both nations. The foreign repercussion is demonstrated in the diagram through a shift to the right in the schedule representing the income level in A. The new position of the schedule for A is $A' = f(B)$. The shift is the result of a change in any of the internal determinants of the income level in A, such as a shift upward in either the investment or government expenditures component of the aggregate demand function. The effect of this is to move the equilibrium income level upward in both A and B, from Y_A to Y'_A in A, and from Y_B to Y'_B in B. The nature of the foreign repercussion effect is indicated by the fact that in the domestic economy the change in the income from Y_A to Y'_A is greater than the difference between old schedule $A = f(B)$ and new schedule $A' = f(B)$. The amount of the change in income in the economy of A that is due solely to internal factors is indicated in the figure by the distance from Y_A to the vertical dashed line.

What determines the size or significance of the foreign repercussion effect? Since it involves the relationship between exports and the national income of the countries involved, the size of the foreign repercussion effect is determined largely by those factors that influence the size of the foreign trade multiplier. For example, the smaller the marginal propensities to save, tax (net), and import in the domestic economy, the larger will be the foreign repercussion effect. When these marginal propensities are small, the multiplier is large; thus, the effect on the domestic income level of any given change in exports will be considerable. In the foreign economy a high marginal propensity to import will, *ceteris paribus*, make for a greater foreign repercussion effect in the domestic economy, although this lowers the value of the multiplier effect abroad. On the other hand, if the marginal propensities to save, tax, and import are low abroad, this will raise the value of the multiplier in the foreign nation and thus cause income to rise quite rapidly as a result of an increase in its exports. But for this increase in income abroad to reverberate back to the domestic economy to any significant degree requires a high value for the marginal propensity to import in the foreign economy. Thus, from the standpoint of the foreign nation, no simple generalization concerning the factors making for a strong foreign repercussion effect in the domestic economy is possible.

Income Changes and the Export-Import Balance

Our analysis has been largely directed toward the effect of a change in exports or imports on income and employment levels in the domestic economy. It is appropriate that we look at the other side of the coin and analyze how internal changes in the income level may affect a nation's export-import balance.

Income equilibrium in an open economy may be defined in terms of an equality between $I + G + X$ *ex ante* and $S + T + M$ *ex ante*. For the sake of simplicity let us assume that government expenditure, G, and net taxes, T, are equal (and therefore eliminate them from the foregoing equality). Thus, in our equilibrium condition, $I + X = S + M$. Transposing the terms in this equation, we get the following:

$$X - M = S - I. \tag{8–11}$$

The meaning of the above equation is that *ex ante* the current account balance must be equal to the difference between saving and investment if an income equilibrium is to exist. Since the values that we have been discussing in this context are *ex ante* in nature, we can express $X - M$ and $S - I$ in the form of schedules that link both of these to the income level. This is done in Figure 8–9. Net national product is measured on the horizontal axis; the net differences between exports and imports, $X - M$, and between saving and investment, $S - I$, are measured on the vertical axis. The $X - M$ schedule slopes downward to the right because, even though the level of exports is presumed to be autonomous with respect to the domestic income level, the level of imports will rise as the domestic income level rises. Thus, as the economy moves from a lower to a higher

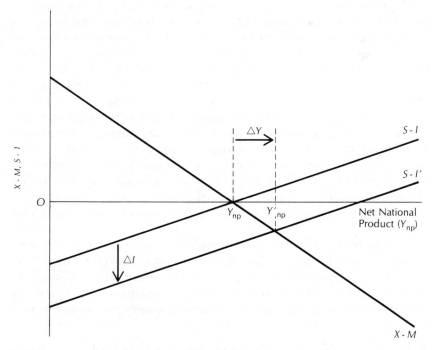

FIGURE 8–9. Income Changes and the Foreign Balance

income level, the export-import balance will shift from a positive to a negative value. The $S-I$ schedule slopes upward to the right because saving increases as the income level rises if investment expenditure is a constant or the marginal propensity to invest is less than the marginal propensity to save.

To illustrate the impact of a change in domestic income on the export-import balance, let us start the analysis with equality between exports and imports. This is shown in Figure 8–9 at the income level Y_{np}. The $X-M$ curve and the $S-I$ curve intersect so that the net difference between exports and imports, $X-M$, and saving and investment, $S-I$, is zero. The effect on the domestic income level as well as the balance of trade of an *increase* in the level of autonomous investment is depicted by a shift downward in the $S-I$ schedule.[6] The new and higher equilibrium income level occurs at Y'_{np}, a point determined by the intersection of schedule $X-M$ and the new and lower schedule $S-I'$. The point of intersection of these two schedules now lies below zero on the vertical axis, which means that $X-M$ is now negative, or that imports exceed exports. We can therefore conclude that a change in the domestic income level—in this instance an increase—has induced an increase in imports sufficient to cause an adverse balance to develop in the nation's balance of trade. Our analysis ignores the foreign repercussion effect that would shift the $X-M$ schedule upward, thus raising the income level even more, but reducing the balance-of-trade deficit.

The preceding discussion of the impact of a change in the domestic income level on the balance-of-trade position has been worked out on the assumption of an increase in the income level, leading to a worsening of the export-import balance. This, of course, is not the only possibility, as study of Figure 8–9 will reveal. The income level may fall, for example, as a result of a shift upward in the saving function. This will raise the $S-I$ curve, and cause it to intersect with the $X-M$ curve at a lower income level. This change, on the assumption that the foreign repercussion effect can be ignored, will lead to an export surplus in the current account. In reality, though, it is unlikely that such a surplus could be maintained for long because the decline in imports will have repercussions abroad that are likely to be felt in the domestic economy. In this instance, the foreign repercussion would take the form of a shift downward in the $X-M$ schedule that would further lower the domestic income level.

Starting from a balanced trade position, an increase in the domestic income level will, *ceteris paribus,* lead to an import surplus and weaken the nation's international payments position. If the trade deficit can be financed on a sustaining basis, no serious problem results. If not, the disequilibrium in the nation's international accounts may sooner or later

---

6. The reason for this is that, at every income level, $S-I$ will be less than it was prior to the increase in autonomous investment. This presumes, of course, that the saving function is unchanged.

force a downward adjustment in the domestic income level. What will happen if, starting from a balanced position, the domestic income level falls? Precisely the opposite of what we have just described.

Exchange Rates and the Export-Import Balance

It is now time to include foreign exchange rates in the analysis, as it makes a great deal of difference to a nation and its international economic position whether it operates with a system of fixed or flexible exchange rates. We shall consider the consequences of each of these alternatives.

A system of fixed exchange rates not only ties a nation's domestic situation closely to its international economic position, but also makes it difficult to secure simultaneously a full-employment equilibrium in the domestic economy and equilibrium with respect to its international economic transactions. A review of the situation shown in Figure 8–9 will clarify this.

As already pointed out, a rise in domestic investment (depicted by a shift downward in the $S - I$ schedule in Figure 8–9) causes a disequilibrium in the nation's export-import balance. If the nation is able to borrow at long term (experience a capital inflow), no serious problems result and the exchange rate can remain fixed. But if long-term capital inflows are not forthcoming, the situation is quite different. As long as the exchange rate is fixed and in the absence of induced (or accommodating) capital transactions, the nation will experience a loss of its international reserves (gold, foreign exchange, and drawing rights in the International Monetary Fund). There is no other way in which a nation can get the necessary foreign exchange to finance an excess of imports.

The continued loss of international reserves by a nation ultimately will force changes in its international economic position.[7] This is so because sooner or later a nation will exhaust its international reserves, including its drawing rights in the International Monetary Fund. What then? The most likely result would be an official devaluation of its currency—a reduction in its price as measured in other national currencies. This was the remedy nations generally opted for during the Bretton Woods era— 1944 to 1973. Since a currency devaluation makes a nation's exports cheaper (in terms of other currencies) and its imports more expensive, exports should rise and imports should fall, thus tending to restore balance in the nation's international economic position. Refer once again to

---

7. There is no generalization about the link between international reserves and a nation's money supply that is valid for all countries. For some nations, especially those which have used the U.S. dollar as a reserve currency, the link may be quite close, as the central banks of such countries are likely to loosen or tighten the money supply on the basis of changes in the nation's inventory of international reserves. For other nations, this is not the case. The United States is in the latter category.

Figure 8–9. If devaluation works as just described, the $X - M$ schedule will shift upward, a change that has the effect of not only increasing the net national product, but also restoring international economic equilibrium. But there is a catch: As the national income rises, imports will also rise, thus tending to nullify somewhat the impact of the devaluation. Furthermore, these developments can take place *only* if the economy is at less than full employment when devaluation takes place. In Figure 8–9, in other words, Y'_{np} must be a less than full-employment net national product. If this were not the situation, an increase in export demand would cause output to bump up against the full capacity ceiling, after which prices would rise. But a rise in the price level would also nullify the effect of the devaluation (in whole or in part), since it would make the nation's exports more expensive. Imports would become more attractive for the nation's residents.[8]

The upshot of all this is that a system of fixed exchange rates makes it largely a matter of chance whether or not simultaneous equilibrium for a full-employment output and the balance of international payments is attained. The two simply may not be compatible, which means the nation will have to choose one at the expense of the other. Of course, if all prices—including the prices of factors of production as well as for goods and services—were flexible both upward and downward, the foregoing conclusion would not hold. Any shift in demand in a nation away from domestic output toward imports would cause the price of the former to fall relative to the latter, thus tending to restore balance between exports and imports. But the real world is simply not like this; most prices are flexible in only one direction—up! Thus, the basic problem remains that, with a fixed exchange system, the nation may have to choose between the pursuit of domestic stability and full employment at the cost of international balance and the pursuit of balance-of-payments equilibrium at the cost of full employment at home. Since most Western nations have committed themselves to maintaining full employment (e.g., the American Employment Act), the realities of politics mean they select the first alternative.

If exchange rates are fully flexible the situation is quite different. In principle, it is impossible for there to be an imbalance between imports and exports, except as a result of lags and other imperfections in the market. The reason is that the rate of exchange would be continuously adjusting to changes in the demand and supply of exports and imports. Thus, if a nation increases its demand for imports relative to the foreign demand for its exports, the foreign exchange value of its currency will fall, causing an immediate increase in the price of imports and a corresponding decrease in the price (for foreigners) of its exports.

8. If devaluation fails to correct a trade imbalance, then a nation may have to resort to more direct, restrictive measures, such as tariffs or quotas. Most economists prefer devaluation to quantitative restrictions on imports (such as quotas) because the former acts through price and permits more scope for consumer choice.

Turn once again to Figure 8–9. A fully flexible exchange rate system means that the $X-M$ line becomes horizontal; it coincides with the horizontal axis in the diagram. If this were the situation, then an increase in domestic investment (depicted by the downward shift of the $S-I$ schedule) would cause the net national product to rise without any impact on the foreign balance. Under such circumstances equilibrium in the output level would be restored at the point of intersection of the $S-I'$ schedule and the horizontal axis. The multiplier effect of a change in investment is much greater in this situation, simply because none of the increase in income is drawn off into imports purchases. This is well and good if the new equilibrium is at or below the full-employment level of net national product, but if beyond it then prices will go up.

The practical consequence of a system of fully flexible exchange rates is to loosen the major ties between the domestic economy of a nation and its international economic situation. A nation's trade balance, in other words, is less affected by domestic disturbances than is the case with fixed exchange rates. It is also true that the domestic economy is more insulated from income and monetary disturbances originating abroad, disturbances which under a system of fixed exchange rates are transmitted from one country to another through their impact on a nation's exports or imports. It also means there is less interdependence with respect to domestic policies pursued by different countries. If country A, for example, wants to pursue a vigorous policy of domestic expansion, it may do so without fear that its actions will cause balance-of-payments problems abroad.

A Summary Comment on the Determination of Aggregate Demand

In this and the three preceding chapters our concern has been with analysis of the component parts of the economy's structure of aggregate demand. As was stressed in Chapter 4, the central thesis of modern employment theory is that, in the short run, when the economy's capacity to produce is relatively fixed, the key to both the income and employment level is demand for the economy's whole output or, more simply, aggregate demand. Expectation of demand leads to the creation of output—and income. Thus, if we can analyze what determines the level of demand for the output of the whole economy, we learn something about the determination of income and employment.

As a result of theoretical developments stemming from the work of Keynes and others and of advances in the field of national income accounting, it is possible to identify the four major components of the economy's aggregate demand structure: consumption, investment, government purchases of goods and services, and the export-import balance. Our purpose has been not only to tie these four forms of demand together into a single integrated structure representing the demand for the economy's total output, but to analyze, too, the determinants of the level of each of these individual parts of the aggregate demand function. Moreover, we have sought to show how changes in the income (and employment) level are linked to changes in the economy's aggregate demand function, and how changes in this function are the result of shifts in any or all of its component parts.

Appendix

Algebraic Determination of the Income Level in an Open Economy

(1) $Y_{np} = C + I + G + X - M =$ the basic identity
(2) $C = C'_0 + a'Y_{np} =$ the consumption function
(3) $I = I'_0 + bY_{np} =$ the investment function
(4) $M = M_0 + mY_{np} =$ the import function
(5) $Y_{np} = C'_0 + a'Y_{np} + I'_0 + bY_{np} + G + X - M_0 - mY_{np}$
(6) $Y_{np} - a'Y_{np} - bY_{np} + mY_{np} = (C'_0 + I'_0 + G + X - M_0)$
(7) $Y_{np} (1 - a' - b + m) = (C'_0 + I'_0 + G + X - M_0)$
(8) $Y_{np} = \dfrac{1}{(1 - a' - b + m)}(C'_0 + I'_0 + G + X - M_0)$

Summary

1. The performance of the domestic economy is affected by the economic transactions undertaken with the rest of the world. These transactions are reflected formally in a nation's balance-of-payments statement, which is an accounting statement that records exports, imports, international transfers, and all major financial transactions with foreign nations.

2. The foreign exchange rate, another major factor affecting the domestic economy through the international sphere, measures the price of the domestic currency in terms of foreign currencies. As this price changes, a nation's export-import balance changes, thereby affecting the domestic economy.

3. Exports are an important element in a nation's aggregate demand structure. In theory, they are generally treated as an exogenous variable, similar to the way investment expenditure is treated. Imports, a function of domestic income, must be subtracted from exports because they represent expenditure directed abroad.

4. In an open economy, both exports and imports must be fitted into the analytical structure involving aggregate demand and aggregate supply. Exports represent a direct demand for domestic output, whereas

imports are, like savings and taxes, a leakage out of the current income stream. In an open economy, aggregate demand *(DD)* is equal to $(C+I+G+X-M)$.

5. As with investment and government expenditure, there is a multiplier effect associated with changes in the export-import balance. An increase in exports, other things being equal, will increase income by some multiple of the initial increase in exports. An increase in imports will also have a multiplier effect, but in the opposite direction.

6. In addition to the multiplier effect associated with changes in a nation's export-import balance, there is also the "foreign repercussion" effect. This shows how a change in the export-import balance in one country affects other countries and reverberates back onto the domestic economy.

7. The line of causation discussed in most of this chapter is from changes in the export-income balance to changes in output and employment. However, changes in the domestic economy will also affect the export-import balance. Other things being equal, a rise in income tends to bring about a trade deficit or a reduction in a trade surplus; a fall in income has the opposite effect.

8. The influence of the foreign exchange rate on the domestic economy depends in part upon whether the nation is operating with a system of fixed or flexible exchange rates.

9

The Roles of Money and Interest Rates

In Chapters 4 through 8 we analyzed the major forms of spending that, when added together, represent total demand for the output that the economy is capable of producing. In the modern *market* economy, however, there really are two broad spheres of economic activity. There is, on the one hand, what economists term the "real" or "goods" sphere, which has to do with the forces of aggregate demand and supply and the conditions under which an equilibrium of output and employment is achieved. On the other hand, there is a "monetary" sphere, an area in which the economic forces at work focus on the demand and supply of money. To comprehend fully how the modern macroeconomy works, we must understand both spheres of economic activity and how they interrelate.

Consequently, in this chapter we shift our analysis to the monetary sphere, the object being to understand the nature of the economic forces that govern the supply and demand for money. Especially since Keynes wrote about money in the 1930s, it has been apparent that what happens in the economy's monetary sphere can have a profound impact upon *real* activity, that is, on the level of output and employment. Money, of course, has been present all along in our analysis, but primarily as a unit of measurement because the spending and output magnitudes discussed in the preceding chapters must be measured in money terms. There is no practical alternative. What we shall be doing in this chapter is analyzing the manner in which money as a *causal* variable enters into the economic picture. It is because money can—and does—play an important causal role in the economy that we are justified in speaking of a monetary sphere where things happen differently from what takes place in the goods sphere.

We shall proceed, first, by an examination of the nature of money and how money comes into existence in the modern economy. After having considered questions that center on the money supply, we shall examine the major theoretical views that economists have developed to explain the demand for money. This is crucial because the *primary* way in which money enters into macroeconomic analysis in a causal sense is through the demand for money. The chapter will conclude with an explanation of how equilibrium is achieved in the monetary sphere.

The ideas about money developed in this chapter are of key importance because they set the stage for an exposition in the following chapter of the general equilibrium model, which is the theoretical centerpiece for the income-expenditure approach to macroeconomic analysis. This is generally known as the "IS-LM" model, the name being derived from the two basic schedules that make up the essence of the model. In the IS-LM model the key ideas about aggregate demand, supply, and money that are analyzed in Chapters 4 through 9 are integrated into a basic theoretical model for the macroeconomy. This model is important for the following reasons: (1) It provides a theoretical basis for most of the policy measures pursued in the post–World War II period; (2) it provides a way to introduce the price level as an important variable into the analysis; and (3) it offers the best frame of reference for examination and discussion of alternative approaches to macroeconomics, the main theme of Part III of this text.

The Nature of Money

There is one fact about money on which there is nearly universal agreement: It is neither easily nor simply defined. Nearly a century ago an economist made the following observation:

> It is a singular and, indeed, a significant fact that, although money was the first economic subject to attract men's thoughtful attention, and has been the focal centre of economic investigation ever since, there is at the present day not even an approximate agreement as to what ought to be designated by the word. The business world makes use of the term in several senses, while among economists there are almost as many different conceptions as there are writers upon the subject.[1]

The situation is not quite that bad today, although the Federal Reserve System regularly publishes data for four major measures of the nation's money stock, the reason being a lack of agreement on a single, all-inclusive definition of money.[2] Probably the best place to start is with the fundamental characteristic of money; it is a generalized *claim* that can be exercised against all other goods, services, and claims of whatever kind

1. A. P. Andrew, "What Ought to be Called Money," *Quarterly Journal of Economics,* January 1899, p. 219.
2. These four measures are discussed subsequently in the section on the supply of money.

and irrespective of their origin. Thus, the essential nature of money does not lie in the physical properties of whatever material substance may happen to fulfill the role of monetary exchange in a society at any particular time; it springs from the fact that the material substance in question is universally accepted as a generalized claim against all other things that possess economic value. The modern demand deposit, a major form of money in many highly developed economic systems, can hardly be said to possess physical properties of value. It consists of nothing more than notations in the ledger of the bank, yet it is something that is almost universally accepted in payment for goods and services, or in the settlement of claims.

Given the nature of money as a generalized claim against all things or entities that possess economic value, it follows that money is the most *liquid* of all assets. *Liquidity* relates to the ease or convenience with which an asset can be converted from one form to another *without loss of value* and with a *minimum* of transactions costs. Money meets this requirement better than any other type of good or claim. Furthermore, the costs of holding money are negligible as compared to the carrying costs that may be involved if one's assets are held in some other form. Understanding the notion of liquidity is a key to understanding a major way in which money may affect the general level of economic activity.

Although money is the asset with the highest degree of liquidity, it suffers from the disadvantage that it does not yield its holder any return—as normally is the case with other kinds of assets. This, too, is a matter of basic importance for understanding how money enters in a causal way into the scheme of things.

The Functions of Money

Economic analysis traditionally states that money performs four major functions. First, money serves as a *standard for the measurement of value.* Without some such standard it would be impossible to reduce the vast and heterogeneous activity of the modern economy to anything meaningful and comprehensible. Unfortunately, money is not a perfect measuring rod because its value will fluctuate as the general price level changes, although this defect can be compensated for (to some extent) by statistical techniques for eliminating the effect of price changes on our measurements. Second, money acts as a *medium of exchange.* In this sense, money is extremely important to the efficient functioning of the economy, because without some medium that everyone is willing to accept in exchange for any good, service, or asset, the economy would have to operate on a barter basis, which would be clumsy and inefficient. Third, money serves as a *store of value.* Since money is essentially a generalized claim to all forms of economic value, this means that economic value can be kept intact over time in the form of money. Of course, any claim or form of wealth that is not highly perishable can serve to store value over time, but money is best suited for performing this function. Finally, money can function as a *standard of deferred payments*. It is customary to measure a debt or promise for future payment in terms of money, rather than some commodity or service.

Of the four functions of money we have outlined, the second and third—money as the medium of exchange and as a store of value—are most germane to the analysis in this chapter.

Alternatives to Money: Debt and Equity Instruments

In a broad sense, each form of wealth represents a claim against every other form of wealth, for it is usually possible to convert items of wealth into money (through sale) and then reconvert the money into a different form of wealth (through purchase). The ease with which this can be accomplished without a loss of economic value varies widely, depending on the nature of the specific items of wealth in question. Of immediate significance to our analysis are certain financial instruments that are in the nature of claims, although of a less generalized character than money. One of the most important of these is the *debt instrument*. A debt instrument is any kind of a note that legally obligates an individual, a business firm, or a government unit to make repayment at some date of a sum borrowed. Normally most debt instruments are interest bearing; the borrower agrees to pay to the lender a sum over and above the specific sum borrowed.

Historically, two broad types of debt instruments are important for economic analysis. There are, first, short-term obligations of which the U.S. Treasury *bill* is a good example and, second, there are long-term obligations generally known as *bonds*.

Short-Term Obligations   An obligation such as a U.S. Treasury bill is a short-term document (usually three months) that promises to pay a specific sum at a future date. This type of instrument normally does not contain an explicit statement of interest, the reason being that Treasury bills are sold at a discount through competitive bidding. In effect, the lender (the person or business purchasing the bill) deducts the interest in advance; when the bill comes due the lender will receive the sum stipulated. The difference between the face (or *par*) value of the bill and the price at which it is sold reflects the current rate of interest for short-term obligations in the "money market." "Money market" is a term applied to all markets within the nation's financial community in which a variety of short-term credit instruments are bought and sold. In addition to Treasury bills, the best-known short-term instruments traded in the money market include high-grade commercial paper, bankers' acceptances, negotiable certificates of deposit (CDs), and federal funds. In general, debt instruments traded in the money market are ones issued by entities with the highest possible credit ratings (like the U.S. government or major corporations and leading banks), and which are characterized by a high degree of safety.[3] Short-term obligations of the type just described are almost as liquid as money and, in addition, have the advantage of yielding the holder a return in the form of interest. Furthermore, there is little risk of a capital loss (or gain) because of fluctuations in the rate of interest, which is not the case for long-term obligations (bonds), as will be explained shortly. The holder of any short-term obligation need only wait a few months at most for the instrument to mature, at which time the face or par value or amount loaned originally will be received.

During the last dozen years or so there has been an explosive growth in a variety of new types of short-term financial instruments that provide the holder with an interest income, and yet are readily transferable into either the more standard forms of money or other types of assets. Since many of these instruments are highly liquid, and since, too, they are usually regarded as safe, they have been termed "near monies." They have, in other words, many of the same characteristics as money and often serve as money substitutes. There have been two facets to this development. One involves the invention of techniques by which traditional thrift institutions such as savings and loan associations, mutual savings banks, and credit unions permit their depositors to transfer their funds by financial instruments that are like the checks used for the transfer of ordinary demand deposits in the nation's commercial banks. Developments like NOW (negotiable order of withdrawal) accounts, POW (payment order of withdrawal) accounts, and other pre-authorized or automatic transfers of funds belong in this category. The other involves the growth of a variety of types of short-term investment pooling arrangements, of which the money market mutual funds are, perhaps, the best example. What happens in this situation is that major financial firms purchase large pools of short-term financial assets of the kind traded in the money market and then sell shares in these pools to individual investors. Usually, the individual funds have a checking option, and shares can be redeemed within 24 hours. What all of the foregoing instruments have in common is that they earn some interest income, which money does not, and they are highly liquid, as money is, of course. Their explosive growth is a major reason why the Federal Reserve System has had to revise its standard definitions of money recently, a subject discussed in the section on "The Supply of Money."

Long-Term Obligations   The second type of debt instrument that is of special importance in economic analysis is the *bond*. Basically, the bond is a document that promises to pay to the holder (that is, the lender) a fixed sum of money as interest at stated intervals and repay the sum initially borrowed at a specific future date. Bonds are considered as long-term debt instruments because normally they have a maturity date of

---

3. For a comprehensive discussion of the "money market" and the large variety of instruments traded in that market, see the Federal Reserve Bank of Richmond, *Instruments of the Money Market*, 5th ed. (Richmond, Va.: Federal Reserve Bank, 1981).

more than a year. This means that the borrower—that is, the entity issuing the bond—does not have to repay the lender—the entity that has "purchased" the bond—for at least a year. As a matter of fact, many bonds in times past were issued for periods of 10 to 20 or more years. This is not as true as it used to be, primarily because persistent inflation since the mid 1960s has made people less willing to lend money at long-term.

As in the situation with short-term financial instruments that are bought and sold in the nation's "money market," there are also highly organized and active markets for the purchase and sale of bonds, both bonds issued by private corporations and bonds issued by federal, state, and local governments. Markets in which fixed income securities with a maturity date of more than one year (i.e., bonds) are bought and sold are called "capital markets." Most bonds issued by corporations as well as by governments can be sold prior to their maturity date. Because of this there is a relationship that has an important bearing on how money enters in a causal way into the economy's performance. This is the relationship between the current market price for a bond in the capital market and the current (long-term) rate of interest.[4] It is useful to examine this relationship at this time. Its full significance will become apparent when we probe more deeply into the theories that involve the demand for money.

Bond Prices and the Rate of Interest   A bond, as pointed out above, is a contractual promise to pay at a future date a specific sum of money, the latter being the amount borrowed initially by the issuer of the bond. This sum represents the bond's maturity value. Furthermore, a bond normally embodies a contractual obligation to pay interest at stipulated intervals on the amount borrowed. This rate, usually called the "coupon" rate, represents the market rate of interest that prevailed at the time the loan was made initially; it is fixed for the life of the bond. Now let us consider what happens if the purchaser of a bond (that is, the lender) should decide that he or she wants to dispose of the bond prior to its maturity date. Let us assume that Mr. Smith purchased 10 years ago several high-grade, 25-year corporate bonds worth $5,000 each, having a coupon rate of 9 percent. Each bond then brings him an annual interest income of $450. Now let us suppose that Mr. Smith decides to sell his bonds, well in advance of their maturity. He can do this because they are marketable and because a well-organized capital market exists for the purchase and sale of such securities. There is a rub, however,

4. One of the convenient simplifications that economists use is to speak of the rate of interest, as if there were but a single rate of interest in the actual economy. This is not true, of course, for there is an entire series or structure of different interest rates. It is also convenient and useful to talk about the long-term rate and the short-term rate, the former applying to rates for loans with a maturity of more than a year, and the latter applying to loans with a maturity of less than a year. Here again it is important to remember that in both instances there are a series of different rates. It is useful, however, to simplify the analysis in this fashion, and no serious harm is done as long as we keep in the back of our minds the complexities of the real-world money and capital markets.

because current market interest rates for long-term loans are much higher than they were when Mr. Smith first acquired his bonds. Assume that the current rate is 14 percent. New bonds being issued will carry this rate as their coupon rate. How will this affect the price that Mr. Smith can get for one of his bonds if he chooses to sell it? What Mr. Smith wants to dispose of in the capital market is a perfectly sound piece of paper (a promise to pay) that will yield the owner $450 per year until maturity and $5,000 when the maturity date is reached. At the current rate of interest (14 percent) would anyone be willing to pay $5,000 for such a promise to pay? The answer is no, because a person with $5,000 to lend at the current market rate of interest of 14 percent could get an annual income of $700 lending the money. Thus, the current market value of Mr. Smith's bond must necessarily be less than its maturity value of $5,000. The crucial question is what is its worth? To answer, we merely ask how much money would one have to invest at a 14 percent rate of interest to obtain an annual income of $450 (the amount guaranteed by Mr. Smith's corporate bond)? To get the answer we divide the annual income from Mr. Smith's bond ($450) by the current interest rate (14 percent), a process commonly referred to as the *capitalization of income.* The result in this case is $3,214, which means that under current market conditions no economically rational person would pay more than this amount for a sound promise to pay (a bond) that yields its holder an annual income of $450 until the maturity date. Of course, if Mr. Smith sells his 9 percent, 25-year bond prior to its maturity at a time when market rates are higher than those which prevailed when he acquired the bond, he will experience a *capital loss.* The greater the amount by which the current market rate exceeds the coupon rate, the greater, too, will be the capital loss if the bond is sold. It is also true that the reverse will hold if current market rate is *below* the coupon rate. In that case, Mr. Smith or any other bondholder selling bonds experiences a *capital gain,* because in this instance the current market value of the promise to pay will be greater than the maturity value (or original purchase price). This brings us, finally, to the basic principle or relationship governing bond prices and current interest rates. Simply put, this principle is that the two are inversely related; that is, the higher the *current* market rate of interest for fixed income securities of any maturity, the lower will be the *current* market value of the securities. This relationship is of primary importance for long-term debt instruments. It also holds for short-term, money-market-type debt instruments, but as pointed out earlier is not of critical importance because a person holding, say, a Treasury bill usually can affort to wait three or nine months until maturity and receive the full amount invested, even if in the meanwhile market interest rates have gone up, causing the current market value of all marketable securities to decline. Later in this chapter we shall examine how this inverse relationship between interest rates and current market values for debt obligations enters into decisions about the form in which people choose to hold their financial wealth.

Equity Instruments   Before we turn to the fundamental question of how the economy gets supplied with money, mention should be made of a second major type of financial claim that is important in economic analysis. This is the *equity* instrument. In contrast to a debt instrument, which always involves a promise to pay because of a loan obligation, an equity instrument is a claim involving the *ownership of wealth,* or real, material assets. Equity instruments have no maturity value and no guaranteed income. The most important type of equity instrument for the purposes of economic analysis is the *share* or certificate of ownership in a joint-stock company. This is what is commonly meant when people refer to "stocks." As most readers are aware, the United States and other modern market economies have highly organized and efficient markets in which equity instruments in the form of shares are bought and sold. The New York Stock Exchange is undoubtedly the best-known example of such a market. Like the money and capital markets, the "stock market" is primarily a "telephone" market of national, not to mention worldwide dimensions, even though its geographic center is in New York City. No part of the nation or globe is removed from this market as long as there is access to the telephone or similar means of almost instant communication. What the stock market does is provide the means whereby ownership claims in the nation's corporations can be easily disposed of or acquired. As readers of the financial pages of the nation's newspapers know, millions of shares of stock are traded daily through the several major stock exchanges located in New York City. Like bonds and even short-term debt instruments, the prices of equities are generally quite volatile, posing always the risk of unforeseen capital gains or losses if financial wealth is held in this form.

Basically, money, debts, and equities represent the three primary ways to hold financial claims that can be converted into spending power or alternative forms of real wealth. They all entail risks of a change in their value, through either changes in the price level in the case of money or changes in their current market values in the case of debts and equities. Money is the most liquid of these three assets forms, because it can be converted instantly without loss in terms of its own value into any other form of wealth-holding or any good or service. Since there are highly organized markets for debts and equities, they too can be readily converted into money and, through money, into goods or services or a different form of wealth-holding. But they differ from money because there is always the risk of a loss in their value at the time such a conversion is made owing to the possibility of a decrease in their prices.

The Supply of Money

There must be an adequate supply of money in an economy to perform the four functions discussed earlier. Money, we have seen, means essentially all things that are generally acceptable in payment of debt and payment for goods and services, and which also serve to measure and store value over time. The supply of money refers to the quantity of things in existence which accord with the foregoing definition. Throughout history the question of not only what constitutes money but where it comes from has been both important and controversial. It is important and controversial because money plays a vital role in how the economy performs; hence, whoever or whatever controls the money supply is in a powerful position to influence economic events. Money today, as we shall see in subsequent discussion, consists of assets or claims created by the financial and banking system. In this system the Federal Reserve, which is America's central bank, plays an important and powerful role, although its power is by no means absolute. The following sections discuss in both theory and actual practice how the actions of the Federal Reserve enter into determination of the money supply.

Before turning to this discussion, some other preliminary comments on money and its nature are in order. Since money is *something*, it must be measured at a particular point in time. This means, in contrast to income, which is measured over time, that money is a *stock*, not a *flow*, phenomenon. Since it is a stock, this also means that amount of money in existence at any point in time must be held by some entity in the economy. This is a point of significance because economists in their analysis of the role played by money make a distinction between the amount of money in existence at any point in time (and which must be held simply because the amount is something that exists) and the amount that people and institutions may want to hold for various reasons. Most people, of course, would like to have more money than they actually have, but this is not the point. In an analytical sense, such a distinction is a useful one, the reason being it enables us to employ the concepts of equilibrium and disequilibrium in conjunction with money, just as we have employed these concepts earlier in conjunction with the income level.

When the amount of money actually being held coincides with the amount that individuals, businesses, and governments actually want to hold, a condition of *monetary equilibrium* exists. This, too, is an important concept, one that is essential for understanding how money as a phenomenon in its own right may significantly influence the level of employment, income, and prices. The counterpart to monetary equilibrium is, of course, *monetary disequilibrium*, a situation in which actual and desired holdings of money are not in balance.

The Measure of Money

While the definition of money and its supply as discussed above is relatively straightforward, the actual measurement of money in the modern economy has become an extremely complex matter. The reason is that there is in practice and in actual circulation in the economy a fairly large variety of financial assets that serve as money in one way or another.

The Federal Reserve System, as indicated earlier, employs four measures for money that actually circulate among the public. The best definition of money, according to the Federal Reserve, is one that is capable of reasonably accurate measurement and that is related in a predictable way to the performance of the economy.[5] It is just because no single monetary measure meets these criteria that the nation's central bank (the Federal Reserve System) must use several different measures of money for its purposes.

The best way to approach the problem of what really constitutes money in the modern economy is to start with two fundamental categories. These are, first, the *monetary base* (or reserve money, as it has been called) and, second, *circulating media*. Before the growth of so many different forms of "near monies," the latter could have been described adequately by the term "deposit" money since a major portion of the money that actually circulated through the economy consisted of demand deposits in the nation's commercial banks. This is too restrictive now because of the recent growth in so many new types of financial assets that play the role of money in the economy. Let us examine these two basic categories.

From the standpoint of monetary control, the most strategic monetary variable is the *monetary base* or, as it is also called, central bank money. It consists essentially of all reserves of financial institutions on deposit with the Federal Reserve banks and all currency in actual circulation or in the vaults of the commercial banks.[6] Currency in the United States now consists entirely of notes issued by the Federal Reserve System. Central bank money, not all of which actually circulates, is also known as "high-powered" money, because it is the primary instrument through which the Federal Reserve can influence the total money supply in the economy. It is called "high-powered" because every dollar of central bank money provides a support base for several dollars of money in actual circulation. Put somewhat differently, the monetary base is strategically important because changes in it have the power to produce multiplied changes in circulating money, a matter we shall consider shortly. The size of the monetary base fluctuates with changes in the assets and liabilities of the central bank. It is primarily through the standard central bank operations of open market purchases, and changes in reserve requirements and the discount rate that the money base changes and, as this happens, the circulating money supply may also change. What the Federal Reserve has under its direct control is the size of the money base. Whether or not changes in the money base actually lead to changes in money in circulation depends upon how the public (including banks and other financial institutions) react to such a change. In the final analysis, it is up to the

5. *Federal Reserve Bulletin,* January 1982, p. 16.
6. Another way to define the monetary base is all the monetary liabilities of the central bank (the Federal Reserve) to the public, including private financial institutions. This would include the deposits of financial institutions with the Federal Reserve banks since a deposit is a liability of the institution in which the deposit is located, as well as currency (bank notes) in circulation. The standard Federal Reserve note is a liability of the Federal Reserve System.

public to decide whether or not to change its holdings of currency, demand deposits, and other financial assets that serve as money in response to any significant change in the monetary base. Thus, the link between the monetary base and the total of money in circulation is a real one, but it is not an exact and mechanical one.

The Federal Reserve definitions of money in circulation begin with the measure of money that is most closely linked to the money base and then proceeds to enlarge this definition by adding specialized types of financial assets that have an important money role, although they are not necessarily of the kind that are used by the general public. Milton Friedman has said that money ought to be thought of as any asset that serves as a "temporary abode for purchasing power," a definition which fits well with the Federal Reserve's most basic definition of money in actual circulation.[7] The latter is what the Federal Reserve now calls M1, and it consists of currency outside the Treasury, demand deposits at all commercial banks, checkable deposits at other financial institutions (NOW and POW accounts), and traveler's checks of non-bank origin. The four major money measures now used by the Federal Reserve System are defined in Table 9–1.

TABLE 9–1.   Measurements of the Nation's Money Supply

M1—This is the most widely used measure of money in circulation and corresponds most closely to the common notion of what money is. It is made up of currency, all deposits that can be transferred by check, and traveler's checks. In August 1983 it totaled $516.7 billion.

M2—This consists of M1 *plus* savings deposits and small time deposits (under $100,000) at all deposit institutions and two types of "overnight" assets, which means assets redeemable the next day. These are "repurchase" agreements by U.S. commercial banks, a form of lending between banks, and "Eurodollar" deposits by U.S. residents in Caribbean branches of member banks. Eurodollar deposits are dollar deposits in banks outside the U.S. M2 was $2,136.9 billion in August 1983.

M3—M2 *plus* large time deposits (more than $100,000) at all deposit institutions and longer than overnight repurchase agreements (loans between banks). M3 in August 1983 was $2,528.5 billion.

L—M3 *plus* other liquid assets such as short-term obligations of the U.S. Treasury (Treasury bills), bankers acceptances and commercial paper (short-term IOUs of business firms), U.S. savings bonds, and Eurodollar deposits held by U.S. citizens. The Federal Reserve regards L as a very broad measure of all liquid assets. In April 1983 it totaled $3,032.1 billion.

7. See the *Federal Reserve Bulletin*, February 1980, for a detailed discussion of the major monetary aggregates used by the central bank.

The Money Multiplier in Theory

It is now time to consider in more detail the relationship between "high-powered" money (the monetary base) and money actually in circulation. We need not at this point undertake a complete review of the process by which commercial banks expand the supply of bank credit (deposit money) on the basis of their reserves, but some summary comments on the key principles involved in the process may prove helpful.[8] The comments apply primarily to M1, the concept of money most appropriate to the basic theme of this text—understanding output, employment, and the price level in the modern market economy.

Since a major part of money in circulation consists of demand deposits,[9] the key to understanding how the money supply changes is the *principle of fractional reserves*. This principle is at the heart of the money supply question in all modern market economies. In essence, it states that normally a bank need only keep a fraction of its total deposit liabilities on hand to meet the withdrawal of deposits by its customers. This being the case, reserves not needed for this purpose become excess reserves; as such they can be used by the bank as a basis for new loans. Commercial banks are in business to make money, and they do so primarily by lending money, most of which is created by the process of lending its excess reserves.

There is, of course, a catch to this. Any single bank in the banking system is limited in its lending—and, hence, money-creating power—to its own excess reserves. But for all banks together the increase in the money supply through the creation of new demand deposits as loans are made is a *multiple* of the reserves banks are required to keep on hand to meet their obligations when customers withdraw or transfer deposits. It is this process that elementary textbooks explain in detail when they describe how the money-creating process takes place in the nation's commercial banking system. The amount of reserves in the form of currency and deposits of the banks with the Federal Reserve System which the banks must maintain is established by the central bank.[10] What is impor-

---

8. Most principles of economics texts contain a detailed explanation of the process of the money-creation process as it takes place through the nation's commercial bank system. See, for example, Campbell R. McConnell, *Economics,* 8th ed. (New York: McGraw-Hill, 1981), Chap. 15.

9. This is less true than it used to be. For example, in 1977, 71.6 percent of M1 consisted of demand deposits, the rest being currency, traveler's checks, and checking accounts at other financial institutions. By the end of 1981, the percentage of demand deposits in the M1 total had declined to 53.8. We shall comment more on the significance of this change, especially in conjunction with the discussion of the data in Table 9–2.

10. Before the Monetary Control Act of 1980 was passed, all banks that were members of the Federal Reserve System (primarily national banks, which are banks chartered by the federal government) were required to hold varying reserve percentages for different types of deposits, but nonmember banks did not have to hold any reserves on deposit with the Federal Reserve System. The new law, which is being phased in gradually until 1989, has varying reserve requirements that by then will apply to *all* deposit institutions. A primary purpose of the 1980 act was to give the Federal Reserve better control over the money supply.

tant to understand, however, is that the fractional reserve principle permits the banking system to expand its deposit liabilities—that is, to create "money"—by some multiple of the total reserves in the system. It is this fact, a principle as old as banking itself, that makes it appropriate to describe reserve money as "high-powered" money. Because of the fractional reserve principle there is, in other words, a *money multiplier* associated with any change in the reserves that banks hold against their deposit liabilities.

The nature of the money multiplier can be illustrated with some simple equations. Initially we shall assume, first, that the ratio of currency to demand deposits in the system is fixed and, second, that the bulk of money in circulation (M1 in the Federal Reserve accounts) consists of demand deposits in the nation's commercial banks. Currency also plays an important role in the money creation process, as we shall see, but for the present we shall look only at the relationship between reserves and demand deposit (or checkbook) money. This will permit us to define in a precise way the nature of the money multiplier.

Let R_a represent the actual reserves in the banking system, D_d the deposit liabilities in the system, and rr the required reserve ratio for the system. The latter is the proportion of deposit liabilities that the banks must hold in reserve against their deposit liabilities. If we assume that the banking system as a whole is "loaned up"—that is, there are no excess reserves—it follows that

$$\frac{R_a}{D_d} = rr. \tag{9-1}$$

Equation (9–1) simply shows that the banking system has no excessive reserves, the reason being that the ratio of actual reserves to deposit liabilities is equal to the required reserve ratio *(rr)*. There cannot be any further expansion in the money supply through the mechanism of demand deposit creation until more reserves are put into the system. To follow up on this process, let us rearrange Equation (9–1) as follows:

$$D_d = \frac{R_a}{rr}. \tag{9-2}$$

What the equation now tells us is that deposits in a fully loaned-up system are equal to the total reserves of the system divided by the required reserve ratio. This is important because from this it follows that an increase in reserves (ΔR_a) will lead to an increase in deposits (ΔD_d), assuming all banks in the system are able to maximize their profits by lending out the newly created reserves. Thus,

$$\Delta D_d = \frac{\Delta R_a}{rr}, \text{ or } \Delta D_d = \Delta R_a \times 1/rr. \tag{9-3}$$

But $1/rr$ is the reciprocal of the required reserve ratio. This we may designate the money multiplier *(km)*. We can now say that

$$\Delta D_d = km \times \Delta R_a. \tag{9-4}$$

In this highly simplified formulation, the injection of more "high-powered" money into the system (ΔR_a) will lead to a multiple expansion of the money supply in the form of expanded demand deposits (ΔD_d).

The foregoing is a useful and simple way to demonstrate the existence of a money multiplier, but it is much too mechanistic to represent reality. The measured money multiplier is not fixed in value, the reason being that the real-world relationship between reserve base and the money stock is much more complicated than is suggested by the above model. One way to illustrate these complications is to introduce currency into the model and drop the assumption that the ratio of currency to demand deposits is fixed. For our expanded model, let us now define the money multiplier *(km)* as the ratio of demand deposits (D_d) to the money base (M_b). The money base (as defined by the Federal Reserve System) includes all reserves of financial institutions at Federal Reserve banks (R_a) plus all currency in circulation and in the vaults of commercial banks (C_u). In symbolic terms,

$$M_b = (R_a + C_u). \tag{9-5}$$

Let us now introduce the ratio of currency (C_u) to demand deposits (D_d), which we can designate as *cr*. Algebraically,

$$cr = \frac{C_u}{D_d}. \tag{9-6}$$

By rearrangement, this equation becomes

$$C_u = cr \times D_d. \tag{9-7}$$

If we rearrange Equation (9–2) we get

$$R_a = rr \times D_u. \tag{9-8}$$

Then, if we substitute the foregoing values for currency (C_u) and reserves (R_a) in the basic definition for the monetary base, Equation (9–5), we have

$$M_b = (cr \times D_d) + (rr \times D_d). \tag{9-9}$$

By simplification and rearrangement, we get

$$M_b = D_d(cr + rr) \tag{9-10}$$

and

$$D_d = M_b \times 1/(cr + rr). \tag{9-11}$$

We are now on the way to deriving a more sophisticated version of the money multiplier which takes into account the fact that, when the public changes the amount of currency it wishes to hold in relation to demand deposits, the relationship between changes in bank reserves ("high-powered" money) and the demand deposit component of the money supply will change. This can be seen in Equation (9–11), since an increase in the ratio of currency to demand deposits *(cr)* will have the effect of reducing the value of the money multiplier, km (the reciprocal of the sum of the ratio of currency to demand deposits and the required reserve ratio).

The Federal Reserve uses, however, a still broader definition of the money multiplier, this being the ratio of the money supply (M1) to the monetary base (M_b). We need to make some further adjustments in our equations to show how we can derive this more complicated measure of the money multiplier. To do this let us start with the basic identity, which says that the money supply (M1) is equal to the sum of currency and demand deposits (C_u+D_d).[11] In Equation (9–7) currency (C_u) was defined as ($cr \times D_d$). If we substitute this for C_u in our basic identity (M1 $=C_u+D_d$) we have

$$M1 = (cr \times D_d) + D_d$$

or

$$M1 = D_d (1 + cr). \qquad (9\text{–}12)$$

From Equation (9–11) recall that $D_d = M_b \times 1/(cr + \bar{r}r)$. If we substitute this for D_d in Equation (9–12), we have

$$M1 = M_b \times \frac{(1+cr)}{(cr+rr)}$$

or

$$\frac{M1}{M_b} = \frac{(1+cr)}{(cr+rr)} = \text{the money multiplier.} \qquad (9\text{–}13)$$

Now we have a sophisticated version of the money multiplier, which we designate as km'. This version takes into account the full impact that a changed desire on the part of the public to hold currency relative to demand deposits has on the relationship between bank reserves ("high-powered" money) and the total of money in circulation. Like the version of the money multiplier given in Equation (9–11), any increase in the ratio of currency to demand deposits will reduce the ultimate impact of any change in bank reserves on the overall money supply. It should also be clear from the equation that a reduction in the required reserve ratio (rr) will raise the value of the money multiplier. An increase will have the opposite effect.

The Money Mutiplier in Practice

How well does this more sophisticated version of the money multiplier accord with experience? Data in Table 9–2 show relevant information

11. Reality is more complicated than this because today money in actual circulation also includes additional forms of deposits transferable by check, as well as traveler's checks. But this does not affect the basic principle, even though it adds more uncertainty to the actual value of the money multiplier, a point discussed near the end of this section on the money multiplier.

TABLE 9–2.   The Money Supply, the Monetary Base, and the Money Multiplier, 1960–82*

(1) Year	(2) Currency (C_u)	(3) Demand Deposits (D_d)	(4) Ratio: $(C_u/D_d =$ cr$)$	(5) Bank Reserves (R_a)	(6) Monetary Base (M_b)	(7) Money Supply $(M1)$	(8) Money Multiplier $(M1/M_b = km')$
1960	$ 29.0	$112.7	0.257	$19.3	$ 48.3	$141.6	2.93
1961	29.6	116.6	0.254	20.1	49.7	146.1	2.94
1962	30.6	118.2	0.259	20.0	50.6	148.8	2.94
1963	32.5	121.7	0.267	20.7	53.2	154.2	2.89
1964	34.2	127.0	0.269	21.6	55.8	161.3	2.89
1965	36.3	132.4	0.274	22.7	59.0	168.8	2.86
1966	38.3	134.5	0.285	23.8	62.1	172.9	2.78
1967	40.4	143.7	0.281	25.3	65.7	184.2	2.65
1968	43.5	154.9	0.281	27.2	70.7	198.5	2.80
1969	46.1	158.6	0.291	28.0	74.1	204.7	2.76
1970	49.1	166.2	0.295	29.3	78.4	215.4	2.75
1971	52.6	176.7	0.298	31.3	83.9	299.4	2.73
1972	56.9	193.6	0.294	31.4	88.3	250.6	2.84
1973	61.6	202.5	0.304	35.0	96.6	264.4	2.74
1974	67.8	207.4	0.326	36.9	104.7	275.7	2.63
1975	73.8	214.1	0.345	34.9	108.7	289.0	2.66
1976	80.7	224.4	0.359	35.1	115.8	307.7	2.66
1977	88.7	239.7	0.370	36.5	125.2	332.5	2.66
1978	97.6	253.9	0.384	41.6	139.2	359.9	2.58
1979	106.3	263.4	0.404	44.0	150.3	386.4	2.57
1980	116.1	267.4	0.434	40.1	156.2	415.6	2.66
1981	123.2	236.4	0.521	42.0	165.2	440.9	2.66
1982	132.8	239.8	0.554	42.1	174.9	478.2	2.73

SOURCE: *Economic Report of the President,* 1981, 1982.
*All dollar amounts are in billions. Money totals are of December of each year.

on the money supply, the monetary base, and the money multiplier for the period 1960 through 1982. The key relationships in the table are the ratio of currency to demand deposits [Column (4)] and the ratio of the money supply (M1 in this case) to the monetary base [Column (8)]. This latter is the money multiplier. What happened over these 22 years was, first, a sharp rise in the ratio of currency to demand deposits, the figure going from .257 in 1960 to .544 in 1982. This amounted to a 111.8 percent increase in currency holdings as a proportion of demand deposits. Why there has been this large increase in the relative importance of currency as compared to demand deposits for money in circulation is not wholly clear, although some observers attribute it to the emergence of the "underground" economy during the years of high inflation. In any event, the change in the currency-demand deposit mix in the money supply has, as Equation (9–11) suggests, brought about a decline in the value of the money multiplier. It fell from 2.93 in 1960 to 2.73 in 1982, a 7 percent change in its value. The changing value for the money multiplier is a major reason why the Federal Reserve finds it difficult to exercise exact control over the money supply, even though it can control the monetary base.

One other aspect of the data contained in Table 9–2 deserves mention. From 1960 to 1970, there was practically no difference between the money supply [M1 in Column (7)] and the sum of currency and demand deposits [Columns (2) + (3)], the reason being that up to this time currency and demand deposits made up practically all of the circulating media. After 1970, however, these two values increasingly began to diverge. By 1982 the money supply total [Column (7)] exceeded the sum of currency and demand deposits by $105.6 billion. What this reflects is the growth in other forms of financial instruments that are now used as money and that are included in M1 (see Table 9–1 on the money supply). Their growth also lessens the reliability of the money multiplier as a guide to the impact of a change in reserves on the overall money supply because the reserve requirements on these deposits (NOW and POW accounts, for example) differ from those required for ordinary demand deposits.

In sum, the fundamental point of the foregoing discussion is that it is through the reserves of financial institutions—especially their excess reserves—that the central bank (the Federal Reserve) gets its leverage over the nation's monetary system. By pumping reserves into or out of the banking system it creates the necessary conditions for either an expansion or contraction of the money supply. Note carefully that the Federal Reserve System cannot force an *increase* in the money supply. It can put more reserves into the banking system, but this does not mean that the public will increase its borrowings. Only if the latter happens will deposits (and the money supply) increase. Contraction is a different story. If the Federal Reserve System puts the squeeze on the reserves of the commercial banks of the system, they will be forced to reduce their liabilities—call in loans when possible and not renew loans as they are paid off—which will reduce the money supply. Thus, the powers of the central bank to force a contraction in money are greater than its powers to force an expansion.

There are three basic means by which the Federal Reserve can affect reserve money in the banking system. They are changing the required reserve ratio *(rr)*; changing the rate it charges commercial banks when it makes loans to them (the discount rate); and, through open market operations, the buying and selling of government securities by the Federal Reserve System. When the Federal Reserve buys government securities the effect is to pump more reserves into the system; when it sells in the open market the effect is the opposite. Open market buying and selling is by far the most frequently used control instrument. Lending by the Federal Reserve (discount rate policy) has been especially important during periods of financial crisis, such as those in 1966, in 1970, during the 1974–75 recession, and again in 1980, at which time the Federal Reserve was called upon at times to "open the discount window" and play the role of lender of "last resort."[12] Changes in the reserve requirements are the least used of the means available to the Federal Reserve System to influence the size of the commercial banking system's reserves of high-powered money.

The Money Supply: Exogenous or Endogenous?

Quite frequently in income and employment analysis the money supply is considered as an exogenous variable, on the assumption that the size of the money stock is determined by administrative action of the central bank. This is a convenient simplification and one which we shall adhere to from time to time in our subsequent analysis. It is not necessary, however, to assume that the money supply is exogenous, that is, unrelated functionally to other variables in the economic system. The trend in recent analysis is to treat the money supply endogenously, as a variable functionally related to other variables in the income system. An interesting and useful approach along these lines has been developed by Professor Ronald Teigen of the University of Michigan. He suggests a money supply function that reflects both the profit maximizing decisions of the commercial banks and the policy actions of the Federal Reserve System. His theory of the money supply is based upon the view that

> commercial banks act in a profit-maximizing way in response to changes in the return from lending relative to the cost. Both the return and the cost are represented by short-term interest rates: in principle, the return is the yield on loans, and the cost is measured by the cost of acquiring the reserves necessary to support the new loans. When it becomes more profitable to make loans, banks are assumed to be willing to supply more deposits and to increase the money stock. However, member banks are constrained in supplying deposits by the reserve requirements imposed by the Federal Reserve System, and if excess reserves are scarce, member banks will tend to increase their borrowings.[13]

In formal terms this hypothesis is expressed as an equation in which the ratio of the existing money supply to money based on unborrowed reserves

12. The "lender of last resort" concept refers to the ultimate responsibility of the Federal Reserve System for the health of the nation's financial system. Thus, when the Franklin National Bank of New York, with assets of over $5 billion, failed in late December 1973, the Federal Reserve provided emergency loans to other financial institutions whose financial health was threatened by the Franklin National collapse. It is a matter, essentially, of providing emergency credit. This is what is meant by the phrase, "opening the discount window." Other recent instances in which the Federal Reserve System intervened in financial markets in its "lender of last resort" role include the Penn-Central railroad financing in 1970, the Real Estate Investment Trust (R.E.I.T.) debacles of 1974–75, the failure of the First of Pennsylvania bank in 1980, and the refinancing of Chrysler Corporation, also in 1980.
13. Ronald L. Teigen, "The Demand for and Supply of Money," in *Readings in Money, National Income, and Stabilization Policy,* Warren L. Smith and Ronald L. Teigen, eds. (Homewood, Ill.: Irwin, 1965), p. 60.

is equated to the rate of return on loans and the cost of acquiring reserves. Specifically, Teigen's money supply function is[14]

$$\frac{M}{M^*} = f(r - r_{\mathrm{d}}). \tag{9-14}$$

In the equation, M is the existing stock of money (currency plus demand deposits) and M^* is defined as the amount of money which could be supported by unborrowed reserves, given the reserve requirements and other institutional characteristics of the Federal Reserve System. Unborrowed reserves are reserves created at the initiative of the Federal Reserve System rather than from member bank borrowing. The significance of M^* in the equation is that it represents the monetary policy variable through which the central bank can affect the money supply. An increase in M^* as a result of Federal Reserve open market operations will lead ultimately to an increase in the money supply *(M)*, assuming no change in either the rate of return from lending *(r)* or the cost of borrowing from the Federal Reserve by the commercial banks (r_{d}). This presumes, of course, that the commercial banks are profit maximizers seeking to increase their loans whenever excess reserves become available. The variables on the right-hand side of the equation reflect market forces that operate directly upon the commercial bank's willingness to expand or contract the money supply. An increase in the return *(r)* on lending, *ceteris paribus*, should lead the banks to expand their loans—and hence the money supply—whereas a rise in the cost of borrowing (r_{d}) from the Federal Reserve, *ceteris paribus*, should have the opposite effect.

Overall, the general tenor of Professor Teigen's analysis is to suggest that if the supply of money responds positively to the rate of interest, the multiplier effect associated with any shift in the aggregate demand schedule will be larger than it would be with a fixed money supply. This is so because any increase in aggregate demand, *ceteris paribus*, tends to raise interest rates, a development which will normally depress investment spending and dampen the multiplier effect. But if the money supply also increases as interest rates rise, the ultimate increase in the rate of interest will be smaller and thus the adverse effect upon investment spending—and the multiplier—will be lessened. A full explanation of the restrictive effect of the money supply on the rate of interest must await the development in the next chapter of the general equilibrium model of the economic system.

The Demand for Money

Let us now turn to the other side of the coin, the demand for money. As pointed out at the beginning of this chapter, the primary means by which

---

14. Ibid., p. 62. Professor Teigen's use of *(r)* should not be confused with our earlier use of this letter to stand for the marginal efficiency of capital.

money in a causal sense is introduced into the analysis is through the demand side. Before we examine how economists have approached this question, some preliminary observations are in order. First, when we speak of the *demand* for money we are speaking of a demand for real balances. People basically want money because of its purchasing power, for what it will buy. This means that we approach the demand for money within the same frame of reference used in analyzing the determinants of aggregate demand, namely, in terms of *real* rather than *nominal* values. Second, the demand for money focuses on the basic question of why people (and institutions) choose to hold money rather than some other type of asset. Money, let us recall, is a stock phenomenon, which means that the amount in existence at any time must be held by someone or some entity, irrespective of its ultimate use.

Historically there have been three major approaches to the question of why people want to hold money. These are (1) the pre-Keynesian (or classical) approach; (2) Keynesian theory; and (3) contemporary portfolio analysis. We shall examine each of these approaches with the intent of distilling from them the essential elements necessary for our basic objective—reaching an understanding of how money enters in a causal way into our analysis of the determinants of output, employment, and the price level.

The Reasons for Holding Money

In *The General Theory* Keynes provided an excellent framework for analyzing the question of why people want to hold money. Money, after all, is in a sense barren, because it does not yield a rate of return, as do most financial assets, and it does not provide directly for the satisfaction of wants. Earlier we examined the major functions that money serves. What Keynes did in *The General Theory* was to go behind these functions and probe into the motives that govern the desire to hold money.[15] Keynes suggested three primary motives for holding money: the transactions motive, the precautionary motive, and the speculative motive.

The Transactions Motive   The transactions motive relates to the need to hold some quantity of money balances to carry on day-to-day economic dealings. Practically all transactions in a money-using economy involve an exchange of money, and, since the receipt of income is not synchronized exactly with all transactions involving money outlays, it is necessary that some money be held in order to meet this need.

Money held to satisfy the transactions motive is related primarily to the medium of exchange function. Money balances held idle in response to this motive provide a means of payment for transactions which will take place in the future. The amount of money in relation to income

15. John Maynard Keynes, *The General Theory of Employment, Interest, and Money* (New York: Harcourt, Brace & World, First Harbinger ed., 1964), pp. 194–99.

that people and business firms find it necessary to hold to satisfy the transactions motive depends on the time interval within which income is received relative to the income. To illustrate with a simple example, let us assume an individual has an annual income of $25,000. If this individual is paid only once a year and, further, if he spends his whole income during the year, his money balance will be $25,000 at the beginning of the year and zero at the end of the year. His *average* holding of money during the year will be $12,500, or 50 percent of his income. Thus, a person paid in this fashion would have to hold, on the average, 50 percent of his annual income in the form of money balances to satisfy the transactions motive. This assumes that income is spent at a uniform rate. Now let us consider what happens if this individual's employer decides to pay him twice a year. Every six months he will receive $12,500 and he will spend the whole of this before the beginning of the next pay period. His money balances will total $12,500 at the beginning of the six-month period and zero at the end. Thus, his average money balance will total $6,250 in each pay period during the year. This means that a person paid twice a year must, on the average, hold but 25 percent of his annual income as money balances in order to satisfy the transactions motive. The more frequent the pay period, the smaller is the proportion of an individual's annual income that must be held to carry on day-to-day transactions.

The Precautionary Motive   The precautionary motive is the desire to hold some quantity of money balances to meet unforeseen emergencies or contingencies. It is, in other words, a desire to set aside some money balances to provide for a "rainy day." The need to hold money to satisfy this particular motive arises out of the fact that we do not have certain knowledge concerning future transactions; a situation may arise in which the need for money balances is much greater than the amount required to carry on normal day-to-day transactions. For the individual this may be the result of unemployment, illness, or some other form of economic misfortune, although it should be stressed that all unforeseen developments that require extraordinary expenditures on the part of either individuals or business firms are not necessarily of an adverse character.

The Speculative Motive   The speculative motive is the most complex and the most important of the three major sources of demand for cash balances postulated by Keynes. Fundamentally, the speculative motive relates to the desire to hold a part of one's assets in the form of cash in order to take advantage of future market movements. It involves, according to Keynes, holding money balances with the objective of "securing profit from knowing better than the market what the future will bring forth."[16] The speculative motive shifts emphasis from the medium of exchange function of money, which dominated classical thinking, and which underlies the transactions and precautionary motives, to the store of value

16. Ibid., p. 170.

function. Under the speculative motive, money is wanted as an asset rather than as a medium of exchange that can be drawn upon as needed at some future date. Money is being held in preference to holding assets in some other form.

Since idle money balances do not, like debt or equity instruments, yield income, why would an individual or a business firm wish to hold on to them? Let Keynes answer:

> Money, it is well known, serves two principal purposes. By acting as a money of account it facilitates exchanges without it being necessary that it should ever itself come into the picture as a substantive object. In this respect it is a convenience which is devoid of significance or real influence. In the second place, it is a store of wealth. So we are told without a smile on the face. But in the world of the classical economy, what an insane use to which to put it! For it is a recognized characteristic of money as a store of wealth that it is barren; whereas practically every other form of storing wealth yields some interest or profit. *Why should anyone outside a lunatic asylum wish to use money as a store of wealth?*
>
> Because, partly on reasonable and partly on instinctive grounds, our desire to hold money is a barometer of the degree of distrust of our own calculations and conventions concerning the future. Even though this feeling about money is itself conventional or instinctive, it operates, so to speak, at a deeper level of our motivation. It takes charge at the moments when the higher, more precarious conventions have weakened. *The possession of actual money lulls our disquietude; and the premium which we require to make us part with money is the measure of our disquietude.*[17]

Basically, the transactions and precautionary motives center on the medium of exchange function of money, whereas the speculative motive relates to money in its role as a store of value or wealth. Each of the three theoretical explanations of the demand for money, the topic to which we now turn, puts a different stress upon these motives and the corresponding functions of money.

The Classical Quantity Theory of Money

Before Keynes's *The General Theory* appeared in the mid-1930s, the thinking of economists about the role of money in the economy was largely summed up in the quantity theory, the roots of which, as pointed out in Chapter 1, stretch back to the sixteenth century. The best starting point for discussion of the quantity theory of money is the equation of exchange, which may be expressed algebraically in the following form:

$$M^0 v = p \cdot Y. \qquad (9\text{--}15)$$

17. John Maynard Keynes, "The General Theory of Employment," *Quarterly Journal of Economics*, February 1937, pp. 215, 216 (italics added). No better example of what Keynes meant exits, perhaps, than the "run" on American banks during the early months of 1933, a crisis which finally led to the temporary closing of the banks. Because their fears about the continued solvency of the banking system were so great people panicked and sought to withdraw their funds.

In the equation, M^0 is the money supply; v the income velocity of circulation (that is, the number of times each unit of money turns over in income and product transactions during a given time period); p the general price level; and Y real income. Expressed in this form, the equation of exchange is simply a truism, for it must follow that the quantity of money multiplied by the number of times each unit of money is used in a period equals the goods and services produced during the period times the average price level for the goods and services. Each side of the equation represents a different way of describing the same thing. A truism, it should be emphasized, does not explain; it is not a "theory." But, as the following comments indicate, it may provide a convenient starting point for development of a theory.

To do this it is necessary to make assumptions about some of the variables contained in the truistic equation of exchange. This is what classical economics did. The result was a theory, the *quantity theory of money*. This theory describes some basic causal relationships with respect to the role of money in the economy. For instance, it was assumed that the velocity of circulation v was relatively stable, the reason being that the velocity of circulation was deeply rooted in the habit patterns of the community and thus slow to change. Since full employment was also an assumption of classical economics, output also had to be a constant. Thus, the only magnitudes that varied in the short run were the money supply, M^0, and the general price level, p.

To understand the classical relationship between the money supply and the general price level, it is also necessary to understand the classical attitude toward money. To the classical economists money was simply a medium of exchange. Its only important function was to facilitate the real process of exchange, which was one of exchanging goods for goods. As a consequence, there was no reason why people would want to hold money as such. If an individual came into possession of additional amounts of money this simply meant that he had additional purchasing power at his disposal and, given the medium-of-exchange function of money, he would choose to spend it. In this view, therefore, more money in circulation in the economy would always mean more spending.

Let us see what this means in view of the assumptions concerning the stability of both v and Y. What will happen, in other words, if there is an increase in the supply of money in the economy? An increase in the money supply means more spending; if output cannot change because the economy is always at full employment, and if the velocity of circulation remains stable, then the only thing that can change is the general price level. In effect, then, the quantity theory of money asserts that the general price level, p, is a function of the supply of money M^0:

$$p = f(M^0). \tag{9-16}$$

It should be noted that this general statement does not tell us exactly how p varies with changes in M^0. A rigid version of the quantity theory holds that prices always vary in exact proportion to changes in the money supply, a view that also implies that v and Y do not vary at all in Equation (9–16). Less rigid versions maintain that the price level tends to vary directly with changes in the money supply, although not necessarily in the same proportion. The latter is the more meaningful interpretation.

The Cambridge Version of the Quantity Theory

The foregoing is the version of the classical quantity theory of money that was largely worked out during the nineteenth century. Later, and primarily because of the work of the great English economist Alfred Marshall of Cambridge University, a more elaborate and sophisticated version of the quantity theory was developed. In this approach, known as the Cambridge version of the quantity theory, emphasis is shifted to the desire of individuals to hold a definite quantity of cash balances. Marshall put the matter as follows:

> In every state of society there is some fraction of their income people find it worthwhile to keep in the form of currency; it may be a fifth, or a tenth, or a twentieth.[18]

While Marshall and other economists recognized that individuals may want to hold money as such, exploration of the motives for holding money had to wait until the appearance of *The General Theory*. Nevertheless, the Cambridge version of the quantity theory represents an important advance over the earlier and more rigidly orthodox concept primarily because it is a step away from the overly simplified classical assumption that money is of real importance only as a medium of exchange.

The essential nature of the Marshallian or Cambridge theory is summarized in the following equation:

$$L = (\phi p Y). \qquad (9\text{--}17)$$

In this equation L is the demand for nominal money balances, p the price level, Y real national income, and ϕ the coefficient that brings the two sides of the equation into balance. Essentially the equation says that society's demand for nominal money balance is linked to its nominal income (the money value of real output). It also follows that the demand for real money balances is linked to real income. This is apparent if Equation (9–17) is rearranged as follows:

$$\frac{L}{p} = \phi Y. \qquad (9\text{--}18)$$

L/p is, of course, the demand for real money balances.

Superficially, ϕ may appear to be nothing more than the reciprocal of

18. Alfred Marshall, *Money, Credit, and Commerce* (New York: Macmillan, 1923), p. 45.

the income velocity of money. The equation of exchange as written in Equation (9–15) may be rearranged as

$$M^0 = \frac{1}{v}(pY).$$ (9–19)

If ϕ is mathematically equal to the reciprocal of velocity ($1/v$), then Equations (9–17) and (9–19) seem essentially the same, assuming monetary equilibrium ($L = M^0$). They may be the same mathematically, but they are not the same in an economic sense. The reason is that ϕ is simply not a numerical coefficient. It represents something else. It is the proportion of the national income (nominal or real) that the residents of a nation wish to hold as cash balances. As such it is basically a psychological propensity that may change. Over the long run the value of ϕ was thought to remain reasonably stable, but in the short run it might shift in a sudden and unpredictable manner as a result of changes in the public's state of confidence. It is this possibility that brings the Cambridge version of the quantity theory much closer to modern thinking on the subject of money.

The distinction between the original classical version of the quantity theory with its emphasis upon money as something to be spent and the more sophisticated Cambridge version with emphasis upon cash balances (real or nominal) may be clarified by using a diagram. This is done in Figure 9–1. Let us begin this analysis with the assumption that there is full employment. This means that real output, Y, is constant. It then follows that the nominal quantity of money people want to hold, L, is proportional to the general price level, p. Thus, we can say

$$L = \phi(p).$$ (9–20)

In Figure 9–1 both the money supply, M^0, and the quantity of money that people want to hold, L, are shown on the horizontal axis, while the general price level, p, is shown on the vertical axis. The curve sloping upward to the right and labeled $L = \phi(p)$ is the geometrical expression of the notion of functional relationship between L and p. The value of the coefficient ϕ is equal to the reciprocal of the slope of this curve. Line M_1^0 depicts the money supply. M_1^0 is shown as a vertical line because the amount of money in circulation (the distance from the origin to the point where M_1^0 meets the horizonal axis) is assumed to be autonomously. determined by the monetary authorities. Monetary equilibrium exists at the point of intersection of the money supply schedule and the $L = \phi(p)$ schedule. The price level at this point is p_1.

In the earlier and more rigid version of the quantity theory a change in the general price level could come about only as a result of a change in the money supply. Such a change would disrupt a preexisting monetary equilibrium and result) in either more (or less) spending with a consequent rise (or fall) in the general price level. To illustrate, let us assume

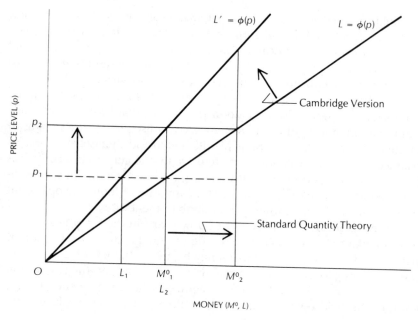

FIGURE 9–1. The Quantity Theory of Money

that the money supply curve in Figure 9–1 shifts to the right. Its new position is given by the schedule labeled M_2^0. This injection of additional money into the economy upsets the prior equilibrium between L and M^0. As a result the amount of money actually in existence is now greater than the amount the people want to hold, L_2, at the existing price level, p_1. Since the rigid version of the quantity theory views money as only a medium of exchange, the new money injected into the economy will be spent. As this happens, prices will rise because of the assumption that real output is a constant. Prices will continue to rise until the normal relationship between the price level, p, and the demand for money to hold, L, is once again restored. This is at a higher level of prices, p_2, and is depicted at the point of intersection of the new and larger money supply curve, M_2^0 and the $L = \phi(p)$ schedule. Opposite effects would ensue if the money supply schedule were shifted to the left. This analysis is properly described as the more traditional version of the quantity theory because the initiative for a change in the price level comes from a change in M^0. There is no question of any change in the value of ϕ. The sequence is $\Delta M^0 \rightarrow \Delta p$.

In the Cambridge version of the quantity theory the general price level may rise from p_1 to p_2, but the manner in which the rise is brought about is altogether different. This is demonstrated in Figure 9–1 by a shift upward in the $L = \phi(p)$ schedule to the level indicated by $L' = \phi(p)$. What is the significance of this shift? Essentially it means a change in the value of ϕ, which is to say a change in the psychological propensity of the public to hold some portion of national income in the form of money. If the $L = \phi(p)$ schedule shifts upward the value of ϕ has declined. Given the new position of $L' = \phi(p)$, the amount of money people want to hold at the price level p_1 *is equal to* L_1. This is the lesser amount than L_2. This disturbs the equilibrium because now the money supply, M_1, is again greater than the cash balances people want to hold, L_1. At this point the Cambridge version falls back upon the notion that money is basically wanted as a medium of exchange, and, as a consequence, the surplus of money, $M_1^0 - L_1$, will be spent as people seek to rid themselves of excess balances. Again this will only serve to drive up the general level of prices because of our assumption that real output is a constant. Thus, equilibrium between the money supply and the amount of money people want to hold will be restored when prices climb to the level p_2.

In the Cambridge analysis, a shift downward in the $L = \phi(p)$ function would mean that the public had decided to hold a larger proportion of national income in the form of money balances. In view of this and on the continuing assumption that real output is a constant, the restoration of equilibrium between M^0 and L requires a fall in the general price level. In the rigid version of the quantity theory, this same result requires a reduction in the supply of money.

The Role of Money in Keynesian Theory

Undoubtedly, the central idea in Keynes's thinking about money is the concept of *liquidity preference*. Liquidity, as we saw earlier, relates to the ease with which an asset can be converted into a different form *without any loss in value*. Money, we also saw, is the most liquid of all assets, a fact that permeates *The General Theory*. In Keynesian theory, therefore, the demand for money is essentially a demand for liquidity, but the nature of this demand differs, depending upon how it is interpreted in the light of the three major motives for holding money balances—the transactions, precautionary, and speculative motives. We turn now to analysis of these.

The Transactions and Speculative Demand for Money

Both logically and for the sake of simplicity in the analysis, the transactions and precautionary demands for money should be lumped together, the reason being that both motives involve holding money to bridge the gap between income and expenditures, either relatively soon in the cause of transactions or for a "rainy day" in the case of the precautionary motive. In any case, the demand for money rooted in these two motives must be related primarily to the medium-of-exchange function of money. Let us call the combined demand for money to satisfy the transaction and precautionary motives the *transactions demand* and designate it by the symbol L_t.[19]

Given the existence of some kind of a normal ratio with respect to the *proportion* of income that the public wants to hold as idle money balances in response to L_t, the actual amount of money held to satisfy this motive will vary directly with income. Thus, L_t is, *ceteris paribus*, a function of income. Algebraically we have

$$L_t = f(Y). \tag{9–21}$$

The fundamental reason for this is not difficult to see. In a complex society the volume of economic transactions of all kinds varies directly with the income level. Consequently, the absolute quantity of money balances needed to carry on these transactions also varies directly with the income level. The amount of money that can be held strictly in response to the precautionary component of the transactions demand schedule is for most people a residual sum which will vary with income. The higher the income level, the easier it will be for individuals and firms to hold idle balances to meet unforeseen contingencies.[20]

The functional relationship between the transactions demand for money, L_t, and the income level is depicted in Figure 9–2. The transactions demand, L_t, is shown on the vertical axis; the income level, Y, on the horizontal axis. The transactions function is the curve labeled $L_t = f(Y)$. The function is a straight line, drawn so that its slope is less than 45°. This indicates, first, that the ratio of money balances held for transactions purposes to income, L_t / Y is normally less than unity (100 percent) and, second, that this ratio is assumed constant. Given these assumptions, the figure shows that the amount of money demanded for transactions purposes, L_t, varies directly with the income level, Y. For example, at the income level Y_1 the transactions demand is L_{t_1}, and at the income level Y_2 the transactions demand is L_{t_2}.

Since idle money balances do not yield any income, should not the amount of money people are willing to hold as balances be related to interest rates? As a matter of fact this is the crucial relationship insofar as the demand for money to satisfy the speculative motive is concerned. But most economists believe the transactions demand is relatively unresponsive to the rate of interest, except, perhaps, at very high interest rates. Then there would be a strong incentive to economize on holding money for ordinary transactions. There is evidence that high interest

19. The analysis which follows is cast in real terms, which is to say the demands for money are for real quantities. This follows because it is presumed that any change in the price level will cause the demand for nominal money balances to change in the same proportion. Thus, it is ultimately real changes which are significant.
20. This should not be confused with saving. Funds held idle to satisfy the precautionary motive may represent one way in which savings are disposed of, but they are not to be mistaken for the act of saving itself.

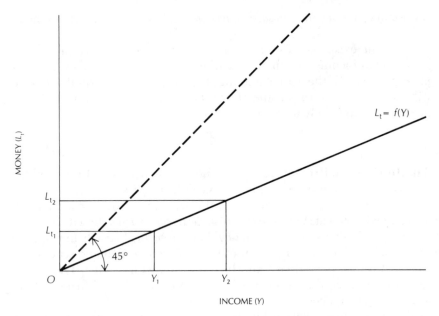

FIGURE 9–2.   The Transactions Demand for Money: Idle Balances as a Function
of the Income Level

rates during 1973–74 and 1979–80 did exactly that.[21] Nevertheless,
linking the demand for money in response to the combined transactions
and precautionary motives to income is a useful, working hypothesis.
The response of money demand to a change in income measures the
income elasticity of the demand for money.

The Asset Demand for Money

The other type of demand for money balances stems from the speculative motive. The essential feature which distinguishes this demand from
the categories considered previously is that it represents demand for
money to hold *as an asset*. In our analysis we will call this demand the
asset demand and designate it by the symbol L_a.

The essence of the asset demand for money is that money is regarded
as a way of holding economic value over time, which is preferable to debt
instruments and equity instruments.[22] Debt instruments normally yield
the holder a fixed income in the form of interest, whereas equity instru-

21. See Richard Porter, Thomas Simpson, and Eileen Mauskopf, "Financial Innovation
and Monetary Aggregates," *Brookings Papers on Economic Activity*, Vol. 1 (Washington, D.C.:
The Brookings Institution, 1979).
22. A person holding either a debt or equity instrument may experience either a capital
gain or a capital loss because of unforeseen changes in the current market value of the
asset. The possibility of a capital loss is a risk a debt or equity instrument-holder assumes.

ments yield the holder an uncertain income in the form of a profit. Although profit can be expressed as a rate of return and thus compared directly with the income derived from a debt instrument, we will simplify our analysis at this stage by assuming that the person who wants to hold economic value over time considers only *two* alternatives: holding money or holding debt instruments. We shall use the bond to represent debt instruments.[23]

Why would an individual hold money, which yields no return, in preference to a fixed-income debt instrument? The answer, as Keynes pointed out, lies in the fact of uncertainty with respect to the future market value of the debt instruments. The corollary of this is that the income foregone by holding money in preference to a fixed-income obligation such as a bond becomes the *opportunity cost* of holding money. If we limit the alternative forms in which economic value may be held to money and bonds, then the rate of interest is the cost of holding money as an asset in satisfaction of the speculative motive, since interest is the income foregone when one chooses to hold money in preference to bonds. This implies that the amount of money held as an asset is a function of the rate of interest, although an *inverse* one. Thus, we have algebraically

$$L_a = f(i). \tag{9–22}$$

The higher the rate of interest, the more costly it becomes to hold money rather than bonds and, consequently, the smaller will be the amount of money held as an asset.[24]

To comprehend fully the nature of the foregoing function, it is essential to understand how Keynes believed people acted when they had to decide between holding money or holding bonds. What is involved in this decision, according to Keynes, is a relationship between the current interest rate, the interest rate that people regard as "normal," and, finally, the current market value of bonds. "Normal" in this context means the level of interest rates that seems appropriate because of past experience.

---

23. Equity instruments involve considerations of future values for the rate of return over cost (the marginal efficiency of capital) as well as for the rate of interest. If persons and firms turn to equities as a means of holding economic value over time they will have to make judgments about the future yields of capital assets and compare these expected yields with the anticipated return from bonds. Holding equities means, too, that economic value may be tied up in real capital assets; thus, in principle wealth-holders should take into account the future value of such capital assets as well as the current rate of return in reaching a decision as to the form in which they want to hold economic value through time. Highly organized markets for buying and selling equities such as the New York Stock Exchange tend to blur the distinction between debts and equities. Nevertheless, a rational wealth-holder would allocate his holdings among the three basic forms in which economic value can be held through time—money, debts, and equities—so that at the margin he would get the same money return, or satisfaction in the event he holds money, from each type of holding.

24. In *The General Theory* Keynes employed the speculative motive to develop a theory of interest rate determination in opposition to the then-dominant classical theory of interest. The nature of Keynes's theory, which is usually called the "liquidity preference theory of interest," is explained in the Appendix to this chapter.

It cannot be defined in an exact numerical manner because of the changing nature of experience. When the decision has to made between holding money and holding bonds, the wealth-holder will be guided by his or her perception of whether the *current* rate of interest lies above or below what is regarded as the *normal* rate. To illustrate, if the wealth-holder believes that current market rates are *below* the normal level of interest rates, the decision will be to hold cash. The reason is this: Believing that current market rates are below normal levels is the same as saying that market rates are expected to rise in the future. But if this happens, bond prices will fall. Hence, it would be unwise to hold bonds since this entails the risk of a capital loss. It is preferable for the wealth-holder to hold cash and wait to see if bond prices actually fall. If the latter happens, then it is appropriate to move from holding cash to holding bonds. On the other hand, if the *current* interest rate lies *below* a rate that is perceived to be normal, the wise thing is to move from holding cash to holding bonds. In this scenario, market rates of interest are expected to fall in the future—or bond prices to rise—and thus the wealth-holder who moves into bonds has the opportunity for capital gains, as well as deriving interest income from the bond.

The foregoing should help explain a vital point about the functional relationship suggested above between the demand for money as an asset and the rate of interest. It is not just the fact that it becomes more costly to hold money as an asset as interest rates go up (remember interest is the "opportunity cost" of holding money); that is important, but expectations about what is going to happen to future interest rates also enter into the relationship. Since expectations are often fragile and based upon highly uncertain knowledge about what may happen in the future, they tend to be volatile. Thus, the entire functional relationship embodied in Equation (9–20) may also be volatile.

In a formal sense, the functional relationship between the asset demand for money and the rate of interest is represented by a schedule as drawn in Figure 9–3. The demand for money as an asset, L_a, appears on the horizontal axis, and the rate of interest, i, on the vertical axis. The curve $L_a = f(i)$ shows the quantity of money that people and firms want to hold *as an asset* at different rates of interest. The schedule depicts the basic relationship discussed earlier, namely, the more costly it is to hold money in terms of interest income foregone, the smaller will be the quantity of money that people want to hold. As depicted in Figure 9–3 every point on the schedule represents a consensus of opinion about the desirability of holding cash, given actual market interest rates (current bond prices) and expectations about future rates (future bond prices). If there is a basic and, perhaps, sudden change in expectations on the part of wealth-holders, the entire schedule shown in Figure 9–3 will shift. Thus, the volatility of expectations for future interest rates relative to notions of what constitutes a "normal" interest rate means that the kind of asset demand schedule for money that Keynes envisaged in *The General Theory*

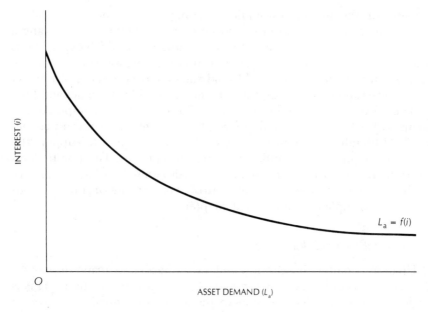

FIGURE 9–3.   The Asset Demand for Money

is volatile. To illustrate, let us suppose a development that causes wealth-holders in general to believe that future interest rates will be higher than previously expected. Such a development occurred, for example, in the spring of 1982 when it became increasingly clear to the financial community that the deficit of the federal government for the upcoming fiscal year was going to be far larger than originally forecast. A development of this sort has the effect of shifting upward the entire demand schedule for money as an asset. Changes in the budgetary outlook changed people's minds about the relative desirability of holding cash and bonds. The expectation that *future* interest rates would be higher than previously anticipated increases the demand for cash. As people shift from holding bonds to holding cash, the price of bonds will decline (current interest rates will rise), thus tending to help bring about the conditions anticipated by the changed expectations.

The asset demand function is also called a *liquidity preference schedule*. Since money is the most liquid of all assets, the demand for the money as an asset is necessarily a demand for liquidity. Although Keynes tended to use the term "liquidity preference" rather loosely to mean the demand for money for all reasons, modern usage restricts the term to the demand for money as an asset. There is one further aspect of the demand for liquidity (money as an asset) which needs to be explored. As drawn in Figure 9–3, the asset demand schedule tends to become perfectly elastic—that is, horizontal—at very low rates of interest. This condition is described as the *liquidity trap*. Keynes suggested that it was theoretically possible for the demand for liquidity (money) to "become virtually absolute in the sense that almost everywhere one prefers cash to holding a debt."[25] What Keynes meant by this was a situation in which expectations about the future value (price) of all income-earning assets have become so pessimistic that no one would hold such an asset because of the risk of a severe capital loss. Thus, the demand for liquidity becomes absolute. Keynes also said that he did not know of any historical examples of the demand for liquidity becoming virtually absolute, but it was a possibility.[26] Although no significant empirical evidence exists to support the existence of an actual liquidity trap, the concept is drawn upon to demonstrate the theoretical possibility of a situation in which monetary authorities have lost all practical control over the rate of interest. This possibility is explained in the next chapter.

The Total Demand for Money

Up to this point we have considered the transactions demand for money, L_t, and the asset demand for money, L_a, as separate functions. This is logical because the determinants of the amount of money held are, in the first instance, income and, in the second, interest. It is possible in theory, though, to combine these two demand functions and obtain a total demand for money. First, we posit the following identity:

$$L = L_t + L_a. \tag{9–23}$$

This equation states that the total demand for money is equal to the sum of the transactions demand and asset demand. This being true, we can posit the following functional relationship:

$$L = f(Y, i). \tag{9–24}$$

In this equation the total demand for money, L, is a function of both the income level, Y, and the rate of interest, i.

The combined transactions and asset demand for money is illustrated in Figure 9–4. The rate of interest is measured on the vertical axis, the total demand for money on the horizontal axis. Income as a variable influencing the level of the overall demand for money is introduced by adding the transactions demand L_t *appropriate to each income level* (see Figure 9–2) to the asset demand function $L_a = f(i)$. The result is a total demand function for money, $L = f(i, Y)$, which combines the asset and transactions demands. As income rises we get a series of demand curves for total money balances, each one of which is associated with a different level of income. The student should note that the L curves shown in Figure 9–4 are drawn so that they begin to bend backward at the upper ranges of the interest rate. This is because even the transactions demand for money becomes sensitive to the rate of interest at very high interest levels.

25. Keynes, *The General Theory*, p. 207.
26. Ibid.

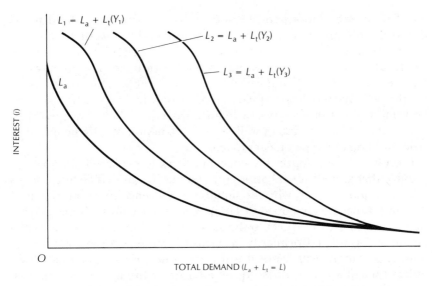

FIGURE 9–4.   The Combined Asset and Transactions Demand for Money

Contemporary Portfolio Theories of Money Demand

The classical and Keynesian ideas about money and its demand traced out in the preceding pages are essentially macroeconomic in character, which is to say they are put in the context of the overall (or total) demand for money. Since Keynes's pathbreaking work on the speculative demand for money, there have been theoretical refinements to the general subject of the demand for money which are closer to the spirit of microeconomics. That is, they begin with the individual (business firm or wealthholder) and treat the demand for money as a theoretical question similar to the demand for any good or service. The results are then generalized to apply to the economy as a whole. Two economists who have made important contributions to our understanding of the demand for money through this approach are Professors James Tobin of Yale and William Baumol of Princeton. Interestingly, their findings are generally in harmony with Keynes's views.

One basic difficulty inherent in the Keynesian explanation of the schedule of liquidity preference and the available supply of money for asset purposes is that it presupposes that persons in the money market will either hold bonds if their expectations are bullish with respect to future bond prices or hold cash if their expectations are bearish. "Bullish" expectations means they believe bond prices will be higher in the future; therefore, capital gains can be expected from holding bonds. "Bearish" expectations means just the opposite with respect to future bond prices. Consequently, holding cash is preferred to holding bonds so that capital losses may be avoided. Individuals will behave in this fashion if their expectations concerning future movements of bond prices (interest rates) are *certain*. But if not, what then? The fact that there may be uncertainty about what may happen to bond prices (interest rates) in the future may lead an individual to hold both bonds and money—he may be led to diversify his portfolio. As a matter of fact, this is the reality, for the personal wealth portfolio of most people includes at any one time both money and other types of financial assets.[27] What is needed is an explanation for this fact, as well as an explanation of why people shift from holding one type of asset to another.

Professor Tobin utilizes the concept of risk to explain, first, how it is possible that an individual's asset portfolio may be divided between bonds and cash and, second, why the liquidity preference function (the asset demand) is negatively sloped.[28] Tobin reaches virtually the same conclusion as Keynes with respect to the shape of this function, but his explanation is formulated primarily in terms of attitudes toward risk rather than expectations with respect to future bond prices. Tobin's analysis, unlike that of Keynes, does not depend upon the notion of a normal rate of interest for understanding why people may choose to hold money rather than bonds (or vice versa). This aspect of Keynes's analysis has been criticized on the grounds that in time the current rate—assuming it is reasonably stable—may come to be regarded as "normal." If this happens, then a key motive for holding assets in money form disappears. Tobin shows that the asset demand for money will still be inversely related to the rate of interest even if the concept of a normal rate is discarded.

In Tobin's view the world of wealth-holders consists of two kinds of people: risk-lovers and risk-averters. These terms come from the fact that, whenever a person holds bonds in preference to cash, he incurs the risk of a capital loss or gain because of uncertain knowledge concerning future bond prices. The larger the proportion of assets held as bonds in preference to money, the greater the risk. The risk-lovers do not have to be induced by higher interest rates to hold bonds instead of cash; they will maximize both risk and interest income by holding all their assets in bonds.[29] If all participants in the money market were risk-lovers an asset demand schedule of the kind shown in Figure 9–3 (p. 311) could not exist.

It would appear, however, that more people in the market are risk-

27. Equities, too, may be included in an individual's portfolio. For purposes of the exposition, though, we will continue to assume the choice is between money and bonds (consols).

28. James Tobin, "Liquidity Preference as Behavior towards Risk," *Review of Economic Studies,* February 1958, pp. 65–86; see also David E. W. Laidler, *The Demand for Money: Theories and Evidence* (Scranton, Pa.: International Textbook, 1969), pp. 67 ff.

29. This is an oversimplification, even though useful for understanding Tobin's basic ideas: It has been shown, however, that even risk-lovers would hold both money and bonds when confronted with uncertainty with respect to both prospective income and expenditures flows. See Roger N. Waud, "Net Outlay Uncertainty and Liquidity Preference as Behavior Toward Risk," *Journal of Money, Credit, and Banking,* November 1975, pp. 499–506.

averters than risk-lovers. The risk-averter will, first of all, diversify his asset holdings. More important, he will assume more risk—that is, hold a greater proportion of his portfolio in bonds—only as the rate of interest increases. Higher interest rates are necessary, in other words, to compensate for the additional risk assumed when more bonds and less cash are held. Since this is the case, the asset demand function assumes the shape shown in Figure 9–3. In reality both attitudes toward risk and expectations with respect to future movements of bond prices—or interest rates—constitute forces at work that determine the nature of the asset demand for money.

Professor Baumol's analysis is addressed to the transactions demand for money. Keynes, as did his classical predecessors, treated the transactions demand (including money held in response to the precautionary motive) as determined essentially by the general level of economic activity (see p. 299). Baumol, however, approaches the matter as a problem in inventory management, the inventory being the stock of money the individual or business firm chooses to keep in hand for transactions purposes.[30] It costs something to hold any inventory, including an inventory of money. Thus, what the firm or individual will attempt is to minimize the cost of holding money in response to the transactions demand.

The amount of money an individual needs to hold for transactions purposes depends on the total values of transactions undertaken over a period of time and the frequency of those transactions. Since the receipt of income for an individual or a business firm does not coincide exactly with expenditures, there must be an inventory of cash on hand. This inventory can be obtained from either holding some portion of income received in the form of cash balances—that is, saving and holding the savings in the form of "immediate liquid command" over goods and services, namely, money—or converting an interest-earning asset (a bond or consol) into cash. These two sources for the cash inventory needed for transactions purposes can be related directly to the costs for maintaining such an inventory—costs which the individual or firm seeks to minimize.

First there is an opportunity cost involved in holding an inventory of cash. This is represented by the current rate of interest, i. This cost exists simply because cash held idle foregoes the opportunity to earn an income through lending at the current rate (purchase of a bond or consol). The larger the inventory of cash held, the greater will be this part of the overall costs for such an inventory. But there are also noninterest transactions (withdrawal) costs which occur each time an income-earning asset is converted into cash. These are broker's fees, as well as any other noninterest cost which may be associated with a conversion to cash transactions (postages, telephone bills, bookkeeping charges, etc.). The more

---

30. W. J. Baumol, "The Transactions Demand for Cash: An Inventory Theoretic Approach," *Quarterly Journal of Economics*, November 1952, pp. 545–56. In his analysis, money held in response to both the speculative and precautionary motive is not considered.

frequently conversion transactions to obtain cash for the inventory are undertaken, the greater will be this aspect of the overall inventory cost. Thus, the total cost for the inventory of cash held for the transactions motive is the sum of interest (opportunity) and transactions (withdrawal) costs.

Now we get to the nub of the problem. If the firm or an individual holds large cash balances, then there will be few withdrawals to get more cash and, hence, transaction costs will be small. But the opportunity costs of foregone interest become large. On the other hand, the latter are reduced by holding down the size of the cash inventory, but this may necessitate more frequent withdrawals, thus raising the transactions part of total inventory cost. To solve the problem, Baumol developed a formula to determine the size of cash withdrawals (conversion of bonds to money) which would minimize the total cost of maintaining an inventory of cash large enough to finance the volume of transactions over a stipulated period of time.[31] Essentially, the formula shows that the demand for cash balances for transactions purposes will vary positively with both the volume of transactions and transactions costs, but inversely with the opportunity costs (the rate of interest). This finding is also in harmony with earlier conclusions about the nature of the transactions demand (p. 306). The Baumol formula also implies that the demand for cash balances will rise less than in proportion to the increase in transactions, a finding which suggests that there are economies in scale in the use of money. The meaning of this is that the richer or more prosperous an individual or business firm is, the greater is their ability to economize in the use of cash. This should not be confused with the tendency of individuals and firms to reduce their cash holdings in response to a rise in interest rates. Both effects may be at work in the modern economy.

Some Empirical Findings

The preceding analysis essentially tells us that the real demand for money will vary inversely with the rate of interest and positively with the level of output. Does the demand for money behave in this fashion? Since Keynes's *The General Theory* first appeared, there have been a large number of empirical investigations into the demand for money relationship. No study has yet been able to come up with an exact statement of this relationship, one that could be used without question for predictive purposes. But most of the studies that have appeared do tend to confirm the general theoretical statements made about the demand for money. They show, first, that the demand for money balances is linked positively to the level of real income and, second, that the relationship between changes in interest rates and the demand for money is an inverse one.

---

31. The formula for the optimum size of withdrawal is $C = 2bT / i$. C is the optimum withdrawal of cash, T is the total transactions in the period, b the costs associated with conversion of earning-assets into cash, and i the appropriate market rate of interest.

Technically, the magnitude of these relationships is a matter of the elasticities of the demand for money with respect to the two key variables, namely, income and interest. The income elasticity of the demand for money is the ratio of the percentage change in money demand to the percentage change in income, and the interest elasticity of the demand for money is the ratio of the percentage change in money demand to the percentage change in the rate of interest. The main empirical findings on the demand for money may be summarized as follows[32]:

1. The demand for money balances is a demand for *real* balances. This is demonstrated by the fact that studies show that the demand for *nominal* money balances rises in proportion to changes in the price level. The practical meaning of this is that people are not victims of a *money illusion.*[33] They will, in other words, adjust their nominal holdings of money whenever the price level changes.

2. The demand for real money balances is related negatively to the rate of interest, meaning that, when interest rates rise, less money will be held and, when interest rates fall, more money will be held. The interest elasticity of the demand for money balances is low, ranging in the short run from -0.16 to -0.4 and in the long run from -0.4 to -0.9, depending upon the definition of money used and the rate of interest selected. To illustrate, an interest elasticity of demand for money of -0.5 means that the demand for idle balances would *decline* by one-half of one percent for every one percent increase in interest rates. Empirical studies have not turned up any significant evidence supporting the existence of a "liquidity trap." In summary, the demand for money balances responds to the rate of interest in the manner suggested by Keynes, but is less sensitive to interest rate changes than Keynes envisioned.

3. The demand for real money balances responds positively to changes in *real* income. Although the income elasticity of demand for money is not particularly high, ranging from 0.5 to 1.0, the empirical findings support the Keynesian hypothesis that income is the primary determinant of the quantity of money held in response to the transactions and precautionary motives. If the income elasticity of demand for money balances is 1.0, this means that the demand for money balances would grow in direct proportion to the growth of real output. In general, however, the empirical evidence suggests that the income elasticity is less than 1, meaning that, while real balances grown as real output expands,

32. Interested students should consult the following studies on this question. H. Latane, "Income Velocity and Interest Rates: A Pragmatic Approach," *Review of Economics and Statistics*, November 1960; C. Christ, "Interest Rates and Portfolio Selection Among Liquid Assets in the U.S.," in Christ et al., *Measurement in Economics* (Stanford, Calif.: Stanford University Press, 1963); R. Teigen, "The Demand for and Supply of Money"; H. R. Heller, "The Demand for Money: The Evidence from Short-Run Data," *Quarterly Journal of Economics*, May 1965; Tong H. Lee, "Alternative Interest Rates and the Demand for Money," *American Economic Review*, December 1967; and Stephen Goldfield, "The Demand for Money Revisited," *Brookings Papers on Economic Activity*, 1973:3.
33. The term *money illusion* was coined by the American economist Irving Fisher and refers to "a failure to perceive that the dollar or any other unit of money expands and shrinks in value." See his *The Money Illusion* (New York: Adelphi, 1928), p. 4.

they do not grow as rapidly. As far as both interest and income elasticities are concerned, the evidence is that long-run elasticities are greater, roughly by a factor of 3.5.[34] The practical meaning of this is that over time the sensitivity of the amount of money people want to hold as idle balances increases with respect to both interest and income. The "long run" in this context is approximately two years.

4. Finally, there is some evidence that the demand for money is influenced by the changes in expected rate of inflation. If the inflation rate is expected to accelerate in the future, this will reduce the demand for real money balances. The reason is that a higher than expected inflation rate increases the opportunity cost of holding money, because the higher rate reduces the *real* value of an individual's nominal money holdings. In effect, this means that the implicit yield on money has been reduced relative to other assets, so less of it will be held. The "implicit yield" of money is the satisfaction (or utility) that an individual derives from holding money in preference to another asset. Keynes, as we have seen, saw this arising out of the uncertainty which surrounds the future market value of other forms for holding wealth. The general message conveyed by Figure 9–3 is that the higher the opportunity cost of holding money, the less will be held. In the figure opportunity cost is measured by the rate of interest, but the idea applies to opportunity cost however measured.

Monetary Equilibrium

Early in this chapter we explained that a condition of *monetary equilibrium* exists when the total amount of money which people want to hold is just equal to the amount of money actually in existence. Now we can pull together the material discussed pertaining to both the demand for and the supply of money to show in a diagrammatic way how monetary equilibrium is achieved in the modern economy. We shall also show how the rate of interest is simultaneously determined, given the fact that the level of interest depends upon the interplay between the demand for and supply of money. The interest rate is the link between the demand for money and its supply, thus making possible equilibrium in the monetary sphere.

The matter of interest rate determination would be relatively simple if there were but a single demand for money schedule. This, however, is not the case. The reader will recall that we constructed the total demand for money by adding the transactions demand prevailing at any given income level to an asset demand schedule (see Figure 9–4). What the Figure 9–4 shows is that we don't have a single curve which relates the total demand for money to the rate of interest and which is independent

34. Stephen Goldfield, "The Demand for Money Revisited," *Brookings Papers on Economic Activity*, 1973:3, pp. 602, 606.

of the income level. The asset demand for money may be independent of the income level, but the transactions demand is not. Thus, we have a series of demand schedules as shown in Figure 9–4, the position of any one of which is determined by the income level.

We need at this point to add to the diagram showing the total demand for money appropriate to different income levels an *endogenous* money supply schedule. By an endogenous money supply schedule we mean one showing that the supply of money is a positive function of the rate of interest, a conclusion reached in our earlier discussion (p. 298). This is done in Figure 9–5. This schedule is labeled M_0 and it slopes upward to the right. Let us examine carefully the significance of this diagram.

Basically, as explained above, monetary equilibrium requires that the total demand for money be equal to the supply. But if we have a series of demand schedules for money such as depicted in Figure 9–5, then there is no single equilibrium rate of interest and no single equilibrium point that equates the total demand for money to the supply. Rather, we have, as Figure 9–5 suggests, a series of equilibrium values with respect to both the rate of interest and money demand and supply, no one of which can be determined until we know the precise level of the total demand schedule for money. This, however, requires that we know the income level. Now we encounter a major complicating element in the theoretical model we have been developing. According to the analysis in the preceding chapters—especially Chapters 5 and 6—we cannot know the income level unless we know the level of investment and the value of

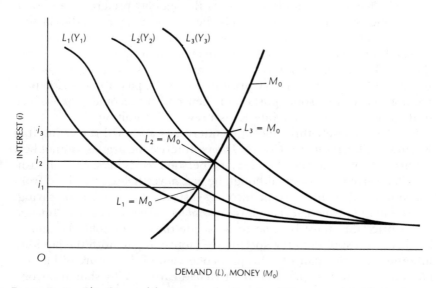

Figure 9–5. The Demand for Money, the Supply of Money, and the Rate of Interest

the multiplier. The latter depends upon consumption, and the former is determined by the rate of interest. What we are confronted with at this point is a chain of interlocking relationships, because the rate of interest cannot be determined until we know the level of income, but the level of income cannot be determined until the rate of interest is known.

The foregoing does not mean that we have a situation for which there is no solution. Rather, the basic conclusion to be drawn from Figure 9–5 is that we cannot arrive at a determination of the interest rate and a state of balance between money demanded and money supplied without a simultaneous determination of the level of output and employment. Thus, we need a more general theoretical model to achieve this objective. We turn to this task in Chapter 10, where we shall demonstrate how the *simultaneous* determination of equilibrium on the *real* or goods sphere and in the monetary sphere resolves the problem.

Appendix

Keynesian Interest Theory

Keynesian interest theory is derived from the idea that money may be wanted as a store of value just as much as it may be wanted as a medium of exchange. Keynes's theory, which is often called "the liquidity preference theory of interest," is based primarily on the asset demand function, although, as we have seen in this chapter, a complete treatment of interest and its determination is not possible without consideration of the transactions demand function.

Fundamental to an understanding of the liquidity preference approach is the concept of interest that is embodied in the analysis. In the classical theory, interest is regarded as the price which equates the supply of and demand for saving; it is considered a phenomenon related to flows rather than stocks. Moreover, interest is seen primarily as the price that is paid for abstinence—the necessary price that must be paid to persuade people not to consume some portion of their current income. The essence of the classical view is that interest is a reward for waiting.

But it is precisely this concept of interest as a reward for saving that Keynes challenges in *The General Theory*. Interest, he argues, cannot be a reward for saving as such because, if a person hoards his savings in cash, he will receive no interest, although he has, nevertheless, refrained from consuming all of his current income. Instead of a reward for saving, interest in the Keynesian analysis is *a reward for parting with liquidity*. Interest is the price that must be paid to persuade those who hold idle money balances in response to the speculative motive to part with the liquidity inherent in such balances. This particular view of the nature of interest takes us back to the question we broached earlier: Why should anyone wish to hold money as an asset in preference to some other form of asset which will yield an income? As we have indicated, the answer is fear and uncertainty with respect to the future value of assets held in forms other than cash. It is necessary to pay people a premium in the form of interest to compensate for the insecurity and diminished liquidity involved in holding assets in other than monetary form at a time of uncertainty. The greater the degree of uncertainty with respect to future economic values, the higher will be the rate of interest.

As stated in *The General Theory*, the rate of interest is "the 'price' which equilibrates the desire to hold wealth in the form of cash with the available quantity of cash."[1] Since we defined the desire to hold wealth in the form of cash in terms of the asset demand function, we can say that the rate of interest is determined by the intersection of the schedule representing the demand for money as an asset—the L_a function—and a schedule representing that portion of the total money supply which is available to hold as an asset. The latter we shall designate with the symbol M_a. This approach to the determination of interest embodies demand and supply concepts, but it is oriented toward stocks rather than flows. For the sake of simplicity in the analysis to follow, we shall assume that the money supply is independent of the interest rate. Assuming, however, that the money supply schedule is a positive function of the rate of interest would not change in any way the essentials of the analysis.

The mechanism through which the rate of interest is determined in the liquidity preference theory is demonstrated in Figure A9–1. Interest is on the vertical axis, while the demand for money for asset purposes, L_a, and the supply of money for asset purposes, M_a^0, are shown on the horizontal axis. The asset demand function, $L_a = f(i)$, slopes downward to the right, as suggested previously, and the money supply function, M_a^0, is shown as a straight line drawn parallel to the vertical axis. This signifies that the supply of money for asset purposes is autonomous with respect to the rate of interest. The reason for this is that the liquidity preference analysis assumes that the supply of asset money, M_a^0, is—given the total supply of money, M^0—a *residual* which is determined by subtracting the quantity of money required to satisfy the transactions demand, L_t, from the total money supply. Given this assumption, the rate of interest is determined by the intersection of the M_a and L_a schedules, for only at this point will the demand for money as an asset be in balance with the quantity of money available to satisfy the speculative motive. This rate is the equilibrium rate and it is designed in the figure as i_e.

In order to understand more fully why the demand for L_a and the supply of M_a^0, must be equilibrated at this particular level of interest rates, let us analyze what will transpire if, momentarily, some other level of the interest rate prevails. For example, what will happen if the interest rate is at the level of i_2, which is higher than the equilibrium rate i_e. At this particular level the asset demand for money L'_a is smaller than the available supply. M_a^0, and, consequently, the rate of interest must fall. Why

1. Keynes, *The General Theory*, p. 167.

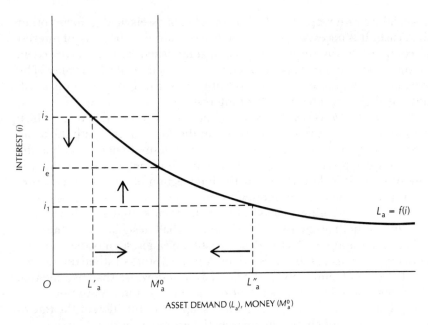

FIGURE A9–1.   The Liquidity Preference Theory of Interest Rate Determination

must they fall? Because at the rate i_2 there exists a situation in which the current price for the surrender of liquidity is so high that people do not want to hold all the asset money that is available. There is, in other words, a surplus of money to hold as an asset, and under such circumstances it is to be expected that the price necessary to persuade people to part with liquidity will come down. This price will continue to fall until a level is reached at which the surplus of asset money is no longer available. This is the equilibrium rate i_e.

The reverse will be true if the rate of interest is below the equilibrium level. Thus, at the rate i_1, the demand for money for asset purposes, L''_a, is in excess of the available supply, M^0_a. The rate of interest i_1 is therefore a disequilibrium rate and must rise, because as long as people want to hold more money as an asset than is currently available for this purpose, they will bid up the price for the surrender of liquidity in an effort to persuade some holders to part with their asset money.

The Significance of the Keynesian Interest Theory

The significance of Keynes's liquidity preference theory of interest does not lie in the fact that it is simply an alternative to the classical theory, an alternative which casts the analysis in terms of stocks rather than flows. The Keynesian theory of interest is important for two major reasons. First it spells out precisely the nature of the monetary sphere of the economic system. Keynesian interest theory makes it clear that monetary equilibrium is the product of forces different from those which produce equilibrium in income and employment. The demand for money as an asset is a major economic force in its own right, but the principles which govern this demand are significantly different from those which govern the demand for goods and services.

Second, Keynes's interest theory provides the necessary theoretical framework to demonstrate that money is not neutral. In the classical theory, money is unimportant precisely because it is neutral, which is to say that money has no role to play in the determination of output and employment. It functions simply as a medium of exchange, in no way affecting the underlying real process of production, exchange, and consumption. Keynes called an economy which uses money merely as "a neutral link between transactions in real things and real assets and does not allow it to enter into motives or decisions . . . a *Real-Exchange Economy*."[2] But in the Keynesian analysis this is not the case. Money, operating through the liquidity preference function, is capable, under the right set of circumstances, of exerting a powerful influence upon the level of both output and employment.

Summary

1. The nature of money and a variety of debt and equity instruments have to be taken into account in the development of the role that sources of finance play in macroeconomic behavior. Interest rates are crucial in the income determination process, and they cannot be understood without knowledge of important financial instruments, especially debt instruments.

2. The supply of money is also crucial for understanding the macro-economy. This entails knowledge of how the central bank—the Federal Reserve System in the United States—can affect the money supply. Key concepts are reserve money, the principle of fractional reserves, and the money multiplier. For analytical purposes, the money supply is often treated as an exogenous variable, but in reality it may be endogenous.

3. The demand for money is also crucial because the primary way in which money in a causal sense is introduced into the analysis is through demand. Analysis of the demand for money involves understanding the reasons why money is held, and how the demand is linked to variables such as income and the rate of interest.

4. Two important theoretical explanations of the demand for money include the classical quantity theory and the Keynesian theory revolving

2. John Maynard Keynes, "On The Theory of a Monetary Economy," reprinted in the *Nebraska Journal of Economics and Business*, Autumn 1963, pp. 7–9. For a comprehensive discussion of Keynes's views on the significance of money, see Dudley Dillard, "The Theory of a Monetary Economy," in Kurihara, ed., *Post Keynesian Economics*, pp. 3–30.

around the demand for money for transactions and the demand for money as an asset. Empirical findings about the link between the demand for money and interest rates show that the demand for money behaves approximately as theory suggests, varying directly with *real* income and inversely with the rate of interest.

5. Monetary equilibrium, the counterpart in the monetary sphere of equilibrium with respect to the output level in the goods sphere, is a condition in which the total demand for money—the amount of money that people want to hold for various reasons—is in balance with the total supply. Changes in the monetary sphere react on equilibrium of aggregate demand and aggregate supply (the "goods" sphere), and vice versa.

10

General Equilibrium in the IS-LM Model

Our analysis in this chapter brings together all the strands in the income-expenditure approach to macroeconomics developed in Part II, providing not only a comprehensive overview of the mainstream ideas in contemporary macroeconomic theory, but also setting the stage for consideration of criticisms and alternative approaches. Our primary objective is to develop a general equilibrium model that shows how equilibrium is obtained simultaneously in the goods and the monetary spheres of the economy. We saw in Chapters 5 through 8 how the demand for goods is created, and in Chapter 9 we saw how the supply and demand of money influence economic activities. Both spheres must be in equilibrium simultaneously, and we see how this is achieved through the IS-LM model. It is generally known as the IS-LM model because of the designation given the two basic curves that constitute the essence of the model—the *IS* curve showing the goods side and the *LM* curve the money side. We shall use the model to demonstrate several things. First, we shall use it to explain the basic principles involved in the application of monetary and fiscal policy to the economy. Second, we shall use it to introduce the price level into the analysis, a development that not only makes the basic model complete and more realistic, but also permits us to construct aggregate demand and supply schedules of a different type than those developed in Chapter 4. The student will find these schedules similar in concept and construction to those normally encountered in the microeconomic aspects of the principles course in that they relate prices to output changes and the demand for the nation's output. Finally, the expanded IS-LM model enables us to demonstrate how prices and output interact with one another, given a change in either aggregate demand or aggregate supply.

The IS-LM Model of General Equilibrium

Aside from its usefulness as an integrating device for all the important elements entering into the theory of income determination, the IS-LM general equilibrium model shows clearly the essential differences between the monetary and goods spheres of activity in the economic system. The stress on the distinction between these two segments of the economy is one of the most fundamental contributions of the income-expenditure analysis. This general equilibrium model also provides a simple and effective means to contrast the effects of fiscal and monetary policy actions. Another important use of the model is to demonstrate through the concept of general equilibrium the manner in which the two spheres of the economy are linked together. The rate of interest provides a bridge between forces affecting the demand for money balances and those which revolve around the demand for goods and services.

The interdependence of the rate of interest and the level of income makes the model truly general; the underlying system of functional relationships operates in such a manner that it is not possible to determine the equilibrium income level without simultaneously determining the rate of interest. The model illustrates this clearly.

The approach that we will use in the development of the IS-LM general model is to show the necessary conditions under which equilibrium may obtain in the goods and monetary spheres of activity taken separately, and then the conditions under which equilibrium may exist in both spheres simultaneously. The latter analysis will provide us with the model that demonstrates the nature of equilibrium in the economic system as a whole.

Equilibrium in the Goods Sphere

The *goods sphere* refers essentially to those economic activities involving the production and use of goods and services. Our concern here is with the forces that center in aggregate demand and supply and with the conditions under which an equilibrium exists with respect to the demand for and the supply of goods and services for the economy as a whole.

The major portion of the analysis pursued prior to this chapter has aimed at defining the various conditions under which income equilibrium exists in the economy. Thus, if we postulate a simple economy without government and without foreign transactions, the necessary condition for equilibrium is that investment and saving *ex ante* be equal (see Figure 5–4). If we introduce government into the analysis, but retain the assumption that there are no international transactions, the necessary condition for equilibrium becomes one in which *ex ante* investment plus government purchases of goods and services, $I + G$, is equal to *ex ante* saving plus net taxes, $S + T$ (see Figure 7–7). Finally, the introduc-

tion of international transactions into the analysis means that the necessary condition for income (and output) equilibrium is one in which the
sum of *ex ante* investment plus government purchases of goods and services plus exports, $I + G + X$, equals the sum of *ex ante* saving plus net
taxes plus imports, $S + T + M$ (see Figure 8–5).

In constructing our general equilibrium model, we shall assume for
the sake of simplicity a closed economy, although the inclusion of foreign transactions changes in no way the basic principles involved. In a
closed economy, the basic condition for equilibrium is the *ex ante* equality
of saving and net taxes $(S + T)$ and investment plus government purchases of goods and services $(I + G)$. Saving and net taxes are a function
of income in the model, whereas investment expenditures are an inverse
function of the rate of interest, and government purchases of goods and
services are assumed to be autonomous with respect to both income and
the rate of interest.[1]

The IS Schedule

The interaction of schedule values for $(I + G)$ and $(S + T)$ in the
determination of an equilibrium value for income is shown in Figure
10–1. In Part A of the figure, an investment demand schedule relating
investment outlays inversely to the rate of interest is shown. To this
schedule at all possible levels of the interest rate is added a fixed amount
representing autonomous government expenditures for goods and services. The result is the schedule $(I + G)$, showing an inverse relationship
to the rate of interest for the combined total of I and G. In Part C of the
figure, the combined saving plus net taxes function is shown, both of
which vary directly with income. By means of the schedules shown in
Part A and Part C, we can link income and the rate of interest in the
goods sphere.

To illustrate, let us assume that initially the rate of interest is at the
level i_4. This rate will yield a combined total of I plus G expenditure
equal to $(I + G)_1$. The latter is measured on the horizontal axis of the
diagram in Part A. Part B in Figure 10–1 shows $(I + G)$ on the horizontal axis and $(S + T)$ on the vertical axis; the 45° line bisecting the figure
in Part B thus represents equality between $(I + G)$ and $(S + T)$. By
projecting vertically from $(I + G)$ in Part A until we intercept the 45°
line in Part B and projecting horizontally from the point until we intercept the $(S + T)$ function in Part C, it is possible to determine graphically
the specific equilibrium value for the net national product that will result
from an interest rate equal to i_4. This equilibrium value is Y_1 on the
horizontal axis of the figure in Part C. Essentially our analysis to this

1. To simplify the construction of the graphic model, we shall not explicitly take into
account investment expenditures induced by a change in the income level, although the
phenomenon of induced investment is built into the model in its graphic form (Figure 10–
1) and the equation system which underlies the model (see the Appendix to this chapter).

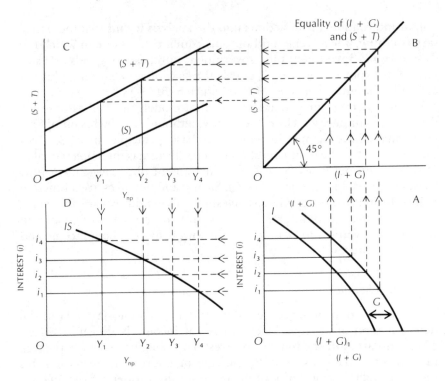

FIGURE 10–1.   Equilibrium in the Goods Sphere

point shows that, given the $(S + T)$ function, a high value for the rate of interest will mean a low level of combined $(I + G)$ expenditures and, hence, a low income level. If we lower the rate of interest, this will increase $(I + G)$ and push the income level higher. Each successively higher equilibrium value for the net national product which results from successive cuts in the rate of interest is one which will prevail after the multiplier effects have worked themselves out.

The main point is that, given both the $(S + T)$ function and the $(I + G)$ function, equilibrium in the goods sphere of the economy is achieved at higher and higher income levels only as the rate of interest declines. This relationship between the rate of interest, the level of income, and successive equilibrium positions in the goods sphere can be expressed in schedule form. In Part D of Figure 10–1 net national product, Y_{np}, is measured on the horizontal axis and the rate of interest, i, on the vertical axis. Since an equality between $(S + T)$ and $(I + G)$ at successively higher income levels results only as the rate of interest declines, the curve that links income and the rate of interest in terms of the $(S + T) = (I + G)$ equilibrium will slope downward to the right. This curve is labeled the *IS* schedule because each point on it relates equilibrium in the goods sphere to income and the rate of interest.

The shape of the *IS* schedule depends upon the essential character of the *(S + T)* function and the investment demand function. If, for example, the investment demand function is assumed to be relatively *interest inelastic,* then it logically follows that the *IS* curve, too, will be relatively interest inelastic because any given changes in the rate of interest will have only a modest effect on the volume of investment spending. As a consequence, the income level will also be little affected by changes in the rate of interest. A change in the position of either the *(S + T)* function or the *(I + G)* schedule shifts the overall position of the *IS* curve. For example, an upward movement in the investment demand schedule will shift the *IS* curve to the right, making possible an equilibrium between *(S + T)* and *(I + G)* at a higher level of income than heretofore. A shift of this type is depicted by the dashed IS_2 curve in Figure 10–2.

Including exports and imports in our analysis does not materially change the nature of the curve describing the relationship between income and the rate of interest in terms of the necessary conditions for equilibrium in the goods sphere. The curve would simply lie further to the right, and our conception of it would have to be enlarged to see each point on it as representing a condition in which $I + G + X$ was equal to $S + T + M$ at specific levels of both income and the rate of interest. Since it can be assumed that G and X are autonomous with respect to both income and the rate of interest, the $I + G + X$ curve would still slope downward to the right; including G and X in the aggregate demand function does not change the inverse functional relationship between investment and the rate of interest.

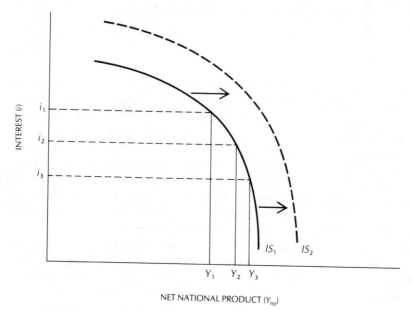

FIGURE 10–2. Shift in the *IS* Curve

Equilibrium in the Monetary Sphere

The *monetary sphere* refers to the economic activities that center around the demand for and the supply of money to hold. These activities are also lumped under the phrase the *money market* because they include the different forms in which wealth-holders seek to hold economic value over time.

As we saw in the previous chapter, monetary equilibrium exists when the total demand for money to hold, L, is equal to the current supply, M^0.[2] The total demand for money, as we have seen, breaks down into two major components, the transactions demand, L_t, and the asset demand, L_a. Thus, $L = L_t + L_a$. The money supply can also be broken down into the quantity needed for transactions purposes, M_t^0, and a residual amount available for holding as an asset, M_a^0. Consequently, $M^0 = M_t^0 + M_a^0$. Therefore, the following equation gives us a symbolic statement of the essential condition for monetary equilibrium:

$$L_t + L_a = M_t^0 + M_a^0.$$

The total demand for money, L, is a function of both income and the rate of interest because one of its components, the transactions demand, is a function of income, whereas its other component, the asset demand, is a function of the rate of interest. This means that equilibrium with respect to the transactions demand is linked to income, and equilibrium with respect to the asset demand is linked to the rate of interest. Consequently, general equilibrium in the monetary sphere must be defined in terms of both the income level and the rate of interest.

The LM Schedule

By combining the asset demand for money and the transactions demand for money and a given money supply, it is possible to derive another curve that is conceptually similar to the *IS* curve but shows equilibrium values in the monetary sphere in relation to the rate of interest and the level of income. This is known as the *LM* curve. From our discussion in Chapter 9, it will be recalled that the asset demand for money is linked functionally to the rate of interest $[L_a = f(i)]$, and the transactions demand for money is linked functionally to the lower level of income $[L_t = f(Y)]$. These two relationships are brought together in Figure 10–3 to show how in combination we can derive the *LM* schedule.

In the figure we begin with Part A in the upper left-hand quadrant. This shows the asset demand for money as a smooth curve sloping downward to the right. Let us begin the analysis with the rate of interest given at the level i_3. At this rate of interest, the demand for money for

2. Remember the analysis is cast in real terms, which is to say that L is the demand for real balances and M the real money supply. Price level considerations will be dealt with later.

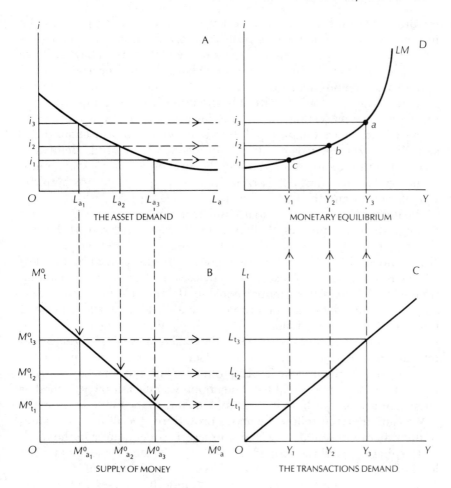

Figure 10–3. Equilibrium in the Monetary Sphere

asset purposes will be equal to L_{a_1}, as depicted on the horizontal axis of the schedule shown in Part A. Move now in a counterclockwise direction to Part B in the figure in the lower left-hand quadrant. In this part of the figure the total supply of money is represented by a straight line that connects the two axes. It is assumed to be exogenous. What this part of the figure shows is that the total money supply can be held either entirely for asset purposes (the point at which the money supply line intersects the horizontal axis), for transactions purposes (the point at which the money supply line intersects the vertical axis), or some combination in between. Return now to our point of departure, namely, a rate of interest of i_3, and an asset demand for money equal to L_{a_1}. This means that $M^0_{a_1}$ of the total money supply (MP) is required to satisfy the demand for money for asset purposes. This leaves, consequently, an amount of money $M^0_{t_3}$ available to support transactions. By projecting this quantity to the demand for money function shown in Part C in the lower right-hand quadrant, we find that an income level of Y_3 can be supported. The income level Y_3, in other words, is the equilibrium income level that gives rise to a transaction demand for money equal to L_{t_3}. Now we have described conditions for equilibrium with respect to both the asset demand and the transactions demand for money. What remains is to link the two together, which is done in Part D in the upper right-hand quadrant of the figure. By projecting the income level Y_3 upward and the rate of interest i_3 across we establish point a where these two projections intersect. Point a represents a condition of monetary equilibrium defined in terms of both the rate of interest and the level of income. It is a point of monetary balance $(L = M^0)$ characterized by unique values for both the rate of interest and the level of income.

Having established this initial equilibrium point, we need to trace through the consequences of changes in the rate of interest. If the rate of interest declines to i_2, the demand for money for asset purposes will rise to the level L_{a_2}. This means that, given a fixed supply of money, less money is available for transactions purposes. In Part B of the diagram we now find a quantity of money equal to M_{t_2} available for transactions, a quantity that will sustain an income level of Y_2. Thus, at a lower rate of interest and with a fixed money supply the equilibrium income level will necessarily be lower because more of the total money supply is absorbed into idle balances (the asset demand), and less is available to sustain income. If we again link the income level Y_2 to the rate of interest i_2 in Part D of the figure in the upper right-hand quadrant, we establish point b, another equilibrium value for both interest and income in the monetary sphere.

We can, in effect, follow the above procedures for all possible values of the rate of interest. This will give us a series of equilibria in the monetary sphere, equilibria defined in terms of the rate of interest and the level of income. This yields the *LM* curve found in Part D of the figure. More precisely, the *LM* curve, given the underlying asset and transactions demand for money, and given, too, the exogenous money supply, describes all possible equilibrium values in the monetary sphere. Equilibrium in the monetary sphere means the demand for and the supply of money are in balance in terms of a relationship between the income level and the rate of interest.

In Figure 10–3 it will be noted that at relatively low income levels the *LM* schedule lies flat or, in technical terms, is perfectly elastic with respect to the rate of interest. On the other hand, at relatively high income levels the *LM* schedule becomes vertical or perfectly inelastic with respect to the rate of interest. What are the reasons for this? The *LM* curve is constructed, it will be recalled, on the assumption that the total supply of money is fixed. This being the case, at low levels of income, the transactions demand for money, L_t, will also be relatively low. Therefore, a large portion of the total money supply will be available for holding as idle balances. But any increase in the quantity of money available to hold as an asset, M_a^0, drives the rate of interest down. There is a limit to the extent that the rate of interest can fall, for as we saw in the analysis in the last chapter the asset demand function becomes perfectly elastic at relatively low rates of interest. This is the liquidity trap. Once we reach the critical level at which interest rates do not respond to any further increases in the quantity of money available for holding as idle balances, then the *LM* curve must become perfectly elastic with respect to the rate of interest. A further decline in income will not, in other words, cause any further decline in interest rates through the impact of money balances released by a declining transactions demand. As pointed out in Chapter 9, there is little empirical evidence to support the idea that the demand for money may become perfectly elastic.[3] We include this possibility in our discussion, however, for the sake of theoretical completeness and to point up later the differences at the extreme between the policy implications of a Keynesianism and a pure classical analysis. The latter involves a total absence of a speculative demand for money balances.

The vertical character of the upper reaches of the *LM* curve is explained by the fact that, without action by the monetary authorities to increase bank reserves, the money supply curve will ultimately become inelastic with respect to the rate of interest. Thus, there is some maximum income level that can be financed with a fixed quantity of money. Money, in other words, can become a bottleneck that will choke off an expansion of income beyond some given level. As the income level rises, the transactions demand for money will obviously increase. A higher level of income means more transactions, and more money will be needed to sustain the larger volume. But if the total money supply does not grow as rapidly as transactions increase, additional quantities of money for transactions purposes can be obtained only by drawing them out of idle balances.[4] The cost of doing this is a higher rate of interest and, as the income level rises, interest rates must rise higher and higher. Eventually the economy will reach a critical level at which any further expansion in the income level becomes impossible because the entire money supply is now held in transactions balances, and M^0 is no longer responsive to increases in the rate of interest. In Figure 10–3 (Part B) Y_5 is assumed to be the maximum income that an amount of money, M^0, can sustain.

3. Even Keynes, who invented the concept of the liquidity trap, recognized its rarity in the real world. In *The General Theory* (p. 207) he said, "There is the possibility . . . that after the rate of interest has fallen to a certain level, liquidity-preference may become virtually absolute in the sense that almost everyone prefers cash to holding a debt which yields so low a rate of interest. . . . *But whilst this limiting case might become practically important in the future, I know of no example hitherto* [italics added]. Indeed, owing to the unwillingness of most monetary authorities to deal boldly in debts of long term, there has not been much opportunity for a test."
4. This assumes, of course, that the income velocity of money is unchanged. An increase in velocity can have the same effect as an increase in the money supply. Our purpose, though, is to analyze the effect on the monetary sphere—particularly interest rates—of a rise in the output level, assuming velocity is relatively constant and the supply is not perfectly elastic.

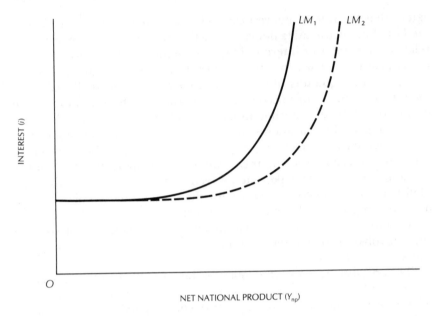

FIGURE 10–4.   Shift in the *LM* Curve

The effect of an increase in the money supply function on the position of the *LM* curve is shown in Figure 10–4. The initial position of the *LM* curve is shown by the solid line *LM*₁. The dashed line $LM_{,2}$ represents a shift in the position of the curve. This type of shift would reflect action by the central bank to increase the money supply, presumably by putting more reserves into the commercial banks. The reason an increase in the money supply will shift the curve to the right can be easily understood by referring once again to Figure 10–3 (Part A). The existence of a fixed money supply schedule meant that monetary equilibrium at each and every possible income level was uniquely associated with a particular rate of interest. An increase in the money supply shifts this curve to the right, thus making possible monetary equilibrium at any particular income level at a lower rate of interest than heretofore. To show this situation in terms of the *LM* curve, it is necessary to shift this curve to the right as is done in Figure 10–4. Each point on the LM_2 curve represents a particular income level that is uniquely correlated with a rate of interest that is lower than the rate correlated with the point representing the same income level on curve LM_1. The effects of a decrease in the money supply would be just the reverse, that is, the *LM* curve will shift to the left.

General Equilibrium

By combining the *LM* and *IS* curves in a single diagram we are able to construct in graphic form a general model of the economic system that shows, particularly, the manner in which the monetary sphere and the goods sphere are linked together through the rate of interest. Such a graphic model is shown in Figure 10–5. This model can be employed to demonstrate how the rate of interest and the income level are mutually determined in the income-expenditure system, and to show a number of different and important situations that may be characteristic of the economic system.

In Figure 10–5 the *IS* and *LM* curves intersect at a point where net national product is at Y_e and the rate of interest is at i_e. These are equilibrium levels with respect to income and the rate of interest, both of which are mutually determined by the intersection of the *IS* and *LM* schedules. At the point of intersection of these curves, the output level, Y_{np}, and the rate of interest, i, are such that $(S + T)$ and $(I + G)$ are in equilibrium, and the demand for money, L, and the supply of money, M^0, are also in equilibrium. There are any number of levels of both the rate of interest and income that are compatible with equilibrium of either $(S + T)$ and $(I + G)$ alone, or the demand for and supply of money also considered alone, but there is only *one* rate of interest and *one* level of income that is consistent with equilibrium in both the monetary and the goods sphere. The actual level of both income and interest that is consistent with equilibrium in the two spheres depends upon the shape and level assumed for the *LM* and *IS* curves, and this, in turn, is dependent upon the characteristics of the functions which lie in back of these schedules.

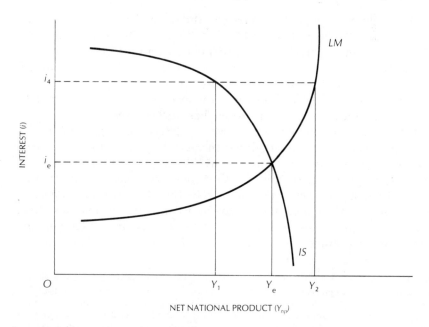

FIGURE 10–5.   A General Equilibrium Model of the Economic System

The reasons why the point of intersection of the *IS* and *LM* schedules depicts a condition of general equilibrium for the whole economy can best be seen if we imagine that income and the rate of interest are, momentarily, at a level different from Y_e and i_e.

Let us assume for a moment that the rate of interest and income are actually at levels represented by i_4 and Y_2 as shown in Figure 10–5. This represents a disequilibrium condition in the system as a whole, for while these values for both income and the rate of interest are compatible with equilibrium in the monetary sphere, they are not compatible with income in the goods sphere. At the interest rate i_4, for instance, income would have to be at the level of Y_1 to bring equilibrium in the goods sphere, as determined by the *IS* curve. The system will of necessity move toward an equilibrium point; at the interest rate i_4 investment expenditure will not be sufficient to maintain an income level of Y_2, and hence the latter will decline. But as the income level declines, a portion of the money supply is released from use in response to the transactions motive, and as this happens the rate of interest declines, thereby making possible equilibrium in the monetary sphere at successively lower rates of both interest and income. This adjustment process will continue until a level of interest rates and income is reached that is compatible with equilibrium in both spheres of economic activity. Then, and only then, will a general equilibrium condition for the whole economy prevail.

Changes in the Equilibrium Values of Income and Interest

A change in the equilibrium level of the net national product and the rate of interest comes about within the framework of our graphic model of the economic system as the consequence of a shift in the position of either the *IS* or *LM* curve. It should be noted carefully that all shifts in equilibrium values for income embody the multiplier process, which is to say that every equilibrium value for income shown in the model is arrived at after the multiplier process has worked itself out.

For convenience in our analysis, we can describe changes which affect the equilibrium values for both income and the rate of interest as being either *real* or *monetary* in origin. By *real* changes we mean those that originate in the goods sector, and that thus come about because the *IS* curve has shifted. *Monetary* changes, on the other hand, refer to developments emanating from the monetary sphere and, consequently, manifest themselves through a change in position of the *LM* schedule.[5] Examination of the major sources of shifts in both the *IS* and *LM* schedules will pro-

---

5. One should be careful not to confuse this use of the terms "real" and "monetary" with the distinction between real and nominal values. In the above discussion we are using real and monetary as a way to distinguish between the two spheres of the economy found in the income-expenditure analysis. In the other usage, the term real refers to values corrected for changes in the price level, whereas nominal refers to values not so corrected. One should always be aware of this distinction.

vide us with the necessary background for a discussion of contemporary economic policy and its application to fluctuations in income and employment.[6]

Shifts in the IS Curve

The fundamental explanation for a rightward shift in the *IS* curve is an increase in the aggregate demand function. Four major explanations for an upward movement of the aggregate demand function can be distinguished. First, there may be an autonomous increase in the investment demand function. In this instance, schedule *I* in Part A of Figure 10–1 shifts to the right, indicating a higher level of investment spending at all ranges of the interest rate. Second, there may be an autonomous increase in government spending for goods and services. If such an increase takes place with no increase in taxes, the maximum shift in the aggregate demand schedule will be obtained. However, even if taxes are increased in an amount equal to an increase in government spending for goods and services, the balanced budget theorem examined in Chapter 7 indicates that the aggregate demand function will still be displaced upward. Third, there may be an autonomous upward shift in the consumption function. This could come about because of an increase in transfer payments, a reduction in personal income taxes, or a general tax reduction with no change in the level of either government expenditures or investment outlays. It might also result from changing attitudes toward thrift, which would have the effect of reducing the propensity to save at all income levels. Finally, the aggregate demand function may shift because of an increase in exports relative to imports. This may result from an absolute increase in exports or a downward shift in the import function. (Refer again to Figure 10–1 and determine how each of the foregoing changes affects the position of the aggregate demand function and, consequently, the position of the *IS* curve. Keep in mind at all times that the *IS* curve is a schedule showing a series of equilibrium values for the output level at alternative values for the rate of interest, given all the underlying relationships which enter into determination of the level of aggregate demand.)

Within the framework of our general equilibrium model, the effect upon income of an upward shift in the aggregate demand schedule depends upon (1) the extent to which the *IS* curve is displaced to the right (the distance *ab* in Part A of Figure 10–6) and (2) the impact that a rising rate of interest will have upon forces which determine equilibrium in the goods sphere (the distance *cd* in the same figure). The factors which govern the magnitude of the shift in the *IS* curve are those which influence the size of the multiplier effect, given an increase (or decrease)

6. In the discussion that follows we shall focus our attention on shifts to the right in both the *IS* and *LM* schedules. The same reasoning and explanations apply with respect to shfits in the opposite direction.

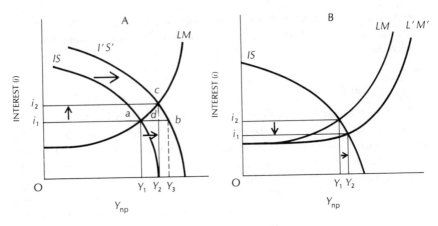

Figure 10–6. Shifts in the *IS* and *LM* Curves

in aggregate demand. These latter are the array of factors that determine the extent of leakages from the income stream. If there is no change in the position of the *LM* schedule with a given shift to the right in the *IS* curve, the result will be a rise in the rate of interest. This is due to the fact that the increase in the transactions demand which accompanies the rightward shift in the *IS* schedule can be met only by drawing money out of the asset sphere, a development that necessarily entails higher interest rates. The overall impact of the rise in the interest rate is to dampen the income-increasing effect of the rightward shift in the *IS* curve. The magnitude of this dampening effect depends upon both the steepness of the *LM* curve at the point of shift in the *IS* schedule and the interest elasticity of the investment component of the aggregate demand function. In later discussions of policy, we shall return to this point.

Shifts in the LM Curve

The effect of a rightward shift in the *LM* curve upon both equilibrium income level and the equilibrium value for the rate of interest is depicted in Part B of Figure 10–6. This shift could take place because of an autonomous increase in the money supply. The reasons why an increase in the money supply shifts the *LM* curve were touched upon in the discussion in conjunction with Figure 10–3. A change in the money supply is most likely to be the source of a shift in the *LM* schedule. The *LM* curve might shift to the right because of a downward shift in the asset demand component, L_a, of the total demand for money. This would be the result of a general decline in the demand for liquidity throughout the economy. The effect of a downward shift in the liquidity preference function is to release funds from idle balances, which spill over into the bond market, pushing up the prices of the latter and thereby reducing interest rates. It follows from this that monetary equilibrium in relation to any given income level will be achieved at a lower rate of interest.[7]

In general, the effect upon the equilibrium income level of a shift to the right in the *LM* curve depends upon (1) the extent to which the rate of interest declines as a result of the shift in the *LM* schedule and (2) the responsiveness of forces in the goods sphere to a decline in the rate of interest. The latter is primarily a matter of the interest elasticity of the investment demand schedule, although other components of aggregate demand may be affected by a change in the rate of interest. We shall elaborate further upon this in our subsequent discussion of policy and its application.

In connection with shifts in the *LM* curve, one additional point should be noted: With the exception of changes taking place in the range of interest rates equal to or below the horizontal portion of the *LM* schedule, a shift to the right in the *LM* schedule will always reduce the rate of interest. The significance of this is that the full multiplier effect will follow; there will be, in other words, no offsetting changes in the rate of interest as is the situation confronting the economy when the *IS* curve shifts.

Public Policy and the IS-LM General Equilibrium Model

Although we shall defer to Chapter 15 a full discussion of the theory and practice of modern macroeconomic policy, at this point we can draw upon the foregoing analysis to describe briefly the nature of monetary and fiscal policy, the differences between them, and how they work. The IS-LM general equilibrium model offers us a succinct and useful vehicle for doing this.

Monetary policy works primarily through controls exercised over the supply of money. In an advanced economy this basically means control over the volume of bank lending. In the United States the Federal Reserve System is the chief agency through which such control is exercised. The objective in controlling the money supply, including bank lending, is indirectly to control spending. More specifically, and within the income-expenditure framework, changes in the money supply will result in changes in interest rates, which, in turn, will have an impact on spending. The brunt of this impact will be borne by investment expenditure, as neither the consumption nor the government expenditures component of aggregate demand is readily linked to the rate of interest. Thus, the question of the efficacy of monetary policy as an instrument of economic stabilization largely turns on the issue of the shape of the investment demand schedule, about which economists are not in full agreement. To modern monetarists, though, this is not the relevant question, for, as

---

7. A third possibility involves a decline in the general price level, a possibility which will be explained in a later section.

we shall see in Chapter 11, they argue that monetary policy works through the impact of changes in the money supply on money balances and the further impact of this on spending for output. Furthermore, the real public policy issue in their view is, in the final analysis, one of persuading the monetary authorities to allow the money supply to grow at a constant rate and do nothing more.

Fiscal policy, on the other hand, involves deliberate changes in government expenditures and taxes as a means of controlling economic activity. The budget of the national government is the key instrument through which fiscal policy is effected. Government expenditures for goods and services directly affect the level of economic activity because such expenditures are a component part of the aggregate demand function; transfer expenditures and taxes, on the other hand, affect disposable income and thus indirectly influence the other two major components of aggregate demand, consumption and investment spending. Fiscal policy therefore works through changes in the government's budget which, in turn, increase or decrease the level of spending in the economy.

Figure 10–7 shows how the economy can move from an underemployment equilibrium by the application of either fiscal or monetary policy or a combination of the two. Let us assume that initially the economy is at an underemployment equilibrium given by the intersection at point

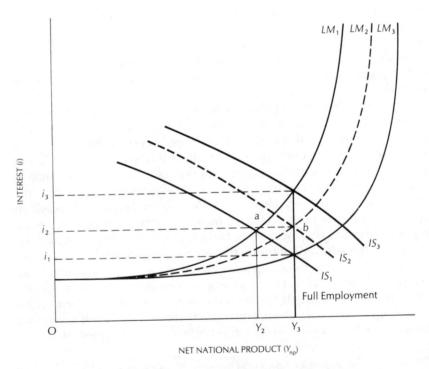

Figure 10–7.   Fiscal Policy, Monetary Policy, and Full Employment

a of *IS* and *LM* schedules designated as IS_1 and LM_1. Fiscal policy measures have the effect of shifting the *IS* curve to the right. If fiscal policy alone is used to get the economy to the full-employment income level of Y_3, the *IS* curve must shift to the position designated in the diagram as IS_3.

The extent to which the *IS* schedule shifts as a result of a given change in either government expenditures, *G*, or net taxes, *T*, depends upon the value of the multiplier. It is the multiplier in combination with the shift in the aggregate demand schedule that determines, *ceteris paribus*, the amount by which equilibrium income changes (See Chapter 7). However, the shift in the *IS* schedule is not the only factor to be taken into account. If there is no change in the money supply curve, then the interest rate will increase as a consequence of a higher level of real output. At IS_3 and LM_1 the equilibrium interest rate has risen to i_3. A rise in the interest rate, *ceteris paribus*, tends to reduce investment outlays and offsets to some extent the effect of more government expenditures for goods and services or of lower taxes on the economy's equilibrium position. Thus, policy-makers must take interest rate changes as well as the value of the multiplier into account in trying to estimate the net effect of a fiscal change on output and employment.

If monetary rather than fiscal policy is chosen as the means to move the economy to the full-employment output Y_3, then the *LM* curve must shift to the position designated as LM_3 in Figure 10–7. This can be brought about by a rightward shift in the money supply curve (see Figure 10–3). For any given shift to the right in the *LM* curve, the response of real output is governed by the interest elasticity of the *IS* curve. This depends primarily on how investment expenditures respond to a change in the rate of interest. If they are sensitive to such changes, then a shift to the right of the *LM* curve will, via the investment multiplier, have a highly favorable effect upon real output. It should be noted, too, that the interest rate effects of monetary policy are the opposite of those associated with fiscal policy changes. Thus, in Figure 10–7, a full-employment equilibrium resulting from the intersection of IS_1 and LM_3 will lower the rate of interest to the equilibrium value of i_1.

The examples just cited show the effects in isolation of fiscal or monetary policy upon real output. Reality is more complex; it may involve a combination of both monetary and fiscal action. It is possible, in principle, at least, to move the economy to the full-employment output of Y_3 without any change in the rate of interest. This outcome is shown by the intersection of the dashed curves IS_2 and LM_2 at point *b*. A combination of fiscal and monetary action means that less stringent measures of either type have to be taken than would be the case if either policy approach is applied separately and in isolation. For the sake of simplicity in the exposition we have assumed that the *IS* and *LM* schedules are independent of one another. In reality this may not be true, a fact which complicates the application of either fiscal or monetary policy. We shall return to this point in Chapter 15.

The Price Level and General Equilibrium

Now that we have constructed the basic IS-LM model of the macroeconomy, it is appropriate to expand the model and at the same time make it more realistic by bringing the price level into the analysis. Up to this point the price level has been taken as a "given" and a constant. As we have seen, this basic assumption has had the effect of putting the analysis in *real* or constant price terms.

Now our objective is to demonstrate how the output (and employment) level may be affected by a change in the price level. The income-expenditure analysis pursued up to this point focuses on the demand side. It has been explicitly assumed that output responds to any change in the level of aggregate demand. As a matter of fact, the constant price assumption means that the only way in which the economy can respond to shifts in the aggregate demand function is through output changes—that is, adjustments in the level of *real* GNP. To a degree this is a reasonable approach, but it is not adequate to deal with the full complexity of the real-world economy. We must recognize that in reality changes in aggregate demand lead to changes in both output and the price level. We must further recognize—as is the case with interest and income (output) in the general IS-LM model—that output and the price level are also determined simultaneously.

To resolve these problems, we shall proceed, first, by the introduction of the price level into the IS-LM model as an *exogenous* variable. This is necessarily an oversimplification, but it is a useful way to proceed. It is useful because from this perspective we can move to the treatment of the price level as an *endogenous* variable—which is the real-world situation—by the development of aggregate demand and supply schedules that link the price level to both the supply of output (the GNP) and the total demand for that output. As we shall see, these particular concepts of aggregate demand and supply are analogous to the concepts of individual demand and supply that microeconomic analysis uses to explain the determination of the price and quantity produced or supplied of an individual good or service. It is important to stress at this point that we shall still be operating within the fundamental framework of macroeconomics, which is that output, employment, and the price level are best explained by the interplay between aggregate demand and aggregate supply. At this point in our analysis we shall be looking at these latter relationships from a somewhat different perspective than we did earlier in Chapter 4 ("A General Model of the Economic System"), but conceptually the approaches are the same.

The Price Level as an Exogenous Variable

To introduce the price level as an exogenous variable into the basic IS-LM model we need to make two simplifying assumptions. The first is that of flexible prices, which is to assume that all prices move freely upward and downward in response to changing economic conditions. Reality, of course, is quite different, but this assumption will enable us to develop our model. The IS-LM model with flexible prices has been described as the "neoclassical synthesis," the reason being it combines classical principles of demand and supply operating in competitive markets with Keynesian principles of output determination.[8] The fully developed neoclassical model also requires that we graft a classical model of the labor market into an IS-LM model with flexible prices, a task we shall turn to subsequently.

Our second simplifying assumption is that when the price level changes all prices change in the same proportion. This, too, is not necessarily true in reality, but it is a useful technique because it enables us to trace through in the most direct fashion how a change in the price level will affect the *IS* and *LM* curves.

Now to proceed. It should be clear that all the key variables that lie behind the *IS* curve—consumption,, investment, government spending, and net exports—are measured in real terms. This is how we have proceeded in the prior chapters as we built up with great care all the variables that enter into the economy's aggregate demand schedule. This also means that households, business firms, and governments do not suffer from a "money illusion." The term "money illusion" was coined by the distinguished American economist Irving Fisher and refers to "a failure to perceive that the dollar or any other unit of money expands and shrinks in value."[9] To put it differently, we are assuming that the key economic actors in our macroeconomic drama—the households, business firms, and governments—clearly understand that the value of money is not stable. Consequently, the relationships that enter into the construction of the aggregate demand schedule are framed in real, not nominal, terms. This being the case, there is no reason why the rise or fall in the general price level should shift any of the underlying real functions—the consumption function or the investment demand function, for example—which determine the position of the *IS* curve. Consequently, we shall assume initially that the *IS* curve does not shift as a result of a change in the general price level.

It is a different story with respect to the *LM* schedule. The demand for money balances is, as we have seen, a demand for real balances, but the amount of money in existence (which is money being held) can only be denominated in nominal terms, as money is the basic unit in which all else is measured. The important question is what happens to the real value (their purchasing power, in other words) of such balances when the price level changes, all else remaining constant? If prices go up, this means that the *real* value of nominal money balances has declined. But this will be the same in an economic sense as a decline in the money

---

8. Paul Samuelson, *Economics, An Introductory Analysis,* 6th ed. (New York: McGraw-Hill, 1955), p. 337.
9. Irving Fisher, *The Money Illusion* (New York: Adelphi, 1928), p. 4.

supply, since persons and firms find themselves with less money available to meet their transactions and other monetary needs. Thus, an increase in the price level, *ceteris paribus,* will pull money out of idle balances into active circulation, thereby causing an increase in the interest rate. There is no difference in this effect between an increase in the price level and a decrease in the money supply, *ceteris paribus.* Since this takes place at any or all values for net national product, the *LM* curve will lie to the left of the position it would occupy at a lower price level. An increase in the price level, in other words, shifts the *LM* curve to the left. A fall in the price level, on the other hand, has the same effect, *ceteris paribus,* as an increase in the money supply. Thus, introduction of a price level variable into the analysis results in a series of *LM* schedules, each one associated with a different price level. These are depicted in Figure 10–8 as $LM(p_3)$, $LM(p_2)$, and $LM(p_1)$.

What we now have in our general equilibrium model is not a single set of equilibrium values for interest and income, as shown earlier in Figure 10–5, but a series of equilibrium values, each one uniquely associated with a different level of prices. But we have something more than this. We now have the mechanism to ensure that equilibrium in the goods market *(IS)* and in the money market *(LM)* is brought into balance at an assumed full-employment level. This mechanism is the price level, assuming *flexibility* in all prices, including money wages.

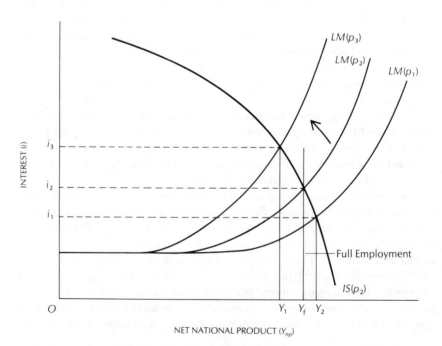

FIGURE 10–8.   General Equilibrium and the Price Level

Turn again to Figure 10–8. If we assume that Y_f is the full-employment output level[10] and that momentarily the price level is at p_1, we now have a disequilibrium condition in terms of the model. This is because, given the price level p_1, the IS and LM curves will intersect at an income level equal to Y_2. But this is not possible, assuming Y_f is the full-employment real income. Consequently, in this situation, the adjusting factor must be a rise in the price level from p_1 to p_2, assuming no changes in the underlying determinants of the system. The income-expenditure model shows, in other words, that, if conditions in the monetary and goods sphere are such that the IS-LM equilibrium output lies beyond the full-employment level, then rising prices are inevitable.

If the price level happens to be p_3 we have an opposite situation. Now the equilibrium output for IS and LM is Y_1, which represents a level of aggregate demand below the full-employment output level, Y_f. Now what will happen? Just the reverse of what took place in the opposite situation. Prices will drop, and they will continue to fall until the system reaches a full-employment equilibrium. In Figure 10–8 this will be at the price level p_2. Flexibility in prices ensures an automatic adjustment of the economic system to full employment.

The Keynes and Pigou Effects

In the foregoing discussion, it is simply price flexibility per se that forces the system to adjust to a stipulated full-employment output, given a fixed quantity of money in nominal terms. We have not to this point specified any specific mechanisms through which these results might be achieved. There are, however, two possible mechanisms by which these results can in theory be brought about, mechanisms which in the literature of economics have come to be known as the "Keynes effect" and the "Pigou effect." These mechanisms are illustrated in Figure 10–9.

The Keynes effect, shown in Part A of the figure, works through the impact that lower prices have on the real value of the economy's money supply. Why is this called the Keynes effect? The answer is that a falling price level, which increases the *real* value of the nation's money supply, will, *ceteris paribus*, lower interest rates. Lower interest rates will, given the negative slope of the investment demand schedule (see Chapter 6), increase investment spending, a change which will also bring the multiplier into play. Thus aggregate demand will increase, which in terms of the IS-LM relationships involves a movement along the IS curve, and the income level will rise. The price level effects that trigger this change are reflected in Figure 10–9 by rightward shifts in the LM curve. If we admit the possibility of a "liquidity trap"—the flat portion of the LM curves—there is a limit to the amount of expansion that can be obtained by reducing prices. In Figure 10–9, this limit is the income level Y'. Since,

10. Later, and by the introduction of a labor market into the model, we shall show how it is the labor market that may ultimately determine the full-employment level of output.

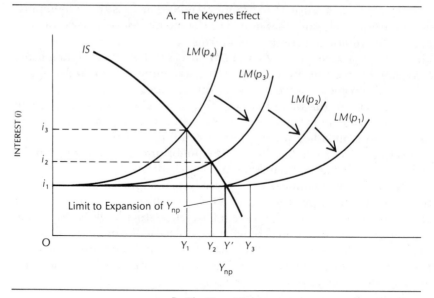

A. The Keynes Effect

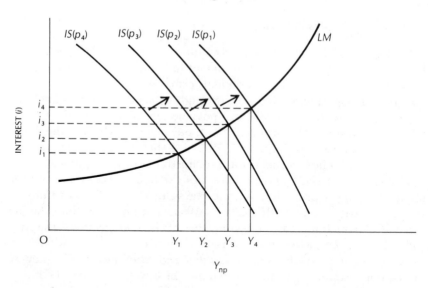

B. The Pigou Effect

FIGURE 10–9.   The Keynes and Pigou Effects

at this income level, the *IS* curve intersects the *LM* curve in the flat portion of the latter, a further reduction in the price level from p_2 to p_1 will not lead to any additional increase in income, even though the *LM* curve would be pushed farther to the right. A word of caution is in order here. This mechanism is called the Keynes effect because it works through the basic Keynesian propensities involving investment and consumption (i.e., the multiplier), but this does not mean that Keynes advocated such a course of action. As a matter of fact, he strongly opposed wage and price deflation as a means of increasing output and employment, believing on practical grounds that an increase in the money supply could achieve the same result with far less resistance and social disharmony. What the idea of the "liquidity trap" did in this situation—granted that Keynes was dubious about its real existence—was to provide theoretical ammunition for Keyne's attack in the 1930s on the prescription of the classical economists that the way out of the depression was to slash wages and prices.

The argument embodied in the Pigou effect is of a different sort and, in principle at least, does not run into any limit on the extent to which output can be expanded by reducing the general level of prices. As pointed out initially in Chapter 5, the Pigou effect asserts that a falling price level will shift the consumption function upward, the reason being that lower prices increase the real value of the consumer's stock of liquid assets and thus lessen the need to save. Hence, real consumption will be higher at all income levels. In terms of the general equilibrium model, this means that the *IS* curve will shift to the right—or upward—as the price level drops. Thus, as shown in Part B of Figure 10–9, the Pigou effect postulates a series of *IS* schedules, each associated with a different level of prices. As a theoretical proposition, the Pigou effect is entirely logical, but most economists do not believe it has any great practical value. Certainly the experience of past depressions and recessions does not offer any convincing evidence that a falling price level will stimulate demand in this fashion.

The Price Level as an Endogenous Variable

In the preceding analysis we have shown how the IS-LM model can be modified to take into account changes in the general level of prices, as well as changes in output and the rate of interest. A problem remains, however, because the model is still basically indeterminate, the reason being that the price level is treated as an *exogenous* variable. As with the earlier version of the IS-LM model that included only the goods and money market and in which output and the rate of interest are determined simultaneously, we now have a model in which output, the rate of interest, *and* the price level are treated simultaneously.

One way to improve on the situation is to modify the model so that the price level becomes an *endogenous* variable. This can be accomplished by the development of aggregate demand and supply schedules that relate the demand for and the supply of output to the general price level. Schedules of this type are analogous to the kind of demand and supply schedules used to explain how the prices and output level for individual goods and services are determined. For construction of an aggregate demand schedule of this type we can employ IS-LM analysis. For development of the aggregate supply schedule, we shall make use of a classical production function and the demand for labor derived from that function.

The Aggregate Demand Schedule   Figure 10–10 shows how the IS-LM model can be used to construct an aggregate demand schedule as described above. In Part A of the figure we show an IS-LM diagram with a series of *LM* curves whose positions are determined by the general price level. In this formulation the money supply is, of course, a given. In Part B of the figure we plot on the horizontal axis the levels of output *(Y)* as derived from the IS-LM equilibrium positions shown in Part A against the price levels *(p)* appropriate to each level of equilibrium output. The result is a downsloping demand curve, except that demand in this instance (the horizontal axis) shows total output and it is the price level, rather than individual prices, which is plotted on the vertical axis. In concept, however, the schedule shown in the lower part of the figure is the same as the demand schedule for any individual good or service. It shows that,

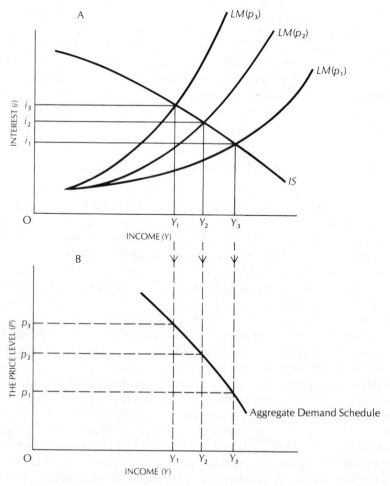

FIGURE 10–10.   *IS-LM* and the Aggregate Demand Schedule

ceteris paribus, the demand for the nation's output will be greater at a lower price level than at a higher price level.

The slope or elasticity of an aggregate demand schedule of the foregoing kind depends primarily upon two sets of forces. First there is the response of the rate of interest to a change in *real* money balances held by the public. When the price level falls, given the stock of money, there will be an increase in the real value of nominal money balances. This will trigger a decline in interest rates, the magnitude of which depends upon the shape of the total demand for money *(L).* The second set of forces embrace the key Keynesian variables that affect the slope of the *IS* curve. Basically what is involved here is the responsiveness of investment spending to a change in the rate of interest (the shape of the investment demand schedule), and the value of the multiplier. The latter determines how total spending (effective demand) will respond to a net change in investment spending. Thus, if the basic Keynesian functions are of a sensitive, responsive nature with respect to their determining variables, aggregate demand will be responsive to changes in the general price level. If not, the opposite will hold, namely, aggregate spending will be inelastic with respect to the price level.

The Aggregate Supply Schedule   To construct an aggregate supply schedule that relates total output *(Y)* to the price level *(p)* we start with the concept of the production function, a concept of fundamental importance in classical economics and one introduced initially in Chapter 3. In its most basic form the production function shows the relationship between the amount of employment *(N)* and the level of output *(Y),* assuming that stock of capital *(K′),* the quantity of natural resources *(R′),* and the level of technology *(T)* are all given. In this formulation, labor is the key variable resource and the relationship between labor used (employment) and output is summarized in the following equation:

$$Y = f(N). \tag{10-1}$$

In graphic form the production function is shown in Part A of Figure 10–11. What the curve shows is that the level of output increases as more labor is employed, but that the rate at which output increases gradually slows down. This is because of the operation of the economic law of *diminishing returns.* At some point output attains a maximum value, which is to say that no more output can be attained even if more labor is employed. The main reason for the operation of this law is that more and more labor is being spread over a fixed quantity of other resources (capital and natural resources), the result being that each successive unit of labor employed is a bit less efficient than prior units. Hence, output cannot grow in the same proportion as the input of labor.

The fact of diminishing returns is also reflected in a falling *marginal* product for labor. The curve which depicts the declining marginal product of labor is shown in Part B of Figure 10–11. The *marginal product of labor* is the extra output provided by each additional unit of labor used.

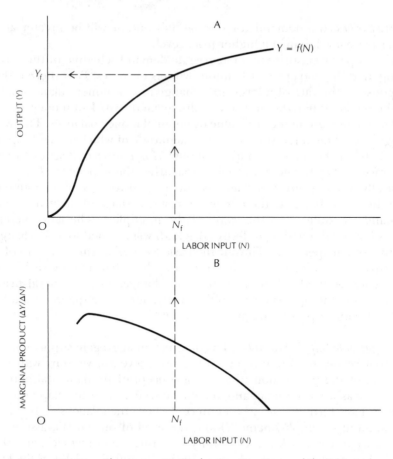

FIGURE 10–11. The Aggregate Production Function and the Marginal Product of Labor Curve

But if each additional unit of labor is a bit less efficient than prior units (diminishing returns), then the marginal product associated with each unit used must decline. Hence, the downward slope of this curve as shown in Figure 10–11, Part B.

Technically, the marginal product for labor for the entire economy is $\Delta Y/\Delta N$, as dividing the increase in total output by the increase in total employment will show how much, on the average, output increases with each additional worker employed. This, of course, is by definition the marginal product of labor. If we assume a competitive economy, all firms will use labor up to the point at which the *value* of output associated with added labor is just equal to its *cost*. When the firm—and by aggregation all firms in the economy—reaches this point it will both maximize its profits and be in equilibrium with respect to the employment of labor. In equation form the necessary condition for profit maximization is

$$\Delta Y p = \Delta N w. \qquad (10-2)$$

In the equation, p is the price level and w is the money wage. By rearrangement of Equation (10–12) we get the following:

$$\frac{\Delta Y}{\Delta N} = \frac{w}{p} . \tag{10-3}$$

But w/p is the real wage (W). Thus, Equation (10–13) says that, in equilibrium and with the assumption of profit maximization, the real wage and the marginal product of labor must be equal. What this means, of course, is that the demand for labor becomes a function of the real wage, a view that Keynes accepted. Thus, we have the basic macroeconomic demand curve for labor expressed as follows:

$$N_d = f(w/p). \tag{10-4}$$

Now that we have developed the classical production function and the downsloping demand curve for labor based upon diminishing marginal productivity, we may employ these concepts to complete construction of an aggregate supply curve that relates output to the price level. This is done in Figure 10–12. Part A of the figure presents a production function of the type just discussed. Note, however, that the axes are reversed, showing labor inputs (N) on the vertical axis and output (Y) on the horizontal axis. Part B shows the demand curve for labor, the quantity of labor being a function of the real wage (W). Again, though, the axes are transposed, the quantity of labor appearing on the vertical axis and the real wage on the horizontal axis.

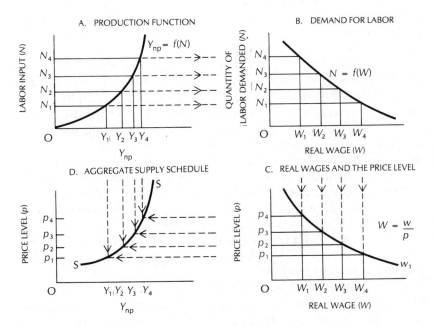

FIGURE 10–12.   Real Output and the Price Level

Part C contains a curve that ties the price level, p, to the real wage, W, by means of the current money wage, w_1. If money wages are given, then the real wage will vary inversely with the price level. This is what the curve w_1 shows. When we combine values for real output (derived from the relationship between the production function and the demand for labor) with the price level (derived from the relationship between real wages and the price level) we obtain in Part D a supply schedule for aggregate output, SS, which relates Y to the price level. What this schedule says, in effect, is that, given a fixed money wage and underlying technical conditions of production, more output will be supplied only as the price level rises. A rising price level is needed to bring about the fall in real wages that must take place to induce producers to use more labor. The reader should recognize the conceptual similarity of SS to the ordinary supply curve.

Aggregate Demand, Aggregate Supply, and the Price Level

The schedules just developed are called *neoclassical*, the reason being that they incorporate classical (or traditional) notions about the relationship of output and prices as well as Keynesian notions about total spending and total output. Now the question is: What specific uses can be made of these schedules? What, in other words, can we show about the economy's performance by using these schedules that we cannot show with the standard IS-LM analysis? There are two broad answers to this. First, the neoclassical aggregate demand and supply schedules provide a convenient mechanism for showing the effect of policy decisions on prices as well as upon output and employment. Second, their use has led to the creation of an income-expenditure (Keynesian) model in what, broadly speaking, is a classical framework.

In Figure 10–13 we bring together in a single diagram the neoclassical schedules of aggregate demand and aggregate supply worked out in the prior section. Earlier (Figure 10–7) we saw that, in principle, we could move the economy to a full-employment output level either by monetary policy, which shifted the LM curve, or by fiscal policy, which shifted the IS curve. Now we duplicate these policy changes in terms of the neoclassical aggregate demand and aggregate supply schedules shown in Figure 10–13. In this figure we assume that initially output is at the level Y_1, and the price level is at p_1. This is less than the full-employment output, which we shall designate in the figure as Y_2. To move the economy to this level of output, we simply have to bring about a rightward shift in the aggregate demand function to the position shown by the curve $D'D'$. How is this to be done, and how will such a shift affect the price level? These are the key questions.

In principle this shift in aggregate demand can be brought about by either monetary or fiscal actions, just as was done in the earlier situation depicted in Figure 10–7. Let us look first at monetary action in the form of an increase in the money supply. Given an initial level of prices (p_1),

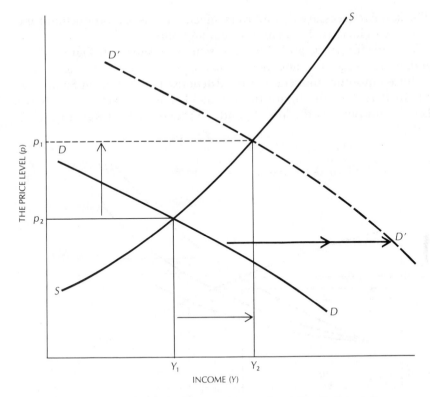

FIGURE 10–13. Neoclassical Aggregate Demand and Supply Schedules

an increase in the money supply will shift the *LM* curve to the right. *Ceteris paribus*, an increase in the money supply causes the rate of interest to fall, which, in terms of the basic IS-LM model (Figure 10–7), leads to an increase in aggregate demand by a move down the *IS* schedule. The policy problem is to increase the money supply sufficiently so that the neoclassical aggregate demand schedule in Figure 10–13 shifts just enough to bring the economy to the full-employment output level *(Y₂)*.

What makes the policy problem more complicated than in the earlier IS-LM model is the positive slope to the aggregate supply curve (*SS*), depicted in Figure 10–13. This means that, when total effective demand is increased, not only will the output level rise, but prices will also rise. The extent to which both output and the price level respond to an increase in aggregate demand depends upon the elasticity of the aggregate supply schedule. The less elastic this schedule the less responsive output and employment are to an increase in the money supply and the greater will be the extent to which more spending dissipates itself in rising prices. We should also recall that the supply schedule *SS* was constructed on the assumption of a fixed money wage. This is not an absolute requirement. What is necessary in this aggregate supply schedule is that prices rise faster than the money wage, for only if this happens will *real* wages decline.

The latter is necessary if employers, given the classical production function, are to increase both employment and output.

We can, in effect, go behind the schedules shown in Figure 10–13 and, using IS-LM diagrams, depict what happens when aggregate demand is shifted by either monetary or fiscal actions. This is done in Figure 10–14. In Part A of the figure the results of monetary action are shown. Initially output is at the level Y_1 and the rate of interest is i_3, an equilib-

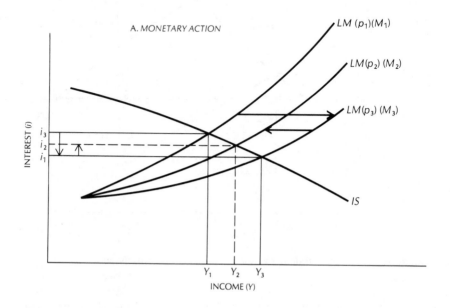

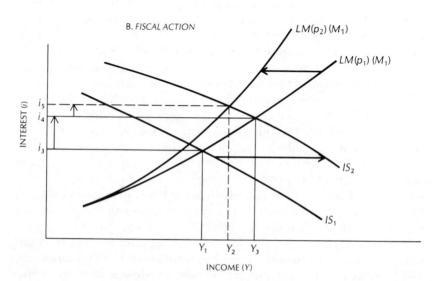

FIGURE 10–14.   *IS-LM* Changes and Shifts in Aggregate Demand and Supply

rium less than the full-employment output of Y_2. The price level associated with the schedule LM_1 is p_1 and the money supply is M_1. Now the money supply is increased to M_2, which with prices momentarily unchanged at p_1 shifts the LM schedule to the level indicated by LM_3. If prices remained stable, the interest rate would fall to i_1, and the equilibrium income level would rise to Y_3. But this is not possible because of the upsloping aggregate supply curve shown in Figure 10–13. Therefore, as expenditure increases because of the rightward shift in the LM curve, the price level also begins to rise. For the reasons discussed earlier in conjunction with Figure 10–8, a rising price level has the effect of shifting the LM curve to the left. Ultimately, a new equilibrium will be established by the intersection of LM_2 and the IS curve, which is the full-employment output Y_2. The price level will now be p_2, interest will be at i_2, and the money supply remains at M_2.

The alternative to monetary moves for shifting the aggregate demand schedule to the $D'D'$ level is fiscal action. Let us assume that this takes the form of an increase in government spending. If we think of the IS curve as embodying not just the private sector (C and I spending), but also the public sector (G spending), then an increase in government spending will shift the IS curve to the right. Again the policy problem is to increase government spending by an amount sufficient to bring output to the full-employment level Y_2 as depicted in Figure 10–13. The complicating factor as before is the price level, since any increase in aggregate spending will cause it to rise. What happens is shown in Part B of Figure 10–14. As indicated, the IS schedule shifts from IS_1 to IS_2, a direct result of the increase in government spending. If the price level remained at p_1, output would rise to a new equilibrium at Y_3, and interest rates would also rise to the level of i_4. But the price level does not remain still. More spending causes it to rise, and as it rises, the LM curve shifts to the left. What this does is raise the interest rate even further, a development which will have the effect of reducing investment spending. To sum up, the net effect of fiscal action in the form of increased government spending with respect to the output level will be smaller than otherwise would be the case because of rising prices. As long as the money supply remains fixed at the M_1 level, there is no offset to the impact that rising prices have on interest rates through a change in the position of the LM curve. Thus, the final equilibrium position of Y_2, which we assume is a full-employment equilibrium, will be one in which interest rates are higher and investment spending is smaller than would be the case if prices had remained stable.

The Neoclassical Synthesis

The term "the neoclassical synthesis" was invented by Professor Paul Samuelson of M.I.T. to describe an economic world in which the classical principles of demand and supply for individual goods and services and competitive markets would apply, once Keynesian principles had been employed to ensure a level of aggregate demand sufficient for full employment. Monetary and fiscal policy can, if necessary, be used to attain this condition.[11] In modern macroeconomic analysis this synthesis has been attained by grafting a classical model of the labor market onto the general equilibrium model (the IS-LM framework) with flexible prices.[12]

The classical labor market embodies the demand schedule for labor described earlier [Equation (10–4)] in which the demand for labor (N_d) is an inverse function of the real wage *(w/p)*. To this we must add the classical labor supply, which holds that the supply of labor *(N_s)* is a positive function of the real wage *(w/p)*. Thus, in equation form we have

$$N_s = f(w/p). \qquad (10\text{--}5)$$

The view that the number of workers seeking employment is a function of the real wage rests partly on the classical assumption that the worker, in offering his services in the labor market, seeks to maximize his income in the same way that the entrepreneur seeks to maximize his profit. Keynes, in speaking of this postulate of the classical analysis, said it means that the utility of the wage associated with a given volume of employment will be just equal to the disutility of that amount of employment.[13] Stated differently, the real wage represents that which is necessary to overcome the irksomeness (or disutility) of work and thus induce people to become employed. What this means is that there must be a "trade-off" between work and leisure, a balancing of the gain to be gotten from consuming the goods and services which the money wage will buy (the real wage) and the value of leisure to the individual. Since leisure has value, a rational person will give some or all of it up only if he or she is rewarded for so doing.

The functional relationship between the supply of labor and the real wage is also based upon the classical assumption that workers and other resource owners do not suffer from the *money illusion* (see p. 343). In other words, the monetary unit is believed to be stable in value, and thus a rise in money income is considered, *ipso facto*, a rise in real income. Under these circumstances—that is, an economy suffering from the money illusion—the supply of labor could just as easily be a function of the money wage as the real wage. But this is not the classical view of the matter. Money, to classical economists, is fundamentally a medium of

11. Paul Samuelson, *Economics, An Introductory Analysis*, 6th ed. (New York: McGraw-Hill, 1955), p. 337.

12. An elegant though somewhat terse exposition of the complete neoclassical model of general equilibrium is found in Martin J. Bailey, *National Income and the Price Level: A Study in Macroeconomic Theory*, 2nd ed. (New York: McGraw-Hill, 1971), Chap. 2, pp. 31–42. This section also draws on Hyman Minsky's study, *John Maynard Keynes* (New York: Columbia University Press, 1975). Professor Minsky is one of the leading critics of the neoclassical synthesis.

13. Keynes, *The General Theory*, p. 12.

exchange, a means to an end; they believe that the use of money should not obscure the fact that basically the economic process is concerned with an exchange of goods for goods. Money is significant only because it is more convenient to have a generally accepted medium of exchange than it is to resort to barter. The implication of such a view is that resource owners, including workers, will value the services of their resources in terms of the real returns they can command.

The Equilibrium Level of Employment

The significance in the classical system of the two schedules discussed—the demand for labor and the supply of labor—is that, when brought together, they uniquely determine both the employment level and the real wage. Moreover, the classical demand and supply schedules for labor necessarily intersect at the level of full employment. The process by which employment and real wage are mutually determined in the classical analysis is depicted in Figure 10–15.

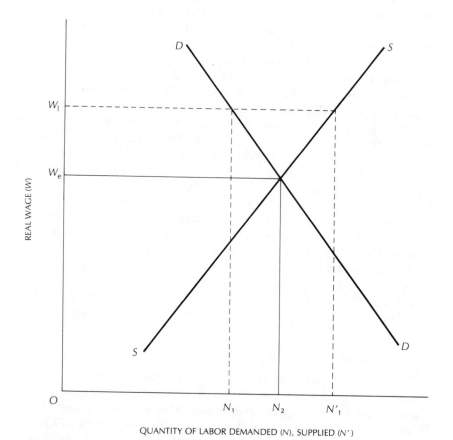

QUANTITY OF LABOR DEMANDED (N), SUPPLIED (N')

FIGURE 10–15. The Equilibrium Level of Employment

In the figure, *DD* represents the demand schedule for labor, and *SS* is the supply schedule for labor. Given these two schedules, competition in the market among employers for workers and among workers for employment will drive the real wage and the employment level to the values represented at the point of intersection of the two schedules. As long as the two schedules do not shift, no other level of either employment or real wages can prevail. If, momentarily, real wages were at the level represented by W_1, the number of workers actually seeking employment would be equal to the distance ON'_1. But at the W_1 level of real wages the amount of labor demanded would be equal only to the distance ON_1. The distance $N_1N'_1$, consequently, represents the surplus of workers seeking employment at the monetarily prevailing level of real wages. Competition for employment among these workers would lead some of them to offer their services to prospective employers at reduced money wages. As this happens, the real wage will decline, assuming other things remain constant, and employment will increase. Equilibrium in the labor market will prevail at the level of real wages W_e and the level of employment N_e. This is the essence of the classical explanation of how the economy's level of employment is determined.

The equilibrium employment level determined by the intersection of the classical demand and supply schedules for labor has to be one of full employment. If any unemployment (aside from frictional unemployment) exists after equilibrium is obtained, it must be voluntary unemployment. This is true for essentially two reasons. First, the classical analysts imply that, if nonfrictional unemployment persists after the equilibrium situation, it must be because some workers are demanding wages too high in relation to the marginal productivity of labor. If these workers are unemployed because of their refusal to accept lower money wages, their unemployment must be regarded as voluntary. If they would accept a reduction in money wages, the real wage would decline, other things being equal, and more employment would be forthcoming.

The second reason why the employment level is one of full employment is simply that the theory maintains that *money* wage bargains between workers and entrepreneurs determine the *real* wage; consequently, the workers in general are in a position to determine their real wage (through money wage bargains) and, therefore, the level of employment. If this is true, it necessarily follows that any unemployment that actually exists at a given level of real wages has to be voluntary unemployment.

The Complete Neoclassical Model

The next and final step is to incorporate the output level as determined by forces at play in the labor market into the IS-LM general equilibrium model of the aggregate economy. This is done in Figure 10–16. What we do is add a vertical line to the standard Keynesian IS-LM diagram at a point on the horizontal axis that is equal to the equilibrium

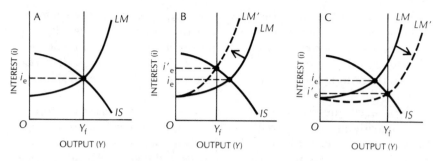

FIGURE 10–16.   The Goods, Money, and Labor Markets Combined

income level (Y_f) determined by the labor market model (Figure 10–15). In Figure 10–16, the labor-market-determined full-employment line is shown for three different sets of circumstances. In Part A of the figure, the vertical line Y_f is drawn so as to pass through the intersection of the IS and LM curves. In Part B it lies to the left of this point of intersection, whereas in Part C it lies to the right.

What does Figure 10–16 show us? In Part A we have a situation in which the three sets of forces at work in the economy—those that pertain to the goods market, those pertaining to the money market, and those pertaining to the labor market—happen to coalesce in such a way that equilibrium in each of the three spheres of the economy is compatible with full employment. But Parts B and C are different. In Part B the intersection of IS and LM lies to the right of the full-employment outuput (Y_f), a situation which implies that the combination of real and monetary forces which lie behind the IS and LM curves add up to a level of aggregate demand that exceeds the real capabilities of the economy. Part C, however, shows just the opposite, as the full-employment output (as determined in the labor market) lies beyond the intersection of IS and LM. What this means is that there is insufficient aggregate demand to get the economy to full employment.

From the standpoint of effective economic performance, the only acceptable situation is the one depicted in Part A, a level of aggregate demand equal to full employment as determined in the labor market sphere. The thrust of Keynesian analysis has been that there is *nothing* inherent in the structure of a market economy that will bring the economy to this situation. On the contrary, Keynes believed that, if the economy got to such a situation *without intervention by government,* it would not only be a rare occurrence, but completely fortuitous. The more normal condition of the market economy under a policy of *laissez faire* was that depicted in Part C of the diagram, a situation in which aggregate demand is chronically deficient.

The foregoing, however, is not the conclusion reached by the neoclassical synthesis. Rather, this approach argues that the economy is inherently stable and market forces can be depended upon to push it either to a short-term full-employment output or to the output path determined by the growth of its productive potential. Thus, although the neoclassical model admits of the possibility of the economy being in the situation depicted by either Part B or C, it does not admit that it can remain there long. Market forces will push it to the situation shown in Part A.

The crucial question is—how? The answer to this was given in conjunction with our discussion of Figure 10–8. It is the mechanism of flexible wages and prices. In our earlier discussion we pointed out that shifts in the *LM* curve brought about by changes in the general level of prices would ensure intersection of the *IS* and *LM* curves at the full-employment income level. All that was lacking in the discussion at that point was a mechanism within the model that would determine the full employment output level. This mechanism is now supplied by the neoclassical synthesis by grafting a classical model of the labor market onto the basic IS-LM model with flexible prices. We have come full circle; the basic Keynesian argument that the economy is inherently unstable and unlikely to attain a full-employment equilibrium on its own has been blunted. Instead, Keynesian mechanisms have been shown to be inherently stabilizing and self-adjusting *if* the classical condition of competitive markets and flexible wages and prices prevails.

To illustrate the foregoing point, consider what will happen if, momentarily, the economy finds itself in the situation depicted by B in Figure 10–16. What the figure shows is that the Keynesian equilibrium as determined by the intersection of *IS* and *LM* adds up to a spending total in excess of the output total determined by the production and equilibrium in the labor market. Something must give. That "something" is, of course, the price level. The excess of demand pulls up prices, rising prices shift the *LM* curve to the left as the figure indicates *(LM'*, interest rates climb (i_e'), and we move backward along the *IS* curve— which indicates a downward adjustment in effective demand as determined by investment spending and the multiplier relationship. Simply put, the goods and money markets adjust to the conditions of equilibrium determined by forces at work in the labor market. If the economy finds itself in the situation depicted in Part C of Figure 10–16, the opposite will happen. When total spending as determined by IS-LM equilibrium falls short of output determined in the labor market, wages and prices will fall, shifting the *LM* curve to the right *(LM')*, which, in turn, brings the rate of interest down (i'_e). The latter change will cause investment to rise, and total demand operating via the multiplier will rise until a full-employment equilibrium is attained.

Intellectually the neoclassical interpretation of the basic income-expenditure model developed in Part II has had a strong appeal to many economists, the reason being that it provides a complete theoretical model that integrates equilibrium in the goods, the money, and the labor markets. Furthermore, it is mathematically complete (see Appendix). It shows that, with wage and price flexibility, the economy becomes self-adjusting; the equations of the labor market ensure that eventually market forces will push the economy to full employment. As we have seen, the labor market dominates in determining output; the more purely Keynesian *IS* and *LM* equilibrium adjusts to conditions in the labor market, not the other way around.

At the level of pure economic theory, the meaning of the neoclassical synthesis is that continuing underemployment equilibrium becomes impossible, except under the special circumstances of downward rigidity in wages and prices or because of the existence of a liquidity trap. Thus, the neoclassical model succeeded in turning Keynes's original analysis upside down, making it a special case in the more general context of an essentially classical view of the world in which the "natural" tendency of the economy is toward full employment, given wage and price flexibility. We should not conclude from the foregoing, however, that the neoclassical analysis does not allow room for an active monetary and fiscal policy. Quite the contrary. It is recognized that wages and prices are often sluggish—especially downward—and thus the process through which the economy will adjust automatically toward a full-employment condition may, politically speaking, take much too long to attain. Consequently, Keynesian-style fiscal and monetary policies are not only necessary but welcome. As one observer has phrased it, "the neoclassical synthesis permits the advocacy of an active full-employment policy to be consistent with an in-theory belief in the self-equilibrating nature of the economy."[14]

In recent years there has emerged a growing number of economists in fundamental disagreement with this particular interpretation of Keynesian ideas. The reasons for this disagreement and the alternative views being developed are the subject of Chapter 13, "Post Keynesian Economics." In the next two chapters, 11 and 12, we shall explore alternatives to the income expenditure approach that have their roots in the classical economic view of how the economy works.

Appendix

Algebraic presentation of the general equilibrium model

Equilibrium in the goods sphere in an open economy.
  (1) $Y_{np} = C + I + G + X - M$ = the basic identity
  (2) $C = C'_0 + a'Y_{np}$ = the consumption function
        $a' = (a - at)$ = the marginal propensity to consume out of net national product
        $C'_0 = (C_0 - aT_0)$ = consumption that is independent of the income level. Taxes are reflected in both a' and C'_0.

14. Hyman Minsky, *John Maynard Keynes* (New York: Columbia University Press, 1975), p. 53.

(3) $I = I'_0 + bY_{np} = $ the investment function

$\quad\quad I'_0 = (I_0 - ci) = $ investment as an inverse function of the rate of interest. I'_0 equals investment which is independent of the income level.

(4) $M = M_0 + mY_{np} = $ the import function

(5) $G = $ autonomous government expenditures for goods and services

(6) $X = $ autonomous exports

(7) $Y_{np} = C'_0 + a'Y_{np} + I'_0 + bY_{np} + G + X - M_0 - mY_{np}$ (Equilibrium in the goods sphere.)

Equilibrium in the monetary sphere

(1) $M^{0'} = $ the nominal autonomous money supply

(2) $L_t = f(pY_{np}) = $ the transactions demand function

$\quad\quad p = $ the price level

(3) $L_a = f'(i) = $ the asset demand function

(4) $L = L_t + L_a = f(pY_{np}) + f'(i) = $ the total demand function

(5) $M^{0'}/p = f(Y_{np}) + f'(i)$ (This defines equilibrium in the monetary sphere in real terms.)

Equilibrium in the labor market

(1) $Y = f(N) = $ the production function

(2) $N = f(w/p) = $ the demand for labor function

$\quad\quad w = $ the money wage

$\quad\quad p = $ the price level

(e) $N' = f'(w/p) = $ the supply of labor function

(4) $N = N' = N_f = $ equilibrium in the labor market.

General equilibrium thus depends upon the solution of three equations—Equation (7) in the goods sphere, Equation (5) in the monetary sphere, and Equation (4) in the labor market—in three unknowns, namely, Y_{np}, N_f, and i.

Summary

1. The model of general equilibrium in terms of two schedules, the *IS* curve and the *LM* curve, is the central theme of the chapter.

2. Equilibrium in the "goods" sphere (the *IS* curve) refers to a balance between the demand for and the supply of total output. It means that aggregate demand and aggregate supply are in balance. For every equilibrium value of output in the "goods" sphere there is a unique value for output and for the rate of interest. The *IS* curve shows all possible equilibrium values for output (and employment) in terms of alternative values for both income and the rate of interest.

3. Equilibrium in the "monetary" sphere (the *LM* curve) refers to a balance between the total demand for money and the total supply of

money. This equilibrium, like equilibrium in the "goods" sphere, can be defined in terms of unique values for both income and the rate of interest. The *LM* curve links all possible equilibrium values for the demand and supply of money to the level of income and the rate of interest.

4. General equilibrium in both the goods and monetary spheres is attained by bringing the *IS* and *LM* curves together in a single diagram. This diagram shows how general equilibrium in the system is possible only if we have equilibrium in both the goods and the monetary spheres. There is, in other words, only one unique value for both money and income that is compatible with equilibrium in the goods and the monetary spheres. Changes in equilibrium are explained by shifts in either the *IS* or *LM* curve.

5. One major use of the IS-LM general equilibrium "model" is to explain the workings of monetary and fiscal policy. Such policy changes can be represented by shifts in the *IS* and *LM* curves with resulting changes in the equilibrium values for income and the rate of interest. The IS-LM model is also useful in showing the conditions under which the effectiveness of monetary and fiscal policy is limited.

6. The IS-LM model was initially constructed in constant prices; hence, it deals on the IS side only with *real* magnitudes. It can be modified, however, to bring in price level changes, thus making it more realistic. Price level changes operate in the model through the *LM* curve, having effects upon the curve similar to changes in the money supply. As developed initially, the price level is treated as an exogenous variable.

7. An alternative way to handle the price level is to treat it as an endogenous variable. This is done by developing aggregate demand and aggregate supply schedules that relate output to the price level, rather than to expenditures and receipts as in the usual income-expenditure approach. When this is done, a more realistic analysis of fiscal and monetary policy can be undertaken, an analysis that involves changes in the inflation rate as well as in output and employment levels.

8. The "neoclassical synthesis" represents an attempt to bring classical and Keynesian principles together, showing how it is possible to allow classical principles of individual price determination and resource allocation to prevail, once full employment is established by the application of Keynesian theories to policy.

III

Alternative Approaches to Macroeconomics

III

Alternative
Approaches to
Macroeconomics

11

The Modern Quantity Theory

For nearly half a century the income-expenditure—or Keynesian—approach to output determination has dominated income and employment analysis. Keynesianism became the reigning orthodoxy, just as was the classical theory in the era prior to the Great Depression of the 1930s. But the commanding position that the Keynesian revolution established in macroeconomics has not gone unopposed. Beginning in the 1960s a formidable challenge to the Keynesian orthodoxy surfaced in the form of a modernized version of the classical quantity theory. Although the "Monetarist Counter-Revolution," so described by one critic,[1] has not succeeded in displacing Keynesian theory as the dominant approach in contemporary macroeconomic analysis, it ranks, nevertheless, as probably the most important theoretical development in aggregate economic analysis since publication of *The General Theory*. This chapter will review the essentials of the modern quantity theory, including analysis of its major points of difference with the more standard income-expenditure approach.

In the next chapter we shall examine an even more recent, more fundamental challenge to the income-expenditure approach, one rooted more deeply in the pre-Keynesian classical analysis than the modern quantity theory. To the extent that there is in contemporary macroeconomic theory a "counter-revolution" against Keynesian ideas, it is to be found in the line of developments discussed in this and the following chapter.

---

1. Harry G. Johnson, "The Keynesian Revolution and the Monetarist Counter-Revolution," *American Economic Review*, May 1971, pp. 1–14.

Origins of the Modern Quantity Theory

The appearance of a significant challenge to the income-expenditure analysis has followed a pattern somewhat similar to the one involved in the successful Keynesian displacement of the classical orthodoxy. First, an important social problem emerged that appeared invulnerable to solution by established theory and, second, an alternative body of theoretical ideas came into prominence at approximately the same time. In the case of the Keynesian revolution, the critical social problem was, of course, mass unemployment, and the body of theoretical ideas waiting in the wings to displace classical thinking was the system of thought Keynes brought together in *The General Theory*.

To some critics the issue which justifies the search for a new theory is the resistance of rapid and persistent inflation to control by conventional policy measures derived from the Keynesian income-expenditure approach to the economy's management. For example, between 1968 and 1981 consumer prices rose 171 percent, even though the economy slid through three recessions in this period. In spite of the Johnson administration surtax in 1968, and in spite of restrictive fiscal and monetary policies pursued by the Nixon, Ford, and Carter administrations, inflation continued unchecked, even reaching double-digit rates in 1979 and 1980. The combination of rising unemployment and continued inflation gave birth to the unlovely term *stagflation* to describe the condition of the economy.[2] Even the Nixon administration's experiment with comprehensive wage and price controls failed to crush the inflation. The pattern of behavior established during this period was depicted graphically in Chapter 1 in Figure 1–8, which shows quite clearly that, prior to the advent of the Reagan administration, recessions have had the effect of slowing the inflation rate, but once recovery came, inflation accelerated once again. Beginning in 1981, the Reagan administration, with the full cooperation of the Federal Reserve System, again pursued a policy of monetary stringency, with predictable results. The economy was plunged into another recession, the fourth in little more than a decade and the most severe since the 1930s. Once again the inflation rate fell, this time more rapidly than in the earlier recessions, but it is yet to be determined whether the secular upward drift of the inflation rate (see Figure 1–8) has been blunted. In 1982, the underlying (or "built-in")

2. In the 1969–70 recession, for example, unemployment reached 4.9 percent of the labor force and the inflation rate (rise in the consumer price index) was 5.9 percent. In the more serious 1974–75 recession (until the 1982 recession, the worst economic downturn since the 1930s), unemployment climbed to 8.5 percent of the labor force and the inflation rate hit a 11.0 percent. In the short but sharp 1980 (Carter) recession unemployment hit 7.1 percent, and the inflation rate was 12.4 percent.

inflation rate was in the neighborhood of 7 percent. The underlying rate is the difference between the rate of increase in productivity (output per person per hour) and the rate of increase in compensation (wages and salaries plus fringe benefits per person per hour).

There are, however, other points worth noting about our present situation that weakens the analogy with the 1930s. For one thing, many economists are not convinced that the policy prescriptions which flow from the Keynesian analysis are fundamentally flawed. It may be argued with considerable justification that our current malaise (excessive unemployment and excessive inflation) resulted not from a basic error in theory, but from a failure to apply the policy prescription at the appropriate time. The 1968 surcharge is a case in point. Professional economic opinion was nearly unanimous that the tax increase was needed in 1966, once it became apparent that a massive military buildup was being imposed on a fully employed economy. In 1966, for example, military outlays jumped $11 billion ($32.7 billion in 1982 prices), a year in which the unemployment rate stood at 3.8 percent. No better formula for economic and social disaster could have been devised than to have stepped up unproductive military outlays under full-employment conditions without a corresponding (and offsetting) increase in taxes.[3] The story of the 1970s might have been quite different if the Johnson administration and the Congress had been willing to apply Keynesian restraints before the economy became overheated and hard-to-control inflationary forces were unleashed.

There is a second point to consider. In the 1930s there was no doubt that mass unemployment was the single, critical economic problem confronting the economy. Among professional economists there was probably as much unanimity on this as there has ever been on any single subject. But this is not true with respect to inflation. Many economists, of course, view persistent inflation as an important social and economic problem, but not necessarily a more serious social evil than unemployment, even when the latter does not approach the magnitudes experienced in the 1930s. The larger society also reflects this ambivalence. Both the Nixon and Ford administrations tended to view inflation as the more serious problem, but neither was willing to put the economy through the wringer of a massive, 1930s-style depression in order to break the upward spiral of prices. When unemployment rose as a result of the recession brought on by stringent monetary and fiscal policies, both administrations reversed their course in an effort to relieve the unemployment problem (see Figure 1–8). The Carter administration came into office vowing to reduce unemployment, so in its first two years it sought to stimulate the economy through monetary and fiscal actions. But when

3. Recall the discussion on the balanced budget thesis in Chapter 7. This suggests that taxes should have been increased by even more than the increase in government outlays if inflationary consequences were to be avoided.

this lead to a new surge of inflation in 1979 and 1982, the monetary and fiscal brakes were applied promptly, again plunging the economy into recession. The Reagan administration does not quite fit the pattern of any of its predecessors. In pursuit of the goal of ending inflation it remained determined to stick with tight money even though this brought about the most severe recession since the 1930s. What really differentiates the Reagan approach from other administrations, however, is the fact that, through the tax cuts enacted in the summer of 1981, its fiscal policy was basically stimulative, whereas its monetary policy was restrictive. Failure to resolve this basic contradiction was partially responsible for the massive federal deficits which have characterized the Reagan administration. In the face of fiscal actions which were expansionary and which would, it was feared, add to inflationary pressures, the administration was forced to pursue a restrictive monetary policy to keep inflation from being rekindled. But the deficits and "crowding out" in the financial markets kept interest rates high and the economy sluggish.

Nobel laureate Milton Friedman[4] is one of those critics who believe that the Keynesian income expenditure approach is not only an inadequate theoretical instrument for dealing with inflation, but is, perhaps, a cause of continuous inflation. In Friedman's view many "Keynesians"—though not necessarily Keynes himself—came to believe that "money didn't matter," the reason being the alleged low interest elasticity of investment spending (see Chapter 6). This led many "Keynesians" to advocate a policy of cheap money—that is, rapid expansion of the money supply to push interest rates down and expand investment. But this also led, in Friedman's view, to the persistent inflation which has plagued too many countries in the post–World War II era.

Thus, for about a quarter of a century Friedman and his followers in the Chicago school worked on both theoretical and empirical levels to develop a modernized version of the quantity theory of money, capable of explaining fluctuations in income, employment, and the price level. The labels, the *modern quantity theory*, or *monetarism*, are attached to Friedman's work mainly because he believes that change in the money supply is the single most important determinant of change in the level of aggregate money income.[5] Until the late 1960s the modern quantity theory was viewed seriously only by Professor Friedman and his most ardent disciples; but since then, it has won acceptance within the economic profession. Another factor in this development has been a heavy flow of

4. Professor Friedman, now retired, spent most of his academic career at the University of Chicago, where for 25 years he conducted a money and banking "workshop" in which he and his students worked out many of the ideas that have become a part of the modern quantity theory.
5. Professor Friedman's views on monetarism have appeared in a wide variety of publications, including his regular column in *Newsweek* magazine. Probably the most authoritative statement of his position is the well-known article, "The Quantity Theory of Money: A Restatement," Milton Friedman, ed., in *Studies in the Quantity Theory of Money* (Chicago: University of Chicago Press, 1956).

empirical research in support of monetarism from the staff of the St. Louis Federal Reserve Bank.[6]

Most important of all, perhaps is that fact that monetarism of the kind advocated by Milton Friedman has had a major influence on policy in recent years, both within the upper echelons of the Reagan administration and in the policies pursued by the Federal Reserve system. When the Federal Reserve, under the leadership of Chairman Paul Volcker, decided in October 1979 to concentrate on the growth of the money supply as a policy target rather than the level of interest rates, it was widely hailed in the press and among academic economists as a victory for the monetarist point of view. Later in this chapter we shall assess the effectiveness of the Federal Reserve's pursuit of monetarism. These achievements, impressive as they are, do not mean that monetarist analysis has succeeded in displacing the income-expenditure approach as the primary theoretical frame of reference for macroeconomics, for such is clearly not the case. But it does mean that it represents an important addition to the economic theorist's kit of intellectual tools for analyzing and understanding the economy's total performance.

The Nature of the Monetarist Challenge

A basic point common to the Keynesian and monetarist analyses is the view that, in the short run, the economy's output and variations in that output must be explained in terms of total expenditure and changes in expenditure. In this sense it may be said that both approaches operate within a common Keynesian framework. But, aside from this common point of departure, the monetarists believe that the modern quantity theory explains both variations in the price level and money income. The Keynesian income-expenditure approach often assumes constant prices, as its focus has been on output and employment. As we saw in Chapter 10, the price level is a variable which can be readily incorporated into a general equilibrium model of the economic system, a model which is essentially Keynesian in its roots.

The crucial difference, though, between monetarism and Keynesianism centers on the issue of what causes changes in expenditures. In the Keynesian model, changes in expenditure—that is, aggregate demand—may be brought about by a variety of factors, including autonomous shifts in the consumption function, increases or decreases in investment as a result of varying interest rates, and tax and public expenditure changes deliberately engineered by public policy measures. But in modern

6. See especially Michael W. Keran, "Monetary and Fiscal Influences on Economic Activity: The Historical Record," *Review,* Federal Reserve Bank of St. Louis, November 1969; Darryl R. Francis, "Has Monetarism Failed: The Record Examined," *Review,* Federal Reserve Bank of St. Louis, March 1972; and Leonall C. Andersen, "The State of the Monetarist Debate," *Review,* Federal Reserve Bank of St. Louis, September 1973.

monetarist theory what really matters are changes in the quantity of money. Money is the key variable. The central idea in the monetarist thesis, in other words, is that changes in the money supply explain changes in money income, real output (in the short run), and the price level. To the modern quantity theorist, the notion that such Keynesian relationships as the consumption function, the investment demand schedule, or the combined transactions and asset demand for money function may shift exogenously and thereby cause changes in output and employment is unacceptable. On the contrary, they hold to the view that any such changes are necessarily endogenous, triggered by prior changes in the quantity of money. The belief that there exists a direct—and causal—link between changes in the quantity of money and changes in money income has been the focus of a major portion of empirical research by contemporary monetarists, including the massive *A Monetary History of the United States, 1867–1960* by Professor Friedman and his co-worker Ann Jacobson Schwartz.[7] It is also their contention that monetary influences are much stronger than fiscal ones—that is, tax and public expenditures changes—in causing changes in the general level of economic activity.

Some of the other differences between the monetarist and income-expenditure approaches are more subtle, but important nevertheless. The monetarist analysis is cast in terms of the nominal value, that is, the current money value, of the relevant variables. This is in contrast to the emphasis in Keynesian analysis upon changes in the underlying real variables of the economic system, especially output and employment. We touched upon this earlier, pointing out that, while the income-expenditure approach does not ignore the price level, employment and output fluctuations as well as real economic growth have generally received more attention from Keynesians than has inflation.

In practical terms, the basic meaning of monetarism is that the impact of money is upon such nominal (or monetary) aggregates as the gross national product in current prices, the price level, money wages, or market rates of interest. Thus, the modern quantity theory is essentially short term, for in the long run monetarists do not believe that real economic aggregates such as output and employment are much influenced by the money supply. In the long run what counts are changes in such real factors as the labor force, supplies of natural resources, investment in capital goods, and technology.[8] But in the short run, in the monetarist view, the money supply can be—and is—a "powerful lever for determining income, employment, and the price level."[9] This may happen under two sets of circumstances. If the output can be expanded, then the increase

7. Milton Friedman and Anna Jacobson Schwartz, *A Monetary History of the United States, 1867–1960* (Princeton: Princeton University Press, 1963). See also Anna Jacobson Schwartz, "Why Money Matters," *Lloyds Bank Review*, October 1969.
8. Leonall C. Andersen, p. 3.
9. David I. Fand, "Monetarism and Fiscalism," *Banca Nazionale Del Lavoro, Quarterly Review*, September 1970.

in money expenditures triggered by an increase in the money supply may expand both output and employment. On the other hand, if output cannot be expanded, then money changes will affect only the price level, not such real values as output or employment. How the monetarists explain these relationships is the matter to which we now turn our attention. What, in other words, is the theoretical framework through which Professor Friedman and other monetarists explain the how and why of the impact of changes in money upon the performance of the economic system?

The Structure of Monetarist Theory

In a nutshell we may characterize income-expenditure theory as a theory of the demand for output as a whole cast in the framework of the aggregate demand function $(C + I + G$, in a closed economy). By analogy, the modern monetarist theory can be characterized as a similar theory cast in the framework of a demand for money function that explains how the money supply affects the performance of the economic system. The demand for money is the fundamental behavioral relationship in monetarist theory.

We shall proceed, first, to an examination of the process by which changes in the money supply affect money income and the price level; and we shall follow this with a detailed analysis of Professor Friedman's demand for money function, the key to the entire process, since the monetarists believe that the functional relationship between the quantity of real money people want to hold and its determinants—primarily income and wealth—is highly stable. Two other assumptions are needed, though, to complete the general picture of how changes in the money supply can influence the current level of economic activity: (1) that the velocity of money is also stable and (2) that the central bank (the Federal Reserve System in the United States) can control the quantity of money. It is interesting to note that Professor Friedman believes that the relationship between the quantity of money demanded and the variables that determine it in the modern quantity theory is more stable than the relationship between consumption and its determinants in the income expenditure (i.e., Keynesian) theory. The practical meaning of this is that the velocity of money is believed to be consistently more stable than the Keynesian multiplier k, the consequence being that there is a much more close and consistent relationship between changes in the stock of money and changes in consumption and income than there is between changes in investment outlays (and other autonomous expenditures) and consumption and income.[10]

10. Milton Friedman and David Meiselman, "The Relative Stability of Monetary Velocity and the Investment Multiplier in the United States, 1897–1958," in Commission on Money and Credit, *Stabilization Policies* (Englewood Cliffs, N.J.: Prentice-Hall, 1963), p. 186.

What will happen then if there is a change in the money supply? Suppose the Federal Reserve creates more money through its open market operations. The initial effect will be to increase money balances in the hands of individuals in the economy. But because an increase in the amount of money will not change the quantity of money that people want to hold in relation to such fundamental determinants as income and wealth, they will seek to readjust their money balances back to the relationship that existed before the Federal Reserve expanded the money supply. To do this they must dispose of the excess money balances, either by spending them or by lending them. As they do this the added spending will bid up prices, expand output, or do both, a process that will continue until the desired balance is restored between money being held and the general level of economic activity. The process just described would, of course, be reversed if the Federal Reserve System chose to reduce the money supply. It is generally agreed by proponents of the modern quantity theory that a lag of six months to a year exists between the initiation of a change in the money supply and its ultimate effects upon money income and the price level.

The essential difference between the Keynesian—or income-expenditure—approach and the modern quantity theory approach to the impact of a change in the money supply on the economy can be illustrated with the aid of a simple diagram, Figure 11–1. In the figure it is assumed that the Federal Reserve is the initiating force for a change in the money supply, a change that in both models works its way into the economic system via the effect of open market operations on the reserves of the commercial banks. Beyond this point, however, the two models display decidedly different *transmission* mechanisms. In the Keynesian model the increase in the money supply operates through the liquidity preference function to influence the rate of interest. Changes in the rate of interest, in turn, impinge upon investment spending via the investment demand function. The ultimate change in total spending—and hence the output level—will depend upon the value of the multiplier (whose size depends upon the consumption function) and the amount by which investment spending changes. A key to the way in which the transmission mechanism works in the Keynesian model is the sensitivity of interest rates to the demand for cash. More money will prompt firms and households to exchange some of the excess money for income-earning assets, a process that pushes down interest rates. Indirectly, then, the demand for real output may be stimulated. But the latter cannot take place in the Keynesian model without a prior adjustment in the financial portfolio of the firm or household.

Monetarism tells a different story, one involving a much shorter transmission mechanism with respect to changes in the money supply and aggregate spending for output. In a nutshell, the monetarist's position is that any increase in the money supply spills over directly into the market for goods and services. Understanding the how and the why of this

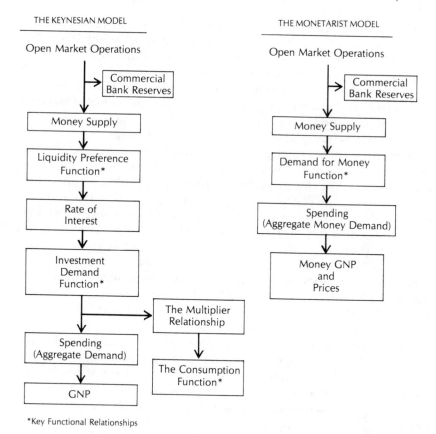

FIGURE 11-1. Keynesian and Monetarist Models Compared

process must wait until we analyze in the next section the nature of Friedman's theory of monetary demand. There is, however, a portfolio adjustment process present in the monetarist's model, but the content of the portfolio differs significantly from that found in the Keynesian model. This, too, we shall explore. In any event, the modern quantity theory with its direct links between money and spending offers a much simpler explanation than does the Keynesian analysis for fluctuations in the general level of economic activity, a fact which, perhaps, accounts for some of its appeal.

The Friedman Theory of the Demand for Money

The point of departure for Friedman's analysis is the fact that people desire to hold money. Friedman is concerned primarily with the factors that determine how much money people want to hold, not, as in the Keynesian analysis, with their motives for holding it. His theory also differs in another significant way from the Keynesian analysis in that he employs a special definition of money. In his view money is anything that will serve as a *"temporary abode for generalized purchasing power,"* a definition that may cover some types of earning assets such as time deposits that do not serve as a medium of exchange.[11] This is not a matter of basic importance for our purpose, except that some critics of monetarism claim that Friedman's empirical findings attesting to the validity of his analysis depend upon his special definition of money.[12]

Friedman identifies three major determinants of the amount of money that households and business firms will hold at any given time. These are (1) the total wealth in all forms of the household or business firm, (2) the opportunity cost of holding money, and (3) the tastes and preferences of the wealth-holding unit. Money in his analysis is viewed like any other commodity or good which yields some utility through its possession. Consequently, the gain—or utility—to be gotten from its possession has to be balanced against the utility foregone by not holding other forms of wealth. In a conceptual sense this view is quite similar to the Keynesian idea that money, through its liquidity, offers utility to its possessor; where it differs significantly is in its specification of the variables that determine the amount of money held.

To flesh out this bare-bones explanation of the quantity of money that households and business firms will hold at any one time, we need to look at all the variables that enter into the three major determinants Professor Friedman postulates. This we can do with the aid of Figure 11–2, which presents in schematic form a formal structure of the variables that determine the demand for money.

The meaning of these variables may be stated as follows:

1. M_d = the demand for nominal money balances. Although the basic functional relationship is expressed in nominal terms, this does not mean that the holders of money are subject to the money illusion. Monetarists view the demand for money balances as ultimately a demand for real balances, which means that nominal balances must be adjusted for changes in the price level.[13]
2. Y_p = money income in Professor Friedman's permanent sense (see Chapter 5).
3. w = the ratio of nonhuman wealth to human wealth.
4. r_b = the rate of return on bonds.
5. r_e = the rate of return on equities.
6. p = the general price level.
7. Δp = the expected change in the price level.
8. u = the tastes and preferences of the wealth-holding units.

11. Stephen W. Rousseas, *Monetary Theory* (New York: Knopf, 1972), p. 161.
12. Dwayne Wrightsman, *An Introduction to Monetary Theory and Policy* (New York: Free Press, 1971), p. 112.
13. In some versions of Friedman's basic equation (shown in the figure) the demand for money is shown as a demand for real balances, which can be done by dividing both sides by p.

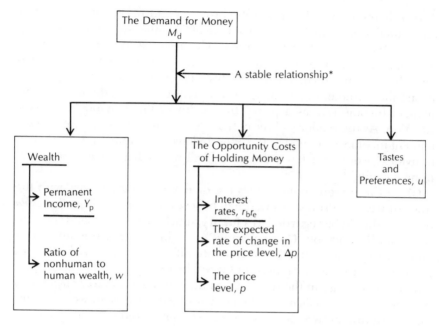

*In equation form the relationship is $M_d = f(Y_p, w; r_b, r_e, p, \Delta p; u)$.

FIGURE 11–2. The Friedman Demand for Money Function

Essentially Professor Friedman holds that, first, the above variables which determine the amount of money that people want to hold do not change much in the short run and, second, the relationship between the demand for money balances and these key determinants is highly stable. We now need to see more specifically how these variables enter into the analysis.

First, there is the matter of wealth. Total wealth in all forms enters into the demand for money function because it represents the upper limit to the amount of money that can be held. No one, in other words, could hold more money than an amount equivalent to the total of the individual's financial worth in all forms. Professor Friedman's concept of wealth includes more than just assets such as cash, bonds, and equities. He also includes in it various types of tangible capital (such as producer and consumer durable goods) and human capital. The latter, as was pointed out in Chapter 5, is the worth of an individual's inherited and acquired skills and training. In principle, the value of human capital would be equal to the discounted value of the future income stream that an individual could expect to obtain from all of his inherited and acquired skills, which would, obviously, include education and training in all forms. The reader will recall from our discussion in Chapter 6 that the present value—or worth—of any asset is found by discounting its expected future income by the appropriate rate of interest.

In Friedman's words, "From the broadest and most general point of view, total wealth includes all sources of 'income' or consumable services."[14] Included in the latter is the productive capacity of human beings, as well as various physical and financial assets (nonhuman wealth) that an individual may own. The rub in this is the extreme difficulty involved in the measurement of human wealth. Therefore, Friedman uses permanent income (Y_p) as a proxy for wealth in his demand for money function. As the reader will recall from the discussion in Chapter 5, permanent income is defined as the expected average annual return that an individual would get from the sum of all his or her wealth, including human capital.[15]

Given the foregoing, how does the demand for money vary with the stock of wealth? Professor Friedman believes that the holding of money balances should be regarded as a luxury, much like the demand for education and recreation. Consequently, he maintains that the amount of money the public wants to hold not only will increase as wealth—that is, permanent income—increases, but it will increase more than in proportion to the increase in the stock of wealth. This means in technical terms that the income elasticity of demand for real cash balances is greater than 1. In testimony before the Joint Economic Committee of the Congress, Professor Friedman suggested that past experience in the United States (at least prior to World War II) indicates that a 1 percent increase in real income per capita tends to be accompanied by nearly a 2 percent increase in the quantity of real cash balances held.[16] In his analysis of the demand for money balances, Professor Friedman clearly regards wealth as a factor that overshadows all the other determinants.

One may ask at this point why is there included in the analysis a variable w representing the ratio of nonhuman to human wealth? Since we do not provide a market for human capital that would establish a rate of return on such capital (this would be possible in a slave society, but we, fortunately, do not live in such a society), there is no simple way in which you can include in the analysis a variable that represents any direct measurement of human wealth, a point of difficulty mentioned earlier. But the individual has some opportunity through education and training to substitute human capital for nonhuman capital (and vice versa) in his total stock of personal wealth. This, though, is a process that takes place

14. Friedman, "The Quantity Theory of Money," p. 4.
15. Recall, too, from the discussion in Chapter 5 that there is no precise and readily available practical measure of "permanent income." Friedman uses a weighted average of past and present measured income (the income an individual actually receives in a year), with less weight being attached to measured income the farther it lies in the past.
16. Milton Friedman, "The Supply of Money and Changes in Prices and Output," in *The Optimum Quantity of Money and Other Essays* (Chicago: Aldine, 1969), p. 175. Friedman's views do not agree with other and more recent findings. For example, a 1973 Brookings Institution study found that the income elasticity of demand for money was less than unity. See Stephen M. Goldfeld, "The Demand for Money Revisited," *Brookings Papers on Economic Activity*, 1973:3.

only with a considerable lapse of time; hence, in the short term the ratio w will be relatively stable. Since as a practical matter it is difficult to turn wealth in the form of human capital into cash—one cannot easily borrow on the strength of future earning power—Friedman argues that this will be compensated for by a greater demand for cash as the human component in the total stock of an individual's wealth increases. Thus, the relationship between M_d and w is an inverse one.

What is the cost of holding money? This portion of Friedman's demand function for money is remarkably similar to the Keynesian liquidity preference function, except that Friedman introduces changes in the price level into the analysis in addition to the rate of interest. Basically, in Friedman's analysis, the cost of holding money is twofold: (1) the rate of interest that could be obtained if bonds or equities were held instead of money and (2) the effect of changes in the price level on nominal money balances. The underlying theoretical relationship is inverse, which is to say that when the cost of holding money rises less will be held and when it falls more will be held.

How this works with respect to the rate of interest should be clear from our earlier discussion of the liquidity preference function. In the income-expenditure approach, it will be recalled, the demand for money for asset purposes (the speculative demand) varies inversely with the rate of interest. Moreover, the interest elasticity of the demand for money balances is relatively high. As a consequence, as we saw in the previous chapter, any change in the money supply will significantly affect the rate of interest and, indirectly, the level of investment spending. Professor Friedman and other monetarists do not deny that interest rates have an influence upon the amount of money held, but, unlike the Keynesians, they maintain that the effect is relatively small.[17] The monetarists, in other words, argue that the interest elasticity of demand for money balances is quite low. Furthermore, they do not make the disctinction found in the income-expenditure approach between money held as an asset and money held for normal transactions purposes.

What about expected changes in the price level? They work in a different fashion. An expected increase in the price level, for example, has the effect of making it more costly to hold money, since both the real value of nominal money balances will be lessened and the market value of other assets will rise. Thus, there will be a smaller demand for nominal money balances. The reverse would take place if the price level was expected to fall.

The matter is quite straightforward with respect to the price level. Since the demand for money function as shown in Figure 11–2 (see also Footnote 13) is formulated in nominal terms, an increase in the price level, p, will result in a proportionate increase in M_d. This must occur if money balances in real terms are to remain constant. Professor Fried-

17. Friedman, op. cit., p. 176.

man believes that this factor is not particularly significant when price changes are small—a few percent a year—but it becomes of major importance when changes in the general price level are large and continue for a long period of time.

The third major determinant is designated as u in the basic schema presented in Figure 11–2. As Friedman says, "The tastes and preferences of wealth-owning units . . . must in general simply be taken for granted in determining the form of the demand function. . . . it will generally have to be supposed that tastes are constant over significant stretches of space and time."[18] The meaning of this is that no significant change in the amount of money people wish to hold can be expected in the short term as a result of any basic change in their attitude toward holding money as compared to other forms of holding wealth.

As a practical matter, Professor Friedman's theory of the demand for nominal money balances can be reduced to the proposition that there are really four major determinants of this demand. These are (1) wealth or permanent income, (2) the price level, (3) the rate of interest, and (4) the rate of increase in the price level. In its most elementary form, his theory holds that the demand for money varies directly with the first two and inversely with the latter two. If we transpose his theory into a demand for real balances, it says, in effect, that this demand varies positively with wealth (permanent income) and inversely with the cost of holding money (interest and expected inflation rates).

Now that we have analyzed the essentials of Friedman's theory of the demand for money, we are in a position to examine more carefully how the modern quantity theory works—how, in other words, we get from changes in money to changes in spending for output. The first point to note is the presumed stability of the money demand relationship; this means that if (for any reason) this relationship is disturbed, an effort will be made by persons and firms to restore the relationship. Since the money demand relationship concerns the amount of real cash balances people and firms desire to hold, anything that increases or decreases these holdings will cause them to try and get back to the level of holdings desired on the basis of the enumerated determinants of these holdings. This is why velocity becomes so important. The stability of the Friedman demand for money relationship requires that the velocity of money be stable. If velocity is not stable, then it is quite possible that a disturbance to the existing cash balances position (more or less money becoming available) may be offset by a change in velocity. If this were to happen, then the close link between the demand for money balances and the other variables—particularly income—is broken. This point can, perhaps, be more clearly seen if it is put in the context of the original quantity theory based upon the equation of exchange ($MV = pY$). If we think of the quantity

---

18. Friedman, "The Quantity Theory of Money," p. 8.

theory as a theory of the demand for money (as Friedman does) rather than a theory of the price level, we have the following equation:

$$M = 1/V(pY). \qquad (11-1)$$

In this equation, the reciprocal of velocity ($1/V$) is a coefficient that links the demand for nominal money balances to nominal income. If there is to be a stable relationship between the demand for money and the general level of economic activity, then V must also be stable. If it is not, then there is no possibility for the kind of relationship suggested by the modern quantity theory, a point to which we shall return subsequently.

A second basic point concerns monetarism's concept of what should be included in the portfolio of persons and firms. It differs from the ideas found in the Keynesian approach. The reason is because Friedman in his theory of the demand for money balances defines wealth to include *all* assets held, including both producer and consumer durable goods. In contrast, the Keynesian approach limits the portfolio of a person or a firm to idle money balances and financial assets (primarily bonds). This is why Friedman's point about the low interest elasticity of demand for money balances becomes crucial. A low interest elasticity of demand for money balances simply means that the willingness of people to hold money as an asset is not especially responsive to the rate of return being obtained on other financial assets, especially bonds. In Keynesian analysis, however, this is a key point, because it is the sensitivity of the demand for money balances to the rate of interest that accounts for the action people or firms take when their monetary equilibrium is disturbed. But if the quantity of money that people want to hold as an asset is not particularly sensitive to changes in the yield on bonds, then excess cash balances are just as likely to be spent for goods and services as for bonds. As a matter of fact, Friedman and the monetarists believe that any excess money balances will spill over directly into the spending stream for goods and services, primarily because the substitution effect between money and the range of financial assets available to the firm or the household is small. Critics of monetarism maintain that they—the monetarists—have not yet demonstrated conclusively the sequence of events whereby excess money finds its way into spending channels. This issue is unresolved.

Policy Implications of the Modern Quantity Theory

Although the theoretical differences between the Keynesian income-expenditure approach and the monetarist position are subtle and complex, the policy implications of these two visions of how the economy really works are, perhaps, even more important.

The modern quantity theory has a deep kinship with classical economics not only because of its stress on the importance of the money supply, but also because it reverts back to the classical idea that a market economy is not inherently unstable, which is to say that it is not subject to abrupt and wide fluctuations in employment and output. One of the leading proponents of the monetarist point of view has succinctly summarized the monetarist position on this point as follows:

> A central monetarist proposition is that the economy is basically stable and not necessarily subject to wide variations in output and employment. In other words, the economy will *naturally* move along a trend path of output determined by growth in its productive potential. Exogenous events such as wars, droughts, strikes, shifts in expectations, changes in preferences, and changes in foreign demand may cause variations in output around the trend path. Such variations will be mild and of relatively short duration. This basic stability is brought about by market forces which change rates of return and the prices of goods and services in response to these exogenous events.[19]

But are exogenous events the only cause of fluctuations in output and employment? The answer is no, for the monetarists—and here their view contrasts most sharply with the Keynesian outlook—hold that the major source of short-run economic instability is mismanagement of the money supply by the monetary authorities, which in the United States is, of course, the Federal Reserve System. In sum, exogenous events over which we have no control emerge in the monetarist view as the explanation of long-term fluctuations in output and employment, whereas government action is seen as the cause rather than the cure for short-term economic instability. It almost goes without saying that this is a point of view 180 degrees out of phase with the Keynesian vision of what the economy is really like. Since the 1930s the fundamental thrust of aggregate theory has been that the private market economy is inherently unstable, primarily because of the volatility of investment spending. Accordingly, government should play a stabilizing role, not only by varying its taxes and expenditures to offset fluctuations in private spending, but also by actions which will influence both private spending for consumption and investment in ways favorable to stabilization.

The monetarist's faith in the underlying stability of the economic system stems from a point already mentioned: their belief that significant variations in real economic variables such as output and employment cannot take place if the trend line of growth for the underlying real determinants—labor, capital, and technology—is stable. And monetarists think this is the case. Professor Friedman stressed essentially this idea in his 1967 presidential address to the American Economic Association in speaking of the "natural rate of unemployment," a rate determined by relationships among such underlying real factors as real wages, the

19. Leonall C. Andersen, "A Monetarist View of Demand Management: The United States Experience," *Review*, Federal Reserve Bank of St. Louis, September 1971.

rate of capital formation, and technological change.[20] It is his firm belief that the economy will over time adjust to the level of output and employment determined by the rate of growth of these underlying real factors. Furthermore, he believes that the process is essentially smooth, except when disturbed by outside forces, including government. The clear implication of his analysis is that changes in any of the important real aggregates of the economy are beyond the reach of the short-term policy instruments of government, fiscal or monetary.

But if this is the case, what policy is appropriate? Given the stable demand function for money, and given, too, the strong belief that only such nominal variables as money GNP and the price level are affected by the money supply, then money alone becomes the appropriate policy instrument for affecting economic activity. Central bank control of the money supply is, in the monetarist's view, the single most powerful means we have to influence the overall level of economic activity, far more powerful in their view than fiscal measures involving changes in taxes or public expenditures.

How should the central bank proceed in the conduct of monetary policy? As the monetarist's basic theoretical proposition—the demand function for money—indicates, the price level is clearly something that the monetary authority can control. But Professor Friedman and the monetarists reject using the price level as a guide for policy, partly because the link between policy decisions by the central bank and the price level is more indirect than the link between these policy decisions and the quantity of money.[21] The more important reason is the existence of time lags of an unpredictable length between changes in the money stock and the variables affected by such changes, including the price level. Therefore, in Professor Friedman's words, "We cannot predict at all accurately just what effect a particular monetary action will have on the price level and, equally important, just when it will have that effect. Attempting to control directly the price level is therefore likely to make monetary policy itself a source of economic disturbance because of false stops and starts."[22]

The time lags are the real rub and, because they exist, the central bank should not attempt to pursue a countercyclical stabilization policy of varying the money supply in response to its reading of current economic conditions. What the monetary authority should do is adopt a rule that would allow the money supply to grow at a rate of between 3 and 5 percent a year and adhere strictly to this rule, ignoring the current state of the economy. Professor Friedman has never ceased to argue for this policy, and has even gone so far as to suggest that there should be a legislated rule requiring the Federal Reserve System to increase the money

20. Milton Friedman, "The Role of Monetary Policy," *American Economic Review,* March 1968, p. 8.
21. Ibid., p. 15.
22. Ibid.

supply at a specified rate. *This has been and remains the essence of the policy recommendations of the modern quantity theory.* From October 1979 to mid-1982, the Federal Reserve under Chairman Paul Volcker pursued such a policy, but after mid-1982 the "Fed" eased up on the money supply, hoping to bring interest rates down.

The Outcome of the Monetarist Challenge

What has been the outcome of the monetarist challenge to the essentially Keynesian structure of modern income and employment theory? In answering this question, it is important to caution the reader that many of the issues raised by the resurgence of the quantity theory in a modern guise have by no means been settled. The exact and proper role of money in modern theory remains in an unsettled state.

The issues raised by the monetarist challenge are both theoretical and empirical, although Professor Friedman believes they are more empirical than theoretical. In any event, there has been a rash of empirical studies since the mid-1960s that aim either to refute or to uphold the contention that the modern quantity theory offers a better guide to the explanation and determination of the income level than the more standard income-expenditure analysis.

Out of the swirl of controversy which has engulfed the economics profession for more than two decades, several major issues have emerged and been clarified, if not resolved—issues important to both the monetarist and the income-expenditure positions. These include (1) the question of whether changes in money or changes in autonomous expenditures in the Keynesian sense are most important in explaining short-term changes in output, employment, and the price level; (2) the basic stability of the demand function for money, a matter primarily of the stability of velocity; (3) the interest elasticity of the demand for money; and (4) the ability of the central bank to control the supply of money. We shall examine each of these.

What Policies Cause Short-Term Changes in Output?

Aside from the massive *A Monetary History of the United States, 1867–1960,* Friedman's most important attempt to find empirical verification for his best argument is the study[23] he completed in collaboration with David Meiselman for the Commission on Money and Credit, a body established in 1957 by the Committee for Economic Development, a private research organization. The basic purpose of the Commission was "to initiate studies into the United States monetary and financial system." Among economists this research has come to be known widely as the Friedman-Meiselman study.

What the authors attempted in this study was to test empirically the

23. Friedman and Meiselman, op. cit. (Ftn. 10).

validity of the Keynesian and monetarist theories, using in each case highly simplified one-equation models.[24] Having established the two models, they proceeded to "test" them by using regression analysis to fit actual data to the equations for the years covered by the study. What did they find? As between the two theories (the Keynesian and the monetarist), Friedman and Meiselman reported:

> The empirical results are remarkably consistent and unambiguous. The evidence is so one-sided that its import is clear without the nice balancing of conflicting bits of evidence, the sophisticated examination of statistical tests of significance, and the introduction of supplementary information that the economic statistician repeatedly finds necessary in trying to decide questionable points. . . .
>
> The income velocity of circulation of money is consistently and decidedly stabler than the investment multiplier except only during the early years of the Great Depression after 1929. . . . Moreover, such relationship as there is between autonomous expenditures and consumption seems simply to reflect the influence of money in disguise. . . .[25]

As expected, the Friedman-Meiselman study aroused a storm of controversy in the economics profession, one which has not yet settled down. Basically, two major criticisms were leveled against Friedman and Meiselman. First, the fundamental basis for the comparison was challenged on the grounds that their one-equation model of the Keynesian system was a wholly inadequate representation of the Keynesian explanation of how income is actually determined. As a result, the findings were held to be "essentially worthless."[26] As we have seen in the earlier chapters, the Keynesian model of income determination is quite complex, involving construction of an aggregate demand schedule by trying to explain how its major components (consumption, investment, government spending, and net exports) are determined. Such a model cannot be represented by a single, simple equation of the type used in the Friedman-Meiselman study.

The second point of challenge is, perhaps, even more fundamental. It involves the difficulty of determining causation even though there is correlation. In the Friedman-Meiselman study this has been described by critics as the problem of reverse causation. It is true that changes in the

---

24. The monetarist equation was $Y = a + V'M$, and the Keynesian equation was $Y = \alpha + K'A$. In these equations Y represents income over time. The monetarist equation expresses income as a linear function of the stock of money, M. V' equals income velocity. The Keynesian equation expresses income as a linear function of autonomous expenditures, A. K' is the multiplier. These equations were their departure point. They were modified before having actual statistical data fitted to them.

25. Friedman and Meiselman, p. 186.

26. Albert Ando and Franco Modigliani, "The Relative Stability of Monetary Velocity and the Investment Multiplier," *American Economic Review*, September 1965, p. 693. In their article, Ando and Modigliani also argue that a properly constructed income-expenditure model meets the test of statistical correlation just as well as does the more simple monetarist model. See also Michael de Prano and Thomas Mayer, "Tests of the Relative Importance of Autonomous Expenditure and Money" in the same issue of *American Economic Review*. There were also responses by Friedman and Meiselman in this issue.

money supply and changes in income are closely correlated. But it is just as plausible to argue that changes in income caused changes in money—after all, more money is needed when income goes up—as it is to argue that changes in money caused the changes in income. Statistical correlation does show how two variables may move together, but it can't tell which variable is the cause and which is the effect. As one critic has said, "theoretical issues cannot be resolved by playing the game of 'correlation, correlation, who's got the highest correlation?' "[27]

A second major effort to demonstrate the validity—as well as the superiority—of the monetarist model came a few years after the Friedman-Meiselman study appeared. This was by the staff of the Federal Reserve Bank in St. Louis. In 1968 two economists from this staff, Leonall C. Andersen and Jerry L. Jordan, published a study similar in design to the Friedman-Meiselman study in which they sought to do two things: first, test the relative effectiveness of monetary and fiscal policies and, second, develop a basic monetarist model for predicting aggregate demand.[28] What they found was that the monetary (as compared to fiscal) actions were generally larger, more predictable, and faster, findings which they believe vindicated the monetarist position. Unfortunately for the state of economic science, the controversy was not so easily settled. Other studies involving econometric models reached different conclusions. One of the most widely used of such models is the one developed jointly by the Federal Reserve System and the Massachusetts Institute of Technology, generally known as the FR/MIT model. In contrast to the monetarist position, in which critics say the transmission mechanism is ill-defined (a sort of "black box" whose workings are hidden from view), the FR/MIT model identifies three channels through which monetary policy works.[29] These include the cost of capital, which affects primarily spending for equipment business structures, and housing; the net worth of consumers, which affects consumer spending; and, finally, credit rationing, which refers to a situation in which lenders ration credit by various nonprice means.[30] It emerges whenever interest rates are sluggish and fail to respond quickly to market forces. Credit rationing was found to be especially important with respect to the link between savings institutions and the housing market. Figure 11–3 is a flow chart developed by the Federal Reserve to show how the first-round effects of monetary policy work in the FR/MIT model. The view incorporated in this flow chart is basically Keynesian, since it shows that changes in money affect spending flows primarily through their impact upon interest rates.

27. Rousseas (Ftn. 11), p. 185.
28. Leonall C. Andersen and Jerry L. Jordan, "Monetary and Fiscal Actions: A Test of Their Relative Importance in Economic Stabilization," *Review*, Federal Reserve Bank of St. Louis, November 1968.
29. For a detailed account of the structure of the FR/MIT models see Frank de Leeuw and Edward M. Gramlich, "The Channels of Monetary Policy," *Federal Reserve Bulletin*, June 1969, pp. 472–91.
30. Ibid.

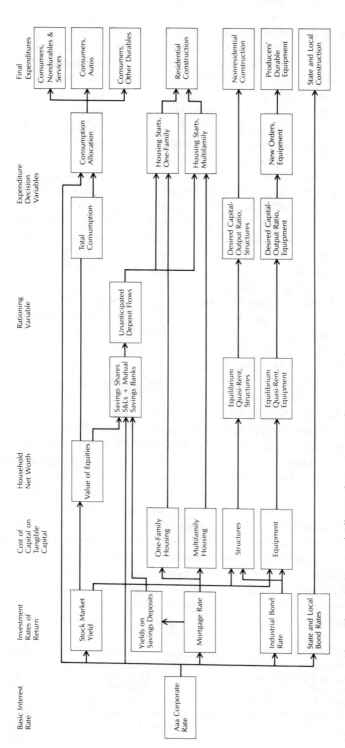

Figure 11-3. Flow Chart: First-round Effects of Monetary Policy

Not only is the FR/MIT econometric model different in structure from the one developed by the St. Louis Federal Reserve Bank, but the results from use of the model are also decidedly different. Essentially, simulation experiments with the FR/MIT model show that the economy will respond as the Keynesian analysis suggests to an expansion of government expenditures which is sustained. It also shows that the impact of changes in the money supply is much smaller than the impact shown in the Andersen-Jordan (St. Louis Federal Reserve) studies, and that monetary policy works more slowly than fiscal policy, the reason being that it takes time before open market operations are reflected in changes in long-term interest rates.[31] In another study which made use of the same measures of fiscal influence used originally in the Andersen and Jordan study, Professor Roger N. Waud of the University of North Carolina found that fiscal measures were as significant as monetary measures in influencing the level of economic activity.[32] The fiscal influences used in the Waud analysis were high-employment federal expenditures and high-employment federal tax receipts. In order to avoid the problem of reverse causation, Waud developed a disaggregated model in which he examined the demand for "production worker man-hours" in several durable goods industries. It was assumed that the demand for production workers in these industries would accurately reflect the general level of economic activity over the period of this study, 1953–68. His basic finding was that *"fiscal influences on economic activity, as measured by the employment of production worker man-hours in durable goods manufacturing industries, are significant and operate in the directions conventionally assumed."*[33]

Where does all the above leave the matter? Basically still unresolved, as the econometric and empirical tests devised to date have not been able to demonstrate conclusively that either the money supply or the Keynesian autonomous variables are the most important determinants of changes in output, employment, and the price level. Certainly the debate will continue, as the monetarist school strongly believes that money is the key to these changes, but Keynesian economists believe that, although money has a role to play, its importance is vastly overrated by the modern quantity theory approach to economic stabilization and management. Perhaps we can put the controversy into somewhat better perspective if we keep in mind that *neither* fiscal nor monetary policies in isolation (or taken together) have yet proved adequate to cope with the serious and persistent problem of *stagflation.* Finding an answer to the

31. For further details on the findings based upon the FR/MIT model see Frank de Leeuw and Edward Gramlich, "The Federal Reserve-MIT Model," *Federal Reserve Bulletin,* January 1968, pp. 11–40; Richard G. Davis, "How Much Does Money Matter? A Look at Some Recent Evidence," *Monthly Review,* Federal Reserve Bank of New York, June 1969, pp. 119–31; and de Leeuw and Gramlich, "The Channels of Monetary Policy."
32. Roger N. Waud, "Monetary and Fiscal Effects on Economic Activity: A Reduced Form Examination of Their Relative Importance," *Review of Economics and Statistics,* May 1974, pp. 177–87.
33. Ibid., p. 186 (italics in original).

chronic malaise of excess unemployment *and* excess inflation remains the most pressing problem that modern macroeconomic analysis confronts.

Stability of the Income Velocity of Money

Let us turn now to the other issues between modern monetarism and the Keynesian analysis. The second point involves the basic stability of the demand function for money, an issue that ultimately involves the question of the stability of the income velocity of money (GNP/M1). Friedman has said that this does not mean that the velocity of circulation of money has to be numerically constant over time; rather, the stability involved in the monetarist position ". . . is in the functional relations between the quantity of money demanded and the variables that determine it."[34] The import of this is not that velocity cannot change, but that the change be gradual and predictable. This may have been the case at times in the past, but it has not been the situation in recent years. Figure 11–4 shows the path of the income velocity of money (GNP/M1) for the years 1960–81. The figures in parentheses indicate the rate of change in income velocity for each year. The chart tells us two important things about the behavior of money in recent years. First, it is clear that there has been a significant increase in the income velocity of money over the last two decades, an increase that accelerated during the 1970s. The reasons for this are not altogether clear, although it is probably due to a

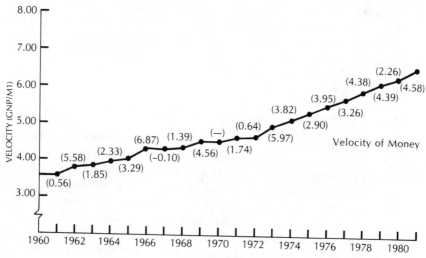

FIGURE 11–4.   Income Velocity of Money (GNP/M1): 1960–81

34. Milton Friedman, "The Quantity Theory of Money—A Restatement" (Ftn. 5), p. 5.

combination of the development of new forms of financial instruments as discussed in Chapter 9 and the high interest rates of recent years. The latter leads to economizing in the use of money. Second, the rate of change in the velocity of money has been erratic rather than stable. This rate of change did accelerate in the 1970s, however. In this period the annual average rate of increase in income velocity was 3.2 percent as compared to 2.9 percent in the 1960s.

The theoretical significance of the data is to raise serious doubts about the stability of the demand function for money, doubts that did not exist some years ago, even among economists not convinced of the overall validity of the monetarist position. Professor Stephen M. Goldfeld of Princeton University said in a recent study[35] that "... the U.S. economy is once again experiencing an apparent shift in the demand for money function. ... when money-demand functions that have been successfully fitted to pre-1974 data are extrapolated into the post-sample period, they consistently and significantly overpredict actual money demand." For example, Goldfeld found that for all of 1975 the actual demand for money was $15.8 billion less than the predicted demand, and for the first two quarters of 1976 the actual demand was $22.3 billion below the prediction. He also found that using an equation of the type developed in the St. Louis Federal Reserve Bank model to predict GNP understated the actual growth in GNP by more than $100 billion. Perhaps J. Charles Partee, a member of the Board of Governors of the Federal Reserve System, summarized the situation correctly when he said, "Velocity is another element of uncertainty in setting money growth targets. There never was all that much certainty between money and GNP, and now there is less."[36] The upshot of this aspect of the monetarist-Keynesian controversy is simply that, if the money demand function is not stable, then the monetary authority (the Federal Reserve System) has—and will continue to have—great difficulty in determining just how much money is needed to keep the economy functioning.

The Interest Elasticity of the Demand for Money

If no consensus has been reached among economists on either the relative importance of fiscal versus monetary measures or the basic stability of the demand for money function, this is not the situation with respect to the link between the rate of interest and the demand for money. On the issue of the interest elasticity of the demand for money, the evidence, as one critic puts it, is overwhelmingly "in favor of the proposition that the demand for money is stable and negatively related to the rate of interest. Of all the issues in monetary economics, this is the one

35. Stephen M. Goldfeld, "The Case of the Missing Money," *Brookings Papers on Economic Activity,* 1976:3, pp. 683, 728.
36. Quoted in *Business Week,* May 30, 1977.

that appears to have been settled most decisively.[37] This finding tends to weaken the monetarist argument that the demand for money is not significantly affected by interest rates. On the other hand, the evidence from the same empirical studies casts doubt on the Keynesian notion that at very low rates of interest the demand for money balances becomes highly elastic. There is no empirical support for the idea of a liquidity trap, in other words. In sum, the evidence suggests that the demand for money is sensitive to the rate of interest, but not nearly so sensitive as the early Keynesian analysis indicated.

The Central Bank's Control of the Money Supply

Finally we turn to the money supply. Here the weight of the evidence is that over the long run the monetary authorities can control with reasonable accuracy the total money supply (M1), but they are less able to do so in the short term. As we saw in Chapter 9, the money multiplier is not constant, reflecting among other things changing attitudes on the part of the public with respect to the relative desirability of holding currency as compared to demand deposits. The actual bank can exercise firm control over the monetary base, which is what gives it control over the money supply in the longer run. But it is also true, as was stressed in Chapter 9, that the money supply responds positively to the rate of interest. The implication of this is that the money supply can accommodate itself to changes in the level of money GNP, as well as influence money GNP, a point of view not favored by the monetarist school.

Monetarism and the Reagan Administration

No administration in recent history has been as openly committed to the monetarist position as the Reagan administration. Not only were prominent monetarists appointed to key positions after the Reagan administration took office,[38] but the administration's basic economic document, *A Program for Economic Recovery*, was explicit in making a reduced rate of monetary growth a key element in the scheme for economic recovery. Specifically, the recovery plan called for the rate of growth in money and credit to be reduced to one-half the 1980 level (6.6 percent for M1) by 1986.[39] As noted earlier, the Federal Reserve shifted to an essentially monetarist position in late 1979, a stance strongly supported by the Reagan administration in its first year in office.

37. David E. W. Laidler, *The Demand for Money: Theories and Evidence*, 2nd ed. (New York: Harper & Row, 1977), p. 130.
38. For example, Beryl Sprinkle, former chief economist for the Harris Trust and Saving Bank in Chicago and a well-known monetarist, was named Under Secretary for Monetary Affairs in the U.S. Treasury.
39. *America's New Beginning: A Program for Economic Recovery* (Washington, D.C.: The White House, February 18, 1981), p. 23.

Once the new administration was in office, the Federal Reserve moved quickly to implement the policy of reduced monetary growth. From an annual rate of increase of more than 10 percent in January 1981, the rate of growth for M1 was reduced to a negative 0.2 percent by September 1981. This sharp reduction in monetary growth was expected, in accord with monetarist doctrine, to bring about an equally sharp break in expectations for continued inflation, a development that was supposed to lead to immediate and significant reductions in interest rates. Monetarists maintain that changes in the inflation rate are reflected quickly in interest rates. When high inflation is expected, lenders will respond by demanding higher interest rates to compensate for the loss in purchasing power of the money they lend. But if inflation is expected to slow, interest rates should decline since lenders have less need for adding an inflation premium to their rates.

At best, the short-term results of the Reagan experiment with monetarism were mixed, certainly not a triumph for monetarism. As in 1969, 1973, and 1980, a substantial slowdown in the rate of monetary growth pushed the economy into a recession, one which in terms of the unemployment rate turned out to be the most severe of all the post–World War II recessions. As is usually the case (see Figure 1–8), recession brought relief from inflation. As the economy turned down, the inflation rate (as measured by the CPI) dropped from an annual rate of 13.2 percent in September 1981 to less than 4 percent in 1982, a rapid decline, which also was a mark of the severity of the recession. From a broader perspective, however, the recession did not have an immediate impact on the underlying (or core) inflation rate; unit labor costs rose at an annual rate of 2.9 percent during 1982. They did begin to drop sharply in 1983, however. During the downswing of any recession markets are weak, a fact which makes it difficult for business firms and trade unions to continue raising prices and wages, but this situation usually changes once the economy turns around and a recovery is under way. Thus, the severity of the 1981–82 recession does not by itself ensure that the economy's wage-price spiral is permanently broken.

The crucial failure in the Reagan administration's experiment with monetarism was the failure of interest rates—especially *real* interest rates—to respond to the slowdown in economic activity. This development did not fit the monetarist scenario and was not readily explained by the monetarists. Figure 11–5 traces the nominal and real "prime" interest rates since 1960.[40] Not only did the real rate begin climbing during 1979, but by the end of 1981 it had reached levels unmatched at any time during the postwar era. The best explanation is simply that the 1982 tax cut in combination with enlarged military expenditures put the economy on a path of large and growing federal deficits. In early 1982 the

---

40. The "prime" interest rate is the rate quoted by leading banks for their best customers. Observers regard it as a good gauge of what is happening in general to interest rates.

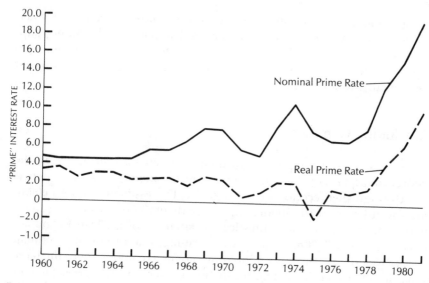

FIGURE 11–5. Nominal and Real Prime Interest Rates: 1960–81

Congressional Budget Office (CBO) estimated that the "baseline" deficit of the federal government would grow from $157 billion in fiscal year 1983 to $248 billion by fiscal year 1987, even while projecting moderate growth in *real* GNP over the period.[41] In the past, periods of growth have seen a reduction in the size of the federal deficit, a consequence of normal countercyclical swings in the government's revenue. What has changed in the picture, according to the Congressional Budget Office, are the massive revenue losses expected in the wake of the 1981 tax cuts, losses that heavily outweigh the usual countercyclical shifts in the government's revenue.[42] Thus, the CBO sees not only permanent and growing deficits, but a permanent expansionary (and inflationary) bias to the budget. In mid-1982, therefore, the economy found itself in a troublesome box: Large and growing deficits and the fears they engendered in the financial community kept interest rates high, which in turn prolonged the recession and generated uncertainty about the durability of a recovery. But any let-up on the monetary brakes to ease the interest rate situation would quickly revive inflationary expectations, which in turn would nullify the impact of easier money on interest rates. The dilemma stemmed from the basic conflict arising from the Reagan administration's simultaneous commitment to both "supply-side" economics (see Chapter 12) and monetarism. Briefly put, supply-side economics holds

41. Congressional Budget Office, *Baseline Budget Projections for the Fiscal Years 1983–1987* (Washington, D.C.: Congress of the United States, February 5, 1982), p. 9. "Baseline" refers to projections designed to show what would happen if existing taxing and spending policies were continued into the future.
42. Revenues usually fall in recession and rebound in the recovery.

that, through major tax cuts, incentives to work, produce, and save would be raised, whereas monetarism requires a firm hand on the money supply to keep inflation under control. There is no easy way that these two approaches to managing the economy can be reconciled, a fact that dogged the Reagan administration during its first two years in office.

Concluding Comments

Before leaving this chapter a few final comments are in order on the theoretical aspects of the controversy over the modern quantity theory. One distinguished economist has said that Professor Friedman's elaborate formulation of the modern quantity theory is really nothing more than "a most elegant and sophisticated statement of modern Keynesian monetary theory."[43] Once the special meanings that Professor Friedman gives to wealth and the costs of holding money are understood, the basic similarities between his demand function for money and the Keynesian demand for money relationship [see Equation (9–24) and Figure 9–4] should be apparent. Of greater importance and theoretical interest was the attempt Friedman made in the early 1970s to develop a theoretical framework which would explain what he believed that he had demonstrated empirically was true—namely, that there is a close and direct link between money and nominal values for the GNP.[44] All along, the chief contention of critics of the modern quantity theory has been that the process by which changes in money get translated into changes in the demand for goods and services is much too vague. Although Friedman's statement helped clarify points which were disputed or unclear in his earlier—and more empirically oriented—statements of the monetarist position, it did not succeed in putting an end to the controversies which surround the modern quantity theory—even at the theoretical level. Even some monetarists were disturbed, as they thought Friedman's effort to clarify the transmission mechanism inherent in monetarist theory only brought him closer to the Keynesian view of this process. Friedman's discussion, they said, is ". . . either misleading or a complete reversal of his often stated position."[45] A strong partisan of Keynesian economics charged that Friedman basically did not really understand the essential character of Keynes's analysis, especially the role that uncertainty plays in the Keynesian system.[46] The debate seems destined to go on—both empirically and theoretically.

43. Don Patinkin, "The Chicago Tradition, the Quantity Theory and Friedman," in Don Patinkin, *Studies in Monetary Economics* (New York: Harper & Row, 1972), p. 108.
44. Milton Friedman, "A Theoretical Framework for Monetary Analysis," in Robert J. Gordon, ed., *Milton Friedman's Monetary Framework: A Debate with His Critics* (Chicago, Ill.: The University of Chicago Press, 1974), pp. 1–62.
45. Karl Brunner and Allan H. Meltzer, "Friedman's Monetary Theory," in Robert J. Gordon, op. cit., p. 72.
46. Paul Davidson, "A Keynesian View of Friedman's Theoretical Framework for Monetary Analysis," in Robert J. Gordon, op. cit., p. 91.

Perhaps the most appropriate note on which to conclude this discussion of the modern quantity theory is by reference to a comment to the effect that the real differences between Friedman and the Keynesians are more ideological than theoretical.[47] And this is probably true, for in a fundamental sense the monetarist counter-revolution is an attack upon the basic Keynesian notion that a market economy is inherently unstable and, if it is to work at all well, government must play a stabilizing role, using to the best of its ability monetary and fiscal means to attain this objective. The Keynesian attack on the classical theory demolished the intellectual foundations for *laissez faire* as acceptable public policy; the monetarist counter-revolution seeks to restore these foundations.

Summary

1. The modern quantity theory differs from the classical quantity theory in two major ways. First, it sees output and employment as well as prices—at least in the short run—as being affected by the quantity of money and, second, the mechanism by which changes in the quantity of money enter into the economic system and affect output, price, and the employment level is more complex than in the original classical theory (see No. 3 below).

2. The key element in the modern quantity theory is Professor Milton Friedman's theory of the demand for money. The demand for money is a stable function that depends upon permanent income, wealth held by customers, including human wealth, the rate of interest, and expected changes in the general level of prices. Velocity is assumed to be stable.

3. Given the stable nature of the monetarist's demand function for money, a change in the quantity of money will disturb the balance between the amount of money being held in response to the variables included in the demand function for money and the money supply. Consequently, individuals and firms will seek to restore the desired balance in their holdings by either spending the excess of money or reducing their spending when the reverse is the case. In either event, imbalance in the demand for and supply of money spills over into spending, thereby affecting output, employment, and the price level.

4. Contemporary monetarists do not believe in either activist monetary or fiscal policy. On the contrary, they regard the economy as inherently stable and believe attempts to influence it by an active fiscal or monetary policy are the cause of cyclical fluctuations. Therefore, they propose a monetary rule, one which requires the central bank (the Federal Reserve System) to allow the money supply to grow at a fixed rate

47. Rousseas (Ftn. 11), p. 196.

based upon the underlying real needs of the economy. The central bank should do nothing more.

5. The outcome of the monetarist challenge to the income-expenditure explanation of macroeconomic behavior remains inconclusive. Empirical tests have not shown conclusively that the money supply is a more important determinant of changes in output, employment, and the price level than are the basic Keynesian variables. Contemporary monetarism has much support in the economics profession and has had a major influence on the Federal Reserve in recent years. The Reagan administration embraced monetarism as part of its "Program for Economic Recovery."

12

The Rebirth of Classical Economics

In this chapter we shall analyze two additional challenges to Keynesian macroeconomics, challenges that are not only more recent than monetarism, but more radical in their nature and implications. Although monetarism, as we have seen, attacks both the fundamental relationships and the basic policy conclusions of the income-expenditure analysis, it accepts the essential framework of that analysis, including the role played by aggregate demand in the short-run determination of output, employment, and the price level. The developments which we now consider, namely, the new classical economics and supply-side economics, go much farther, rejecting in a fundamental way the Keynesian approach and philosophy. They turn instead to the pre-Keynesian classical school for ideas and inspiration.

Because these theoretical approaches are so deeply rooted in classical ideas, it is crucial that the basic nature of classical macroeconomics be understood. We have used the term "classical economics" from time to time in the text, including a brief explanation of its meaning in Chapter 1, but we have not to this point offered a more formal exposition of classical macroeconomic theory. Now it is appropriate to do so, given the dependence of the theories we are about to discuss on the classical view of how the economy works.

The Classical Macroeconomics in Broad Outline

In *The General Theory*, Keynes used the term "classical economics" to characterize the whole body of economic theorizing that preceded his work and that stretches back at least to Adam Smith. Technically this was not correct; historians of economic thought distinguish classical economics from neoclassical economics. Roughly speaking, the former embraces economic thought from David Ricardo (1772–1823) to John Stuart Mill (1806–73), whereas the latter refers to the theories of economists who came after John Stuart Mill. For our purposes, however, this distinction is not of major importance, the reason being that contemporary macroeconomics generally uses the term "classical" as Keynes used it, namely, to describe pre-Keynesian theorizing about the determinants of output, employment, and the price level.

No single work contains the whole body of classical economics, although Alfred Marshall's *Principles of Economics* comes close to doing so. The theories and concepts that make up classical economics explain how an economy organized on the basis of free, competitive markets and the private ownership of land and man-made capital (i.e., structure and machines) is supposed to work. In the classical lexicon, a "competitive" market is one in which neither buyers nor sellers can by their own actions determine or in any way influence the prices which the market establishes through the interaction of the buyers and sellers. To explain how the system works means to explain how through markets the system establishes prices for everything that is produced and prices for the resources required so that production can take place; how efficiency in the use of resources is obtained; and how the material welfare or well-being of all participants in the system is maximized. In a sense, the classical economics as developed and refined throughout the nineteenth century was really concerned with explaining in a formal way how Adam Smith's "invisible hand" working through markets harnessed personal greed (viz., the pursuit of self-interest) to the social good (viz., the maximum production of the things people want).

Classical employment theory consists of three basic propositions. First, the level of employment is determined by the total demand for and supply of labor. A corollary to this is that, once employment is determined, output is also determined since the production function ties the two together. In classical macroeconomic theory the labor market is essentially the labor market for the individual business firm writ large and applied to the whole economy. Practically speaking, the classical school regarded the full employment of labor as a normal state for the economy, a proposition mocked by the mass unemployment confronting the economy in the 1930s. The second classical proposition involves Say's law of markets, which we encountered in Chapter 1. Even though the level of employment is determined by the total demand for and supply of labor, and this level utilizes all workers seeking work, the possibility exists that the output produced with this labor might not be sold. In its simplest form, Say's law asserts that "supply creates its own demand," which means that every act of production creates income and therefore demand equal to the value of that production. No general overproduction is possible. In a crude form, Say's law is valid in a barter economy, since no person would bring goods to market except to exchange them for other goods. In an economy that uses money, matters are not so simple. Production generates money income for the producers, but one of the virtues of money is that one doesn't have to spend it immediately. Thus, in a money-using economy, the possibility exists that some income arising from production may not be spent immediately—it might, in other words, be saved. Classical economics got around this problem by adding a corollary theory to Say's Law, namely, a theory that links the supply of savings to the rate of interest and the latter to borrowing by the businessman to purchase new capital goods, that is, structures and equipment. Therefore, if more is saved, interest rates will fall, and more borrowing and spending for real capital will take place. If less is saved, the reverse will happen. The essential point is that, in the classical theory, saving cannot cause a decline in spending and thus be responsible for more being produced than could be sold. Say's law works in a money-using economy as well as in a barter economy. At least this was the classical view, echoes of which are heard today in the argument that the economy is suffering from a shortage of saving.

This brings us to the third classical proposition, namely, the role of money in the theory. Basically, money's purpose is to make the economy more efficient by avoiding the clumsiness of barter. Money serves, primarily, as a medium of exchange, which is to say that it is generalized purchasing power readily convertible into almost anything. This being the case, any change in the amount of money will lead to more or less spending, but since resources are normally fully employed, more or less spending primarily affects the price level. The idea that prices are linked directly to the money supply is, of course, the quantity theory of money. It is an old idea, dating back to the eighteenth century or earlier, but, as we saw in Chapter 11, it has been reconstituted in modern dress by Milton Friedman.

Combining the foregoing propositions with competitive markets and the free play of self-interest by businessmen, workers, and consumers gives us all the necessary ingredients for a self-regulating economic system, one which employs all resources fully and in the most efficient way possible. The logical—or "natural"—policy conclusion derived from this view is that of *laissez faire*, or noninterference by government in the running of the economy. Classical economics thus did what any good economic theory should do: It explained—how employment, output, and prices were determined; it predicted—full employment would be the norm; and it prescribed—governments should keep their hands off the economy.

A Formal Classical Model

The key propositions of classical employment theory come together in a formal model. We shall do this in terms of, first, a series of simple algebraic equations that sum up the key elements in classical theory and, second, through a diagram that draws these elements together. Basically, the formal classical model embodies the labor market, a theory of the price level, and a theory linking both saving and investment to the rate of interest. The latter is essential to preserve the working of Say's law in a money-using economy.

The Labor Market

As we have seen from the discussion in Chapter 10, the classical labor market involves the demand for and the supply of labor and the production function. Employment is determined by the interaction of the demand for and the supply of labor, and output through the production function is determined by the employment level. The latter is normally a full-employment level. In equation form we have the following:

$N_d = f(w/p)$	The demand for labor	(12–1)
$N_s = f(w/p)$	The supply of labor	(12–2)
$N_d = N_s$	Equilibrium in the labor market	(12–3)
$Y = f(N, K', R', T)$	The production function	(12–4)

In the above equations, w is the money wage, p is the price level, N, is the level of employment, K' is the stock of capital, R' represents natural resources, and T is technology.

The Theory of the Price Level

Classical economic thinking about the role of money in the economy and the determination of the price level is summed up in the quantity theory of money. The quantity theory of money is rooted in the equation of exchange, a truistic statement which says that the monetary value of output (Yp) is equal to the quantity of money in circulation times its average rate of turnover (Mv). If we assume that Y is a given because the normal state of the economy is one of full employment—hence Y is fixed by the amount of employment—and that turnover (the velocity of circulation, v) is stable because it is rooted in payment habits which are slow to change, the price level will vary directly with the amount of money. This follows from the classical view that the *primary* function of money is to serve as a medium of exchange. Hence, more money means more spending and less money means less spending. In equation form we have

$Mv = Yp$	The equation of exchange	(12–5)
$p = f(M)$	The quantity theory	(12–6)

Saving, Investment, and the Rate of Interest

Output (Y) in classical theory is determined via the production function by what happens in the labor market. Involuntary unemployment is impossible in this situation, given the nature of the classical demand and supply schedules for labor. But there remains the logical possibility that some of the output produced by the fully employed labor force won't be sold, that there might be a "glut" of goods. Say's law, however, makes this impossible, asserting that every act of production in effect constitutes a demand for something. There is no problem with Say's law in a barter economy. But once money is introduced into the picture (as with the quantity theory) difficulties may ensue. In a money-using economy production always generates sufficient income in the aggregate to buy back what is produced. To this extent Say's law holds when money enters the picture. But when we resort to the use of money rather than barter, a loophole opens. This is because a part of money income can be saved rather than spent; if this happens demand for what is produced (spending) may turn out to be less than the money income generated by production (supply). At this point the classical theory of interest enters the picture. By making both saving (S) and investment (I) functions of the rate of interest, the integrity of Say's law in a money-using society is preserved. Saving via changes in the rate of interest will always translate into more or less investment spending. Thus, there cannot be any interruption to the flow of spending (demand) because of saving. As Keynes said in *The General Theory* the rate of interest in classical thought is the nexus that unites decisions to abstain from consumption—that is, to save—with decisions to provide for future consumption—that is, to invest.[1] As long as this is the case, Say's law is intact. In equation form we may summarize these ideas as follows:

$S = f(i)$ The supply of saving   (12–7)

$I = f(i)$ The demand for saving for investment   (12–8)

$I = S$ Equilibrium of saving and investment   (12–9)

Now that we have discussed the major propositions that enter into the classical theory of employment, it is useful to draw these propositions together and show how they interact to provide a formal model for the classical theory. This is done in diagrammatic form in Figure 12–1, which we may summarize as follows:

1. Part A in the diagram has two parts. The upper diagram depicts the classical production function. Its purpose is to show that with a *given* technology and a *fixed* quantity of resources other than labor, output depends uniquely upon the level of employment. To explain what determines the employment level, we must turn to the bottom portion of Part A, where are found the classical demand and supply curves for labor. Interaction between demand and supply as shown here determines both the level of employment and the real wage. The classical equilibrium shown in Part A is a unique one involving output, employment, and the real wage.

1. John Maynard Keynes, *The General Theory of Employment, Interest and Money* (New York: Harcourt Brace & World, First Harbinger ed., 1964), p. 21.

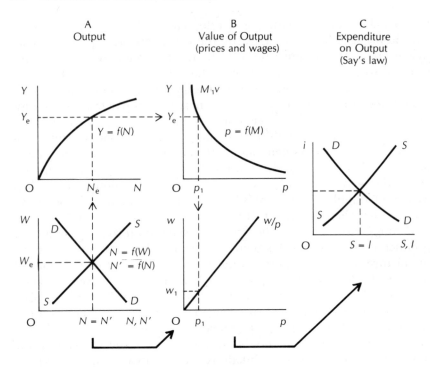

FIGURE 12–1.   The Complete Classical System

2. Turn now to Part B. In the lower portion of Part B we introduce a new curve, one labeled w/p. This shows the price level on the horizontal axis and the money wage on the vertical axis. The slope of the line (w/p) measures the real wage as determined by the demand for and supply of labor given in the lower portion of Part A. The upper portion of Part B shows how the monetary value of the real output level—determined from the production function in Part A—depends upon the money supply and velocity. If the latter is given, then the money supply becomes the prime determinant of the price level and hence the monetary value of any real output level. By changing any of the variables in the classical system or shifting a relevant function, it is possible to trace through the impact of any such change upon output, real wages, employment, the price level, or money wages. To gain familiarity with the workings of the classical "model," the reader should work out such changes on his or her own.

3. Finally, Part C shows how Say's law fits into the analysis by assuring the necessary equality between savings and investment so that there is no interruption in spending flows because of any deficiency in total demand. Note that in the classical model the rate of interest cannot have any impact upon the output level; its role is to determine the division of output between investment and consumption, as well as to ensure that all savings flow into investment spending.

Before we turn to a discussion of the broad policy implications of the classical analysis, two things need to be said in summary about the model we have been discussing. In the first place, the system is constructed so that it tends automatically toward a level of full employment. The demand for and the supply of labor curves have the role of determining the actual employment level, but they are conceived so that this employment level is by definition one of full employment. Moreover, Say's law of markets, in conjunction with the classical theory of interest, makes certain that there is no possibility of involuntary unemployment in the system because of any deficiency of aggregate demand. Second, if there is within the system any temporary deviation away from the full-employment equilibrium, the appropriate remedy is clearly indicated. This is a reduction in the real wage, which can be brought about either by an increase in the money supply, with its consequent effects on the general price level, or by a cut in money wages.

Policy Implications of the Classical Theory

The classical theory of employment implies a *laissez faire,* "hands-off" (or noninterference) policy that minimizes the extent to which government intervenes in the operation of the economy. In a broad sense there are two major reasons why government might intervene in the economy. The first is that imperfections in the market economy may lead to an undue concentration of economic power in private hands. The second is that the private or market sector of the economy may not function sufficiently well to provide jobs for all members of the labor force actively seeking employment.

Actually both of the above possibilities are denied by the classical system. As we saw earlier, classical economists assumed that competition is a normal characteristic of the economy. The kind of competition they envisioned as being dominant in the economy was the *atomistic* variety, in which the number of firms in every industry is so great in relation to the demand for the output of the industry that no single firm can exercise any control over the price at which its product is sold. If no firm is in a position to exercise any control whatsoever over price, no firm (or person) can possess any real economic power over other firms (or persons). All firms and persons are at the mercy of the impersonal market forces of supply and demand. If this is a correct evaluation of the situation in the economy, then there is no basis for intervention by the state for the sake of redressing any abuse of private economic power. The latter does not exist in the classical scheme.

The second reason for state intervention is the continued existence of a significant amount of *involuntary* unemployment. As we have seen, classical employment theory leads to the conclusion that involuntary unemployment on a large scale for anything more than brief periods is an impossibility. If the economy has an inherent and automatic tendency toward equilibrium at full employment, then there is no real need for public intervention on the ground that employment is inadequate. Under such circumstances *laissez faire* is the appropriate policy.

Competition plays a vital role in this respect because its presence within the economic system ensures the flexibility of wages and prices, including the rate of interest. The system will move toward an equilibrium at full employment only if wages respond instantly to the least discrepancy between the demand for and supply of labor in the market. The same holds true for the rate of interest, for, unless interest responds to any discrepancy between the demand for and supply of saving, the system will not attain the equality between saving and investment necessary to ensure the working of Say's law in a monetary economy. Price and wage flexibility stems from competition, and the more highly competitive the system, the more responsive wages and prices will be to market forces.

The New Classical Economics

As pointed out at the beginning of Chapter 11, it was the alleged failure of policies based upon the Keynesian income-expenditure model of the economy to control inflation from the mid-1960s onward which stimulated the growth of contemporary monetarism. The same policy failures have also given rise to the more fundamental challenge to the structure and premises of contemporary macroeconomic theory known as the "new classical economics."[2] Specifically, the policy failures which led to these challenges are rooted in the collapse of the Phillips curve relationship.

The Phillips curve, named after the British economist A. W. Phillips, who initially presented the idea in an article published in 1958, shows an inverse relationship between the inflation rate and the unemployment rate.[3] Figure 12–2 contains a scatter diagram relating inflation (measured by the annual rate of change in the GNP deflator) and unemployment for the period 1960 through 1982. The solid-line curve labeled *ee*, which covers the years 1960 through 1969, illustrates the basic hypothesis embodied in the curve. This is that there exists a short-term "trade-off" between the unemployment rate and the inflation rate, a decrease in one leading to an increase in the other and vice versa. What was so important about the early data (1960–69) was that they strongly suggested the possibility that by the judicious use of monetary and fiscal policy society could achieve a low level of unemployment (say 4 percent) at an acceptable inflation rate—say 3 percent or less. It was believed, in other words, that it would be possible through "fine tuning" to reconcile

2. James Tobin, *Asset Accumulation and Economic Activity* (Chicago: The University of Chicago Press, 1980), p. 20.
3. A. W. Phillips, "The Relation between Unemployment and the Rate of Change of Money Wages in the United Kingdom, 1861–1957," *Economica*, November 1958, pp. 283–99.

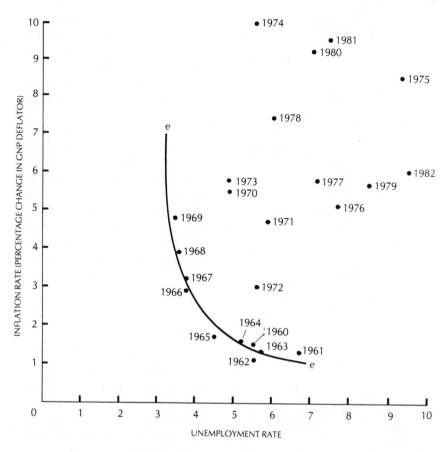

FIGURE 12–2. The Inflation-Unemployment Trade-off, 1960–82

the goals of both price stability and full employment. Unfortunately, this was not to be. As the data in Figure 12–2 show, after 1970 the possibility for any "trade-off" between inflation and unemployment at rates for either variables which were socially and economically acceptable totally vanished. Thus, critics of the income-expenditure approach to macroeconomics argued that policies based upon such an analysis were simply not workable.

Although the new classical economics did not begin to have an impact upon macroeconomics and the economic profession until the mid-1970s or later, its roots trace back to a 1961 article by Professor John F. Muth, now of Indiana University. In this article Professor Muth developed what has become the core idea in the new classical economics, the *theory of rational expectations*.[4] Initially, the theory was used to explain behavior in

---

4. John F. Muth, "Rational Expectations and the Theory of Price Movements," *Econometrica*, Vol. 29, No. 3 (July 1961), pp. 315–335.

financial markets, but subsequently it was applied to macroeconomic theory. The leader in this later development was Professor Robert Lucas of the University of Chicago. In addition to Professor Lucas, important contributions to the new classical economics have been made by Professors Thomas Sargent and Neil Wallace of the University of Minnesota, Robert Barro of the University of Chicago, and Bennett McCallum of the University of Virginia.

The new classical economics rests upon two basic theoretical propositions. The first we just mentioned, namely, the *theory of rational expectations,* originally developed by John Muth. The second is the *theory of continuous market clearing,* a fundamental premise of classical economics as it existed before Keynes. Rational expectations is the new element, but it is the older idea of market clearing, which, according to Nobel laureate James Tobin, gives the new classical school such far-reaching implications.[5] We shall first examine each of these theories separately; second, examine their implications when brought together; and, finally, analyze and evaluate the criticisms levied against the new classical economics.

The Theory of Rational Expectations

The logical point of departure for an analysis of this theory is to examine the role that expectations play in economics. Expectations are important, for three principal reasons. First, expectations have to do with views about future values for economic variables—prices, output, employment, and others. Second, these views exert an influence—often a strong influence—upon what happens today. For example, our expectations about the future inflation rate will undoubtedly influence current buying decisions. Some people may decide to buy now if they expect future prices to be higher, whereas others may decide that they should save more. Third, expectations have a crucial relationship to one of the fundamental ideas employed in economic analysis, namely, the concept of an equilibrium. *All* schedules used in economic analysis represent *ex ante* or expected (anticipated) values for the variables concerned. This is true at both the micro and macro levels of economic analysis. What equilibrium means, therefore, is a state or condition in which actual *(ex post)* and expected values coincide. To put it differently, in equilibrium events turn out as people expect.

How are expectations formed? This is one of the most difficult problems in economics, one for which economists have not found a satisfactory answer. Before we examine in detail the answer to this question offered by the new classical economics, a brief review of two alternative approaches is in order.

One approach is known as the method of adaptive expectations. It is

5. Tobin, op. cit., p. 22.

the approach that has been incorporated into most of the large econometric models employed to forecast the economic future. Simply put, the term "adaptive expectations" means that expectations are determined primarily by recent experience, giving events of the recent past a greater weight than events more distant in time. In a technical or statistical sense, adaptive expectations can be measured by constructing a weighted average of past changes in some variable—the consumer price index, for example—in which the most recent data carry the greatest weight. What is involved in this method is the extrapolation of recent trends into the future, always a procedure fraught with some risk. The reason, of course, is that expectations formed in this way are tied to past behavior, but such behavior can change, a point of key importance made by the rational expectations theorists.

Another way to determine expectations is simply to ask people, which is to say to attempt to measure them directly by a survey technique. This particular method has been extensively developed and pursued by the Survey Research Center at the University of Michigan. One of its most important efforts in this direction is the Index of Consumer Sentiment, designed to measure the consumer's confidence as it affects future spending plans. This index is shown in Figure 12–3.

The rational expectations hypothesis takes an entirely different approach. Whereas the foregoing methods for measuring expectations are empirically oriented, being derived either from recent experience (adaptive) or direct questioning (surveys), the rational expectations approach is based upon what is, perhaps, the most fundamental premise of classical economics, that of individual rationality. What does this mean? Rationality in the context of classical economics means maximizing—or optimizing—behavior, that is, obtaining the best or most favorable results in a given situation. In making their economic decisions people always try to achieve the maximum results, whether their objective is profit, income, or simply satisfaction from consumption. Maximizing must take

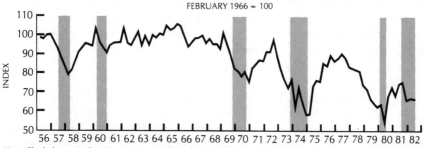

FIGURE 12–3. Index of Consumer Sentiment.
SOURCE: Survey Research Center, The University of Michigan

place of course, within the limits of the individual or the business firm's income and the prevailing technology.

The roots of this principle trace back to the philosophy of *utilitarianism,* a doctrine espoused by Jeremy Bentham (1748–1832). The object of mankind, Bentham said, should be to secure the greatest happiness for the greatest number or, in economic terms, to maximize utility for the largest number of individuals. This is what a rational individual will do when confronted with the choice between "pleasure and pain," to use Bentham's words, and this is what society ought to do. Thus, Bentham's "principle of utility" provides the philosophical foundation for the classical idea that an individual acts rationally when he or she maximizes advantages in a situation and minimizes the disadvantages. More specifically, the consumer maximizes utility, that is, satisfaction from consuming goods and services; the businessperson maximizes profit; and the worker maximizes his or her real wage, which is an offset to the disutility involved in work.

In forming their expectations, people, or economic agents as rational expectations theorists call them, use all available and relevant information and they use this information efficiently. This sounds both simple and obvious, but it is neither so simple nor obvious as it may appear. In using all available and relevant information people reflect upon past errors and adjust their information accordingly. Any errors that remain in their expectations are thus of a random nature and hence unpredictable.

There is a second point which is even more fundamental, especially for the policy implications of the theory. This is that, in forming expectations, people have knowledge of the relevant economic model which policy-makers use in making their decisions. This is not quite as esoteric as it sounds. It does not mean that every person is a trained economist, but that people learn from experience how economic variables are related to one another. For example, if the government indicates that it is going to increase the money supply in an effort to stimulate the economy, people who form their expectations rationally will expect wages and prices to go up. Why? Because they have learned from observing such action in the past that an increase in the money supply is followed by an increase in wages and prices. Consequently, they will act in response to their expectations, namely, raise prices and wages to the extent possible since this is what the "relevant economic model" tells them will happen if the money supply is increased.

The Policy Implications   Now we come to the fundamental policy implication of rational expectations theory. Basically, it is that no policy action by the government can be successful if expectations are formed rationally. The reason, of course, is that people—economic agents—anticipate the policy's effect and alter their behavior accordingly, thus distorting the policy's intended effect. The only circumstance under which a policy action can succeed, according to this theory, is when the policy action is unanticipated. This has led the rational expectations theorists to make the appealing argument that unless the government systematically tries to "fool people" its policies cannot succeed. We must be careful not to overstate what is being claimed. Rational expectations theory applies primarily to the macro policy actions of the government, not to other policies, such as the enforcement of antitrust laws, establishment of minimum wages, regulation of public utilities, and all other traditional actions of government, most of which affect economic activity at the micro level. To sum up, application of the theory of rational expectations to macroeconomic policy formation means that the government should not attempt any activist countercyclical measures to control output, employment, or the general level of prices. Even worse, according to the theory, attempts by the government to pursue an activist countercyclical policy will bring about expectational errors, which, as we shall explain more fully shortly, are the main source of variations in output, employment, and the price level over the course of the business cycle. Thus, any macroeconomic policy that attempts to "fine-tune" the economy with short-term stimuli will not only fail, but, worse yet, it may bring about the very thing it seeks to correct, namely, fluctuations in output and employment. This is the fundamental and devastating policy conclusion to be drawn from the theory of rational expectations.

The Theory of Continuous Market Clearing

Now we come to the second crucial proposition of the new classical economics. The theory of continuous market clearing combines the older Walrasian general equilibrium theory with the more recent theory of efficient markets. The former was developed in the latter half of the nineteenth century by Leon Walras (1834–1910), a French-born economist whose academic career was spent in Switzerland at the University of Lausanne. The latter theory emerged from Professor Muth's seminal article in which he first formulated the concept of rational expectations. Efficient market theory has been concerned primarily with prices and equilibrium in financial and commodity markets—markets often described as "auction" markets.

What Walras did was to develop a basic mathematical model to show how, in an economy characterized by competitive markets, a general equilibrium will be established in which all prices are equilibrium prices and these prices will be determined *simultaneously*. The prices so established are equilibrium prices in that in every market quantity demanded and quantity supplied are in balance—there is, in other words, neither excess demand nor excess supply in any market, including the market for labor. In mathematical terms, the Walrasian system of general equilibrium involves solving a set of simultaneous equations in which there are the same number of prices as supply and demand functions (that is, schedules) to determine these prices. To explain how equilibrium is brought about Walras posited the existence of a fictional "auctioneer" who cries out the price of the goods being traded and continues to do so until an equilibrium—that is, a market clearing—price is established for every good traded in the market. This process by which a general equilibrium was established Walras described as *tatonnement,* a French word which literally means "groping." To put it differently, the process is one of trial and error, in which eventually all trading takes place at equilibrium prices. From a macroeconomic point of view, the general equilibrium envisioned by Walras is one in which there are no unsold quantities of goods and services left in the market, including the supply of labor services. Thus, the general equilibrium model necessarily involves full employment.

In a general way, the efficient market theory is a refinement of Walrasian general equilibrium theory in the sense that it tells us something more about the nature of equilibrium prices in a Walrasian world. It has to do with the relationship between prices and information. A market is efficient when the prices established in that market reflect *all* the available information about the good or service being traded. An efficient market not only processes all relevant information, but it does so quickly, almost instantaneously. This is why in the stock market, for example, one is rarely able to "beat the market"—that is, to profit from knowing something that no one else knows. Financial markets are presumed to be highly efficient in this sense. They quickly process all available information about the security traded, and this information finds its way into the price of the security. A significant amount of evidence has been accumulated to show that financial markets, such as the long-term bond market, are efficient in the sense that we have been using the term.[6] Tests of the hypothesis have generally shown that it is *not* possible to explain changes in yields in these markets on the basis of information available prior to the change in price (that is, yield). Thus, such changes have to be accounted for by new information. What is not evident, however, is that the efficient market theory can be applied more broadly, that is to say to the market for goods and services generally, including labor. This, however, is one of the key assumptions of the new classical economics.

The New Classical Economics and the Business Cycle

Although both the theory of rational expectations and the theory of continuous market clearing are key elements in the new classical economics, the latter is especially crucial. Why? Because its real meaning is that if, in effect, markets—including the labor market—do continuously clear, then full employment is always the norm. In the classical analysis the "natural" rate of employment—and the corresponding "natural" rate

6. William Poole, "Rational Expectations in the Macro Model," *Brookings Papers on Economic Activity,* 1976:2, p. 467.

of unemployment—is the level at which the quantity of labor demanded and supplied are in balance at an equilibrium *real* wage (Figure 12–1). The "natural" rate hypothesis originated with Milton Friedman.[7] Professor Friedman and the monetarists do not argue, however, that the actual unemployment rate cannot differ from the "natural" unemployment rate for substantial periods of real calendar time. But with the assumption of the new classical economists that at "each point in time" markets clear and "agents" act in their own self interest,[8] the logical conclusion is that, at most, any deviation of the actual unemployment rate from the "natural" rate is extremely short-lived. Therefore, with continuous market clearing there is no room for any systematic policy action designed to influence the actual unemployment rate.

This theoretical conclusion confronts a formidable challenge, because it must be reconciled with the fact of the business cycle—those ups and downs in economic life which characterize the economy's behavior over real, calendar time. It is a formidable challenge because the new classical economics must not only explain the reality of the business cycle, but it must do so in a manner that is consistent with its fundamental tenets— namely, the theory of rational expectations and the theory of continuous market clearing. The new classical economists have provided such an explanation, one that is both ingenious and rooted in classical microeconomic theory.

In standard classical microeconomic theory the supply curve for a seller of either goods and services or of labor slopes upward, showing that, in general, sellers (that is, producers) will offer more of their product or service as the price goes up. The reverse holds true when the price goes down. The immediate concern of any seller is with the price of the particular good or service he is selling, which economic theory identifies as a *relative* price, which is to say his price in comparison to other prices. Any seller also has some concern about prices in general—that is, the price level—but as far as the individual, optimizing decision of a particular seller is concerned what counts initially is *relative* price rather than prices in general. This point is crucial to an understanding of how the new classical economists explain the reality of the business cycle.

Before proceeding further, a word is in order about the meaning of the business cycle in this context. Presumably there is a long-term trend path that the economy would follow for real output if that output were always in balance with the economy's productive potential. The latter is determined by the long-term growth of resources, especially labor and capital, and changing technology. But as we saw in Chapter 1, the actual path of real GNP is seldom smooth, departing over time in both direc-

---

7. Milton Friedman, "The Role of Monetary Policy," *The American Economic Review*, March 1968, pp. 1–17.
8. Robert E. Lucas and Thomas J. Sargent, "After Keynesian Macroeconomics," in *After the Phillips Curve: Persistence of High Inflation and High Unemployment* (Boston: Federal Reserve Bank of Boston, 1978), p. 58.

tions from the trend representing potential output. These departures in both directions from the trend are not smooth, but there is enough regularity to them to warrant the name "business cycle."

With these remarks as a backdrop, let us proceed to examine how the new classical economics explains the cycle. We shall begin with a period of rising prices, brought about either by an expansion of the money supply or simply by an increase in nominal demand. Since suppliers (including workers) have good knowledge of their own prices (wages) but limited knowledge of the general level of prices (wages), they will interpret the price (wage) increases initially as a *relative* change, meaning that the demand for their good or service has increased. Given, then, the nature of the classical supply curve for a good or service, including the supply of labor, output will be expanded or more labor will be offered on the market. This response is shown in Part A of Figure 12–4, which shows in idealized fashion the swing of output over time around the basic, underlying trend line for real GNP. What happens in this phase, according to the new classical economists, is an information lag, a period in which sellers are generally unaware that prices (and wages) in general are rising. This means that there has not in fact been any change in the *relative* price for the good or service being supplied. If every seller, including workers, understood from the start that all prices (and wages) were going up together, they would not respond because nothing had really changed. For the supplier of a good or service, *relative* prices would

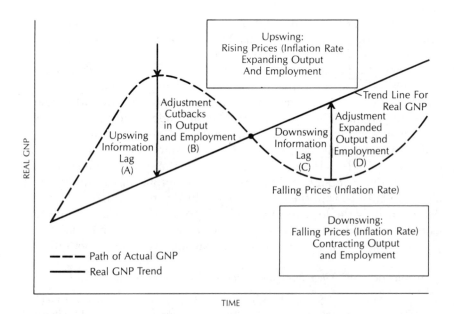

Figure 12–4. The New Classical Economics and the Business Cycle

be unchanged, and for the supplier of labor, the *real* wage would be unchanged. As a leading proponent of the new classical economics says, "This scenario . . . depends crucially on the confusion on the part of agents between relative and general price movements."[9] Furthermore, it is argued that the kind of response described above applies to invest- ment goods, as well as goods and services in general. Thus, they argue that the investment boom which is often characteristic of the upswing phase of the business cycle can be explained in the same way. By the time it is recognized that general rather than relative price changes are taking place, it is too late—more capacity has been added than is neces- sary to meet actual demand.

Consider now what happens. In the downturn phase of the cycle, Part B in Figure 12–4, adjustments are being made as producers begin to see that they were mistaken, that what they took to be a change in *relative* prices in their favor turns out not to be the case. Over time the infor- mation about what is really happening to prices (and wages) in general permeates through the economy, leading to cutbacks in production and in labor supplied. The presumption is that economic "agents," now that they have the correct information, try to adjust back to their original positions on their supply curves—points where they were before prices in general started to rise. What happens after this is suggested by the area designated as C. Now prices (and wages) are falling,[10] but once again this change is perceived initially as a change in *relative* prices (and wages), rather than a general movement. Consequently, suppliers reduce their output, labor is withdrawn from the market, and actual output falls below the trend line for real GNP. We have a recession or a depression. This process will continue until producers once again are aware that relative prices (wages) are not changing, but only prices (wages) in gen- eral. Then the reduction in output will end, as will the withdrawal of labor from the market, and a recovery will begin as suppliers seek to return to their original positions.

Thus, the new classical economics maintains that it is possible to explain the business cycle—which they concede is a reality—without having to abandon the essential tenets of classical equilibrium economics, namely, that all behavior is rational and that markets clear continuously in the Walrasian sense. It turns out that basically the business cycle is a product of misinformation by economic "agents" who are presumed to act ration- ally at all times. This is especially crucial for the problem of unemploy- ment. Since the supply of labor is a function of the real wages, any withdrawal of labor from the market turns out to be voluntary. Workers,

9. Robert E. Lucas, Jr., "Understanding Business Cycles," in Karl Brunner and Alan Meltzer, eds., *Stabilization of the Domestic and International Economy* (Amsterdam: North-Holland, 1977), p. 22.
10. It would be more correct to speak of the inflation rate as falling rather than wages and prices, for rarely since World War II have prices and wages actually declined. But the principle is the same.

misreading the fall in money wages as a decline in real wages because they don't perceive that prices in general are also falling, withdraw from the labor market. Since they are not immediately aware of what is happening in other labor markets, assuming that the decline in their wage is a relative one, they continue to search for employment elsewhere. But, nevertheless, their withdrawal and continued search are perceived as a voluntary act, resulting primarily from an informational failure.

Some Critical Observations

The new classical economics has a strong appeal, especially because, by linking expectations to traditional classical ideas about rational behavior, it seems to provide the bridge between micro- and macroeconomics that economists have sought for so long. But as a theory capable of explaining the real-world behavior of complex market economies, it has serious limitations. Critics point to three major weaknesses in the theory.

The most fundamental weakness, perhaps is the assumption that markets clear continuously. In reality this is nothing more than a restatement of the old classical view that markets are purely competitive, that prices (and wages) are flexible, and that the movement in the market is always toward an equilibrium of price and planned quantities. We must remember, however, that the market-clearing assumption is, as Professor Tobin says, "just that, an assumption. It is not justified by any new direct evidence that a Walrasian auctioneer process generates the prices observed from day to day or month to month or year to year."[11] Furthermore, as Professor Tobin has also said:

> We must therefore remind ourselves how severe a draft on credulity is the literal application of the market-clearing area. The Walrasian Auctioneer is a great myth; I emphasize both words. She must collect all the demand and supply schedules for the m commodities and n agents. She must solve the simultaneous equations, announce the market-clearing prices, and see that the scheduled transactions are consummated at those prices. For continuous market clearing the whole process must be repeated every quarter or day or second.[12]

Reality, of course, is vastly different. The majority of markets in the real world do not have the characteristics of "auction" markets, that is, markets in which prices are set by the interaction of many buyers and sellers, no one of whom has any control over the outcome. Participants in auction markets are known as "price-takers," simply because as either a buyer or a seller they have no choice but to respond to the prices established in the market. Most markets in the real world, according to the late Arthur Okun, a former chairman of the Council of Economic Advis-

11. James Tobin, "Are New Classical Models Plausible Enough to Guide Policy?" *Journal of Money, Credit, and Banking,* November 1980, p. 788.
12. James Tobin, *Asset Accumulation and Economic Activity,* op. cit., p. 34.

ers, are ones in which sellers (or suppliers) of both commodities and labor are "price-makers," which is to say that they *do* have control over the process by which prices and wages are determined.[13] Prices and wages are not necessarily set to clear the markets in the short run. For goods and services, customer-supplier relations are a major factor in the establishment of prices, a factor which leads to stability and durability, rather than volatility in price as in the auction model. The same is true for wages, for in labor markets the stability of employer-workers relations over the long term is usually of primary importance. The practical impact of "price-making" rather than "price-taking" as a characteristic of markets is to insulate prices and wages to a significant degree from shifts in demand, leading to adjustments in output and employment when there are such shifts. This is quite in contrast to the views of the new classical economists, who hold that relative price adjustments occur practically instantaneously in response to changes or disturbances in demand and supply in particular markets.

Why is it, one may ask, that the classical economists insist on a view that is as much at odds with reality? In the older classical economics, the Walrasian general equilibrium solution was in practical terms seen as a long-run outcome, not a condition present at every moment of time. The answer seems to lie, in part, in a very strong feeling among the new classical economists that macroeconomics must be rooted in the optimizing individual behavior which is characteristic of microeconomics. Keynesian theoretical propositions, such as the consumption function, have been criticized for not having such a link. It also has a strong appeal because the Walrasian general equilibrium outcome is one in which there is an optimal allocation of resources and a maximum production of the goods and services wanted by people in the economy. Since no satisfactory alternative model exists for dealing with fundamental issues of resource use and output composition, the Walrasian general equilibrium model holds great appeal, even though it simply is not possible to describe the real world in terms of continuous clearing in competitive markets. Mathematical models are useful because they can help to discover relationships among variables, but they can never yield results other than those which are embodied in their initial assumptions. As other critics have said, the rational expectations hypothesis is nothing more than a "mathematical method of incorporating expectations into economic models. It is no more and no less. It is especially not . . . a proof that people behave rationally."[14]

A second critical thrust centers on the other half of the new classical economics, namely, the theory of rational expectations. There are, it is said, serious deficiencies in this hypothesis, especially in the matter of

13. Arthur Okun, *Prices & Quantities: A Macroeconomic Analysis* (Washington, D.C.: The Brookings Institution, 1981), p. 138.
14. David C. Colander and Robert S. Guthrie, "Great Expectations: What the Dickens Do 'Rational Expectations' Mean?" *Journal of Post Keynesian Economics*, Winter 1980–81, p. 232.

how expectations are actually formed in the real-world economy. One major deficiency in the rational expectations approach is that it requires that people know much more about how the economy works and the significance of all the data generated than reasonably can be expected. Given the fact that there is so much fundamental disagreement among professional economists about how the economy works, how can it be expected that the public at large have the necessary knowledge to engage in the kind of rational expectation formation envisioned by the new classical economics? There is no answer to this question other, perhaps, than to fall back on the argument that eventually people do learn enough about the way the economy works to avoid being fooled when policy decisions are made. The difficulty is, however, that economic relationships, even though they may be well-established on the basis of historical data, can and do change, sometimes in unpredictable ways. This, of course, changes the nature of the relevant economic models that the policy-makers use.

It is also argued by critics of the rational expectations hypothesis that the notion that people use all information efficiently by incorporating it into their expectations ignores the fact that information is not a free good. On the contrary, the gathering and the processing of the kind of information necessary to understand what is going on in the economy and to interpret what decision-makers are doing are a costly process. It is quite possible that the benefits to be derived from doing this may not, in many instances, outweigh the costs involved. Often the best way people have to deal with the complexities and uncertainties of the economy is to fall back on relatively simple rules-of-thumb behavior which take into account what has happened recently. Decision-making may be truly rational in the sense in which the new classical economists employ the term in the securities markets. They are highly organized, centrally located, and deal with a "commodity" which is basically homogeneous, all of which makes for a quick and comprehensive flow of information to all participants in the market. But these characteristics are not typical of most other markets in the economy, including labor markets.

More fundamental, perhaps, is the criticism leveled against the rational expectations hypothesis by the late George Katona, long associated with the Institute for Social Research at the University of Michigan. The formation of expectations, Professor Katona argues, is a psychological process, one rooted in habits derived from repeated and rewarded past experiences.[15] In order to understand in a meaningful way how expectations are actually formed, economists must consider the theories and findings of psychologists, not begin with an unsubstantiated assumption about the way human beings behave, namely, the rationality postulate of the classical economics. Our behavior is rooted in the past and generally

---

15. George Katona, "How Expectations Are Really Formed," *Challenge,* November-December 1980, p. 32.

expectations are derived from the experiences of the past. But conditions change and humans are capable of learning as well as changing their attitudes and beliefs, including their expectations about the future. When something new enters the picture, people may change both their behavior and their expectations. One cannot simply assume, however, that expectations are always modified sufficiently to take into account new elements in any situation. The rational expectations approach makes such an assumption. As a practical matter, the only way to resolve this difficulty is by empirical research, which means going out and asking about expectations.

Finally, critics of the theory of rational expectations argue that, even if valid, it has limited applicability because it can deal only with situations in which the economic events that enter into the formation of expectations involve situations of "risk" and not "uncertainty." "Risk" applies to a situation in which events repeat themselves—such as the presumed regularities of the business cycle—with enough certainty that a probability calculus can be applied to determine the likelihood of any particular event occurring. This limitation of the rational expectations hypothesis is readily granted by its advocates. "In situations of risk, the hypothesis of rational behavior on the part of agents will have useable content, so that behavior may be explainable in terms of economic theory. . . . In cases of uncertainty, economic reasoning will be of no value."[16] What this means is that the rational expectations theorists have constructed a world in which events repeat themselves in logical time—the world of neoclassical general equilibrium economics. Risk is an appropriate concept for such a world, and in it "economic agents" can form their expectations on the basis of appropriate probability calculations. The real world, according to the critics, is one of *nonrepetitive* events occurring in *historical* time. Uncertainty, not risk, is the appropriate concept to be applied to such a world.[17] Uncertainty pervades economic life, the reason being that the economy exists in historical, not logical, time. When we deal with real, historic time, we are dealing not only with the past and present, but also with the future, and the future is uncertain. Major economic events— such as investment spending—are tied to an uncertain and unknowable future, not to events that tend to be repetitive. The problem, as Keynes pointed out many years ago, is when we are dealing with uncertainty— such as the yield of a new factory over its lifetime—"there is *no scientific basis* on which to form any capable probability whatever. We simply do not know."[18] Thus, we have to fall back on such flimsy and uncertain foundations as recent and present conditions and majority opinion as guides to the future.

16. Robert E. Lucas, Jr., "Understanding Business Cycles," op. cit., p. 15.
17. Leonard Forman, "Rational Expectations and the Real World," *Challenge,* November-December 1980, p. 36.
18. John Maynard Keynes, "The General Theory of Employment," *Quarterly Journal of Economics,* February 1937, p. 213.

The final criticism of the new classical economics centers on its explanation of the business cycle. Two things should be said about this explanation of the cycle. First, it really strains the imagination to believe that long periods of unemployment, such as the economy experienced in the 1930s and even at times in the post–World War II period, can be explained by a persistent failure to understand not only what is happening in other markets, but also what is happening in the economy overall. As Arthur Okun has said, the "theory is weak, however, in explaining why any demand disturbances . . . should be so poorly perceived for so long that they create pronounced cycles in real activity."[19] The response of the new classical economics to this is basically that it simply may take a long time for the economy to adjust to and reverse any output changes which result from misinformation, even though it will not necessarily take a long time for producers and workers to realize what is happening in other markets and to the economy overall. Second, the new classical economics is criticized for failing to provide any direct empirical evidence that sellers of both goods and labor do not have any relevant and timely information about other prices which bear on their own decisions. "Any theory that attributes decision-making errors by private agents to missing information implies that there exists, in principle, some set of correct, timely information that would eliminate these errors. That information needs to be identified specifically."[20] This has not been done.

In concluding this discussion of rational expectations and the market-clearing postulate, two points need to be made. Granted that the logic and mathematical completeness of the new classical economics has a strong appeal to many economists, empirical evidence, which after all is the ultimate test for the validity of any theory, does not support the argument of the new classical school that *all* macro policy measures are ineffective. To verify this one should look again at Figure 1–3 in Chapter 1 Output (and employment) have been much more stable in the post–World War II period than they were before the war. This has been the period of active stabilization policy, and the overall results have been more beneficial than detrimental. What has given the most credence to the resurgence of classical ideas has been the failure of conventional macroeconomic policies to cope with the dominant problem of the 1970s—the simultaneous existence of excess inflation and excess unemployment. The correct lesson of this experience is that we do not yet have successful policies for attaining full employment—especially full employment over time—with stable prices. But the answer to this dilemma is not to abandon the basic income-expenditure model in favor of reinvented classical theories found wanting in the past. Rather, it is to expand and improve the model, bringing into it elements which can account for the observed fact of rising prices and wages along with slack markets and excess capacity. We shall examine these elements in Chapters 13 and 14.

19. Arthur Okun, *Prices & Quantities*, op. cit., p. 172.
20. Arthur Okun, "Rational-Expectations with Misperceptions as a Theory of the Business Cycle," op. it., p. 820.

Supply-Side Economics

The second major development representing a rebirth of classical thinking is popularly known as "supply-side" economics. It is far better known
to the general public than the new classical economics, primarily because
it provided the basic theoretical rationale for the Reagan administration's 1981 "Program for Economic Recovery."[21] As a body of theoretical
ideas, however, it has far less substance or elegance than either the standard Keynesian income-expenditure analysis or the new classical economics just discussed. Actually, supply-side economics does not constitute
a coherent set of relationships like the Keynesian model, relationships
which purport to explain how the macroeconomy works. Rather, it consists of two propositions, roughly related to one another, and which look
to classical economics for their origin and inspiration. These propositions are, first, full faith in the validity of Say's law of markets and, second, a belief that tax rates are the prime determinant of incentives, which
in turn are the prime determinant of production. These are linked to a
deep and abiding hostility toward government. Basically, "supply-side"
economics is as much, if not more, ideological than it is economic.

Why do supply-side economists insist on the validity of Say's law, particularly when no empirical evidence is produced to support this validity? As with the earlier classical economists, it is in part an article of faith,
a belief in the beneficent workings of the market system. It is also a
logical necessity for their basic argument, namely, that it is possible to
explain how the economy works by approaching it from the standpoint
of aggregate supply rather than aggregate demand. Concentrating on
supply as the key determinant of aggregate output makes sense *only* if
there is assurance that everything produced ultimately can be sold. Say's
law provides this guarantee, logically, if not empirically. Finally, it reflects
the fact that classical economics deals with what Keynes called a *real-
exchange economy.* Such an economy is one which uses money, but only as
a neutral link between transactions in things. It does not allow money to
enter into motives or decisions, as money does in Keynesian theory.[22]
Contemporary supply-side economists, by restating their faith in Say's
law, are also saying that savings always lead to investment spending, a
proposition not supported by empirical evidence.

Taxes, Incentives, and Production

The real theoretical core of supply-side economics resides in the belief
that the major factor holding back production, causing unemployment,
creating inflation, and leaving the government with insufficient reve-

21. Details of this program are discussed in Chapter 15, "Managing the Macroeconomy."
22. John Maynard Keynes, "On the Theory of a Monetary Economy," *Nebraska Journal of
Economics and Business,* Autumn 1963, pp. 7–9.

nues and large deficits is taxation. More specifically, supply-side economics argues that *marginal* tax rates are the real source of the economy's problems. The marginal tax rate is the progressive increase in the tax rate applied to each increment of income as the taxpayer moves into a higher tax bracket every time his nominal (money) income increases. Jude Wanniski, former editorial writer for *The Wall Street Journal* and a leading proponent of supply-side economics, argues that the principle of the margin can be called upon to explain almost the totality of economic behavior.[23] "The concept of marginality," he says, "is crucial to an understanding of economic behavior. . . . Very few people *think* on the margin, but everyone *acts* on the margin."[24] Production comes about, according to Wanniski, "because people are willing to work, and people work for only one reason—to maximize their welfare."[25] It is at this point that taxes enter the picture, particularly the marginal tax rate. Taxes are a *disincentive* to produce. Taxes on capital discourage investment and taxes on people discourage work. This is the essential message of supply-side economics.

The theoretical centerpiece in supply-side economics is the concept of the Laffer curve, named for economist Arthur Laffer of the University of Southern California. Professor Laffer's now-famous curve purports to show the relationship between tax rates and tax revenue.[26] Figure 12–5 depicts a standard version of the Laffer curve, showing on the vertical axis the tax rate, and on the horizontal axis the revenues of the government associated with different tax rates. First, it should be noted, there are two tax rates which produce no revenue for the government—namely, a 100 percent rate and a zero rate. Presumably if income were taxed at 100 percent, there would be no production and hence no revenue. If the tax rate were zero, there would be no revenue, irrespective of the level of production.

A second point about the curve is of far greater significance. This is that between the extremes of a zero and 100 percent tax rate, there are *always two* rates of taxation which will produce the same revenue—a high rate and a low rate. In the figure, for example, the tax rate TX_2 (a higher rate) yields a revenue of R_1, as does the tax rate TX_1 (a lower rate). This brings us to the heart of the supply-side argument about taxation. It has been the contention of supply-side economists that the economy is operating in the tax range between TX^* and TX_2. In the curve, the rate represented by TX^* produces the maximum revenue for the government. It is, in other words, the optimum tax rate. If taxes are above this optimum, as is the case if the actual tax rate is at TX_2, then clearly the government can increase its revenues from R_1 to R_m by a reduction in the

23. Jude Wanniski, *The Way the World Works* (New York: Basic Books, 1978), p. 42.
24. Ibid., p. 43.
25. Ibid., p. 71.
26. The story is that Professor Laffer first sketched out his curve on a napkin at a Washington, D.C., restaurant. See Fred Barnes, "The Story of 'Supply-Side,' a Revolution in Economic Thinking," *The Baltimore Sun*, February 17, 1981.

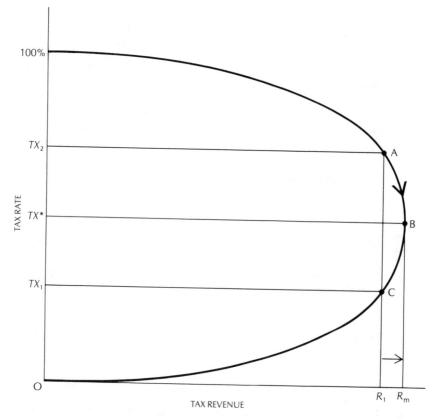

FIGURE 12–5.   The Laffer Curve

tax rate from TX_2 to TX^*. Such a reduction in tax rates will move the economy along the Laffer curve from point A to B. In this range of the curve, tax revenues are *elastic* because a cut in the tax rate leads to a more than proportionate increase in taxable income and hence in a *rise* in the government's revenue. Cutting taxes below the level TX^* would reduce revenues, for in the range from B through C (and beyond to a zero rate) tax revenues are *inelastic*, since at rates below TX^* any increases in taxable revenues from tax cuts will lead to a less than proportionate increase in taxable revenue and thus a decline in total tax receipts.

The Laffer curve presents in abstract form a theoretical argument for a tax reduction which presumably will lead to more rather than less government revenue. This argument was the basis for the Reagan administration's across-the-board three-year cut (5-10-10) in the personal income tax, a major part of the administration's 1981 "Program for Economic Recovery." We shall discuss these policy decisions fully in Chapter 15 ("Managing the Macroeconomy"); at this point it will suffice to say that no important empirical evidence was forthcoming from the supply-side economists to support their contention that the economy was, in reality, actually operating in the upper ranges of the Laffer curve (between points A and B) at the time the 1981 tax cuts were enacted. It was an argument based upon faith in the validity of the curve, not factual knowledge about the actual impact of existing tax rates upon incentives to produce.[27]

A second important theoretical idea developed by Professor Laffer is the concept of the "wedge," especially the tax "wedge." This is the gap that government through its power to tax and to regulate introduces between what an individual gets for working and what the individual is allowed to keep. Anything that government does—minimum-wage laws, regulations, tariffs, etc.—might be a part of this "wedge," but taxes are by far the most important. As Professor Laffer has said:

> Marginal tax rates of all sorts stand as a *wedge* between what an employer pays his factors of production and what they ultimately receive in after-tax income. . . . In order to increase total output, policy measures must have the effect of both increasing the firms' demand for productive factors and increasing the productive factors' desire to be employed. Taxes of all sorts must be reduced. These reductions will be most effective where they lower marginal tax rates the most.[28]

The "wedge" argument is, of course, another way to underscore the basic argument of the supply-side perspective, namely, that taxes are the chief barrier to higher production and higher productivity.

Supply-Side Economics and Government

From the "wedge" analysis it is an easy step to understand the hostility of supply-side economics to governmental activity. Since the only and ultimate source of productive activity lies in the individual's drive to maximize personal satisfaction or welfare, anything which detracts from this necessarily reduces productive effort. Government and its taxes belong in this category. Government is perceived as essentially nonproductive, if not positively wasteful. There is a presumption in the supply-side view of the world that anything produced in the private sector, if it sells and hence survives the test of the market, cannot be in any sense wasteful. In the supply-side view the ultimate test of the "legitimacy" of production, so to speak, is the market. Productive activity is basically market-determined activity. Therefore, it follows logically that governments should only do those minimally necessary things for a lawful and orderly society, including protecting that society from its external enemies. All else is waste.

---

27. In the 1981 *Economic Report of the President* (the last report of the Carter administration), the Council of Economic Advisers estimated that a 10 percent cut in personal income tax rates would produce an increase in potential GNP of 0.2 percent to at most 0.6 percent. See *Economic Report of the President* (Washington, D.C.: U.S. Government Printing Office, 1981), p. 81.
28. Memorandum to the U.S. Secretary of the Treasury, November 1974, as quoted by Jude Wanniski, op. cit., p. 85.

Summary

1. The new classical economics and supply-side economics are two additional challenges to the income-expenditure approach to the macroeconomy. Both have deep roots in classical economic theory.

2. Classical economics involves three fundamental propositions: (1) a theory of the demand for and supply of labor which explains the employment level; (2) Say's "law of markets," which explains why general overproduction—a "glut" of goods—is impossible; and (3) the quantity theory of money, which explains how and why the price level is determined by the money supply.

3. Like all economic theory, the classical theory contains important policy implications. The most important of these is *laissez faire,* or noninterference in the economy by the government. The thrust of classical economics is that full employment is the normal state of affairs, and no policy actions by the government are necessary to attain this condition.

4. The new classical economics is the most recent challenge to the Keynesian-oriented income-expenditure approach to macroeconomics. It arose in part because of the alleged policy failures of Keynesian economics during the 1970s, a period when the economy experienced simultaneously too much inflation and too much unemployment. It rests upon two basic propositions, namely, the theory of rational expectations and the theory of continuous market clearing.

5. The theory of rational expectations argues that all economic "agents" form expectations rationally by taking into account all relevant information, including how policy will affect the economy. The consequence of this is that, unless a policy action is not foreseen, the results of any policy will be anticipated and therefore the policy will be ineffective. Because the rational expectations theorists believe that the economy is inherently stable, and because of the way in which they believe expectations are formed, they do not believe *any* policy action by the government can affect output, employment, or the price level.

6. The other key element in the new classical economics is the theory of continuous market clearing. This involves the principles involved in Walrasian general equilibrium theory, which show how equilibrium can be established simultaneously in all markets, if competition is present. This theory includes equilibrium in the labor market, which means that full employment is the normal state of affairs.

7. The new classical economics recognizes the existence of the business cycle, but explains it in terms of misinformation on the part of producers and wage-earners who fail to perceive what is happening in specific markets and thus temporarily supply more goods and labor than needed.

Critics argue that this is insufficient to explain the depth and duration of most cycles.

8. Supply-side economics consists of two basic propositions: (1) faith in the validity under contemporary conditions of Say's law of markets and (2) a belief that incentives to work, invest, and save are badly impaired by taxes being too high. The latter is based upon the Laffer curve. The basic policy recommendation of supply-side economics is to cut taxes sharply. Supply-side economics formed a part of the theoretical base of the Reagan administration's "Program for Economic Recovery."

13

Post Keynesian Economics

The modern quantity theory, the new classical economics, and supply-side economics, all discussed in the last two chapters, have two basic ideas in common. First, they reject the Keynesian relationships contained in the income-expenditure approach developed in Part II of this text, even when the overall framework of Keynesian analysis is accepted, as is the case with contemporary monetarism. Second, they represent a return in one form or another to classical economic principles, to belief in the *inherent* stability of a market economy and its self-correcting tendencies.

In contrast to the above dissenters from the standard post–World War II macroeconomic analysis, there are the "Post Keynesians." Not only do they reject all attempts to revive classical economics as applied to the whole economy as being both unworkable and unrealistic, they also are sharply critical of the standard post–World War II interpretations of Keynes, particularly the "neoclassical" synthesis. The latter they regard as an attempt to push the ideas of Keynes into a classical mold, thus stripping the Keynesian "revolution" of all significance. Instead of looking to a pre-Keynesian classical past for ideas and inspiration, they look, first, to important elements in Keynes's thinking that post–World War II interpretations have neglected. But they go beyond this, because they also seek to develop new theoretical insights into the workings of contemporary systems of market capitalism, economies far removed in time and structure from the simple competitive models that characterize the classical counter-revolutions. Their insights and theories are "Keynesian" in their origin and inspiration, but, the Post Keynesians argue, they involve much more than an attempt to update *The General Theory*.

Fundamental Concerns of the Post Keynesians

The Post Keynesian economists are a diverse group, more so, perhaps, than the monetarists, the new classical economists, or the supply-siders. In one major subgroup we find economists like Robert Clower and Alexis L. Leijonhufvud, of the University of California, Los Angeles, who have challenged the Walrasian system of general equilibrium, which is one of the two key elements in the new classical economics. A second group, largely but not wholly centered at Cambridge University in England, has concentrated on the dynamics of full-employment growth, paying special attention to the linkages between income distribution and growth. Among the economists in this subgroup we find Roy Harrod, Nicholas Kaldor, the late Joan Robinson, and Jan Kregel, as well as Alfred Eichner of Rutgers University. Finally, there is a third group whose interests are directed toward the workings of the real-world market economy, not an idealized vision of a market such as is found in the new classical economics. The real-world market economy operates in *historic* time, is characterized by a high degree of uncertainty, and is one in which both financial institutions and the power of organized groups play a crucial role. Economists who fit into this subcategory include, among others, Paul Davidson of Rutgers University, Hyman Minsky of Washington University, the late Sidney Weintraub of the University of Pennsylvania, and John Kenneth Galbraith of Harvard University.

Rejection of Walrasian General Equilibrium Theory

Perhaps the most fundamental proposition common to all Post Keynesian economists, irrespective of the particular subgroup to which they belong, is a rejection of the Walrasian theory of general equilibrium as the micro-foundation for macroeconomic theory. As seen from prior discussion of both the neoclassical synthesis and the new classical economics, Walrasian general equilibrium theory is the basis for the belief that, when competition is present, a market system is inherently self-correcting and will automatically lead to the full utilization of labor and all other resources.

Post Keynesians, led by Professors Clower and Leijonhufvud, find the Walrasian theory incompatible with Keynesian economics. To see how, we begin with a brief review of the key ideas in Walrasian general equilibrium theory. In the Walrasian model, planned excess demand represents the goods and services that people want to obtain through exchange in order to satisfy their wants. Planned excess supply, on the other hand, represents the goods and services—including labor services—that people bring to the marketplace to exchange for those things they want. In this context all supply, following Say's law, represents the demand for something. The quantities of goods and services demanded cannot be determined, however, in the absence of prices. To put it differently, the quantity of excess demand or excess supply for anything depends upon the price that must be paid for it when it is acquired or the price received for it when it is given up. This principle applies to labor as well as to goods and services. Prices must be known, and when prices are known, the demand and supply functions (that is, schedules) are established for all goods and services (including labor) traded in the marketplace.

Now the famous Walrasian auctioneer enters the picture.[1] A demand or a supply schedule always represents the planned (or *ex ante*) purchases or sales of any good or service at an array of all possible prices. The role of the auctioneer is to continue to call out prices until *planned* demand and supply are in balance in *every single market*. The auctioneer, in other words, supplies the basic information that makes it possible for all participants in the market to act and in acting be on their demand or supply schedules. Only when the participants have information about prices in every other market can they act.

In the Walrasian system it is crucial to understand that *no* trading or exchange can take place until planned demand and planned supply match in every market. The job of the auctioneer is to continue to call out new sets of prices for everything being traded until prices are found that will *clear* all markets simultaneously. This is what Walras meant by the process of *tatonnement*, of groping toward a general equilibrium solution for the whole economy.

Now we come to a crucial point in Walrasian theory, crucial both to the theory itself and to the Clower and Leijonhufvud criticisms of that theory. In a Walrasian general equilibrium situation, there can be no *false trading*. False trading is the exchange of goods and services at other than equilibrium prices. The miracle that the Walrasian auctioneer works is to have everyone in the market hold off making any exchange until equilibrium prices are known for everything being traded. Then all trade takes place instantaneously.

Here is the entry point for the Clower-Leijonhufvud criticism. Walrasian general equilibrium theory is an idealized picture, far removed from real-world markets and exchange. In the real world, false trading takes place all the time. As a practical matter, it is nearly impossible to determine whether any price in any particular market is an equilibrium price; nevertheless, prices exist and exchange takes place. What is the consequence of this? If false trading takes place, then there is exchange at other than equilibrium prices. But if this happens, then *effective* demand may depart from planned demand (Professor Clower calls planned demand "notional" demand). This opens up the possibility for disequilibrium states because insufficient information is being conveyed to all

1. Walras invented the idea of the auctioneer to explain in nonmathematical language what he was attempting to demonstrate by mathematics. At that time few economists understood mathematics. Walras was originally trained as an engineer, hence his interest in explaining the economy in mathematical terms.

participants in the market. Why this is so can be readily illustrated through a simple supply and demand diagram representing the labor market, as shown in Figure 13–1. Before we see how this works, however, we need to understand another principle, one that Professor Clower terms "Say's principle." This is the idea that a buyer always plans to finance his purchases from the sale of goods or services. As far as workers are concerned, in common-sense terms this means that it is the wage obtained through the sale of a year's labor service that will finance their purchases of goods and services. In Walrasian terms, the workers' planned (notional) demand for goods and services is dependent upon the income they expect to receive from the sale of their labor services. The latter is their planned sale and is derived from the supply schedule for labor.

In Figure 13–1 the wage is W_1. At this wage, which is not an equilibrium wage, firms will use only ON_1 units of labor. This will be their effective demand for labor, assuming that an exchange actually takes place at the wage W_1. In the Walrasian system, of course, no exchange would take place at this wage since it would amount to false trading. Workers, given the wage W_1, will supply labor in the amount ON_2. This is their planned (or notional) supply. Now, in a Walrasian world, they plan to

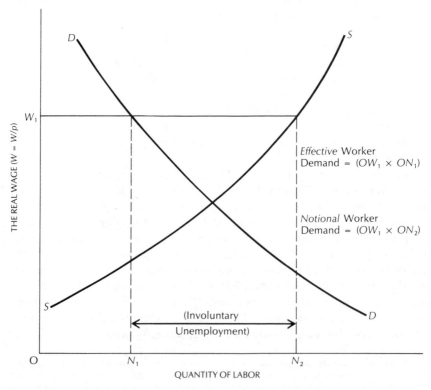

FIGURE 13–1. Effective Demand Failure in the Labor Market

spend on the basis of their planned supply of work, since this supply represents the demand for goods and services, assuming that their planned supply of work is translated into realized employment. Here comes the rub. The workers' planned (notional) demand for goods and services depends upon their expectation that they will have a realized income based upon their planned (notional) supply of labor. In the figure this is equal to $(OW_1 \times ON_2)$. Because in the real world there is no Walrasian auctioneer, workers have no way to convey to prospective employers the information that, if ON_2 workers are hired, they will spend this income and it will justify employers hiring at this level. Instead, employers, confronted with the wage W_1, will only hire ON_1 workers, whose total income—and hence effective demand—will be equal to $(OW_1 \times ON_1)$. Thus, we have a clear case of *effective demand failure*. There is involuntary unemployment—the distance N_1N_2 in the figure—because it is the realized current income of the workers derived from actual employment $(OW_1 \times ON_1)$ that governs the amount of employment firms can offer. Unemployment emerges and may persist, perhaps for a long period of time.

The Economy and Historic Time

One of the crucial weaknesses of Walrasian general equilibrium theory is its inability to deal with real, historic time. Models based upon Walrasian theory are static and timeless. This follows from the basic nature of equilibrium. Equilibrium, as Nobel laureate and British economist Sir John Hicks has pointed out, is by definition a state in which the relevant variables are not changing; hence, time is not involved in equilibrium analysis.[2]

The absence of time in classical economics and in the Walrasian general equilibrium model leads to a second major proposition concerning which there is basic agreement among Post Keynesian economists. This is that the economy is seen as an ongoing process that exists in *real*, historic time. This is a simple idea yet it has far-reaching ramifications for economics and economic theorizing. When we say that the economy and economic processes exist in real, historic time we are saying that they exist in a world in which the past is known and irrevocable, but the future is unknown. The economy, in other words, moves continuously from a known past through the present to an unknown future. Furthermore, the process is irreversible, a view basically different from what exists in equilibrium analysis, wherein a system when disturbed returns to its original state. The knowledge observers can have about the future is, at best, no more than the knowledge of probabilities; they may surmise, guess, or speculate what might happen, but they can never know for

2. Sir John R. Hicks, "Some Questions of Time in Economics," in *Evolution, Welfare, and Time in Economics*, Anthony M. Tang, ed. (Lexington, Mass.: D. C. Heath, 1976), p. 140.

sure what will happen. This is especially relevant for the investment decision, since such decisions are entirely future-oriented.

Not only is the economic process one-directional, but often it is cumulative in character, especially during the up- and downswings of the business cycle. This means that, when economy is disturbed for any reason, it may tend to expand or contract at an accelerating pace. Furthermore, in Keynesian theory generally, money, saving, and investment play key roles in the determination of output and employment. Once real time is introduced into the picture their roles become even more important. This is because they provide vital links between the economy's historic past and its uncertain future. The fact that the economy has a historic past also means that the economic process can't be understood without knowledge of this history. To put it somewhat differently, the economic process is both evolutionary and cultural, which is to say that we cannot detach the economy and economic behavior from the cultural environment in which it takes place. To an extent, then, economic principles are necessarily limited by time, place, and culture, a fact that some may find disturbing because it limits the possibility of developing a general theory of the economic process that could be applied to any society at any time, irrespective of its technology or institutions. In sum, evolutionary change is the normal state of affairs, not movement toward a state of rest at some fixed level of economic activity.

Uncertainty and Expectations

The real world of historic time is dominated by uncertainty, the third key proposition that unites Post Keynesian economists. Uncertainty exists simply because we cannot know the future, no matter how good our knowledge of the past may be. In *The General Theory,* uncertainty emerges as, perhaps, the key element in economic life. It follows from the basic fact of uncertainty that expectations play a critical role in the economic process. What we do economically and how we do it are strongly influenced by our expectations concerning the future. What distinguishes the Post Keynesians in this respect is their belief that the foundations for expectations are uncertain and volatile. As we saw in the previous chapter, the new classical economists also emphasize strongly the role expectations play in determination of economic activity, but their view shows that the foundations are built on carefully analyzed statistical certainty.

To underscore this difference and to emphasize as strongly as possible how uncertainty and expectations enter into Post Keynesian economic thinking, it is instructive to review explicitly how Keynes viewed the matter. The problem with the classical economists, according to Keynes, was that they assumed a certainty of knowledge where such certainty was simply not possible. The classical economists held that "facts and expectations were assumed to be given in a definite and calculable form; and risks, of which, though admitted, not much notice was taken, were supposed to be capable of an exact actuarial computation. The calculus of probability . . . was supposed to be capable of reducing uncertainty to the same calculable status as that of certainty itself."[3]

Unfortunately, Keynes maintained, human beings most of the time have only the vaguest idea of any but the most direct consequences of their acts. Moreover, the consequences with which we may be most concerned are often remote in time. This is especially true for one of the most important acts with which economics is concerned, namely, the accumulation of wealth—that is, investment. As Keynes went on to say, "the whole object of the accumulation of wealth is to produce results, or potential results, at a comparatively distant, and sometimes *indefinitely* distant, date."[4] Unfortunately, the knowledge on which decisions involving the accumulation of wealth (investment) must be based is highly uncertain. Keynes explained what he meant by "uncertain" knowledge as follows:

> By "uncertain" knowledge let me explain. I do not mean merely to distinguish what is known for certain from what is only probable. The game of roulette is not subject, in this sense, to uncertainty; nor is the prospect of a Victory bond being drawn. Or again the expectation of life is only slightly uncertain. Even the weather is only moderately uncertain. The sense in which I am using the term is that in which the prospect of a European war is uncertain, or the price of copper and the rate of interest twenty years hence, or the obsolescence of a new invention, or the position of private wealth holders in the social system in 1970. *About these matters there is no scientific basis on which to form any calculable probability whatever. We simply do not know* [italics added].[5]

Yet decisions must be made, and they must be made on the basis of expectations held about future outcomes for which, as Keynes said, there are no scientific grounds for calculable probability. What, then, do we do? In answer Keynes suggested we fall back on conventions that (1) assume that the present is a "more serviceable guide to the future than past experience has shown it to have been"; (2) assume that existing market conditions are a sound guide to future market conditions; and (3) assume that average or majority opinion is better than our own as a guide to the future. The practical meaning of this is that expectations formed in this fashion rest on flimsy foundation, subject to "sudden and violent changes. . . . All these pretty, polite techniques, made for a well-panelled board room and a nicely regulated market, are liable to collapse."[6]

There are two critical points at which uncertainty and the volatility of expectations based upon uncertainty enter into the economic process. They enter, first, into the decisions that households, firms, and financial

3. John Maynard Keynes, "The General Theory of Employment," *The Quarterly Journal of Economics*, February 1937, p. 213.
4. Ibid.
5. Ibid.
6. Ibid., p. 215.

institutions make concerning their portfolio decisions, that is, decisions on the kind of assets they wish to hold. Second, they enter the formation of views held by business firms and lending institutions about the prospective yield for new capital assets. Liquidity and investment decisions—decisions which are key factors in explaining the ups and downs of the market economy—rest upon expectations that are intimately bound up with an uncertain and unknowable future. The inescapable and practical conclusion to be drawn from this fact is that instability is *endemic* to the economic system; it is not something imposed upon it by random events external to how the system functions.

In contrast to the Post Keynesian view with respect to the pervasive influence of uncertainty and the manner in which expectations are formed, the new classical economics, in effect, deals with uncertainty as if it were the same as predictable risk. As one critic, Paul Davidson, has said, these economists "assume that the uncertainty of the future can be adequately represented by probability statements about an economic world which, without being absolutely determinate, is at least statistically predictable."[7] What this means, according to Professor Davidson, is that the new classical economists are simply replacing the certainty about the future which was built into traditional classical economics with the concept of "a known probability distribution." Instead of perfect foreknowledge, "economic agents" now possess actuarial knowledge, which means that they can calculate actuarial costs and benefits and thus act in the same manner as if they had perfect foreknowledge. Human behavior, therefore, fits into the general equilibrium mold, since it is not only rational in the sense in which this term was explained in Chapter 12, but all expectations are eventually realized, also an essential outcome in the Walrasian general equilibrium model.

Finally, there is an even more fundamental point that flows out of Keynes's ideas about uncertainty. Professor G. L. S. Shackle says that in *The General Theory* Keynes challenged the central tenet of traditional economics, which is that men pursue their interests by applying reason to their circumstances. This, of course, is the meaning of rational behavior in the classical sense. But, according to Professor Shackle, reason cannot achieve practical results unless information is complete. Only if this is the case can it be assumed that maximizing behavior is an accurate representation of the way human beings actually behave. This, perhaps, is one of the most disturbing of all the implications that flow from the Keynesian view of uncertainty, striking as it does at the central organizing principle for nearly the entire corpus of contemporary economic theory. We are not, says Professor Shackle, the "assured masters of known circumstance via reason, but the prisoners of time."[8] It would not be

7. Paul Davidson, "Post Keynesian Economics: Solving the Crisis in Economic Theory," in *The Crisis in Economic Theory*, Special Issue, *The Public Interest*, 1980, p. 160.
8. G. L. S. Shackle, "Keynes and Today's Establishment in Economic Theory: A View," *Journal of Economic Literature*, June 1973, pp. 516–19.

correct to argue that at this stage the Post Keynesians have arrived at a more suitable approach to human behavior than is found in the classical thinking. This is not the case. They do take a different approach, however. They do not start with the *a priori* assumption as in classical economics that human behavior in the economic sphere is of necessity rational—that is, it involves maximizing. In the face of uncertainty of the kind described by Keynes, the Post Keynesians argue that human behavior is largely shaped or determined by the social, cultural, and economic institutions through which people act. Thus, to understand human behavior we must begin by understanding the dominant institutions of a society.

Institutions and the Economy

Post Keynesian economists stress institutions—especially economic and political institutions—for two major reasons. First, this follows logically from their rejection of neoclassical general equilibrium theory. In the latter theory, as Professor Davidson has pointed out, there are no institutions of any significance, save the institution of the market itself. Given markets, price flexibility, and atomistic competition—all essential ingredients in the Walrasian view of the economic universe—other institutions have no theoretical significance. They do not affect the outcome of events, which, as we have seen, is a general equilibrium situation in which all resources are fully utilized. But if this is not a true view of the world, then institutions count. Here we have the second reason for the stress that the Post Keynesians place upon institutions. In their view, human behavior is shaped by and filtered through institutions, the effect frequently being to give such behavior a collective rather than an individualistic character. This contrasts sharply with the neoclassical view in which human behavior is always individualistic and free of institutional influences. Consequently, if we want to understand what happens in the economy, we must understand the institutions that shape and influence human behavior.

What are the institutions that are of major concern to the Post Keynesian economists? They are found in two major areas of economic life. First, there are those that revolve around money and finance, including the institution of money itself. They are crucial to the functioning of capitalistic, market economies. Second, there are institutions that reflect the importance that organized groups play in the life of the economy. The modern large corporation and the trade union belong in this category.

The Institution of Money   Of all the institutions that color the Post Keynesian view of the economy, none is more central than money. Why is money so important to the Post Keynesians? Why is it seen as *the* central institution in economy? These are the questions of key importance for understanding the Post Keynesian preoccupation with money. One of Keynes's major criticisms of classical economics was that it was a theory which applied only to a *real exchange economy*, Keynes's description of an economy in which money, while an instrument of great convenience, is "transitory and neutral in its effect."[9] Money is merely a link between transactions, and is not supposed to either affect the essential nature of transactions, which always involve real things (hence the term "real exchange economy"), or modify the motives and decisions of the parties involved in any transactions. But Keynes saw the matter in a fundamentally different way. Money, in his view, is *not* neutral; its role is not limited to merely facilitating the exchange of real things. Keynes anticipated that *The General Theory* would not only offer an explanation for the determination of output and employment, but that it would also constitute a "monetary theory of production." This is a key point, because the standard, post–World War II interpretation of Keynes (the "neoclassical synthesis") has been criticized for holding that "money doesn't matter."[10] Such a viewpoint, according to the Post Keynesian perspective, runs counter to the real spirit of *The General Theory*.

By a "monetary theory of production," Keynes meant an economy in which money "plays a part of its own and affects motives and decisions and is, in short, one of the operative factors in the situation, so that the course of events cannot be predicted, either in the long period or in the short, without a knowledge of the behavior of money between the first state and the last. And it is this which we ought to mean when we speak of a *Monetary Economy*."[11] In short, money is *not* neutral, it is not a mere convenience, something that facilitates an underlying, *real* process of exchange. Rather, it dominates the economic process. "Making money" is seen as the end objective of economic activity, and production is a means to this end, rather than the other way around as in the classical analysis.

Several significant corollary ideas flow from the foregoing perspective. In a pecuniary society money becomes the ultimate consumer good, the thing that is valued above all else. This is so because it opens the door to power, to wealth, to attention, to status and prestige, to all the things that humans value along with and often to a greater extent than consumption. Production is, of course, crucial, but it is seen in a different perspective than it is seen in classical economics. In a monetary economy in the above sense, money flows to people who control those things that command a price, that have value in the marketplace. Marketplace value can originate in productive activity—in classical analysis this appears to

9. John Maynard Keynes, "On the Theory of a Monetary Economy," *Nebraska Journal of Economics and Business*, Autumn 1963, p. 7.
10. The argument was that "money did not matter" in a policy sense because of the interest inelasticity of the investment demand schedule and, perhaps, the interest elasticity of the demand for money.
11. John Maynard Keynes, "On the Theory of a Monetary Economy," op. cit.

be the only source of value—but it can also result from the activities of persons skilled in the arts of manipulation (what Keynes described as a "speculative" in contrast to an "enterprise" type of activity), or through the acquisition of sufficient power to control the terms upon which an exchange takes place.

Money is crucially important, too, because it provides the necessary link between the present and the future, a future which, as we have seen, is shrouded in uncertainty and hence unknowable. What the possession of money does, according to Keynes, is "lull our disquietude" about the future. The desire to hold money as a form of wealth is a barometer of "the degree of our distrust of our own calculations and conventions concerning the future."[12] This involves the role that money plays as a source of liquidity. In the standard IS-LM model of the economy (Chapter 10), the distinction is made between the "real" sphere—the *IS* curve—and the "monetary" sphere—the *LM* curve. In the Post Keynesian view, the IS-LM model, while useful, fails to capture the essential properties of money that make the economic system inherently unstable. What may happen, according to Keynes, is that, periodically, fear and uncertainty about the future create such a strong demand for the safety found in money—a demand for "liquidity"—that collapse in the real sector of the economy is brought about. The problem lies in the institutional peculiarities of money. It is not like other commodities. It does not obey the "normal laws" of the market, increasing in supply when the demand for it goes up—as when there is a scramble for liquidity—or by having other things substitute for it when its price (the rate of interest) goes up. The demand for money, because of its peculiar ability to calm our fears with respect to an uncertain future, is a systemic flaw in the system. "Unemployment develops," according to Keynes, "because people want the moon;—men cannot be employed when the object of desire (i.e., money) is something which cannot be produced and the demand for which cannot be readily choked off."[13]

One more aspect of a monetary economy needs to be stressed. In all modern economies, as Professor Davidson points out, production is organized on a "forward money-contracting basis." This means that when production takes place future dates are specified for both delivery and payment. Production, of course, takes time, and during this time labor must be paid and materials used in production must be purchased. Both these activities require money or "finance." This is not the case in the world of Walrasian general equilibrium, for there it is assumed that all goods are traded simultaneously and that all payments are made at the instant trade takes place. In the actual economic world producers incur obligations to make payments to labor and to suppliers while production is taking place. Unless they were able to do this, efficient production

12. John Maynard Keynes, "The General Theory of Employment," op. cit., p. 216.
13. John Maynard Keynes, *The General Theory of Employment, Interest, and Money* (New York: Harcourt Brace & World, First Harbinger ed., 1964), p. 235.

planning would not be possible in the world of real, historic time. The expectation is that the sale of output will supply the necessary proceeds to cover all the costs incurred in production. Meanwhile it is crucial that entrepreneurs have the necessary "liquidity"—that is, money on hand—or access to necessary finance through borrowing to sustain the production process until such time as the product is finished and sold. Then—but not until then—obligations incurred in order for production to take place can be liquidated. For any of this to happen, including production itself, there must be an array of money and finance-creating institutions.

Trade Unions, Large Corporations, and Other Institutions Professor Davidson's emphasis on the practice of "forward contracting" in today's market economy leads us logically to consider the second major area in which institutions play a critical role—the domain of organized groups. Of all the types of "forward contracting" taking place in the economy, none is more widespread than the money wage contract. Money wages are crucial because the relationship between them and the productivity of labor largely determines prices for newly produced goods and services. Unlike the classical economists, the Post Keynesians believe that the level of money wages is strongly influenced—if not largely determined—by trade unions, particularly in the central core of the economy where production is concentrated in large corporate enterprise. Put differently, it is the institution of the trade union more than the institution of the market that is chiefly responsible for the level of money wages in the modern, technologically advanced economy. Wages then become an exogenous rather than an endogenous variable. And what about prices? Here again the Post Keynesians view the economy from a different perspective. In the economy's central core where large, oligopolistic firms are dominant, prices are administered, the basic technique being a "markup" over labor costs per unit produced. Thus, trade unions and the large corporation are institutions crucial to the determination of both individual prices for much of the nation's output, and for prices in general.

Other corollaries follow from the foregoing. The distribution of income and power is a central concern of most Post Keynesians. This stems in part directly from *The General Theory*, since Keynes held that the inequitable distribution of income and wealth along with the failure to provide for full employment were the outstanding faults of the economy. It also stems from the fact that the Post Keynesians recognize that a dominant characteristic of the society in which we actually live—not the hypothetical world of Walrasian general equilibrium—is the ongoing struggle of people to gain greater control over their own lives. In the economic context this means control over their incomes, which involves, as Professor Galbraith has phrased it, an escape from "the impersonal tyranny of the market." How is this to be done? Unless one possesses unique personal characteristics that offer a degree of monopoly power—artists and athletes come to mind—the alternative is either organization or recourse to the power of the state, the end in either instance being to bend market forces in one's favor. In the modern economy the trade union and the large corporations reflect the thrust toward organization as a way to modify the forces that determine incomes.

More than personal control over one's income is at stake. Both inflation and economic growth are linked in the minds of the Post Keynesians to administered wage and price behavior. This follows because the struggle to exercise control over the money wage engenders a competitive struggle among organized groups, each seeking to obtain both control and a larger share of the national output for members of the group. This leads to what one observer terms"competitive inflation," a situation in which groups (organized or not) compete with one another to raise the prices of the goods and services they sell (including labor services), the objective being to raise their real incomes.[14] Even Keynes in *The General Theory* recognized that the struggle about money wages primarily affected the *distribution* of the aggregate real wages among different labor groups, not the average wage per worker. The Post Keynesians have expanded on this idea, making the drive to get control of one's income a major factor in the economy's endemic inflation. Economic growth is affected because of its linkage to investment, which, in turn, is linked to the pricing behavior of the large corporation. If internal funds are required for investment expenditure, as is the practice in reality, then by raising prices through a higher markup the corporation can increase the flow of internal savings for investment purposes.

Minsky's Financial Instability Hypothesis

Professor Hyman Minsky of Washington University has come closest to formulating a fully developed theoretical model characteristic of Post Keynesian work.[15] This is his "financial instability" explanation for the systematic instability of contemporary market capitalism. We shall conclude this chapter on the Post Keynesians with an analysis of the salient features of the Minsky model. (A review of the section on "The Financing of Investment," pp. 195–201 in Chapter 6, may be useful prior to reading this section on Minsky's theory.)

Professor Minsky's point of departure is the basic argument of Keynes in *The General Theory* that the economy is characterized by both persistent unemployment and persistent instability. The latter is systemic, not the result of random, external shocks. It is this perspective of *The General Theory* that was lost when the "neoclassical synthesis" emerged as a major school of macroeconomics in the post–World War II era. As we have seen, the neoclassical synthesis forced the Keynesian revolution back into a classical mold by demonstrating that, in the absence of rigidities in

14. W. David Slawson, *The New Inflation: The Collapse of Free Markets* (Princeton, N.J.: Princeton University Press, 1981), p. 13.
15. See esp. Hyman P. Minsky, *John Maynard Keynes* (New York: Columbia University Press, 1975), and *Can "It" Happen Again?* (Armonk, N.Y.: M. E. Sharpe, 1982).

either wages and prices (or both), the system is ultimately self-correcting, and, given sufficient time, it will reach a full-employment equilibrium. The existence of wage and price rigidities may justify the use of fiscal and monetary policy to attain full employment for the pragmatic reason that it may take longer than is politically feasible for the self-correcting features of the system to bring about a full-employment equilibrium. Thus, the neoclassical synthesis denies that the Keynesian revolution was a revolution in theory. Keynes, it has been said, may have won the policy war, but he did not win the theoretical war.

The foregoing viewpoint is rejected by Minsky, both because experience since the mid-1960s flatly contradicts the neoclassical interpretation of the economy's macroeconomic behavior and because it ignores vital elements in *The General Theory* which are necessary for understanding how the economy really works. Not only have we had four recessions since the 1960s (1969–70, 1974–75, 1980, and 1981–82), as well as excessive inflation, but we have had a series of financial crises (like the Franklin National Bank collapse in 1975), each one of which threatened to degenerate into a full-blown debt-deflation process with catastrophic results for the economy.[16] Only the timely intervention by the Federal Reserve System as "lender of last resort" prevented this from happening. Professor Minsky's model is designed to explain why the economy behaved this way.

What is fundamentally wrong with the neoclassical synthesis is that it ignores the importance that Keynes in *The General Theory* attributed to financial factors in explaining how market capitalism works. In Keynes's theory, fluctuations in investment spending are the primary cause of economic instability, a viewpoint common to most post–World War II interpretations of Keynes. There is, in other words, no serious disagreement with the basically Keynesian view that the investment decision is the key to the level of aggregate demand. What is wrong with the standard interpretations of Keynes, according to Professor Minsky, is that the crucial elements that account for the chronic instability of investment spending are neglected. These are the disequilibrating forces at work in the economy's financial markets. Such forces affect primarily the valuation—that is, the present value or demand price—of capital assets relative to the cost (or supply price) for newly produced capital. As in *The General Theory*, it is the ratio of these two variables which is the key to the level of investment activity. In *The General Theory* Keynes saw money and the demand for liquidity as the primary sources of financial instability, the major elements around which financial forces operate. Today the economy is far more complex because the financial system embraces many

16. See Irving Fisher, "The Debt-Deflation Theory of Great Depressions," *Econometrica*, 1933:1, pp. 337–57. The debt-deflation process is brought on by the economy getting into a state of over-indebtedness in the sense that payment commitments for debt exceed the ability of firms and individuals to meet their obligations. This leads to debt liquidation through distress selling, the contraction of the money supply as bank loans are paid off or defaulted, falling prices and falling profits, bankruptcies, and ultimately reductions in output and employment. The whole process tends to be cumulative once it gets started.

more types of financial instruments than originally envisioned by Keynes. It is the complexity and sophistication of the financial system that must be taken into account if we are to gain a true understanding of how investment decisions are actually made in the real world of market capitalism.

The basic problem with standard economic theory—especially the neoclassical synthesis—is that it starts from what Minsky terms a "village fair" perspective.[17] This means that economic analysis originates with the idea of barter, as implied by Say's law, and then proceeds to elaborate on the basic process of exchange by adding production, capital goods, and money and financial assets to the process. In this way it can be shown how a decentralized market mechanism may lead to "coherent"—that is, nonchaotic—results. Basically this is what Keynes had in mind when he said that the difficulty with the classical theory was that it applied only to a "real exchange economy," one in which money and financial institutions did not make any real difference to the underlying, "real" economic process of production and exchange. What is wrong with the "village fair" paradigm is that it cannot explain why there are periodic disruptions to the process—why, in other words, we have the business cycle.

It is Professor Minsky's contention that the proper starting point for understanding the economy's behavior is what he describes as a "Wall Street" perspective. From this perspective the economic world is not one dominated by the exchange of goods for goods, as in the "village fair" paradigm, but a world dominated by commitments to obtain cash today and pay cash in the future. It is a world in which the distinction between "making goods" and "making money" has great relevance. What is of crucial importance in this paper world are cash flows. Cash flows are a legacy of past contracts in which money is obtained (by issuing debt) in exchange for a commitment to make money payments in the future by repayment of debt. In this view, investment decisions are bound up with deals that involve commitments to pay cash in the future in exchange for getting cash today. In the world of "Wall Street" the investment process flows from money to real investment to money, not from investment to money to consumption, as in the classical view. To put the matter differently, the cash flows that are the bedrock of the "Wall Street" perspective have two primary dimensions. First, cash obtained today is exchanged for the expectation of getting cash in the future. This is what happens when investment takes place. Second, the cash obtained today is also exchanged for a *promise* to pay cash in the future. This is what happens when borrowing takes place in order to finance investment.

If "cash flows" are at the center of a "Wall Street" perspective on the economy, how does the "real" economy of production and exchange fit into the picture? The viability of the paper world of Wall Street rests upon the cash flows that business firms, households, and governments

17. Hyman P. Minsky, "The Financial Instability Hypothesis: An Interpretation of Keynes and an Alternative to 'Standard' Theory," *Nebraska Journal of Economics and Business,* Winter 1977, p. 7.

receive through the income-generating process. Income in the form of profits, wages and salaries, and taxes generates the cash flows that sustain the commitments to repay debt contracted in the past. The real economy of production and employment must sustain the paper economy that is dominant in a "Wall Street" view of the world. The basic problem of market capitalism is that periodically the real world of production and employment goes sour because of what happens in the paper world of money and finance. Unlike the classical world, in which money is a mere convenience that has no effect upon the "real exchange economy," in the paper world of Wall Street developments that center around debt, finance, and cash flows are the "tail" which frequently wags the "dog" of output and employment.

Essential Elements in the Working of Market Capitalism

Now that we have examined the "Wall Street" perspective that Professor Minsky argues is the proper way to approach an understanding of how a system of market capitalism with sophisticated financial institutions works, we are in a position to examine key elements that explain how the economy behaves over time and why it is subject to periodic breakdowns. The key to this process is a knowledge of how the liability structures of firms, banks, and other financial institutions evolve *over time* and the manner in which these affect investment spending, the key to fluctuations in the private economy.

In a capitalist economy every economic unit has a portfolio, that is, a set of tangible and financial assets owned and the financial liabilities which it owes. Every unit also must make portfolio decisions, decisions that have two facets. First, there is a decision as to the kind of assets to be held or acquired and, second, there is the decision as to how ownership or control of these assets is to be financed. In the world of money and finance the latter decision is described as how one's "position" in assets is to be financed. The assets and liabilities in the portfolio of an economic unit may also be viewed as annuities in that they set up a series of cash receipts and cash payments which are expected and which must be met over some fixed or variable future time period. In the modern capitalist economy there is an enormous variety of both assets and liabilities that yield future income or incur future payments obligations.

In its essentials, a capitalist economy works through the process of acquiring tangible assets—that is, real investment—which are expected over time to yield a cash flow. This cash flow results from the sale of the final goods and services that are to be produced in the future with the aid of the capital. This cash flow, as we saw in the analysis of the investment decision in Chapter 6, must be large enough to cover the actual supply price of the new item of capital plus the costs involved in financing it. This brings us to a second point. Assets are acquired by the creation of financial liabilities. The latter may take a variety of forms, including shares and the many different forms of debt. Unless an economic unit (business firms and households) finances its investment outlays wholly from internal sources—retained earnings, in other words—what "buys" real capital for the unit in a system of market capitalism is a stream of commitments the unit makes for making future payments. It is expected that ordinarily these payments will be met from the income-producing operations of the economic unit, that is, wages and salaries in the case of households and gross sales or profits in the case of the business firm. Money—and other highly liquid assets which are near monies—plays a peculiar role in this situation. As Professor Minsky points out, the possession of money (or liquidity in general) acts as a kind of "insurance" against the economy's malperformance, that is, a possible economic downturn which would make it difficult for economic units to continue to meet their payment obligations from the cash flows generated by income-producing operations. Then the possession of money can keep the economic unit afloat, at least temporarily. Money, in other words, is a cushion against adversity.

The portfolio decisions which lie at the heart of the capitalistic economic process are significantly affected by two sets of institutions that are of strategic importance. There are, first, the pricing institutions, especially those which affect investment. Second, there are the financial institutions through which borrowing and lending take place and which control the terms upon which positions in assets are financed.

In the realm of pricing, a capitalistic economy is characterized by two sets of *relative* prices: one relating to the production and distribution of current output and the other to capital assets. Classical economics focused its attention almost exclusively on the former set of prices, but it is the latter set which is crucial to the investment decision and an understanding of the basic instability of the system. Both sets of prices have a role to play in the investment decision, however. The demand price for newly produced capital goods is, as we saw in Chapter 6, the discounted present value of the expected income stream for newly acquired capital assets. This depends upon long-term expectations, which, as we have seen, are rooted in uncertainty. Prices for current output enter into the investment decision because they relate to the supply price for newly produced capital assets. Prices for goods and services currently being produced, including capital assets, are based upon demand conditions in the short term. The interplay between these two sets of prices with vastly different time horizons is a major determinant in the investment decision. The other is financing conditions, to which we now turn.

Financial institutions, such as banks, are organizations which take a position in (that is, acquire) financial assets by emitting their own liabilities. Thus, when a bank creates a new demand deposit by making a loan, it, in effect, acquires a financial asset, namely, a note from the borrower to pay off the loan, in exchange for creating a liability in the form of a demand deposit. The liabilities of financial institutions usually involve a commitment to pay cash on demand, as is the case with the demand deposit. Financial institutions differ from ordinary business firms in that the latter take positions in real capital assets, for which they issue liabilities—that is, debt—whereas the financial institutions take positions in financial rather than real assets.

Because positions are financed, both for the business firm and for financial institutions, by issuing liabilities within the banking system, the process involves not only the creation of demand deposit money, but the almost continuous innovation with respect to new types of instruments that increase the amount of financing available. A second point is that, whenever liabilities are issued to finance positions in assets, both financial and real—future cash—payment commitments are created. Every business firm and every financial institution engage in speculation when they make such commitments. As Professor Minsky says, "The firm in accepting a liability structure in order to hold assets is betting that the ruling situation at future dates will be such that the cash payment commitments can be met; it is estimating that the odds in an uncertain future are favorable."[18] Decisions made in this manner rest upon some "margin of safety," some estimate of just how much of the firm's future income can be safely committed to meeting the cash payment commitments which grow out of the liability side of the firm's balance sheet. This "margin of safety" lies in the excess of the firm's receipts and holdings of liquid assets over its payments commitments. Whenever the margin of safety erodes, the firm is in financial trouble. Such erosion may come about from a collapse of its current receipts because of a downturn in economic activity, or as a result of going too deeply in debt—creating new liabilities—in order to finance additional assets.

The Sequence of Events

To pull all the foregoing elements together and show how a financial crisis develops, we should begin at a point in the business cycle when the economy is doing reasonably well. What we want to show is how a boom develops and how the boom carries within itself the seeds for its own destruction. From a Keynesian perspective, an expansion will get under way whenever conditions are favorable to a high level of investment spending. This requires that the demand price for capital goods (D_k) exceed the supply price (S_k), or that the marginal efficiency of capital (r) exceed the rate of interest (i). If an expansion is under way it may also be assumed that the liability structures which a firm has inherited from the past are not yet a problem, which is to say that the margins of safety are for the time being adequate. Given this setting, what will take place as good times continue and an expansion turns into a boom? According to Professor Minsky's financial instability hypothesis, events can be expected to unfold in roughly the following sequence.

1. *Investment and Profits:* A high and growing volume of investment spending is the key to the gross profits of business firms. Figure 13–2 shows the close correlation between investment spending and gross prof-

18. Hyman Minsky, *John Maynard Keynes,* op. cit., p. 87.

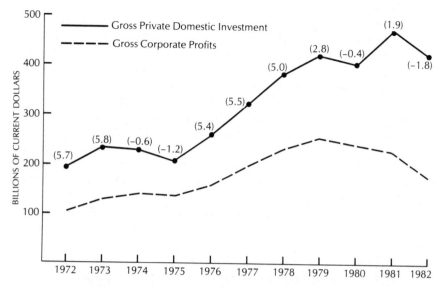

FIGURE 13–2. Gross Private Domestic Investment and Gross Corporate Profits: 1972–82

Note: Figures in parentheses are the percentage change in *real* GNP

its. It also shows through the figures in parentheses the close relationship between fluctuations in gross investment spending and the rate of growth of real GNP. Gross profits play two roles in the boom. First, they provide the cash flows to meet current commitments for the repayment of debt and, second, through the dividends paid to stockholders they help determine in the stock market the valuation of the firms and their assets. Shareholders in boom conditions enjoy capital gains on their holdings, a development which affects favorably the prospects for further investment. High profits, in other words, reverberate back through the stock market and boost the demand price for more new capital.

2. *Unfolding of a Boom:* As the boom continues it becomes apparent to the managers of firms and financial institutions that existing debts and their payments commitments are being easily managed. This means that borrowing to acquire new assets turns out to have been worthwhile. Business and financial units that were heavily in debt prospered, a sign to managers that their existing margins of safety are, perhaps, too conservative. This leads to further leveraging, or an increase in the ratio of total debt to total assets. This, of course, increases the commitment to make payments in the future. The capital gains being experienced by shareholders as prosperity continues reinforce this process, sometimes at a feverish pitch. In his discussion of how a boom unfolds and its effect upon the asset and liability structure of firms, Professor Minsky distinguishes between "hedge" and "speculative" finance. "Hedge" finance takes place when the cash flows from current operations are large enough to meet the payments obligations on the existing debt structure. It is the safest position for the firm. "Speculative" finance, on the other hand,

takes place when the cash flows from current operations are not large enough to meet current payments commitments, even though overall the present value of expected receipts is greater than the present value of the firm's payment commitments. In the long run, in other words, the asset-liability position of the firm is sound, but in the short run the firm may have difficulties. Firms that engage in speculative finance find it necessary continually to refinance debt—that is, borrow anew—to obtain the funds necessary to meet current payment obligations. Speculative finance does not cause trouble as long as the economy is expanding, but any units which engage in speculative finance are increasingly vulnerable as the boom lengthens. They are vulnerable because they may find that they must pay higher interest rates for their refinancing operations (something which raises the magnitude of their payment obligations) and because any shortfall in cash receipts relative to payment commitments can cause rapid changes in what the financial community regards as acceptable margins of safety. The latter are highly subjective.

3. *The End of a Boom:* Why does the boom end? This is the crucial question. The essence of Professor Minsky's thesis is that, as a boom continues, firms and financial institutions increasingly create for themselves financial structures that are vulnerable to any rise in interest rates, or any slowdown in the pace of economic activity. Excessive leveraging continuously leads to an increase in the commitments to make future payments, an increase not necessarily matched by the ability of firms in the economy to meet these commitments from their current operations. The process is wholly endogenous and results from the normal functioning of financial markets. A financial crisis may explode quite suddenly as interest rates rise, sources for new loans dry up, or expectations about the continued profitability of additional investment collapse. Margins of safety with respect to the liability structure of firms which seemed perfectly secure during the boom are quickly and dramatically reduced. Runs on banks and other financial institutions take place as firms and financial institutions scramble for additional liquidity so that they can secure cash to meet their commitments. Borrowing to finance new investment will cease and firms will use whatever internal funds they are able to obtain for meeting existing payment commitments. In this way the investment boom comes to an end, bringing with it a downturn in the level of economic activity and rising unemployment.

4. *Avoidance of Depression:* The final question that Professor Minsky addresses is: Why, in the post–World War II era, does the endogenous financial crisis generated by boom conditions *not* degenerate into a full-blown debt-inflation crisis and depression on the scale of the 1929 debacle? He argues that the most significant economic event since World War II is something that has not happened—namely, a deep and long-lasting depression. There are two basic reasons why it has not. First, the Federal Reserve in its role of lender of last resort can feed money into the financial system and prevent a full-blown debt-deflation process from developing. Unfortunately, such intervention at times during the 1970s was

not accompanied by any serious financial reforms, the result being a legacy of liquidity that fueled a new round of inflation once the crisis was past. As Professor Minsky has said, a big depression was avoided in the 1970s by "floating off untenable debt structure through inflation. Stagflation is a substitute for a big depression." The second reason is big government and the many built-in stabilizers that lead to massive government deficits as production and factor incomes fall. This puts a floor under the economy, keeping it from tumbling into a deep and long-lasting depression on the scale of the 1930s. The price, however, has been continued fragility in the nation's financial structure and vulnerability to inflation.

Some Conclusions

Two broad conclusions emerge from Professor Minsky's financial instability hypothesis. The first is that our system of market capitalism is inherently and inescapably flawed because the forces that periodically generate financial and output crises are rooted in the system's structure. This does not mean, according to Minsky, that capitalism should be rejected. But it does underscore the importance of institutions for shaping the economy's behavior. If we want to modify that behavior in a fundamental way, we shall have to change the institutions. It also shows that the economy must be managed, that the neoclassical view of a self-regulating system is an illusion.

The theory also points toward some specific policy changes. In Minsky's view, as was the case with Keynes earlier, investment is the source of the instability. But Minsky goes beyond Keynes and argues that the periodic need to bail out threatened financial structures by Federal Reserve action is one of the major causes of inflation. Both instability and inflation might be lessened if the economy were more oriented toward the production of consumer goods through techniques less capital-intensive than those now in use. Policy, in other words, should be directed toward growth through consumption rather than through investment, as has been the practice since the 1970s. Any such policy switch should be accompanied by policies that would simplify financial structures, although this may be difficult to achieve.

Summary

1. Post Keynesian economics is the term applied to the beliefs of a diverse group of economists who look to Keynes's *The General Theory* for inspiration, but reject efforts to push the ideas of Keynes into a classical mold, as the "neoclassical synthesis" has done. They are concerned with developing a macroeconomic theory appropriate to contemporary market capitalism with its strong tendencies toward concentration of economic power in a relatively small number of giant corporations.

2. The Post Keynesians reject Walrasian general equilibrium theory as a valid explanation of how the market economy works in reality. One specific reason for this is that Walrasian theory is not able to deal with an economy that exists in real, historic time. Emphasis upon economic activity as a *process* that exists in real, historic time is a key characteristic of the Post Keynesians.

3. The Post Keynesian viewpoint also stresses uncertainty and expectations formed on the basis of uncertain knowledge. Uncertain knowledge of a kind that cannot be reduced to calculable probabilities is a fundamental feature in the economic world in which we actually live, not the ideal world of general equilibrium theory. Expectations—particularly expectations that govern the creation of new wealth—are highly volatile because they rest upon expectations which themselves are volatile and uncertain.

4. In the Post Keynesian view, the roots of inflation are found in the behavior patterns shaped by key institutions. Key institutions shaping the economy are those revolving around money and finance, including money itself, and institutions like trade unions and large corporations which have a pervasive influence upon the process by which money wages and prices are determined.

5. There does not exist a single "model" which can be said to be the dominant Post Keynesian model. The most comprehensive effort in this direction is the financial instability hypothesis, developed by Professor Hyman Minsky of Washington University. Minsky's model seeks to explain the *systemic* instability of market capitalism because of the dominant role that financing and financial institutions play in accounting for investment behavior, the major source of fluctuations in output and employment.

6. Minsky's model is dominated by a "Wall Street" perspective, by which he means that the "paper" world of money and finance, in which the basic objective is to make money by lending and borrowing, dominates the *real* world of actual investment in structures and equipment. Because the paper world of money and finance frequently overextends itself— the process is seen as endogenous to a system of market capitalism— booms followed by busts are a frequent occurrence.

7. Since the end of World War II, two factors have kept recessions from turning into major depressions on the scale of the collapse of the 1930s. The first is the role that the Federal Reserve System plays as a "lender of last resort," bailing out when necessary large banks and other firms to prevent the kind of collapse that could trigger a general debt-deflation process through the entire economy. The second is the sheer size of the federal government, whose large deficits in a downturn provide a substantial floor for the economic system.

14

The Economics of
Inflation

No Western nation has yet discovered how to get full or high employment without encountering unacceptable inflation rates. In 1982 the U.S. inflation rate, as measured by the consumer price index (CPI), dipped to 3.9 percent, the lowest rate since 1967. The price for bringing inflation down to this level, however, was the most severe recession since World War II, one that cost millions of workers their jobs and billions of dollars in lost output. Since it is by no means certain that the pattern of the recent past—in which inflation comes down during a recession but accelerates again once recovery comes (see Figure 14–15)—will not continue into the future, it is appropriate that we now examine the forces that determine the general level of prices in the economy.

At the outset it is vital to stress that *no* single theory of the price level is agreed upon by economists. What we have are a number of well-established approaches to the problem of changes in the general level of prices. We shall examine each of these separately, although it is crucial to bear in mind that the inflationary process in the real-world economy is exceedingly complex. At any particular time when prices are rising, a variety of forces may be at work. What we shall attempt in this chapter is to identify such forces and explain how they fit into the inflationary process at different times and under different circumstances.

The History of the Price Level in the United States

Let us begin by looking at what has happened to the price level since World War II, contrasting this period with all previous periods in our

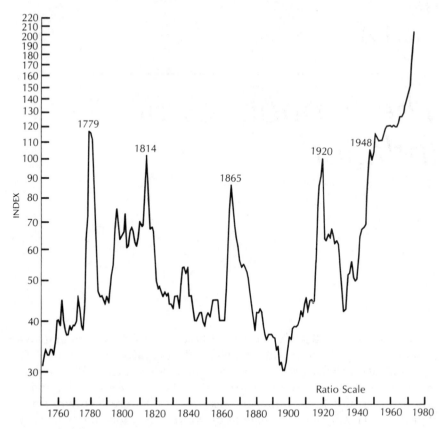

FIGURE 14–1.   The Wholesale Price Index, 1750–1974 (1947–49 = 100)

SOURCE: Economic Society of South Florida

history. Figure 14–1 shows an index for wholesale prices (now called producer prices) for the period 1750–1974. Historically in the United States inflation has been a phenomenon closely associated with war, the rate rising sharply during wartime and falling equally sharply once the war is ended. The reason is not hard to discover, since we have chosen, in effect, to pay for most of our wars by running the printing press or engaging in somewhat more sophisticated forms of debt financing, although the economic effects are about the same. Figure 14–1 also shows that inflation over the long term has not been the norm for the American economy, as there have been periods of falling prices, notably after the War of 1812 and the Civil War.

The period after World War II has been different. Not only did prices fail to collapse after the war, as happened following every previous war in the nation's history, but they have risen continuously since 1945. Figure 14–2 traces the post–World War II inflation, using the GNP implicit price deflator as a measure of the inflation rate. In the 37-year period from 1945 to 1982, prices jumped more than fivefold, or by 446 percent, making this period one of the longest and most severe inflationary eras in our history. If the 1930s are known as the years of the "Great Depression," it is possible that historians someday will call the era after World War II the time of the "Great Inflation."

Although the general trend in prices was upward throughout this period, the rate at which prices advanced was by no means even. To some extent what happened was in line with our historic experience, since there were sharp price increases because of war. When price controls were removed prematurely after World War II, the price level

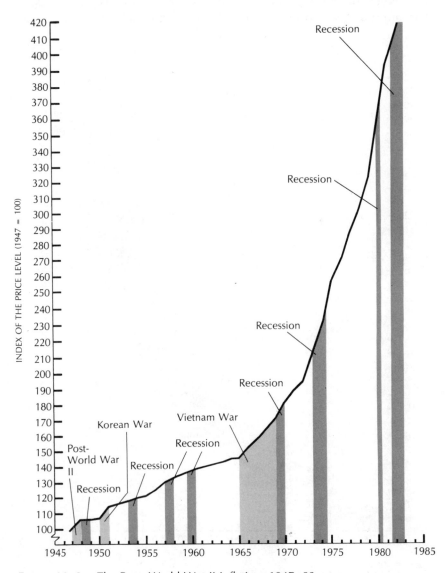

FIGURE 14–2.   The Post–World War II Inflation: 1947–82

jumped 21 percent in two years (1946–48). Again during the Korean war (1950–53) prices shot up by 9.8 percent before controls were imposed, and in the Vietnam war period (1965–69) prices jumped by 16.7 percent. But the really explosive price increases came during peacetime. In the four years from 1973 to 1976, prices climbed by 25 percent. They went up even somewhat more in the four years from 1977 to 1980. Unlike all previous war experience, prices did not fall during *any* of the post–World War II recessions, even though recession brought a slowdown in the inflation rate.

Figures 14–3 and 14–4 offer some additional empirical insights into price behavior in the post–World War II era. Figure 14–3 is a scatter diagram that plots an index for *real* GNP, using 1947 as the base year,

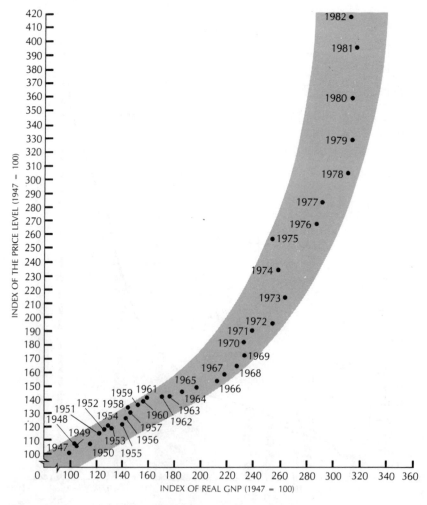

FIGURE 14–3.   Real GNP and the Price Level: 1947–82

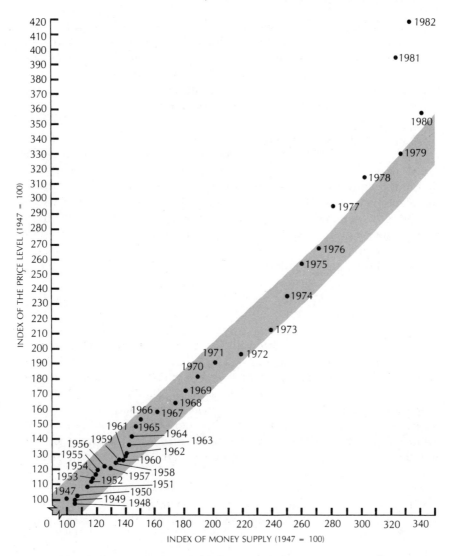

FIGURE 14–4. Money Supply and the Price Level: 1947–82

against an index for the price level, also using 1947 as the base year and using the implicit GNP price deflator as a measure of the price level. This figure tells us two things of importance. First, it shows that over time increases in real GNP are accompanied by significant increases in the price level. Thus, the data in the figure provide some rough empirical verification for the type of theoretical aggregate supply curve developed in Chapter 10, a curve that related real income (Y) to the price level (p). Second, these data suggest that the slope of the aggregate supply curve is increasing, a fact that reflects the economy's increased vulnerability to inflation.

Figure 14–4 shows another scatter diagram, although in this case the price level index is plotted against an index of the money supply, using 1947 again as the base period for both indexes. The money supply variable used in this index is the former M1 measure, namely, currency plus demand deposits. What the scatter diagram shows is the close correlation between increases in the money supply and increases in the price level. What are we to make of this? It is useful to know that such a correlation exists, but we should not read too much into it. If it is presumed that changes in *real* GNP are a consequence of shifts in the Keynesian $C+I+G$ schedule, and that changes in the money supply largely reflect decisions of the monetary authority—that is, the Federal Reserve—then it appears that empirical support exists for either a simplistic Keynesian or a simplistic monetarist explanation of inflation. The former involves an excess of aggregate demand and the latter an excess of money. Actually, inflation is a much more complex phenomenon, and, at minimum, any general theory of the price level must show how the money supply can be related to both aggregate demand and the price level.

The Meaning of Inflation

We have used the terms *inflation* and a *rise in the price level* in a manner that suggests they are synonymous. This is not quite correct. While inflation normally involves an upward movement in the general level of prices, all price level increases are not of the same magnitude, nor is their economic consequence and duration always the same. This is readily seen if we examine the data in Table 14–1. The periods shown are, of course, arbitrary, but they permit us to be more specific about what the term inflation means. They correspond to the broad divisions established for discussion of post–World War II policy actions.

As data in the table indicate, there were wide variations in the rate at which prices went up during this period. The index used is the consumer price index (CPI). Many people would say that for all practical

TABLE 14–1. Inflation Rates in the Post–World War II American Economy (Annual Average Percentage Increase)

Period	Inflation Rate (%)
Truman-Eisenhower Years (1948–60)	2.2
The Kennedy Era (1961–65)	1.3
Vietnam and Its Aftermath (1966–70)	4.3
The 1970s (1971–80)	7.9
The Reagan Administration (1981–82)	6.4
35-Year Average (1948–82)	4.4

SOURCE: *Economic Report of the President,* 1983.

purposes we had price stability in the Kennedy era. The rate of increase was a modest 1.3 percent, and given the fact that there was undoubtedly some improvement in the quality of the goods and services produced in these years, inflation in a real sense was probably close to zero. The more recent data also show that the rate at which prices are going up has accelerated. In the 1970s the rate was more than three times what it was in the first half of the postwar period. For the period as a whole, prices went up at an annual average rate of 4.4 percent. During these three and a half decades, there were 14 years in which prices rose at a rate higher than the average for the whole period, and 21 years in which the rate was below the average.

What is the moral of this? Essentially—and in the absence of any techniques whereby price changes can be corrected for quality changes—it is that we cannot define inflation in terms of any *specific* rate of change in the price level. We simply have to fall back on the common-sense idea that inflation is a persistent or sustained rise in the general level of prices. This is a less satisfactory situation than exists with respect to full employment, for at least there is agreement among economists that full employment lies somewhere between a 4 and 5.5 percent unemployment rate. By the standard just enunciated we thus had inflation even during the Kennedy era, although it was much more moderate—and hence easier to live with—than what we have experienced in recent years. The "official" definition of an appropriate inflation rate is given by the "Full Employment and Balanced Growth Act of 1978," which stipulated as a national goal the reduction of the inflation rate to no more than 3 percent annually within five years after enactment of the act. Unfortunately, this remains a pious statement of intent rather than a program for action, since the act contained no effective machinery for its enforcement.

Types of Inflation

Keynes defined true inflation as a condition in which any additional increase in aggregate demand produces no further increase in output.[1] When the economy reaches this point any increase in aggregate demand expends itself wholly in price increases. Inflation such as this is the kind envisioned by the classical quantity theorists, although it should be noted that this definition does not preclude some price increases prior to the point at which the economy has reached the absolute upper limit of its output potential. In speaking of true inflation Keynes meant to emphasize only that there is some point in the short run when the elasticity of output with respect to changes in aggregate demand falls to zero, and it is at this point that it is proper to talk of a true inflationary condition.

Several decades ago it was fashionable to speak of "creeping" or "gradual" inflation, such as the nation experienced during the Truman-Eisen-

---

1. John Maynard Keynes, *The General Theory of Employment, Interest and Money* (New York: Harcourt, Brace, & World, First Harbinger ed., 1946), p. 303.

hower years or the Kennedy era. This was a type of inflation in which there was a slow but persistent upward movement of the general price level, even though the economy was not necessarily operating at full employment. Actually some economists looked with considerable favor on such a situation because it was believed that a mild inflation was not only a good stimulus to output and employment gains, but probably necessary in a society characterized by downward rigidities in prices, wages, and costs in general.

No handy tag has been found to characterize or describe the kind of inflation experienced in the 1970s, an inflation too rapid to be described as "creeping" and yet not so out of control as to warrant the adjective "hyper" (see below). It is perhaps premature to speak of a permanent inflation, although it has been suggested that an underlying, 5 to 6 percent "basic" inflation rate has become built into the economy. This results from a combination of money incomes outrunning productivity and expectations that inflation will continue. In any event, the post–World War II inflation is different. Prior to the last three and a half decades— and from the sixteenth century onward—inflations were temporary and generally limited in the number of countries affected. Now inflation is persistent and worldwide.[2]

Inflation is sometimes described as suppressed. There is no inflation in the technical sense of the word here, because prices do not rise. Suppressed inflation is a situation in which, by one means or another, the general price level is held down, but at the cost of a buildup of forces that may make for an explosive surge upward in prices at some later date. Suppressed inflation is most common during wartime when controls and rationing limit spending and prevent price increases but do not prevent the public from accumulating large amounts of liquid assets that can be readily turned into purchasing power at some future date. This clearly happened after World War II when consumer prices jumped by 24 percent in 1946 and 1947. It is not so clear that this happened during the wage-price control experiment carried out by the Nixon administration from August 1971 through April 1974. The reason is that prices began going up long before price controls were removed, even during the more stringent phases of the program (see the last section in this chapter for full details).

Finally, there is hyperinflation, which is best described as a situation in which the value of the monetary unit is totally destroyed. Under conditions of hyperinflation, prices rise to astronomical heights, and the velocity of circulation of money becomes almost infinitely great. Money ceases to serve as a store of value and is used only as a medium of exchange. Money that has become almost worthless is still more efficient than barter. If the hyperinflation goes far enough, there may be a com-

2. Irving S. Friedman, *Inflation: A World-Wide Disaster* (Garden City, N.Y.: Anchor Press/Doubleday, 1975), p. 5.

plete collapse of the monetary system and people will have to resort to barter. Hyperinflation is almost always associated with defeat in war, the revolutionary destruction of an existing government, or some other equally catastrophic event that brings normal productive processes to a halt, forcing a government to resort to uncontrolled use of the printing press to finance its needs.

What Is Wrong with Inflation?

It is not necessary to belabor the point that hyperinflation—an inflation that totally destroys the currency of a nation—is a major social disaster. We only need to recall the great German inflation of the early 1920s, an inflation which many economists believe helped destroy the Weimar Republic and pave the way for Hitler and the ascent of Naziism.[3] However, this is not the kind of inflation we face. Even so, we need to understand why, next to persistent unemployment, persistent inflation is a social evil of major proportions. Keynes has said that "there is no subtler, no surer means of overturning the existing basis of Society than to debauch the currency. The process engages all the hidden forces of economic law on the side of destruction, and does so in a manner which not one man in a million is able to diagnose."[4] Let us examine some of the things Keynes may have had in mind.

We must always be careful about making generalizations on the basis of a limited number of observations. Nevertheless, the experience of the 1970s strongly suggests that persistent inflation looms as a major barrier to high employment and prosperity. An unchecked inflation sooner or later chokes off a business boom because too many people find that their money incomes are not keeping pace with soaring prices. Thus, *real* incomes fall, buying is curtailed, and an economic collapse is triggered. Among expert observers—economists, business forecasters, and corporate executives—there was near unanimous belief that inflation was one of the prime causes of the 1974–75 economic collapse.[5]

What inflation does is to redistribute income and wealth in an arbitrary, capricious, and usually unjust fashion. "Throughout history," it has been said, "inflation, social injustice, and political upheaval have been strongly correlated; this association is neither coincidental nor arbitrary, but has much to do with the impact of inflation on the distribution of income and wealth between the various classes of society."[6] More often than not the redistribution wrought by inflation is from the poor to the

---

3. For a recent discussion of the link between the German hyperinflation of the 1920s and the rise of Hitler see L. E. Hill, C. E. Butler, and S. A. Lorenzen, "Inflation and the Destruction of Democracy: The Weimar Republic," *Journal of Economic Issues*, June 1977, pp. 299–313.
4. John Maynard Keynes, *Essays in Persuasion* (New York: Norton, 1963), p. 78.
5. *The Wall Street Journal*, April 25, 1975.
6. Sylvia Ann Hewlett, "Inflation and Inequality," *Journal of Economic Issues*, June 1977, p. 353.

affluent, from the ordinary citizen to the government, a fact not widely understood.

Among the groups that suffer the most in an inflation are the aged and the poor. The aged suffer because most of them are on fixed incomes, incomes that are derived from savings, private pensions, insurance, or Social Security benefits. Since 1972 the latter have been "indexed," which is to say that benefits are adjusted upward along with changes in the consumer price index. But because the income many retired couples get from Social Security is quite low, indexing does not solve the inflation problem for the aged. The aged—and the poor generally—also suffer because in an inflation all prices do not rise at the same rate. In the 1970s prices for basic necessities—food, shelter, medical care, and transportation—went up faster than most other prices. Since families of low or moderate means spend on the average three-fourths of their budget for such necessities, this aspect of inflation may be especially devastating.

Workers, too, are often among the losers in an inflation, even though some workers through unions may be able to protect themselves somewhat against inflation through "cost of living agreements" (or COLAs), in their wage contracts. The U.S. Department of Labor estimated at the close of 1982 that 58 percent of all workers with collective bargaining agreements are covered by COLAs. Usually they provide for automatic wage increases based upon changes in the consumer price index, although COLAs don't always allow for increases equal to the full change in the price index. (During the 1970s average gross weekly earnings for all nonagricultural workers in current dollars rose by 122 percent. In constant dollars, however, gross weekly earnings in 1982 were 10 percent below their 1970 level.[7]) What such clauses do is allow the better-organized workers to secure gains at the expense of the less organized, one example of how inflation redistributes income perversely.

But inflation may play a cruel joke on all workers, organized or unorganized, by thrusting them into a "Catch 22" situation. In fact, most families may find themselves in this situation. Because their money incomes go up during inflation, they are pushed into a higher tax bracket. But the increase in their money incomes is not sufficient to keep pace with both rising prices and rising taxes. This is known as "bracket creep." During the 1974–75 economic slump, the Joint Economic Committee of the Congress reported that taxes calculated as a percentage of personal income actually rose from 17.8 percent at the peak of the boom in 1973 to 18.3 percent as the recession reached bottom in late 1974.[8] Rising prices plus increased taxes caused the consumer's *real* take-home or spendable income to drop off more sharply than in any economic down-

7. *Economic Report of the President* (Washington, D.C.: U.S. Government Printing Office, 1982), p. 277.
8. "Inflation and the Consumer in 1974," Joint Economic Committee, Congress of the United States (Washington, D.C.: U.S. Government Printing Office, February 10, 1974), p. 12.

turn since the 1930s. It should be noted that this perverse working of the tax system—a feature of its progressive character—tends to offset the stabilizing effects of built-in stabilizers. Milton Friedman calls this aspect of inflation the "inflation tax." Inflation, he says, "is the only form of taxation that can be imposed without anybody having to vote for it."[9] The Reagan administration's Economic Recovery Tax Act, which became law in August 1981, provided for indexing of the personal income tax, effective in 1984. This is designed to eliminate "bracket creep."

It is not just income which is rearranged in a capricious and usually unjust fashion by inflation. The same thing happens to personal wealth, especially monetary wealth in the form of savings deposits, cash holdings, bonds, the value of life insurance policies, pension rights, and other claims on present and future purchasing power. Basically, inflation redistributes wealth from creditors to debtors, provided debts are stated in fixed money terms, as is usually the case. The reason there is redistribution is that inflation enables the debtor to pay off his obligation in money whose real value has declined.

Professor G. L. Bach of Stanford University investigated how much redistribution of wealth resulted from inflation following World War II. From the end of the war until the beginning of the 1970s, Bach found that there was a massive transfer of wealth from households—ordinary citizens, in other words—to governments and to business. The magnitude of this transfer has been staggering—between one-half and two-thirds of a trillion dollars.[10] The reason why the transfer has been *from* households to government and business is because households have been net creditors in this era. Their assets exceeded their liabilities.

But this is not the whole story. Inflation has also been responsible for significant transfers of wealth *between* households. Bach found these to be of two kinds. First, wealth was transferred from both the very poor and the very rich to households in the middle-income range. This happened because the latter are often, on balance, debtors, especially for houses and automobiles. The poor, on the other hand, have few debts and usually do not own assets whose value appreciates in an inflation (land or houses), whereas the rich are usually without debts simply because they are rich. Also their assets are often of a monetary nature (such as bonds), and hence vulnerable to inflation. What few assets the poor have are also in monetary form. Second, there was a large transfer of wealth from the old to the young, the reason being that young families are often heavily in debt. They borrow to set up a household, to buy houses and cars, and to finance education. On balance, a large proportion of the assets of the old are in a fixed value form.

The foregoing represent concrete, measurable ways in which inflation

9. Milton Friedman, *Is Inflation a Curable Disease?* Graduate School of Business, University of Pittsburgh, May 1975, p. 8.
10. G. L. Bach, "Inflation: Who Gains and Who Loses?" *Challenge,* July / August 1974, pp. 48–55.

is damaging. But its ultimate threat is more intangible, more subtle, though nonetheless real. It arises out of the fact that modern society is a future-oriented society. No individual, no family, no business, or no government lives wholly in the present, disregarding the future. More perhaps than many realize, money and assets valued in money are our link which the economy has to the future. This, perhaps, is the most insidious danger of inflation. Between 1939 and 1982—43 years—the U.S. dollar lost 86 percent of its purchasing power. In the 1970s alone the value of the dollar shrank by 49 percent.

Destruction of the value of a nation's currency is serious. Besides being a link to the future, money is part of the glue holding a society together. When confidence in the value of money erodes, a pernicious and corrosive element enters into the nation's economic life. People are robbed of a dependable yardstick for understanding and evaluating what is happening around them. Further, there tends to be within a society a subtle but dangerous tilt away from productive activities toward those which are primarily speculative. Inflation provides an ideal milieu for the fast-buck operator—often more money can be made by dealing in things that already exist than by producing new wealth. It is also true that inflation exacerbates the struggle over the distribution of income. As individuals and families catch on to the adverse effects that inflation has on relative income positions, they become aroused, aggressive, and angry, ready to deploy all the economic power they command to protect or enlarge their share of the income pie. A vicious circle ensues. Inflation worsens income distribution, but the struggle over distributive shares that it unleashes feeds the inflationary spiral.

Theories of Inflation

Since the end of World War II there has been much discussion concerning the cause and cure of the persistent inflationary trend that has characterized the economies of most nations. As a consequence of such discussions, as well as extensive analysis and empirical research, three broad theoretical explanations for the phenomenon of inflation have emerged. These may be described as the *demand-pull* hypothesis, the *cost-push* hypothesis, and the *structural* hypothesis. We shall examine each of these in turn, but the reader is cautioned at the outset that postulating three theories of the inflationary process does not mean that they are mutually exclusive or that any one of them will suffice to explain the inflationary process. The upward trend of the general price level that appears to be an important characteristic of most modern economies is neither wholly understood nor readily controlled.[11]

The Demand-Pull Hypothesis   The demand-pull hypothesis relates to what may be called the traditional theory of inflation. The theory holds that

---

11. The development of incomes policies as a technique for the control of inflation is discussed in the latter part of this chapter.

inflation is caused by an excess of demand (spending) relative to the available supply of goods and services at existing prices. In both the traditional and modern quantity theories the factor of key significance is the money supply; only an increase in the money supply is capable of driving the general price level upward. In income-expenditure theory, demand-pull is interpreted to mean an excess of aggregate money demand relative to the economy's full-employment output level. This is similar to the Keynesian definition of true inflation, although the demand-pull hypothesis should not be interpreted to mean that no upward movement in the general level of prices is possible prior to the point of full employment. The basic idea is that whatever upward pressure may exist on the price level emanates from demand. The theory further presumes that prices for goods and services as well as for economic resources are responsive to supply and demand forces, and will thus move readily upward under the pressure of a high level of aggregate demand.

The presumed cure for inflation in the demand-pull category is quite obvious; if there is an excess of spending, it must be cured by the vigorous pursuit of monetary and fiscal policies that will reduce total spending and thus lessen the upward pressure on the price level. The demand-pull thesis presumes, too, that prices and other costs are flexible downward as well as upward and, therefore, that policy measures necessary to reduce total spending will not adversely affect employment levels. However, if money wages and prices are not flexible downward, then it is not possible to control excess spending without significant reductions in employment. This point was verified by the experiences in 1969–70, in 1974–75, in 1980, and in 1981–82 when the fiscal and monetary brakes were applied successively by the Nixon, the Ford, the Carter and the Reagan administrations. The results were recessions but continued inflation, although the rate was slowed.

The Cost-Push Hypothesis   The cost-push explanation of the source of inflation has come into favor since World War II, especially in the 1970s.[12] This theory finds the basic explanation for inflation in the fact that some producers, groups of workers, or both succeed in raising the prices for either their products or their services above the levels that would prevail under more competitive conditions. Inflationary pressure originates, in other words, with supply rather than demand and spreads throughout the economy. An inflation of this type is possible in theory because in the aggregate prices and wages are not only costs as seen from the standpoint of buyers, but also income when viewed from the standpoint of sellers of goods and labor. For any single commodity or factor service an increase in its price will reduce the quantity of the good or services demanded, but this is not necessarily true for the whole economy.

Inflation of the cost-push variety is most likely to originate in industries that are relatively concentrated, and in which sellers can exercise

---

12. This type of inflation is also described as market power inflation, income share inflation, and administrative inflation.

considerable discretion in the formulation of both prices and wages. Competitive conditions must be such that either business firms or trade unions have some control over the prices of their products or services. Cost-push inflation would not be possible in an economy characterized by pure competition. If recent inflationary pressures in the United States and other economies can really be attributed to cost-push factors, serious and difficult problems of policy are raised. An inflation caused by cost-push is not susceptible to control by traditional monetary and fiscal measures directed at the level of aggregate demand and spending because administered prices and wages by their very nature are insensitive to changes in demand. Thus, measures that reduce overall demand may not affect prices, but can affect quite adversely the economy's real output and employment level. On the other hand, policy measures that involve direct controls over either wages or prices are strongly resisted by both organized labor and the business community under peacetime conditions. Although initially there was broad public support for the Nixon administration's program of wage-price controls (introduced in August 1971), business groups, organized labor, and the general public became increasingly disillusioned with such controls the longer they were in effect.

The Structural Hypothesis   The structural thesis was developed by Charles Schultze to explain the inflation experienced by the American economy in the late 1950s,[13] a time when considerable slack existed in the economy. Schultze was chairman of President Carter's Council of Economic Advisers.

It shows that inflation may be the consequence of internal changes in the structure of demand, even though overall demand may not be excessive and there are no undue concentrations of economic power within the economy. This particular theory of inflation has its origin in the fact that in many areas of the economy wages and prices are flexible upward in response to increases in demand, but not flexible downward when demand declines. If this is the situation, it follows that inflationary pressure can be generated by internal changes in the composition of demand alone. In a dynamic economy such changes are an inherent part of the economic process, consequent upon continuous changes in the structure of consumer tastes and desires. The mechanism by which such changes can generate inflationary pressure in the absence of any marked excess of aggregate demand or aggressive exploitation of positions of market power is relatively clear-cut. The expansion of demand for the output of particular industries or sectors will lead to wage and price increases in these areas because wages and prices have an upward sensitivity when demand is rising. But the contraction of demand in other sectors will not

13. Charles L. Schultze, *Recent Inflation in the United States*, Study Paper no. 1, Joint Economic Committee, Study of Employment, Growth, and Price Levels (Washington, D.C.: U.S. Government Printing Office, 1959). This is also described as intersectoral or demand shift inflation.

lead to any corresponding downward movement of prices. Thus, over-all, the average level of prices will necessarily rise. The structural thesis makes price inflation inherent in the process of resource allocation, if wages and prices are flexible upward but not downward.

The Inflationary Process

No single explanation will suffice when we deal with a phenomenon as complex as inflation in the modern economy. The theories just described should not be construed as alternatives in any absolute sense, but rather as approaches that lay stress on one factor relatively more than another. In the inflation characteristic of the contemporary American economy, elements present in each of the theories have been at work. Thus, it is not so much the question of one theory being better, or more valid, than another as it is of the emphasis that should be placed on demand, cost, or structural factors.

Except for the convinced monetarists, most economists do not see the problem of inflation as basically a matter of too much money in circulation. But this does not mean that the money supply is not in the picture. Barring unprecedented shifts in the velocity of circulation, all the theories of the inflationary process that we have discussed predicate increases in the money supply if the inflation is to continue. The income-expenditure approach sees these increases in money as a secondary consequence of other changes that in themselves are primarily responsible for the increases in prices, whereas the classical view (traditional and modern) regards changes in the money supply itself as the basic cause of inflation.

Crucial to any understanding of the nature of the inflationary process, as well as the causes of inflation, is a knowledge of the sensitivity of prices and wages to changes in demand. Two possibilities are present: Wages and prices may be flexible or inflexible. By flexible we mean that both wages and prices respond readily and quickly to changes in demand. Wages and prices that are inflexible, on the other hand, are said to be *cost determined;* that is, they do not respond to changes in demand. Wages are cost determined in the sense that they are fixed in relation to some index of living costs, such as the consumer price index, and change only as the latter changes. Prices are cost determined in the sense that they are determined on the basis of a "markup" over cost and remain relatively fixed as long as costs do not change.

Demand-Pull Inflation

Let us begin our analysis of the inflationary process with the assumption that inflation gets under way with an excess of aggregate demand over *current supply at existing prices.* The Vietnam-induced inflation provides an almost perfect textbook example of such a situation. During 1965 the economy was near full employment—at the end of the year the unemployment rate had dropped to 4.1 percent of the civilian labor force—and the price level was nearly stable. In 1966, however, and as part of the Vietnam military buildup, expenditures for goods and services for military purposes jumped $10.9 billion, a spending surge that sent the economy on an inflationary surge that was still going strong at the start of the 1970s. Given the type of aggregate supply curve described in Figure 4–3 (Chapter 4, p. 103), any excess of aggregate demand will drive the price level up, even if the economy is not initially at the full-employment level. The price level rises because the elasticity of output has a value of less than unity, and the elasticity of the price level has a value greater than zero.[14] This initial increase in prices and costs does not mean that all prices and wages are affected equally. There will be some groups that register a net gain from the initial inflationary spurt in the economy because their money incomes have increased more than the prices of things they buy. Other groups find their real position unchanged; their money incomes and the prices of the things they buy have changed in the same proportion. Still others are net losers because prices increase more swiftly than their money incomes.

The extent to which an upward movement in the price level generated initially by aggregate demand continues depends basically upon whether or not all groups in the economy attempt to maintain their real income and expenditure positions. If all groups, in the face of inflation, try to maintain real expenditure positions, real aggregate demand is unaffected by changes in the price level. But real expenditure positions can be maintained only if aggregate money demand—that is, expenditure—continues to rise at the same rate as the general price level. For example, if the groups that initially saw their real economic position adversely affected by the original inflationary spurt succeed in raising either the prices of the things they sell or their money wages, their real income and expenditure position remains intact. But this, of course, will boost prices to still higher levels, and thus require additional upward adjustments in money income and expenditure on the part of still other groups that now seek to maintain intact their real expenditure positions. From the viewpoint of the whole economy, an added increase in the level of aggregate money expenditure is inevitable if the level of real aggregate demand is to remain constant.[15]

---

14. Technically, the elasticity of output is the ratio of a percentage change in output to a percentage change in aggregate demand and the elasticity of the price level is the ratio of a percentage change in the price level to a percentage change in aggregate demand.

15. In a dynamic setting in which output is rising, aggregate real demand must rise, not remain constant. See Schultze, Footnote 13. The student should note most carefully at this point that the analysis is attempting to spell out the circumstances under which the price level will continue to rise, given an initial excess of aggregate demand over supply at current prices. A continued expansion of demand is much the simpler case. Recent experience provides empirical verification on the point. Aggregate real demand slowed sharply in 1969 and actually declined in 1970, but money national income continued to rise in both years. The same thing happened again in 1974, 1975, 1980, and 1982. In all these years real GNP fell, but GNP valued in current prices continued to rise. This happened even though the 1981–82 slump was the most severe since the Great Depression of the 1930s.

The reader should not forget that it is the level of aggregate demand in real terms—that is, constant prices—which is of significance with respect to the employment level. The key to an understanding of the inflationary process lies in the impact that a rising price level has on real aggregate demand. An upward movement of the general price level can continue, irrespective of whether the initial inflationary impulse came from demand-pull, cost-push, or structural factors, only if aggregate real demand remains unchanged, or does not drop too severely. This requires that aggregate money expenditures rise at about the same rate as the general price level. The experience of the 1974–75 and 1981–82 recessions is instructive on this point, as it suggests that under present conditions a severe drop in aggregate real demand—that is, a deep recession—may be necessary to slow the inflation rate, once inflation is under way.

There are a number of possible ways in which a rising price level may have a dampening effect upon aggregate real demand. For example, a progressive tax system can lead to a reduction in real consumption because money income in the hands of the economy's spending units does not rise in proportion to a change in prices. As pointed out in the discussion on the effects of inflation, this clearly happened in the 1974–75 recession. It is possible, too, that a rising price level will reduce the real value of liquid assets held by consumers, and thus lead to a slackening of real consumer demand as households attempt to bring their asset holding back to what they consider a desirable level. This is the Pigou effect at work in reverse. If, in addition, it is assumed that the money supply is fixed, an increase in the price level may have a depressing effect upon real investment outlays because under these circumstances the rate of interest will rise.

Granted that the possibility exists that aggregate real demand may decline—or, alternatively, that aggregate money demand may not rise in proportion to the change in the price level—the significance of this for a continuation of the inflationary process depends upon the sensitivity of prices and money wages to changes in demand. If we assume, first, that a rising general price level tends to depress the level of real demand and, second, that both money wages and prices are flexible, then the economy contains a kind of built-in corrective factor that makes a continued upward movement of the general price level difficult to sustain. More particularly, a cost-push type of inflation is practically impossible under these conditions, because the decline in the level of aggregate real demand means a decline in the demand both for the different categories of output and for the services of different economic resources, particularly labor. In the short run this will lead to growing unemployment of labor and excess plant capacity. But if prices and wages are sensitive to the state of demand, it will be impossible for any upward movement of either to continue. If wage and price sensitivity exists, in other words, the inflationary process will come to a halt unless there is a constant renewal of excess aggregate money demand. This is not likely if restraint is exercised by the government in the face of the downward pressure on the price level that will develop once the force of the initial volume of excess expenditure exhausts itself. Recent experience provides mixed evidence on this point. There is not much evidence that wages and prices are flexible downward, and the ability of the federal government to exercise restraint in spending is doubtful. The initial impetus to inflation from Vietnam war spending was largely exhausted by 1969, when military outlays stabilized, and then dropped to lower levels for four years (1970–73). But total federal expenditures (in current prices) for goods and services continued to mount, going from $95.7 billion in 1970 to $129.2 billion in 1976, a 35 percent increase in seven years. In the first two years of the Reagan administration, federal spending for goods and services rose by 31 percent, despite the administration's well-publicized intent to pare back the size of the federal establishment. Most of this increase was accounted for by the administration's buildup in military outlays, although the 1981–82 recession also brought about a large increase in transfer outlays.

Cost-Push Inflation

The results are different if money wages and prices are not particularly sensitive to a change in demand, even though aggregate real demand is adversely affected by a general upward movement of the price level. Under these conditions the economy no longer contains any kind of internal corrective factor to limit the extent to which an initial excess of aggregate demand may push up the price level. A reduction in real aggregate demand, given inflexible wages and prices, leads chiefly to a reduction in employment and to excess capacity. Prices and wages will not decline, and thus the inflation may continue. If unemployment and idle capacity lead to demands from organized labor and business that the government adopt monetary and fiscal policies that will increase aggregate money demand sufficiently to restore real aggregate demand to its prior level, a cost-push type of inflationary process is possible. This clearly was the case in early 1971, at which time the Nixon administration junked the game plan that called for a gradual slowdown in the pace of economic activity in the hope of containing inflation. The same scenario was played over again in the spring of 1975 when the Ford administration changed its policy stance and called for a tax cut as part of a package to stimulate the economy. The Carter administration did the same in the spring of 1977, even though the economy then was in the recovery stage from the 1974–75 recession. The Reagan administration did not follow this pattern as the 1981–82 recession unfolded. Its 1981 tax cut package of a 5 percent reduction in 1981, followed by 10 percent in both 1982 and 1983, was originally proposed to the Congress and to the public as a "supply-side" measure that would raise productivity and production. Ironically, however, as the recession dragged on through 1982, the tax cut came to be viewed from a Keynesian perspective. For example, a *Business Week* "Commentary" in March 1983 argued that, in fact, "Reaganomics" had in early 1983 become more Keynesian than supply side in its basic thrust.[16]

In general, however, the circumstances described above set the stage for a continuous upward movement of the price level, particularly because all groups do not share equally in the initial round of price increases. When the price level begins to rise, aggregate real demand may fall. But this does not bring prices down. As a consequence, groups that did not gain from the initial price rise now seek to boost their money incomes so as to maintain real expenditure positions. This creates more upward pressure on the price level and, indirectly, puts pressure on government to take the necessary steps to sustain aggregate real demand and prevent unemployment. Both the 1970 and 1974–75 recessions and the sluggish recoveries that followed these economic downturns illustrate this process. As Table 14–2 shows, hourly earnings in current dollars continued to rise in the recession years at rates which were only slightly less than those in the preceding boom periods. In 1970, for example, gross hourly earnings in private nonagricultural activity increased by 6.3 percent, compared to 6.7 percent in 1969—a year of fiscal and monetary restraint— and 6.3 percent in 1968, a boom year. Again in 1974, a recession year, hourly earnings rose more rapidly than they did in 1972 and 1973, both boom years. The pattern was not quite so clear-cut during the 1981–82

TABLE 14–2. Annual Average Increase in Hourly Earnings in Nonagricultural Employment: 1968–82

Year	Economic Conditions	Percentage Increase in Hourly Earnings	Unemployment Rate
1968	Boom	6.3%	3.6%
1969	Boom + restraint	6.7	3.5
1970	Recession	6.3	4.9
1971	Recovery—slow	6.8	5.9
1972	Boom	7.2	5.6
1973	Boom + restraint	6.5	4.9
1974	Recession	7.6	5.6
1975	Recession + stimulus	6.8	8.5
1976	Recovery—slow	7.3	7.7
1977	Expansion	8.0	6.9
1978	Expansion	8.4	6.0
1979	Slowdown in expansion	8.3	5.8
1980	Recession	8.1	7.0
1981	Recession	8.9	7.5
1982	Recession	5.8	9.5

SOURCE: *Economic Report of the President,* 1983.

16. "Reaganomics II: More Keynes than Laffer," *Business Week,* March 21, 1983.

recession, although hourly wages continued to rise in spite of the recession. The rate of increase in 1982 (5.8 percent) was the lowest since 1968, a fact that can be attributed to the severity of the slump.

In the situation described above, both the elasticity of the price level and the elasticity of money wages[17] have values that are high with respect to any increase in aggregate money demand, but low with respect to a decrease in aggregate real demand. Beyond this, the mechanism must exist through which pressure can be generated to raise the level of aggregate money demand and thus prevent unemployment and idle capacity from developing. It is clear from recent experience that the political process provides that mechanism.

If we drop the assumption that a rise in the general price level tends to reduce real aggregate demand, then there is less reason to assert that any kind of a built-in corrective factor is present in the economy. Under the assumption that aggregate real demand is not adversely affected by a rise in the general price level, no downward pressure on either prices or wages will develop in the event of an initial rise, irrespective of whether the first impulse toward higher prices resulted from demand-pull or cost-push forces. However, a cost-push type of inflation is easier to sustain if a rising price level does not depress aggregate real demand. Then, no downward pressure on either prices and wages or employment levels will develop as various groups push prices and costs upward in an effort to maintain their real expenditure levels. From the point of view of the whole economy, rising costs (and prices) can generate an equal increase in aggregate monetary demand as long as we assume that aggregate real demand is unaffected by a rise in the general price level. Thus, a cost-push inflationary process can, in theory, continue indefinitely without any necessarily adverse effects on the employment level. Under the foregoing circumstances, the degree of flexibility or inflexibility of both wages and prices loses much of its significance, for this is a matter of importance chiefly when we assume that a rise in the price level will depress aggregate real demand.

Structural Inflation

The third theoretical explanation offered for the inflation was described earlier as the structural thesis. As noted, it differs from both the demand-pull and cost-push analyses primarily in that it stresses changes in the composition of demand.

In this analysis the starting point for inflation is a change in the structure of demand which leads to an increase in the demand for the products of particular industries. There is nothing unusual in this, for in a

17. The elasticity of money wages is the ratio of a percentage change in money wages to a percentage change in aggregate demand.

dynamic economy it is presumed that a process of changing demand and resource reallocation is continuously under way. What is significant, though, is that both money wages and prices in the modern American economy are flexible upward in response to shifts in demand, but rigid downward. Prices will therefore move upward in those industries that experience an increase in the demand for their output, but prices will not fall in those industries where there is either an absolute or a relative fall in demand. Not only will prices fail to fall in the industries where demand declines, they may actually rise. The increase in wages and other prices in the industries with an expanding demand will force the demand-deficient industries to pay higher wages for labor and higher prices for other materials in order to get the economic resources they need to continue in production, even though these industries are confronted with a decline in the demand for their output. Wage and price rigidity downward is basically the cause for this type of behavior, for it would not be possible for prices to move significantly upward in the industries which have an increase in demand if wages and prices elsewhere moved downward in response to a declining demand situation. Consequently, wage and price increases in particular sectors gradually spread out and permeate the whole economy.

The most important single implication of the structural explanation of the inflationary process is that monetary and fiscal measures of a general character are not capable of coping with this type of an inflationary situation. General monetary and fiscal measures aim basically at the control of aggregate demand, but this is much too blunt an approach for an inflation that has its origin in changes in the composition of demand. Restrictive measures designed to reduce the overall level of demand may simply lead to unemployment of labor and idle plant capacity without any significant impact on the price level. Schultze has suggested that an inflation which results from changes in the composition of demand is a means by which an economy characterized by downward rigidities in its cost-price structure brings about the necessary reallocation of resources in response to changing conditions of demand. In the development of any policy measures designed to cope with this type of inflation, care would have to be exercised not to control prices at the cost of blunting the process of resource allocation. The difficulty with this is that there is no way of knowing just how much inflation is necessary and acceptable for this purpose. We cannot distinguish, in other words, between this type of inflation and inflation that results from other causes.

The phenomenon of inflation in the modern economy cannot be fully explained in terms of either the demand-pull or the cost-push theory. The major distinction between these two theories of the inflationary process centers on the sensitivity of both money wages and prices to changes in demand. Those who believe that significant price and wage flexibility exists in the economy would generally argue in favor of the demand-pull thesis as the basic cause of inflation because such flexibility makes it virtually impossible for any cost-induced inflationary trend to sustain itself if the level of aggregate real demand is sensitive to a rising price level. On the other hand, economists who are skeptical concerning the extent of wage and price flexibility in the economy are inclined to place more emphasis upon the cost-push theory as basic to an explanation and understanding of inflation. Such theorists do not deny the importance of demand factors, but they take the view that the basic insensitivity of wages and prices to demand conditions means that a substantial—and probably intolerable—level of unemployment and idle capacity would be required before the general price level was stabilized. In essence, the cost-push theorists see inflation as a consequence of market power, a phenomenon that cannot be dealt with by traditional fiscal and monetary tools. In a cost-push situation the pressure on the price level does not have to come solely from wages or other costs. It may originate with prices themselves, given the existence of market power in key sectors of the economy. Many large trade unions have the power to push wages up in the face of a falling demand, but many large corporations have the same power with respect to prices. In a 1974 report on the causes of the economy's inflation, the Joint Economic Committee of the Congress said that "increasingly, a significant part of the current inflation can be understood only in the context of administered prices in concentrated industries which typically increase despite falling demand."[18] Concentrated industries, the Committee asserted, have the power to resist competitive forces and achieve a target rate of return on investment in good times and bad. To do this they must have power to control prices. To cope with inflation caused by private market power, administrative and legislative action should be taken to break up such power and to eliminate, as well, government regulations and practices that restrict competition. This was a key recommendation of the Committee. Among economists, John Kenneth Galbraith and Gardner C. Means are probably the best-known advocates of the thesis that concentrated market power in the oligopolistic sectors of the economy is a major factor in the contemporary inflation, particularly inflation when unemployment is high.[19] Both also believe that the basic remedy is for the government to control prices in the few hundred giant corporations that dominate the American economy. In the long run, Means is willing to experiment with policies that would reduce market power by breaking up oligopolistic enterprises, but Galbraith is skeptical of this approach.

18. "An Action Program to Reduce Inflation and Restore Economic Growth," Joint Economic Committee, Congress of the United States (Washington, D.C.: U.S. Government Printing Office, September 21, 1974), p. 3. See also Howard M. Wachtel and Peter D. Adelsheim, "How Recession Feeds Inflation: Price Markups in a Concentrated Economy," *Challenge*, September / October, 1977.
19. The best statement of Galbraith's position on this question is found in his *Economics and the Public Purpose* (Boston: Houghton Mifflin Company, 1973), especially Chapters 19 and 26. See also Gardner C. Means, "Simultaneous Inflation and Unemployment," in *The Roots of Inflation* (New York: Burt Franklin & Co., 1975), pp. 1–30.

The Microeconomic Roots of Inflation

The theories we have examined, as well as our analysis of the inflationary process, point to the conclusion that, whatever the ultimate explanation for any sustained rise in the price level, the modern market economy experiences significant upward pressure on the price level well before the full-employment output is reached. Empirical verification for this is to be found in examination of the relationship between the rate of wage and price increases and unemployment rates by means of the Phillips curve, an analytical technique we shall discuss later in this chapter. In the meantime, though, it is appropriate that we look at some of the forces at work at the microeconomic level—that is, within the firm and the industry—to help explain this process.

As suggested earlier in this chapter, contemporary income expenditure analysis argues that the relationship between the price level and output takes the form of a curve of the kind shown in Figure 14–5. As output rises toward full employment (Y_f), increases in the price level become more and more pronounced until eventually the curve depicting the relationship of the general price level to income becomes vertical. This happens at Y_f and signifies that at this point any further increase in aggregate demand will not lead to additional output, but simply to an increase in the price level. This is what Keynes designated as true inflation.

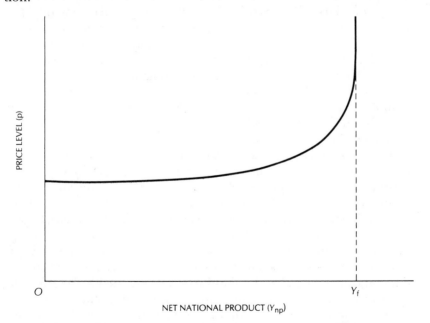

Figure 14–5.   The Price-Output Relationship: Aggregate Supply Curve

To understand why the general price level tends to vary in the manner shown in Figure 14–5, we need to analyze the forces that determine prices at the level of the firm and the industry. The behavior of the general price level in response to changing levels of aggregate demand depends upon how individual prices respond to output changes that are brought about by changes in demand. Therefore, we can employ the same key analytical concepts of demand and supply that we use to explain the process of individual price determination to explain the process through which the general price level is determined.

Traditionally, the body of economic analysis called price theory or microeconomics teaches that prices are governed by demand and supply conditions. In our analysis we have been concerned primarily with demand for the whole output of the economy. In a conceptual sense, aggregate demand represents the sum of all the individual industry (or product) demand schedules that exist in the economy at any given moment. There is associated, in other words, with any given level of aggregate demand an underlying structure of demand schedules for all the different industries that make up the economy. It logically follows that some or all of the individual demand curves will shift when there is a change in aggregate demand, although the individual schedules will not necessarily shift to the same degree as the total demand. If we thus assume some change in an industry demand schedule consequent upon a shift in aggregate demand, our problem reduces itself to one of explaining how output and price will respond at the industry level to such a change.

In Figure 14–6 we present a typical demand and supply diagram showing how market price is determined for some given commodity. Let us call this commodity A. Given the existence of the industry supply curve SS and the industry demand curve DD, the equilibrium price is P_1 and the equilibrium output is A_1. Since we are interested in the impact of a change in demand on both price and output, let us see what happens if we shift the demand curve to the right, from DD to $D'D'$. The result of this shift is an increase in output to the level of A_2 and an increase in price to the level of P_2. There have been both output and price responses to the change in demand.

Why has this increase in price accompanied the higher level of output? If we are going to explain the price change depicted in Figure 14–6, it is necessary to go behind the schedules, so to speak, and analyze the factors that underlie supply. With an assumed shift in demand, the manner in which both price and output will change depends primarily upon supply considerations.

The position and shape of a typical supply schedule, such as SS in Figure 14–6, reflect the behavior of costs as output changes. From the standpoint of the individual business firm costs are the key determinant of the supply function. The most important cost element in the short run is *marginal cost,* defined as the cost of producing an additional unit of output. Since marginal cost represents cost associated with changes in output, it is apparent that the behavior of marginal costs is crucial to an

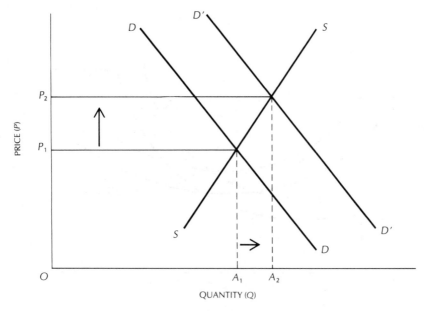

FIGURE 14–6. Determination of Market Price

understanding of the behavior of prices in response to changes in output. In the short run, with fixed plant capacity, marginal cost is the same thing as a change in variable costs, which are costs that vary directly with changes in output. The most important variable costs are the wages of labor and the cost of materials.

Modern economic analysis asserts that, typically, the costs of the business firm are not constant as output expands toward the capacity level; rather, the presumption is that increases in output eventually lead to increases in variable costs per unit of output—and hence marginal costs—and that this will occur prior to the point at which the absolute upper limit of the firm's productive capacity is reached. The short run is characterized, in other words, by a rising level of both variable and marginal costs. Figure 14–7 depicts the shape of the variable and marginal cost curves for the typical business firm in the short run.

There are three reasons why variable costs may rise prior to the point of maximum capacity. The first of these involves the classic principle of diminishing returns. Even if we assume that all resources are homogeneous, additional inputs of a variable resource such as labor eventually lead to a less than proportionate increase in output as long as productive capacity remains fixed. This is the essence of the principle of diminishing returns. If the price of our variable resource, labor, is fixed—that is, money wages are constant—a decline in physical productivity is tantamount to a rise in variable costs per unit produced.[20] Thus, diminishing

20. The reader should recognize that this is essentially the same analysis as developed in Chapter 10, where the relationship of the demand for labor and a falling real wage (productivity) to the supply of output and the price level was shown (Figure 10–12). They are different routes to the same objective—showing why prices rise with increased output.

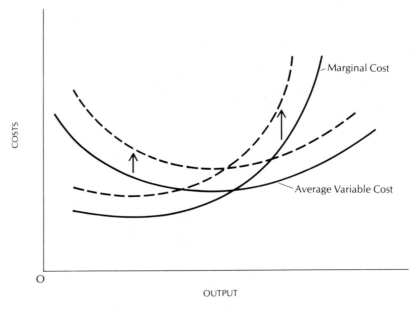

COSTS

OUTPUT

Figure 14–7.   The Costs of the Business Firm

productivity means that ultimately the firm will be faced with rising labor costs per unit of output.

A second major reason for the increase of variable and marginal costs as output expands is the nonhomogeneity of resources that are variable in the short run. This is stressed by Keynes.[21] In reality, labor and other resources are neither homogeneous nor fully interchangeable in the productive process. An expansion of output within the limits of ultimate productive capacity may require the use of labor units that are less and less. efficient in relation to the going wage rate. This will cause an increase in the labor cost per unit of output even though the firm's capital equipment is not fully utilized. Rising labor costs may result in spite of the fact that suitable equipment is available for use in conjunction with added labor—if the labor units are not of the same degree of efficiency.

The third explanation for rising costs—and prices—as output expands is simply that the prices the firm must pay for its variable resources are unlikely to remain constant as output expands. If an expansion of output is general in the economy, it is most likely that the prices that firms must pay for labor and other resources will rise prior to attainment of the full-employment level. There are two reasons for this. First, the elasticity of supply of all commodities and services is not the same; thus, for some resources supply may become perfectly inelastic before output as a whole has become perfectly inelastic, that is, before the full-employment level for the economy as a whole is reached. The emergence of

21. John Maynard Keynes, *The General Theory*, pp. 42, 299–300.

bottlenecks in particular industries and for particular goods and services will cause the price of various *intermediate goods and services* to rise and will thus ultimately affect the price of final goods and services. Second, a period of expanding demand and output will lead to increased pressure by organized labor for wage increases. Wages are flexible upward but not downward. If the economic outlook is generally favorable, business firms are not likely to resist these demands very strenuously. Changes in the prices that the business firm must pay for its variable resources will cause a change in its unit costs over the entire range of output possible within the limits of the firm's capacity. Thus, changes of the type we have just been describing are subsumed in shifts in the position of both the variable and marginal cost curves of the firm, such as those depicted by the dashed lines in Figure 14–7.

The Keynesian Theory of the Price Level

The foregoing discussion leads us directly into the theory Keynes developed to explain the price level. In a chapter in *The General Theory*[22] that never received from economists the attention it deserves, Keynes attempted to show that the same forces which economists stress in their explanation of how individual prices are determined (see prior section) also determine prices in general. As Keynes put it, one of his objectives was "to bring the theory of prices as a whole back to close contact with the theory of value."[23] What classical economics had done, according to Keynes, was explain prices at the level of the firm and industry by conditions of supply and demand, but introduce an entirely different kind of explanation into the picture when it came to prices in general—namely, the quantity theory of money. This Keynes viewed as a false division. Keynes sums up his basic argument quite succinctly as follows:

> In a single industry its particular price-level depends partly on the rate of remuneration of the factors of production which enter into its marginal cost and partly on the scale of output. There is no reason to modify this conclusion when we pass to industry as a whole. The general price level depends partly on the rate of remuneration of the factors of production which enter into marginal cost and partly on the scale of output as a whole, i.e. (taking equipment and technique as given) on the volume of employment.[24]

Here in a nutshell are the essential ideas we discussed in the previous section. By scale of output Keynes means to encompass all those factors which influence the shape of the cost curves (Figure 14–7) as the output level changes. By remuneration of the factors of production, Keynes is pointing to all the forces that may cause the prices businessmen have to

22. Chapter 21, "The Theory of Prices."
23. Keynes, *The General Theory*, p. 293.
24. Ibid., p. 294.

pay (wages, interest, rents, etc.) to get resources to rise as they use more resources. In Figure 14–7 these forces influence the level of the cost curves—shown by the dashed lines.

To complete his explanation of how prices in general vary with changes in output, Keynes brought into the analysis all the key elements which enter into his own explanation of income and employment. Starting with an increase in the quantity of money,[25] Keynes asked how and by what process does such a change get to the price level? The answer he gave runs as follows. A change in the money supply will affect, first, the rate of interest. How interest changes depends on the schedule of liquidity preference, which in turn depends upon expectations concerning the future as well as the current level of economic activity. Next, a change in the interest rate will lead to a change in investment spending. How much investment spending changes is a matter of the sensitivity of the latter to changes in the rate of interest. This is a question involving *all* the variables which enter into the investment demand schedule (see Chapter 6), including expectations and the state of business confidence. A change in investment spending will lead to a change in aggregate demand, but the magnitude of the latter depends upon the value of the multiplier. This, it will be recalled, is determined by the various "leak-ages" from the income stream (Chapters 7, 8, and 9). Once aggregate demand has increased, it will exhaust itself in either an increase in out-put (and employment), an increase in the price level, or both. This brings us full circle to Keynes's basic argument: The way in which more spend-ing divides itself between higher prices and more output depends on the strength of the underlying forces which operate through the scale of output and which determine the rate of remuneration for the factors of production. Figure 14–8 shows these relationships in a diagram.

In the short run Keynes believed strongly that the principle of dimin-ishing returns (or productivity) was a major factor in explaining why marginal and variable costs rise as output expands (see Figure 14–7), the reason being that technology and equipment (i.e., capital) are fixed. In this respect he was very much a classical economist. But, in the long run, he believed that the level of money wages and their relationship to changes in productivity are the more important. As he put it, "And the long-run stability or instability of prices will depend upon the strength of the upward trend of the wage unit (or, more precisely, of the cost unit) compared with the rate of increase in the efficiency of the productive system."[26]

---

25. This in a way is a classical stance, but presumably he used this as a starting point in developing his theory because he wanted to show that the link between money and the price level had to take into account not only his basic theory of output determination, but also essentially classical ideas of how individual prices are determined. Only in this way could he bring the "theory of prices as a whole back to close contact with the theory of value."

26. Keynes, *The General Theory*, p. 309. By the wage unit Keynes means the money wage. The cost unit would be all unit costs. But money wages are of major importance, account-ing for two-thirds to three-fourths of production costs.

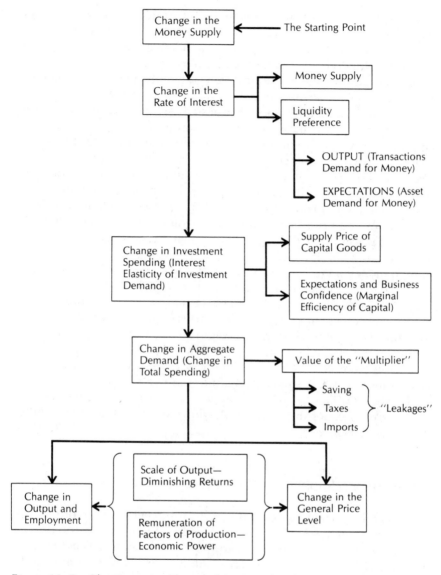

FIGURE 14–8.   The Keynesian Theory of the Price Level

The British economist Joan Robinson has called the idea that in an industrial economy the level of prices is determined primarily by the level of money wages "the other half of the Keynesian Revolution," the first half being the principle that aggregate demand determines the level of output.[27] She believes that this view seriously undermines the neo-

27. Joan Robinson, "What Has Become of the Keynesian Revolution?" *Challenge*, January / February 1974, p. 9.

classical belief that the economy is inherently stable, tending toward an equilibrium of full employment. "The level of money wages in any country at any time is more or less a historical accident going back to a remote past and influenced by recent events affecting the balance of power between employers and trade unions in the labor market."[28] Another economist, the late Professor Sidney Weintraub of the University of Pennsylvania, has drawn upon Keynes's basic analysis to develop a theory which is particularly appropriate to the pricing process in concentrated industries. Weintraub argues that typically the large firms add a standard "markup" to their wage bill, the "markup" being large enough to cover all other costs and ensure the firm of a target rate of return on its investment.[29] Thus, when wages go up as a result of collective bargaining, prices will follow accordingly. This approach presumes that both trade unions and firms have sufficient economic power to push up both wages and prices even when aggregate demand is depressed.

Confirmation of Keynes's view about the longer-term relationship between money wages and the price level is found in Table 14–3, which gives in index number form the link since 1965 between increases in hourly compensation (money wages plus employer contributions to public and private benefit programs for workers), productivity, unit labor costs, and the price level. If money wages go up faster than productivity (Keynes's "the rate of increase in the efficiency of the productive system"), unit labor costs will rise. If there is a markup factor at work as Weintraub suggests, then prices ought to rise at about the same pace as unit labor costs. This is what has happened since 1965. Readers should note the close relationship between the index of unit labor costs and the index of the price level.

The Aggregate Supply Function Revisited

There is an important aspect of the relationship between the price level and output (real GNP) that is *not* revealed by the data and the theory examined so far. This is that the output-price relationship is not reversible. This is an extremely important finding. Prices rise when output rises, but they *do not fall when output falls*. As a matter of fact, prices continue to rise when output falls, even though the *rate* at which they are rising (the inflation rate) slows down. This has been the pattern ever since 1965. Whether or not it will continue to be the pattern in the future remains uncertain, although there is no evidence to suggest that the trend shown in Table 14–3 of money wages continuing to outrun productivity improvements is changing.

28. Ibid., p. 9.
29. Sidney Weintraub, *Classical Keynesianism, Monetary Theory, and the Price Level* (Philadelphia: Chilton, 1961), esp. Chap. 3, "The Theory of the Price Level and the Analysis of Inflation."

TABLE 14–3.   Productivity, Wages, Labor Costs, and Prices: 1965–82
(1965 = 100)

Year	Productivity*	Wages†	Unit Labor Costs	Consumer Prices‡
1965	100.0	100.0	100.0	100.0
1966	102.5	106.1	103.6	102.9
1967	104.5	111.7	107.1	105.8
1968	107.8	120.1	111.5	110.3
1969	107.7	128.0	119.2	116.2
1970	107.8	137.1	127.1	123.1
1971 (R)	111.4	146.0	131.0	128.4
1972	115.7	155.8	135.0	132.6
1973	118.5	167.5	141.5	140.8
1974 (R)	115.8	183.4	158.8	156.3
1975 (R)	118.2	200.9	170.7	170.6
1976	122.0	217.3	178.8	180.4
1977	124.4	233.6	187.9	192.6
1978	125.1	253.7	203.0	206.8
1979	123.5	277.6	224.8	230.6
1980 (R)	122.5	305.8	250.0	261.2
1981	124.2	335.5	270.3	289.3
1982 (R)	124.4	359.8	289.5	305.9

SOURCE: *Economic Report of the President,* 1983.
*Output per man hour in the private, nonfarm economy.
†Total hourly compensation (wages and salaries plus employer contributions to social insurance and private benefit plans) per person.
‡The Consumer Price Index.
Note: (R) = recession year.

What the foregoing suggests is that when the economy is expanding—that is, when *real* GNP is rising—the price level moves upward in the fashion suggested in Figure 14–5. But when recession comes and real output falls, the entire price-output relationship is displaced upward. The reason for this lies in a combination of rising labor costs per unit produced, as suggested by the data in Table 14–3, plus "markup" pricing, which is characteristic of large, oligopolistic firms. Thus, we find that the nonreversibility of the output-price relationship stems from periodic upward shifts in the aggregate supply function, shifts that apparently take place whenever expansion is interrupted and the economy falls into a recession.

Is the foregoing simply hypothetical, or does evidence exist to support such an interpretation? The answer to the latter question is yes. Empirical evidence supporting this answer is found in Figure 14–9, which shows a scatter diagram relating real output (measured in 1972 prices) to an index of the price level as measured by the consumer price index (1965 = 100). Beginning in 1965 the economy grew steadily through 1969, a five-year expansion period. Real GNP rose by 17 percent and the price level rose by 16 percent. Then came the 1970 recession, when real GNP

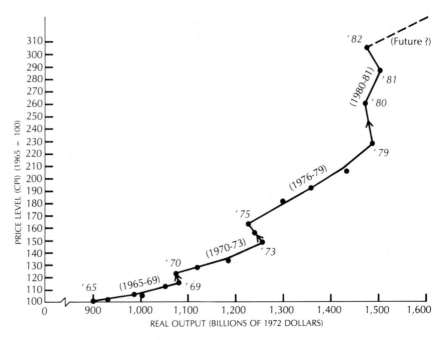

FIGURE 14–9.   An Aggregate Supply Curve—Real Output and the Price Level: 1965–82

SOURCE: *Economic Report of the President, 1983*

declined slightly. But prices continued to rise and, when expansion resumed the following year, the process of both output and prices rising started from a new and higher price plateau. There was, in effect, a kind of "ratcheting" effect that, as Figure 14–9 suggests, can be interpreted as an upward shift in the aggregate supply function. Then, in the 1971– 73 expansion, the process repeated itself. Real output rose by 16.5 percent and the price level jumped another 14.4 percent. Output fell for two years (1974 and 1975), but the price level continued to rise. Consequently, once again the aggregate supply function was displaced upward. In the third distinct expansion period shown in the figure (1977–79), output (real GNP) rose by 20 percent and prices climbed even more sharply, increasing by 35 percent. After 1979 the pattern is more erratic, since there was a short but sharp recession in 1980 followed by barely a year of expansion (from mid-1980 to mid-1981), and then a new and deeper recession (1981–82). What the future pattern will be is uncertain, as suggested by the dashed line and question mark. The strongest probability is that, once expansion is again under way, the price level will again rise, although whether prices will rise as rapidly as in the past is yet to be determined. Nothing has happened in the last few years to suggest any fundamental change in this pattern.

There is one other possible way in which we can relate real output changes to prices. In place of an index of the price level, we can link output to the inflation rate. Since prices overall have not declined in any year since the mid-1960s, there is some merit in seeing how the inflation rate is affected by changes in the output level. This is done in Figure 14–10. Here too, is a scatter diagram, but one in which the inflation rate is plotted on the vertical axis and real output on the horizontal axis, and the data are for the period 1965–1982. What does this figure tell us? The message is straightforward. Generally, when output is rising, the inflation rate is also rising, and when output is falling, there is a corresponding decline in the inflation rate. The correlation, however, is only approximate, for in some years the decline in the inflation rate lagged significantly behind the change in real GNP. Since it is apparent from the data in both Table 14–3 and Figure 14–9 that prices overall simply have not fallen at any time since the mid-1960s, the conclusion is inescapable that the aggregate supply function, while showing the general shape depicted in Figure 14–5, has been shifting upward in rather erratic fashion.

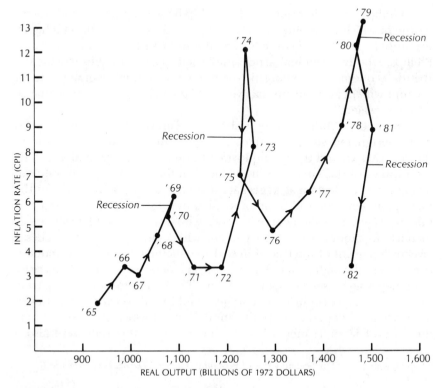

FIGURE 14–10.   Real Output and the Inflation Rate: 1965–82

SOURCE: *Economic Report of the President, 1983*

The explanation for this upward shift in the aggregate supply function lies in a combination of downward wage and price rigidity—at no time in the entire post–World War II period have average hourly wages dropped—and the ability of workers and oligopolistic firms in the economy's central core to push up wages and prices under nearly all demand conditions. In spite of four recessions since 1965, wages and prices continued to rise, although the rate of increase was slowed by the recessions (Figure 14–10). Aside from external shocks, such as came from OPEC-administered oil prices in the 1970s, the data from Table 14–3 and Figure 14–9 show that trade union pressure and administered prices based upon markups are the basic source for the inflation side of the "stagflation" of the 1970s. As Joan Robinson said in her 1971 Ely Lecture to the American Economic Association, the "Experience of inflation has destroyed the conventions governing the acceptance of the existing distribution [of income]. Everyone can see that his relative earnings depend upon the bargaining power of the group that he belongs to."[30]

The Phillips Curve

The Phillips curve describes a relationship between inflation and unemployment which for a time in the 1960s showed promise of being a highly useful policy tool. The curve is named after a British economist, A. W. Phillips, who in a seminal article published in 1958 established for the British economy a relationship between the annual average rate of unemployment and the annual average rate of change in money (that is, nominal) wages.[31]

A theoretical Phillips curve is shown in Figure 14–11. It is the solid curve designated *aa*. The rate of change in money wages is shown on the vertical axis and the unemployment rate on the horizontal axis. The significance of this curve lies in the fact that the unemployment rate can be expected to decline as aggregate demand increases, but a fall in the unemployment rate will be accompanied by a higher rate of increase in money wages. The solid curve is drawn with a slope such that the rate of increase in money wages is 3 percent when unemployment reaches a level of 5 percent of the labor force. If the unemployment rate is reduced to 4 percent through an increase in aggregate demand, the rate of increase in money wages rises to about 5 percent. The extent to which any particular rate of increase in money wages would tend to cause increases in the price level depends upon the annual rate at which the average productivity of labor is increasing. If, for example, this rate were also 3

30. Joan Robinson, "The Second Crisis of Economic Theory," *The American Economic Review*, May 1972, p. 9.
31. A. W. Phillips, "The Relation between Unemployment and the Rate of Change of Money Wages in the United Kingdom, 1861–1957," *Economica*, November 1958, pp. 283–99.

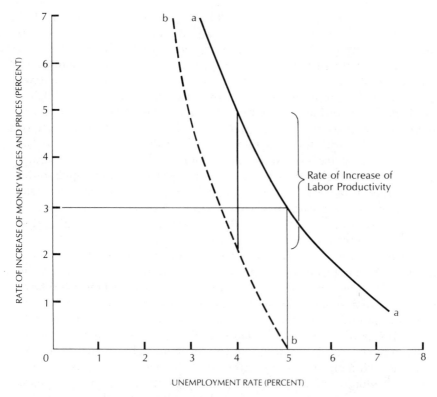

FIGURE 14–11. The Phillips Curve

percent, then it would be theoretically possible for the economy to attain an unemployment rate of 5 percent of its labor force and have money wages increase at an annual average rate of 3 percent without any increase in the general price level. Any reduction of the unemployment rate below the 5 percent level would generate upward pressure on prices.

What is the significance of the Phillips curve? One of the most important conclusions drawn from the establishment of an apparently stable empirical relationship between the rate of change in money wages and the rate of unemployment is the possibility of the simultaneous existence of both unemployment and inflation, a condition that has in fact been with us for a long time. To illustrate, if 4 percent unemployment is an assumed measure of full employment, and if, too, the actual Phillips curve occupied the position shown in Figure 14–11, then the economy might be confronted with a significant amount of inflation, even though the unemployment rate climbed to 5 or 6 percent.

The matter can be put in slightly different form. What the Phillips curve really means is that the policy-makers are confronted with an uncomfortable dilemma—a trade-off between unemployment and inflation. It is impossible, in other words, to have both full employment and price level stability; the two are simply incompatible goals. If full employment is the prime policy objective, then the social cost of attaining this objective is a rise in the price level. The exact inflation rate depends upon transforming the rate of the wage increase–unemployment curve into a rate of increase in the general price level–unemployment curve. This can be done quite simply, if we know the annual rate at which labor productivity is growing. For example, if the latter is 3 percent and money wages are increasing at an annual rate of 5 percent, then the rate of increase in the price level will be 2 percent. In Figure 14–11 the rate of increase in the price level–unemployment curve is obtained by subtracting from the curve *aa* at each employment level an amount equal to the annual rate of increase in productivity. The result is the curve *bb*. This curve tells us that an unemployment rate of 5 percent is the necessary trade-off for absolute stability in the general price level, assuming that the rate of increase in labor productivity remains at 3 percent.

As we shall see, events of the 1970s cast deep doubt on the idea that there is a stable, trade-off relationship between unemployment and the price level. However, if we accept momentarily as a working hypothesis the notion of a stable Phillips curve, some policy problems of the modern economy can be illuminated. It means, for example, that policy-makers must choose between more inflation and less unemployment or more unemployment and less inflation, an unhappy choice in any event. Whether reducing inflation is stressed at the cost of rising unemployment or reduced unemployment is preferred over higher prices depends obviously upon the values and social philosophy of the administration in power at any particular time. Presumably, too, an administration will try and develop the right combination of monetary and fiscal policies designed to move the economy along the Phillips curve in the direction of more or less unemployment or inflation.

There is, though, another difficult problem in public policy that the Phillips curve analysis helps to illuminate. This stems from the possibility that if the economy succeeds, on the one hand, in bringing the unemployment rate down to an acceptable level, it may be confronted with an unacceptable rate of inflation, and, on the other hand, if it gets the price level under control, the unemployment rate may be too high. This possibility implies that there are maximum rates for both unemployment and increases in the price level that are socially—or politically—acceptable. Rates above these maxima simply will not be tolerated. If such rates exist, this poses another difficult—or cruel—dilemma for policy-makers.[32]

The situation is illustrated in Figure 14–12. The shaded area represents a "zone of socially tolerable outcomes," derived from the combination of the acceptable rate of inflation and the acceptable rate of

32. For an excellent survey of the development of the Phillips curve analysis, see Thomas M. Humphrey, "Changing Views of the Phillips Curve," *Monthly Review*, Federal Reserve Bank of Richmond, July 1973.

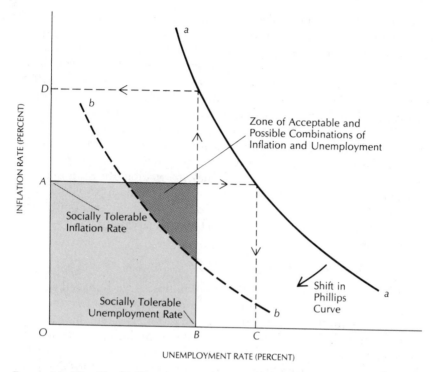

FIGURE 14–12.   The Phillips Curve and Socially Tolerable Rates of Inflation and Unemployment

unemployment. If the Phillips curve lies above and to the right of this zone, then there is *no* combination of unemployment and inflation that is politically or socially acceptable. It seems the economy has been in this fix much of the time in recent years. That is what "stagflation" is all about. In the figure this is the situation depicted by the solid line Phillips curve labeled *aa*. If the inflation rate is brought down to a level that the society is willing to tolerate—point *A* in the diagram—then the unemployment rate rises to an intolerable level, point *C* on the horizontal axis. On the other hand, if the unemployment rate is reduced to the tolerable level, as indicated by point *B* in the figure, then the inflation rate is pushed beyond an acceptable rate to point *D* on the vertical axis.

What is to be done? If it is impossible by means of fiscal and monetary policies to attain an acceptable combination of inflation and unemployment, then different policy alternatives must be found. Monetary and fiscal policies can move the economy along a given Phillips curve such as *aa*, but they cannot shift the curve downward and to the left into the zone representing an acceptable combination of unemployment and inflation rates. How can such a move be brought about? One approach is through adoption of an incomes policy, a term that has come to refer to measures designed to limit the rate at which wages and prices rise as the economy approaches full employment. In the late 1960s the Johnson administration developed an incomes policy in the form of wage-price guideposts, and the Nixon administration had its own incomes policy in the form of direct wage-price controls, beginning in mid-1971. The Carter administration also experimented briefly with an incomes policy in 1978. We shall discuss both forms of income policies later in the chapter. Another approach lies in the development of manpower programs to train and retrain unskilled, semiskilled, and displaced workers so that the economy has a better supply of trained workers as it moves toward higher employment levels. If such policies succeeded, the Phillips curve might shift downward and to the left, thus making possible the attainment of some combination of unemployment and inflation that is socially acceptable. The dashed curve *bb* shows this. To date, however, manpower programs have not demonstrated any spectacular successes.

Challenges to the Phillips Curve Analysis

Until the late 1960s the idea that the Phillips curve reflected a stable trade-off relationship between inflation and unemployment was not subject to serious question. This is no longer the case. For one thing, recent data on both inflation and unemployment cast doubt upon the stability of this relationship. Figure 14–13 contains a scatter diagram relating the inflation rate as measured by the annual rate of change in the GNP price deflator and the unemployment rate for the period 1960 through 1982. The solid-line curve *ee* is sketched in to indicate that the data for the years 1960 through 1969 roughly approximate the behavior pattern suggested by the Phillips hypothesis. More specifically, there appears to be a close correlation between falling unemployment and a rising price level from the beginning of the decade through 1966. For the next three years—1967 through 1969—prices rose very sharply with only minimal effects upon the unemployment rate. But the most noticeable—and damaging—departure from the Phillips hypothesis occurred in the 1970 through 1982 period. In each of these years the unemployment rate was much higher for any given inflation rate than it ought to have been, given the relationship shown by the curve *ee*. What, therefore, are we to conclude? One possible explanation is that the data for 1970 through 1982 are to be found on Phillips curves that lie to the right of and above the curve *ee*. If this is the case, it means that there may not be one basically stable functional relationship between inflation and unemployment, but possibly a series of short-run Phillips curves of a volatile nature. Another is simply that the curve has shifted steadily upward in recent years. But the data are too erratic to support this view.

Bolstered by empirical findings that indicate a shifting Phillips curve, monetarists launched a strong theoretical attack in the late 1960s on one of the fundamental premises of the Phillips curve analysis, namely, that it is possible to reduce permanently the unemployment rate to some

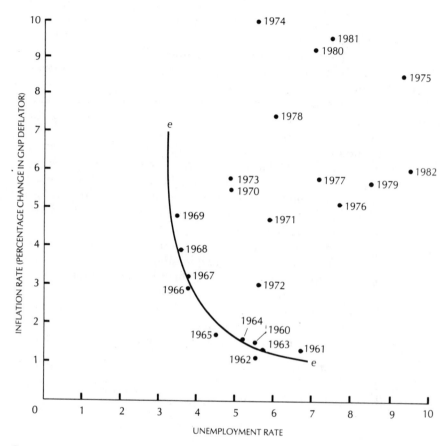

FIGURE 14–13. The Inflation-Unemployment Trade-off, 1960–82

desired level by driving up the price level. On the contrary, according to the monetarists, there is no permanent trade-off between inflation and unemployment. Policy measures based upon such an assumed trade-off will, in the long run, only result in an acceleration in the inflation rate, with no permanent change in the unemployment level.

As in the case of the controversy over the role of money in aggregate economic analysis, this monetarist challenge to the Phillips curve analysis has been led by Professor Milton Friedman of the University of Chicago. He has argued, first, that there exists a natural unemployment rate, determined by underlying real factors such as capital formation and technological change, and, second, that the Phillips curve is a short, transitory relationship, valid only as long as the wage-earners adhere to the money illusion and have no expectations prices will continue to rise.

Once wage-earners, though, lose the money illusion and develop expectations about continued inflation, they will begin to bargain for real wages by attempting to take the anticipated inflation rate into account in their wage negotiations. If, under these circumstances, the attempt is made to reduce the unemployment rate by increases in the price level, all that will happen is an acceleration in the inflation rate, but with no effect upon the long-term natural rate of unemployment. It is for this reason that the monetarist critique of the Phillips curve theory is sometimes called the accelerationist thesis.

The manner in which this works is shown in Figure 14–14. According to the accelerationist thesis, the Phillips curve becomes, in the long run, perfectly inelastic with respect to the rate of change in the price level at the natural rate of unemployment. This is the vertical line labeled the "Long-Run Phillips Curve" that intersects the horizontal axis at the natural rate of unemployment, U_n. The curves PC_1, PC_2, etc., represent a series of short-term Phillips curves, each one of which incorporates a different *expected* rate of inflation. An increase in the expected inflation rate will cause the Phillips curve to shift upward. The point at which a particular short-term curve intersects the long-run curve represents equality between the expected and actual inflation rates. Let us suppose that the policy objective is one of reducing the unemployment rate to U_t, a level below the presumed natural rate. If we assume, further, that the economy was in equilibrium with stable prices, then aggregate demand would have to increase to bring the economy closer to the target level of unemployment, U_t. The increase in aggregate demand will trigger a rise

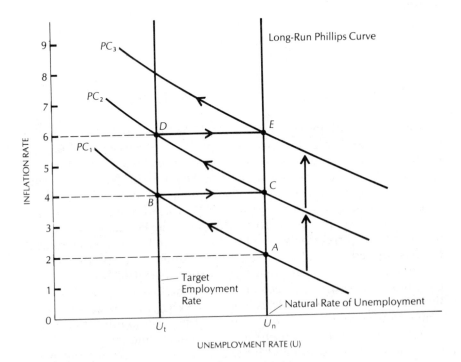

FIGURE 14–14.   The Accelerationist Thesis

in prices, which will be reflected in a movement of the economy along the short-term Phillips curve labeled PC_1. Prices must rise faster than money wages—that is, real wages must fall—if unemployment is to be reduced.

According to the accelerationist thesis, however, the rise in the price level cannot keep the economy permanently at a level of unemployment below the natural rate. This is true for two reasons. First, money wages will begin to catch up with the price level, thus pushing the real wage back toward its original level. This tends to cause the unemployment rate to move back toward the natural rate, U_n. But the inflation rate will have accelerated to 4 percent. Second, wage-earners soon abandon the money illusion in the face of a rising price level and begin to bargain for money wages that take into account anticipated increases in the price level. If this happens the short-term Phillips curve will shift upward in response to expectations that inflation will continue. It will now be at the level PC_2, a level which incorporates a new set of expectations (4 percent) about the inflation rate in the future. But the target goal of a reduction of unemployment to the level of U_t has not been reached. If aggregate demand is stimulated once again the process will repeat itself, except this time the movement will be along the curve PC_2, and the inflation rate will rise to 6 percent. Once again employment will sink back to the natural rate as money wages catch up with the rising price level. But 6 percent now becomes the expected rate and the Phillips curve shifts once more, this time to the level PC_3. The conclusion of the monetarists is quite clear: The unemployment rate can be kept below the natural rate only by a *continuously accelerating* inflation rate. The inflation and unemployment rates will follow the zigzag path marked *ABCDE*. What Figure 14–14 shows is that the short-term Phillips curve must move continuously upward for unemployment to remain at the level U_t. Since it is unlikely that a society will tolerate a continuous acceleration in the inflation rate for the sake of marginal gains in unemployment, the short-term Phillips curve should eventually stabilize. But when this happens, the unemployment rate will move back to its natural level and the inflation rate will be at a permanently higher level. In the figure this is 6 percent. This is the essence of the accelerationist thesis. In the view of Professor Friedman and other monetarists, the only way in which the unemployment rate can be permanently lowered is through structural changes that reduce the natural unemployment rate. These would include measures to improve the mobility of labor through better information systems relating to labor demand and supply, improved vocational and on-the-job training, less discrimination in hiring, getting rid of legal minimum wages, and the reduction or elimination of import quotas and tariffs. Some of these measures tend to make the labor market more effective and others, such as the elimination of tariffs, put downward pressure on the domestic price level. It may be noted, too, that supporters of the Phillips curve hypothesis endorse some of these measures, for, as pointed out earlier, improvements in the skill and knowledge of the work force tend to push the curve to the left.

Like much of the controversy surrounding the role of money in the economy, the disputes over the viability of the Phillips curve hypothesis continue. Many economists are not ready to accept wholly the accelerationist critique on the basis of the rather erratic behavior of prices and unemployment during the 1970s. Evidence accumulated for much longer periods of time supports the thesis of a trade-off between inflation and unemployment, although most economists will now concede that the relationship is probably less stable than they once thought. Professor James Tobin suggests that a Phillips curve relationship exists which is quite flat at high levels of unemployment, but tends to become vertical as the economy approaches critically low levels of unemployment.[33] His view involves a blending of the original Phillips curve hypothesis with elements of the monetarist critique, although it does not require the postulate of a natural rate of unemployment.

More recently it has been suggested that because of the severity of the 1981–82 recession and its impact upon the rate of increase in money wages, new opportunities exist to use the Phillips curve trade-off idea in policy-making. It is possible, one observer suggests, that the 1980s may more closely resemble the early 1960s than the 1970s.[34] If this is true, there is room to employ discretionary policies of a stimulative nature in order to bring down the unemployment rate without causing an immediate rise in the price level. Whether or not this is the reality remains to be seen.

Incomes Policy in the 1960s

The emergence of the Phillips curve hypothesis in the early 1960s gave a strong impetus to the development of incomes policies as complements to the older and more traditional fiscal and monetary approaches to influencing the level of output and employment. In its essentials, an *incomes policy* deals with the development of mechanisms through which money wage and price increases can be held within tolerable levels as an economy approaches full employment. As indicated in the prior discussion, the lesson of the Phillips curve analysis is that, unless something is done about the matter, the economy cannot expect to get to full employment without high—and probably unacceptable—rates of inflation.

In the United States the first serious attempt to develop an incomes policy was made in 1962, when the President's Council of Economic Advisers established a series of guideposts for noninflationary wage and price behavior.[35] The principles of the guideposts were relatively simple.

33. James Tobin, "Inflation and Unemployment," *American Economic Review,* March 1972.
34. Norman Jonas, "Commentary," *Business Week,* March 28, 1983.
35. *Economic Report of the President* (Washington, D.C.: Government Printing Office, 1962).

The Council asserted in effect that if gains in wages and other forms of money incomes were to be noninflationary, then they should be no greater, on the average, than the annual average gain in productivity (output per worker-hour) for the economy as a whole. If all increases in money income were held within this limit, then factor costs per unit of output for the economy as a whole would be stabilized, thus eliminating any tendency for market forces to bring about an increase in the general price level. In its analysis of the stiuation, the Council of Economic Advisers put primary stress upon increases in money wages, since they account for 65 to 70 percent of the national income. The principle, though, applied to all forms of money income, including profits.

The Council made allowance for appropriate adjustments in individual industries, if their conditions varied from the conditions prevailing in the economy as a whole. For example, if an industry experienced a rate of increase in productivity that was greater than the national average, the prices of its product should decline, because a higher than average rate of productivity increase implies falling labor costs. The reverse would be true if productivity lagged behind the national average. At the time the guidepost policy was proclaimed, the Council believed that productivity was rising on the average at a rate of 3.5 to 4 percent a year; hence, wages and other forms of income could advance at this rate without being inflationary.

The guidepost policy expressed the view that society should enjoy the benefits of improved productivity through higher money incomes and stable prices rather than through stable money incomes and falling prices. Given the distribution of income, the benefits of productivity gains would spread more evenly over the whole society if stability in money incomes was coupled with a declining price level. But in a world in which prices and costs are generally flexible upward and inflexible downward, such an outcome was not likely. The Council was no doubt being realistic in arguing that the most practical way to translate advances in productivity into improved material well-being is through a policy that permits money income in all forms to increase at the same pace as output per worker-hour.

How well did the guidepost policy work? From 1962 through 1965 it was moderately successful, as the data in Table 14–4 indicate. In these years, annual average percentage increases in compensation per worker-hour (wages and salaries plus employer contributions to social security and private benefit plans) were only slightly higher than the annual average gain in productivity, with consequent mild effects upon unit labor costs. But beginning in mid-1966, when the unemployment rate fell below 4 percent of the civilian labor force and the expenditure buildup for Vietnam accelerated, the guidepost policy broke down as pressures mounted for wage and salary adjustments in excess of productivity gains. Since 1966 wage and salary adjustments have shown very little relationship to productivity changes.

One reason for the breakdown of the guidepost policy was the fact

TABLE 14–4. Changes in Productivity, Compensation per Worker-Hour, and Unit Labor Costs: 1962–82 (percentage change from previous year)*

Year	Productivity*	Compensation Per Worker-Hour	Unit Labor Costs
1962	3.6	4.0	0.4
1963	3.2	3.5	0.2
1964	3.9	4.5	0.6
1965	3.1	3.4	0.3
1966	2.5	6.0	3.5
1967	1.9	5.5	3.5
1968	3.3	7.5	4.1
1969	− 0.3	6.5	6.8
1970	0.3	7.0	6.6
1971	3.3	6.6	3.1
1972	3.7	6.7	2.8
1973	2.5	7.6	5.4
1974	− 2.4	9.4	12.1
1975	2.1	9.6	7.4
1976	3.2	8.1	4.7
1977	2.0	7.6	5.5
1978	− 0.2	8.5	8.7
1979	− 0.7	9.7	10.4
1980	− 0.3	9.9	10.3
1981	1.4	9.7	8.1
1982	0.1	7.3	7.1

SOURCE: *Economic Report of the President,* 1983.
*All data are for the private, nonfarm economy.

that the government had no effective means for forcing business and industry to adhere to productivity guidelines in wage and salary settlements. The government's power was largely limited to persuasion and exhortation, which derisively was termed *jawboning.* This apparently worked only as long as organized labor and the management of large and powerful business firms were willing to adhere voluntarily to the guidelines, a condition that rapidly evaporated when the economy began to heat up as a consequence of the expanded war in Vietnam.

Incomes Policy in the 1970s

Although the Nixon administration came to power in 1969 firmly convinced that an incomes policy was unnecessary and that inflation could be brought under control by the delicate applications of monetary and fiscal policy, in mid-1971 it completely reversed its stance. On August 15, 1971 the president announced to a startled nation his "New Economic Policy," a program which, among other things, contained a ninety-day absolute freeze on wages, prices, and rents. This date marks the beginning of the nation's most comprehensive and longest experiment with an incomes policy involving strong controls over wages and prices backed by the enforcement power of the federal government, an experiment that ran its full course by April 1974. Authority for the control system came from the Economic Stabilization Act, first passed in 1970 and extended in 1972 for another two years. The act has since expired and thus a president no longer has the authority to impose wage and price controls without going to the Congress and asking for such authority.

Incomes policy in the Nixon administration evolved through four stages, or phases, as they came to be known to the public. The headline-catching element of Phase I was the ninety-day freeze on wages and prices but the package also included tax cuts, a slowdown in federal spending and employment, and a devaluation of the dollar in the foreign exchange markets. A Cost of Living Council, headed by the secretary of the treasury, was created, charged with the task of developing a permanent incomes policy.

In November 1971 Phase II went into effect. The freeze was lifted, but mandatory guidelines were set for wage and price increases. Wage increases of 5.5 percent were to be allowed and price increases of 2.5 percent. Administration of these controls was through a five-member Pay Board and a seven-member Price Commission, two agencies established at the time the New Economic Policy first went into effect. Phase II lasted until January 1973, at which time it was replaced by a system of voluntary controls. This was the beginning of Phase III. The decision to abandon mandatory controls was nearly as much of a surprise as President Nixon's earlier decision to impose controls in August 1971, as most observers had expected Phase II to continue well into 1973. Although a majority of business firms and trade unions were freed from restraints under Phase II, controls were left in effect in three particularly troublesome areas: food prices, health costs, and the construction industry. Voluntary guidelines for wage adjustments were still pegged at 5.5 percent and price increases were not supposed to exceed cost increases, although the latter were not clearly defined.

The voluntary control program was short-lived, for in June 1973, in another startling reversal of economic policy, the Nixon administration imposed a new sixty-day freeze on prices. The new freeze, which was dubbed by the press Phase III-B or Phase III½, was clearly a stop-gap measure designed to buy some time as the administration struggled to contain an accelerating price level and work out new policies to control inflation. At the time the new freeze was imposed the consumer price index (CPI) stood at 131.5, more than 10 percentage points above the level of a year earlier. In mid-July the president announced the outlines for Phase IV, which the administration said would take the nation out of the freeze on a sector-by-sector basis. Food prices were exempted from the freeze at the time the Phase IV program was announced. Phase IV, in essence, amounted to a return to a tougher system of mandatory controls administered on a selective basis. The key principle for price increases was to permit prices to rise as costs rose, providing there were no increases in profit margins. Standards for wage increases were the same as in Phases I and II. Large firms, defined as those with annual sales in excess of $1 million, were required to notify the Cost of Living Council of intended price increases; such increases could not be put into effect for thirty days, during which time the Council could suspend or deny the increases. The president stated that Phase IV was designed to move the nation back to a control-free economy. Phase IV ended in April 1974. As one observer said, "By the time the controls expired . . . they had outlived their usefulness. Public support, evident throughout Phases I and II, had evaporated."[36]

When Phase IV ended in April 1974 the nation also ended its first major peacetime experiment with wage and price controls. Neither the Ford nor the Carter administration had any interest in a renewal of the experiment. It is nearly inconceivable that the Reagan administration, with its strong commitment to a free market ideology, would ever seriously consider controls on wages or prices. One should remember, however, that it was believed that the Nixon administration had an equally strong hostility to controls. How successful was the Nixon "New Economic Policy"? No definitive answer is possible to this question, given the impossibility of knowing what would have happened to price levels in the absence of a control system during this period. At best, though, the results are mixed, and at worst they suggest that mandatory wage and price controls are not especially effective in peacetime in containing powerful inflationary pressures. Figure 14–15 is instructive in this respect. It contains data showing, on a monthly basis, the percentage change in the consumer price index for the prior six months converted to an annual basis. These data give us a moving average of changes in this index and thus are most useful for showing trends.

Two significant points concerning the effectiveness of the control system are suggested by the data of Figure 14–15. First, it is evident that the peak of the Vietnam-induced inflation was reached in January 1970, about twenty months before the first freeze was imposed. At the time the freeze was imposed—August 1971—the trend for the rate of increases in the price level was clearly downward. Inflation was not being eliminated, but it was slowing down. The probable reason for this was the recession in 1970, which followed the economic slowdown measures taken by the Nixon administration in 1969 (Chapter 15). Thus, the imposition of controls was not responsible for the lessened rate of inflation, but did coincide with a reduction in the inflation rate, a reduction that was the lagged response to the 1969 actions. The second point is that these data also indicate that the trend in the inflation rate had moved strongly upward

36. Jerry E. Pohlman, *Inflation Under Control* (Reston, Va.: Reston Publishing Company, 1976), p. 218.

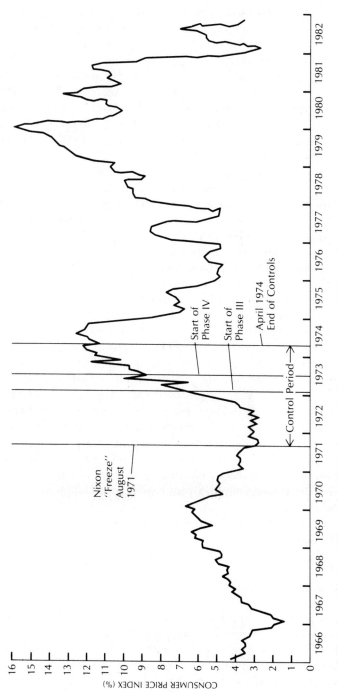

FIGURE 14–15. Consumer Price Index (Annual Rate of Change of Six-Month Intervals)

long before Phase II was dropped in favor of the voluntary system of Phase III. Thus, the argument that Phase II was dropped too soon and this is the reason for the wild upsurge in prices during 1973 does not stand up under close scrutiny. A vigorous boom was under way by mid-1972 and this, in combination with such other factors as worldwide economic prosperity, higher exports stemming from successive devaluations of the dollar, bad weather and droughts that hurt food production all over the world, and no strong anti-inflationary fiscal policy, is much more responsible for the record-breaking inflation of 1973 than the premature abandonment of Phase II.

The last experiment in the United States with an incomes policy came during the Carter administration. In its first year in office (1977) the administration paid little attention to prices, preferring to concentrate on bringing the unemployment rate down. At the beginning of 1978, however, the administration began to show concern with inflation, the rate of increase in the consumer price index having gone from 4.8 percent in 1976 to 6.8 percent in 1977. Consequently, in his 1978 economic report, President Carter called upon the business community and the nation's workers to participate in a voluntary program to decelerate the rate of price and wage increases. No standards were established, but it was hoped that both wage and price increases would be kept below the rate at which they had risen in the previous year. The latter did not happen; by mid-year consumer prices were advancing at double-digit rates. Consequently, in October the administration announced a new program that included explicit wage and price standards. Wages and fringe benefits were to rise no more than 7 percent per year, and business firms were requested to keep their price increases to a rate one and a half percentage points below the annual average rate of increase in their prices during the period 1966–77. Like the Johnson administration guideposts, the program was voluntary, except that the Carter administration sought to use the federal government's purchasing as a means to favor firm's that complied with the program. There is no evidence that this approach was particularly successful. Furthermore, it aroused considerable resentment in the business community.

The Future of Incomes Policies

Do incomes policies have a future? In spite of the less than satisfactory experience to date in this country with incomes policies, it remains doubtful that modern industries can avoid indefinitely facing the fact that inflation has become endemic in the system, heating up once a recovery is under way. If monetary and fiscal policies are to be the primary instruments through which the elusive goal of full employment is sought, then some complementary type of an incomes policy is essential to contain inflationary pressures as the economy approaches a full-employment output.

Two recent approaches to the problem are worthy of mention, although there are no immediate prospects of either being enacted into law. Both come under the rubric of "tax-based" incomes policies—or TIP for short—because they propose using the tax system as a device to restrain wage and price increases. One proposal was developed jointly by Henry C. Wallich, currently a member of the Board of Governors of the Federal Reserve System, and the late Sidney Weintraub, professor of economics at the University of Pennsylvania. The other was developed by the late Arthur M. Okun of the Brookings Institution who was also chairman of President Carter's Council of Economic Advisers.[37]

The two plans are basically similar, except that the Wallich-Weintraub plan operates on a penalty principle whereas the Okun plan operates on the basis of a reward. Both use taxes as the mechanism of control, but both also operate through the price system, thereby avoiding the charge that any direct intervention into the wage and price setting process will impair efficiency and distort the allocation of resources. Both plans claim to be relatively inexpensive to administer because of the way in which they are tied into the tax system.

Keynes's belief that in the long run the prime factor in inflation is the relationship between money wages and "efficiency"—that is, productivity—provides the theoretical jumping-off place for the Wallich-Weintraub approach. In their view, wage settlements in excess of productivity gains plus markup pricing in the economy's oligopolistic core are the sources of inflation. The remedy is to persuade corporate managements to resist wage settlements that exceed some set of noninflationary guidelines. To achieve this objective, Wallich and Weintraub would establish a system whereby the corporate tax rate is automatically increased for any firm whose wage settlements were in excess of the allowable amount. Suppose, for example, that noninflationary wage increases were pegged at 4 percent, but Corporation X concluded a collective agreement with its workers for a 6 percent wage increase. The corporation's tax liability would then be increased automatically by some multiple of the amount by which the wage settlement exceeded the allowable increase. If this multiple were 4, then there would be a surcharge of 8 percent (4 × the 2 percent excess) added to the corporation's normal tax liability. The amount of the multiple would depend upon how severe the government wanted the penalty to be for a wage settlement in excess of the guidelines. Since it is hoped that a TIP approach would lead to settlements within the guidelines, the administrative costs would be small. Neither organized labor nor business management has shown any great enthusiasm for such a plan. This, perhaps, is one of the major drawbacks to the Wallich-Weintraub approach, since the political support of both labor and management will be necessary to get any incomes policy put into effect.

The Okun plan is also based upon the tax system, but rather than

37. Henry C. Wallich and Sidney Weintraub, "A Tax-Based Incomes Policy," *Journal of Economic Issues*, June 1971, pp. 1–19. Arthur M. Okun, "The Great Stagflation Swamp," *Challenge*, November–December, 1977, pp. 6–13.

penalize firms that exceed the noninflationary guidelines for wage settle-ments, it would reward both workers and firms that followed the guide-lines. At the start of the year the government would announce acceptable rates of increase for both money wages and prices. If a firm and its work-ers adhered to these guidelines during the year, the workers would receive a rebate equal to a certain percentage of their wage or salary, and the firm would receive a tax rebate calculated as a percentage of its tax lia-bilities. When Professor Okun first unveiled his scheme in 1977, he sug-gested that for 1978 an appropriate wage increase would be 6 percent and the price increase 4 percent. Workers who participated would get 1.5 percent of their wage or salary as a rebate, up to a maximum of $225, and firms would get a rebate equal to 5 percent of their tax liabilities.[38] These figures would have to be set anew each year, depending on infla-tionary conditions at the time the decision was made and the outlook for the coming year. The Carter administration tried unsuccessfully to develop a version of TIP with its proposal for "real wage insurance." Employees would have received a tax credit if their wages rose no faster than a stipulated standard.

A final comment on the incomes policy approach to inflation control is in order. The arithmetic behind this approach is irrefutable. If money incomes in all forms continue to exceed productivity gains, then, on the average, costs of production—especially labor costs—per unit produced will rise and inflation is inevitable. Consequently, the basic idea of a set of guidelines (or guideposts) that seek, on the average, to keep wage and salary incomes in line with productivity gains is sound. The real rub comes from the fact that it means that the *relative* income position of every group in the economy remains unchanged. If there is satisfaction with the existing distribution of income, then such a policy will work. But if such satisfaction does not exist, it will break down, once groups find that they can begin to exercise whatever economic power they can muster to improve their standing *relative* to the rest of the economy. The fundamental lesson, then, that we should draw from our experience to date with an incomes policy is that no such policy can hope to succeed, no matter how it is designed, unless the income distribution issue is addressed at the same time.

Summary

1. Inflation remains one of the unsolved economic problems of mar-ket capitalism, as no modern industrial nation has been able to achieve both full employment and a low rate of inflation. Over the long term (since 1750), inflation has not been the norm for the American economy, but since World War II the price level has risen almost continuously.

---

38. Okun, op. cit., p. 13.

2. There are different types of inflation, such as gradual, suppressed, and hyper. Inflation is bad because of its arbitrary and uneven impact on different groups in our society, especially those on fixed incomes and with little economic power. Inflation redistributes income and wealth in an unfair manner.

3. Economists are not in agreement on the causes of inflation—which may be many and varied—but they do agree on at least two broad frames of reference for approaching the inflation problem. These approaches are described as the demand-pull hypothesis and the cost-push hypothesis. They provide a framework in which forces responsible for inflation that originate on either the demand or the cost side of the process can be examined.

4. Inflation has roots in microeconomics and must, therefore, be explained partly in terms of what happens at the microeconomic level. There are two factors at work. The first involves the behavior of costs because of the shape of the costs curves typical of the firm. Economists assume that increasing costs are the norm, which means that, as output and employment approach capacity levels in the individual firms, costs will increase. Thus, prices must rise to cover rising costs. The other factor is that the prices firms must pay to get resources, including labor, will rise as output expands. This, too, pushes up prices.

5. The theory of the price level developed by Keynes in *The General Theory* draws directly upon the foregoing analysis. In contrast to the classical analysis, which sees the money supply as the primary determinant of the price level, Keynes in *The General Theory* argued that the price level depends upon (1) the scale of output, which means diminishing returns play a key role, and (2) the remuneration of the factors of production. Thus, Keynes argues for the microeconomic roots of inflation, asserting that the general price level can be explained by the same forces that explain how individual (or relative) prices are determined.

6. The Phillips curve was developed in the 1950s and shows the relationship between the unemployment rate and the rate of increase in money wages (or the rate of increase in the price level). Until simultaneous inflation and unemployment at high rates for both appeared in the 1970s, economists generally thought that the Phillips curve provided guidance for a satisfactory "trade-off" between inflation and unemployment. This notion disappeared in the 1970s, especially in the face of challenges by monetarists to the effect that no such trade-off existed.

7. Out of the Phillips curve analysis and other theoretical developments in the post–World War II period the idea of an incomes policy emerged. Such a policy is directed at keeping the rate of increase in money incomes, especially wage income, in line with productivity gains. The Kennedy-Johnson and the Carter administrations attempted an incomes policy, but without notable success.

15

Managing the Macroeconomy

This chapter has two basic purposes, one essentially theoretical and the other historical. First, we shall draw together and discuss in detail the major policy instruments at the disposal of modern governments, showing how the instruments of policy can be used to cope with fluctuations in output, employment, and the price level. In doing so we shall draw heavily upon the basic Keynesian general equilibrium model (IS-LM) developed in Chapter 10. Second, we shall review and appraise the use and effectiveness of policy actions the United States government has taken during the post–World War II era, the object being to provide the reader with a historical account of success and failure in the overall management of the American economy. Although adherents to the new classical school may argue that *no* policy actions can be successful with respect to the economy's overall and short-term management, this view has not won acceptance outside some academic circles. Every post–World War II administration—from Harry Truman to Ronald Reagan—has come to power believing that it could influence the economy's course, and every administration has tried to do so. Success has, of course, varied, but there is no indication that this attitude will change.

The Principles of Economic Policy

The formation of economic policy is a difficult and subtle art and involves, as Edwin G. Nourse, first chairman of the President's Council of Economic Advisers, has said, choice among conflicting values and judgment as to what is best in a total situation.[1] To be effective, economic policy

1. Edwin G. Nourse, *Economics in the Public Service* (New York: Harcourt, Brace, 1953), p. 18.

must be grounded in sound economic theory. Therefore, we need to understand the policy implications that flow out of the theoretical analysis developed in preceding chapters.

Economic stabilization is a major social goal believed to be within the control of government in modern society. The economic power inherent in the public sector puts government in a position to promote stability, full employment, and maximum production. In the United States, the Employment Act of 1946 gave congressional sanction to the idea that the national government has a responsibility for income and employment levels in the economy. Although neither price stability nor economic growth—nor full employment *per se*—is mentioned in the act, the tacit assumption was often made by economists as well as the federal government that these goals, too, were a part of the intent of the act. Later, the "Full Employment and Balanced Growth Act of 1978" established a 3 percent unemployment rate for workers age 20 and over and a 3 percent inflation rate as goals to be reached by 1983. But lack of any realistic means to attain these goals is a major short-coming of this act. Thus, it remains essentially a statement of pious intent, rather than a basis for effective policy action.

As we have seen, monetary and fiscal measures are the two chief instruments at the disposal of the central government for attainment of economic stabilization. Since, in Keynesian analysis, fluctuations in income and employment are primarily matters of too much or too little spending in relation to existing supply or capacity, stabilization policy involves the exercise of influence on the economy's overall expenditure level. Both monetary and fiscal policy measures must therefore be evaluated in terms of their impact on expenditure levels, which is to say in terms of their impact upon aggregate demand. To put the matter somewhat differently, the goal of policy is full employment with stable prices, a goal which governments strive to reach by pulling on the levers marked "monetary" or "fiscal" policy. Difficulty in the mid-1960s in getting to full employment without pushing the price level up at too rapid a pace gave rise to a third type of policy, generally known as *incomes policy,* discussed in the previous chapter.

Monetary Policy and Its Application

As we have seen, (Chapter 10), monetary policy involves changing the money supply with the expectation that such changes will influence total spending and thus output, employment, and the price level. The central bank, which in the United States means the Federal Reserve System, is the body responsible for carrying out monetary policy. From a strictly Keynesian viewpoint, monetary policy works indirectly through the impact of money on the rates of interest, whereas the monetarists hold that changes in money affect aggregate demand directly. These points have been discussed previously. There are, however, other matters to consider.

To begin, monetary policy operates through two broad sets of controls. First, there are general or indirect controls, which include changes in the reserve requirement of the commercial banks, changes in the rediscount rate, and open market operations by the central bank—that is, the Federal Reserve System. Second, there are selective or direct controls aimed at specific types of credit, such as installment credit, mortgage credit, or credit extended for the financing of stock market transactions. Indirect controls are used to alter the overall volume of credit available to the economy; they do not seek to influence the allocation of credit (that is, money funds) among alternative uses. As discussed in Chapter 9, the primary instruments for the exercise of indirect monetary controls are open market operations, changes in the discount rate, and control over reserve requirements. The locus for these powers is the Board of Governors of the Federal Reserve System. General (or indirect) credit controls have been by far the most important policy instrument used by the Federal Reserve System. Thus, any general discussion of monetary policy must be directed primarily toward the use and effectiveness of these controls.

The foregoing is but a part of the story. In order to carry out monetary policy, the monetary authority (the Federal Reserve System in the United States) must depend upon some economic variable as a policy guide, as an *indicator* which will signal the necessity for a policy change. Such a policy guide or indicator ought to tell the monetary authority something of what is going on in the economy currently. But it ought to do more than that. It should be a variable that has an impact upon the goals of policy (i.e., full employment or price stability) and it should be one that changes in response to changes in policy. In practice, two such guides have been important in recent years. These are the money supply itself (or a variable closely related to the money supply, such as the volume of commercial bank reserves), or the general state of credit conditions, often represented by one or more rates of interest. To put the matter as succinctly as possible, the question is: Should the Federal Reserve as the custodian of monetary policy pay the most attention to the money supply (however defined) or interest rates as a guide to its policy decisions? The answer is neither obvious nor simple. Figure 15–1 shows the linkages involved in this question.

If either the money supply or interest rates are to be used as guides to monetary policy, two things are essential. First, changes in either should lead to changes in total spending (and hence output, employment, and the price level) and, second, they (money and interest rates) should be subject to control by the Federal Reserve System. The difficulty is that there is no agreement among monetary specialists—as well as economists in general—on either of these points. Take the matter of Federal Reserve control over either the money supply or interest rates. Proponents in favor of using the money supply as the basic policy guide (usually monetarists) argue that in short term the Federal Reserve does not have good control over interest rates, the primary reason being that credit markets

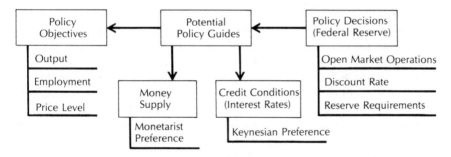

Figure 15–1. Policy Guides and Monetary Policy

are quite sensitive to other factors besides actions taken by the Federal Reserve (open market operations, for example). On the other hand, advocates of the interest rate as a policy guide (generally Keynesians) say essentially the same thing about the money supply, namely, that the money supply is not under control of the Federal Reserve System to the degree required to make it a good policy indicator. One reason for this is the existence of *near monies* (Chapter 9, p. 284).

As a practical matter, the choice of a policy guide really comes down to the question of how the transmission mechanism works, which is, in effect, a question of which monetary theory is valid—contemporary monetarism or Keynesianism. Since monetarists believe that there is a close, causal link between the money supply and the general level of economic activity, their preference is for using money as the primary policy indicator. As the matter of fact, Friedman and other monetarists fear that use of interest rates as an indicator may actually be destabilizing rather than stabilizing. For example, if interest rates are rising because of high employment and rapid economic expansion, any attempt by the Federal Reserve System to stabilize or bring interest rates down by *adding* to the money supply would be self-defeating. More money, in their view, would fuel more spending, which would cause interest rates to go up even faster. Nonmonetarists, on the other hand, adopt what is essentially a Keynesian position, namely, that the link between money and the general level of economic activity is through the interest rate (see discussion in Chapter 11 on the Keynesian view of the channels of monetary policy, pp. 374–75). Thus, the preference of Keynesians is for using interest rates as a policy guide. Prior to the late 1970s the Federal Reserve System relied almost exclusively on credit conditions (interest rates) as a policy indicator. In October of 1979, however, the Federal Reserve announced a major policy switch in its management of monetary policy. Henceforth, the agency said it would try to achieve better control of the money supply by shifting the emphasis in its day-to-day operations from controlling credit conditions through the federal funds rate (the rate charged for intrabank short-term loans, usually for one day) to the supply of bank reserves. The move was hailed generally by monetarists as an appropriate shift in Federal Reserve policy toward their position.

Basically the Federal Reserve continued to focus on the money supply until mid-1982 when, in response to pressures to bring interest rates down, the money supply was allowed to increase at a relatively rapid pace. The policy of controlling the money supply was not wholly successful, as the annual rate of growth has been quite erratic most of the time. This is shown in Figure 15–2. In February 1983 the chairman of the Federal Reserve System, Paul A. Volcker, told the Senate Banking Committee that rather than be tied specifically to the money supply as its target for policy-making, the Federal Reserve would use real GNP growth as the determinant of whether or not money was too tight or too loose. As a "Commentary" in *Business Week* phrased it, "The Fed is, in a sense, getting back to basics. The Fed has long been mandated to fix its gaze on overall economic performance."[2] Thus ended the experiment undertaken by the Federal Reserve in the post–World War II period that came closest to the monetarist idea of concentrating wholly on the growth of the money supply as a means of controlling the economy's overall, short-term performance.

There are other concerns in the application of monetary policy. One of these is the matter of lags, which involves the length of time between a change in policy and its effect upon the economy. The problem is that there is no exact statistical information on the length of such lags—what information we do have suggests, further, that they may be highly variable, ranging, perhaps, from a few months to nearly two years. The lack of precise information on the length of policy lags is another reason why monetarists such as Friedman prefer that the monetary authority adhere to a fixed rule for expansion of the money supply. Two basic types of lags are important, *inside* lags and *outside* lags. The former refers to the length of time which passes between the need for action and the actual taking of action by the Federal Reserve System. The latter pertains to the time involved between the taking of action by the Federal Reserve

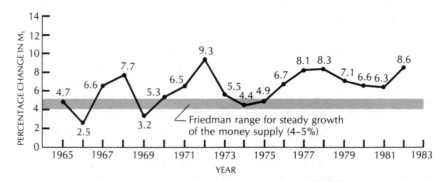

FIGURE 15–2.   Annual Percentage Rate of Change in the Money Supply (M1): 1965–82

2. G. David Wallace, "Commentary," *Business Week,* February 26, 1983.

and the effect of that action on the goals of policy, namely, the employment or price levels.

Another problem affecting monetary policy is that its ultimate impact
may be both uneven and unfair. A large corporation often has adequate
financial reserves, and thus is not forced to go into the money market to
get funds for expansion. On the other hand, the small firm has fewer
internal financing resources and must depend upon bank credit for some
of its operations. Consequently, in a period of tight money, the pressure
of monetary policy may be felt most acutely by small businesses, leaving
large corporations relatively unaffected by central bank policies. Since
the spending decisions of large corporations generally have more impact
on the economy than those of small businesses, some of the effectiveness
of monetary policy may be lost. Industrial concentration—the tendency
for industries to be dominated by a handful of large firms—may also be
furthered under these circumstances.

Economists recognize that different investment expenditures differ
significantly in their sensitivity to a change in the rate of interest. For
example, expenditures for buildings, including residential housing, are
much more sensitive to a change in the rate of interest than are business
expenditures for inventories, or even new equipment. Table 15–1 shows
mortgage interest rates and new (private) housing starts for the 18-year
period 1965 through 1982. Note the sharp downturn in new housing

TABLE 15–1.   Interest Rates and New Housing: 1965–82

Year	Mortage Rates (in percent)	Housing Starts (in thousands of units)
1965	5.81	1,473
1966	6.25 ↑	1,165 ↓
1967	6.46	1,292
1968	6.97	1,508
1969	7.81 ↑	1,467 ↓
1970	8.45	1,433
1971	7.74	2,052
1972	7.60	2,357
1973	7.95 ↑	2,045 ↓
1974	8.92 ↑	1,338 ↓
1975	9.00 ↑	1,160 ↓
1976	9.00	1,538
1977	9.02	1,987
1978	9.56	2,020
1979	10.78 ↑	1,745 ↓
1980	12.66 ↑	1,292 ↓
1981	14.70 ↑	1,084 ↓
1982	15.14 ↑	1,061 ↓

SOURCE: *Economic Report of the President,* 1983.

construction in the years in which money "tightened"—1966, 1969, 1973–75, 1979, 1980, and 1981. Mortgage rates continued to rise in 1982, even though monetary conditions eased somewhat. This reflects both lags and the fact that the correlation between money supply growth and interest rates is not perfect. Thus, a stringent monetary policy that leads to a sharp rise in the rate of interest affects investment spending unevenly. Whether such uneven effects are desirable from the standpoint of a social policy is a matter of key importance.

Monetary policy has also been criticized because, if it is applied with sufficient vigor in a period of inflation to bring about a contraction in investment spending, it will push the economy into a recession. This has been the experience in every recession since 1970. Table 15–2 gives, for the period 1968–82, the rate of change in the money supply (M1) and the rate of change in real gross domestic investment. In each year in which the rate of growth in the money supply slowed, real investment fell in the following year. The volatility of investment spending as well as its sensitivity to changes in monetary growth are reflected in these data. The most recent recession began in mid-1982, but for the year as a whole *real* gross national product did not fall.

On the other hand, monetary policy cannot be relied upon to bring the economy out of a serious depression, because even a drastic change in the interest rate is not enough of an incentive to stimulate investment spending when aggregate demand is at a low level. Proponents of monetary policy are likely to point in reply to the indirect character of mon-

TABLE 15–2. The Money Supply and Real Investment: 1968–82

Year	Rate of Change in the Money Supply (M1)	Rate of Change in Real Gross Investment*
1968	7.7%	4.3$
1969	3.2	6.0
1970 (R)	5.3	− 7.5
1971	6.5	9.7
1972	9.3	12.1
1973	5.5	11.5
1974 (R)	4.4	−10.1
1975 (R)	4.9	−20.8
1976	6.7	19.2
1977	8.1	15.8
1978	8.3	7.6
1979	7.1	1.3
1980 (R)	6.6	−12.6
1981	6.2	5.5
1982 (R)	8.5	− 8.4

SOURCE: *Economic Report of the President,* 1983.
*In 1972 prices.
Note: (R) = recession year.

etary policy as one of its chief virtues because the government is not involved directly in the regulation of economic activity. Monetary policy can be said to possess the virtues of speed and flexibility since normally it is administered by central banks and thus does not require legislative action.

To sum up, economists are by no means in agreement with respect to either the effectiveness or the desirability of monetary policy. From roughly the end of World War II to the mid-1960s a clear majority of economists held that fiscal policy was the more powerful, the more effective instrument for the overall control of economic activity. No longer is this the case, primarily because of the impact that the monetarist "Counter-revolution" has had on economic thinking. But it would not be accurate, either, to suggest that a majority of economists now regard monetary policy as a more effective control instrument. Rather, modern macro-economic theory sees *both* fiscal and monetary policies as having important roles to play in any stabilization program. They should not be regarded as rivals, but complementary approaches to the problem of economic stabilization. No doubt an even more accurate view is that a growing number of economists believe that, as the economy is presently structured, neither monetary nor fiscal instruments seem well suited for the control of inflation.

Fiscal Policy and Its Application

Fiscal policy, as we have seen, involves *deliberate* changes in the taxes government collects and the money it spends as a means to influence the economy. Taxes and spending are the means and the government's budget is the instrument through which fiscal policy is carried out. In the definition the word deliberate must be stressed. Governments collect taxes and spend money for a variety of purposes, ranging from building highways to providing for the common defense. Only when they deliberately change their spending or taxes to try and affect the economy's performance is it correct to speak of fiscal policy. In the United States, the locus of fiscal policy is in the administration in power (the president) and the Congress. Usually, the president initiates fiscal policy—a tax or spending change—but nothing can happen until such changes are approved by the Congress.

Prior to the 1960s two widely different viewpoints held sway among professional economists as to the proper role and scope for fiscal policy. At one extreme was the concept of *functional finance*, which asserted that the primary consideration of the government in all its operations should be the effects of its actions on income and employment levels.[3] Advocates of functional finance argue, for example, that government should raise (or lower) taxes not because it needs more (or less) money, but

---

3. The late Abba P. Lerner was the chief proponent of this idea. See his *The Economics of Control* (New York: Macmillan, 1949), pp. 302 ff.

because it wants to decrease (or increase) consumption spending. Proposals embodied in the notion of functional finance rest upon the assumption that economic stabilization is the one really important function of the modern government, a point of view that will be disputed by those who are keenly interested in the problem of an adequate supply of social goods and services in an expanding and affluent society. We may note parenthetically that here is a point of potential conflict and contradiction, because a growing need and demand for social goods may make it difficult if not impossible at times to adjust the tax and expenditure budgets of the public sector to the requirements of stabilization policy.

At the other extreme were proposals that suggested that the budget of the federal government ought to be constructed so that taxes and expenditures would be automatically in balance at an income level somewhat below that of full employment. If this were done, and if, further, tax rates and government expenditures remained constant, then a budgetary surplus would automatically be generated as the economy approached the full-employment level. But if income fell below the level at which taxes and expenditures were in balance, an automatic deficit would ensue.[4] A budgetary policy that leads to a surplus in prosperity and a deficit in recession or depression is generally recognized as countercyclical because the surplus draws funds out of the current income stream and the deficit adds funds to the income flow. Such a policy relies entirely upon the built-in characteristics of the tax structure that cause taxes automatically to rise in periods of income expansion and to fall in periods of income contraction. It allows no room for discretionary fiscal action by either the executive or legislative branch of the government. The similarity of this sort of arrangement to Professor Friedman's desire for a fixed rate of growth in the money supply should be recognized. What both approaches have in common is a distaste for discretionary action and a faith that somehow the economy can be made to perform automatically if only the proper, self-regulating instrument can be discovered. The real-world economy is unlike this, though. It is untidy, irregular, and requires some form of public intervention if it is to function well. This is the fundamental viewpoint of Keynes.

If a poll had been taken among economists in the 1940s and 1950s the view of a majority on the proper scope of fiscal policy probably would have been bound to lie midway between the extremes of functional finance and the notion of an automatic countercyclical budget. A point, though, upon which there would have been near unanimity of opinion is that there is no sound economic reason why the budget of the national government should be balanced on an annual basis. It is only desirable, according to the rules of modern fiscal policy, that deficits incurred dur-

4. This idea is generally credited to the Committee on Economic Development. For further details see the studies issued by the CED: *Taxes and the Budget,* November 1947, and *Monetary and Fiscal Policy for Greater Economic Stability,* December 1948.

ing a depression or recession be offset by surpluses acquired in subsequent periods of prosperity. The economy's track record on this point is not good. In twenty-five of the last thirty-four years (1949–82) the federal government has had a deficit, even though many of these years were marked by prosperity. Even so there is no general consensus among economists on the proper mix of automatic stabilizers and discretionary action by appropriate authorities.

Beginning in the 1960s, though, the focus of fiscal policy shifted away from the idea of minimizing the ups and downs of cyclical fluctuations in both income and employment. Largely because of the persuasive influence exerted by Professor Walter Heller of the University of Minnesota, who served as chairman of the Council of Economic Advisers in the Kennedy administration, the primary emphasis became one of using discretionary fiscal policy, especially changes in individual and corporate tax rates, as a means of keeping the economy growing at its full potential. Heller described this shift as follows:

> As part of the reshaping of stabilization policy, then, our fiscal policy targets have been recast in terms of "full" or "high" employment levels of output, specifically the level of GNP associated with a 4-percent rate of unemployment. *So the target is no longer budget balance every year or over the cycle* [italics added], but balance . . . at full employment. And in modern stabilization policy . . . even this target does not remain fixed.[5]

The budget of the federal government is the primary instrument for the implementation of fiscal policy. The mechanics of this are relatively simple. If the federal government at full employment spends more for goods and services, G_f, than it receives in net taxes, T_f, then it will be operating at a deficit, which is to say that it will be putting more into the income stream via its expenditures than it is pulling out through net taxes.[6] Consequently, the overall effect of the federal budget will be expansionary. On the other hand, a surplus would have a contractive economic effect, since it entails an excess of net taxes, T_f, over spending for goods and services, G_f, which in turn means that the federal government is pulling more out of the income flow than it is putting in. The overall expansionary or contractive effect of the federal budget depends, of course, on the absence of offsetting changes in the private sector, such as a fall in private investment when a federal deficit emerges.

The way of looking at the federal budget which Heller described above has come to be known as the *full-employment budget*. It offers a different and presumably more meaningful way of looking at the economic effects of a surplus or deficit in the federal budget. It is, in other words, a better

5. Walter W. Heller, *New Dimensions of Political Economy* (New York: Norton, 1967), p. 66. What Heller meant by the full-employment target not being fixed was that the economy would grow over time, since a growing labor force and a rising productivity for the labor force would increase continuously the output level associated with a 4 percent unemployment rate.

6. The subscript f is used to denote spending and taxes at the federal level.

guide to the real economic impact of the federal government's fiscal behavior than the state of balance of the budget in any given year. Essentially, the full-employment budget attempts to estimate the federal deficit or surplus that would emerge if the economy were operating at the full-employment level, a procedure that not only involves estimating the economy's full-employment output potential (see Chapter 3), but the federal tax revenue this level of output will generate, as well as the amount of expenditures that will be forthcoming. Table 15–3 shows the actual and estimated full-employment surplus and deficit for 1970–80. The Carter administration was the last administration to mention and make use of the full- or high-employment budget in its annual *Economic Report*. There is no mention of this concept in the first *Economic Report* (1982) of the Reagan administration. In view of this administration's strong opposition to the entire idea of continuous economic management through fiscal and monetary policy, this omission is not surprising.

TABLE 15–3.   Actual and Full-Employment Federal Government Receipts and Expenditures: 1970–80 (billions of current dollars)

Calendar Year	Receipts	Expenditures	Surplus or Deficit (−)	
			Amount	Change
Actual				
1970 (R)	192.1	204.2	− 12.1	− 20.6
1971	198.6	220.6	− 22.0	− 9.9
1972	227.5	244.7	− 17.3	4.7
1973	258.6	264.2	− 5.6	10.6
1974 (R)	287.8	299.3	− 11.5	− 4.8
1975 (R)	287.3	356.6	− 69.3	− 59.7
1976	331.8	384.8	− 53.1	12.9
1977	375.1	421.5	− 46.4	6.7
1978	431.5	460.7	− 29.2	17.2
1979	494.4	509.2	− 14.8	14.4
1980 (R)	538.9	601.2	− 62.3	− 97.5
Full- or High-Employment Budget				
1970 (R)	201.0	203.6	− 2.6	6.3
1971	210.0	219.1	− 9.2	− 6.6
1972	222.1	243.6	− 21.5	− 12.3
1973	252.7	264.0	11.3	32.8
1974 (R)	296.9	297.6	0.7	10.6
1975 (R)	315.8	344.9	− 29.1	− 28.4
1976	354.7	374.8	− 20.1	9.0
1977	390.7	413.8	− 23.0	− 2.9
1978	441.1	456.8	− 15.7	7.3
1979	504.2	506.5	− 2.2	13.5
1980 (R)	573.2	591.6	− 18.3	− 16.1

SOURCE: *Economic Report of the President,* 1977, 1981.
Note: Detail may not add to totals because of rounding. (R) = recession year.

The basic rationale for this budget concept is that the true inflationary or deflationary potential of the federal budget is apparent only when the economy is at full employment. The reasoning behind this is quite simple. If the economy is at full employment, and if, too, there is a deficit $(G_f > T_f)$, then the government's fiscal activities (tax and expenditure policies) are clearly inflationary. The reverse is, of course, the case if there is a surplus $(T_f > G_f)$. On the other hand, the situation is not clearcut with respect to the real effects of either a current surplus or deficit when the economy is not at full employment. To illustrate, suppose in the current year the federal government runs a deficit. But if this deficit happened because of a recession and the resulting falloff in taxes, it would mean that the deficit was an induced consequence of changing economic conditions rather than a force deliberately designed to change economic conditions. The figures in Table 15–3 for 1974 illustrate clearly these two situations. In this year the actual budget was in deficit by $11.5 billion. This was the year in which the economy was sliding downhill into a recession, and, as expected, the deficit increased over the previous year. But the full- or high-employment budget for 1974 shows a slight surplus ($0.7 billion), which means that the federal budget was basically restrictive. More important in the analysis is the swing from one year to the next in the magnitude of the full (or high)-employment budget surplus or deficit. Note that in 1972 the full-employment budget showed a deficit of $21.5 billion, an expansionary situation. By 1973, this full-employment deficit had been replaced by a full-employment surplus of $11.3 billion. The swing from a deficit to a surplus was $32.8 billion, which indicates that between 1972 and 1973 the budget had gone from an expansionary to a restrictive position. Thus, the budget was clearly a major factor in bringing on the 1974–75 recession. The figures in the column labeled "Change" are helpful in interpreting what happened to the budget in any one year, particularly for the full (or high)-employment budget. Positive values show that the budget became more restrictive, whereas negative figures show the opposite, namely, that the budget was expansionary. Even though there are serious limitations inherent in the concept of a full-employment budget—especially because of difficulties involved in estimating and measurement—many economists believe it is a much better tool for indicating the probable impact of discretionary fiscal policy than a simple calculation of the current surplus or deficit of the federal sector.

Toward New Budgetary Policies

Prospects for the efficient administration of fiscal policy improved when the Congress passed the Congressional Budget and Impoundment Control Act of 1974, a historic piece of legislation which is designed to help the Congress—in contrast to the administration—develop an overall budget policy. For the first time in our history, the Congress will be required to look at the federal budget in total, with respect to both expenditures and receipts. Heretofore, both spending proposals and appropriation measures were considered separately, not only for the spending and taxing totals, but for their component parts. It was a piecemeal process that never permitted the Congress to view the budget in its taxing and spending aspects as an entity in relation to its impact on the economy. That has now changed. The 1974 Budget Act provides, first, that the entire Congress adopt in May of each year spending and revenue targets. This is done by a concurrent resolution. Later in September, just prior to the beginning of the new fiscal year on October 1, a second concurrent resolution is adopted which either affirms or revises these targets. This second resolution becomes binding. The reform act also established committees on the budget in both houses of the Congress, committees which have the responsibility for developing a comprehensive budget policy each year. To help in doing this, the 1974 legislation also established the Congressional Budget Office, a body roughly designed to serve the Congress in the same way that the Council of Economic Advisers serves the president.

Even if fiscal policy is a powerful instrument for economic stabilization it, like monetary policy, is subject to difficulties and limitations. First fiscal policy measures which involve changes in public expenditures may conflict with the long-term character of many governmental expenditure programs. It is not possible continually to adjust expenditures for basic social goods and services to meet the shifting exigencies of economic stabilization. Second, the political process through which changes in expenditures and taxes are effected is so long, drawn out, and fraught with so many uncertainties that it is nearly impossible in a democratic society to obtain the necessary speed and flexibility that fiscal policy requires if it is to be successful as an instrument for economic stabilization. This is probably true in spite of the passage of the Budget Reform Act in 1974. This act will undoubtedly give the Congress a better understanding of the economic consequence of the budget, but it probably won't speed up the political progress significantly. The exception to this view, perhaps, is tax reduction, as the Congress has shown it can act with a fair amount of speed when tax cuts are involved. It took about two months for the Congress to pass the Ford administration's tax reduction proposals in 1975, but a somewhat longer period before it acted on the Carter administration requests in 1977. The Reagan tax cut package of 1981 took longer, as the act did not become law until August 1981. The longer period was due to the fact that it represented the largest and most controversial tax reduction act in our history. Our limited experience to date suggests two to three months appears to be the norm for Congressional action involving a tax reduction. This should be contrasted to the possibility that the Federal Reserve can literally act within a week if necessary. To some extent discussion of future tax cuts may be academic because the Reagan administration's 1981 actions have put the federal government in a position of having large—and possibly growing—deficits far into the forseeable future.

To give fiscal policy the same speed and flexibility characteristic of monetary policy, it has been suggested that the president be given limited authority to vary tax rates within limits laid down by the Congress, and subject, as well, to a congressional veto.[7] Both the Kennedy and Johnson administrations made such a recommendation. In his last budget message, President Johnson proposed that the president have the authority to vary rates on personal and corporate income taxes (up or down) by 5 percent. To date the Congress has resisted strongly the idea of giving the president authority to vary tax rates within guidelines laid down by the legislative body. Since Watergate the surge of hostility toward any more delegation of legislative power to the president makes the possibility of an arrangement of this type even more remote.

Finally, it is averred that one concept of modern fiscal policy, the cyclically balanced budget at the national level, simply won't work politically. There is no serious objection to a governmental deficit in a recession or depression, because nearly everyone will benefit from the stimulus this brings to the economy. But opposition to the kind of tax policy necessary to generate a surplus may be so strong that the required budgetary surplus fails to appear in period of prosperity.[8] As already pointed out, deficits appear to be the norm, no matter what the state of the economy.

The Application of Fiscal and Monetary Policies

It is now appropriate that we turn to a deeper analysis of the workings of fiscal and monetary policies. For this purpose we shall use the Keynesian general equilibrium model as our primary expository device. In a brief introduction to this topic in Chapter 9, it was pointed out that the workings of either fiscal or monetary policy or both in combination can be demonstrated by shifts in either the *IS* or *LM* curve. We shall continue in this vein. Initially we shall disregard changes in the general price level, as our first objective is to concentrate on the effects of monetary and fiscal policy actions on real output (and employment). After we have

7. The president is not without some power to act without congressional approval. He can in a small way vary the timing for expenditures within the budget limits set by the Congress. This works in either direction, which is to say he can speed up or slow down spending. President Nixon attempted to "impound" funds already appropriated by the Congress, his object being to cut back on spending. This involved him in an ongoing battle with the Congress over its constitutional right to control the "purse strings," and was a factor that led to the passage of the 1974 Congressional Budget Act.

8. This difficulty is dramatically illustrated by the obvious reluctance of the Johnson administration to request a tax increase at any time during 1966, even though the rising level of military expenditures for the war in Vietnam put the economy under strong inflationary pressures. The Nixon administration was equally unwilling to raise taxes to combat inflation.

done this, we can introduce price level changes into the analysis and see how the impact of various policies is affected.

In *The General Theory* there is a statement by Keynes that most appropriately describes the procedure we shall be following. In economic analysis we have to consider various relationships in isolation from one another and then, after we understand them, bring other relationships into the picture. In doing this, Keynes said:

> The object of our analysis is, not to provide a machine, or method of blind manipulation, which will furnish an infallible answer, *but to provide ourselves with an organized and orderly method of thinking out particular problems;* and after we have reached a provisional conclusion by isolating the complicating factors one by one, we then have to go back on ourselves and allow, as well as we can, for the probable interaction of the factors amongst themselves. *This is the nature of economic thinking.*[9]

Theoretical Limits to Fiscal and Monetary Policies

As a backdrop to our subsequent discussion of the practical workings of both fiscal and monetary policy measures, an explanation of the theoretical limits to the effectiveness of either policy approach is in order. In reality, it is unlikely that the economy will get into a situation in which these theoretical limits are actually present; yet we may approach them, and thus some knowledge of them is important for understanding the circumstances under which one policy approach may be more effective than the other.

In the post–World War II literature of macroeconomics these possible limits to the effectiveness of either fiscal or monetary policy have come to be known as the Keynesian range (or case) and the classical range (or case). The Keynesian general equilibrium model offers an ideal vehicle for dramatizing these two alternatives. Figure 15–3 illustrates these extremes of viewpoint. In the figure, IS_1 intersects the LM curve in the range in which the latter is perfectly elastic with respect to the rate of interest (the Keynesian range), and IS_2 intersects the LM curve in the range in which this curve becomes perfectly inelastic with respect to the rate of interest (the classical range).

If the IS curve intersects the LM schedule in the range in which the latter is perfectly elastic with respect to the rate of interest, certain significant policy implications follow. Such a situation might arise because the economy is in a deep depression, with both income and the rate of interest declining to relatively low levels. In this situation monetary policy involving an increase in the money supply will be completely ineffective. An increase in the money supply shifts the LM curve to the right, and this will, *ceteris paribus*, tend to raise the income level, but only if the

---

9. John Maynard Keynes, *The General Theory of Employment, Interest, and Money* (New York: Harcourt, Brace & World, First Harbinger ed., 1964), p. 297 (italics added).

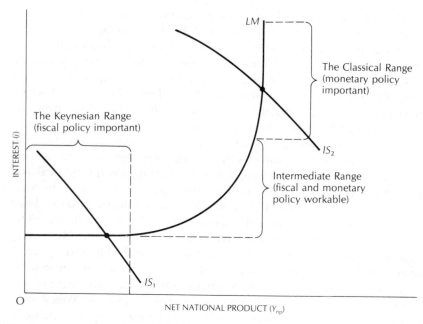

FIGURE 15–3.   Theoretical Limits to Fiscal and Monetary Policies

rate of interest lies above the critical level at which the LM schedule is perfectly elastic. The point of intersection of IS_1 and the LM curve typifies a situation in which the demand for liquidity is so great that any increase in the money supply simply is added to existing idle balances. The increase, in other words, drops into the *liquidity trap;* consequently no change in either the rate of interest, investment expenditure, or the income level will ensue. Under these circumstances it might be said that "money doesn't matter." A rise in the income level must wait upon a higher position of the IS curve, which would require an upward shift in the aggregate demand function. The obvious implication of this analysis is that fiscal rather than monetary policy measures are needed.

A situation quite the opposite of the one just described prevails if the IS curve intersects the LM curve at a point at which the latter is perfectly inelastic with respect to the rate of interest. This is shown in Figure 15–3 by the intersection of IS_2 and the LM schedule in the inelastic range of the latter. This is a classic case of a situation in which the only effective means to increase income is through monetary policy. Hence, we might say that "only money matters." If the money supply is increased, the interest rate will fall, and the income level will rise as investment expenditure responds to a lower rate of interest. If the intersection of the IS and LM curves in the range in which the latter is perfectly interest inelastic implies the desirability of monetary policy, it is equally true that intersection in this range implies the complete unworkability of fiscal policy. Fiscal policy measures that induce an upward shift in the aggregate demand function without any corresponding change in the money supply are bound to be self-defeating. The only consequence of fiscal action is an increase in the rate of interest. An upward shift in the aggregate demand function, assuming no change in the money supply, merely drives interest rates higher because of the rising transactions demand induced by the original shift in the aggregate demand function. The net result ultimately is no change in the income level, but equilibrium of saving and investment at a higher rate of interest.

As a practical matter it is the area that lies between the extreme Keynesian and classical positions that is important for policy in the real world. In terms of the diagram, this is the area in which *both* fiscal and monetary policy are workable in the sense that they can affect the level of real output—net national product (Y_{np}) in the diagram. The closer the economy lies to the classical position the greater is the relative effectiveness of monetary policy, whereas the closer it is to the Keynesian range, fiscal policy becomes relatively more effective. When we speak of the economy being close to either of these extremes it is not meant literally. We don't have any machines that can tell us the exact state of our economic health or where we stand at any particular time. Policy-makers, in the final analysis, exercise their own judgment on these matters, deciding the proper mix of fiscal and monetary actions to reach desired ends. As stated at the beginning of this chapter, the formulation of economic policy is a difficult and subtle art, involving choice among conflicting values and judgment as to what is best in a total situation. The reader should not forget that our discussion and analysis pertain to what takes place within the confines of a graphic model of the economy, and thus the conclusions offered with respect to the effectiveness of both monetary and fiscal policies should not be thought of as providing definitive answers to the complex problems of policy that exist in the real economic world. At best they represent insights into the workings of the economy and suggest only the broadest sort of guidelines to actual policy formulation.

Fiscal and Monetary Policies Compared

Let us now compare the effectiveness of the fiscal and monetary approaches to economic stabilization. Since fiscal policy involves changes in government spending or taxes, its impact is upon the basic components of aggregate demand—government spending for goods and services, consumption spending, and investment spending. In the framework of the Keynesian general equilibrium model, the effect of fiscal policy is shown by shifts in the *IS* curve. Monetary policy centers on increases or decreases in the money supply; consequently it works through changes in the *LM* curve, again within the context of the Keynesian general equilibrium model. All this is not new, but it is of such fundamental importance that it bears repeating. In making these comparisons we shall, initially, assume *pure* fiscal and monetary policies. A *pure fiscal action* changes the spending stream without directly affecting the money supply curve, whereas a *pure monetary action* changes the money supply curve without directly affecting the spending stream. If fiscal and monetary policies are *pure* in this sense, then either the *IS* or *LM* curve can shift without affecting the position of the other curve. The curves become independent of one another, in other words. Later we shall drop the *pure* assumption. Resorting to such an assumption is another example of what Keynes meant when he said that after reaching a "provisional conclusion by isolating the complicating factors one by one, we have to go back on ourselves and allow . . . for the probable interaction of the factors amongst themselves."

Figure 15–4 shows graphically the basic differences between fiscal and monetary policies, assuming that the objective is to raise real national income. Part A of the diagram illustrates the *pure fiscal policy* case and Part B the *pure monetary policy* case. We shall examine each of these in turn.

Initially the economy is at Y_1, a level of income determined by the intersection of IS_1 and the *LM* curve. Assume now that we have a shift to the right (upward) in the *IS* curve, the reason being either an increase in government expenditures or a cut in taxes. The extent to which the *IS* curve shifts depends upon the value of the Keynesian multiplier and the amount by which the aggregate demand schedule changes because of either the increase in government expenditures or the cut in taxes. As analyzed in Chapter 7 (p. 223), a tax cut has a smaller initial impact upon aggregate demand than an increase in government expenditures, the reason being that it (the tax cut) affects aggregate demand indirectly. In any event, the new equilibrium income level will be determined by

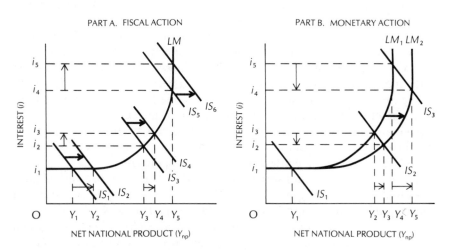

FIGURE 15–4. Fiscal and Monetary Policies Compared

the intersection of IS_2 and the *LM* curve. This shift takes place in the Keynesian range of the model, which means that the rate of interest doesn't rise. If the economy is in a liquidity trap situation, potential spenders—governments, business firms, and even consumers—presumably have idle balances that they can activate to sustain higher levels of spending. For a while, then, more borrowing would not be necessary to permit output to expand. Under these circumstances the economy will experience the full multiplier effect from either an increase in government spending or a cut in taxes. The closest our society has actually come to this situation was in the depths of the Great Depression, in 1932 and 1933.

Much more normal is the situation depicted by the intersection of IS_3 and the *LM* curve, where income is at the level Y_3, a level presumably less than full employment. The rightward shift of the *IS* curve is the same in magnitude as in the prior instance, but the impact on the income level will be less (the difference between Y_4 and Y_3 is smaller than the difference between Y_2 and Y_1). The reason for this is that some of the increased government spending (or added private spending induced by a tax cut) will be offset by the rise in interest rates from i_2 to i_3. Some spending (private) has been "crowded out" by the fiscal stimulus, a development which means that the overall impact is less than it was in the prior instance when the interest rate was unaffected by increased spending. As pointed out in Chapter 7, "crowding out" is associated with the financing of a government deficit. In the example being considered, the rise in interest rates could result from the sale by the government of new securities to the public—that is, government borrowing—an act which would depress existing security prices (bonds), thereby forcing up the rate of interest. This process may be viewed as involving either an addition by government to the supply of bonds or an offer of higher rates of interest to persuade some wealth-holders to switch from holding money to holding bonds. In either case the result is the same—higher interest rates and some offsetting declines in private investment (and consumption) spending. In a purely Keynesian perspective all that needs to happen is for interest rates to rise and pull some money out of inactive balances into active circulation. But more is involved because wealth-holders have to be persuaded to hold their wealth in some form other than money. This is why lending and borrowing must come into the picture. The "crowding out" that occurs in this example is only partial, as the stimulus to output resulting from more government spending (or a tax cut) is not wholly offset by induced declines in private spending.

A completely different situation exists when the economy's initial position is shown by the intersection of IS_5 and the *LM* curve. At this point this equilibrium income level is Y_5. Once again the *IS* curve shifts in response to fiscal actions, a cut in taxes or an increase in government spending for goods and service. But the output level does not change. In terms of the diagram the increase in the rate of interest is great enough to cause a fall in private investment (and consumption) spending which just offsets the effects of the fiscal stimulus. Note carefully that this analysis does not imply that Y_5 is a full-employment output. That is to say, it is not a ceiling on real output which confronts the economy, but offsetting declines in private spending induced by higher interest rates—declines which wholly nullify the effects of the fiscal actions. Why does it happen this way? Since these changes are taking place within the vertical range of the LM curve, it means that there are no idle balances out of which the increased spending can be financed. Hence, the only way in which the government can get funds through borrowing is to push interest rates high enough so that the return wealth-holders can get from government bonds is greater than they can get from private investment projects. In this way investment spending will be cut back ultimately by an amount equal to the increase in government spending (or the private spending induced by a tax cut). Under the circumstances just described, "crowding out" is complete. We have a "pure" classical case, one in which fiscal policy has become totally ineffective. What will happen, however, is a change in the composition of output; the application of fiscal measures under these circumstances means there will be more public spending and less private spending, but the overall output level will be unchanged.

Let us now turn to the monetary side of the question as illustrated by Part B in Figure 15–4. We shall start again with the intersection of IS_1 and LM_1, which gives us a low-level equilibrium income level, Y_1. Monetary policy works by changing the money supply, which in the framework of the Keynesian general model is reflected through shifts in the LM curve. In our analysis we shall be concerned only with an increase in the money supply; thus, the LM curve shifts from LM_1 to LM_2. But in this instance nothing happens. The reason is that the economy has sunk into the liquidity trap, a situation in which the demand for money has become perfectly elastic. There is so much uncertainty—and fear—about future bond prices that the public (wealth-holders) is quite willing to exchange the bonds it is now holding for additional cash without the price of bonds having to increase. When the government pumps more money into the economy, all that happens is that the public winds up holding more cash and fewer securities. Monetary policy cannot drive down the rate of interest further, and therefore it has no effect upon the level of aggregate demand. Parenthetically, let us note that the situation just described—one in which monetary policy is wholly ineffective—is not recognized as valid by monetarists. It exists only within a Keynesian perspective. This requires that the demand for liquidity (money) may become absolute and that changes in the money supply always be transmitted to aggregate demand through the interest rate, propositions rejected by monetarism.

Turn now to the intersection of IS_2 and LM_1. Equilibrium income is Y_2. Now the economy is operating in a range in which monetary policy is effective. The analysis is quite straightforward. As the money supply is increased, the *LM* curve shifts to the right (LM_2), which brings the rate of interest down from i_3 to i_2. The mechanism for doing this is the purchase of securities (bonds) by the central bank, an action which drives up their prices and pushes down the rate of interest. Since the economy is in the range in which the *LM* curve is neither wholly horizontal nor wholly vertical, some of the new money will be absorbed into speculative balances and some into active (transactions) balances. As long as any of the money spills over into idle balances, the increases in aggregate demand will be less than the increase in the money supply, assuming no change in velocity. The increase in income is measured by the distance from Y_2 to Y_3.

The last situation we shall examine is depicted by the intersection of IS_3 and LM_1, which gives us an equilibrium income equal to Y_4. As we pointed out earlier, the vertical segment of the *LM* curve means a condition in which there are no idle or speculative balances—all money is in active circulation. Interest rates are extremely high ("extremely" in this case means relative to general perceptions of what is a "normal" level for the rate of interest). The rightward shift in the *LM* curve means, once again, that the government is buying securities, an action which will increase the money supply in the hands of the public and drive down the rate of interest. In the diagram, IS_3 intersects LM_2 in the vertical range of the former. This means that the rate of interest will have to fall far enough to absorb *all* the new money into active circulation, since the economy is still in a "pure" classical world in which no balances are being held for speculative purposes. If this happens, the increase in aggregate demand will be equal to the increase in the money supply, again assuming no change in velocity. Thus, monetary policy will be totally effective.

In the foregoing analysis we traced out the income effects of policy-induced shifts in either the *IS* or *LM* curve. There is one final point to consider. If we assume the two curves are independent of one another (as we have done) then the extent to which income responds to a shift in either the *IS* or *LM* curve depends upon the shape of the other curve. This becomes a matter of the interest elasticity of the curves—that is, the sensitivity of the underlying determinants of the two curves to changes in the rate of interest. For example, for any given change in the *IS* curve, the income effect will be greater as the *LM* curve approaches the horizontal—as it becomes more interest elastic. Furthermore, the "crowding-out" effect of interest rate changes will be minimized the *less* responsive investment (and consumption) spending is to changes in the rate of interest—or the more interest inelastic is the *IS* curve. For a change in the *LM* curve, on the other hand, the income effect will increase as the *IS* curve becomes more interest elastic—as its slope becomes more horizontal. Furthermore, the effectiveness of monetary policy becomes greater as the *LM* curve becomes less interest elastic—as it approaches the ver-

Effectiveness of:	INTEREST ELASTICITY	
	High	Low
Fiscal Policy	LM Curve	IS Curve
Monetary Policy	IS Curve	LM Curve

FIGURE 15–5.   Interest Elasticity and Effectiveness of Fiscal and Monetary Policies

tical. The overall effectiveness of fiscal and monetary policies and the cross-relationships between these two important curves—IS and LM— are summarized in the matrix arrangement shown in Figure 15–5. It should be studied carefully in relation to the analysis developed in connection with Figure 15–4.

Crowding Out Revisited

In the foregoing comparison of fiscal and monetary policies, the phenomenon of crowding out was discussed under the assumption that the IS and LM curves are independent. Except for the extreme classical case (which is not likely to be encountered in reality), crowding out would only be partial most of the time (see Chapter 7, p. 246). This, however, does not satisfy advocates of the crowding-out thesis (monetarists primarily). It is argued that, if a wealth effect is taken into account, or if the assumption of stable prices is dropped, then crowding out may occur even if the economy is operating between the extremes of the Keynesian and classical ranges. Figure 15–6 examines how this may come about.

In Part A of Figure 15–6 the economy is originally at income level Y_1, a result of the intersection of IS_1 and LM_2. Now it is assumed that through fiscal policy the IS curve is shifted to the right to the position IS_2. To understand how complete crowding out may occur, let us recall Friedman's theory of the demand for money (Chapter 11, pp. 375–81). The demand for money varies positively with the quantity of wealth people hold. Included in such wealth will be government bonds which are newly issued to finance the added government expenditures (or a tax cut). But this means that the demand for money will increase. In the context of the Keynesian general equilibrium model, an increase in the demand for money envisioned in this way shifts the entire series of money demand curves upward, assuming no change in the money supply curve. The consequence of this will be an upward (leftward) shift in the LM curve to the position of LM_1 in Figure 15–6. In the example shown, the LM curve has shifted sufficiently to just offset the effect of an increase in government spending (or a tax cut). Crowding out is complete, and the only change of consequence is a rise in interest rates from i_1 to i_3. Friedman characterizes the changes which result from a shift in the IS

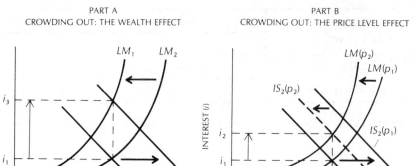

FIGURE 15–6.   Crowding Out: Wealth and Price Effects

curve as "first round effects." Changes which show the impact of increased wealth upon the demand for money and subsequently the position of the *LM* curve represent the "ultimate effects." Friedman believes that the latter are, in the final analysis, stronger than the first-round changes, although they have not been put to empirical testing.[10]

There is yet another way in which crowding out may occur. This requires dropping the assumption of stable prices, an approach illustrated in Part B of Figure 15–6. As before, the *IS* curve shifts to the right, a result of either more government spending or increased private spending because of a tax cut. The shift is from $IS_1(p_1)$ to $IS_2(p_1)$. Now, however, the increased aggregate demand pushes the price level up, which has two consequences. First, higher prices reduce the real value of the assets people hold, causing the consumption function to shift downward, a "Pigou effect" in reverse. This is shown in Figure 15–6 by a second shift of the *IS* curve to the level shown by the dashed line $IS_2(p_2)$. But higher prices also have the same effect as a decrease in the money supply; thus, the *LM* curve will shift upward (leftward) to the position of $LM(p_2)$. The combined consequence of these two changes is to leave the income level unchanged, but cause interest rates to rise from i_1 to i_2. Interest rates have not increased as much as in the situation in which crowding out is induced by the wealth effect, but they have gone up, nevertheless.

10. Robert J. Gordon, ed. *Milton Friedman's Monetary Framework: A Debate with His Critics* (Chicago: University of Chicago Press, 1974), p. 147. See also Alan S. Blinder and Robert M. Solow, "Does Fiscal Policy Matter?" *Journal of Public Economics,* 2 (1973), pp. 319–37, and W. Silber, "Fiscal Policy in IS-LM Analysis: A Correction," *Journal of Money, Credit, and Banking,* November 1970, pp. 461–72. Note: there is agreement among both Keynesians and monetarists that a deficit financed by printing money (or direct sale of government bonds to the treasury) will be expansionary.

Crowding out is obviously an issue of both theoretical and empirical importance. If it occurs on any appreciable scale, then the effectiveness of fiscal policy as an instrument for economic expansion is seriously weakened. But the controversy is by no means settled. As matters now stand, the monetarists have failed to develop adequate empirical evidence to support the crowding-out hypothesis, even though a theoretical case can be made for its existence. History has not yet thrown up sufficient experiments to allow the controversy to be decided.[11]

With the advent of the Reagan administration's enormous tax cuts, the crowding-out issue again came to the forefront of discussion, both among academic economists and government policy-makers. The reason, of course, is the massive budget deficits generated by the combination of the 1981 tax cuts and the 1981–82 recession. Interest rates failed to fall to the same degree as the slowdown in the inflation rate during the recession, the reason being, it was argued, excessively high government demands for credit. Deficits in the range of $150 to $200 billion raised anew fears of crowding out of a magnitude great enough to absorb all or most of personal saving in the economy.

Stabilization Policy in Perspective

In this section we shall take a broad look at some of the major policy decisions made during the post–World War II era from the Truman through Reagan administrations. Our intent is not to examine these in detail,[12] but to convey to the reader some sense of the major developments that required policy decisions, some feel for the political and economic climates in which these decisions were made. We shall conclude the chapter with some comments on the present state of stabilization policy, including some suggestion for changes in the economy.

The Truman-Eisenhower Years

In the 15 years from the end of World War II to the election of John Kennedy as president in 1960, the nation experienced four measurable recessions,[13] although the period in retrospect is generally viewed as one of prosperity and rising real income for most Americans. The latter is true to a degree, although not to the extent that recent nostalgia for the

11. For a concise survey and analysis of the state of the crowding-out controversy prior to the budget deficits of the Reagan administration, see Keith M. Carlson and Roger W. Spencer, "Crowding Out and Its Critics," Federal Reserve Bank of St. Louis *Review,* December 1975, pp. 2–17.
12. The annual *Economic Reports of the President,* which contain the president's annual economic message to the Congress and the much lengthier *Annual Report* of the Council of Economic Advisers, are the best sources for details of key policy decisions each year.
13. Technically a recession exists when *real* gross national product declines for two successive quarters. For more details, see Chapter 17.

less turbulent 1950s has made it seem. In this period *real* GNP grew by 31.5 percent, a figure which translates into an annual average rate of growth of 2 percent. This is well below the long-term historic average for the American economy (see Table 16–1, Chapter 16). *Real* per capita disposable income grew by 12.1 percent in this period—a solid though not spectacular gain. In spite of the Employment Act being passed in 1946, and in spite, too, of the obvious example of World War II as a successful application of Keynesian ideas, little effort was made during the Truman-Eisenhower years to apply the lessons of the Keynesian "Revolution" to the peacetime management of the economy. Four recessions—mild through they may have been in comparison to the Great Depression of the 1930s—attest to this.

In the spring of 1948 the Congress passed a substantial reduction in the personal income tax over President Truman's veto. The tax cut was not aimed at the state of the economy, but turned out fortuitously to be the right thing to do. The reason was that later in the year the economy slid into the first of the mild postwar recessions it was to undergo between 1946 and 1960. President Truman believed at the time that inflation was a much more serious threat than deflation, so much so that he asked for a substantial tax increase in his 1949 budget message, even though by then the economy had definitely turned down. It was not until mid-year that the administration recognized that a recession was under way. In its mid-year economic report the request for a tax increase was withdrawn. The president also gave up his hope for a balanced budget, suggesting that a deficit would be a source of support against the factors making for decline in the economy.[14] The deficit was the result of the recession, not a policy-inspired deficit. No major fiscal policy measures were called for to deal with the recession, which reached a trough in the fourth quarter of 1949. Expansion got under way in the spring of 1950 and the Korean war boosted the economy into boom conditions through 1953.

The Eisenhower administration, which took office in January 1953, was even more committed to a balanced budget philosophy than its predecessor. In his 1960 *Economic Report*, President Eisenhower said that the appropriate budget policy is one that "not merely balances expenditures with revenues, but achieves a significant surplus for debt retirement."[15] This statement fairly well sums up the budget philosophy characteristic of the Eisenhower years. Behind this view appears to have been a persistent fear of inflation coupled with a belief that budget deficits were the prime source of inflation. There simply is not any evidence that the Eisenhower administration understood—or wanted to understand—how Keynesian ideas might be used for effective economic management. The

14. Wilfred Lewis, Jr., *Federal Fiscal Policy in the Postwar Recessions* (Washington, D.C.: The Brookings Institution, 1962), p. 113.
15. *Economic Report of the President* (Washington, D.C.: U.S. Government Printing Office, 1960), p. 54.

result was three more recessions—1953–54, 1957–58, and 1960–61—of which at least the first was probably the direct result of the administration's near-continuous preoccupation with a balanced budget. In an effort to cut down on the deficits incurred during the Korean war (1950–53), the new Eisenhower administration sharply curtailed federal spending in 1953–54. As a result, the federal budget as measured on a full-employment basis became sharply restrictive and the economy in mid-1953 dropped into a second postwar recession. Unemployment rose from a Korean war low of 2.9 percent in 1953 to 5.5 percent in 1954. Once again a fortuitous development helped bail the economy out, as both individual and business taxes were cut in 1954. But these tax reductions were not put into effect as an anti-recession measure; they had been planned and scheduled earlier as a part of the administration's efforts to reduce the size of the federal budget.[16] In the last two recessions of the Eisenhower years, primary blame for the recessions cannot be laid at the door of the federal government. The administration did not, however, initiate vigorous policy measures in either 1957–58 or 1960–61[17] to get the economy out of the recessions.

The same fear of inflation that dominated the Eisenhower administration's thinking about the budget is apparent in monetary policy during these years. In most of the Truman portion of the 1946–60 period there was, in effect, no possibility of any monetary policy. This was because of the wartime "accord" between the Federal Reserve and the Treasury. In order to hold down interest rates—and with them the financial cost of government borrowing—the Federal Reserve agreed in 1941 to buy an unlimited quantity of government securities in the open market at fixed prices. This, in effect, put a floor under the price of government securities and a ceiling on interest rates. If the price of bonds could not fall, then interest rates could not rise. Thus, it was impossible to have a monetary policy since the "accord" would not allow the Federal Reserve to take action to raise interest rates—that is, enter the open market and sell securities. This accord continued until 1951, when it was abandoned.

From 1951 onward monetary policy was restrictive. Figure 15–7 shows this clearly. Except for the Korean war years when deficit financing gave it a spurt, the money supply grew very slowly through most of the Eisenhower years. As Figure 15–7 also shows, the annual average rate of change in the money supply $(M1)$[18] was below the rate of 4 to 5 percent Friedman recommends for policy. During the eight Eisenhower years (1953–60), the money supply grew at an annual average of 1.6 percent. Compare Figure 15–7 with Figure 15–2, which shows the rate of change in

16. Lewis, p. 182.
17. By 1961 the Eisenhower administration was out of office. In his last budget message, sent to the Congress in January 1961, President Eisenhower took an optimistic view of the state of the economy (unemployment in 1960 was 5.5 percent) and said that it was essential to maintain fiscal integrity. He continued to argue the need for a budget surplus.
18. This is the "old" M1, namely, currency and demand deposits. The concept is adequate to illustrate the point, even though the definition has been changed.

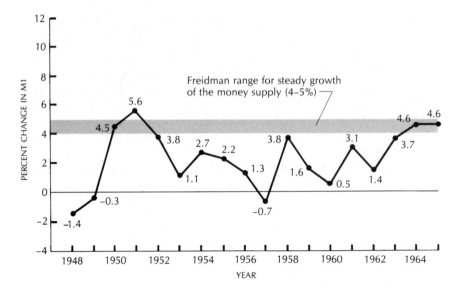

FIGURE 15–7.   Annual Percentage Rate of Change in the Money Supply (M1): 1948–65

M1 (new definition) after 1964. The contrast is stark, in spite of slightly different definitions for M1 in the two diagrams. The basic attitude of the Board of Governors at this time is aptly summed up in the statement that the then chairman, William McChesney Martin, made to the Joint Economic Committee of the Congress early in 1961: "The flexible monetary policy that has been in effect for a full decade . . . is one of leaning against the winds of inflation and deflation with equal vigor."[19] Translated, this meant that, when inflation threatened, the Federal Reserve System would clamp down on the money supply and, when recession loomed, the money supply would be expanded. Although the Board of Governors is not officially on record with respect to its primary objectives, it has traditionally placed more emphasis upon stable prices as a policy goal than any other objective,[20] a point of view that fit in well with the inflationary fears that dominated the Eisenhower years.

One final question remains concerning the Truman-Eisenhower years. It seems clear that neither the Truman nor Eisenhower administration had either a clear understanding of Keynesian principles or a willingness to pursue a vigorous anticyclical policy. The question then is: Why did not any of the four recessions in this 15-year period turn into a major, post-World War II depression? The answer is not found in the policies followed by either administration—except for the fortuitous fiscal mea-

19. Quoted by Sherman J. Maisel in his *Managing the Dollar* (New York: Norton, 1973), p. 63. Dr. Maisel, a former governor of the Federal Reserve System, is now a professor of economics at the University of California at Berkeley.
20. Ibid., p. 66.

sures—but partly in the effectiveness of the economy's built-in stabilizers, a topic first discussed in Chapter 7 (pp. 240–43). As one observer comments, the "built-in fiscal stabilizers have made a substantial contribution to the stability of the postwar economy. They have pushed the federal budget strongly toward a deficit when that was needed in each postwar recession, thus helping to slow the economic decline."[21] The other relevant factor was the strength of the postwar demand for consumer goods, a carryover from wartime shortages.

The Kennedy Era

When the Kennedy administration came to power in early 1961, the entire intellectual climate as well as the character of economic policy-making changed drastically. Essentially there were two fundamental changes. First, the Kennedy administration intended to pursue a policy of aggressive economic management. President Kennedy, after all, had campaigned on the promise to "get the country moving again," and he was determined to carry out this campaign pledge. Second, the new president was a bright man, willing, even eager, to learn what modern macroeconomics had to say about the economy. John Kennedy was not knowledgeable about Keynesian economics when he assumed office, but he was a quick learner. Since the period 1961–65 represents a time when the prestige of economics and economic policy attained a post–World War II high, what happened in this period is worth close analysis.

In January 1961 the major economic problem that confronted President Kennedy and his Council of Economic Advisers[22] was the stagnant state of the economy, still floundering in the fourth recession since the end of the war. During the preceding Eisenhower years, unemployment averaged 4.9 percent of the labor force, a figure judged excessive by the 4 percent minimum that the Kennedy Council regarded as the desirable objective of stabilization policy. Just how the new administration planned to resolve this persistent problem of a sluggish economy and excessive unemployment did not become fully apparent until a year later when the first *Economic Report* of the new administration appeared.

In its first full report, the Kennedy CEA stated that since mid-1955 the rate of growth of actual output was significantly below the economy's potential. The consequence of this lag in economic growth below the potential was a gap of $40 billion between the actual output in 1961 and the value of the goods and services that could have been produced if there had been full employment in 1961.[23] Figure 15–8 reproduces the CEA's charts from the historic 1962 report showing the gap between

21. Lewis, p. 15.
22. Members of the original Kennedy Council at that time were Professor Walter W. Heller, chairman; Professor Kermit Gordon; and Professor James Tobin.
23. *Economic Report of the President* (Washington, D.C.: U.S. Government Printing Office, 1962), p. 51.

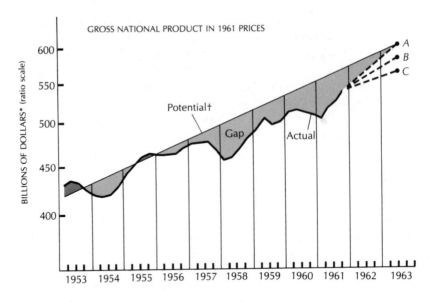

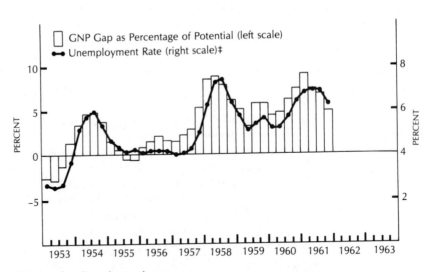

*Seasonally adjusted annual rates
†3½% trend line through middle of 1955
‡Unemployment as percentage of civilian labor force; seasonally adjusted
Note: A, B, and C represent GNP in the middle of 1963 assuming unemployment rates of
    4%, 5%, and 6%, respectively

FIGURE 15—8.   Gross National Product (Actual and Potential) and Unemployment
              Rate: 1953–63

SOURCE: *Economic Report of the President,* 1962

actual and *potential* GNP and unemployment rates (as a percentage of the civilian labor force) for 1955 through 1965.

The CEA got its measure of potential output by the simple technique of projecting a trend for the actual GNP in mid-1955 forward at an annual average rate of growth from 3¼ to 3½ percent. Mid-1955 was used as the base year for those calculations because, with unemployment down to 4 percent of the labor force, actual output was equal to potential output. In determining the growth rate to be used to measure the trend of potential output, the CEA took into account the rate of growth in the potential labor force, the annual average rate of growth in labor productivity for the entire labor force, and the downward trend in hours worked per year. The reader may wish at this point to review the discussion in Chapter 3 of the determinants of productive capacity as well as the concept of the output gap.

This concept of an output, or performance, gap emerged in the early 1960s as one of the key tools used by the CEA for analysis of the economy's performance. To explain the serious performance gap which characterized the American economy from mid-1955 onward, the CEA developed a theory of fiscal stagnation. The Council argued that the failure of the economy to expand at a rate sufficient to provide full employment was not due primarily to a deficiency of either private consumption or investment demand, but to the restrictive impact of the federal tax structure on the overall level of demand.

The major analytical tool utilized by the Council of Economic Advisers to demonstrate the restrictive effect of the federal tax structure upon the economy was the concept of the full-employment surplus. Earlier in this chapter we defined the full-employment budget. The full-employment surplus is a variant of this concept. In the 1962 *Economic Report* the CEA used it to mean the budgetary surplus of the federal government that would be generated by a given budget program under conditions of full employment (a 4 percent unemployment rate). Figure 15–9 is from the 1962 CEA report and illustrates this concept. In the diagram the ratio of actual GNP to potential GNP is shown on the horizontal axis. This axis is labeled the "Utilization Rate"; the 100 percent point represents full employment. It will be recalled that potential GNP is based on projecting a trend that embodies a 4 percent unemployment rate. Thus, when the ratio of *actual* to *potential* GNP equals 100, the economy must be operating at full employment. On the vertical axis, the federal surplus or deficit is measured as a percentage of the potential GNP.

Two schedules are shown in the diagram, one of which reflects the tax and expenditure program of the federal government for the fiscal year 1960 and the other for the fiscal year 1962. Both of these schedules slope upward to the right, which indicates that the surplus or deficit associated with any given budget program will depend upon the level of economic activity prevailing in the economy. By a "given budget program" is meant a particular pattern and level of expenditures combined with a particu-

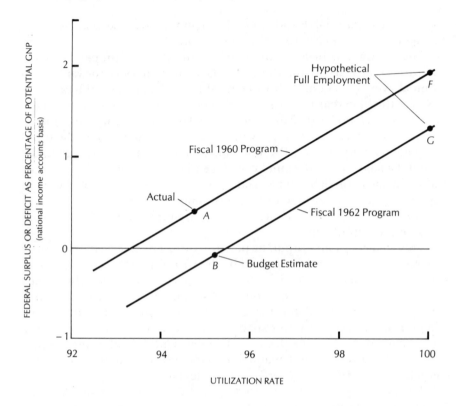

FEDERAL SURPLUS OR DEFICIT AS PERCENTAGE OF POTENTIAL GNP (national income accounts basis)

UTILIZATION RATE

FIGURE 15–9.   Effect of Level of Economic Activity on Federal Surplus or Deficit

lar structure of tax rates. With fixed expenditures and a given rate structure for the tax system, a deficit will decline or a surplus will increase as
the economy's utilization rate increases—or as the economy approaches
full employment. The height and steepness of the schedule depend upon
the character of the budget program that exists at any given time—namely,
the level of expenditures, tax rates, and the degree of progression present in the system.

Discretionary fiscal policy—action that deliberately changes the level
of government expenditures or tax rates—has the effect of shifting the
schedule up or down. For example, a reduction in tax rates would lower
the schedule, thus either increasing a deficit or reducing the surplus
associated with a specific level of economic activity—the utilization rate
shown on the horizontal axis. The effects of built-in stabilizers, on the
other hand, are reflected in a movement along the schedule as the level
of economic activity changes. A rise in the income level will automatically
generate a surplus sooner or later, as long as there is no change in
expenditures. It should be noted, too, that if tax rates and expenditure
programs remain constant, the full-employment surplus will rise over
time. The reason for this is that over time the full-employment potential

GNP grows, simply because a growing labor force which is fully employed and whose productivity is improving inevitably means a larger output. As long as tax rates are unchanged, the absolute volume of tax revenues yielded by a full-employment economy must increase over time. This being the case and with expenditures unchanged, the budgetary surplus should grow.

The economic significance of a full-employment budget surplus lies in the fact that the actual achievement of full employment requires that gross investment expenditures (including net foreign investment in an open economy) must be large enough to offset the total private saving plus the net surplus of the public sector which the economic system generates at full employment. In equation form, $I = S + (T - G)$, in which the variables represent full-employment, *ex ante* (or planned) values. The actual situation between 1955 and the early 1960s, according to analysis of the Council of Economic Advisers, was a tendency for full-employment saving (including government saving or the full-employment surplus) to run ahead of gross investment, including net foreign investment. In symbolic terms, $S + (T - G) > I$.

The Remedy for Fiscal Stagnation   The solution proposed by the Kennedy administration to fiscal stagnation was a massive reduction in both personal and corporate income taxes. President Kennedy in a 1963 special message on tax reform requested that the tax rates on personal income be reduced from a range of 20 to 91 percent to a range of 14 to 65 percent, and that the rate on corporate income be reduced from 95 to 47 percent. The Congress did not act on President Kennedy's request, but, following his assassination, essentially the same proposals were presented to the Congress in January 1964. Speedy action was forthcoming and the Revenue Act of 1964 was signed into law on February 16, 1964. In its 1965 *Annual Report* the CEA estimated that the total of tax reductions taking effect in 1964 and 1965 would be $11 billion for individuals and $3 billion for corporations.[24]

It was expected that the tax cuts would operate to stimulate both consumption and investment spending, thus bringing output closer to the full-employment potential. The reduction in the personal income tax would add directly to the personal disposable income of consumers and, since most of this added income would be spent, the multiplier would come into play and generate a cumulative expansion in consumption. Investment spending would rise both because the after-tax profit on new facilities would be increased and because more internal funds would be available to firms for investment purposes.

In its 1963 *Annual Report*, the CEA presented a textbook-like explanation of the multiplier effects that could be expected to flow from the

24. *Economic Report of the President* (Washington, D.C.: U.S. Government Printing Office, 1965), p. 65. The Excise Tax Reduction Act of 1965 called for a reduction in excise taxes totaling $4.6 billion over several stages through 1969.

reduction in rate on the personal income tax. After taking into account all the various leakages at work in the economic system, the Council concluded that each additional dollar of GNP generated initially by the tax cut would generate an additional $0.50 of consumption expenditures. In other words, the marginal propensity to consume out of the GNP is 0.50, which yields a multiplier of 2 to be applied against the initial increase in consumption spending stimulated by the increase in disposable income.[25] The ultimate expansionary effect was expected to be even greater because of the stimulus to investment resulting both from the initial reduction in the corporate rate and from the expansion in consumption generated by the cut in personal income tax rates.

The Effectiveness of the 1964 Tax Cut   While there are no absolutely conclusive tests that can be employed to determine the effectiveness of the 1964 tax cut, the available evidence is strong that the tax cuts did, in fact, achieve the results expected. In the first place, the gap between actual and potential output, which reached a peak of $50 billion at an annual rate in the first quarter of 1961, was reduced to an annual rate of $10 billion in the last quarter of 1965. The unemployment rate declined to 4.1 percent by the end of 1965; in September 1966, the rate stood at 3.8 percent of the civilian labor force. These changes largely took place before the Vietnam military buildup had begun to have much effect upon the economy. Figure 15–10, taken from the 1966 *Economic Report of the President,* shows these gains. It should be compared to Figure 15–8.

Additional evidence for the effectiveness of the tax cut is to be found in the performance of GNP. In 1964, GNP (in current prices) increased by $41.0 billion, in contrast to an increase of $31.7 billion (in current prices) in 1963. The CEA stated in its 1966 *Annual Report* that statistical analysis of the impact of the tax cut indicates that it was responsible for nearly $10 billion of the gain in the annual increase of the GNP. The increase continued in 1965. With respect to the entire expansion, the CEA estimated that, by the end of 1965, the contribution of the tax cut reached $30 billion.[26]

The third piece of evidence that can be cited in support of the effectiveness of the tax cut is the fact that, from the close of 1964 to the close of 1965, federal revenues increased by $9.4 billion, in spite of the fact that in this same period tax reductions effected by both the Revenue Act of 1964 and the Excise Tax Reduction Act of 1965 totaled about $16 billion.[27] This experience bears out the claim of the CEA that a tax reduction, if it succeeds in stimulating economic growth, would lead to an increase rather than a decline in revenues. Thus, it is apparent that,

25. *Economic Report of the President* (Washington, D.C.: U.S. Government Printing Office, 1963), pp. 45–51.
26. *Economic Report of the President* (Washington, D.C.: U.S. Government Printing Office, 1966), p. 34.
27. *Economic Report of the President* (Washington, D.C.: U.S. Government Printing Office, 1977), p. 271.

GROSS NATIONAL PRODUCT IN 1958 PRICES

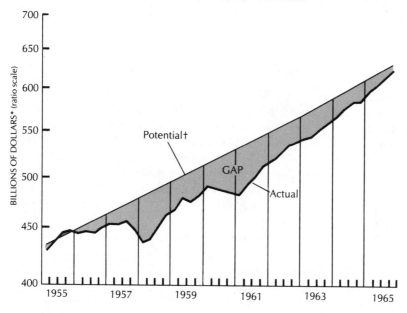

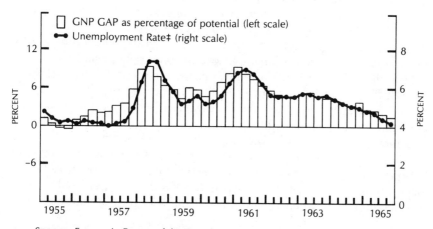

SOURCE: Economic Report of the President, 1966

*Seasonally adjusted annual rates

†Trend line of 3½% through middle of 1955 to 1962 IV; trend line of 3¼% thereafter

‡Unemployment as percentage of civilian labor force, seasonally adjusted

FIGURE 15–10. Gross national Product (Actual and Potential) and Unemployment Rate: 1955–65

if the level of government expenditures had remained constant during this period, the federal government would have experienced a substantial surplus by the end of 1965. Actually, total expenditures (including transfers) of the federal government rose from $118.2 billion in 1964 (on a national income accounts basis) to $123.8 billion in 1965, an increase of $5.6 billion, a figure slightly more than the increase in revenues in the same period. The federal government attained a small surplus of $0.5 billion in 1965.[28]

Vietnam and Its Aftermath

From 1966 to the early 1970s economic effects of the Vietnam war and its inflationary aftermath dominated the economy and economic policy. By the end of 1966 the unemployment level fell below 4 percent, the target figure the Council of Economic Advisers established in the early 1960s as representing full employment. During 1969 unemployment averaged 3.5 percent, the lowest figure in the entire post–World War II years except for the Korean war years. Also in 1966 the GNP gap disappeared, not to reappear until the 1970 recession. With reduction of the unemployment rate below the target level and the disappearance of the GNP gap, inflation quickly became the number one aggregate—and domestic—economic problem.

During the Vietnam period economic policy was directed almost totally toward the control of inflation.[29] The major policy moves included imposition of a 10 percent surcharge on corporate and individual income taxes in 1968, the 1969 game plan of the Nixon administration for inflation control, and the experiment with an incomes policy which began in mid-1971. The latter is discussed in detail in Chapter 14. Here we shall discuss the 1968 surtax and the policies pursued to control inflation by the Nixon administration during its pre-incomes policy phase.

By mid-1966 it was evident to most economists that the heating up of the economy consequent to the escalation in Vietnam required the application of a restrictive fiscal policy,[30] although it was not until two years later that the Johnson administration and a reluctant Congress enacted a tax increase. The Revenue and Expenditure Control Act of 1968, signed into law at the end of June, provided for a 10 percent surcharge on personal and corporate income taxes, retroactive to January 1, 1968, for corporate income taxes and to April 1, 1968, for the personal income tax. Through subsequent action by the Congress, the surcharge on per-

---

28. Monetary policy played a much less dramatic role than did fiscal policy in the Kennedy era. Nevertheless, the Federal Reserve stepped up the rate of growth in the money supply (M_1) in 1963 and 1964, a development which is the basis of the claim of some monetarists that the increase in the money supply rather than the 1964 tax cut was responsible for improved economic conditions in the Kennedy era. This is an issue which will probably never be settled.

29. The major economic stimulus from the war came from 1966 through 1968 in the form of rising military expenditures, but the inflationary aftermath lasted through 1973. Thus, economically, the Vietnam war period runs from 1966 through 1973.

30. In 1966 the purchase of goods and services by the federal government for military purposes jumped by $10.9 billion, an increase that took place in a fully employed economy. No new taxes were imposed to finance this vast and sudden increase in federal outlays, a development that caused the federal government's deficit to rise to $13.2 billion on a national income accounts basis the following year. It would be difficult to find a more perfect example of irresponsible government action that inevitably would have serious inflationary consequences.

sonal income was extended at a 10 percent rate through 1969, dropped to a 5 percent rate in the first half of 1970, and allowed to expire on June 30, 1970. The same provisions applied to the corporate income tax.

The 1968 surcharge was a fiscal policy counterpart to the tax reductions of 1964, as it was expected via its impact upon disposable income and corporate profits to dampen spending and thus contribute to bringing inflationary pressures under control. Was the 1968 tax increase as successful in holding down aggregate demand as its predecessor tax cut apparently had been in stimulating aggregate demand? The answer, unfortunately, is by no means clear-cut. Consumer prices rose at an annual average rate of 4.2 percent in 1968, 5.4 percent in 1969, and 5.9 percent in 1970. It was not until the economy went into the 1969–70 recession that a slowdown in the inflation rate became evident. This happened in 1971, when the annual rate of price increase dropped to 4.3 percent. Since the surcharge was allowed to expire in mid-1970, we really do not know what might have happened under circumstances in which the tax remained in effect. Furthermore, as critics of the surcharge maintain— especially some proponents of the permanent income hypothesis—consumers were well aware of the temporary nature of the tax. Consequently, they adjusted to it by reducing their saving rather than their spending when the tax increase cut into their disposable income. Personal saving as a percentage of disposable income declined from 8.1 in 1967 to 7.1 in 1968 and 6.4 in 1969, and then climbed back to 8.0 in 1970, the year in which the surcharge was lifted. But 1970 was also a recession year, marked by a good deal of consumer caution and uncertainty, so the evidence on the saving ratio is not definitive.

A highly comprehensive study of the effectiveness of the 1968 surcharge was completed in 1971 by the late Arthur Okun, a former chairman of the Council of Economic Advisers.[31] Professor Okun used four different econometric models to test the hypothesis that the surcharge was expected to curb consumer demand, then compared the results obtained with the estimated actual impact on consumption. He did find that, with the exception of the demand for automobiles, the surcharge was effective during the 1968–70 period in curbing consumer demand for other durables, as well as nondurables and services. Automobile demand, for reasons that are not entirely clear, displayed great strength during this period, as did business investment (including residential construction) in spite of the surcharge on corporate income. Professor Okun's general conclusion is that, overall, consumer demand responded about as expected to the reduction in disposable income, but the expansionary and inflationary forces let loose by the Vietnam war were much greater than recognized at the time. As he says, "The medicine of the personal tax surcharge did lower the patient's fever. To be sure, the patient was more feverish than the doctors recognized and consequently their anti-

31. Arthur M. Okun, "The Personal Tax Surcharge and Consumer Demand, 1968–70," *Brookings Papers on Economic Activity*, No. 1, 1971.

fever prescription was inadequate. But don't blame the medicine; it did most of what it should have been reasonably expected to do. In short, the evidence of the surcharge period provides further confirmation of the general efficacy and continued desirability of flexible changes in personal income tax rates—upward or downward, permanent or temporary."[32] The most damaging weakness of the surcharge was its application approximately two years too late, a failing of the political system rather than in economic diagnosis.

The stance of the Nixon administration when it assumed power at the beginning of 1969 was that the first priority was to bring inflation under control. This, it was thought, could be done by a gradualist approach which would try and slow down the economy sufficiently to dampen the inflationary psychology that the Nixon economists believed three years of rising prices had engendered. In 1969 the administration was confident that this could be done without bringing on a recession or too much unemployment. Under the leadership of Professor Paul McCracken of the University of Michigan, the Nixon CEA put together a combination of fiscal and monetary restraints designed to accomplish this, a package that came to be known as the administration's "game plan." In 1969 the rate of growth of federal expenditures for goods and services slowed sharply—from 7.8 percent in 1968 to an actual decline of 0.5 percent in 1969—as did the rate of growth in the money supply—dropping from 7.7 percent in 1968 to 3.2 percent in 1969. The percentages are for M1, new definition. We shall return to the subject of monetary policy shortly.

What were the results? Since there is a normal lag of six to twelve months between the initiation of economic policy and ultimate results, 1970 was the decisive test year for the effectiveness of the 1969 game plan. By the end of the year, it was apparent that gradualism had not done the job of stopping inflation. It has already been pointed out that consumer prices rose by 5.9 percent in 1970, as compared to 5.4 percent in 1969 and 4.2 percent in 1968. Yet unemployment rose from the 3.5 percent level of 1969 to a rate of 6 percent by December 1970. The failure of the gradualist approach was abetted by the Nixon administration's strongly voiced unwillingness at the start of 1969 to give any consideration to having an incomes policy. Furthermore, the administration was openly hostile to the surcharge, making no move to ask the Congress to extend it beyond the planned expiration date of June 30, 1970. During the first half of 1971 the Nixon administration largely marked time in terms of economic policy, uncertain as to how to cope with the growing problem of both unemployment and inflation. Finally in mid-August President Nixon made his bombshell announcement that with a wage-price freeze his administration had embarked on an experiment with a comprehensive incomes policy, an approach the administration had scornfully rejected in early 1969. The results of this phase of the Nixon administration economic policies were discussed in the preceding chapter.

32. Ibid.

In the meanwhile, what role did monetary policy play in the Vietnam period? In general, the acceleration in the rate of growth in the money supply that began in the Kennedy era continued, but with two important exceptions—1966 and 1969. In late 1965 and early 1966, the Federal Reserve System, worried about the growing inflationary pressures because of Vietnam, slammed on the monetary brakes. The discount rate was raised and growth in the money supply sharply curtailed (in 1966, overall, the rate of monetary growth dropped to 2.5 percent, compared to 4.7 percent in 1965). The result was a severe credit squeeze, generally known as the "credit crunch" of 1966. Particularly hard hit was the housing industry, because the rise in open market interest rates exceeded the rates that financial intermediaries such as savings and loan associations, mutual saivng banks, and life insurance companies were able to pay. Consequently, the flow of savings to these intermediaries dropped, which in turn dried up the flow of money into home mortgages.[33] Thus, the construction of new houses slumped badly (new housing starts were off by more than 300,000 in 1966). In many respects 1969 was a repeat of 1966. As part of the Nixon game plan the money supply was tightened— the rate of growth of M1 dropped to 3.2 percent in 1969 as compared to 7.7 percent the prior year. And again as in 1966 housing was hurt as the flow of savings to financial intermediaries began to dry up. The crunch was not so severe as earlier, however, because the Federal Reserve moved to a less restrictive stance early in 1970. The experiences in 1966 and in 1969 demonstrate dramatically the point made earlier in this chapter about the uneven impact of monetary policy (p. 503).

In the view of one knowledgeable observer, 1966 was a year crucial in significance in the post–World War II development of monetary policy. That year, according to Sherman J. Maisel, former member of the Board of Governors of the Federal Reserve System, marked the end of the "age of innocence" for the system.[34] What he meant was that henceforth the system had to abandon the simplistic view of former chairman William McChesney Martin that its main task in an inflationary era was to restrict the money supply; rather, it had to be equally mindful of how its credit and monetary policies would affect the different sectors of the economy, a lesson driven home by the severe—and adverse—effect that monetary restriction during 1966 had on the flow of funds into the housing market.

After 1966, in short, the Federal Reserve recognized that the effective use of monetary policy required that the Board take into account the actual workings of financial markets in terms of traditional channels of lending and borrowing as well as the total quantity of money and commercial bank reserves available to the economy.

33. This process is called *disintermediation*. The reason is that the financial institutions just mentioned operate essentially as channels for the transfer of funds from savers to borrowers. Hence, they are serving as intermediaries. When the process slows down or stops, we have disintermediation.
34. Maisel (Footnote 19), p. 69.

The 1970s

There is no clear line of demarcation that indicates precisely when the Vietnam war ceased to be the dominating factor in policy-making for the economy. In a sense, because of the continued pressure on the price level, we are still feeling the effects of that historic national misadventure. But for practical policy-making, the failure of the 1969 Nixon game plan and the shift to an incomes policy in mid-1971 represent a rough turning point. From then onward, the fiscal and monetary policies of the ill-fated Nixon administration were geared toward bringing down the unemployment rate, particularly with a presidential election in the offing.

In both 1971 and 1972 fiscal and monetary policies became aggressively expansive. To illustrate, the deficit on the full-employment budget rose from $2.6 billion in 1970 to $9.2 billion in 1971 and $21.5 billion in 1972, an $18.9-billion swing in two years.[35] This resulted from a combination of tax cuts and rising expenditures. Equally expansive was monetary policy, as the money supply (M1) increased by 6.5 percent in 1971 and a phenomenal 9.3 percent in 1972, a higher rate of growth than any year since 1948. The administration was confident that the system of wage and price controls instituted in mid-1971 (called "The New Economic Policy" in the press) would contain any added inflationary pressures resulting from the fiscal and monetary stimuli.

What were the results of the switch from a policy of restraint (1969) to all-out expansion (1971 and 1972)? They were mixed, an outcome that reflects the fact that it is becoming increasingly difficult to deal adequately with either inflation or unemployment in our economy by fiscal and monetary means. The unemployment rate continued to rise through 1971, reaching a rate of 5.9 percent for the year. In 1972 it came down slightly—to 5.6 percent—but the decline was far less than expected in view of the strong fiscal and monetary stimuli applied to the economy. The stubborn resistance of unemployment to improvement by applying the usual Keynesian remedies turned out to be one of the more persistent and difficult problems of the 1970s. It is rooted in the structure of the labor force, since some groups—minorities and teenagers especially—benefit only in a marginal way from higher levels of aggregate demand (see Figure 4–1, p. 98). With respect to the price level, there was improvement in both 1971 and 1972, a development which appeared to indicate that controls were working. In 1971 the inflation rate dropped to 4.3 percent and it fell further in 1972 to 3.3 percent, a low for the 1970s. There is evidence, however, (see Chapter 14), that these gains

35. In a news conference early in 1971 President Nixon said "I am a Keynesian," a remark widely interpreted as indicating the willingness of his administration to use fiscal measures to stimulate the economy. This view was strengthened by his endorsement of the concept of the full-employment budget in his 1971 Economic Message to the Congress.

were nothing more than a lagged consequence of the 1969–70 recession.

When Gerald Ford became president in the late summer of 1974 he inherited fiscal and monetary policies which had once again turned restrictive. The new president, if anything, was even more concerned than his predecessor with an inflation which was accelerating rapidly. In the first half of the year consumer prices rose at an annual rate slightly in excess of 10 percent. Americans began to hear more and more about a new economic menace—"double-digit" inflation. Even though the Arab oil embargo in late 1973 and poor crops were in part responsible for the acceleration in the inflation rate, the Ford administration continued to pursue policies which were strongly restrictive. This took place in spite of the fact that the crucial business cycle indicators of the Department of Commerce were pointing downward (see Chapter 17). In 1974 the money supply (M1) grew at an annual rate of 4.4 percent, down from the 5.5 percent growth rate of 1973 and well below the record rate of expansion in 1972. Fiscal policy, too, continued to be restrictive, a fact reflected in the swing of the full-employment budget from a deficit of $11.3 billion in 1973 to a surplus of $0.7 billion in 1974. Overall this was a swing in a restrictive direction of $12 billion. Inflation plus the combination of highly restrictive fiscal and monetary policies led to the second most severe economic slump since the Great Depression of the 1930s. Real gross national product declined in both 1974 and 1975, and the unemployment rate rose to a post–World War II high of 8.9 percent in May 1976.

Recovery began in the spring of 1975, coincident with the passage of a tax cut bill proposed by the Ford administration—a package which overall contained tax cuts on the order of $15 billion. Since then events moved along a path which is becoming distressingly familiar, even though there was a change in administrations at the start of 1977. Real output expanded after the turnaround came in the third quarter of 1975, but not rapidly enough to bring the unemployment rate down to even the Ford administration's suggested target of 5.5 percent for "full employment." Two years after the recovery got under way (May 1977), unemployment was still at the excessively high figure of 6.9 percent of the labor force. Inflation was down from the double-digit range which alarmed so many people in 1974, but the situation was not satisfactory. In the first four months of 1977 consumer prices rose at an annual rate of nearly 10 percent, a development that the Carter administration attributed to bad weather in the early part of the year.

In many ways the Carter administration policies were not much different from those of the predecessor Ford administration, in spite of the rhetoric of the 1976 campaign. The high unemployment from the 1974–75 recession lingered on through 1976, making unemployment the major focus for administration policy during its first two years in office. In 1977 the unemployment rate was 7.1 percent down only slightly from the 1976 rate of 7.7 percent. This led the new administration to propose a two-year program of tax reductions in the amount of $31 billion, including a one-time $50 rebate on 1976 taxes. Although the idea of a tax rebate was dropped in April 1977, when it became apparent that there had been a larger than expected boost in consumer spending in the early part of the year, the administration proposed additional personal tax reductions during 1978. In his January 1978 *Economic Report* President Carter asked for a tax reduction of $25 billion, to take effect in October. In May this request was scaled back to $20 billion, not to take effect until January 1979, cuts which were eventually incorporated into the Revenue Act of 1978.[36] The postponement of the tax cut in combination with a slower rate of growth in federal spending than anticipated by the administration helped reduce the full-employment deficit in the latter part of the year, a development welcomed by the administration because the inflation rate had started back up during the year.

During the last two years of the Carter administration the focus of policy shifted from stimulating the economy to bring down the unemployment rate to instituting restrictive measures because of the acceleration in inflation. During 1979 consumer prices rose at an annual average rate of over 13 percent; in the first three months of 1980 the rate accelerated to nearly 17 percent. As already pointed out, the Federal Reserve made a major policy shift in October 1979, targeting from then on the money supply rather than interest rates and seeking to curtail sharply the growth in the money supply. From October through June of 1980 the growth of M1 (currency plus demand deposits) was practically halted. The seriousness of the inflation threat caused the administration to take even more drastic measures to control the growth of money and credit. In March 1980 the president, using the authority of the Credit Control Act of 1969, authorized the Federal Reserve to institute certain direct controls on consumer credit and some of the lending activities of larger banks. Two consequences followed from the actions of both the Federal Reserve and the Carter administration. First, there was a sharp curtailment in the first half of 1980 in the expansion of both money and credit. Consumer credit outstanding dropped by $9.8 billion in the second quarter of 1980.[37] Second, the restrictive measures taken in late 1979 and the spring of 1980 plunged the economy into one of the sharpest but shortest recessions on record. During the second quarter of 1980, *real* gross national product dropped at an annual rate of 9.9 percent.[38] The unexpected sharpness of the downturn led the Federal Reserve to ease up on the money supply and in July the direct controls were ended as the president revoked the authority of the Federal Reserve to institute these controls. Once again, however, the potency of monetary policy to push the

36. *Economic Report of the President* (Washington, D.C.: U.S. Government Printing Office, 1979), p. 93.
37. *Economic Report of the President,* (Washington, D.C.: U.S. Government Printing Office, 1981), p. 310.
38. Ibid., p. 235.

economy into recession had been demonstrated. As in prior recessions, there was a deceleration in the inflation rate (see Figure 14–15). The upturn that began in the second half of 1980 continued until the second quarter of 1981, when the restrictive effects of the Reagan administration's fiscal and monetary policies began to be felt.

The Reagan Experiment

Ronald Reagan's economic advisors come from the new classical and supply-side school. As a result, his economic program differs drastically from the Keynesian and, to some extent, monetarist policies we have seen used by other administrations. Supply-side economists, such as Arthur Laffer of the University of Southern California, assert that the tax burden on individuals is so high in this country that incentives to work and save are badly hurt. Consequently, a reduction in taxes would unleash an explosion of work and saving so great that federal tax revenues ultimately would increase. Not surprisingly, a significant element in the Reagan strategy was a major reduction in personal and business taxes. Initially the president asked that tax rates on personal income be reduced by 10 percent "across the board" for three years, beginning July 1, 1981. This was basically the Kemp-Roth approach to tax reduction. For a number of years Representative Jack Kemp and Senator William Roth jointly introduced legislation in the Congress calling for a 30 percent reduction in federal taxes, spread over a three-year period. As we saw in Chapter 12, the intellectual basis for the Kemp-Roth proposals comes from the supply-side theories of Arthur Laffer. As finally approved by the Congress in the Economic Recovery Tax Act of 1981, personal income tax rates were reduced by 5 percent in the first year, effective October 1, 1981, and by 10 percent each in 1982 and 1983, effective July 1 in each year. The legislation also lowered the top rate on earned income from 70 to 50 percent and, beginning in 1985, tax brackets are to be indexed to prevent "bracket creep"—higher taxes caused by inflation alone. With respect to business taxes, the act established a new system of accelerated depreciation, called the *accelerated cost recovery system* (ACRS), and increased the investment tax credit for certain types of investments. The Reagan tax package, irrespective of its intended supply-side effects, also was designed to bring about a major redistribution of the tax burden in favor of business and upper-income groups. The reason was that Reagan's policy aimed to stimulate investment specifically, and more money in the hands of business and upper-income groups was thought to be the most effective way to achieve this. They would invest in new capital, the capital would create jobs, and the tax cut's benefits would "trickle down" to the rest of the taxpayers in the form of more jobs and a growing economy.

The Reagan administration sought strong support from the Federal Reserve System as the overall program was implemented. The administration asked the Federal Reserve to cut the rate of growth of the money supply in half by 1986, a proposal that reflected the president's firm commitment to the monetarist position. Reagan has also sought to cut the costs government imposes on business, primarily by lessening or eliminating government regulations. The belief that federal regulatory activity has become excessively burdensome for business and thus a major factor in inflation is largely the handiwork of Murray L. Weidenbaum, economics professor at Washington University and first chairman of the Reagan Council of Economic Advisers. Professor Weidenbaum is the source of the widely circulated figure that federal regulation costs taxpayers, business firms, and consumers about $100 billion a year, a figure by no means accepted by other economists.

A Critique of the Reagan Experiment

When the president signed into law in August 1981 the Economic Recovery Tax Act of 1981, he was extremely optimistic, predicting that the act would bring about stable prices, rising employment, economic growth, and a substantial reduction in the size and influence of the federal government in the economy. With the exception of a sharp decline in the inflation rate during 1982, none of these lofty goals of the Reagan administration was attained during the administration's first two years. We shall conclude this section with an examination of some of the reasons why the results to date have been disappointing.

Central to the entire thrust of the Reagan program for economic recovery was the assumption that federal spending is out of control. As put in the President's *A Program for Economic Recovery,* "The *uncontrolled* growth of government spending has been a primary cause of the sustained high rate of inflation experienced by the American economy. . . . Thus, a central goal of the economic program is to reduce the rate at which government spending increases."[39] The problem with this is that essentially it is not correct, resting upon a misreading of recent trends in government spending in relation to spending in general. In reaching its conclusions about what was happening to federal spending—especially federal spending in relation to the gross national product—the administration examined only very recent data. Longer-term trends were not examined, trends which do not support the idea that federal spending is "out of control."

The basis for this viewpoint is found in Table 15–4, showing rates of growth of federal spending and total spending (as measured by nominal gross national product), and also federal spending as a percentage of the gross national product. These data cover the period 1965–1982.

A close examination of the data reveals a most important fact. In the table the years in which the figures are in italics and underlined are years

---

39. *A Program for Economic Recovery,* op. cit., p. 10 (italics added).

TABLE 15–4. The Annual Rate of Growth of Total Spending and Federal Spending; Federal Spending as a Percentage of GNP: 1965–82

Year	Total Spending*	Federal Spending*	Federal Spending as a Percentage of GNP†	Comment
1965	8.4%	4.7%	17.9%	
1966	9.4	16.0	18.9	Vietnam War
1967	5.8	14.0	20.5	Vietnam War
1968	9.2	10.3	20.7	Vietnam War
1969	8.1	4.3	19.6	
1970	5.2	8.4	20.5	Recession
1971	8.6	8.0	20.5	
1972	10.1	10.7	20.6	Nixon recession
1973	11.8	8.2	19.9	
1974	8.1	13.2	20.9	Recession
1975	8.0	19.1	23.0	Recession
1976	10.9	7.9	22.4	
1977	11.6	9.5	21.9	
1978	12.4	9.2	21.4	
1979	12.0	10.5	21.1	
1980	8.9	16.4	22.9	Recession
1981	11.6	15.6	22.7	
1982	4.1	11.0	24.2	Recession

SOURCE: *Economic Report of the President,* 1983.
*As measured by GNP in current dollars.
†For goods and services and transfer payments in current dollars.
Note: Years in italics are years in which the percentage growth of federal spending exceeded the percentage growth of total spending.

in which federal spending did grow more rapidly than spending in general, leading, consequently, to a rise in the ratio of federal spending to the gross national product. The important fact revealed by these data is that, with the sole exception of 1972, the years in which federal spending grew more rapidly than spending in general were either war years (the Vietnam war) or recession years. The reasons for such growth are easy to understand. As we saw earlier, there was a major expansion in federal spending during the Vietnam war. Recessions lead to sharp increases in transfer payments because of rising unemployment. Consequently, we have more spending for unemployment compensation, welfare, food stamps, earlier retirement, and other purposes. In each of the last four recessions this happened. It was the Vietnam war that boosted federal spending to a level 20 percent higher than the gross national product. Subsequent boosts have come about because of recessions.

Two additional observations may be made about these data, both tinged with irony. In the 1980 presidential campaign, Mr. Reagan was largely successful in convincing the public that the Carter administration had lost control of the budget. Yet the facts indicate otherwise; in the three nonrecession years of the Carter administration, the ratio of federal spending to the gross national product declined. It rose only in 1980, again a result of the short but sharp recession in the spring of the year. In its economic recovery program, the Reagan administration set as a target a reduction in the federal spending–gross national product ratio to 19.0 by 1986. Yet, under the Reagan administration, the ratio is now higher (24.2 percent) than at any time since 1965. Again this is a consequence of the recession. Because supply-side effects failed to deliver a balanced budget, Reagan's tax program has become the kind of deficit-financed expansionary program Keynesian theorists advocate. As one commentator pointed out, by the end of 1982, the effect of "Reaganomics" was more Keynesian than Laffer.[40] As a consequence, the real effect of the program was to pull the economy simultaneously in two opposite directions, toward expansion because of the fiscal side and toward contraction because stringent monetary restraint was also a part of the plan. Reducing the rate of growth of the money supply to one-half the 1980 rate (6.6 percent for M1 in 1980 and 9.0 percent for M2) was essential both for bringing down the inflation rate and for inducing a decline in inflationary expectations. Unfortunately, monetary restraint proved during the first two years of the Reagan experiment to be a stronger force than the expansionary thrust flowing from the fiscal actions. Consequently, the economy fell into its fourth recession since 1969.[41]

Table 15–5, labeled "The Reagan Economic Experiment in Brief," gives data in support of the foregoing arguments. All the data in the table were taken from the president's original plan, *A Program For Economic Recovery*. These data are on a fiscal rather than an annual year basis, covering the years 1981 through 1986. The (C) pertains to the last budget for which the Carter administration was primarily responsible (the fiscal year which ended September 30, 1981), while the four years labeled (R) are the budgets for which the Reagan administration is responsible. Since it is not now known who will be president after 1984, the budget for fiscal 1986—the first budget for which a president elected in 1984 will be fully responsible—is labeled (?).

The first six lines in the table show the sources of the problems confronting the Reagan economic program during the administration's first two years in office. The next seven lines show some key projections made in the president's economic program and the actual results to date.

40. Seymour Zucker, "Commentary," *Business Week,* March 21, 1983.
41. Some have argued that the 1981–82 recession was a consequence of monetary restraint which began when the Federal Reserve changed its policy in October 1979. This is not strictly correct. From October 1979 through June 1980 it is true that monetary policy was restrictive as measured by the rate of change in M1, but from July to December 1980 it was expansive. Beginning in January 1981, and with the full approval of the Reagan administration, the policy again turned highly restrictive. This continued through October 1981. The onset of the recession was in August 1981. From November 1981 to July 1982, the trend was mixed, although still tending to be more restrictive than expansionary. After August 1982, as the severity of the recession became more and more apparent, monetary policy again turned expansive. The annual rate of increase in M1 went from a low of 3 percent in June 1982 to 12.7 percent in January 1983.

TABLE 15—5.   The Reagan Economic Experiment in Brief* (Fiscal Years 1981–86)

Item	(C) 1981	(R) 1982	(R) 1983	(R) 1984	(R) 1985	(?) 1986	Total
1. Additional military spending	1.3	7.2	20.7	27.0	50.2	63.1	169.5
2. Tax reduction	8.9	53.9	100.0	148.1	185.7	221.7	718.3
3. Total of 1 + 2	10.2	61.1	120.7	175.1	235.9	284.8	887.8
4. Targeted budget reductions	4.4	41.4	79.7	104.4	117.6	123.8	471.3
5. Difference of 3 − 4	5.8	19.7	41.0	70.7	118.3	161.0	416.5
6. Expected revenue gains from economic growth	—	48.3	57.1	58.9	75.3	87.2	326.8
7. Estimated federal receipts after new tax policy	600.2	650.5	710.2	772.1	850.9	942.0	4,525.9
8. Actual revenue receipts	559.3	617.8	597.5†	659.7†	n.a.	n.a.	n.a.
9. Shortfall	0.9	32.7	112.7	112.4	—	—	—
10. Targeted budget deficit (−) or surplus (+)	−54.9	−45.0	−22.9	+0.5	+6.9	+29.9	—
11. Actual budget deficit (−) or surplus (+)	−57.9	−110.6	−207.7†	−188.8†	—	—	—
12. Planned federal expenditures as a percentage of GNP‡	23.0	21.8	20.4	19.3	19.2	19.0	—
13. Actual federal expenditures as a percentage of GNP‡	22.7	24.2	—	—	—	—	—

*All numbers are taken from the president's *A Program for Economic Recovery*, February 18, 1981, and are in billions of dollars.
†Estimated.
‡Calendar year basis.

Lines 1 and 2 in the Table are crucial, for they show, first, the planned increase in military spending over this six-year period and the planned reduction in taxes. The sum of these two, shown in Line 3, represents the amount of revenue needed either to finance the military buildup or to offset the revenue lost through tax reduction. One way to achieve this is by reductions in the nonmilitary parts of the budget. The reductions originally targeted in the economic recovery program are shown in Line 4. The difference between Lines 3 and 4 represents, therefore, the amount of revenue needed to offset revenue lost through the tax reduction and revenue needed because of larger military outlays (Line 5). This difference is of key importance because it yields a rough quantitative measure of the task faced by supply-side economics. As we have seen, the basic rationale for the 5–10–10 tax cut was that it would improve incentives to such an extent that production would rise dramatically and with it there would be an actual increase in the revenue of the federal government. The actual increases in tax revenues projected from the workings of supply-side economics contained in the economic recovery document are shown in Line 6. These gains were predicated on annual average rates of growth in real GNP of 1.1 percent in 1981, 4.2 percent in 1982, 5.0 percent in 1983, 4.5 percent in 1984, and 4.2 percent in 1985 and 1986.[42] The amounts of added revenue to be gained from the supply-side effects (Line 6) did not match fully the needs for more revenue (Line 5), but, if the plan had worked out as intended, the differences would not have been overwhelming. Unfortunately, this did not happen, one reason being that many believed that the entire program rested upon projected rates of growth in real GNP that were wholly unrealistic.[43]

The failure of supply-side economics to deliver on the promised growth meant that during at least the first two years of the Reagan administration the economy's actual performance fell far short of the projected performance in key areas. As indicated, some of these results are reflected in Lines 7 through 13 in Table 15–5. Line 7 shows estimated receipts after the tax changes were in effect, whereas Line 8 shows actual and estimated revenue through fiscal 1984. As shown in Line 9, there has been a cumulative revenue shortfall of nearly $259 billion in this period, a development that accounts in large part for the expansionist thrust of the fiscal side of the recovery program. Because of this shortfall, targeted budget deficits (−) or surpluses (+) (shown in Line 10) failed to materialize. Rather, the result is large actual (or expected) budget deficits through fiscal 1984 (Line 11). Finally, the recession brought about by tight money caused planned and actual federal expenditures as percentages of the GNP to rise significantly above the planned ratio. These figures are shown in Lines 12 and 13, respectively.

While all the evidence to date indicates that the administration's 5–10–10 percent cut in personal income tax rates has not had the intended supply-side effects, there are other effects whose long-term consequences may significantly affect the economy's macroeconomic performance. These are the redistributional effects of the combined impact of the income tax cuts and the reductions in transfer spending for social and welfare purposes. As *The Wall Street Journal* stated on December 6, 1982, the debate over how to cure the recession may overlook an impor-

---

42. *A Program for Economic Recovery*, op. cit., p. 25.
43. The arithmetic of the Reagan program is such that added revenue expected from the supply-side effect worked out at about 45 cents for every dollar of tax income lost through the tax cuts (the total shown in Line 6 divided by the total shown in Line 2).

tant impact of President Reagan's tax and budget cuts: "The rich are getting richer and the poor are getting poorer."[44]

This conclusion of *The Wall Street Journal* is thoroughly documented in a special study by the Congressional Budget Office completed in February 1982. The combined effect of tax cuts and reductions in benefits flowing to individuals is to bring about a *net* transfer from the lowest to the highest income groups. The data in the CBO study pertained to 1983 and was based upon the first two stages of the tax cut (the 5 percent cut effective October 1, 1981, and the 10 percent cut effective July 1, 1982).

The results of this study are found in Table 15–6, which shows on a per-household basis for five different household income classes the reduction in cash and in "in-kind" benefits, the increase in income because of the tax reduction, and the net change in the household income because of the combined effect of these changes.

Although the long-term consequences of the Reagan budgets are still to be determined, some probable effects are clearly evident. There already has been a decided increase in the poverty population, partly as a result of the 1981–82 recession and partly as a consequence of the budgetary trends reflected in Table 15–6. In 1979 the incidence of poverty in the United States was 11.6 percent, down from the 17.3 percent that prevailed in 1965, before most of President Johnson's "war on poverty" legislation was passed. The poverty ratio rose to 14 percent in 1981 and rose again to 15 percent in 1982. Even with recovery, this trend may continue. Second—and most important—it is possible that for the first time since the end of World War II there may be a significant change in the distribution of personal income in this country. For three and a half decades there has been a remarkable stability in this distribution, but the long-term effect of the Reagan tax and expenditure program is likely to change the distribution significantly in the direction of *greater inequality of income*. This could have a profound and probably adverse effect upon the economy's performance. It will be recalled from our discussion in

TABLE 15–6. Net Change in Federal Individual Income Taxes and Federal Benefit Payments for Individuals by Household Income Class: 1983

	Less than $10,000	$10,000– 20,000	$20,000– 40,000	$40,000– 80,000	Over $80,000
Cash benefits	− $270	− 140	− 90	− 70	− 70
"In-kind" benefits	− $90	− 80	− 50	− 60	− 50
Taxes	$120	440	950	1,830	15,250
Net change	− $240	220	810	1,700	15,130

SOURCE: Congressional Budget Office, Special Study, 1982.

44. *The Wall Street Journal,* December 6, 1982, "The Outlook" column.

Chapter 5 ("Consumption, Saving, and the Multiplier") that the overall distribution of income is an important factor in determining the position and shape of the consumption function. A significant tilt in the direction of greater inequality in the distribution of money incomes could lower the consumption function, thereby making it more difficult on both a short- and long-term basis to generate sufficient investment spending to attain full employment.

Finally, we will look at some additional overall results of the Reagan experiment, primarily with respect to the gross national product and key components. Before reviewing these data, we should note again that the major accomplishment of the Reagan administration in terms of key macroeconomic variables was to bring the inflation rate down from an annual rate of 12.4 percent (as measured by the consumer price index) in 1980 to 3.9 percent in 1982. This gain, however, was the consequence of the recession, and, as we saw earlier in Chapter 14 (Figure 14–15), the pattern was similar to what the economy experienced in each of the previous three post-1969 recessions. The unanswered question is whether or not the inflation rate will stay low once a strong recovery is under way.

Table 15–7 compares the first two years of the Reagan economic experiment with the first two years of the Carter administration. For this comparison, fourth-quarter data are used. What these figures reveal is that none of the optimistic expectations that accompanied the launching of the "Program for Economic Recovery" was achieved during the first two years of the Reagan administration. In every major category of real expenditure except military outlays, the first two years of the Reagan

TABLE 15–7.   The Reagan and Carter Administration Compared: The First Two Years (Gross National Product Data in billions of 1972 prices)

	First Two Carter Years			First Two Reagan Years		
	1976–IV	1978–IV	Percentage Change	1980–IV	1982–IV	Percentage Change
Gross National Product	$1,315.4	$1,468.4	11.6%	$1,479.4	$1,473.9	− 0.4%
Personal Consumption Expenditure	$ 839.4	$ 919.2	9.5%	$ 941.0	$ 967.5	2.8%
Gross Private Domestic Investment	$ 186.3	$ 242.2	30.0%	$ 209.6	$ 183.8	−12.3%
Investment in Durable Equipment	$ 89.4	$ 119.0	33.1%	$ 118.9	$ 107.9	− 9.3%
Exports (net)	$ 23.4	$ 29.3	25.2%	$ 45.6	$ 23.3	−48.9%
Government Purchase of Goods and Services	$ 266.4	$ 277.7	4.3%	$ 283.2	$ 299.2	5.6%
Military Purchases	$ 65.5	$ 66.2	0.9%	$ 69.6	$ 81.2	16.7%

SOURCE: Survey of Current Business, July 1983.

experiment were inferior to the same period in the Carter administration. Little beyond this can be said with accuracy at this point. The longer-term effects of the Reagan "counter-revolution" may be more salutary, but this remains to be seen. To date, however, the results of the Reagan "experiment" show, first, that supply-side economics is of doubtful validity and, second, that monetary policy, stringently applied, can reduce the inflation rate, but the price is high in terms of unemployment and lost output.

Some Summary Comments

What has been learned from the experience with economic policy in the post–World War II period, especially the turbulent years since the onset of the Vietnam war? Several points are important. First, it seems clear that we have the economic knowledge necessary to manage the economy in a manner which will prevent another major depression on the order of the 1930s. None of the seven recorded recessions since 1945 has been allowed to develop into a long and damaging depression. That is a plus. What we don't have is the knowledge or skill to "fine tune" the economy. "Fine tuning" is a phrase which came into vogue after the success of the Kennedy tax cut. It meant the continuous use of fine adjustments in fiscal and monetary policy to keep the economy moving on a full-employment path of economic growth without excessive inflation. The experiences of the last decade have disabused most economists—not to mention the public—of the notion that through "fine tuning" the business cycle has been banished from our economic life. As we have already indicated, the business cycle is far from dead. We shall examine this fact further in Chapter 17.

Second, it should be quite plain from the experience since 1965 that through fiscal and monetary policies inflation cannot be ended or even brought under control—at least not without costs in terms of unemployment that are largely unacceptable to our society. The jury is still out on the question of whether the 1981–82 recession brought the inflation rate down permanently. Putting on the fiscal and monetary brakes pushes the economy into a recession much faster than it brings down the inflation rate. That is the sad lesson of the Nixon, Ford, Carter, and, perhaps, Reagan administrations. We shall never know, of course, *if* the prompt imposition of a tax increase in 1966 might have held the Vietnam inflation in check. What we do know is that once inflation gets started and persists, then inflationary expectations become built into the economy, expectations which tend to be cumulative in their effects. No doubt a recession (or depression) deeper and more prolonged than anything experienced since World War II could permanently break the back of such expectations, but such a policy might destroy the economy in the process.

Third—and this is a corollary of the above—the social ineffectiveness of a restrictive monetary and fiscal policy stems from wage and price rigidities deeply rooted in the structure of the economy—the power of trade unions and the giant corporations. This makes for a situation in which prices and wages—as well as other costs—are readily flexible upward, but not flexible downward. Under such conditions the results that we have been discussing are almost inevitable when the money supply is tightened or taxes are increased. Oligopolistic firms and strong trade unions will react to a falloff in demand by raising prices and wages. Worse yet, the impact of restrictive monetary and fiscal measures may add directly to inflationary pressures because higher interest rates become a part of the cost structure and higher taxes may lead workers to bargain for higher money wages to maintain take-home pay.[45] The foregoing would not work in a highly competitive economic environment, such as Keynes assumed, but it surely works when there is a substantial amount of economic power in the hands of both firms and workers.

As a fourth point, the experience of the last dozen years casts doubt upon our ability as a society to submit to the social discipline necessary to make fiscal and monetary policy work *in both directions*. This is aside from the necessity of creating conditions under which we can "dampen down" the economy without plunging it into a recession. Admittedly this is more a political than an economic problem, yet it is one which economists cannot ignore. The realities of our political life suggest that policy is one-directional—expansionary in the form of tax cuts. Worse yet, it seems we as a society are unwilling to finance through taxes what we demand out of the national government. In 25 of the last 37 years the federal government has run a deficit (on a national income and accounts basis); since 1965 there have been only two years in which the federal budget was in balance or registered a surplus. This is not to suggest a return to an outmoded fiscal philosophy which says the budget must be balanced annually, but serious questions are raised about the efficacy of modern fiscal and monetary policies *if* the norm has become one of deficits in good years and bad. Federal red ink is not the sole cause of inflation as many conservative thinkers believe, but when conditions are relatively prosperous and employment high (as has been the case over much of the post–World War II era), they do contribute to inflation.

Finally, we need to realize and keep in perspective just how far we have come in our understanding of the economy as compared to where we were in the early 1930s. Then there was no real understanding of what could and should be done in the face of the collapse that began in 1929 and quickly spread to most of the world. This was so in spite of the impressive body of theoretical analysis which had been developing over the prior century—classical economics. We have not yet found the exact-

---

45. Robert Eisner, "What Went Wrong?" *Journal of Political Economy*, May / June 1971, p. 633.

key to the problem which is now most vexing—stagflation—but in modern macroeconomic analysis we do have the necessary theoretical tools to do the job. Furthermore, our policy instruments, imperfect as they may be, are being used to prevent our having to face another bout with mass unemployment 1930s style while we struggle to cure an equally damaging social evil—chronic inflation.

Summary

1. Monetary and fiscal policies are the two major policy instruments utilized by contemporary systems of market capitalism. Monetary policy focuses on the money supply and interest rates, using either as a policy guide. If the monetary authorities (i.e., the Board of Governors of the Federal Reserve System) are oriented toward monetarism, they will focus on the money supply. If not, their focus will be on interest rates.

2. Fiscal policy operates primarily through the budget of the federal government, using changes in taxes or changes in expenditures to achieve the desired budgetary effects. A budgetary surplus has a restrictive effect on the economy, whereas a deficit is expansionary. The full (or high)-employment budget emerged in the post–World War II period as the primary tool for the implementation of fiscal policy.

3. There are important theoretical limits to the application of both fiscal and monetary policies. Monetary policy becomes ineffective in theory when the demand for money becomes totally elastic—the flat range in the *LM* curve—whereas fiscal policy becomes ineffective when no more money is available for transactions purposes—the vertical portion of the *LM* curve.

4. In the Truman-Eisenhower years (1945–60) no conscious efforts were made to apply the principles of modern macroeconomics to the overall management of the economy. In general, this period, especially the Eisenhower era, was dominated by fears of inflation; consequently, budgetary policy tended to be restrictive. As a result, there were several recessions during the period, unemployment was relatively high, and growth was sluggish.

5. The Kennedy-Johnson era (1961–68) represents the first time that an administration actively embraced contemporary macroeconomics and sought to use it for the effective management of the economy. The Kennedy administration developed the rationale for what became the 1964 tax cut entirely on the basis of the Keynesian income-expenditure approach to the economy. Evidence indicates that the tax cut was successful. The Johnson administration failed to follow through by applying the same principles to the economy in 1966, when the buildup in military expenditures called for a tax increase.

6. During the Nixon, Ford, and Carter presidencies (1969–80) inflation was the primary concern most of the time. All three administrations sought to control inflation by restrictive monetary and fiscal policies, but with results which were generally less than satisfactory. Restrictive policies produced recessions which brought the inflation rate down, but the change was not permanent, as each recovery saw a new surge in inflation. The result was a decade of "stagflation," excessive unemployment and excessive inflation at the same time.

7. The Reagan administration introduced the most far-reaching change in policy of any of the post–World War II administrations. It abandoned the view characteristic of the economy from the 1960s onward to the effect that overall management was necessary and that fiscal and monetary policies were the instruments for this management. Rather, it adopted a major tax cut on the basis of supply-side economic principles in the expectation that this would stimulate production. At the same time the administration embraced monetarism, opting for a restrictive monetary stance. The net result was a serious recession, then a sharp drop in the inflation, followed by the beginnings of a recovery in early 1983.

IV

Economic Growth and Fluctuations

16

Productivity and Growth

We now turn our attention to some of the principles and problems of a growing economy. Up to this point we have examined output, employment, and the price level on the assumption of a relatively fixed productive capacity. Now we shall shift from an essentially static to a dynamic approach, analyzing what happens over time when there are continuous changes in both the economy's productive capacity and its aggregate demand function.

We shall proceed to approach the problem from two perspectives. First, we shall look at the supply side of the matter. This means we examine the basic determinants of the economy's productive capacity and how that capacity may change over time. We first encountered this issue in Chapter 3 when we discussed the relationship between employment and output. Now we shall explore this in depth. The analysis will focus, first, on the production function concept, which provides us with the formal, theoretical basis for identifying the sources of growth in the modern economy, and, second, on the concept of potential output, which provides a practical and useful way to translate the theoretical basis for output into a measured magnitude.

Second, if the productive capacity of the economy is growing over time, how can the use of this capacity—especially its full-employment use—be assured? This is the basic theoretical problem posed by growth, one that has been looked at in different ways in the post–World War II era. The quite simple but nonetheless fundamental fact about such an economy is that the economy's productive potential is utilized *only* if demand (actual or expected) exists for the goods and services produced. If there is no market for what is being produced, a market economy won't work, a point often neglected by supply-side theorists. Resources and technology make output possible, but it is through demand that potential output is transformed into actual output.

The Nature of Economic Growth

Economic growth can be defined as the expansion of a nation's capability to produce the goods and services its people want. Since the productive capacity of an economy depends basically on the quantity and quality of its resources as well as on its level of technological attainment, economic growth involves the process of expanding and improving these determinants of productive capacity.

Although a fundamental definition of economic growth is the economy's potential for the production of goods and services, this is not a sufficient definition. Productive capacity is crucially important to the concept of economic growth, but actual growth depends not only upon change in the economy's potential for production, but also upon the extent to which that capacity is utilized. Economic growth involves, in other words, an increase over time in the actual output of goods and services as well as an increase in the economy's capability to produce goods and services.

Interest in economic growth stems in large part from our concern with the material welfare of human beings. There is no acceptable set of criteria for measurement of such a subjective matter as welfare, but there is general agreement that material welfare (or well-being), in the last analysis, depends upon the availability of goods and services. A rising level of economic well-being for any society requires an expansion in its output of goods and services.

If we are interested in economic growth because of its significance for our material well-being, then what counts is not just an increase in capacity and output per se, but output per capita. What is important from a welfare standpoint is the availability of goods and services per person; it is reasonable to talk of an improvement in the material well-being of a people only if, over time, each person has a growing volume of goods and services at his disposal. Thus, the measure of economic growth that is most meaningful is the level of real output per capita. Analysis of economic growth on a per-person basis requires that we take into account not only changes in a nation's productive potential and its use of that potential, but also changes in its population. If population grows at a faster rate than either output or capacity, no improvement in the average standard of material well-being on a per capita basis is possible (see Table 16–1).

Why is economic growth important? Growth certainly is not an end in itself. It is a means to an end. It provides a society with the means—resources plus goods and services—whereby it can do more things for itself and for its citizens. Growth makes more goods and services available to consumers for their private use, and more resources available to the public sector for its purpose and responsibilities. The ways in which private citizens and governments use the added output may be wise or foolish, but one cannot gainsay the fact that without economic growth prospects for a better life for everyone would be much grimmer. In the developed nations of the West standards of life are affluent enough so that some of the population can afford the luxury of discussing whether or not more growth is desirable. But for most of mankind this is not possible. The overwhelming proportion of the world's people live on the edge of grinding poverty. For them growth is an absolute imperative if they are to survive.

The Growth Record of the American Economy

A brief review of the growth record of the American economy shows that over the long run its performance has been highly impressive. The overall record of growth for the period 1839–1981 is summarized in Table 16–1. The data for 1839 through 1959 are taken from an analysis of the American economy prepared in 1960 for the Joint Economic Committee of the U.S. Congress. Separate data for the period 1960–81 are shown in Column 5 of the table. They are taken from the 1982 *Economic Report of the President.*

As the table shows, the data for 1839 through 1959 are broken down into three subperiods, each of 40 years' length. The average annual rate of growth for the real GNP of the American economy over the whole 120-year period (1839–1959) was 3.66 percent, a record unmatched by any other country for so long a period. These data also show that there was some slowing down in the rate of total real output in the third period, although when the data are reduced to a per capita basis there does not

TABLE 16–1.   Growth Trends in the American Economy, 1839–81 (average percentage increase per year)

	(1) Entire Period	(2)	(3)	(4)	(5)
	1839–1959	1839–79	1879–1919	1919–59	1960–81
		40-Year Subperiods			
Price level	1.15	−0.16	1.91	1.40	4.92
GNP in constant prices	3.66	4.31	3.72	2.97	3.44
Population	1.97	2.71	1.91	1.30	1.04
Per capita GNP in constant prices	1.64	1.55	1.76	1.64	2.46

SOURCE: Joint Economic Committee, Congress of the United States, *Staff Report on Employment, Growth and Price Levels,* 1960, *Economic Report of the President,* 1982.

appear to be any significant change in the long-term trends. Real GNP rose at an annual average rate of 4.31 percent during the first 40-year period (1839–79). In the period 1879–1919 the growth rate fell to 3.72 percent per year, and then for the next 40 years (1919–59) declined further to an annual average rate of 2.97 percent. The per capita data do not show the same long-term decline. During the first 40-year period GNP per capita in constant prices increased at an annual average rate of 1.55 percent. This period, though, was the one in which population increased most rapidly; population grew at an annual average rate of 2.71 percent, as compared to 1.91 percent in the second 40-year period and 1.30 percent in the third 40-year period. The slower rate of population growth is reflected in the fact that real GNP per capita in constant prices actually increased at a more rapid rate in the second and third 40-year periods, even though this was not true for the aggregate GNP. In the period 1879–1919 real GNP per capita rose at an annual average rate of 1.76 percent. During the next 40-year period (1919–59) the rate declined to an annual average of 1.64 percent, although this figure is still above the average of 1.55 percent per year for the first one-third of the whole 120-year period.

And what of the more recent period, 1960–81? The data do suggest some shifts in the long-term trends, although it is, perhaps, premature to say that they are permanent. More likely they reflect in part some of the turbulence of the last two decades. Real GNP grew more slowly than the long-term historic average, a development resulting in part from four recessions. The most dramatic change is in the price level, as its rate of growth is significantly above the average for any of the pre-1960 periods covered by the data in the table. This clearly reflects both the severity of the recent inflation and its uniqueness as compared to the nation's historical experience. The trend for population growth continued to decline, a development that is in line with past experience. Since 1970 the rate of growth of population had dropped to less than 1 percent the actual rate being 0.86 percent for 1970–81. This is close to the zero population growth (ZPG) rate, a development some anti-growth advocates welcome. Finally, real per capita GNP rose at a rate faster than any previous period in span covered by the table. Was this a real gain? Given the fact of an unpopular war and the social turbulence of the 1960s and early 1970s one would, indeed, have to be bold to assert that *all* of this increase represented real gains in social and economic welfare.

Economic Growth and the Production Function

In Chapter 3, the idea of the production function was introduced, a concept which offers a useful way to organize thinking about the sources of growth in the modern economy. In a formal, theoretical sense, the production function sets forth the relationship between the quantities of resources used during a period of time and the output produced during the same period of time. Conceptually, the relationship applies to a single commodity or service or to the entire economy. Our concern is with the latter, namely, the relationship between the national output (GNP) and the resources needed to produce that output.

In the form presented originally in Chapter 3 (see pp. 88–90), the production function showed how output (GNP) varied in response to changing levels of employment *(N)*, given known values for the economy's stock of natural resources *(R')*, capital equipment *(K')*, and the state of technology *(T)*. Such a production function is shown in Part A of Figure 16–1. As more people are employed *(N)*, the level of output (GNP) rises, but not proportionally because the principle of diminishing productivity applies when only one input varies. In the diagram this is reflected in the gradual leveling off of the output curve. Note that the diagram shows that there are two possible ways in which output can be increased from GNP_1 to GNP_2. The first is simply by increasing the quantity of labor used from N_1 to N_2. This, of course, reflects the basic relationship represented by the production function. The other way comes from a shift upward in the entire function—from the curve GNP_a to GNP_b in the diagram—a development which comes about through either a change in the stock of capital and natural resources, an improvement in technology, or some combination of both. An upward shift in the production function means that the economy has become more efficient—that there has been an improvement in the productivity of labor—since more output is being produced with the same quantity of labor. This is the basic meaning of an improvement in efficiency.

The foregoing represents a standard and well-known way of depicting the production function. Another useful way is to describe it in terms of a relationship between the quantity of capital per worker *(K/N)* and the output per worker (GNP/N). This approach puts the focus on a key con-

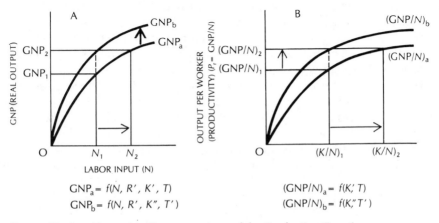

FIGURE 16–1. Alternative Representations of the Production Function

cept, namely, the average productivity of labor, a variable identified in Chapter 3 by the symbol (P_r). As pointed out earlier (see p. 88), the productivity of labor is a convenient measure of the efficiency with which labor is being used in production. We must be cautious in the use of this concept, for it does not simply measure the average skill or efficiency of the individual worker as such; rather, it is a useful way to express in terms of the input of a single resource—namely, labor—all of the factors that have a bearing on the efficiency of the economic system. Output per worker can be measured on a worker-hour basis, as when GNP is divided by total hours worked by the labor force, or on a worker-year basis, when GNP is divided simply by the number of people at work in a given year. In concept both are the same; only the time unit differs. If P_r above stands for *output per worker-year*, then the economy's productive capacity is equal to $P_r \times N'$, the economy's fully employed labor force.

A key factor in determining worker productivity as defined above is the amount of capital per worker (K/N). If we think of capital essentially as tools—basically this is the nature of capital—then, in general, the more capital (tools) workers on the average have at their disposition, the more efficient each worker will be. It is reasonable, therefore, to conclude that the output per worker per unit of time will increase as the quantity of capital available per worker increases. This observation permits us to express the production function as a relationship between capital per worker (which is also called the capital-labor ratio) and the productivity of labor. This version of the production function is shown in Part B of Figure 16–1. On the vertical axis worker productivity is shown and on the horizontal axis capital per worker. Note that the curve is similar in shape to the curve depicting how total output varies as quantity of labor used in production increases (Part A of Figure 16–1). The reason again is diminishing productivity. Worker productivity will increase as the capital-labor ratio increases, but not without limit. As long as all other resources and technology remain fixed, the gains in worker productivity attained by increasing the ratio of capital to labor will eventually level off. Two curves are also shown in Part B of Figure 16–1, and they mean that output per worker can be increased from GNP/N_1 to GNP/N_2 in one of two ways: The first is simply by increasing the capital/labor ratio from K/N_1 to K/N_2, a process precisely analogous to increasing employment from N_1 to N_2, as depicted in Part A of Figure 16–1. Alternatively, the increase may come through an upward shift in the entire production function, a result that can come about only through an increase in the efficiency of capital, given no change in the quantity of labor being employed. This represents technological change, which has its impact primarily on the efficiency with which capital is used in the economy.

Theoretical Sources of Economic Growth

One important result that flows from the foregoing discussion of the production function is a precise identification of the primary sources of growth in the modern economy, of which there are basically three. First, there is growth in the supply of labor. As first discussed, the production function shows that output will increase as more labor is employed, *other things being equal*. The latter applies primarily to capital and technology. If we put this into the context of increases in the economy's productive capacity *(Q)*, then changes in the size of the labor force are an important source for such increases, again assuming the stock of capital and technology to be a given.

A second major source of growth in the modern economy is physical capital—the tools with which the labor force has to work. Our analysis of the production function concept has shown that, as long as capital is growing more rapidly than the labor force, worker productivity will rise, even though at a decreasing rate because of diminishing returns. Other things being equal, however, this means that normally an increase in the capital stock will increase the economy's productive potential. The same line of reasoning applies to natural resources *(R')*, which historically in the United States have been an important source of growth. Today this is far less true than it used to be, given the settlement of the continent and the absence of new lands to be opened to settlement. As we have seen from our discussion of investment spending in Chapter 6, the factors which influence spending for capital goods in a market economy are both numerous and complex. But there is one basic point to be kept in mind: Utlimately it is the expected profitability of capital goods which determines whether or not they will be produced and used. This is true whether we approach the question from the capacity side or the demand side. More capital is created only through spending for capital goods by entrepreneurs, and more spending for capital goods takes place only if the profit prospects for the new capital are favorable.

The third and final source of growth is technological change, depicted in both types of the production function shown in Figure 16–1 by shifts in the functions. Technological change means that more output can be produced with the same quantity of labor, given the stock of capital *(K')* and the available natural resources *(R')*, or that, with no change in capital per worker *(K/N)*, more goods and services can be produced. To put the matter somewhat differently, technical progress means that more output can be produced with the same inputs. Like the determinants of investment spending, which adds to the capital stock, the determinants of technological changes are many and complex. But two factors are of particular importance. The first is research and development, that is, the deliberate employment of scientific and engineering talent and other resources for the discovery and implementation of new knowledge. The second is capital. For analytical purposes it is useful, as we have done, to identify capital as a source of growth distinct from technological change. But in the real world this distinction is often blurred, if not impossible to make. The reason is that technical changes do not take place in the abstract; frequently, they must be embodied in new equipment if they are to become a viable part of the real-world economy.

Sources of Economic Growth in the American Economy

Now that we have examined the theoretical sources of growth for an advanced market economy, let us turn to this question: What do we know about the actual sources of growth for the American economy, including their relative importance? A number of economists have investigated this question, but none more extensively than Edward F. Denison, Senior Fellow with the Brookings Institution in Washington, D. C. In Table 16–2 the major sources of economic growth in the United States are identified. The data cover two periods, a 47-year span from 1929 to 1976 and a more recent period of 25 years from 1948 to 1973. The latter is presumably typical of the post–World War II period, whereas the former covers the years of the "Great Depression," as well as those in the postwar era.

The first line in the table shows for each of the periods the annual average rate of growth for potential *real* national income. *Real* national income differs from *real* GNP because it excludes depreciation and indirect business taxes. For each period the growth rates shown are broken down, in terms of percentage points, into basic sources of growth. These consist of either more input of labor and capital or advances in output per unit of input (productivity). The latter reflects technological changes. These percentage points are then converted (Columns 3 and 5) into percentage figures showing the relative importance of each source, using the annual average rate of growth appropriate to the period as 100 per-

TABLE 16–2.   Sources of Growth of Potential Real National Income in the United States: 1929–76 (in percentage points)

(1) *Source*	*(2)* *Period* *1929–76*	*(3)* *Percentage* *Distribution*	*(4)* *Period* *1948–73*	*(5)* *Percentage* *Distribution*
Rate of Growth for potential real national income	3.18	100.0%	3.87	100.0%
Total factor inputs	1.93	60.7	2.19	56.6
1. Labor	1.46	45.9	1.48	38.2
2. Capital	0.47	14.8	0.71	18.4
Output per unit of input (productivity)	1.25	39.3	1.68	43.4
1. Better resource allocation	0.28	8.8	0.30	7.8
2. Economies of scale	0.27	8.5	0.32	8.3
3. Advances in knowledge and "residual"	0.70	22.0	1.06	27.3

SOURCE: Edward F. Denison, *Accounting for Slower Growth* (Washington, D.C.: Brookings Institution, 1978), p. 105.

cent. What do Denison's figures tell us about the sources of growth in the American economy? For the longer period (1929–76) a little more than 60 percent of the growth in potential output came from using more resources, mostly labor. Somewhat surprisingly, only about 15 percent of growth is explained by the use of more capital, although we should not forget that the longer period includes the depression years, a time when capital investment was drastically curtailed. Improved productivity accounted for 39.3 percent of growth during this period, most of which was due to advances in knowledge. Better use of resources and economies of scale are included under this category; they fit the concept of an improved technology since the latter means using resources more efficiently.

If we shift to the more recent period (1948–73), the most important development is the increased role that technological change (improved productivity) played in the growth process. In this period, 43.3 percent of the growth in the economy's potential was due to greater output per unit of input, as contrasted to 39.3 percent for the longer period (1929–76). Because of the overlap between the two periods, the contribution of advances in knowledge to growth—the "knowledge explosion" of the post–World War II period—was actually much greater after World War II than is indicated by these figures. In the period before the war (1929–41), improved productivity was responsible for only 28.6 percent of the growth in the economy's productive potential.[1] What is reflected in these figures is the gradual but continued transformation of the modern market economy in the direction that Harvard sociologist Daniel Bell has described as a "post-industrial society." The latter, according to Bell, is one in which improvements in knowledge increasingly loom more important in explaining growth than simply the use of more labor and capital.[2] This is a complicated matter since advances in knowledge also transform the nature of both capital and labor as resources (factor inputs), a transformation which cannot be readily measured statistically. Nonetheless, this is the direction in which Denison's statistical findings point, a development which means that now and in the future research and development activity and education are of critical importance for continued growth in the economy's productive capacity.

Measuring Potential Output

In a practical sense the most important use made of the foregoing theoretical and empirical material on the production function is in the form of statistical estimates of the economy's potential output. Two questions are involved here: (1) How is potential output measured? (2) What use has been made of measures of potential output?

1. Edward F. Denison, *Accounting for Slower Growth* (Washington, D. C.: Brookings Institution, 1978), p. 105.
2. Daniel Bell, *The Coming of Post-Industrial Society* (New York: Basic Books, 1973), p. 112.

It was in the early 1960s that the Kennedy administration through its Council of Economic Advisers started using a measure of potential GNP as a key policy-making tool. Basically two techniques have been used for the calculation of potential GNP. In its 1962 *Economic Report,* the Kennedy Council of Economic Advisers computed potential GNP by extrapolating a trend rate of growth for *real* GNP from a year which, in their judgment, represented a full-employment output. For the latter, the Kennedy Council used a 4 percent unemployment rate (see p. 83). The trend rate of growth used in their extrapolation was 3½ percent, the real average rate of growth of the economy in the post–Korean war period. Mid-1955 was chosen as the starting point for the extrapolation, since unemployment stood at 4 percent is that time.[3] The result was the chart shown in Figure 16–2, which plots potential GNP through 1963 as determined by the method just described, and actual output through most of 1961. The basic point of this statistical exercise was to demonstrate the existence of a growing "gap" between the economy's potential and actual output, a gap in output caused by the failure of the economy to achieve and maintain a full-employment (4 percent unemployment) output level. The "gap" analysis developed in the 1962 *Economic Report* set the stage for the administration's later package of tax cuts designed to stimulate growth, matters discussed in the prior chapter.

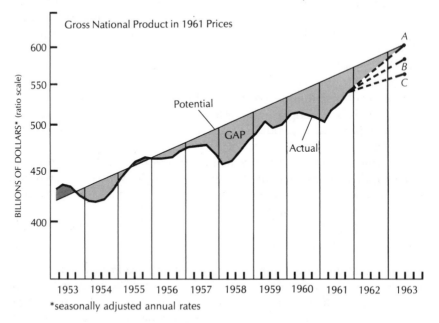

FIGURE 16–2.   Gross National Product (Actual and Potential), Kennedy Administration Estimates, 1953–63

3. *Economic Report of the President* (Washington, D. C.: U. S. Government Printing Office, 1962), p. 51.

The alternative method for calculating potential output, a method favored by subsequent Councils, adheres most closely to the theoretical material discussed earlier. Basically, this method involves multiplying the average productivity of labor (P_r)—measured on either a worker-hour or worker-year basis—by the fully employed labor force. In equation form, this is

$$GNP' = P_r \times N'. \tag{16-1}$$

In the equation, GNP' represents potential output, P_r represents labor productivity, and N' represents the fully employed labor force. The values for P_r and N' will depend upon assumptions made about the rate of technological growth, as this will govern the annual average rate of change in labor productivity, the appropriate measure of a fully employed labor force, and the rate at which the labor force can be expected to grow. During the 1970s there were a number of revisions in estimates of the economy's potential GNP, primarily for two reasons. First, during the decade there was a sharp decline in the rate at which productivity was increasing and, second, there were several upward revisions in the unemployment rate which measured "full" or "high" employment. In 1977, for example, the Ford administration in its final *Economic Report* revised downward the rate of growth of labor productivity to 2.0 percent, and revised upward the "full-employment" benchmark for the labor force from 4.0 to 4.9 percent.[4] One consequence of these revisions was a reduction in the size of the GNP "gap," a not unwelcome political development. Subsequently, the Carter Council in 1979 again revised downward its estimates of the rate of growth of productivity, while raising the benchmark unemployment rate to 5.1 percent.[5] In its final *Economic Report* (published in January 1981), the Carter administration made a slight upward adjustment in its estimates, primarily because productivity performance as reflected in revised GNP data was slightly better after 1973 than earlier estimates indicated. The 1979 adjustments made by the Carter administration in potential GNP are shown in Figure 16–3. In the figure, three different trend lines for potential output are shown, reflecting adjustments made by different Councils since the late 1960s. The trend lines are extrapolated through 1981, permitting us to bring up to date the magnitude of the GNP "gap." Of course, the latter varies, depending on which trend line for potential GNP is the most accurate.

From the time the concept of potential output was introduced into the reports of the Council of Economic Advisers by the Kennedy administration until the Carter administration left office in January 1981, every administration utilized the concept as a tool for economic policy-making. Primarily, the emphasis was placed upon the growth of the economy's

4. *Economic Report of the President* (Washington, D. C.: U. S. Government Printing Office, 1977), pp. 53–54.
5. *Economic Report of the President* (Washington, D. C.: U. S. Government Printing Office, 1979), p. 75.

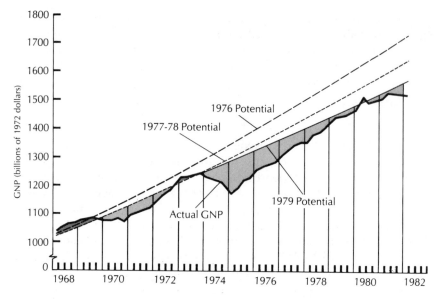

FIGURE 16–3.   Gross National Product (Actual and Potential), Carter
Administration Estimates, 1968–81

basic potential for production in relation to actual output, thereby setting up a backdrop against which policies could be discussed for bringing the two trends—potential and actual output—closer together. With
the advent of the Reagan administration, "gap" analysis and references
to the economy's potential disappeared from the *Economic Report.* In view
of the Reagan administration's strong philosophic thrust toward less
government and basic distrust of the ability of the federal government
to employ monetary and fiscal policies in the effective short-term management of the economy, such a development is not surprising. In its
first *Economic Report,* the major innovation of the Reagan Council of Economic Advisers was the exposition of the basic philosophic attitude of
the administration toward the economy, a statement which stressed primarily the limited economic role that government should undertake,
including analysis of the limited ability of the government to manage the
economy in a macroeconomic sense.[6] It remains to be seen whether the
Reagan administration, or any future administration for that matter, will
return to using potential GNP and the GNP "gap" as a technique of
analysis and basis for policy decisions.

The Productivity Crisis

One basic conclusion to emerge from the foregoing analysis is that, in
the long run, the rate of growth in labor productivity is the single most

---

6. *Economic Report of the President* (Washington, D. C.: U. S. Government Printing Office,
1982), esp. Chap. 2, pp. 27–46.

important determinant of the economy's productive potential. In this figure we find subsumed the underlying real forces—technological change, the growth of capital, the quality and availability of natural resources, not to mention the skill and training of the labor force—which ultimately determine how rapidly the economy can grow. In a simple but nonetheless profound sense the annual rate of advance labor productivity is the key to how rapidly the economy can improve its real standard of living, how fast money incomes can grow without persistent inflation. Table 16–3 illustrates these crucial relationships. It shows for the years since 1960 annual average rates of change in output per worker-hour (worker productivity); compensation per worker-hour, which includes hourly pay plus all fringe benefits (paid by both employee and employer); labor costs per unit of output; and the inflation rate as measured by the con-

TABLE 16–3.   Productivity, Money Incomes, and Inflation: 1960–82
(annual average rates of change)

Year	Productivity*	Compensation†	Labor Costs‡	Inflation Rate§
1960	0.8%	4.3%	3.5%	1.6%
1961	2.9	3.2	0.3	1.0
1962	3.6	4.0	0.4	1.1
1963	3.2	3.5	0.2	1.2
1964	3.9	4.5	0.6	1.3
1965	3.1	3.4	0.3	1.7
1966	2.5	6.0	3.5	2.9
1967	1.9	5.15	3.15	2.9
1968	3.3	7.15	4.1	4.2
1969	−0.3	6.5	6.8	5.4
1970 (R)	0.3	7.0	6.6	5.9
1971	3.3	6.6	3.2	4.3
1972	3.7	6.7	2.9	3.3
1973	2.4	7.6	5.0	6.2
1974 (R)	−2.5	9.4	12.2	11.0
1975 (R)	2.0	9.6	7.5	9.1
1976	3.2	8.1	4.7	5.8
1977	2.2	7.6	5.2	6.5
1978	0.6	8.6	8.0	7.7
1979	−1.3	9.3	10.7	11.3
1980 (R)	−0.9	10.2	11.2	13.5
1981	1.4	9.7	8.1	10.4
1982	0.2	7.3	7.1	6.1

SOURCE: *Economic Report of the President* (Washington, D.C.: United States Government Printing Office, 1983).
*Output per worker-hour in nonfarm business sector.
†Hourly wages plus all fringe benefits.
‡Per unit of output.
§From consumer price index.
Note: (R) = recession year.

sumer price index. It is the close correlation of the latter two which shows how crucial productivity growth is for making possible real advances and containing inflation. When the rate of increase in money incomes—measured in the table by the compensation per worker-hour—exceeds the rate of gain in worker productivity, the inevitable result will be rising labor costs per unit of output. Since, on the average, wages and salaries plus fringe benefits make 60 to 70 percent of total production costs, and since, too, most business firms in the economy set their prices on a markup over cost basis, higher labor costs per unit produced translate into higher prices. The data in Table 16–3 clearly reflect this. One particularly instructive segment in the table is the period 1961–65. During these years productivity and compensation increases were very close, the result being near stability in the general price level. As discussed in Chapter 15, it was during these years that the Kennedy administration formulated its "guidepost" policy for noninflationary wage increases. The data in the table also show clearly the deterioration in the general price level that set in after 1966 as worker-hour increases in compensation consistently outpaced productivity gains.

What also is shown in the table is the slowdown in the rate of gain in productivity in the American economy, a slowdown that became especially pronounced during the 1970s. It is this slowdown which gave rise to the fear that the United States is facing a "productivity crisis." There is no doubt that the slowdown is real, although there is no agreement among economists as to the cause of the slowdown. Table 16–4 gives for the post–World War II period the magnitude of the slowdown.

A variety of reasons have been offered by economists to explain the lagging productivity situation. Among the more important are the following: (1) a slowdown in the rate of capital formation, causing the capital-labor ratio to grow less rapidly than earlier; (2) an influx of less-experienced workers into the labor force, especially young workers, because of the "baby boom," the children of which have come of age, and of women because of changing attitudes toward and from women in the work force; (3) a shift in the composition of output away from the goods-producing industries toward the service sectors, areas where allegedly productivity growth has been historically less vigorous; (4) a decline in the spending for research and development; and (5) excessive

TABLE 16–4. Output per Worker-Hour in the American Economy: 1950–82 (annual average rates of change)

	1950–59	1960–69	1970–82
Rate of productivity increase	3.5%	2.9%	1.0%

SOURCE: *Economic Report of the President* (Washington, D.C.: U.S. Government Printing Office, 1983).

regulation of business, an explanation favored by the Reagan administration. Comments on these explanations are in order.

In a recent study published by the Brookings Institution, three economists from the Bureau of Labor Statistics of the United States Department of Labor attempted to identify the factors responsible for the
productivity slowdown.[7] In their study the post–World War II period
was divided into three subperiods: 1948–65, 1965–73, and 1973–78. It
was during the latter of these three periods that they uncovered a distinct slowdown in productivity growth, a finding similar to the data contained in Table 16–4. Basically, the economists of the Bureau of Labor
Statistics concluded that the slowdown in productivity growth in the latter periods came from different sources. For the first slowdown period
(1965–73), they failed to find any strong evidence linking the productivity lag to insufficient capital formation. There was a slight indication that
the influx of young workers into the labor force had some effect on
productivity, but in general the authors of the Brookings study concluded that the 1965–73 slowdown was not explained by either insufficient capital investment or a change in the composition of the labor force.[8]

For the second slowdown period (1973–78) their results were different. In this period, which is relatively short and includes the 1974–75
recession (the most severe of those in the post–World War II period up
to that time), they found that a slowdown in the rate of growth of capital
relative to labor was the factor most responsible for the productivity
decline.[9] Rising energy costs may have been a factor in the reduced rate
of capital formation, but the Brookings study did not find that required
investments in pollution-abatement equipment—a cause which would fit
the excessive regulation explanation—were a significant factor in the
productivity slowdown.

In another study three academic economists challenged some of the
reasons cited above for the productivity decline, reasons that have tended
to become a part of the "conventional wisdom" with respect to the problem.[10] In this study it was found that, contrary to popular belief, the
slowdown in productivity growth was more pronounced in the goods-
producing industries than in the services sector, even though in general
productivity is lower in the service areas of the economy than in the
goods sector. Thus, the shift in the composition of output away from
goods and toward services is not necessarily a major cause of the economy's lagging productivity. Similar results were found by these econo-

7. J. R. Norsworthy, Michael J. Harper, and Kent Kunze, "The Slowdown in Productivity
Growth: Analysis of Some Contributing Factors," *Brookings Papers on Economic Activity*, 1979,
No. 2, pp. 387–421.
8. Ibid., p. 421.
9. Ibid., p. 417.
10. The economists are Samuel Bowles, David M. Gordon, and Thomas E. Weisskopf of
the University of Massachusetts at Amherst, the New School for Social Research, and the
University of Michigan, respectively. See their article "Falling Productivity: At the Heart
of Economic Decline," *The Nation*, July 10–17, 1982.

mists with respect to the "capital shortage" explanation, one especially favored by the Reagan administration. Except for the recession years of the 1970s, there does not appear to be any significant change in the proportion of the nation's *real* GNP being devoted to fixed investment. As a matter of fact, the share of *real* GNP going into investment into equipment—the kind of investment most likely to reflect technological advance—actually rose in the 1970s as compared to the two previous decades. For the period 1970–81, fixed equipment investment averaged 7.0 percent of *real* GNP, compared to 5.6 percent from 1960 through 1969, and 5.3 percent in the 1950–59 period.[11]

One explanation for the productivity decline that has received comparatively little attention but which may be of greatest importance stems from the impact of military spending on the economy. Between 1950 and 1981 the United States spent more than $2 trillion for military purposes, much of it for complex and costly weapons systems that diverted scarce resources from the civilian economy. Lloyd J. Dumas of the University of Texas at Dallas reported in 1980 that military budgets had had an "enormously negative long term impact on the functioning of the United States economy."[12] A major reason was that since the 1950s the United States has channeled from 30 to 33 percent of the work of its scientific and engineering manpower into military activity, a development that Professor Dumas argues has played a key role in slowing the nation's rate of productivity growth. Furthermore, according to Professor Dumas and also contrary to the "conventional wisdom," there is little effective "spinoff" of military-related research into the civilian economy. As Professor Dumas concluded, "The effects of severe structural damage to the competitiveness of United States industry done by three decades of persistently high military spending have surfaced with a vengence in the 1970s. Collapsing productivity, high inflation and high unemployment are the sad legacy of our participation in the ongoing international arms race."[13]

Theories of Economic Growth

The basic thrust of the preceding analysis is that over time the economy's potential for production grows, not necessarily smoothly, but nonetheless persistently. This being the case, the fundamental theoretical question becomes how will aggregate demand in a market system adjust continuously upward so as to ensure the full utilization over time of the economy's growing productive capacity? Within the income-expenditure

11. *Economic Report of the President,* 1982, p. 234.
12. Lloyd J. Dumas, "The Impact of the Military Budget on the Domestic Economy," paper presented at the annual meeting of the American Association for the Advancement of Science, San Francisco, January 1980.
13. Ibid.

theoretical framework developed in Part II, two economists, Evsey Domar, an American, and Roy F. Harrod, an Englishman, developed similar theoretical analyses directed toward this question.[14] The Harrod-Domar approach, as their theories have come to be known in the literature of economics, puts the equilibrium analysis developed in Part II into a dynamic setting, showing in particular why progress over time in a market system is never smooth. The Harrod-Domar analysis is important because it provides the necessary theoretical explanation for the reality observed in Chapter 1—the historic fluctuations in a market system of output, employment, and prices.

The appropriate point of departure for discussion of these theories is a brief review of the full-employment equilibrium in a short-run setting. Parenthetically, it is important to remember that the basic model developed in Chapter 4 is static simply because it does not involve any change over time in the fundamental determinants of the economy's productive potential. As Keynes pointed out in *The General Theory*, the analysis takes as given "the existing skill and quantity of available labour, the existing quality and quantity of available equipment, the existing technique, the degree of competition, the tastes and habits of the consumer."[15] With capacity known and fixed, the central problem is the determination of the level of aggregate demand; in static analysis the level of aggregate demand determines the output and employment level, and shifts in the aggregate demand schedule bring about shifts in both output and employment.

In the simplest income-expenditure model, aggregate demand consists of consumption and investment expenditure. The basic condition for equilibrium at any level of income and employment is that investment expenditure be sufficiently large to absorb the saving forthcoming at the income level in question. Consequently, the necessary condition for a full-employment equilibrium income level is that investment expenditure be sufficient to absorb the saving made at the full-employment income.

There is nothing wrong with this analysis since it expresses an idea fundamental to all modern income and employment theory: namely, income paid out or created during the productive process must be returned in one form or another to the income stream if the expectations of producers are to be satisfied and equilibrium maintained. But, as both Domar and Harrod observe, the equilibrium so obtained has

14. Professor Harrod developed his ideas in a series of lectures given at the University of London in 1947. Professor Domar's model appeared in the *American Economic Review* in the same year. For details, see R. F. Harrod, *Towards a Dynamic Economics* (New York: St. Martin's Press, 1966), especially Lecture Three, pp. 63–100, and E. D. Domar, "Expansion and Employment," *American Economic Review*, March 1947, pp. 34–55. For both the intermediate and advanced student of macroeconomics, the Harrod-Domar "models" have been and are the basic introduction to the theoretical questions involving growth in the modern, market-based economic system.
15. John Maynard Keynes, *The General Theory of Employment, Interest and Money* (New York: Harcourt, Brace & World, First Harbinger ed., 1964), p. 245.

meaning only for a relatively short period of time because the *capacity-creating* effects of investment expenditure will cause the income level that is appropriate to the full employment of both labor and other resources to rise over time.

To facilitate our understanding of why a level of income sufficient to achieve full employment of all resources today may not be sufficient to achieve full employment of all resources tomorrow, let us discuss income, investment, and saving in the net sense, that is, after proper allowance has been made for the replacement of capital goods used up in the current production process. If the discussion is cast in net rather than gross terms, it does not change the underlying principle: Full-employment equilibrium requires that investment expenditure be equal to full-employment saving. The key difference is that now the basic statement describing the necessary condition for achieving and maintaining a full-employment income level must be modified to read that *ex ante* net investment must equal *ex ante* net saving at full employment.

But when we put the analysis in net terms and define full-employment equilibrium in terms of an equality between net saving and investment, we are faced with a serious dilemma because the analytical system no longer retains its static character. Net saving is a dynamic concept, for if a society steadily saves some portion of its net income and just as steadily invests the income saved in productive capital, it follows that the stock of productive capital equipment, one of the basic determinants of both capacity and output, will change. Static analysis does not concern itself with a situation in which a basic determinant of productive capacity such as the capital stock changes. The paradox of the situation arises from the fact that net investment is by definition an addition to the economy's stock of wealth in the form of productive capital, and thus net investment must logically increase the economy's productive capacity. But if productive capacity is increasing, the analysis can no longer be static.

Domar's Analysis of Economic Growth

The paradox that net investment is, on the one hand, a necessary offset to net saving if full employment is to be maintained and, on the other, an addition to the economy's stock of capital provides a setting for Domar's analysis of the problem of growth in an advanced economy. The dominant theme in his theoretical treatment of economic growth is that net investment raises productive capacity and thus causes the economy to grow. Given the capacity-creating impact of net investment, Domar attempts to determine the rate at which income must grow if full employment is to be maintained over time.

To explore this problem, Domar develops an analytical model which seeks to show how growth in capacity over time can be linked to growth in aggregate demand, output, and employment. Domar's analytical framework is essentially Keynesian, although it is placed in the long run and includes some new elements.

Before we examine Domar's analysis of the growth process, we must define the concepts he employs and state the assumptions underlying the analysis. The key concepts and assumptions are as follows:

1. *The propensity to save.* This is the ratio of saving to income at any given level of income. Domar assumes that S/Y is constant, which means he is working with a long-run saving function. Also, the marginal propensity to save, $\Delta S/\Delta Y$, is equal to the average propensity to save, since mathematically the average propensity to save could not be a constant unless it was equal to the marginal propensity to save. In the analysis both the marginal and the average propensity to save are designated by α. In Domar's analytical system, as in the basic income-expenditure model, the significance of the average propensity to save is that it determines the amount of saving that must be absorbed by investment at the full-employment income level, while the significance of the marginal propensity to save is that it is the key to the value of the multiplier.

2. *The capital-output ratio.* This magnitude, which is sometimes called the capital coefficient, is the ratio of the capital stock of the economy, K, to full capacity output, Y. Basically, K/Y is a way of defining the economy's capacity in terms of its capital stock; given the existing level of technology, there will be, on the average, a certain physical quantity of capital required to obtain a given quantity of output. Since both capital (a stock phenomenon) and output (a flow phenomenon) must be measured in terms of their monetary values, the capital-output ratio becomes, as a practical matter, the number of dollars' worth of capital required on the average to get a dollar's worth of output. Domar bases his analysis on the average capital-output ratio for the whole economy, although the actual capital-output ratio may vary widely from industry to industry.

3. *The marginal capital-output ratio.* This ratio represents the relationship between changes in the capital stock, ΔK, and changes in the output level, ΔY. Since a change in the capital stock is the same thing as net investment, $\Delta K/\Delta Y$ tells us how much added capital or investment is needed to get an additional unit of output. The marginal capital-output ratio or capital coefficient may or may not be equal to the average capital-output ratio, but if the marginal ratio is constant and equal to the average ratio, technological change is said to be neutral.[16] Technological change that is not neutral alters both the average and marginal capital-output ratios, but especially the latter, because new developments make themselves felt primarily at the time when additions to the capital stock are being made. Technological change may, moreover, lower or raise these ratios by reducing the amount of capital required to obtain a unit of output. If the capital requirement has been reduced, capital saving is

---

16. Neutral technological change leaves the capital-output ratio unchanged. See R. F. Harrod, op. cit., p. 83.

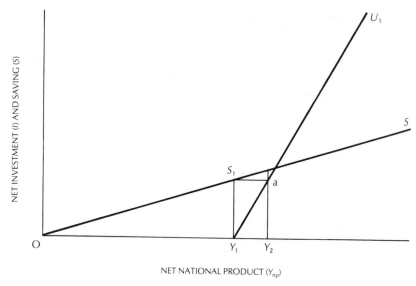

NET NATIONAL PRODUCT (Y_{np})

FIGURE 16–4. The Marginal Capital-Output Ratio

said to have taken place; if it has been increased, the result has been capital deepening.

The nature of the marginal capital-output ratio can be shown by means of a diagram. In Figure 16–4, with output and capacity on the horizontal axis and net savings and investment on the vertical axis, OS represents the long-run saving function, the slope of which is such that the average and marginal propensities to save are equal.[17] If Y_1 is the full-employment income, then the full-employment requirement is that net investment be equal to saving at this income level. This is the distance Y_1S_1. The marginal capital coefficient is represented by Y_1U_1, the slope of which is equal to the ratio of an increment of capital to an increment of output. Thus, if investment in the income period proceeds at the rate Y_1S_1, the impact on the economy's productive capacity is shown by projecting a horizontal line from S_1 to the point at which it intersects the Y_1U_1 line (point a in the diagram), and then dropping a vertical line from this point to the horizontal axis. The distance Y_1Y_2 represents the increase in capacity that has resulted from net investment in the amount Y_1S_1 in the present income period.

4. *The productivity of capital coefficient.* In Domar's analysis, and in growth economics generally, the ratio Y/K (the reciprocal of the capital-output ratio) is a measure of the average productivity of capital in the same sense that a full-employment output, Y, divided by the labor force, N', is a measure of the average productivity of labor. The ratio Y/N', which

17. This diagram was developed by Harold Pilvin. See "A Geometric Analysis of Recent Growth Models," *American Economic Review*, September 1952, pp. 594–99.

may be called the *average productivity of labor,* has frequently been used to determine the economy's potential for production, as it is necessary only to multiply the average productity of labor by the assumed labor force to get a measure of potential output. The ratio Y/K shifts the emphasis from labor productivity to capital productivity in the determination of capacity.

In Domar's analysis the ratio of an increment of output, ΔY, to an increment in the capital stock, ΔK, is designated by s. If the average and marginal ratios are assumed equal, s is both a measure of the average productivity of capital *ex post* and a measure of the amount by which each dollar's worth of newly created capital, taken by itself, will add to the productive capacity of the economy. Viewed in the latter sense Domar's s is simply the reciprocal of the marginal capital-output ratio, because, if, on the average, three dollars' worth of capital equipment is required to produce one dollar's worth of additional output, s will have a value of 0.33. In other words, the average productivity of capital will be 0.33, because each dollar's worth of new capital will increase capacity by this amount.

Although Domar employs the symbol s to describe the immediate and direct effect on capacity that results from added capital, this particular ratio is not the appropriate ratio for the whole economy, because normally some newly created capital goods will be brought into use at the expense of existing capital. Thus, the amount by which overall capacity is increased for each new dollar's worth of capital equipment will be less than s. To designate the amount by which productive capacity for the whole economy is actually increased for each dollar's worth of new capital Domar uses σ, which he calls the *potential social average productivity of investment.* Normally σ is smaller than s. As we shall see shortly, σ is the most important single concept employed by Domar in his analysis of the growth process.

5. *Some simplifying assumptions.* The concepts discussed in the foregoing paragraphs constitute the key ideas Domar employs in the construction of his growth theory, but there are some simplifying assumptions that should be made clear before we turn to discussion of the theory itself. In the first place, he assumes an economy in which there is neither government nor international economic transactions. This does not imply that public activity and international transactions have no role to play in the growth process, but simply reflects Domar's desire to concentrate the whole of his analysis on the growth potential embodied in the capacity-creating effect of net investment in the private sector. Second, the analysis assumes that there are no lags in adjustment, which is to say that output is assumed to respond immediately to changes in expenditure and expenditure is assumed to respond immediately to changes in income. The absence of lags permits us to see as clearly as possible the key relationships involved in the growth process. Finally, the analysis starts with the assumption that a full-employment income level has been attained.

The Capacity-Creating Process

Having discussed Domar's key concepts, we can now examine the way in which he describes the capacity-creating process associated with a given amount of net investment. In Figure 16–4 the full-employment income level is assumed to be Y_1, and the amount of net investment required at this income level is given by the distance Y_1S_1. If investment expenditure proceeds during the income period at this rate, we can use σ to determine the effect of this amount of investment on productive capacity. Specifically, if net investment in the income period is equal to I dollars, the subsequent increase in the productive capacity of the whole economy is

$$\Delta Y_Q = I\sigma. \qquad (16\text{--}2)$$

ΔY_Q represents the increase in the *productive potential* of the economy; it does not represent any actual increase in output. The expression $I\sigma$ reflects the supply side of the economic system, for it describes the extent to which productive capacity has been increased as a consequence of a specific amount of net investment. In terms of standard diagrammatic analysis this means that the full capacity output level has been pushed farther to the right along the horizontal axis. If, to refer back to Figure 16–4, Y_1 represented a full-employment income level at the beginning of the current income period, it no longer represents the full-employment income level at the end of this period.

The nature of the capacity-creating process of net investment can be clearly illustrated by a simple numerical example. Let us assume, first, that σ has a value of 0.3 and, second, that the average (and marginal) propensity to save out of net income is 0.10. Let us assume further that the full-employment income in the present period (the Y_1 of Figure 16–4) is $2,400 billion. Then, for full employment, investment expenditure must equal 240 billion (or 10 percent of $2,400 billion). If the net investment of the economy is at the rate of $240 billion during the current income period, what effect does this have on productive capacity? The potential social average productivity of investment coefficient, σ, supplies the answer; if, on the average, every dollar's worth of new capital increases productive capacity by $0.30, then $240 billion of new capital will increase the overall productive capacity of the economy by $72 billion ($240 billion $\times$ 0.3 = $72 billion).

What are the consequences of the above process? Although $2,400 billion represented the full-employment output level at the start of the income period, this is no longer the case. Capacity has grown and with it the full-employment output level. This fact underscores the fundamental necessity for output to grow if full employment is to be maintained over time in an economy in which there is positive net saving and positive net investment. What would happen if, in the next income period, income remained at $2,400 billion? As Domar points out, the creation of new capital will result in one of three possible effects, assuming the level of income remains unchanged[18]: (1) The new capital remains unused, in which case it should not have been produced in the first place; (2) the new capital is used at the expense of previously constructed capital, which also may represent a waste of resources if net investment is large; and (3) the new capital may be substituted for labor, which may lead to a substantial amount of involuntary unemployment if the introduction of the new equipment is not accompanied by a voluntary reduction in either the size of the labor force or the length of the work week. If income remains at the same level in the next period, even though there has been net investment in the present period, the result will be either unemployed labor, unemployed capital, or both.

The Demand Requirement

The key point of the foregoing analysis is that, if net investment increases the economy's productive capacity, it is essential that output grow through time to ensure that the added capacity created by the investment process is continually absorbed into use. The problem is therefore to determine, first, how output can be made to expand so as to bring into use the added capacity and, second, the necessary rate at which output must expand to achieve the continued full utilization of additional capacity.

Domar's analysis of the growth process is carried out within the basic framework of aggregate demand and aggregate supply, wherein the most important role played by aggregate demand is to bring capacity into use. Both output and employment result from the use of capacity, and it is the expectation of demand that leads the entrepreneur to make use of the productive capacity at his disposal. It follows that *it is necessary for aggregate demand to rise if added productive capacity is to be brought into use.*

Since we have eliminated government expenditure and international transactions from the analysis, and since consumption is a dependent variable (in that it is a function of income), investment is the key determinant of the level of aggregate demand. Thus, investment will have to increase if there is to be an upward shift in the aggregate demand function; the shift must be great enough to bring about an overall increase in aggregate expenditure sufficient to utilize—and thus justify—the added productive capacity. This aspect of the problem is easy to understand, for the reader need only recall the multiplier analysis to realize that any given total increase in aggregate expenditure depends upon the amount by which investment itself has risen as well as upon the value of the multiplier. The latter, of course, is dependent upon the marginal propensity to save.

If the utilization of additional capacity requires an increase in aggre-

18. Domar, p. 37.

gate expenditure equal to the amount by which capacity has increased, and if changes in investment expenditure are the ultimate source of changes in effective demand, we can express the required increase in effective demand in equation form as

$$\Delta Y_D = \Delta I \times \frac{1}{\alpha}. \tag{16-3}$$

This equation is simply the multiplier formula applied to an increase in investment expenditure. ΔY_D represents the overall increase in effective demand or total expenditure brought about by the given increment in investment expenditure. $1/\alpha$ is the simple investment multiplier, since α represents the marginal propensity to save.

In conjunction with the equation depicting the demand side of his system, Domar places great stress on what he terms the *dual nature of the investment process.* By this he means that the capacity-creating effects and the demand-creating effects of investment expenditure are dissimilar, because *all* net investment expenditure adds to the economy's capital stock and thus increases the economy's productive capacity, but only increments to investment expenditure, operating through the multiplier effect, raise the level of effective demand. This, in short, is the real paradox of investment; if net investment expenditure simply remains constant through time, the income level will not change—that is, equilibrium will be maintained—but the result will be idle capacity and a growing volume of unemployed labor. Investment and income must grow in each succeeding income period if net investment expenditures in any specific income period are to justify themselves.

The Required Rate of Income Growth

If the maintenance of full employment for both the economy's labor force and stock of productive capital requires that output grow at the same rate at which productive capacity is increasing because of net investment, we can bring together the equations discussed above and compute the necessary rate at which output must grow. The basic condition is that, over time, increments of effective demand must equal increments of capacity. Symbolically, this can be stated as

$$\Delta Y_Q = \Delta Y_D. \tag{16-4}$$

In the above definition equation we can substitute the earlier values for ΔY_Q and ΔY_D. hus:

$$I\sigma = \Delta I \times \frac{1}{\alpha}. \tag{16-5}$$

$I\sigma$ represents the supply side of the system, for it shows the potential increase in supply that results from current investment, whereas $\Delta I \times (1/\alpha)$ represents the demand side, since it depicts the amount by which aggregate effective demand must rise if the added capacity is to be utilized.

Domar solves the above fundamental equation by multiplying both sides by α and then dividing both sides by I. The result of this is the following growth equation:

$$\frac{\Delta I}{I} = \sigma\alpha. \qquad (16\text{–}6)$$

The left side of this equation shows the absolute increment in investment expenditure divided by the total volume of investment expenditure. It is expressive of the percentage rate of growth of investment. Thus, Equation (16–6) means basically that *investment expenditure must grow at an annual rate equal to the product of the marginal propensity to save, α, and the potential social average productivity of investment, σ,* if a state of continuous full employment is to be maintained. Since Domar assumes that the average and marginal propensities to save are equal and that the average and marginal values of σ are equal, it is easy to demonstrate algebraically that income as well as investment must grow at a constant annual percentage rate equal to the product of α and σ.[19] Thus:

$$\frac{Y}{\Delta Y} = \sigma\alpha. \qquad (16\text{–}7)$$

The above equation, like Equation (16–6), indicates in a simple and direct way the necessary condition for the maintenance of full-employment output over time. It shows, to quote Domar, "that it is not sufficient, in Keynesian terms, that savings of yesterday be invested today, or, as it is so often expressed, that investment offset saving. Investment of today must always exceed savings of yesterday. . . . The economy must continuously expand."[20]

A Numerical Representation of the Growth Process

The nature of this growth process may be illustrated by numerical example. Tables 16–5 and 16–6 contain hypothetical data pertaining to the growth of net national output, consumption, and investment over a five-year period, assuming different sets of values for both α and σ. In Table 16–5, the propensity to save, α, has a value of 0.10, while the value of the productivity of capital coefficient, σ, is 0.30. The required rate of growth is thus 3 percent per year, since $\alpha \times \sigma = 0.03$. If the net national income of the economy is \$2,400 billion in the first year, a 3 percent annual rate of growth will raise income to the level of \$2,702 billion at

19. This can be shown algebraically as follows:
   (1) $I = \alpha Y$ [This assumes that the saving of the period is invested.]
   (2) $\Delta Y_Q = \sigma\alpha Y$ [This is from Equation (16–2).]
   (3) $\Delta Y_D = \sigma\alpha Y$ [This on the assumption that the change in aggregate effective demand must equal the change in capacity.]
   (4) $\dfrac{\Delta Y}{Y} = \sigma\alpha$ [This follows algebraically from above.]

20. Domar, p. 42.

TABLE 16–5.   The Required Growth of Income: I (in billions of dollars)*
$\alpha = 0.10$
$\sigma = 0.30$
$\sigma\alpha = 0.03/\text{yr}$

(1)	(2)	(3)	(4)	(5)
				Increase in
	Income	Consumption	Investment	Capacity
Year	(Y)	(C)	(I)	(Iσ)
1	$2,400	$2,160	$240	$72
2	2,472	2,225	247	74
3	2,546	2,291	255	77
4	2,623	2,361	262	79
5	2,702	2,432	270	81

*All figures are rounded to the nearest whole number.

TABLE 16–6.   The Required Growth of Income: II (in billions of dollars)*
$\alpha = 0.12$
$\sigma = 0.40$
$\sigma\alpha = 0.048/\text{yr}$

(1)	(2)	(3)	(4)	(5)
				Increase in
	Income	Consumption	Investment	Capacity
Year	(Y)	(C)	(I)	(Iσ)
1	$2,400	$2,112	$288	$115
2	2,515	2,213	302	121
3	2,636	2,320	316	127
4	2,763	2,408	328	131
5	2,894	2,547	347	139

*All figures are rounded to the nearest whole number.

the end of five years. The effect of investment upon capacity in each income period is shown in Column (5). The figures in this column are the product of $I\sigma$, for we assume that the net saving of each income period is invested. The amount of such saving is determined by the average propensity to consume. Investment (and saving) remain a constant proportion of income, but the absolute amount of investment is greater in each subsequent income period. This is a clear example of what Domar means when he states, as quoted above, that the investment of today must always exceed the savings of yesterday. This simple example offers considerable insight into the dynamic behavior inherent in maintaining full employment over time in an advanced economy; the economy must not only expand continuously in order to avoid unemployment but in order to do this it must constantly find outlets in investment expenditure for a rising absolute amount of saving.

Table 16–6 contains similar hypothetical data, except in this instance we are assuming higher values for both the propensity to save and the productivity of capital coefficient. Specifically, α is assumed to have a value of 0.12, and σ a value of 0.40. This means, first, that this hypothetical economy saves, on the average, a higher proportion of its net income and, second, that the productivity of capital is, also on the average, higher. As a consequence, investment expenditure equal to the saving at any particular income level will have a greater impact on the economy's productive capacity than was the case in the prior example. This is not only because the absolute amount of saving will be greater at each and every income level, but also because the higher value for the productivity of capital coefficient means, in effect, that every dollar of investment expenditure increases productive capacity by a greater amount. Thus, the overall effect of higher values for both the propensity to save and the productivity of capital coefficient is to increase the necessary growth rate for our hypothetical economy. With the above assumed values for these coefficients, the necessary growth rate for maintenance of full-employment output level over time becomes 4.8 percent. The data of Table 16–6 show that such a growth rate, if sustained for a five-year period, would raise the output level from $2,400 billion in the first year to $2,894 billion in the fifth year. The reader should compare the impact of investment on productive capacity in each period, Column (5) in Table 16–6, with the same data in Table 16–5. In each period I_Q is greater.

A Diagrammatic Representation of the Growth Process

The growth process envisioned by Domar can also be illustrated by means of a diagram. Figure 16–5 is similiar to Figure 16–4; the line *OS* represents the long-run saving function, and its slope is such that the average and marginal propensities to save are equal.

Let us assume initially that the full-employment income level is equal to Y_1, and investment expenditure is such as to absorb the saving at this income level. Investment is thus equal to Y_1S_1. Since investment is autonomous with respect to income, the investment function is represented by the schedule labeled I_1. The impact of this amount of investment on the economy's productive capacity is depicted by the line Y_1U_1, the slope of which is equal to the marginal capital-output ratio. Since the marginal capital-output ratio is the ratio of a change in the capital stock (after account has been taken of the displacement of some existing capital by new capital) to a change in the output level, the reciprocal of Y_1U_1 is the productivity of capital coefficient, σ.

If net investment proceeds in the first income period at a rate equal to Y_1S_1, productive capacity will be increased by an amount equal to the distance Y_1Y_2. This distance is determined, in Figure 16–5, by projecting a horizontal line from point S_1 to the point at which it intersects the Y_1U_1 line, and then dropping a vertical line from this point to the horizontal axis. Consequently, Y_2 now represents the economy's full-employment

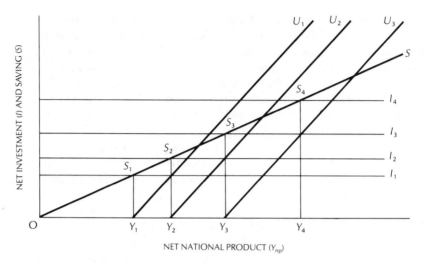

FIGURE 16–5. Net Investment and the Growth Process

income level. But if this is the case, and given the saving function OS, the absolute amount of saving that will be forthcoming at the new full-employment income level has risen to the amount Y_2S_2. Since equilibrium requires equality between saving and investment *ex ante*, investment expenditure must rise to the level depicted by the investment schedule I_2 if the economy is to maintain full employment. This shift of the equilibrium income to the level represented by Y_2 requires, too, a shift in the curve representing the productivity of investment coefficient to the position Y_2U_2, because net investment in the amount Y_2S_2 will result in further additions to the economy's capital stock. Since σ remained constant during the time interval involved in raising income from Y_1 to Y_2, Y_2U_2 can be drawn parallel to Y_1U_1. Net investment in the second income period equal to Y_2S_2 will cause productive capacity to rise by an amount equal to the distance Y_2Y_3. Once again investment will have to increase if a full-employment income level is to be maintained, because the saving at Y_3 is greater than the saving at Y_2. Investment must now rise to the level shown by the investment function I_3.

Inspection of this model reveals a number of interesting aspects of the growth process. If we assume fixed values for both the propensity to save and the productivity of investment coefficient, not only must investment expenditure rise continuously through time if full employment is to be maintained, but also the absolute increments of investment required in such subsequent income periods must become larger and larger. The logic of this is readily apparent, for if capacity increases through time by increasing absolute amounts, and if the investment multiplier is constant because of a constant marginal propensity to save, effective demand will increase through time in an amount equal to the increase in capacity only if the increments to investment expenditure become absolutely larger in each successive income period. Figure 16–5 clearly shows the difficulties facing an advanced economy that habitually saves some significant portion of its net income. Such an economy must continuously find new outlets for not just a constant but a growing absolute volume of saving. For this reason, advanced economies have frequently found it exceedingly difficult to sustain a constant rate of growth over relatively long periods of time.

The above analysis may strike the reader as unduly restrictive because of the underlying assumption that both the propensity to save and the productivity of investment coefficient have constant values. Different results will ensue with different values of either α or σ. For example, the investment function would not have to shift upward continuously (as shown in Figure 16–5) if the long-term propensity to save were to undergo a decline. This possibility is depicted in Figure 16–6, which shows the saving function, *OS*, pivoting downward with each successive increase in capacity. This decline in the value of the propensity to save does not eliminate the capacity-creating effect of net investment, but means merely that the absolute increases in capacity, ΔY_Q, in each income period would be constant because investment remains constant in each income period. It is scarcely realistic, however, to assume that the secular saving function undergoes a downward shift; this would mean that over time the economy saved a smaller and smaller proportion of its net income, but empirical research indicates that the proportion of net income saved remains constant over the long run.

A final possibility has to do with changes in the value of the productivity of capital coefficient. A decline in the value of σ means that the impact

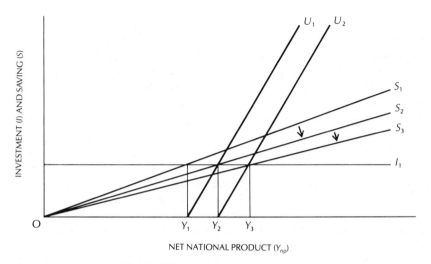

FIGURE 16–6. Downward Shift in the Saving Function

on capacity of any specific amount of investment is smaller, and therefore the extent to which income would have to grow to absorb into use the additions to capacity would also be lessened. A reduction in σ would, in other words, make the problem of attaining a constantly rising volume of investment expenditures less difficult, because, with a slower rate of growth of capacity and income, the growth of saving in an absolute sense also will be slower. A decline in σ is the same as a rise in the capital-output ratio, for, if a given quantity of investment expenditure has a smaller effect on capacity than heretofore, more capital per unit of output is required. Unfortunately, it is quite unlikely that an advanced economy can easily resolve the problem of maintaining continuous full employment by a downward adjustment in the value σ. For one thing, the productivity of capital coefficient is basically a technological coefficient and, as such, is not easily adjusted to whatever value might be required for maintenance of a full-employment equilibrium. In addition, the long-term trend for the actual capital-output ratio in the United States appears to be downward. If such a trend is characteristic of advanced economies in general, it means higher rather than lower values for the productivity of capital coefficient. Thus, the impact on capacity for any given amount of investment has tended to become greater rather than smaller.

Significance and Limitations of the Domar Analysis of Economic Growth

The analytical system that we have been discussing can be described as dynamic primarily because it goes beyond the assumption of a fixed productive capacity and examines the consequences of an increase in the quantity of a key economic resource, the economy's stock of real capital instruments. Domar's concern with the capacity-creating effect of net investment has a dual significance for economic analysis. First, the analysis follows an old tradition, for nearly all economists who have had something meaningful to say about economic development have accorded the accumulation of capital a priority role in this process.[21] Second, the analysis demonstrates that economic growth is not merely a desirable phenomenon for an advanced capitalistic economy, but an absolute necessity if the economy is to avoid a growing volume of unemployment of both labor and other economic resources. The analysis, moreover, shows that, while the economy may grow at a satisfactory rate, there is no reason to expect it to do so automatically.

Our appraisal of Domar's analysis would not be complete if we did not point out some of its important limitations. For one thing, the derivation of the required rate obviously depends upon the existence of known and

21. See especially Benjamin Higgins, *Economic Development: Principles, Problems, and Policies,* 2nd ed. (New York: Norton, 1959), p. 204.

constant values for such crucial factors as the propensity to save and the productivity of capital coefficient. In reality, it is unlikely that either of these are constant all the time. But the difficulty of deriving a required rate does not in any way invalidate the basic theme of the analysis—that there exists *some* rate of growth that will ensure a full-employment equilibrium over time.

A second limitation is Domar's use of a productivity of investment coefficient that is an average for the whole economy. The capital-output ratio, both on the average and at the margin, varies widely from industry to industry because of differences in the capital requirements for different kinds of production. This means that it will be very difficult to determine the exact impact of a given volume of investment on capacity unless we know the composition in an industrial sense of the investment. For example, a given quantity of investment expenditure in an industry characterized by a high capital-output ratio will obviously have a smaller overall impact on productive capacity than the same amount of investment expenditure in an industry with a lower capital-output ratio.

Finally, Domar's analysis fails to distinguish between a rate of growth of income which will ensure full employment of the labor force and a rate of growth of income which will ensure full utilization of the economy's stock of capital. This has been a matter of concern for some economists, who argue that the rate of growth sufficient to absorb additions to the economy's stock of capital will not necessarily provide full employment for a growing labor force.

In spite of these limitations, attention should not be detracted from the important and positive contribution that the Domar type of analysis has made to an understanding of the process of economic development in an advanced economy. Admittedly, Domar's system is overly simplified and, perhaps, overly rigid. But this is a criticism that could be justly leveled at most facets of contemporary economic theory. The real task of economic theory is to direct our attention to a few strategic relationships as a means of understanding somewhat better the vast complexities of the economy in the real world. Not many economists would deny that an enlargement of the economy's productive potential is a factor of key strategic significance in the process of economic growth.

Harrod's Analysis of Economic Growth

Since Harrod's analysis of the growth process in an advanced economy is in many respects similar to Domar's it has become fashionable for economists to speak of the Harrod-Domar theory when they are discussing developments which extend the basic concepts of income and employment theory to the general area of economic growth. But there are also enough fundamental differences in their approaches to warrant separate discussion of the ideas of each.

Harrod, like Domar, is concerned with the necessary conditions under which the equality of *ex ante* saving and investment can be maintained over time, but he treats the central element in the growth process, investment expenditure, in a different manner. In Domar's schema we look to the effect that current investment expenditure has on future productive capacity, assuming that this investment expenditure is sufficient to offset the saving of the current income level. In a sense, Domar's analysis is forward looking because such a procedure requires us to determine how much both income and investment will have to grow in the next income period in order to absorb into use at that time the added capacity that is the consequence of investment in the present income period.

Harrod, on the other hand, constructs his analysis in terms of the response of current investment expenditure to a change in the economy's output or real income level. He seeks to determine whether the rate at which income has grown in the immediate past is high enough to induce an amount of investment expenditure sufficient to absorb the saving in the current income period.

The key analytical tool that Harrod employs in his analysis is the *accelerator*, which is defined symbolically as the ratio of a change in the capital stock, ΔK, to a change in the output level, ΔY. Since the change in the capital stock is the same as the net investment, I_n, the ratio $\Delta K/\Delta Y$, or $I_n/\Delta Y$, when defined as the accelerator, represents a behavior coefficient in the sense that it seeks to express as a coefficient the investment response of entrepreneurs to a change in the output level. The acceleration approach makes current net investment a function of the rate of change in output. Fundamental to the notion of the acceleration coefficient, however, is the concept of the capital-output ratio conceived as a technical relationship, for if a relatively fixed relationship did not exist between output and the quantity of capital necessary for the production of that output, there would be no point in asserting that investment expenditure may be induced by changes in output.

Although the treatment of investment expenditure differs in the two analyses, both Domar and Harrod accord identical roles to the saving function. Both analyses are based on the long-run saving function, on an equality between the average and the marginal propensity to save. In both analyses saving *ex ante* and saving *ex post* are presumed to be equal, which means that saving calls the tune. Other variables such as investment, the productivity of capital coefficient, and the accelerator must adjust to the rate of saving if full employment over time is to be maintained.

The basic procedure employed by Harrod is to postulate a series of fundamental equations, each of which embodies a carefully defined rate of growth. By means of comparisons between these growth rates, it is possible to determine the conditions under which a steady rate of advance is possible for the economy.

The Warranted Rate of Growth

The most important growth rate developed by Harrod in his analysis is the *warranted rate of growth*, G_w, which he defines precisely as "that overall rate of advance which, if executed, will leave entrepreneurs in a state of mind in which they are prepared to carry on a similar advance."[22] In algebraic terms we have

$$G_w = \frac{\Delta Y}{Y}. \qquad (16\text{--}8)$$

More explicitly, the warranted rate of growth concept refers to a rate of advance for the economy as a whole that will leave entrepreneurs (in the aggregate or on the average) satisfied with the outcome of economic activity. Within the framework of equilibrium analysis, a condition of entrepreneurial satisfaction is a situation in which investment and saving *ex ante* are in equilibrium. This is basically what Harrod means by the warranted rate of growth, except that he is talking of a developing rather than a static situation. The concept of a warranted rate of growth refers to a situation in which a growing absolute volume of *ex ante* investment is in equilibrium with a growing absolute volume of full employment, *ex ante* saving. To express the necessary condition for equilibrium in a steadily advancing economy, Harrod postulates the following equation, which, he says, describes the condition in which producers will be content with what they are doing[23]:

$$G_w \times C_r = s. \qquad (16\text{--}9)$$

Before we examine the significance of this equation, it is necessary to explain the key concepts employed by Harrod in his analysis. We have already discussed G_w. The variable s represents the long-run propensity to save and is the same as α in Domar's analysis. Thus, the average and the marginal propensities to save are identical. Harrod assumes that saving intentions are always realized; consequently saving *ex ante* and saving *ex post* are always equal. Algebraically,

$$s = \frac{S}{Y} = \frac{\Delta S}{\Delta Y}. \qquad (16\text{--}10)$$

The variable C_r in Equation (16–9) is somewhat more complex and requires a more detailed explanation. Harrod describes C_r as the symbol for the *capital requirement*, by which is meant "the requirement for new capital divided by the increment of output to sustain which the new capital is required."[24] Harrod conceives the capital-output ratio as a techni-

22. Harrod, *Towards a Dynamic Economics*, p. 82.
23. Ibid., p. 81.
24. Ibid., p. 82.

cal relationship, for, as he says, the above definition is "based upon the idea that existing output can be sustained by existing capital that additional capital is only required to sustain additional output."[25] The capital requirement concept must be interpreted with care, for if interpreted too literally it leads to the absurd conclusion that more capital is needed to increase output by the amount that output has just increased. Actually, since capacity is not a precise magnitude, the technical relationship embodied in the capital-output ratio means that, at some point near the absolute upper limit of the individual firm's productive capacity, entrepreneurs will feel that more capacity will be required to provide additional output to meet a rising level of demand. Algebraically, we have

$$C_r = \frac{\Delta K}{\Delta Y} = \frac{I_n}{\Delta Y}. \qquad (16\text{--}11)$$

Although C_r as defined above may be said to represent the capital requirement of the economy, the above ratio may also be defined as the accelerator. In this sense, C_r becomes an expression of entrepreneurial behavior, for it represents the coefficient which describes the amount of investment that will be induced by a change in the output level. Investment in the above equation is, in other words, *ex ante* or planned investment, the amount of which depends upon a prior change in output.

Which of these definitions of C_r is appropriate in the context of Equation (16–9), which purports to describe the condition under which equilibrium in a growing economy is possible? Basically, both are appropriate, for although the acceleration concept may be used to explain why investment has attained a particular level in the current income period, it can have no meaning unless an underlying technical relationship between capital and output is assumed.

To clarify this statement, let us make the following algebraic substitutions in Equation (16–9): $\Delta Y/Y$ for G_w; $I_n/\Delta Y$ for C_r; and S/Y for s: Then we have

$$\frac{\Delta Y}{Y} \times \frac{I_n}{\Delta Y} = \frac{S}{Y}. \qquad (16\text{--}12)$$

Since the ΔY's on the left-hand side of the equation will cancel out, we then have

$$\frac{I_n}{Y} = \frac{S}{Y}. \qquad (16\text{--}13)$$

The basic meaning, therefore, of Harrod's equation that expresses the equilibrium of a steady advance is that the rate of growth must be such that *ex ante* investment is equal to *ex ante* saving. Since, in accord with the accelerator concept, *ex ante* investment depends upon the rise in output, the necessary condition for equilibrium is that output (or income) rise sufficiently to induce enough investment to absorb the saving of the cur-

25. Ibid.

rent income period. If this happens, then we can properly speak, as Harrod does, of the growth rate being a *warranted growth rate.*

The Actual Rate of Growth

The second crucial rate of growth in Harrod's analysis is the *actual rate of growth,* which represents the *ex post* percentage change in output between the present and the past income periods. Algebraically, the actual rate of growth is

$$G = \frac{\Delta Y}{Y}. \tag{16-14}$$

The actual rate of growth, G, to quote Harrod, is "the increment of total production in any unit period expressed as a fraction of total production."[26]

Harrod's fundamental equation pertaining to the actual, or *ex post,* performance of the economy is as follows:

$$G \times C = s. \tag{16-15}$$

G represents the actual rate of growth as defined above, while s is the actual saving ratio, which is assumed in Harrod's analysis to be the same always as the *ex ante* saving ratio. C may be defined as the actual (or *ex post*), as distinct from the intended (or *ex ante*), capital requirement (or accelerator). In other words, C is simply the ratio of the actual increase in the capital stock, ΔK or I'_n, to the actual change in output, ΔY. If we substitute algebraically in Equation (16–15) in the same way as we did earlier in equation (16–9), we have

$$\frac{\Delta Y}{Y} \times \frac{I'_n}{\Delta Y} = \frac{S}{Y}. \tag{16-16}$$

Since once again the ΔY's on the left-hand side of the equation cancel out, we now have

$$\frac{I'_n}{Y} = \frac{S}{Y}. \tag{16-17}$$

This equation simply means that investment *ex post* is equal to saving *ex post*. This is always true, irrespective of the income level. What Harrod has done is simply to place this truism in a growth context.

The Growth Process: Actual and Warranted Rates Compared

It should be apparent that, algebraically, the expression $G_w \times C_r$ equals the expression $G \times C$, since both are equal to s, the *ex ante* and *ex post*

26. Ibid., p. 77.

propensity to save. However, it does not follow that G_w necessarily equals G or C_r equals C. There is no inherent reason, in other words, why the actual rate of growth experienced by the economy should correspond with the warranted rate. Nor need the actual change in the capital stock in an income period coincide with the intended change in capital stock in the same income period. Let us analyze what the results will be if G and G_w do not coincide.

We shall assume, first, that the actual rate of growth is greater than the warranted rate, that is, $G > G_w$. It then follows algebraically that C_r is greater than C. But if this is true it means that *ex ante* (planned) investment is greater than *ex post* (actual) investment in the current income period, because C_r conceived of as the accelerator shows the amount of intended investment induced by a given change in income. Thus, if C_r is really greater than C, it has to mean that $C_r \times \Delta Y$ is greater than $C \times \Delta Y$ because ΔY is the same in both instances.

When investment *ex ante* is in excess of investment *ex post*, aggregate demand is greater than aggregate supply, a condition that will lead to an expansion in income and employment. To put the matter differently, we can say that when G is greater than G_w the economy is in a situation in which output has grown, but aggregate demand has grown even faster. Under such circumstances the economy will experience a chronic shortage of capital, as investment *ex post* continuously falls short of investment *ex ante*. The outcome will be further pressure on planned, or *ex ante*, investment as entrepreneurs seek to make good the economy's capital shortage, but such a reaction only serves to drive the actual rate of growth farther and farther from the warranted rate. Thus, it is Harrod's contention that any movement away from the line of steady advance represented by his warranted rate of growth tends to be cumulative in its effect; departures of the actual growth rate from the warranted or equilibrium rate do not, in other words, set in motion forces tending toward a restoration of equilibrium. Equilibrium once disturbed leads to a disequilibrium which becomes progressively worse.

The nature of the process of cumulative expansion envisioned by Harrod when G is in excess of G_w can be demonstrated diagrammatically. For this we can utilize the standard income determination diagram, as is done in Figure 16–7. Let us assume that the income level, which initially is at Y_1, moves to the level Y_2. The change in income is thus equal to the distance Y_1Y_2, while the actual rate of growth, G, is equal to the ratio Y_1Y_2/Y_1. Since this growth rate is greater than the warranted rate, C_r is greater than C. As a consequence, the amount of investment induced by the change in income from Y_1 to Y_2 is seen to be equal to the distance C_2D_2. But since this amount of investment is greater than the amount prevailing at the prior income level, the aggregate demand schedule has, in effect, shifted from $C + I_1$ to $C + I_2$. Aggregated demand now exceeds aggregate supply at the income level Y_2, and this in turn tends to drive the economy toward the income level Y_3. Again the change in income

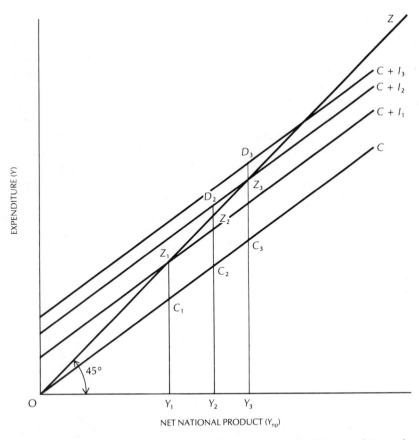

FIGURE 16–7.   The Actual Rate of Growth in Excess of the Warranted Rate of Growth

from Y_2 to Y_3 induces an amount of investment expenditure, C_3D_3, that is greater than necessary to achieve equilibrium at the income level Y_3. Investment *ex ante*, in other words, once again exceeds investment *ex post*, and thus the income level will be driven still higher. The departure from the initial equilibrium, the income level Y_1, has not, as shown in the hypothetical model, brought a restoration of equilibrium; rather, forces have been set in motion that drive the economy farther and farther from the initial equilibrium position. In this situation, saving becomes a virtue, in that a higher rate of saving means, algebraically, an increase in the warranted rate of growth, and thus restoration of equality between the actual rate and the warranted rate. More saving will permit a greater amount of actual investment in each income period, and this will tend to reduce the economy's capital shortage which, in turn, is the main reason why aggregate demand continuously runs ahead of aggregate supply.

The alternative to the situation just described is one in which the warranted rate of growth is greater than the actual rate of growth, that is,

$G_w > G$. If this is the case, it must follow that C is greater than C_r; the ratio of actual investment to the change in income is greater than the ratio of intended (planned) investment to the change in income. Investment *ex ante* in the current period falls short of investment *ex post* and, consequently, excess capacity will appear, making it impossible for the economy to continue to advance at the same rate as in the past. In other words, a situation in which G_w is greater than G indicates a tendency in the economy toward stagnation and a chronic excess of productive capacity. Under such circumstances it will be difficult enough to sustain any growth at all for a significant length of time, let alone at a rate that will justify itself only if net investment is continually increasing in absolute amount.

For a better understanding of what takes place when G_w is greater than G let us refer once again to an income determination diagram. In Figure 16–8 we will begin, as we have done previously, with an assumed full-employment equilibrium income level, Y_1. Now if income rises to the

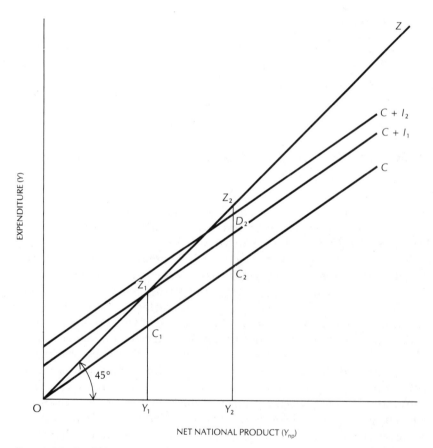

FIGURE 16–8.   The Warranted Rate of Growth in Excess of the Actual Rate of Growth

level Y_2, the actual rate of growth, G, again is equal to the ratio Y_1Y_2/Y_1. Since, however, the accelerator, C_r, is smaller than the actual capital coefficient, C, the amount of investment induced by the change in income falls short of the *ex post* investment at the higher income level.

Ex post investment at the income level Y_2 is represented by the distance C_2Z_2, which is also equal to both *ex post* and *ex ante* saving at this income level. The change in income from Y_1 to Y_2, however, induces an amount of investment equal to the distance C_2D_2, which falls short of actual investment at the Y_2 income level. Aggregate demand has shifted upward from $C+I_1$ to $C+I_2$ but the shift is not great enough to sustain the actual growth experienced by the economy when income moved from Y_1 to Y_2. At Y_2, aggregate demand now falls short of aggregate supply, so this income level cannot be sustained.

To summarize Harrod's analysis briefly at this point we can say that the necessary condition for an equilibrium rate of growth is that the actual rate be equal to the warranted rate. This means that, in each income period, investment, which is linked to the rate at which income has grown in the immediate past, will be equal to the planned saving of the income period. Furthermore, Harrod's analysis asserts that, if G and G_w are not equal, which is a condition of disequilibrium, the result will not be a restoration of equilibrium or a return to conditions in which G and G_w are equal but rather a greater and greater divergence between G and G_w. The growth process in Harrod's view is an inherently unstable phenomenon, as even the slightest departure from the exceedingly narrow path of an equilibrium rate of growth sets in motion forces making for either secular expansion and inflation or secular stagnation.

The Natural Rate of Growth

For a complete picture of the growth process as seen in Harrod it is necessary to introduce still another rate of growth. This is the *natural rate of growth,* which Harrod describes as "the rate of advance which the increase of population and technological improvements allow."[27] The use of the term *natural* is somewhat misleading. Harrod is not referring to any growth rate that comes about automatically as a consequence of the free play of market forces. It would be more accurate to describe this particular growth rate as the potential or even *maximum feasible rate of growth,* since Harrod is really talking about the rate of growth required for the full employment of a growing labor force. Such a rate of growth depends upon, first, the average annual rate of increase in the labor force and, second, the average annual rate of increase in the productivity of labor. If, for example, population and the labor force are growing at an annual average rate of 1 percent while output per worker is increasing, on the average, at the rate of 2 percent per year, the rate of growth necessary to maintain full employment of labor is 3 percent per year.

27. Ibid., p. 87.

Introduction of the concept of a natural, or feasible, rate of growth into his analysis better enables Harrod to describe the conditions under which the economy will tend toward a condition of either secular stagnation or secular exhilaration. This is possible because there is no inherent reason, in Harrod's view, for the natural growth rate, G_n, and the warranted growth rate, G_w, to coincide. These two rates may be equal, but the more normal situation, in Harrod's view, is one of divergence between the natural and the warranted rates of growth. For example, Harrod asserts that the economy will tend toward secular stagnation if G_w is greater than G_n. The logic of Harrod's position is that, other than for short intervals of time, G cannot exceed G_n because, given the rate at which the productivity of labor is increasing, the available labor supply will set a ceiling on the rate at which output can actually grow. If this is true, and if G_w is greater than G_n, it follows that G_w will be greater than G. Most of the time, in other words, the actual rate of growth will be below the warranted rate of growth.

But the above condition is one in which investment *ex post* will run ahead of investment *ex ante* and, consequently, excess capacity will appear. Because the accelerator is weak, the increase in aggregate demand is not sufficient to absorb into use all additions to the economy's capital stock. Such additions, of course, are determined by net *ex post* investment in the income period. If this is the economy's situation, it means basically that over time the economy will tend toward chronic underemployment of all resources, that is, secular stagnation.

Another way in which we can describe this situation is to say that the rate of growth required for the full utilization of a growing capital stock is greater than the rate of growth required for full employment of a growing labor force. This will foster excess capacity and with it the impossibility of sustaining the existing growth rate, even though this rate is below the warranted rate.

The warranted rate of growth is interpreted as a full capacity (as distinct from a full employment of labor) rate of growth. In what sense is this true? The concept of the warranted rate of growth is concerned with the amount of added capital needed to sustain added output. Therefore, the warranted (or justifiable) rate of growth is one that induces just enough of an upward shift in the schedule of aggregate demand (see Figure 16–7) so that the added capacity represented by net *ex post* investment at each successively higher level of income will be utilized. But the rate of growth that will induce a sufficient shift upward in the aggregate demand schedule to absorb into use a growing productive capacity does not necessarily have to be equal to a rate of growth that will give full employment to a growing labor force. This is basically what Harrod is attempting to demonstrate by asserting that the natural rate of growth does not necessarily have to equal the warranted rate.

The alternative situation suggested by Harrod is one in which the natural rate is greater than the warranted rate. In this instance, Harrod reasons that the actual rate of growth will stay above the warranted rate most of the time. As described earlier, *ex post* investment will continuously fall short of *ex ante* investment, with a consequent chronic shortage of real capital. Aggregate demand will run ahead of aggregate supply, the inducement to invest will remain high, and thus the economy will find itself in a state of secular exhilaration.

Concluding Observations on the Harrod-Domar Analysis of Economic Growth

Both the Domar and Harrod approaches to the broad problem of economic growth in an advanced market economy accord investment the central role in the growth process. Furthermore, both Domar and Harrod undertake their analyses of the process of growth within the income-expenditure framework. They agree that the central problem in the growth process in an advanced economy is that of the conditions under which planned investment will be continuously equated with a growing absolute volume of planned saving. Domar and Harrod are also in agreement with respect to the key role of saving, since their analyses are based on the assumption of a constant average and marginal propensity to save, and on the further assumption that actual and planned savings are always equal.

The two analyses differ mainly in the ways in which they look at the investment process. Domar's analysis looks ahead in the sense that he stresses the effect of today's net investment on tomorrow's capacity or productive potential, and thus seeks to determine the rate at which the economy must grow if this productive capacity is to be absorbed into use in the future. He is concerned primarily with the essentially technical question of the effect of present investment on future capacity. Harrod's analysis, on the other hand, tends to look backward in the sense that he is seeking to determine if output has actually grown enough between yesterday and today so as to induce an amount of net investment sufficient to absorb today's full-employment saving. Although his analysis rests in a fundamental sense on a technological relationship between output and capital, Harrod's key analytical tool is the concept of the accelerator, since this is the coefficient that links current investment to changes in the output level. Harrod's analysis centers primarily on the reaction of entrepreneurs to past changes in the income level and assumes that, if entrepreneurs in the aggregate are satisfied with the past rate of growth, they will act in such a way as to promote future growth in the economy at the same rate.

Both the Domar and the Harrod analyses of the growth process are subject to the same general criticism of being perhaps excessively abstract and too dependent (insofar as their conclusions with respect to the economy's ability to achieve a satisfactory rate of growth are concerned) on some rather rigid assumptions concerning the values and fixity of such critical determinants as the propensity to save and the capital coefficient. Harrod, in particular, can be criticized for placing too much stress on the phenomenon of induced investment as the crucial factor in the growth process. As a consequence, there emerges a picture of the economy tied tightly to a very narrow path of growth—with the twin disasters of either secular exhilaration and inflation or secular stagnation threatening in the event of the slightest divergence from the precisely determined path of advance.[28] This has been described as movement along a razor's edge equilibrium path of output.

Despite the shortcomings we have noted, the analyses of Domar and Harrod, by directing our attention to such strategically important ideas as the capacity-creating efforts of net investment and the phenomenon of accelerator-induced investment, do succeed in providing important insights into the operation of the real-world economy. More specifically, their theories enable us to understand, first, why the economy must grow if full employment is to be maintained and, second, why the economy cannot be expected to grow automatically at a rate that will ensure full employment.

Neoclassical Growth Theory

The razor-edge character of the Harrod-Domar analysis has been attacked by a number of economists as being excessively rigid and unrealistic.[29] The basic point of contention is the assumption in the Harrod-Domar analysis of a fixed value for the capital-output ratio (K/Y) and its reciprocal, the productivity of capital coefficient—Domar's σ. It is this feature which gives the analysis its razor-edge character, as the economy is tied tightly to a narrow equilibrium path. As Harrod demonstrates, any departure from this equilibrium $(G_w = G)$ leads to either a surging expansion or a plunging collapse.

What the neoclassical critics of the Harrod-Domar analysis seek to show is that the economy in a growth context is stable and that it will, if left to

28. Harrod's analysis appears unnecessarily rigid because it is built almost entirely around the concept of induced investment. He does recognize, however, that some investment is autonomous in that it is not directly linked to immediate output requirements. The existence of such investment obviously reduces the amount of current saving that must be absorbed into investment as a consequence of past changes in the income level. The same is also true for net foreign investment, as the excess of exports over imports may also provide an outlet for current saving through foreign lending. The introduction of autonomous investment and the foreign balance makes the economy's growth path somewhat less precarious than originally suggested by Harrod.
29. See especially Robert M. Solow, "A Contribution to the Theory of Economic Growth," *Quarterly Journal of Economics*, February 1956, and T. W. Swan, "Economic Growth and Capital Accumulation," *Economic Record*, November 1956. The model discussed in this final section of Chapter 16 is a simplified version of the one developed by Professor Swan in the latter article.

its own devices, seek out a steady-state equilibrium growth path. There is a basic similarity here to the monetarist approach to the economy's behavior, for, like the monetarists, the neoclassical theorists are challenging the Keynesian notion that the economy is inherently unstable.

This approach is called neoclassical for several reasons. It assumes that full employment is normally present as the economy grows; hence, savings are continuously absorbed by investment. A competitive economy, diminishing returns, and returns to the factors of production equal to their marginal products are also assumed. But most important for our purposes is the key assumption of the substitutability of capital for labor—and vice versa. In contrast to Harrod-Domar, the capital-output ratio and its converse, the productivity of capital, σ, are variable. It is this feature of the neoclassical theory that permits the system to move toward a steady-state equilibrium path of growth.

The essentials of the neoclassical model can be demonstrated with a simple diagram, as shown in Figure 16–9. The horizontal axis in the diagram shows different values for the output-capital ratio (Domar's σ), and the vertical axis represents the rate of growth of output ($\Delta Y/Y$) and the capital stock ($\Delta K/K$). Given a positive value for the propensity to save, the rate of growth will be greater, the greater is the value of the output-capital ratio. Domar's analysis should make this clear, for if all saving is

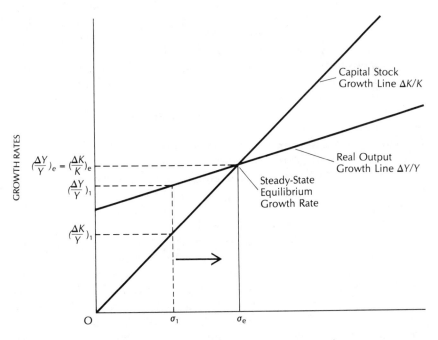

FIGURE 16–9.   The Neoclassical Growth Model

invested (an assumption of the neoclassical analysis), then the larger the amount of saving the greater will be the effect on productive capacity as the value of σ increases. Since full employment is assumed, it necessarily follows that the rate of growth of real output will be a positive function of σ. The real output growth line $(\Delta Y/Y)$ crosses the vertical axis at a positive growth rate because some growth will take place as a result of a growing labor force and independently of the value of σ.[30]

The rate of growth of the capital stock $(\Delta K/K)$ will be proportional to the output-capital ratio $(Y/K$, or $\sigma)$, given a fixed value for the propensity to save. This can be shown quite simply. If s is the long-term propensity to save, then S (saving) will be equal to sY. But since the neoclassical model assumes that full employment is the norm and that full-employment savings are absorbed by investment, it follows that $sY = I = \Delta K$. If we divide $sY = \Delta K$ by K, we have sY/K or $s\sigma = \Delta K/K$, which shows that, given the propensity to save, s, the rate of growth of the capital stock is proportional to the output-capital rate $(Y/K$, or $\sigma)$.

Now let us examine what happens in terms of the model shown in Figure 16–9. Suppose the economy is initially at a point at which the value of the productivity of capital coefficient is σ_1. What does this show? If this is the situation it means that output is growing faster than the capital stock, that is, $(\Delta Y/Y)_1 > (\Delta K/K)_1$. In the neoclassical world, when this happens, the productivity of capital will rise and capital will be substituted for labor. This will tend to accelerate the rate of growth of both capital and output, but, as long as the productivity of capital (σ) is increasing, the rate of increase in output will have to accelerate more than the rate of increase in the capital stock. This will continue until the two growth rates become equal—the point of intersection of the capital stock growth line and the real output growth line—and a steady-state equilibrium growth rate will prevail.

Contrast this with the Harrod analysis. If output is growing more rapidly than the capital stock, it means the economy faces a chronic shortage of capital. In Harrod's terminology, G is greater than G_w, which means an explosive upward surge in planned investment and the system moves farther and farther away from the equilibrium growth rate of $G = G_w$. Only the full-employment ceiling set by the natural growth rate G_n halts the upsurge.

What happens in the neoclassical model when the output-capital ratio is at a value which has the capital stock growing faster than output? This would be to the right of σ_e in Figure 16–9. In this case, the productivity of capital will decline, labor will be substituted for capital, and this process will continue until the income-capital ratio has fallen sufficiently to bring the rate of growth of the capital stock into line with the rate of growth of output; a steady-state equilibrium will again prevail. In the Harrod analysis, however, this situation is one in which excess capacity

30. See the Swan article for elaboration on this point.

develops $(G_w > G)$, and a cumulative downward movement gets under way, a collapse that will continue until the system works off its excess capacity. Without public intervention this might take a long while.

Neither the Harrod-Domar nor the neoclassical approach taken in isolation provides a wholly adequate theoretical analysis of the problems an advanced market economy confronts in attempting to attain both growth and full employment over time. Even though its underlying assumptions are more rigid than can be justified, the Harrod-Domar analysis underscores two important aspects of the economy. The first is the capacity-creating effect of net investment, and the second is the inherent instability typical of a market system. Experience tends to confirm this view more than it does the neoclassical (and monetarist) view that the system is inherently stable. On the other hand, the neoclassical analysis helps us understand that the kind of precarious knife-edge equilibrium found in Harrod-Domar is probably much too extreme a view of how the system really works. Perfect substitutability of capital for labor does not exist in reality, but neither do absolutely rigid capital-output ratios in most instances. Thus, there must be some blending of the two approaches if we are to obtain a workable and realistic theory.

Summary

1. Economic growth concerns the long-term performance of the economy, having to do with both the ability of the economy to expand over time its productive capacity and the ability to use that productive capacity. The former is a supply-side problem, whereas the latter involves aggregate demand.

2. The production function is a useful concept for getting into the subject of economic growth, as it enables us to focus on the key variables that determine over time the economy's productive capacity. These include the supply of labor (N), the quantity of capital (K), natural resources (R), and the level of technology (T).

3. Additional key concepts important in analyzing growth are productivity (output per worker-hour) and the ratio of capital to labor (K/N). Long-term historical evidence indicates that technological change, which involves using resources more efficiently, is a major factor in explaining the growth in the economy's potential for production.

4. The economy's output potential can be determined by multiplying the average output per worker per year by the labor force. This is a useful measure which most post–World War II administrations have employed in making policy decisions.

5. One post–World War II development that has had serious consequences for the American economy is the productivity crisis, the slow-

down in the rate of growth in American productivity, which became evident in the 1970s. This has been a major factor in the inflation, since inflation is inevitable if wage increases run ahead of productivity gains. This was the situation during most of the 1970s. There is no agreement among economists on the sources of the productivity crisis, although there is agreement that it is serious.

6. Within the income-expenditure framework, there are two major theoretical models of economic growth. These are known as the Domar and Harrod models. Both theories are concerned essentially with this basic question: In a dynamic economy with an ever-expanding production potential, how and at what rate must aggregate demand increase in order to keep the capacity utilized and fully employ the economy's labor force?

7. Professor Domar's model focuses primarily upon the capacity-creating effects of net investment. When investment (net) takes place, the economy has added capacity, which means that in subsequent income periods the economy must grow if that capacity is to be utilized. Since, in the Keynesian income-expenditure framework, investment is the basic source of income change, Domar determines the rate at which investment must grow in order to keep the added capacity fully employed. In this sense his analysis is said to be forward looking.

8. Professor Harrod's approach is slightly different, even though outcome is essentially the same as in the Domar model. Both models explain theoretically why growth is an absolute necessity in a system of market capitalism. If stagnation and chronic unemployment are to be avoided, Harrod's model draws upon the theory of the accelerator and poses the question of whether or not past growth has been sufficient to induce investment equal to full-employment savings. If so, the economy will continue along a full-employment equilibrium in either an upward or a downward direction, which will be cumulative, leading either to chronic inflation or chronic stagnation. Professor Harrod believes the latter is the dominant tendency.

9. Neoclassical growth theory was developed in part as an answer to the precarious "knife-edge" state of equilibrium found in the Harrod model. By assuming flexibility in all prices, including wages and the return on capital, plus mobility and adaptability of resources, the neoclassical model shows how the economy can settle down over time to a growth path that fully utilizes all resources.

17

Business Cycles
and Forecasting

In a broad sense this chapter extends the theme of the last chapter—
economic growth. The difference is that we are concerned now with
historical patterns of growth and the tools economists use to predict future
changes in the economy. Economic growth does not occur at a steady
rate; it proceeds by fluctuations—ups and downs if you will.

Figure 17–1 plots the uneven nature of the economy's performance
over nearly two centuries. This chart shows the deviations of an index
of general business activity from the long-term trend of the economy.
The latter, of course, has been upward; as we saw in the preceding chapter the long-term rate of growth of the American economy has been
around 3.5 percent per year. But this is a trend, not the reality of any
given year. What Figure 17–1 reveals is that progress over time is spo-
radic, proceeding in a rough cyclical fashion in which a period of expansion is always followed by a period of contraction.

Historically the term "business cycle" has been used to describe the
periodic ups and downs that characterize the actual movement through
time of the real economy. The reason for using the word *cycle* is because
economic activity over the long pull does follow a wavelike pattern with
a significant amount of regularity. But there is some danger in using this
term because it carries the connotation of more regularity than is the
reality. For a period of time after World War II the term "business cycle"
fell out of favor among economists, in part because the long postwar
economic upswing gave rise to a belief—now seen as naive—that the
business cycle was a thing of the past. "Fluctuations" came to be the preferred term, particularly because it does not imply a regular wavelike
motion as does the word *cycles*. As a result of the experiences of the

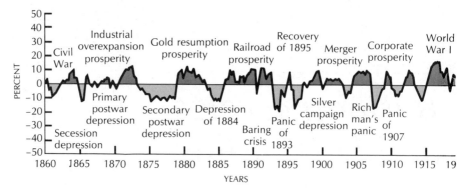

FIGURE 17–1. Business Activity in the United States, 1860–1982. Percentage
Deviation from the Long-term Trend

1970s—especially the severe downturns in 1974–75 and 1981–82—the
idea of the business cycle has come back into fashion. In the final analysis, the name used is less important than the reality; our economy has
not experienced a smooth growth path in the past nor is it likely to in
the foreseeable future.

Our objectives in this chapter are basically three. First, we shall examine the nature of the business cycle—how it is defined, how it is measured, and what happens during the course of a typical cycle. Second,
we shall take a broad, historical look at some of the ideas economists
have stressed as explanations for the cycle. Finally, we shall examine the
general area of economic forecasting, including a review of the nature
and effectiveness of the major forecasting techniques. Forecasting exists
because the business cycle exists. If the economy always proceeded upward
along a smooth trend line, then it would only be necessary to extrapolate
the past in order to know what would happen in the future. Unhappily,
the world is not that simple. Hence, there is a necessity for economic
forecasting.

The Nature of the Business Cycle

We have, in fact, already defined the business cycle. A formal definition
would be *a wavelike movement in the general level of economic activity that takes
place over time.* Such a definition is broad enough to apply to the business
cycle as a general phenomenon encompassing the entire economy, or to
the many individual types of economic activity that are a part of a more
general picture. A couple of important points need to be stressed. First,
the business cycle is wavelike, but it is not regular in an exact periodic
sense. Motions of the latter sort are characteristic of many physical phenomena—electrical current, for example—but not of economic activity.
Second, the business cycle is an economic phenomenon characteristic of

SOURCE: Data from the Cleveland Trust Company

all countries organized on market principles, which is to say organized on the basis of private property and the pursuit of private gain. Furthermore, major business cycles occur at the same time in the leading industrial nations. Business cycle research shows, for example that this has been true in both the nineteenth and twentieth centuries for such major industrial powers as Germany, France, Great Britain, and the United States. It is not true for the minor cycles, and it is not true that all major industrial nations have had the same number of business cycles. But in a broad, historical sense it is clear that the business cycle is an international phenomenon deeply rooted in the behavior patterns of market economies.

In the United States the most important work in defining, measuring, and understanding the business cycle has been done by the National Bureau of Economic Research, a privately funded research organization located in New York City. In Chapter 2 it was pointed out that the National Bureau pioneered in the development of national income accounting in this country. Wesley Mitchell, a long-time leader in business cycle research, was instrumental in the creation of the National Bureau. Mitchell was the foremost advocate of the view that the cycle involves a continuing, self-generating process that is inherent in a capital-using economy organized around the exchange of money for goods and goods for money in private markets. In his classic study of fluctuations, *What Happens during Business Cycles*, Mitchell defined the cycle as follows (his definition remains as the working concept of the cycle used by the National Bureau of Economic Research):

> Business cycles are a type of fluctuation found in the aggregate economic activity of nations that organize their work mainly in business enterprises: a cycle consists of expansion occurring at about the same time in many economic activities, followed by similarly general recessions, contractions, and revivals which merge into the expansion phase of the next cycle; this sequence of events is recurrent, but not periodic; in duration business cycles vary from more than

one year to ten or twelve years; they are not divisible into shorter cycles of similar character with amplitudes approximating their own.[1]

Thus, the business cycle as seen by Mitchell pertains primarily to fluctuations in the overall level of economic activity, affecting most industries and activities at about the same time. It is a recurrent process, but not regular in either the magnitude of fluctuations or the frequency with which they occur.

Measuring the Business Cycle

There are various possible ways in which the business cycle can be measured, but the one most widely used is the method developed by the National Bureau of Economic Research. This method is also used by the U.S. Department of Commerce, which, in its monthly periodical *Business Conditions Digest*, publishes the most comprehensive volume of data from any source on what is happening to the economy in a cyclical sense. For its purposes the National Bureau measures the business cycle from trough to peak to trough, although it is just as possible to measure it from peak to trough to peak.

Figure 17–2 shows a simmplified, "idealized" cycle in which real GNP moves from point *A* (an initial trough or lower turning point) through point *B* (the peak or upper turning point) and back down to point *C* (a second trough), from whence a new cycle will begin. The fluctuations take place around a trend line that incorporates the economy's long-term growth rate. Because the economy is growing, each peak and each trough normally will be at a higher level than the prior peak or trough. The word "normally" is used advisedly in this context, as a glance at the long-term behavior of the economy shown in Figure 17–1 shows that it does not always happen this way, especially when the economy collapses to the extent it did during the Great Depression of the 1930s.

Figure 17–2 includes additional technical information on the nature of the business cycle. The phase from point *A* to *B* is generally called *upswing,* a period in which output is rising faster than its long-term trend. Normally an upswing will encompass both a recovery period, which involves getting from the low of the trough to a level of output reached at the previous peak, and a period of expansion or boom, which involves output rising to levels beyond the previous peak. From point *B* to point *C* the economy is in the *downswing* of the cycle, a period which involves an actual decline of output. In the downswing the economy finds itself in either a recession or depression. Technically, the National Bureau defines a recession as any period in which *real* GNP has dropped for two successive quarters (six months). Beyond this, there is no precise defini-

1. Wesley C. Mitchell, *What Happens during Business Cycles.* (New York: National Bureau of Economic Research, 1951), p. 6.

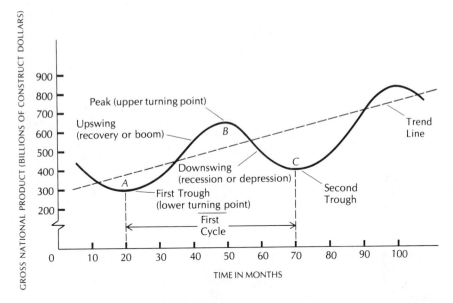

GROSS NATIONAL PRODUCT (BILLIONS OF CONSTRUCT DOLLARS)

TIME IN MONTHS

FIGURE 17–2. A Simplified Cycle Pattern

tion of what constitutes a *recession* and what constitutes a *depression*. The difference between the two is a matter of judgment, depending upon the depth of the fall in output (the rise in unemployment) and the length of the downswing or slump in economic activity. Most citizens have no trouble identifying the collapse of the 1930s as a depression because of its length and severity. Since World War II, however, the term recession has generally been used, the reason being the relative mildness of downturns, except for the 1974–75 and 1981–82 slumps. The extent to which output—or any other economic variable—departs from the long-term trend is described as the *amplitude* of the cycle. It is normally measured as the average deviation (expressed as a percentage) of the series from its trend. Amplitude may be measured with respect to the entire cycle or for specific periods (a month, for example) within the cycle.

How frequent and how lengthy are business cycles in the United States? Although no precise answer can be given to this question because satisfactory data are lacking for the early years of the nation, reasonably good estimates are available. Table 17–1 gives business cycle data as measured by the trough to trough method from 1854 to 1983.

In the period covered by the data of Table 17–1 there have been 30 full cycles, averaging 57 months in length (from trough to trough). The expansion phase has been almost twice as long as the contraction phase. On the average, since 1854, periods of expanding economic activity have averaged 33 months—or nearly three years—while the downturns typically have been slightly less than two years, averaging 18 months. The data of Table 17–1 also indicate some significant changes in the cyclical

TABLE 17–1. Duration of Business Cycle Expansions and Contractions in the United States, 1854–1982

Business Cycle			Duration (in months) of		
Trough	·Peak·	Trough	Expansion	Contraction	Full Cycle
Dec. 1854	June 1857	Dec. 1858	30	18	48
Dec. 1858	Oct. 1860	June 1861	22	8	30
June 1861	Apr. 1865	Dec. 1867	46	32	78
Dec. 1867	June 1869	Dec. 1870	18	18	36
Dec. 1870	Oct. 1873	Mar. 1879	34	65	99
Mar. 1879	Mar. 1882	May 1885	36	38	74
May 1885	Mar. 1887	Apr. 1888	22	13	35
Apr. 1888	July 1890	May 1891	27	10	37
May 1891	Jan. 1893	June 1894	20	17	37
June 1894	Dec. 1895	June 1897	18	18	36
June 1897	June 1899	Dec. 1900	24	18	42
Dec. 1900	Sept. 1902	Aug. 1904	21	23	44
Aug. 1904	May 1907	June 1908	33	13	46
June 1908	Jan. 1910	Jan. 1912	19	24	43
Jan. 1912	Jan. 1913	Dec. 1914	12	23	35
Dec. 1914	Aug. 1918	Mar. 1919	44	7	51
Mar. 1919	Jan. 1920	July 1921	10	18	28
July 1921	May 1923	July 1924	22	14	36
July 1924	Oct. 1926	Nov. 1927	27	13	40
Nov. 1927	Aug. 1929	Mar. 1933	21	43	64
Mar. 1933	May 1937	June 1938	50	13	63
June 1938	Feb. 1945	Oct. 1945	80	8	88
Oct. 1945	Nov. 1948	Oct. 1949	37	11	48
Oct. 1949	July 1953	Aug. 1954	45	13	58
Aug. 1954	July 1957	Apr. 1958	35	9	44
Apr. 1958	May 1960	Feb. 1961	25	9	34
Feb. 1961	Nov. 1969	Nov. 1970	105	12	117
Nov. 1970	Nov. 1973	Mar. 1975	36	16	52
Mar. 1975	Jan. 1980	July 1980	63	6	69
July 1980	July 1981	Jan. 1983	12	18	30
Average, all cycles:					
30 cycles, 1854–1983			33	18	51
14 cycles, 1919–83			41	15	55
8 cycles, 1945–1983			45	12	51

SOURCE: *Business Conditions Digest*, April 1973, p. 115; May 1977, p. 11; January 1983, p. 10.

pattern of the economy following World War II. Since 1945 we have had eight measurable business cycles, but the significant development has been an increase in the length of the expansion and prosperity phase of the cycle and a reduction in the average length of the downturn. After World War II expansions were 36 percent longer and contractions 33 percent shorter than the long-term average for the economy (1845–1983).

In part this was the result of the unusually long upswing of the 1960s, but not wholly since upswings for six out of the eight cycles recorded between 1945 and 1983 were longer than the historic average.

It was the mildness of cycles—especially the downswings—in the post–World War II era which gave rise to the belief that the business cycle had been tamed by modern monetary and fiscal policies. This attitude was summed up by the Kansas City Federal Reserve Bank in the following comment:

> Ironically, in the late 1960s, after nearly a decade of almost uninterrupted growth, a widespread notion developed that the old-style business cycle was extinct. It was suggested that the definition of the business cycle be expanded to include periods of retarded growth. The title of a government publication was changed from *Business Cycle Developments* to *Business Conditions Digest*. Unfortunately, the business cycle was not dead.[2]

As mentioned, belief that the business cycle was dead collapsed in the face of the unexpected severity of the 1974–75 and 1981–82 slumps, the worst economic downturns experienced by the economy since the 1930s. Not only was the falloff in output in these recessions more severe than any of the other post–World War II recessions, but the contraction phase in the 1981–82 recession lasted 18 months, a period equal to the long-term historic average for bad times. Clearly the 1974–75 and 1981–82 recessions were old-fashioned business cycles of the sort that was not supposed to happen, according to optimistic observers of the post–World War II economy. But they did.

Inflation and the Business Cycle

In one important sense, however, the most recent cycles differ significantly from the "old-fashioned" business cycle of the pre–World War II years. This difference is inflation and its persistence through *all* phases of the cycle—the downswing as well as the upswing. This change led the Conference Board to suggest that we are observing a new type of cyclical experience, one characterized by fluctuations of widening intensity not only in output and employment, but also in the inflation rate.[3] In the view of the Conference Board economists, the cycle has changed in a way which makes it increasingly difficult to control by deployment of monetary and fiscal policies in the conventional countercyclical fashion. Figure 17–3 uses fluctuations in the industrial production index to illustrate the widening intensity of the cycle.

The root of the problem appears to be the new inflation, an inflation which does not seem to be "fundamentally cyclical; rather, it looks like a new strain, highly resistant to conventional anti-inflationary policy, and

---

2. Federal Reserve Bank of Kansas City, *Business Conditions*, March 1975, p. 11.
3. Albert T. Sommers with Lucie R. Blau, *The Widening Cycle: An Examination of U.S. Experience with Stabilization Policy in the Last Decade* (New York: The Conference Board, 1975).

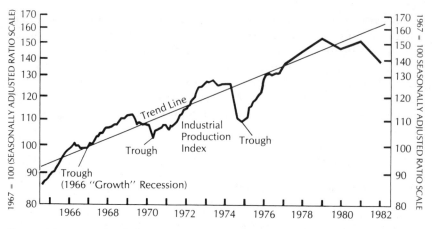

Figure 17–3.   Cyclical Fluctuations in Industrial Production: 1965–82

flagrantly in violation of theoretical explanations of price behavior. . . ."[4]
What happens in the face of a persistent upward thrust in the price level
is that attempts to bring inflation under control by putting on the monetary and fiscal brakes push the economy into a recession before they
have any significant impact on prices. The recession may slow down the
rate of inflation, but it does not bring about an actual decline in prices
(see Figure 14–15). This is the major difference from earlier experiences. But since the public will no longer tolerate a significant rise in the
unemployment rate, restrictive policies not only have to be abandoned,
but must be thrown into reverse to pull the economy out of the recession. This, of course, was the situation prior to the advent of the Reagan
program. The Reagan administration did not explicitly reverse course,
but *de facto* this happened. As the recession deepened, the Federal Reserve
let up on the monetary brakes in mid-1982, and the 1981 tax cuts came
to be viewed as a stimulus to demand, a needed stimulus. This, clearly,
is a Keynesian perspective. For the most part in the 1970s policy alter-
nated between "stop and go," which, as the Conference Board research
suggests, pushes the economy into intensifying recessions as a consequence of the struggle against mounting inflation. It is clear that the
1970s experienced a resurgence and intensification of the economy's
cyclical behavior, but it is not certain that this is the pattern of the future.
This is yet to be determined, although the Conference Board believes
that the renewal of the strength of the business cycle is associated with
an inflationary trend that goes deeper than the cycle itself. In its view,
the roots of the inflation lie not in any single cause—such as federal
deficit spending, for example—but in the multiple public and private
demands placed upon the system from 1965 onward.[5] These demands

4. Ibid., p. 3.
5. See also Wallace C. Peterson, *Our Overloaded Economy: Inflation, Unemployment, and the
Crisis in American Capitalism* (Armonk, New York: M. E. Sharpe, 1982).

mounted rapidly and, in effect, outran the economy's real capacity to satisfy them. Our goals, in other words, have outdistanced our means. Since society has not developed adequate political mechanisms to adjudicate excessive claims upon a limited national output—fiscal and monetary policies were not adequate for this task—inflation has been the inevitable result. Stable growth and stable prices will continue to elude us until we undertake a tough-minded critical review of our national goals and discipline ourselves so that these goals do not exceed our real resource capabilities. It remains to be seen if our democratic society can meet this challenge.

Long Waves in Economic Life

Typically the business cycle as defined and measured by the National Bureau of Economic Research lasts from three to five years. Most business cycle research has centered on this type of a cycle, although from the time research into the cyclical behavior of the economy first began in the nineteenth century there have been scholars intrigued with the idea that there are much longer economic waves at work in market economies. One of the earliest serious students of the businesss cycle was Clement Juglar, a French medical doctor who became so fascinated with the idea that it was possible through statistics to isolate and measure the ebb and flow of economic life that he gave up the practice of medicine and became an economist. Juglar was an early advocate of the idea that there were commercial cycles that occurred with considerable regularity. He saw that each cycle had a similar pattern, even though there was no uniformity with respect to either frequency or length. He suggested that cycles had three parts—prosperity, crisis, and liquidation—and that they always followed one another in the same order.[6] Juglar did think, however, that the average length of a cycle was 9 to 10 years, which is two to three times longer than the cycles recognized by contemporary theorists.

It was a Russian economist, Nikolai D. Kondratieff, whose name has become almost synonymous with the idea of long waves in economic life.[7] Kondratieff developed his theory of long waves by studying data on wholesale prices, interest rates, wage rates, and physical production for the French, British, and American economies. His studies covered the period from about 1780 to 1920, or almost a century and a half.

6. Wesley C. Mitchell, *Business Cycles: The Problem and the Setting* (New York: National Bureau of Economic Research, 1927), p. 452.
7. Kondratieff developed his ideas about long waves in the early 1920s. He published a paper on the subject in Russian in 1925 which was subsequently translated into both German and English. The English version of his article may be found in *Readings in Business Cycle Theory* (Philadelphia: Blakiston, 1944), pp. 20–42. Kondratieff was a Marxist economist, but he disappeared from the Soviet scene sometime in the late 1920s. It has been reported that he incurred the displeasure of Stalin, was arrested, and banished to a Soviet labor camp. His real fate remains unknown.

From these studies he concluded that Western—that is, market or capitalistic—economies are subject to very long waves of a distinct cyclical character. These "Kondratieff cycles" are approximately 50 to 60 years in length with an upswing and downswing of about equal length. Furthermore, they are international in scope and appeared about the same time in the major industrial states of Europe as well as the United States. Kondratieff did not offer any theoretical explanation to account for the existence of long waves, but he did suggest that they are inherent in a capitalistic economy.[8] Table 17–2 shows an "idealized" version of the Kondratieff long waves extrapolated to the present. These data are termed "idealized" because specific dates are shown for the turning points of the cycles, although Kondratieff's research specified a range of four or five years, rather than a specific year for the turning points.

   Joseph A. Schumpeter, best known, perhaps, for his theory linking investment to innovation and invention (Chapter 6), developed a "model" of the business cycle which involved an integration of Kondratieff's long-wave theory with the ideas of Juglar and a third economist, Joseph Kitchin, who, writing in the early 1920s, developed a theory involving major and minor cycles.[9] His minor cycle averaged 40 months in duration and his major cycle consisted of three minor cycles, which made the Kitchin major about the same length as the cycle Juglar thought he had discovered (9

TABLE 17–2.   "Idealized" Kondratieff Cycles: 1790–1970s

First Long Wave: 1790–1845		(55 years)
Expansion: 1790–1815		
Contraction: 1815–1845		
Second Long Wave: 1845–1895		(50 years)
Expansion: 1845–1870		
Contraction: 1870–1895		
Third Long Wave*: 1895–1940		(45 years)
Expansion: 1895–1920		
Contraction: 1920–1935–40		
Fourth Long Wave: 1940–??		(?? years)
Expansion: 1940–70s		
Contraction: 1970s–??		

SOURCE: Nikolai D. Kondratieff, "The Long Waves in Economic Life," in *Reading in Business Cycle Theory* (Philadelphia: Blakiston, 1944), pp. 20–42.
*Published research by Kondratieff covered only 2½ cycles, 1790 to 1920.

8. Wesley C. Mitchell, *Business Cycles*, p. 228.
9. Joseph Kitchin, "Cycles and Trends in Economic Factors," *Review of Economic Statistics*, January 1923, pp. 10–16.

to 10 years). What Schumpeter did was combine the 40-month Kitchin cycle and the 10-year Juglar cycle with Kondratieff's long wave. In Schumpeter's scheme the Juglar cycle provided the link between the Kondratieff long wave and the much shorter Kitchin cycle. No special significance attaches to this, except in those rare instances when the downswings of all three cycles coincide. As Schumpeter said, "No claims are made for our three cycle scheme except that it is a useful descriptive or illustrative device. Using it, however, we in fact got *ex visu* of 1929, a 'forecast' of a serious depression embodied in the formula: coincidence of the depression phase of all three cycles."[10]

Many contemporary students of the business cycle flatly reject the notion of long waves in economic life, of either the Kondratieff variety or the shorter Juglar type. There are cycles—of this there is little doubt—but the general consensus among economists is that they average between three and five years in length, as is suggested by the data in Table 17–1. Minor cycles do exist, but most of these appear to be the result of inventory adjustments. Economists do not believe that there is any systematic relationship such as Kitchin described between minor cycles and a longer cycle of perhaps 10 years.

An economic historian, W. W. Rostow of the University of Texas, gives credence to the Kondratieff concept of long waves, but interprets the phenomenon differently from most business cycles theorists. He sees the long-wave theory primarily in terms of a price cycle whose true significance is found in the movement of the price of basic commodities (raw materials and food) *relative* to other prices. According to Rostow, there have been five times in the past 200 years when a rise in the relative price of basic commodities occurred, the most recent being the surge in energy, other raw materials, and food prices which began about 1972. The other four occasions began in the 1790s, the early 1850s, the latter part of the 1890s, and the late 1930s.[11] What happened in each of these earlier periods was that food and raw material prices rose sharply and then fluctuated in a relatively high range for approximately a quarter of a century. Figure 17–4 plots an "idealized" Kondratieff cycle against the index for wholesale prices in the United States (1967 = 100) for the period 1790–1975. As indicated earlier, the path of the Kondratieff cycle from 1920 onward is an extrapolation, as Kondratieff's original findings covered the two and a half cycles which he had actually measured through the early 1920s. In Rostow's analysis the upsurge of food and raw material prices (the upswings of the Kondratieff's cycle shown in Figure 17–4) was followed by a period of approximately equal length in which food and raw material prices were *relatively* cheap. Down to 1914, Rostow argues, the classic response of the world economy to the Kondratieff

10. Joseph A. Schumpeter, *Business Cycles* (New York: McGraw-Hill, 1939), Vol. I, p. 174.
11. W. W. Rostow, "Caught by Kondratieff," *The Wall Street Journal*, March 8, 1977. See also "The Bankruptcy of Neo-Keynesian Economics," *Intermountain Economic Review*, Spring 1976, pp. 6–7.

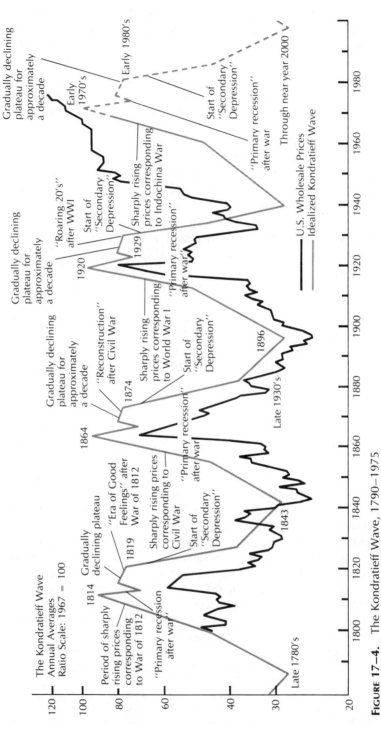

The Kondratieff Wave
Annual Averages
Ratio Scale: 1967 = 100

Period of sharply rising prices corresponding to War of 1812

"Primary recession" after war

Gradually declining plateau

1814

1819 "Era of Good Feelings" after War of 1812

Sharply rising prices corresponding to Civil War

Start of "Secondary Depression"

"Primary recession" after war

1864

Gradually declining plateau for approximately a decade

1874 "Reconstruction" after Civil War

Sharply rising prices corresponding to World War I

Start of "Secondary Depression"

1896

Late 1930's

1843

Late 1780's

Gradually declining plateau for approximately a decade

1920 "Roaring 20's" after WWI

Start of "Secondary Depression"

1929

Sharply rising prices corresponding to Indochina War

"Primary recession" after war

"Primary recession" after war

Through near year 2000

Gradually declining plateau for approximately a decade

Early 1970's

Early 1980's

Start of "Secondary Depression"

120
100
80
60
40
30
20

1800   1820   1840   1860   1880   1900   1920   1940   1960   1980

—— U.S. Wholesale Prices
—— Idealized Kondratieff Wave

FIGURE 17–4. The Kondratieff Wave, 1790–1975

SOURCE: *International Moneyline*, January 1977

upswing was to open new agricultural lands to production (the American West, Canada, Australia, Argentina, and the Ukraine). In the fourth upswing, which began in the late 1930s, the response took the form of more investment and a diffusion of technology, which brought rapid productivity gains to food and other raw materials production. What is the lesson in this? Rostow believes that, in the face of a Kondratieff upswing in the *relative* price of basic materials, an industrialized nation must increase or redirect investment in ways which will expand the supply of basic products or economize on their use. "The central operational fact about Kondratieff upswing is that the pattern of investment, the directions of investment, must change."[12] If we are in a Kondratieff upswing, it is fundamentally different from the past because it involves not just changes in the relative price of food and raw materials generally, but quite a new situation with respect not only to the price but also to the supply of such absolutely fundamental resources as energy and water, not to mention a livable environment. One consequence, according to Rostow, is that we will have to depend relatively more on government and less on the workings of the market system for the necessary response to price movements during the most recent Kondratieff upswing.[13]

What Happens in a Typical Business Cycle

While it is true that no two business cycles are the same with respect to length, intensity, or other developments, it is also true that there is a basic pattern of events that is similar in all cycles. Thanks largely to the long, painstaking research of Wesley Mitchell, we have a clear picture of the most important things that happen in a business cycle. To arrive at a composite picture of the cycle, Mitchell examined the behavior of more than eight hundred time series.[14] He never did develop a precise theory of the business cycle, although when viewed overall his findings provide a reasonable and coherent explanation of the cyclical process.

There are two important points to note and understand with respect

12. Rostow, "Caught by Kondratieff."
13. Economists use the phrase "terms of trade" to refer to the movement of the prices for one group of commodities *relative* to another. Thus, a rise in food and raw material prices relative to other prices (as happens in a Kondratieff upswing) means a change in the terms of trade in favor of agricultural commodities and other raw material prices. The reason is easily understood. If, for example, the price of a bushel of wheat is going up faster than the price of other goods and services, then each bushel of wheat has more *real* purchasing power in terms of other goods and services. This is what Rostow says happens in the upswing of the Kondratieff cycle—the terms of trade turn in favor of food and other raw materials.
14. Right up to the time of his death, Mitchell was still trying to find out empirically what actually happened in the cycle. His work over the years is summarized in his last book, published after his death. See Wesley G. Mitchell, *What Happens during Business Cycles: A Progress Report* (New York: National Bureau of Economic Research, Studies in Business Cycles 5, 1951). Our account of the sequence of events in a typical cycle is based largely on Mitchell's findings.

to Mitchell's view of the cycle. First, Mitchell—like many other econo-mists—found the cycle to be inherent in money-using, market econom-ies in which the quest for money profits by business enterprises is the dominant fact of economic life. Second, the processes at work in the typical cycle are cumulative and carry within themselves the seeds by which one phase of the cycle is transformed into the next phase. These processes are not only cumulative, but repetitive, and from this comes the fact that *all* cycles have certain common characteristics.

A convenient point of departure is a recession or depression. In the absence of deliberate policy actions by a central government (a tax cut, more spending, lowered interest rates, or any combination of these) what will bring a recovery? In a recession prices drop (or the inflation rate lessens), labor is in ample supply because of unemployment, wages and other costs go down (or at least go up less rapidly), while money and credit become increasingly available as bank reserves grow. Profits, of course, are low or nonexistent in many cases. Profits, however, are the key to a recovery. Somewhere, in some sector of the economy, a recovery will start when the profit picture changes, usually because costs in a recession—or depression—eventually drop farther than prices. Although a recovery tends to be slow at first, once started it spreads throughout the economy and becomes cumulative in effect. Prices start rising once a recovery is well under way. Here we encounter one of Mitchell's key statistical findings, which is that as a recovery merges into an expansion or boom the prices of finished goods and services rise more rapidly than the prices of those things which enter directly into production costs—wages for labor, rents for land and buildings, and interest on loans. There is no guarantee that this pattern will hold in a recovery, but to the extent that it does, profits improve and the expansion gathers momentum. An improved profit picture not only stimulates current production, which puts people back to work, it also stimulates investment spending as pes-simism in the business community gives way to optimism.

Why doesn't prosperity continue indefinitely? What brings an expan-sion to an end? Basically what happens is that the cumulative process of recovery and expansion (or boom) is subject to two fundamental stresses, both built into market systems organized around profit-seeking business enterprises. One pertains to the production process itself and the other to the financial structure. We must keep in mind that the business cycle is a short-term phenomenon, which means that it takes place within a time period (three to five years) that does not permit large increases in productive capacity. Thus, as an expansion proceeds, the costs of doing business will begin to rise, slowly at first but at an accelerating pace as prosperity proceeds. This comes about in part as firms push up against capacity limits set by the existing stock of equipment. The cost of labor will rise, not only because prosperity pushes up standard wage rates as firms scramble for increasingly scarce labor, but also because more over-time will be paid. Furthermore, labor efficiency (worker productivity) declines as less skilled workers are pulled into the job market and older and less efficient equipment is pressed into use, while longer hours and pressure to turn out goods at an even faster pace cause more mistakes, waste, and numerous small inefficiencies, all of which increase the costs of doing business. At some point in an upswing prices of raw materials begin to rise faster than the selling prices for finished products, a development which puts further pressure on cost-price relationships and the profit picture.

In the meanwhile, parallel stresses are developing in the investment and money markets. Essentially what Mitchell found was that the supply of funds available for lending through the usual financial channels (the bond and mortgage markets) fails to keep pace with the demand. Neither does the supply of bank loans, which are necessarily limited by the reserves banks must hold against their expanding liabilities. Firms find that it becomes more and more difficult to negotiate new security issues— bonds especially—except on increasingly onerous terms. High levels of employment and economic activity generally soak up most of the money in circulation, leaving little available for lending or to meet liquidity needs. The demand for bank loans continues to grow, not only because of expanded levels of activity, but also because prices are rising. For a time at least this demand is not responsive to higher interest rates, since profit expectations remain high and firms are optimistic that they can turn borrowed money over rapidly enough to come out ahead. The growing tensions in the financial markets are a threat to continued expansion simply because sooner or later higher interest rates will cut into both actual and expected profit margins. When this happens both current production and investment for future production will suffer.

As the foregoing pressures and tensions mount in both the real (goods) and financial (money) spheres of the economy, only one route is open to prevent disaster from overwhelming the economy. This is to continue to push up prices fast enough to keep rising costs from encroaching upon profits. But this proves to be impossible. Some prices, such as those set by law, by long-term contracts, by custom, or even by business policy, simply cannot move up rapidly. Incomes, too, may not keep pace with prices, a factor responsible for the 1974–75 recession. In any event, the accumulated stresses imposed on both the production and financial sides of the economy during an expansion end sooner or later in a *crisis*. In Mitchell's view a crisis initially is a situation in which business firms attempt to liquidate some or all of the debts they have incurred during the expansion and prosperity phase of the cycle. The crisis, which marks the upper turning point of the cycle, may be mild or severe, even turning into a full-fledged monetary panic of the sort which led to the temporary closing of the banks in 1933. But once an expansion or boom slides into a crisis, the situation again becomes cumulative, spreading from the banking community to business firms to the entire community. Business firms are forced to concentrate on looking after their outstanding liabilities and husbanding their financial resources, instead of pushing sales and continuing to expand production. Thus, the volume of new orders and, with it, production and employment begin to fall, a process which is cumulative downward just as a recovery and expansion is cumulative upward. Unless checked by government intervention or some other unforeseen outside event (such as a war), the economy slides into a recession or depression, from whence, according to Mitchell, the cycle will begin all over again.

Are there limits to the amplitude of the cycle? This is a question which Mitchell never addressed directly, although his notion that each phase of the cycle carries within it the forces which lead the economy into the next phase implies the existence of limits. Professor J. R. Hicks developed a theory of a "constrained" cycle in which the magnitude of fluctuations is limited by both a ceiling and a floor.[15] In Professor Hicks's analysis the cycle results from an interaction between the Keynesian multiplier and the accelerator in a fashion similar to the example developed in Chapter 6. Figure 17–5 depicts the Hicksian cycle "model" with the built-in floor and ceiling. The ceiling is set by the rate of growth of the full-employment labor force plus the rate of growth in its productivity. Thus, if the fully employed labor force grew at an annual average rate of 1 percent and labor productivity increased annually on the average at 2.5 percent, the ceiling at which output could grow over time would be 3.5 percent. Actual output could not exceed this figure except for a brief interval. Thus, there is an effective upper limit to cyclical fluctuations in the economy.

The floor below which output during its cyclical path cannot fall is determined differently. It results in part from the fact that the working of the accelerator over the course of the cycle is not symmetrical. The accelerator, it will be recalled, leads to more or less investment spending as a consequence of a *change in the rate* at which output is changing. Dur-

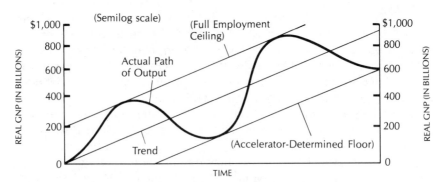

FIGURE 17–5. The "Constrained" Business Cycle of J. R. Hicks

15. J. R. Hicks, *A Contribution to the Theory of the Trade Cycle* (London: Oxford University Press, 1950), especially Chaps. VII and VIII, pp. 83–107.

ing a downswing the fall in output will, of course, lead to a decline in induced investment, but there will be a limit to the amount by which total investment will fall. The reason is that all investment is not induced. Even in a severe depression some autonomous investment is likely; hence total investment will not normally fall to zero or even become negative (except for very short periods). This means, in effect, that the effective value of the accelerator may be smaller in a downswing than it is in an upswing, a fact that automatically tends to put a floor under the downswing. Furthermore, we must reckon with the Keynesian fact that, as income (that is, real output) falls, consumption does not fall as fast. Even, therefore, if gross investment fell to zero—or became negative for a short period of time—consumption spending would eventually act to place a limit to the fall in output. This is so simply because at some point it will begin to exceed output. When this happens the floor will have been reached. It almost goes without saying that the economy may experience a level of unemployment that is not acceptable politically long before the "floor" is reached, but this does not change the theoretical fact that such a floor may exist. It merely means that positive policy actions will be taken before this point is reached.

Causes of the Business Cycle

Although some economists have tried to understand and explain the business cycle ever since the existence of cycles in economic activity was recognized, most of this effort took place outside the mainstream of theoretical economics. The reason, of course, was the dominant position of the classical approach to economic understanding right up until the crash of 1929. Classical economics, dominated by Say's law and belief that full employment was the normal state of affairs, simply had no place for a view of the world in which serious ups and downs in economic activity were the norm. As a consequence, most theorizing about the business cycle in the nineteenth century did not have much academic respectability, being seen mostly as a part of an "underworld" of economics populated by cranks, crackpots, and assorted charlatans pushing their pet nostrums for the world's economic ills.[16] The situation did not change until the early 1900s, at which time the work of Mitchell, Schumpeter, and a few others began to have a recognized impact. Still, business cycle theorizing continued largely outside the mainstream of economic analysis until Keynes's monumental study appeared in the mid-1930s.

Even though there is no agreement today among economists on *the*

16. Karl Marx is, of course, an exception to this, as he is one of the commanding figures in the history of economic thought and a man of the nineteenth century, as well. Marx believed that the business cycle was so ingrained in the capitalistic system of ownership and production that the only possible cure was a complete change in the nature of the system. The classical economists did not accept Marx's analysis of capitalism.

cause of the business cycle, one very important thing happened because of Keynes's work: *The General Theory* brought the business cycle into the mainstream of economic analysis. Keynes did not develop a definitive theory of the business cycle.[17] But cycles are a phenomenon characteristic of the aggregate economy. Furthermore, they have been viewed historically as an inherent characteristic of profit-oriented, market-based economic systems. Since these viewpoints are in harmony with the content and spirit of *The General Theory*, it follows naturally that analysis of the business cycle can—and should—take place within the unified theoretical framework that Keynes developed.

Explanations for the cycle have fallen into one of two quite broad categories, an approach we shall follow in this discussion. First, there is an approach usually described as *external* or *exogenous*. This view, which is characteristic of much thinking about the cycle during the nineteenth century, looks upon external shocks—such as a war or a bad harvest—as the fundamental cause of the business cycle. Technically such shocks are said to be stochastic, which means random. It is true, of course, that the way in which the economy reacts to an external shock is important for understanding and explaining the cycle, but the basic cause is held to be external to the system itself. Philosophically, this approach fits in with classical thinking since the classical economists saw the economic system primarily as a self-regulating mechanism that tended (if left alone) toward an equilibrium of full employment. In their view this was its "natural state."

The second stream of thought is much more in tune with modern Keynesian thinking about the nature and behavior of the economic system. It involves the belief that cycles are inherent in the economic system, that their existence is not dependent upon any external forces. This clearly is the spirit of *The General Theory*. Such *internal* or *endogenous* theories of the cycle may be wholly mechanistic, as is the case with the purely formal multiplier-accelerator model developed in Chapter 7, or they may be loose and relatively unstructured, as is a theory which revolves around the key role that Keynes accords to expectations and uncertainty. In any event, all such internal explanations of the cycle have in common a belief that profit-based, market-oriented economic systems are inherently unstable.

External Causes

One of the oldest of the external—or *stochastic*—attempts to explain the cycle is the "sunspot theory," an approach developed by the English

---

17. As we have seen, the purpose of *The General Theory* was to develop a systematic explanation of the forces which determine the level of output and employment in the mature, market (i.e., capitalistic) economy. Keynes did not set out to establish a theory of the business cycle, but he did believe that the theoretical framework which he developed in his classic work could also be used to explain this phenomenon. See Chapter 22, "Notes on the Trade Cycle," in his *The General Theory, Interest and Money* (New York: Harcourt, Brace & World, First Harbinger ed., 1964).

classical economist W. Stanley Jevons.[18] His investigations into fluctuations led him to suggest a cycle of approximately 10 or 11 years' duration. But the main causes of such cycles were periodic upheavals in weather conditions, a development that he thought was traceable to variations in the intensity of sunspots. If there were a strong correlation between sunspots and cycles in the weather, such a theory of the business cycle might make sense for a predominantly agricultural economy, but it would not suffice to explain the business cycle in an economy in which agriculture accounts for only a small part of the output total. Subsequent research doesn't support the close correlation between sunspots and business cycles that Jevons thought existed, although the subject of the impact of sunspots on the earth's climate continues to fascinate scientists and laymen alike. It remains an open scientific question.

Money—especially gold—has sometimes been seen as the source of an exogenous shock capable of initiating a cyclical reaction in the economy. Gold discoveries in California and Alaska are examples of monetary shocks. The difficulty with this view is that such events happen only once in a great while, whereas cycles are a more or less regular occurrence. Under modern conditions a monetary shock theory of the cycle simply will not do, for the money supply is no longer dependent upon such chance happenings as the discovery of a new gold field in the nation or abroad. Although critics of the Federal Reserve maintain that the actions of the men who manage the nation's central bank are often counterproductive, they do not claim that these actions are wholly capricious, unrelated to what is happening in the economy. Thus, there is no real basis for a modern theory of the cycle based upon monetary shocks.

Joseph A. Schumpeter not only studied the business cycle and its length in detail, but he also developed a theory of the cycle which should be classified with other external or exogenous explanations. Briefly, Schumpeter believed that innovation was the major external shock that would start the economy on a cyclical path. Schumpeter is at one with other theorists who see the business cycle as a continuing process, one that moves through successive phases with considerable regularity. But innovation is the key originating cause in such fluctuations. He described the process as follows in an important 1927 article:

> These booms consist in the carrying out of innovations in the industrial and commercial organism. By innovations I understand such changes of the combination of factors of production as cannot be effected by infinitesimal steps or variations on the margin. They consist primarily in changes in methods of production and transportation, or in changes in industrial organization, or in the production of a new article, or in the opening up of new markets of new sources of material. The recurring periods of prosperity of the cyclical movement are the form progress takes in capitalistic society.[19]

18. Jevons is perhaps best known for his role in the development of the law of diminishing marginal utility.
19. Joseph A. Schumpeter, "The Explanation of the Business Cycle," *Economica*, December 1927, p. 295.

In this article and in his subsequent voluminous writings, Schumpeter made it clear, first, that innovations originate in irregular fashion because a single individual or a relative handful of businessmen see possibilities for gain not seen by the vast majority and, second, that the cycle of boom followed by collapse is the mechanism through which the benefits of any innovation get spread throughout the economy. The cycle, in other words, is the price of progress. Schumpeter's theory is classified as an external or exogenous approach because the individual entrepreneur (or a small band of entrepreneurs) who gets the process started is, in a sense, outside the system. The act of innovation is an extraordinary act, one not normally forthcoming because of the usual, routine operation of the economy. It is in this sense that innovation is an external or exogenous cause of the cycle.

Before we look at the alternative set of explanations for the cycle—those that define it as wholly an internal affair in a market system—let us consider briefly a thoroughly modern version of the external or exogenous approach, a version that puts government in the role of the external cause. This view grows out of the neoclassical and monetarist views of the economy as being inherently stable, tending when left alone toward a full-employment equilibrium.[20] Some external shock is required to dislodge the economy from its natural, equilibrium state. When this happens, there will be public pressure for government action to restore equilibrium. But, because of lags, the government policy reaction will not only come too late, but its response is likely to be too strong in view of the fact that the forces that tend to restore equilibrium start working even before a policy decision is made. What government intervention does is exaggerate the natural corrective response of the economic system to an external shock, thus worsening rather than correcting the effect of the shock. Government is seen as a cause of, not a corrective to, cyclical fluctuations. Milton Friedman is one of the leading proponents of this viewpoint, especially in the realm of monetary policy. The Federal Reserve System, he argues, usually does the wrong thing because it misreads what is happening in the economy, failing to pay enough heed to the economy's self-correcting mechanism. For example, the Federal Reserve usually interprets rising interest rates as a sign of insufficient money rather than of excess spending. It reacts—wrongly, according to Friedman—by increasing the money supply, which only worsens the situation by leading to more spending. Government action is destabilizing rather than stabilizing.

---

20. See, for example, Merton H. Miller and Charles W. Upton, *Macroeconomics: A Neoclassical Introduction* (Homewood, Ill.: Richard D. Irwin, Inc., 1974). In their preface, Miller and Upton say "We believe that the course in macroeconomics should emphasize . . . that a market economy left to its own devices will settle into a full employment equilibrium. External shocks, of a variety of kinds, will dislodge it from equilibrium from time to time, but the economy's internal defenses will speedily return it to equilibrium barring new shocks or actively destabilizing policies by the government."

Internal Causes

In spite of the often persuasive arguments of Professor Friedman, a majority of economists are not ready to accept the view that the economy is inherently stable. Consequently, cycle theories of an *internal* or *endogenous* character are more in tune with contemporary thinking about the economy's behavior than are external shock theories. Here again, however, there is no single theory, no consensus among economists on how to explain the business cycle. For simplicity in exposition we shall consider, first, some pre-Keynesian views of the internal causes of the cycle and follow that with a brief examination of the cyclical process as seen by Keynes in *The General Theory*.

Pre-Keynesian theorizing about the business cycle may be divided into two broad categories. These are, first, a group of theories usually labeled "underconsumptionist" and, second, another group generally described as "overinvestment" theories. We shall take a brief look at some of the main ideas and economic personalities associated with each of these broad categories.

Although the term "underconsumption" lacks a precise meaning, the "underconsumptionist" approach to the business cycle sees the ultimate collapse in boom conditions as being caused by a failure of spending by consumers to keep pace with production, leading eventually to a "glut" of unsold goods. The reasons why consumption fails to keep pace are not always clear, sometimes being the result of hoarding, sometimes of an excess of savings, or sometimes simply because it is believed that the system does not pay out sufficient funds to buy back what is being produced. Why the latter happens is not always clear, although it is a theme that runs through the underconsumptionist literature. The roots of the underconsumptionist viewpoint trace back to Thomas Malthus, one of the early classical economists. In one of the many letters he exchanged with David Ricardo, Malthus pointed out that it was possible for demand to be deficient if a society attempts to save at a pace in excess of the willingness to invest (to employ modern terminology), but his arguments made no impression on Ricardo and other classical economists. Say's law won out over what Keynes called "plain sense."[21]

Prior to Keynes, the most complete development of the underconsumption approach to business cycles came from John A. Hobson, a British economist writing near the end of the nineteenth century. Hobson took issue with Say's law, asserting that the business cycle resulted from a combination of oversaving and underconsumption. He did not deny the fundamental premise that production (that is, supply) creates the means to make payments or buy back what is produced, but he did argue that

21. See Keynes's essay on Malthus entitled "Thomas Malthus: The First of the Cambridge Economists," in John Maynard Keynes, *Essays in Biography* (New York: Norton, 1951), p. 117.

many persons produced more (that is, got more income) than they needed to consume, so their production did not translate into an equal amount of effective demand. Consequently, demand could be insufficient in the aggregate. The remedy was in less saving, an end that could be attained by some redistribution of income and wealth. Hobson recognized that redistribution could go too far, thereby impairing saving and ultimately economic progress, but progress was also hurt by the periodic failures of demand to keep pace with the growth in productive power because income was too unequal. Thus, society had to thread its way toward a more equal distribution of income, but not one so equal as to threaten all saving and the progress it made possible.

In a way the "overinvestment" theories are a mirror image of the underconsumptionist approach to the cycle. Like the latter, prosperity collapses because of an excess of production—a glut of goods. But in this case the goods in excess supply are capital goods, not consumer goods. Basically what happens is that an upswing in activity is set in motion by a rising tide of spending for new capital goods, a surge that eventually saturates the economy with more new capital than it can profitably employ. When this happens the investment boom collapses, dragging down the rest of the economy.

What causes the overinvestment boom? No specific answer exists for this question, although the practice in the theoretical literature is to lump the causes of the investment boom into two broad categories—monetary and nonmonetary. Frederick A. Hayek, an Austrian-born economist and Nobel laureate, is the best-known exponent of the monetary overinvestment theory of the business cycle. At the root of the problem is the willingness of the banking and financial system to create new bank credit and make this credit available to business enterprises on favorable terms. It is, in other words, an expansion of money and credit that gets the investment boom rolling. For investment to take place, however, there must be "real" savings, which involves a diversion of resources from consumer to investment goods output. In Hayek's scheme the necessary savings are *forced*, not voluntary. This is what eventually causes the investment boom to collapse. Savings are "forced" by the process of rising prices brought about by producers of investment goods bidding for increasingly scarce resources as the boom accelerates. The boom can continue as long as investment spending is fed by expanding bank credit and forced saving. But ultimately this leads to maladjustments in the structure of production—there are too many new capital goods in relation to the real ability of consumers to buy. Forced savings means that consumers are being priced out of the market by higher prices, a process that must sooner or later lead to a glut of both investment and consumer goods. The inevitable collapse is hastened by growing stringency in the financial markets as the banking system exhausts its excess reserves and interest rates begin to rise. Thus, firms find it more and more difficult to secure on favorable terms the credit needed to keep the investment boom rolling. What the crisis and downturn do, in Hayek's view, is force the economy back into a more normal situation, which is one in which the structure of production—that is, the relationship between investment and consumption goods output—is adjusted to the level at which voluntary savings are forthcoming. Recession or depression is the price the economy pays for the excesses of an investment boom generated initially by easy money conditions.

Nonmonetary overinvestment theories of the business cycle suggest a similar sequence of events—too much investment, too little consumption demand, and an eventual turning point or collapse when the investment goods produced during the boom begin turning out increased quantities of consumer goods and services. The basic difference is that much less stress is placed upon money and credit as the ultimate causal factors in the investment boom. What is common to all such theories is a belief that the cycle is caused by overproduction that results from overinvestment. Money of necessity plays a role, for no expansion is possible without more money, but the nonmonetary theorists view the money and financial system primarily as a part of the response mechanism rather than a fundamental causative factor. Leading exponents of a nonmonetary overinvestment approach to the cycle have been a Russian economist, Michel Tugan-Baranowsky, a German, Arthur Spiethoff, and Gustav Cassel, a Swedish engineer who became an economist. The key studies of these and other overinvestment theorists appeared before publication of Keynes's *The General Theory*.

The General Theory

Keynes did not set out to develop a theory of the business cycle (in *The General Theory*), but he did think about the phenomenon and draw upon the theoretical apparatus that he developed in his classic work to suggest why cycles existed in a market economy. Most of the ideas discussed previously in this section can be fitted into the sequence of events that Keynes envisioned. We shall conclude this discussion of the causes of the business cycle with a brief summary of Keynes's views on the phenomenon.

In his "Notes on the Trade Cycle" (Chapter 22 in *The General Theory*) Keynes says that the essential character of the trade cycle—the regularity and the duration of the economy's ups and downs which justify the notion of a cycle—is due mainly to "the way in which the marginal efficiency of capital fluctuates."[22] This, of course, puts investment at the heart of the matter, for the marginal efficiency of capital is the key to what happens to investment spending. Keynes approaches the question of the cycle by asking what happens in the later stages of a typical boom. As with most business cycle theorists, Keynes sees the boom carried forward mainly

22. Keynes, *The General Theory*, p. 313.

by investment spending, given the essentially passive role of consumption spending. But investment spending, Keynes reminds us, depends not only on the existing scarcity and cost of capital goods, but on expectations as to the future yield of newly produced capital goods. However, "the basis for such expectations is very precarious. Being based upon shifting and unreliable evidence they are subject to sudden and violent change."[23] The future and its uncertainty is a theme to which Keynes returns again and again in *The General Theory*. And here we have the basic reason for the sudden and unpredictable collapse of the marginal efficiency of capital, an event which marks the onset of the "crisis" and the downward plunge of the economy. In the latter stages of any investment boom, expectations of future yields must be optimistic enough to offset the growing abundance of capital, the rising supply price for new capital, and increases in interest rates. At some point, however, all this may collapse; the longer the boom goes on, the more fragile and uncertain becomes the basis upon which expectations for future yields rest. Thus, as Keynes says, the "predominant explanation of the crisis is, not primarily a rise in the rate of interest, but a sudden collapse in the marginal efficiency of capital."[24] All else flows from this fundamental fact.

Following the collapse of the marginal efficiency of capital, there will be a sharp increase in liquidity preference, a consequence of the dismay and uncertainty about the future that the crisis precipitates. For a time interest rates will be high, but even after the immediate crisis passes the marginal efficiency of capital remains so low that there is no practical way in which interest rates can be reduced enough to bring investment spending out of a slump. For a period the slump will be intractable. Unless there is outside intervention—government action, for example—some time must elapse before a recovery can begin. But there cannot be a general recovery from the slump until there is a revival in the marginal efficiency of capital. This will not happen, however, until the economy rids itself of surplus inventories of all goods carried over from the crisis and ensuing slump and until normal forces of growth begin to make the stock of fixed capital assets (equipment and buildings) *relatively* less abundant.

Keynes distinguishes his analysis from earlier "overinvestment" theories of the cycle by pointing out that in his opinion the term "overinvestment" should be used only to describe a state of affairs in which every kind of capital good is so abundant that no new investment in any kind of capital could earn more than its replacement cost—a condition in which capital ceased to have any true scarcity value. This, of course, is not the situation he is describing, for a collapse in the marginal efficiency of capital means a collapse in the expected returns based upon uncertain and flimsy knowledge about the future. Such expectations may or may

23. Ibid., p. 315.
24. Ibid.

not reflect the scarcity of capital in a more enduring and fundamental sense. It is the relative scarcity of capital in a subjective sense that governs the marginal efficiency and thus determines the pace of investment. This is the true meaning of Keynes's theory, which sees wide swings in the marginal efficiency of capital as the key to understanding the business cycle.

The Political Business Cycle

Before we leave the subject of causes of the business cycle, a brief word is in order about a related idea—the political business cycle. In a remarkably prescient article published in 1943, Michal Kalecki foresaw that once governments learned how to control the business (or trade) cycle, they might find themselves confronted with a political cycle.[25] The gist of Kalecki's argument was that attempts to ensure full employment by large-scale government spending during a slump would sooner or later encounter strong opposition from the business community. Such opposition would arise in part because of straightforward hostility by business to deficit spending as a matter of principle, and in part because of the fear that a prolonged period of full employment would strengthen the economic position of the wage-earner *vis à vis* the property owner and businessman. But the general public will not tolerate a prolonged slump with high unemployment; consequently, political pressure mounts until the government acts to bring the economy out of the slump by either cutting taxes, increasing public spending, or both. In any event, the policy measures taken to counter the slump involve deficit spending, a development which sooner or later arouses the opposition of the business community and forces the government to return to a more orthodox policy of reducing deficits. A new slump follows. Kalecki foresaw a situation in which government policy (fiscal and monetary) was whipsawed continuously between forces demanding action to end slumps and unemployment and forces fearful of the consequences of prolonged deficit spending. In many ways Kalecki's vision of a political business cycle is very much like what both Britain and the United States have experienced in recent years. The basic difference is that it is primarily inflation (not deficit spending) which leads to alternating policies of *stop* (putting on the fiscal and monetary brakes) and *go* (stepping on the fiscal and monetary accelerator) in an effort to cope with the contemporary malaise—

25. Originally from Poland, Michal Kalecki visited England in the 1930s, remained there during the war years, and returned to Poland after World War II. He died in 1970. The article in question is entitled "The Political Aspects of Full Employment," *The Political Quarterly*, October-December 1943, pp. 322–31. It is now generally recognized that Kalecki developed in the early 1930s an analysis of the workings of a market economy which in its broad outline is remarkably similar to Keynes's theory. Because his ideas were first published in Polish they did not become generally known among Western economists until after *The General Theory* appeared in 1936.

stagflation. Modern governments have not been notoriously successful to date in solving the problem of stagflation.

Economic Forecasting

We shall conclude this chapter with a few observations on economic forecasting. What is economic forecasting? The answer is simple but important. Forecasting is an attempt to determine what will happen in the economy over the near term, which is to say what will happen in the next quarter or the next year. Most forecasting does not extend further into the future. Forecasting involves, in other words, an attempt to foresee or estimate changes in the major aggregate economic variables—output, employment, and the price level, for example—in the period immediately ahead. Forecasting requires a knowledge and understanding of what has happened in the recent past, what is happening now in the economy, and the *why* of such happenings. The latter implies a need for economic theory, for we cannot understand and interpret the observed performance of the economy without a theoretical frame of reference. Forecasting is both an art and a science, although it is probably more of an art than a science, the reason being the uncertainty that surrounds the economic future. Thus, we touch once again on a key theme that threads its way through the Keynesian view of the economic universe.

Forecasting is necessary because the economy moves forward in irregular fashion—in the kind of cyclical or wavelike movements that have been the subject of this chapter. If the economy's path through time were regular, then forecasting would not be necessary. We should merely have to extrapolate past trends to know what tomorrow would bring. Unfortunately, the world in general and the economic world in particular do not work this way. Yet man wants to know what is going to happen next week, next month, or next year. Thus, forecasting meets an important human need. Furthermore, accurate forecasting is essential if economic stabilization is to work. We know from the available evidence that the economy is inherently unstable, but we also believe that this instability can be minimized by a judicious use of the policy tools that are the legacy of contemporary macroeconomic theory. But unless we can forecast with a reasonable accuracy forthcoming ups and downs of the economic system, our knowledge of how to apply economic theory to improve the economy's performance will not do us much good.

This brings us to a more specific question: What do we expect from economic forecasting? Basically, forecasting should accomplish two things. First, it should tell us that the economy is approaching a turning point, which is to say that forecasting ought to send out some kind of a signal that a major change in the economic weather is coming. It should, in other words, tell us that a downturn or an upturn is in sight. Ideally, forecasts ought to tell us exactly when a turning point can be expected, but this is beyond the current capabilities of the art. Second, a forecast should have something to say about the magnitude of a forthcoming change. For example, if the economic signals say a recession is coming, they also ought to give some indication of the severity or depth of the recession.

There are some knotty problems involved in the foregoing matters that are worth pointing out, although we shall not explore them in depth. For example, if correct policy action is taken in the face of a forecast, the forecast is thereby rendered incorrect. What does this do to the belief in the accuracy of subsequent forecasts? Another and different problem may arise if business firms and private individuals react to a forecast in ways that bring about the conditions being forecast. For example, the forecast of a downturn in economic activity may lead business firms to trim costs in anticipation of hard times by laying off some workers or persuade consumers to save more and spend less. Such actions could make future conditions worse than they might have been in the absence of a forecast. There are no ready answers to these problems although most economic forecasting is probably not yet accurate enough for these possibilities to affect seriously the economy's performance.

Methods of Forecasting

There is no one technique widely recognized among economists as *the method* for forecasting. The techniques actually used range from the subjective judgment of a single competent individual to the use of elaborate econometric models involving large numbers of sophisticated equations. We shall review some of the more widely used techniques, although no claim is made that our list is exhaustive.

Extrapolation

The technique that is both the simplest and the most widely used by the nonspecialist is to project into the future what is happening currently or has happened in the recent past. Possibly a simple extrapolation of the present into the future should not be designated as a "technique," but this method is probably used—consciously or unconsciously—more than most people realize. Keynes believed that this was largely the way in which businessmen form their expectations about the future, since he argued there was no scientific basis whatsoever they could employ for the calculation of future values. What they do, he argued, is assume— even though past experience shows this to be risky—that the present is a serviceable guide to the future. In addition, the individual businessman seeks support for his judgment by falling back on the judgments of other businessmen. Unfortunately, they also are doing exactly the same thing—assuming that the present is a serviceable guide to the future.[26]

26. John Maynard Keynes, "The General Theory of Employment," *The Quarterly Journal of Economics*, February 1937, p. 214.

What this means, of course, is that such forecasts are based on a flimsy foundation, subject to "sudden and violent change." This technique may work for a while because of the cumulative character of most expansions and contractions, but it cannot—except by chance—forecast turning points in the cycle or provide evidence on the magnitude of the cyclical swing.

The Consensus Approach

Another commonly used forecasting technique is the consensus method. This method is widely employed in the press, especially by business and financial publications. It is labeled concensus because it involves getting opinions from a large number of observers as to what is likely to happen to the economy in the months or year ahead. A consensus outlook is then constructed based on these opinions. This technique is most often employed at the start of a new year. General-circulation newspapers tend to develop their forecasts by surveying leaders in business, labor, government, and education, whereas the business and financial press is more likely to direct its probing at professional economists in business and the universities. *Business Week* magazine, for example, normally publishes at the end of the year a major article on the economic outlook for the next twelve months. Their analysis typically pulls together the opinions of a broad sample of academic and business economists and compares their outlook with forecasts turned out by the best known econometric models. Table 17–3 contains the average of the forecasted percentage changes made by 30 economists and 10 econometric models for 1983 as reported in *Business Week*. The average of the changes predicted by the 30 economists is a good example of consensus-type forecasting.

TABLE 17–3. Economic Forecasts for 1983 (in percent)

	Real GNP	Inflation Rate	Unemployment Rate
Estimates of 30 economists	3.8	5.3	10.1
Estimates of 10 econometric models	3.7	5.5	10.2

SOURCE: *Business Week*, December 27, 1982.

Indicators

One of the most important forecasting tools developed in recent years are the indexes of *leading, coincident,* and *lagging* indicators. These terms refer to statistical series which either lead, coincide, or lag behind the general cycle movement of economic activity. For forecasting purposes the index of leading indicators is most important, because it is designed to tell us that either a downturn or an upswing in economic activity is in the offing.

The National Bureau of Economic Research in cooperation with the federal government has been primarily responsible for development of this particular forecasting technique. For more than two decades, Geoffrey H. Moore and Julius Shiskin conducted an intensive study of the behavior of several hundred time series for economic variables, seeking always to discover those series which would enable economists to forecast changes in economic activity. Out of these studies they narrowed the analysis to 88 indicators, of which 36 were placed in the leading category, 25 were put in the coincident group, 11 were classified as lagging, and 16 were not classified with respect to timing. The list was further refined and shortened, leading ultimately to the development of a composite index for each of these three categories—leading, coincident, and lagging. These composite indexes are published monthly by the U.S. Department of Commerce in *Business Conditions Digest*. Table 17–4 lists the economic time series included in each of these three composite indexes

TABLE 17–4. Composite Indexes and Their Composition

Index and Series
  Composite Leading Index (12 series)
    1. Average workweek for manufacturing production workers
    2. Layoff rate in manufacturing (per 100 workers)
    3. New orders for consumers goods and materials
    4. Percentage of companies reporting slower deliveries
    5. Net business formation
    6. Contracts and orders for plant and equipment
    7. New building permits for private housing
    8. Net changes in inventories
    9. Changes in sensitive prices
    10. Prices for 500 common stocks
    11. Changes in total liquid assets
    12. Money supply (M1)
  Composite Coincident Index (4 series)
    1. Employees on nonagricultural payrolls
    2. Personal income less transfer payments
    3. Industrial production
    4. Manufacturing and trade sales
  Composite Lagging Index (6 series)
    1. Average duration of unemployment
    2. Manufacturing and trade inventories
    3. Labor cost per unit of output in manufacturing
    4. Commercial and industrial loans outstanding as reported by large commercial banks (weekly)
    5. Average prime rate charged by banks
    6. Ratio of consumer installment debt to personal income

SOURCE: *Business Conditions Digest, January 1983.*

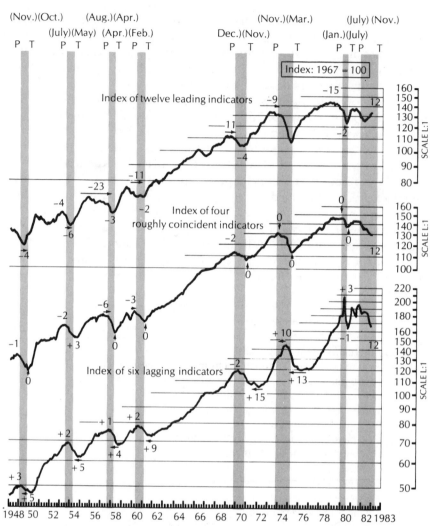

FIGURE 17–6.   Major Composite Indexes: 1948–83 (1967 = 100)

SOURCE: *Business Conditions Digest*

and Figure 17–6 shows their behavior for the period 1948–83. This chart shows clearly that the downturn in the composite index for leading indicators foreshadowed a recession, although there is a wide variation in the 1948–83 period in the number of months by which the downturn in this index led the overall downturn in economic activity. The average forecast lead time for the last 5 recessions was 10.8 months, although the actual lead time ranged from a maximum of 23 to a minimum of 4 months. If the index of leading indicators turns down for two consecutive months, trouble may lie ahead. This is the current thinking of the Department of Commerce.

Econometric Models

Finally some comments are in order about forecasting with econometric models of the economy. Basically, an econometric model is a mathematical representation of the economy that consists of a series of equations involving dependent (endogenous) and independent (exogenous) variables. The relationships presented in the equations are developed on the basis of a statistical investigation into the economy's past performance, using correlation analysis to determine the relationships. Judgment and skill are obviously required to determine the extent to which an empirically observed correlation between economic variables also involves a causal relationship. If an econometric model is to be used successfully in economic forecasting, then the fundamental equations that enter into the model must involve true causal relationships—not just a statistical correlation.

Econometric models developed from the fundamental structure of Keynesian economics, particularly the income-expenditure model. The procedure has been to break the major elements that enter into the aggregate demand function into their different components—to disaggregate them to a degree—and develop for each of these parts appropriate regression equations which reflect the underlying causal relationships. The result is a system of simultaneous equations that can be employed for forecasting. Since some econometric models involve sixty or more equations, an electronic computer is mandatory for their successful operation. This points up a dilemma which confronts the econometric modelbuilder. As the econometrician strives for greater authenticity he is forced toward more disaggregation, but this increases the number of equations in the model and makes it increasingly ponderous to use. Furthermore, it may require a staff of individuals simply to keep the model up to date in the light of the fact that observed data from the past are often revised as more information becomes available. This may lead to changes in some of the basic causal relationships embodied in the equations of the model, which, in turn, may force the econometrician to reconstruct some substantial portion of his model. In short, an elaborate econometric model is an expensive undertaking that requires the support of a highly trained staff. This is the basic reason why only a handful of major econometric models have been constructed in the United States. The best-known ones are those developed by the Federal Reserve Board and MIT, the Wharton School of Finance at the University of Pennsylvania, the University of Michigan, Princeton University, and the Brookings Institution. There are also two well-known models developed by private business firms: Chase Econometrics (a subsidiary of the Chase Manhattan Bank) and Data Resource Incorporated.

The Effectiveness of Forecasting

Just as there is no single technique for economic forecasting, there is no simple answer to the question of its effectiveness. There has been significant forward progress in this field since World War II, but much remains to be done to improve the accuracy and effectiveness of the art. Numerous studies in recent years have sought to answer this question of the accuracy of economic forecasts.[27] We shall conclude this chapter with some observations on a few of these.

In an analysis of the performance of econometric models in forecasting GNP and changes in GNP over the 1953–64 period, Victor Zarnowitz found that forecast values for GNP were off by only about 2 percent on the average, not an excessively large error. But much larger errors were made by the econometric models in forecasting the actual change in GNP. Here the range was from 28 to 56 percent, with the average error being about 40 percent.

One important body engaged in making forecasts is the Council of Economic Advisers. Since 1962 it has included in the annual *Economic Report* forecasts of current and constant dollar value for the GNP as well as the inflation rate as measured by the GNP deflator. The Council employs a variety of forecasting techniques—including econometric models—to develop its projections. In general, according to Geoffrey Moore's analysis, the track record of the Council in forecasting change in the rate of growth of *real* GNP is pretty good. In ten out of the thirteen forecast years, the Council's forecasts of changes in the rate of growth for real GNP were in the right direction, which is to say that they correctly forecast that the rate of growth would either increase or decrease. Their record on forecasting changes in the inflation rate was not satisfactory, for in only four of the thirteen years was the Council able to forecast correctly whether the inflation rate would rise or fall. In four years its forecasts were in the wrong direction, and in the other five years the results were ambiguous because either the forecast rate or the actual rate (but not both) remained constant. With respect to forecasts for actual GNP (real and current dollar amounts), Moore found that the Council's errors were about one-half as large as they would have been if it had been assumed that last year's change was the same as this year (used a single extrapolation, in other words). For inflation, the results were much

---

27. Readers interested in this question should consult one or more of the following studies. Victor Zarnowitz, *An Appraisal of Short-Term Economic Forecasts* (New York: National Bureau of Economic Research, 1967); Stephen K. McNees, "An Evaluation of Economic Forecasts," *New England Economic Review,* November/December 1975, and an update of the subject by the same author in the September/October 1976 issue of the *New England Economic Review;* Geoffrey H. Moore, "Economic Forecasting—How Good a Track Record?" in *The Morgan Guaranty Survey,* January 1975; and Maury N. Harris and Deborah Jamroz, "Evaluating the Leading Indicators," Federal Reserve Bank of New York, *Monthly Review.* Other references will be found in these studies.

less satisfactory, since the Council consistently tended to underestimate the inflation rate. Actually, according to Moore, an assumption that the previous year's inflation rate would repeat itself would have produced forecasts as accurate as those found in the *Economic Report*.

Probably the forecasting tool which has proved to be accurate more consistently than any other is the composite index of leading indicators. According to the Harris-Jamroz study cited above, this particular index has never failed to signal any of the post–World War II downturns (Figure 17–6), although on occasion when it has dropped no recession followed. As pointed out earlier, the chief weakness of this index is not that it does not give an accurate signal of an impending change, but that there is no consistency to length of the lag between the downturn (or upturn) in the indicator and the subsequent change in the economy's direction.

What these various findings indicate is that no wholly satisfactory technique has evolved for forecasting either the timing or the strength of major changes in the aggregate economy. All the various techniques have a role—the National Bureau concluded that there are no major differences between the accuracy of forecasts based upon informal consensus models, econometric models, and leading indicators. That is, perhaps, to be expected, since all techniques must depend in greater or lesser degree on some extrapolation of present or recent past conditions into the future. But since humans can learn from their experience, the future will never be exactly like the past. Forecasting is a useful art, and efforts should continue to improve it. But given the uncertainties that attach to an unknown future, we can never make it into a "science" in which we push a few buttons on a computer and get an accurate reading of tomorrow's economic weather.

Summary

1. The business cycle is a term that is used by economists to describe the fluctuations in output, employment, and the price level which characterize the time-path of the economy. The term "cycle" is used because in a rough way these fluctuations have a wavelike character, even though the cycles are highly irregular in both amplitude and length.

2. The business cycle typically has four major phases. These include the peak, or upper turning point, a downswing, a trough or lower turning point, and a recovery or upswing. Historic records, both statistical and written, indicate that the business cycle is at least as old as market capitalism. Since 1854, the National Bureau of Economic Research finds that the United States has experienced 30 cycles. A full cycle is normally measured from trough to trough.

3. Data on the business cycle also indicate that in the post–World War II period the cycle is both less frequent and less severe. The comparative

mildness of cycles prior to the 1970s gave rise to a belief that the cycle had been conquered once and for all. Experience since the 1970s has shown, however, that this is not true. Since 1969, the economy has experienced four cycles, two of which (1974–75 and 1981–82) were exceptionally severe.

4. In addition to the normal business cycle, with an average duration of 51 months, some economists believe that there is evidence of very long waves in economic life. The best known of these stems from the work of a Russian economist, Nikolai D. Kondratieff, who suggested that systems of market capitalism experience a cycle of approximately 50 to 60 years in length, half of which consist of an upswing and the other half of a downswing. In the downswing phase of a Kondratieff cycle, the normal business downtown is deeper and more prolonged than is the case when the cycle is superimposed on a Kondratieff upswing.

5. There is no simple explanation of the business cycle. One of the most thorough students of this phenomenon, Wesley C. Mitchell, spent his professional life studying what happens during the cycle, but never ventured a basic theoretical explanation. Theories of the cycle are sometimes divided into those which explain it in terms of the economic system's reaction to external events and those which see the cycle as inherent (or internal) to a system of market capitalism.

6. Joseph P. Schumpeter is a major business cycle theorist who explained the phenomenon in terms of shocks to the economy that came from innovations and that started the economy on a cyclical path.

7. Keynes, in *The General Theory,* did not develop a theory of the cycle as such, but he did show how the instability of investment spending was a major source of the economy's cyclical behavior.

8. Economic forecasting has become an important economic activity that attempts to foresee what will happen to the economy in the near term, usually a year or less. Methods of forecasting are both informal and formal. The U.S. Department of Commerce has developed several statistical series that have proved to be useful in forecasting. The index of leading indicators is a part of this series. It is an index which tends to tell in advance when the economy will turn up or down.

9. Econometric models are the most elaborate and complex of the forecasting tools used by economists. They are essentially mathematical representations of the economy involving many different economic relationships expressed in equation form. They rest upon the belief that past economic behavior can readily and accurately be extrapolated into the future. Economic forecasting, irrespective of the technique used, has proved useful but is far from perfect.

Index